45-57
book focuses on 3 aspects of material
culture in each of the Tudor reigns
① texts   ③ state spectacles
② visual depictions   & rituals

SELLING THE TUDOR MONARCHY

p XXIV - the materiality of what
he's studying & the consumption
of these in Tudor / Renaissance.

XXV - from H8 on, new attempts at   (Thesis)
✓ image control — Tudors constructed a
"cult of monarchy" how material culture
could leverage new media & or politics of representation

p 5 scholars who "travel freely
from past to present"
[like us → quote]

p6 adv as central to cons culture
p7 why the Tudors remain so powerful
in our present culture

(P8) purpose of bk - blueprint

p10 Bagehot - monarch as individuals

11 RF connecting w/ families of the
people (USE)   ⟶

P 64 Henry VII understands the politics
of display & the PR machine. But H7
didn't capitalize on this b/c he didn't
actually *perform* in his own theater of
power.

"failed the postcard recognition test" 65

(H8) - The 1st one who exploit theatrics of (P 85)
royalty as a rhetorical device

FCG Field of the Cloth of Gold

68- H8's constructing/disseminating his
Royal image the 1st act of Royal propaganda
in England

69→ process of sacralizing monarchy

70. Holbein's famous frontal portrait
of Henry - awe, fear, reverence

SELLING THE TUDOR MONARCHY

AUTHORITY AND IMAGE IN SIXTEENTH-CENTURY ENGLAND

KEVIN SHARPE

p 85 - Shakespeare & sacredness of royal
authority thru text

p 97 - how the people learned of
royal proclamations nailed on the mkt cross.

103 H8 writes a bestseller - 30 COPIES

110 - genre of "succession poems" -
written after death of monarch to reassure
ppl. about the lineage -

126 ballads & plays as popular genres
about the monarch &
divine authority of kingship

YALE UNIVERSITY PRESS
NEW HAVEN AND LONDON

p 130 - portraits & need to be seen
& recognized emerge in the Renaissance

p130 long galleries (portraits) newly constructed
reinforced dynasties. artists w/ nnH
rep'sations attracted nnlen

As the ruler w/ most est'd visual rep
(Holbein) is the reason

140 H8 opened his palace at Greenwch
to all honest persons to view tapestries
& silverware — a few days a year. ⚡ for
(& p 172 — more on this)   use for
                                                    only
141 copies of royal portraits in the
                              noble houses

The right of Kevin Sharpe to be identified as the author of this work has been asserted by him in accordance with the Copyright, Designs and Patents Act 1988.

For information about this and other Yale University Press publications, please contact:
U.S. Office: sales.press@yale.edu   www.yalebooks.com
Europe Office: sales@yaleup.co.uk   www.yaleup.co.uk

Set in Minion by IDSUK (DataConnection) Ltd
Printed in Great Britain by TJ International Ltd, Padstow, Cornwall

Library of Congress Control Number: 2009920918

ISBN 978-0-300-14098-9

Published with assistance from the foundation established in memory of Oliver Baty Cunningham of the Class of 1917, Yale College

A catalogue record for this book is available from the British Library.
10 9 8 7 6 5 4 3 2 1

141 illustrations of H8 as biblical figs in
Bibles of the time during his reign
(at H8's authorization)

146 Evidently Henry attached great importance to
objects that bore his likeness.

For Alex

149- how H8's royal arms were displayed on
"moveables" - everyday items of material culture
<logos> - The Tudor rose & also on lots of
religious objects to reaffirm Head g C of E
portrayed him as "a King of piety as well
as prowess" - connected himself to St George
the Dragon

152- seals, medals, coins → most likely ways
the common ppl saw H8's image
"medallic history of England opens w/ H8'
commemoratives

p154
(H7) - 1st currency to bear true likeness of a
monarch
H8 had multiple coins minted commemorating
aspects of his reign / engravers also made them
on their own

p157 The most impt presentation of
Kingship was the King himself

p 158 H8 as young, vigorous jock until 38 /
his an act of courage & skill advertised the
might of the nation. / commoners would watch
159 conspicuous pageantry crucial to H8's reign
160 "Henry's whole govt rested on
    conspicuous consumption & display"
160 resuscitates Order of the garter &
    the ceremonies

161 public devotion to rituals
163 Field of the Cloth of Gold - most famous
pageant in H8's reign
    164 extravaganza of "special cultural
significance & authenticity"

166 retailers & merchants f London &
Italy planned & executed the pageants
when Emperer Chas V visited London
in 1522

166 coronation entry to legitimize Anne
    B as queen. 1533 barges & a pageant
dragon
    167 describes coronation pageant (to
                                        back)

CONTENTS

ILLUSTRATIONS

Preface and Acknowledgements

This study of the past was very much influenced by my experience of the present – or what was the present when I began thinking about it. During the 1980s, when I lived at times both in England and America, I was struck by how politics in both countries was changing, how political campaigns, elections and broadcasts were emphasizing appearance and image more than substantive issues. Speeches were being carefully crafted to convey good feelings as much as information; and political leaders seemed very concerned to stage-manage images of themselves – be it Ronald Reagan at home in his check shirt on his ranch or Mrs Thatcher at the helm of a British tank.

Yet though this felt new to me as a citizen of the twentieth century, I soon reflected as a historian that there was little in this that was novel. In particular in my field, the Renaissance and early modern period, rulers had taken great pains to craft rhetorically effective addresses and to recruit the finest portrait artists to represent their majesty – even to help to construct their authority. Given that, at the time, I was finishing a study of Charles I that I had been engaged on for ten years, I could not but be struck by the importance to Charles not only aesthetically but also politically of his image and the philosophy of government and kingship that it represented. I included in what was a conventional political history of the 1630s a section on the image of the king and its relation to his values and style of governance. But I had a sense, stimulated by later developments, that there was a larger subject and indeed approach to the past here which had not received full attention. Images of rulers, of course, had not been neglected. But, often studied by literary scholars and art historians, they had at best been confined to the margins of political history, historians regarding them as something other and less than the 'real business' of politics and power.

During the 1990s, however, it became ever more apparent that rhetoric and image were emerging as the real business of power and politics. Certainly, newspaper and TV coverage of events was paying considerable attention to appearances, in every sense; and political figures were recruiting media advisers and public relations teams to present themselves in the best light to readers and viewers. Even those who greatly disapproved of such developments were quick to acknowledge them through criticism. The entirely pejorative terms (they were then pejorative – times change) 'spin', 'photo-opportunity' and 'image manipulation' began to enter the political lexicon as critics bemoaned the decline of an old politics of issues, honest and robust debate and critical scrutiny. In 1992 the Tory leader John Major shrewdly intuited, perhaps, that the people at large were not as enamoured of the new 'dark arts' of the media men as were the political leaders themselves. Famously Major fought that election with a campaign that publicly renounced the 'makeover' and the PR adviser and, as 'honest John', he toured the country addressing the voters from a humble (and we would now say deliberately retro) soapbox. It is not certain what part his politics of nostalgia played in his narrow, but unexpected, victory. But 1992 was also the year of Neil Kinnock's infamous rally at Sheffield which, it has been argued, cost him many votes by alienating the people with a triumphalist style that did not then accord with English sensibilities. Whatever the truth of such assessments or the causes of Major's surprise victory, it would be naïve to read it as the victory of substance and old politics over spin and new politics. For Major by no means neglected image. His self-presentation as an 'ordinary bloke' was cleverly pitched against noisy triumphalism; and he evoked too, as has become famous, an image of an England of warm beer, shadows over cricket fields and old ladies cycling to country churches – not the past but Betjeman's England as refashioned by the media men. Spin and image fuelled counter-spin and alternative images, even if these were advertised as having no artifice but as representing a simple and honest past and politics.

Things have come a long way since 1992. New Labour, itself more a rebranding exercise than anything else, developed a politics of style beyond anything seen in England before; and, in attempting to recapture power from them, the Conservatives have devoted all their energy to refashioning their image, to the neglect, it is still being argued as I write, of any clear policies. Meanwhile Blair's successor, Gordon Brown, has adopted some of Major's self-representation as a man of business uninterested in his image; indeed, he has exploited his reputation for being dour and colourless and made it his image. Today political parties are formed as much around images as around policies; and party politics and the struggle for power are as much about contesting representations as about programmes for government; indeed, the two have become inseparable. They are perhaps an essential aspect of the political condition in a divided polity where the support of the citizens needs to be courted.

As I reflected on this, it occurred to me that such was the condition of England after the Reformation or Henry VIII's break from Rome. Though he was the king of a sovereign monarchy, Henry, after his divorce, confronted a new and desperate situation. Not only did he face the threat of foreign invasion by Catholic powers dedicated to upholding papal authority and the Roman church, but also the danger that some of his subjects would consider him a heretic and therefore begin to question the nature of their allegiance and whether loyalty was owed first to the king or their conscience. The Reformation introduced fundamental ideological divisions within the English polity and, consequently, a need not just to state authority but to argue it: through words, images and spectacle. Henry understood the need to represent himself and so began a new chapter not only in the history of the church and government but in the arts of royal representation. Henry and his successors, because they had to, made themselves public figures who impressed themselves on their subjects in order to maintain their authority. But at the same time they exposed themselves to the counter-presentations of those of different faiths and beliefs. The struggle to win hearts and minds that, I will argue, began with the Reformation only eased at the end of the seventeenth century with the gradual acceptance of toleration, in an England that by then had institutionalized political differences in parties, clubs and social habits.

The more I thought about this, the more it seemed to me that, though not unfamiliar, this perspective had not much influenced the traditional histories of sixteenth- and seventeenth-century politics; indeed, I argue, historians continued to think of politics in older, nineteenth- and earlier twentieth-century terms, sidelining rhetoric and image as things of little importance in the past as they were and are (to many) disagreeable in the present. I decided in about 1992 to embark on a study of representations of authority and images of power in early modern England, from the Reformation to the 1688 Revolution and its aftermath.

When I began, I intended to write one large book, because I knew that, as well as making particular arguments, I wanted to posit theses about the whole period. As I began working, I was overwhelmed by the amount of material I needed to read – a problem compounded by my determination not to define 'politics' (especially for what was a Renaissance state) narrowly but to recognize the political in places and genres of writing not usually considered as materials for the political historian – in poems and plays, translations and travel writing, as well as sermons and treatises. And the problem was further compounded by my inclination towards an interdisciplinary scholarly practice, the only approach in my view that can make sense of the early modern period and especially of a subject such as this.

As I began to research on a year's leave at the Huntington Library in 1992–3, I began to get a sense of just what I had taken on. For reigns or aspects of reigns that were well studied, I had much secondary reading to do, as well as readings and re-readings of primary materials (albeit, as my subject is about public discourse, mostly in print).[1] For other rulers, Edward VI and Mary or Charles II and James II, say, there was little in the secondary literature and the research had to be done virtually from scratch. Needless to say, it was research not only in periods with which I was less well acquainted but on materials – portraits, engravings, medals, coins and rituals – which I had never studied systematically. Even so, I had not fully grasped by the end of 1993 that I was taking on a fifteen-year project and even then one that has only been made possible by having half of that period on research leave.

When I came to write, I still intended one large book. But as soon as I had drafted over 70,000 words on Henry VIII and Edward VI (and that with a very keen sense of what I had not been able to include), I knew that a one-volume study would not be feasible. I have therefore written this study as three volumes. They stand alone and independently: in each book, as indeed in each section or chapter, as well as adding to our knowledge and understanding of rulers and reigns, I hope I have larger arguments to contribute to the continuing debates about sixteenth- and seventeenth-century English history. But bigger arguments still are made across the three volumes, arguments some of which might suggest the need to rethink this period as a whole, as well as to reconsider what politics meant and was. Certainly, as I hope I make clear, I have become convinced that study of monarchical images underlines, rather than counters, the arguments for the centrality of the people in politics, which scholars have begun to argue recently. A study of representation questions any simple choice between elite history or history from below.

This study then ranges over an unusually long historical period, pursues an interdisciplinary approach and, rather than viewing them as the top-down impositions of authority, considers representations as dialogues with subjects.

While each of the volumes stands alone – and each has its own introduction and epilogue or conclusion – I have prefaced the whole project with a fairly full methodological discussion. Though this is not a common (or welcome) practice among historians, I was convinced, especially with a subject such as this, that it was important to be open about the way I understood terms, and to explain the approach I took and the scholarship, from different periods and disciplines as well as early modern history, that had influenced me. It will be interesting to learn how various readers respond to that discussion and whether those readers of only the second or third volumes (which do not begin with the methodological introduction) feel deprived or advantaged without it (though in some cases I can already hazard a good guess).[2]

This study of representations of early modern rule represents a huge labour and years of long, hard reflection. But no one is more aware than I of its deficiencies and faults.

It hardly needs saying that the image of early modern English kings and queens owed – increasingly – a considerable debt to European artists and rulers, with whom English monarchs competed and who were often an intended audience for their representations. If space, the state of scholarship, and my own expertise had permitted, I would have explored this European context more fully; all I can say by way of mitigating this failing is that my essential subject is the relations of English rulers with their native subjects and it is how they represented themselves to them that most concerns me. As I wrote, I had to abandon early plans to include music and dance and, both on account of the mass of other material and the deficiency of scholarship, discussion of dress and jewels is given far less attention in the seventeenth-century volumes. I often felt that many a section or chapter deserved to be a book – one or two are close to being short books. As a reader observed, though there have been specialized studies of aspects of my subject, each form of representation for each reign could – and perhaps should – be the subject of a monograph. If here I, perforce, for all the research that underpins my studies, sacrifice depth for breadth, it is because I seek to make comparisons and arguments across the two centuries and must hope that other scholars might be stimulated by them to return to individual topics and reigns. In particular for each reign, though I end with a brief glance at counter-representations, I wished I had had much more space to consider more fully reaction and opposition to official scripts and images and to pursue them into gentry houses, town halls and parish alehouses. To effect that satisfactorily, however, would be to attempt a full social history of early modern authority – for which I am not qualified and which could certainly not be written across this period even within three large volumes. In the absence of that, I urge readers to place the findings and arguments of my studies in the context of recent work on the culture of authority in the early modern locales and communities, the counties, courts and parishes in which, as we have come to appreciate, royal authority was absorbed, interpreted, debated and contested by magistrates and people whose own politics was shaped by local (as well as national) customs and expectations. Most of all, I was always conscious of my lack of expertise in many areas that I had to discuss. But, as I argue below, I have been encouraged by scholars who have celebrated bravery and even amateurism. And I have always been certain that, whatever my deficiencies in subject matter or skill, this study had to embrace and bring together both texts and approaches usually studied and pursued in other disciplines or sub-specialisms. In both the usual and more archaic meanings, this is an essay – a sketch towards a larger treatment and an effort: my best shot, to return to the modern argot from which I began thinking about my subject.

One of the things that this study has taught me is how image-making in the past, as in the present, is the work of many contributors who contribute in very different ways, with ideas, advice, labour, finance, organization and so on. The same is true of these books. To a greater extent than my previous publications this study depended upon resources: research expenses and, most of all, time. Over the last decade or so large increases in student numbers, together with the bureaucratic administration that has followed endless assessments, reviews and appraisals, has often inhibited large-scale research projects. I owe my opportunity to work on this scale to the generosity of a number of organizations and individuals. As I indicated, my first work was begun on a Huntington Library fellowship and a Mellon fellowship at the California Institute of Technology in 1992–3. I would like to thank the Huntington and Caltech and the late Martin Ridge, Robert Ritchie and John Ledyard for that vital year. On return to England, I was in 1994 seconded for five years from undergraduate teaching to the School of Research and Graduate Studies at the University of Southampton and I am deeply grateful to the late Professor Peter Ucko who persuaded me to stay and take advantage of a period of interdisciplinary graduate teaching. In 2001–2 I was awarded a Fletcher Jones Senior Fellowship at the Huntington, where I began to draft chapters of the first volume and to get a sense of the direction of my study. For 2003–4 I was awarded a prize fellowship by the Humboldt Foundation to be held at the Max Planck Institute for History at Göttingen. I am enormously grateful to the Humboldt Stiftung, to Professor Hartmut Lehman who sponsored me for it and to Dr Georg Schütte who provided both academic support and generous hospitality which made a year in Germany as enjoyable as it was productive. In Göttingen I carried out much of the research for the later seventeenth century with excellent and efficient library provision.

But what finally enabled me to embark on writing three volumes was an award of a Major Research Fellowship by the Leverhulme Trust. This three-year research award made what would otherwise have been an impossibility seem at least nearly possible and has enabled me, as I write, to complete two volumes and to make considerable headway with the third. Words cannot express my gratitude to the Trustees for the award of this fellowship which, as well as time and funds, gave me the confidence that the assessors in a highly competitive process could see the importance of what I was attempting.

For permission to take up these awards, I would like to thank the Universities of Southampton and Warwick and especially Queen Mary, University of London.

More personally, I would like to thank all those colleagues and friends who continue to provide advice, suggestions and a willing ear: George Bernard, Tom Corns, Neil Gregor, Annabel Patterson, Joad Raymond and Mark Stoyle, and my new colleagues Julia Boffey, Warren Boutcher, Jerry Brotton, David Colclough, Lisa Jardine and Evelyn Welch. I am especially grateful to Steve Zwicker who has without any complaint indulged me in countless discussions of this subject and provided myriad helpful suggestions and Greg Walker who nobly and most helpfully read and commented on the whole first volume, giving me the great benefit of his considerable knowledge, insight and eye for a sloppy thought or formulation. Peter Lake has not only been a wonderful sounding board to my project over several years, but also kindly surrendered his anonymity as a press reader and made very helpful suggestions for improving the argument.

Once again I have been fortunate to benefit from the encouragement and skills of the staff at Yale University Press. Tom Buhler read the entire script very carefully, made several very helpful suggestions and saved me from some errors and slips. Robert Baldock has, as always, been a supportive editor and friend from the beginning of this project – even when he discovered he was getting three books not one; and my agent Peter Robinson has been good enough to take care of yet another book which has made neither him nor me any beyond intellectual profit. I would also like to thank, at Yale, Beth Humphries who copyedited the script, drawing attention to any lack of clarity; Rachael Lonsdale who with ingenuity and good humour tracked down the illustrations; and especially Candida Brazil who oversaw the book's path to production with her customary skill, attention to detail and helpfulness.

The dedication is deceptively short and simple but really does speak volumes.

December 2007

INTRODUCTION

Politics may appear to be a timeless business and art, but in reality much has changed even in our own time. Since the 1980s, and even more latterly, politics has appeared less the business of ministries, elections and parliamentary oratory, more a matter of spin, news management, image manipulation and photo opportunities, of focus groups and internet blogs. Historians, however, still writing about politics in the past, in nineteenth- and early twentieth-century terms, have failed to explore these aspects of the political process. Though from antiquity politics has always been about image, the modes of representation and media of communication, we have been slow to explore or analyse them or relate these aspects of rule to the success or failure of past governments. Yet the age of the Renaissance, as well as the age of learning, magnificence and display, was an age of new technologies in print and portraiture that transformed the presentations and perceptions of princes.

The Tudor and Stuart period is one of the best known and most popular periods of British history. The characters of Henry VIII, Queen Elizabeth and Charles I are the subject of frequent biographies and TV programmes, not least because they were charismatic figures who imprinted themselves on their own age and on our memories. And yet, though we have many histories of events and personalities, there has been no full examination of how, or the ways in which, successful rulers impressed themselves upon their subjects: that is, of how they persuaded sometimes reluctant people to follow controversial courses and not only to obey them but regard them as sacred. Similarly, we have not fully examined how and why the monarchs who failed got the message wrong. Though we are generally familiar with images of early modern monarchs, there has been little analysis of the verbal and visual representations of rulers as arts essential to their authority in dangerous and divided times.

This is the subject of my study of representations of early modern rule. My purpose has been to study all the means by which rulers from Henry VIII to

Queen Anne sought to establish and sustain their authority, enhance their standing and reputation, and refute or neuter criticism and opposition, through changing and often difficult circumstances. Though there has been some work, of course, on royal speeches, portraits and ceremonies, my study differs fundamentally in scope and approach. First, unlike any earlier work, it is an interdisciplinary study which embraces words, images in all their forms, and rituals and performances; by bringing them together I hope I have cast light on how programmes to represent rulers were devised, who constructed them, and the role of monarchs themselves in the fashioning and disseminating of their image. As well as bringing together research too often separated into the sub-fields of political, cultural, social and economic history, I also engage with new methods and interests in the history of visual culture, literary studies and the history of consumption, and some critical work on the nature of representations and textual performances. What follows is based on study of the texts, modes and forms of representation, and images, especially the neglected engravings, woodcuts, medals and coins, which circulated images of authority to a consuming public which was increasingly eager to acquire them.

Secondly, rather than take a top-down view of representation as propaganda devised to manipulate subjects (as does much of the older work on this subject), this study reinforces the argument that subjects participated in the construction of images of power and responded variously to those images. Counsel and criticism, satire and mockery, the burning of books and desecration of pictures, civic ritual and popular festivity, were all dialogues with representations of rule, as much as with authority itself. Though this is a vast subject which I cannot hope to tackle as it deserves, I have attempted to sample and assess how images performed by locating them in the discourses, aesthetic and religious, social and political, and in the particular circumstances which shaped their production and reception among different communities at different times.

Thirdly, this study of representations of rule deals with a long period, from the early sixteenth to the early eighteenth centuries. Though this does not permit a full monographic study of each form of representation for each ruler, it enables us to see how rulers fashioned their image in relation to that of predecessors and to compare and contrast the ways in which Tudor and Stuart rulers, male and female sovereigns, adults and minors, Catholic and Protestant monarchs both shared vocabularies and styles of self-representation and yet differed in the ways in which they projected themselves and their authority to their subjects. Furthermore, addressing to the long period from the Reformation to the Augustan age facilitates a reconsideration of the Tudors and early Stuarts from a longer perspective, enables a fresh re-evaluation of the Reformation, the Civil War and 1688 revolution as crises of representation, and places early modern

England in the context of recent work on the emerging image of the monarch as a focus of national identity in the eighteenth century.

The authority of monarchy in early modern England was not founded on any new institutional or military developments. The business of government was the art of securing compliance. While patronage was central to that process, compliance depended to a large extent on images and changes in the perceptions of authority. Of course, monarchs had always been concerned with their image. But from the reign of Henry VIII, scholars have (rightly) argued, there was new emphasis on, and new attempts to control, images of power – through the royal word, portraits, buildings and festivals. The break from Rome made necessary the constitution of a new political culture, and it was arguably this new political culture that secured the Tudor dynasty and the English state. Where elsewhere in Europe Reformation undermined royal authority, in England Catholic rituals were appropriated and secularized as liturgies for the worship of the ruler and the mystification of power. Queen Elizabeth, it is said, drew on the cult of the Virgin Mary in representations of her rule and, not least through such representations, turned the disadvantages of her situation and sex into effective strategies of governance. Through speech and writing, palaces and progresses, coins and seals, the arts of portraiture and miniature, the Tudors, scholars have agreed, constructed a cult of monarchy that was the foundation of a strong dynasty.

James I, from his experience in Scotland where the arts of majesty were less developed and mystification of rule suspected, seemed less concerned with magnificence and display. James represented his kingship primarily through the word. That he failed to win the same affection from his subjects evidences less the failure of his policies – historians have begun to regard him as an astute ruler – than the importance of image and James's failure to appreciate it. Where the Tudors and especially Elizabeth had responded to what the public desired to see and hear of their sovereign, James never got the message right. And the more sophisticated court of his son, for all its attention to the arts of representation, failed, the scholarly consensus has it, because it appeared foreign and popish.

While we may agree in general about the Tudors' success and the Stuarts' failure, many of these assertions require interrogation and complication. Fundamental questions remain about the representations of early modern rulers (Queen Mary in particular) and the relation of representation to effective rule. How did rulers shape the language and rhetoric of their pamphlets and proclamations to the shifting circumstances of their reign? How was the royal image refigured through decades of mounting religious and factional division and of popular unrest? How did a burgeoning print culture and an increasing appetite for news destabilize the royal image and give rise to new genres and modes of representation?

If important questions remain about the Tudors and early Stuarts, work on the second half of the seventeenth century has only recently begun. The Civil War and republic raise important questions about representation: how, we need to ask, did Royalists and Parliamentarians compete for the languages and symbols that validated rule? Was the collapse of republican government a failure to devise a republican culture that erased the powerful memories of monarchy? And how, as Lord Protector, did Oliver Cromwell redeploy a quasi-regal court culture to validate his rule?

For much of the period after 1660 the issues of royal image and representation remain largely uncharted. How, we must ask, did Charles II adapt his representation to a world in which, for all the restoration of old forms, regicide had partially demystified authority and republicanism had bequeathed new political languages and perceptions? Memories of civil war, ideas of Davidic kingship, genres of romance, even debauchery and pornography, all need to be studied as representations of Charles II's monarchy in a transformed culture of politics. Hitherto there has been no study of James II's representation, of the attempts he made to reconstitute the image of monarchy, or of the centrality of Catholicism to his notions of spectacle and display; nor, indeed, of the role of Dutch and Whig visual propaganda in undermining James's authority. While recent scholarship has begun to elucidate the image of William III, we have yet to explain the ways in which Whig political supremacy was secured through a dominance of all the modes of representation – literature and history, portrait and cartoon, texts of morality and memory. And though the image of Anne as mother has recently been addressed, her evocation of Elizabethan style, her publicization of Stuart dynasty, and yet her celebration of an almost bourgeois domesticity all require explication as strategies of rule in the circumstances of Augustan culture and post-revolutionary politics. By 1700, it would seem that the arts of demystification had become as important to monarchy as the sacred mysteries of Gloriana had been a century earlier.

Throughout the early modern period, the age which produced some of the most powerful and enduring images of monarchy in our history, image was central to the exercise of authority; but what constituted a successful image? How did different monarchs (including a boy and women), consorts and princes deploy and revise established images of monarchy through their reigns? To what extent did rulers oversee or control the texts and icons of rule, and how far were they manipulated by others? How far were words and images targeted at different audiences, and what part did the desires and expectations of subjects play in the construction of royal representations? How far is it appropriate to talk about a struggle for representation, either at court or in the country, and what was the relation of that struggle to political contest? It is such questions that these books seek to begin to answer.

In the books in which I map this subject, each section or chapter will deal with a reign and will be subdivided. I will examine the principal genres of royal representation – texts, images and pageants – the divisions over and challenges to official words and images, and the success in (sometimes literally) selling an image of the ruler. Under words, I explore royal speeches, proclamations and declarations not just (as is usual) for their content, but as artful rhetorical performances designed to persuade, as modern political addresses do, by invoking patriotism, self-interest and anxiety by various devices. I also analyse, often for the first time, royal writings, such as songs, poems, prayers, transla- tions and biblical commentaries, as images of monarchical rule and represen- tations of the particular person of the king or queen. The chapters on images embrace not only portraits but engravings and woodcuts, which have been neglected, and seals, medals and coins which often specifically connect visual images to moments and events in the reign. The chapters on ceremonies and rituals discuss the state occasions on which the monarch was presented to the people – the funeral of his or her predecessor, coronation, marriage, state entries to parliament and so forth – and also the daily rounds of court ritual (Garter festivals, for example) and royal progresses throughout the country. For each reign, a brief discussion endeavours to begin to gauge the responses to these official scripts, images and performances by sampling the reactions reported and the evidence of resistance and counter-propaganda. By bringing together subjects usually studied separately and by scholars in different departments, I hope that we gain a clearer picture of the themes of represen- tation and are better able to reinterpret individual texts and portraits in the light of them.

The royal image, of course, was not fixed, even for the course of a lifetime. For each monarch, especially the long reigns of Henry VIII, Elizabeth and Charles II, I endeavour, in so far as space allows, to convey a sense of how the image and representation of the sovereign were reconstituted both by the normal passage of time that changed vigorous youth to old age or, say, single to married status, and by events, enacted by design or happenstance, that compelled the ruler to change image as well as policy. Obvious examples here, of course, are the break from Rome under Henry, the civil war in Charles I's reign, and the 1688 revolution for both James II and William III. But as important, though less obvious, in redirecting representations of the ruler were events such as the Armada and Gunpowder Plot, rebellions and revolts, and scandals and scares, such as the Overbury murder or the Popish Plot.

The books are chronologically arranged and the sections and chapters bring together the media that fashioned the image of each ruler and were intricately connected with their style of rule, policies, reputation and success. But throughout each volume and across all three I will be plotting a long historical arc that will also help to identify shifts in the technologies and genres of representation. Importantly, I wish to argue how, on the one side, the wider dissemination of print and news, new forms of portrait and engraving, and more refined minting techniques, and, on the other, growing literacy, a market economy, habits of collecting and widespread discussion of politics in inns and coffee-houses transformed the nature of, and contest over, representation and image.

As well as making contributions to our understanding of each reign, then, this study has a number of large arguments to make that will refine and revise recent scholarship. It reassesses the role of print in disseminating and criticizing authority; it traces changes in the style of royal portraiture in relation to shifting tastes and the emergence of bourgeois (and even popular) interest in collecting; it documents shifts in forms of spectacle (the increased use of fireworks, for instance) and the ways in which audiences shaped as well as witnessed ceremonial occasions. Most of all, revisiting from a very different perspective the subject of the king's two bodies, the books explore the dichotomy that existed throughout the period between the need for the mystification of authority and the equal necessity for the ruler to be popular and 'accessible'. Only those rulers, I argue, who successfully negotiated that dichotomy – notably Elizabeth and Charles II – enjoyed a reputation that enabled them to survive crises and even enhanced their authority.

Originally I set out to write one large book. But the chronological range, the depth of original research necessitated by whole areas where there is no secondary literature to draw on, and the range of media examined has made anything beyond the most superficial survey impossible within the pages of one volume. I have therefore written my project as three books. While each will contribute to the large argument about *both* the sacralization and demystification of regality in early modernity, the separate volumes each constitute an independent study of, respectively, images of Tudor monarchy, representations of seventeenth-century kings and commonwealths, and of late seventeenth-century royal rulers.

The central subject of *Selling the Tudor Monarchy: Authority and Image in Sixteenth-Century England* is the consequences for monarchical representation of Henry VIII's break from Rome: the need to sacralize secular authority and the person of the monarch and the challenge that presented to Henry's successors, a minor and two women, one Protestant, one Catholic. As well as offering important revisions of our understanding of Henry and Elizabeth, this is the first serious study of the image of Edward VI and Mary Tudor and of the relationship of their representations to their reputations and rule.

The second volume, on images of seventeenth-century kings and commonwealths, is concerned with how the early Stuarts endeavoured to represent their authority and how political conflict was inseparable from a mounting competition for public support – a contest for representation. It seeks to explain why the day of regicide also saw the publication of a text that both raised kingship to the most sacred heights and was also the bestseller of the century. It will trace how the Commonwealth failed to free itself from the cult of personality and from monarchical forms and how the success of the Cromwellian Protectorate lay in its appropriating them.

The third volume, on images of later seventeenth-century monarchy, deals with the implications of revolution and republic, Restoration and 1688 for representations of rule and new styles of kingship. It considers the Restoration impulse to continuity and change, Charles II's skilful embrace of new and ambiguous styles of kingship, and the ways in which his successors fashioned their image in a rapidly changing culture. It endeavours to explain how James, who had successfully cultivated popularity as Duke of York, lost the initiative as king, but also describes a fierce battle for hearts and minds waged between Williamites and Jacobites for long after 1688. A chapter on Queen Anne looks at a woman who borrowed Elizabethan modes of representation and who was the last monarch to touch for the king's evil but who also signals the end of a cult of monarchy that passed with the succession of a foreign dynasty which was the first to be the subject of scatological cartoons.

Though each contributes to large arguments about the whole period of early modern English history, each book has its own distinct period, subject and argument. Though I retain a historian's inclination to chronological organization, sections and chapters each study a form of representation and revisit the history of the royal image from a different perspective. While the books are thus arranged for the sake of clarity and so that readers interested in, say, following visual representations might read the relevant sections across reigns – and indeed across the volumes – my purpose has been for each reign to bring royal words, images and rituals together and to explicate them in conversation with each other and with other contesting representations. In the chapter that follows, I present a review of my own conversations with a variety of disciplines and scholars of different periods which and who have stimulated the questions I have asked and influenced my approaches to texts and terms – indeed to the subject of representation itself.

PART I

CONCEPTS AND METHODS

There are no natural symbols.
Mary Douglas, *Natural Symbols* (1970)

CHAPTER 1

Representing Rule
TERMS, PREMISES, APPROACHES

I

It is a truism, frequently stated (if seldom acted upon) that the present has much to learn from the past.[1] But the reverse is also true: our present experiences may open questions about and perspectives upon the past that lay unasked or unexplored by earlier generations. Many historians will be suspicious of such a claim and, rightly, wary of the risk of presentism: the imposition upon the past of our own preoccupations, values and vocabularies. Yet a dialogue between past and present has always been intrinsic to the study of history and often beneficial to it. The history of women, the family and sexuality, for example, unquestionably emerged from twentieth-century questioning and refiguring of gender roles, yet opened rich new understandings of aspects of the past which had remained unknown, or had even seemed unknowable. The recently fashionable field of enquiry known as the history of the book was similarly born out of late twentieth-century developments such as the computer and internet, and questions about the long-term survival of the printed word as the privileged medium of communication. Far, however, from distorting the past (a problematic notion to which I shall return), contemporary engagement with the book, the commerce of print, the production of meaning, and the reception and reading of texts has stimulated some of the most interesting historical writing of the last two decades and even begun to change approaches to the most traditional of historiographies – political history. An ever-changing present opens new insights into our past, not least by relocating seemingly timeless things – books or the family, for instance – in the changing past, in history.

The subject of this study derives directly from my experience of politics in the last quarter of the twentieth century and first years of the twenty-first. This may seem oddly specific. Politics, after all, has always been part of our lives and has traditionally been the most studied aspect of the past. However, to anyone who is late middle-aged, living in England or America especially (and doubt-less other countries I know less well), there has been a major shift in the nature, meaning and conduct of politics that we might characterize as a shift from institutions, issues and policies, or parliamentary and democratic procedures, to an emphasis on image, appearance, representation and the media and modes of self-presentation, self-projection and advertisement. Critics depict these changes as a shift from substance to style, honest debate to spin, even from a politics of representation (in both senses of appealing to and standing for the people) to that of misrepresentation. Whatever one's attitude to such changes, they have only recently, and by no means even now broadly, influ-enced historians' approaches to the history of politics. Whether writing about medieval barons, early modern monarchs or modern parliaments and parties, historians – and especially perhaps nineteenth- and twentieth-century English historians brought up with a circumscribed notion of the political – have in the main studied politics as affiliations, struggles for place and ideological contests. Such concepts of the political are, of course, themselves bound by time, are part of history. What are central to our experience today – carefully crafted rhetoric, posed images, choreographed spectacles – have more traditionally been the subjects of intellectual and cultural history, or, as often, been studied by other disciplines. Even when it has been recognized that ideas, images and rituals are not separable from an understanding of power and authority in the past, they have been subordinated, at least until very recently, to an emphasis on 'real power', the proper subject of the historian.

From their very different perspectives, Marxist scholars and students of intellectual history tended, by respectively subordinating or reifying, to sepa-rate ideas from the daily thrust of political struggle – as endless old textbooks (and some not so old) with closing chapters on culture and ideas testify.[2] While scholars of the Warburg School were certainly and fruitfully interested in the connections between ideas and politics (and in the cases of Frances Yates and Roy Strong contributed greatly to a historical understanding of monarchical ceremonies), they concentrated on the elite classical tradition and arcane Platonic and hermetic philosophies that all but excluded the ordinary people from the domains of ideas – or politics. From a rather different approach, the historians of mentalités have also tended to write a cultural history with politics either left out or on the margins.[3]

Rather than academic historians, it has been scholars of other disciplines who, over the last two or three decades, have theorized, and led an insistence on, the porous interconnections of culture and politics, representation and authority, in the present and the past. Far from feeling a need to protect the distinction between past and present concerns, many critics have questioned the existence of any history that claims not to have been written out of present concerns; in some cases they have self-consciously rewritten history to support contemporary causes or campaigns: for women's or gay rights, for example. Even research without such obvious polemical agenda has freely moved between periods, applying the perspectives of one to another and of the present to all. The work of the influential ethnographer, the late Clifford Geertz, has moved between studies of nineteenth-century Bali and Elizabethan England, applying to each a theory of the theatricality of power which clearly owed much to a late twentieth-century preoccupation with social roles, performance and play.[4] A variety of literary scholars and cultural critics, fascinated with the personality, performance and perceptions of Princess Diana, in life and after death, have readily compared her with earlier figures, such as Elizabeth I, and been drawn to psychological researches on charisma and on the importance to authority of affective bonds, personations and myths, none the traditional materials of the historian.[5] Studying another queen of hearts, a literary scholar has written of Queen Victoria that 'the adulation around her . . . looked back to the courtly adoration of Elizabeth I and forward to the manufactured glamour of Hollywood stars'.[6] Modern cinema, it is suggested, may have something to offer the historian of modern and early modern monarchy.

The reference to 'manufactured glamour' hints at very different working practices, and premises, to those of most historians. Scholars from other disciplines who have travelled freely from present to past (and vice versa), and who espouse rather than eschew the politics of culture and of their own writing, have tended to take a very different approach to the materials of the past – both which materials we admit or privilege as sources and the ways in which we interpret them. Influenced by a variety of theoretical pronouncements and reflections (often too simply herded together under the label postmodernism), many critics, especially literary critics and art historians, have argued that representations, misrepresentations, myths and fictions are as much the proper materials of historical study as the 'facts' and 'truths' historians claim – which more radical critics (notoriously) describe as just another set of representations or stories devised out of, and for, present concerns.[7] Critics have tended to read such materials not as documents with one meaning to be excavated and communicated but as unstable texts containing a multiplicity of meanings and significations and open to various, shifting and contesting interpretations. Though I have been charged with underestimating their willingness to embrace such approaches, I still believe that, though there is some sign of change, this is not how historians approach their documents.[8]

But it is through their address to the present, to representations, to multiplicity and instability, to the rhetoricity of all texts and the textuality of all performances of power that, I argue, other disciplines have much to contribute to the study of the pre-modern past – because it was a past concerned with just such matters. Central to the culture of modern consumer capitalism is the act of advertising – to entice, persuade and draw consumers to a product by selling a lifestyle that it promises. The effectiveness of an advertising campaign, its use of words or slogans, logo or design, its evocations of past or future, of hope or anxiety, its manipulation of fear and desire, is essential to the fortune and social standing of a company.[9] No less modern capitalist polities have drawn on the advertiser's arts to sell policies or personalities by means of soundbites, photo-opportunities, media manipulation and moments of carefully staged informality and intimacy.[10] In the most pessimistic view, modern politicians do not use these media to advance a programme or even a party; rather, some claim, the political process is reduced to nothing but a series of reconstructions and re-presentations devised from analysis and focus groups – a surrender of content to process and of real authority to image and fashion.[11]

Such diagnoses are not only too pessimistic and fail to explain how new and initially unpopular ideas do take hold; they also fail to understand or historicize our present condition. For though the modern media of communication, television, cinema and the internet, have enabled and increased a politics of representation and image, they are arguably also essential to a participatory democracy. In a modern democratic state (and, as the collapse of the old Eastern bloc might suggest, ultimately in many non-democratic states) the exercise of authority depends upon communication with, appeal to, the people. Because, at least in the West, the authoritative icons of popular culture are sporting heroes, rock musicians, models and celebrities – including ordinary, formerly uncelebrated people made famous by reality TV – politicians, seeking to influence and gain power, draw on the texts of popular culture and seek association with its champions. Moreover, for all the cult of celebrity and fashion, which politicians depend upon as much as manipulate, cultural authority still depends, and is seen to depend, on traditions, histories and memories. These too, albeit often repackaged for the present as heritage or nostalgia, also form essential elements of the advertiser's and politician's rhetoric of persuasion and authority.[12]

What strikes a scholar of my interests, with thirty years' experience of working on early modern England, is not how alien but how familiar this brand of cultural politics is. For in their effort to establish security for their dynasty and authority for the monarch, the early Tudors had to persuade the subjects of an England which had been divided by over a century of internal conflict of their right to rule. To remain on their thrones, as well as acquiring wealth and fostering good relations with nobles who could provide armies, they needed to secure, and secure in a polity increasingly divided by confessional differences, the compliance of subjects through careful acts of representation – in words, images and spectacular performances that did not simply reflect or enact power but helped to construct it.[13] In their need to present and re-present themselves and to construct their authority, the Tudors, and their Stuart successors, were by no means unique. But I shall suggest that the reason they remain so powerful *in our present culture*, the reason almost all of us can imagine, picture or quote several of them, is that the circumstances in which they found themselves, especially after the break from Rome, the publicization of and contest for authority, and the rise of new media of communication, combined to impel and enable a politics of representation different in kind as well as degree to what had gone before or what immediately followed them.

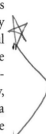

In this study, I examine the images and representations of the Tudor and Stuart rulers and the relationship of their representations to the success of their rule, to the authority they wielded and to the political struggles of their reigns. At first reading this may seem like a rehearsal of a very familiar story. A huge amount has been published by historians and biographers on the Tudor and Stuart monarchs, especially Henry VIII, Elizabeth I and Charles I. Art historians and literary scholars have worked extensively on portraits and panegyrics, on processions and festivals. However, to a regrettably great extent, scholarship has remained compartmentalized and fragmented. Historians have, perhaps on account of their methodological differences, been reluctant to take up the work of critics on the rhetorics and symbolics of power; and among many (especially left-leaning) critics, the study of high politics has for long been unfashionable: suspect and subordinate to the recovery of the subjected and marginal. Moreover, since the earlier work of Roy Strong, Stephen Orgel and others on early modern culture and politics, new scholarly developments and approaches have complicated questions of authorship and production and directed greater attention to the audiences and reception of texts and performances. Recent work on aspects of visual culture neglected by traditions of connoisseurship – the engraved print or woodcut, for example – and on material culture has shifted the emphasis from hegemonic elite proclamations to languages, symbols and objects that circulated between elites and the populace.[14] Other texts and materials – early modern coins and medals – little studied for decades outside the professional circles of specialists and collectors, yet await a full integration into the history of the representation and commerce of authority.

What distinguishes this study, then, is first an attempt to bring together the scholarship on culture and politics, on words, images and spectacle in all their forms, and to deploy in analysis of them the methods and perspectives of a variety of disciplines as well as my training as a historian. Secondly, rather than taking a view of representations as propaganda devised to manipulate subjects, the model that informs this project and emerges from it is a model of early modern authority as a negotiation rather than autocratic enactment.[15] Thirdly, though I am concerned in each section and chapter with the specific circumstances of a reign or (in the Commonwealth's or Oliver Cromwell's case) regimen, each volume (and the books taken together) posits a number of large arguments about the whole period from 1500 to 1700. If the scope and range of this study are unusually broad, it is because I believe that only an address to the *longue durée* from the Reformation to the Augustan age enables those large arguments and places the history of each ruler in the longer arc which offers fresh perspectives on individual rulers and particular moments. Here the English Reformation, Civil War and 1688 revolution are reconsidered as crises of representation as well as state; the 'success' of Elizabeth I is evaluated by the criteria of her memory as well as monarchy; and Queen Anne's efforts to re-establish Stuart dynasty are traced through the contested representations and memories of Elizabeth I and Charles I and of the events of 1642 and 1688. Throughout I shall explore how and to what extent the rhetoric and style of each ruler shaped the politics of the reign; how different monarchs appropriated, revised and redeployed vocabularies and symbols that conveyed authority; and, necessarily more briefly, how others received and contested such representations. We shall also consider the economic, technological and social changes that, across this whole period and at particular moments, fashioned or influenced the construction, the media, and the distribution of, and the audiences for and consumers of, royal representations.

It is early modern English rulers and a long early modern age that I wish to re-examine from the perspectives of modern experience and modern and postmodern scholarship. Later, I shall argue the special place and importance of the sixteenth and seventeenth centuries and their monarchs in *any* history of the representation of rule and culture of authority. First, however, I want to turn to a number of ill-defined and contentious terms and concepts already used here too loosely. And I shall glance at how scholarly work on periods long before and after the early modern and on polities other than England has grappled with the questions of central concern to me: the nature of power and authority, their representation and reception. Some recent studies by scholars of other periods, whether historians, art historians or critics, raise questions and take approaches that have not been pursued by early modernists; and they invite us to rethink what was common, as well as exceptional, for early modern kings and queens in the history of the arts and technologies of representing rule and constructing authority.

In any discussions of the culture of authority and images of power, a number of terms and concepts arise that require, if not exact definition, interrogation. The most obvious are the words power and authority themselves. Once asked to distinguish the two, I responded by characterizing power as the effective means by which a ruler could enforce his will: I listed armies, law enforcement agents and instruments of force and punishments as the constituents of power.

Authority, I suggested, was more a cultural construction: a set of codes and norms worked out by communities, small and large, that, to give an example, enables the chairman of a committee to steer the proceedings or a lecturer to expect silence and attention until the end of his discourse. While I still think the distinction I then endeavoured to formulate is helpful, as well as being simplistic (even armies are cultural communities) it is not supported by the etymology of the terms: power from the old Norman French *poeir* literally meant to be able, without any definition of means; while authority stems from the same root as author (*auctor*), one who possesses agency. The use of both terms has shifted over time and I suspect that my attempt to make a distinction owed something to a post-war upbringing, the cultural memories of armed conflict and experience of the Cold War arms race. Interestingly, in more recent historical work, in a variety of fields, the use of the terms has been rather different. In his magisterial study of Old Regime Europe, when several regimes had mighty armies at their disposal, Tim Blanning boldly states, 'Power depends as much on perception as reality'; and his title and book locate power very much in cultural constructions and practices.[16] In a recent book on George III, John Barrell sees the power the king exercised as rooted, in an age of sensibility, in an affective bond between king and people, strengthened by the violent regicide in France and the personal tragedy of George's madness.[17] The affective component of power informs recent books on rulers as far apart as Julius Caesar and Queen Victoria whose power is located in the people's need for 'a central focus of imaginative and affective investment'.[18] John Plunkett's location of a ruler's power in the needs and desires of subjects is echoed in other recent work on the Bayeux Tapestry and indeed on early modern England, especially Queen Elizabeth, whom one scholar has described as 'the subject of a bourgeois fantasy'.[19] Such discussions of 'the problematics of power' and emphasis on the role of subjects in its construction and conferral mark a shift in our understanding that has surely been influenced by the collapse of the Soviet bloc and a media enfranchisement of the people.[20] In studies of different periods I have sampled from recent writings, power and authority are no longer construed simply as the capacity of sovereign agents to enact their will, but as complex negotiations between rulers and subjects. Such negotiations are not fixed but contingent; and they also complicate the contrast we used to draw between authority and opposition. For, if the people are not merely subject to but the shared authors, that is makers, of power, opposition itself involves negotiation. Writing of the embracing of Queen Victoria by her subjects, Plunkett astutely observes: 'This condition is the key to both her power and her powerlessness'.[21] What one might add is that the need of subjects to embrace and appropriate her is similarly the key to their impotence as well as agency. Of course, Victorian England was a very different polity to early modern England. Yet the new emphases on the affective bonds of rulers and subjects, on (and the language is now common) the psychology of power, on the complex constructions of and negotiations over power and authority, most of all the insistence on power (as well as authority) as a cultural phenomenon (rather than a force outside, even dominant over, culture) opens helpful insights into the exercise and representation of rule in early modern England. Such new insights will inform the general approach taken in this study.

Most of the examples I have used while discussing power and authority are the examples of monarchs; and the monarch, of course, is an institution, a member of a dynasty or family, and an individual person, male or female, adult or child. Walter Bagehot laid emphasis on the humanity of regal authority when he defined monarchy as 'a government in which the attention of the nation is concentrated on one person doing interesting actions'.[22] Bagehot's focus on the 'one person' and his or her performance directs us to both the private and the public, the human and the mystical aspects of monarchical rule – to what long ago Ernst Kantorowicz discussed as the king's two bodies.[23] Kantorowicz's model is familiar to students of medieval history but has perhaps been inadequately explored for later periods. Yet it would seem that the affective bond that scholars have lately discerned as a vital aspect of power was intimately bound up with the ruler's possession and representation of a body: a sexual body that was generative and human as well as mystical. Responding to what one scholar of coronations requested – an analysis of rule that transcended 'the traditional political history of great events' – as well as to our own cultural moment, several historians of monarchy, and still more myriad biographers of kings and queens, have focused on the sex lives of great rulers.[24] While this at times, especially in popular biographies, may appear a gratuitous bid for readers, such work has illuminated the similar preoccupations of subjects in the past with the amorous and sexual lives of their sovereigns. Henry VIII and Charles II were infamous for their sexual relationships in their own day; Queen Elizabeth, we have learned recently, was the subject of widespread gossip about illicit pregnancies, malformed genitalia and lesbian inclinations.[25] The historian of Victoria's image finds 'a very lurid attention to [her] sexuality'; and the image and memory of Edward II and James I, to name but two, are inseparable from contemporary knowledge and disapproval of their transgressive sexuality.[26] Though such negative images evidence the failure of these rulers to control their representation, they also indicate how, in a monarchical rule that was both public and private, the representation of the royal body was essential to rule – that is to the construction of a bond between ruler and subject. Almost throughout history, the concept and language of the body politic have expressed the need for a corporeal, personal, as well as mystical, bond; and, at least for an age of chivalry, amorous language has been part of the discourse of state.[27] Following Aristotle's exposition in the *Ethics* and *Politics* of the family as the origin of the polis, the monarch's own marriage and family have been (and remain) vital aspects of successful rule. Family, marriage and sexuality were in a monarchy public as well as private spheres; it was by their personal circumstances, and through representation of their personal circumstances, that rulers might succeed in conjoining their public and private bodies and bridge the distance between ruler and subject. Or not. John Plunkett, analysing Victoria's publicization of idealized, intimate, married life in photographs and the queen's own *Journal of Our Life in the Highlands*, concludes that 'the British royal family was able to dominate the imagined community of the nation' and to help to cohere the polity by such means.[28] Marital and sexual circumstances being 'contingent and personal', not every ruler could present such an idealized vision of marriage that connected the royal family to the family of the realm.[29] But we are again invited by such studies to reconsider how each of the rulers of our period – males married (once or several times), women (married, or single), a boy, a bisexual, fathers, mothers, the childless or infertile – personified and deployed the tropes of family, marriage and body so as to make an intimate connection with the people, as well as to represent a dynasty. In our study of representation, we must always remember that it is the personal body as well as the public body of the ruler that is being publicized and displayed, and that the texts of the private, interior life are as much (albeit different) representations of rule as the more obvious public declarations and proclamations. Love poems, we shall see, not only expressed a relationship between royal wooer and the object of desire, but figured and helped form affective bonds with subjects that were essential to the exercise of authority in a personal monarchy.

All authority requires legitimation but the need to legitimize and the challenge of legitimizing applied especially to new dynasties, new forms of rule, or to those who acquired authority or exercised it in unusual circumstances – after the break from Rome, the regicide, or the 1688 revolution, for example. As the origin of the term implies, the legitimate is that which conforms to the laws or the rules and traditions of the polity. Rulers could, and needed to, appeal to those laws and codes and could claim them to support their regimen. But we need to see legitimation as more than a legal process and as one by no means controlled by authority.

Indeed, more even than a historical process, legitimation was, as recent scholars of diverse periods and geographies insist, a cultural process. Andrew Bell, in his study of spectacle in the Greek and Roman cities, writes of 'the abstract legitimation of the populus' and specifically discusses the legitimation of Octavian through carefully devised popular spectacles.[30] Discussing the problems faced by a foreign dynasty with a highly controversial claim to the throne of England, Suzanne Lewis reads the Bayeux Tapestry as an elaborate pictorial and material legitimation of Norman rule, one which, by drawing on genres of epic and crusade, presented a historical narrative that helped to effect the 'process of cultural and political transformation from Anglo Saxon to Anglo Norman'.[31] Lewis argues that, while the message and purpose of the tapestry are certain, by making his own viewing and reading the viewer becomes complicit in the representation and thereby legitimizes the revolutionary change to feudal rule; indeed effaces its revolutionary aspect to accept Norman rule as the natural course.[32] Coming back to our period, a historian of early modern coronations, discussing the doubts surrounding the titles of a series of monarchs from Richard III to William III, demonstrated how, rather than a matter of laws or codes, 'no myth was too implausible to be availed of in the process of legitimation'.[33] Legitimation unquestionably involved an *appeal to the past*, to tradition; but, necessarily, at moments of crisis or change, legitimation might require a *departure from tradition*, if a departure not publicly proclaimed. Lois Schwoerer, analysing the modes of legitimizing the 1688 revolution which removed the Stuarts from the throne, described ceremony and spectacle as having 'wrapped change in traditional forms'.[34] More than a narrowly legal or constitutional process, the legitimation of a ruler necessitated the (more or less) difficult process of establishing an interpretation of the past, as well as present, texts of the culture which subjects were willing to endorse; at times even to create a shared myth. Legitimation I take in this study to be a cultural process enacted in and through histories, paintings, legends and prophecies as much as the usual political pronouncements, enacted that is by means of fictions as much as truths.

The legitimation, exercise, representation and perception of authority are inextricably connected to cultural memory. Memory has recently become a fashionable field of enquiry that has probably been stimulated by our twentieth-century experiences of world war, atrocities and the Holocaust, of a perceived need to remember in order to prevent repetition, and by a hope that remembering and commemorating might refashion or strengthen a shared moral vision.[35] Memory can indeed be a powerful moral force; but, as Neo-Nazism, Holocaust denial, or even the privileging of some atrocities over others have shown, memory is contentious and divided, deployable as partisan rhetoric rather than in forming collective consciousness. Memory, memories we should say, because they are not merely or predominantly archival but personal, psychological imaginings and constructions as well as unmediated recollections, are never removed from the present self, society or state but are part of the formation and legitimation of selves, communities and polities. Who could doubt that modern Germany has emerged out of memories as much as history (used here, as historians prefer, to mean some objective past)? Or, for that matter, that the twenty-first century USA has been built on (latterly bitterly contested) legends and myths? Though historical studies of memory have contributed invaluable insights to modern and medieval history, work on the early modern period from this perspective is only just, and tentatively, beginning and early modern historians have much to learn from practitioners in other periods.[36] For memory is often a historical force that does not leave its mark in the archive. Mark Antony may have toppled the statues of Caesar and lit fires where they had stood, but, as his own symbolic act acknowledged, the removal of material forms could not itself erase memory; absence could not easily erase presence.[37] Both the invocation and the attempted erasures of memory are part of the history of legitimation and authority. In a dazzling study of Westminster Cathedral, Paul Binski showed how a succession of monarchs from Henry III onwards sought to enhance their authority by fostering and attaching themselves to the memory of Edward the Confessor, who had become a symbol of ancient laws and liberties as well as of English kingship.[38] Such memories of Edward, or at least the materials of memory, were probably manufactured: the cult surrounding the Confessor's regalia emerged only in the thirteenth century and it was not until Henry IV's use of it in 1399 that we find reference to Edward's chair, ever after the official throne for coronation services.[39] Memory, like tradition, involved invention as well as selection; the 'repositories of memory' combined history and invention to validate present persons and policies through representations and performances that connected the present to an actual *and* imagined past.[40] Queen Victoria and Prince Albert's dressing as Edward II and Philippa nicely captures the extent to which successful kings and queens strove to embody the nation's memory, or such aspects of it as they believed endowed them with greater imperial sway and popularity.[41]

In the early modern period, the age of the Renaissance in England, we need hardly be reminded of the moral, polemical and political force of the past and of precedents: as a source of lessons, as ammunition in argument, and as a mode of validation.[42] Histories, as some antiquarians and writers of history found to their cost, came too close to the problematics of power and political dispute. The Reformation in England, as in Europe, impelled rival narrations of history and contesting claims to memory that were inseparable from denominational and political struggles.[43] But early modern memories were not just represented and contested in written histories. As Jonathan Brown has shown, Philip IV, in commissioning Velázquez for his portrait, was more concerned to evoke and locate himself within a pattern of memory than to present his own appearance in a flattering light.[44] Late-Stuart medals gestured back to the cult of the martyr Charles I, while the Whig pope burnings of the 1680s drew on memories of the Spanish Armada of 1588 to fan anti-Catholicism.[45] Memories formed one of the discourses and symbols that were used to validate authority. Like other symbols and discourses, however, they were, for all the wishes of rulers other-wise, unstable, contested and virtually impossible to control. As Paul Strohm argued, though Henry IV refused to see Richard II buried in Westminster Abbey and interred him far away at Langley, 'as former monarch Richard could not be wholly expelled from the symbolic' and Henry V reburied his remains at Westminster not simply out of respect for his predecessor but in order to harness tradition to the cause of advertising his own legitimacy.[46] Not least because they could not be censored like books, or even policed like libels, memories could destabilize authority and its representation. Historians of the English Reformation with Catholic sympathies have recently argued persuasively for a popular attachment to familiar artefacts and rituals of faith and demonstrated in some areas communities clinging to them.[47] Long after they had been removed, long after Tudor arms had replaced crucifixes on rood screens, memories sustained faiths and allegiances beyond the reach of authority. Queen Elizabeth's famous reluctance to make windows into men's souls, their inner being, may have expressed, as well as a concern about what she might discover, a shrewd acceptance of the power of memory and the limitations of authority to control it. As I have argued elsewhere, it was emblematic of the overall failure of the English Commonwealth that it was unable to eradicate the memory of monarchy: that a decade after regicide Londoners still referred to the Royal Exchange, as indeed they continued to view the world with a cultural memory shaped by regal forms.[48]

Authority's invocation of memory, then, was, though a necessary, also a risky aspect of representing authority: the representation in pageant of Elizabeth as Truth might have been intended to sweep away memories of a Catholic predecessor who made the same claim, but it might just as easily have led some to ask who had the better claim to be the custodian of veracity.[49] Similarly, Charles II's direct appropriation of the iconography of his father, though it endowed him with the authority of sacred memory, also risked reopening the public imagination to the possibilities of civil war and regicide.

Not only were early modern monarchs unable to control the memories and representations of their predecessors which they regarded as essential to their dynastic security, but they were also unable, for all their efforts, to secure their own memories. In a dynastic age and a personal monarchy, rulers knew that the manner of their death, their entombment, posthumous reputation and memory, were vital to their successor. Royal wills, bequests, instructions regarding burial, were not just pious preparations for death, they were texts of dynasty and state. The fate of a monarch after death, however, lay not only with his or her successor whose first public performance was usually the funeral of a predecessor – we think again of Richard II excluded from a royal sepulchre or of Mary, Queen of Scots buried by Elizabeth far away at Peterborough (whence her remains were later removed to Westminster by her son).[50] The memory of a king or queen was also and as much in the hands of the people. As well as official sermons and elegies, the death of an early modern sovereign usually called forth popular ballads which summed the vices and virtues of the reign and ruler in brief moral tales or lines of verse that helped to script the new reign and were often obviously intended to counsel, even admonish, the new ruler. The memory that was essential to regality was simultaneously public property. Indeed, ironically, it was the monarchs who most impressed themselves on the imagination of their subjects, even the most popular rulers, whose memories were least controlled and most appropriated. The obvious example here is Elizabeth I, whose speeches and portraits evidence as great a desire to control the perception of her memory as her person. Yet, just as in her lifetime, scandals contested the official image of the Virgin Queen after her death: not least because so much authority had become attached to her name, almost all protagonists of innumerable contesting causes sought to appropriate the queen and claim her as their champion.[51] Where the first rulers of a new and foreign dynasty, James I and Charles I, invoked her as the queen ruling a realm of religious orthodoxy and social consensus, puritans, in a manner that would have shocked and dismayed her, claimed Elizabeth as the patron of their preferred ecclesiology and church. Where Charles II consciously re-enacted her coronation pageant to represent divine kingship, after 1649 some sought to figure her as a supporter of a commonwealth – a distorted polemic that still finds its followers among some republican historians today.[52] The Elizabeth who was invoked by Queen Victoria and the Suffragettes, who has charmed elderly male historians and fired feminists, is a paradigm of the instability and multivalence of memory. Her authority may have been built in part on memory; but memories of her have authorized multiple agents and so deconstructed her sovereign image – perhaps sovereign authority itself.

Power and authority, the legitimation of monarchy and dynasty, depended on representations – of both living and deceased kings and queens. The concept of representation needs explication because it is both old and new to historical studies. At the simple level of meaning display or ceremonial publication, the term might be synonymous with what Walter Bagehot long ago defined as the 'dignified' aspect of monarchy. But as an approach to the study of the past and the materials for study of the past, the concept of representation that underlies this study is relatively recent and has been – and still remains – controversial. As used in several theoretical studies and in the title of an influential journal that emerged from New Historicist critical circles in 1983, the turn to representation signalled a shift in the study of history based on a Nietzschean philosophy that humans do not have access to truth or reality but construct them.[53] Rather than using a language of truths or facts, or pursuing, say, the 'real' Henry VIII or Louis XIV, such a new approach takes the rigid distinction made between the represented and the real to be a false one. As a consequence, rather than being excluded from the traditionally privileged category of 'evidence', all the texts and performances, including the myths and stories, fables and fictions of past society, are viewed as materials for the historian who anyway, it is argued, has no other access to a 'real' past. To approach the past as an unfolding of shifting representations is to write a different political history: one that conceives all social organizations and the structures of power as constructs endowed with authority by the discourses and signs the culture at any given time authorizes. 'History as the study of representations collapses the boundaries traditionally placed between rhetoric and truth, play and politics; it makes all accounts of the past a cultural history and politics itself a set of discourses and performances in the process of construction, deconstruction and reconstruction.'[54] Many historians have – perhaps understandably – reacted with hostility to an approach to the past that apparently challenges their cherished working practices and their claims to be able, through hard work, to sift the truth from 'false' testimonies. For long, with the pioneering exception of Roger Chartier, it was critics rather than historians who enthusiastically pursued such an approach.[55] But, not least because process, image and signification constitute the 'real politics' of our own experience, several scholars are now taking a representational approach to study of the past. History, a scholar now writes as though it were self-evident, is the story of things done and their representations: 'history is not reflected in images but produced by them'.[56] In similar vein, John Plunkett approached his study of Queen Victoria from the sense that 'the experience of monarchy was invariably an experience of the media through which it was communicated'.[57] As Helen Hackett observed in a review of recent historical writing, one discerns a new interest in façades and their construction different from an older concern with some supposed reality that lay beneath them, which historians believed they could recover.[58]

Though what we might call a representational approach holds out great promise for historians of an early modern period preoccupied with play, display and artful construction, and has influenced important studies of early modern European monarchy and ritual, it has not until very recently found much favour with historians of Tudor and Stuart England. However, John Guy, a scholar of the most conventional training at the feet of Geoffrey Elton, eschewed a conventional historical biography of Sir Thomas More for a study of the multiple personations and representations of a man whose 'real self' was indistinguishable from them.[59] Very recently a young scholar of later Stuart England has revolutionized our approach to, as well as understanding of, politics by a move from a narrative of parties and plots to a study of political culture and the contested representations that were central to party formation and conflict.[60] Mark Knights devotes as much attention to linguistic tropes and literary styles as to the content of texts and insists on the status of opinions and fictions as historical evidence and materials for the construction of individual, party and national identities; and he argues that the most material of revolutions, that which produced a fiscal-military state in England, was 'also a representational one'.[61] Politics in Knights's study is a communicative, representational process. At the core of his argument is the relationship between representation and representativeness. The claim, necessary for parties in later Stuart and Augustan England, to represent the people involved acts of representation *to* the people. Knights's thesis has a historical specificity pertinent to an age of more frequent elections, a broader electorate, and a partisan politics performing in a public sphere. However, as well as his rich approach, his unfolding of the relationship, the interdependency, between standing for and representing to the people has applications to earlier periods. Not least, in the mounting sixteenth- and seventeenth-century quarrels between crown and parliament, both claimed to be more representative of the people (albeit in different ways) and used vocabularies and signs to support their claims. Rulers represented the realm, that is all the members of the commonweal of which they were the head, and often needed to demonstrate their position as representative as well as sovereign head. While the effective extent to which they could claim to be representative was most clearly demonstrated after the outbreak of the Civil War, in the speeches of Charles I from the disputes over the militia to his trial and execution, early modern kings and queens often made their representativeness part of their representation.

Indeed it may be – and I shall later develop the suggestion – that acts of representation made rulers more representative of, more accountable to, the people.[62] Plunkett sees Queen Victoria's 'ubiquitous presence' through representation as stimulating criticisms of her monarchy.[63] 'Victoria's media making,' he writes, 'helps to explain why she was simultaneously revered, reviled, fetishised . . . and gossiped about', and so constructed, owned in some measure, by her subjects.[64] It was Elizabeth I's immense publicity, John Watkins reminds us, that rendered her available to interpretation, that is available to represent whatever subjects thought fit – and ultimately to represent them.[65] David Kastan some time ago made a related but different point about the doubleness of representation in sustaining and undermining authority through study of a prominent early modern medium of royal representation – the theatre. From the Reformation (if not earlier), rulers and/or their ministers favoured plays as a means of persuading audiences to adopt a position, or of proclaiming and publicizing power. At the same time and later, a succession of Tudor and Stuart monarchs had occasion to lament the staging of plays critical of the royal policy or person.

The danger Kastan identified, however, lay in theatrical representation itself. On the stage, a boy performed the role of a king (or queen) and so drew attention to regality itself as play and performance. On the stage, too, royal words (scripted by another) were refuted or disputed and the actor playing the king depended, no less than his fellows, on the reaction, the approval and applause, of the audience. Because, Kastan wrote, theatrical 'representation offers an inherent challenge to the fundamental categories of a culture that would organise itself hierarchically and present that organisation as inevitable', such representations, by refiguring all as performed and enacted, was inherently 'subversive'.[66]

Though restricted to theatre, Kastan's observations identify the central dilemma in all acts of representation that underlies my whole story. Authority in all ages has needed – and still needs – to be performed, written and displayed: to be publicized. But publication and publicization render authority public, that is constructed and determined by public audiences as well as communicated to them. By authoring and presenting themselves, rulers made themselves available to interpretation and so made readers and spectators of the scripts and spectacles of state into critics of government – or citizens. Later we shall examine Habermas's thesis that contrasted a public sphere which emerged, as he posited, in the Augustan age with the representational state which preceded it. Here, I want to observe that the representational state depended upon a public and so fostered a public sphere as each ruler, necessarily, strove to be a focus of public attention. Well before the age of party contest or a wide franchise, there was a real sense that through (re)presenting themselves to the people rulers came to be their representative, to share an authority that was reciprocally endowed and enacted.

The use of words like 'shared' and 'reciprocal' may not only appear inappropriate in characterizing a monarchical state, they also take us far away from a term that was once freely used in studies of royal addresses, images and rituals: propaganda. The shifting meanings of the word have caused such problems for historians that some have excised it from their writings on the early modern period. The term originated from a committee of Roman cardinals responsible for foreign missions, for propagating the faith, and so implied no misrepresentation or insincerity – rather the opposite. Twentieth-century experience, however, of Fascist regimes and the Communist bloc, has led Western liberals, if sometimes from a reluctance to appreciate the sincerity of unattractive ideologies, to take propaganda as an entirely negative, immoral attempt to persuade people to courses that even the propagandists know they are misrepresenting.[67] One might say that, even if we take such a definition or usage, one person's propaganda may be another's faith. And though such an axiom may sound flippant, it directs us to exactly such differences and uncertainties in early modern Europe, many of which were a consequence of denominational conflict. In an age of war for the survival of one's faith, an age that effectively spans the whole period of our study, it was virtually impossible to accept another religion's profession of faith as legitimate or sincere. Most obviously, Jesuit proselytizers who were dedicated to spreading the Catholic faith were a synonym in Protestant circles for dissimulation and manipulation, while, from Luther on, Catholics regularly accused Protestants of masking self-interest and self-indulgence under the rhetorical cloak of election and salvation. In an age of violent religious conflict, a preoccupation with faith meant a preoccupation with lies: in religious terms a concern with presenting and representing the true faith implied anxieties about misrepresentation and false witness.[68] The Reformation, that is, led contemporaries to understand propaganda, although they almost never used the term other than in Latin and as a verb, in *both* our senses of sincere pronouncement and cynical attempt to mislead. Nor was this just a matter of faith. In terms of the state, the figure who revolutionized early modern politics also introduced an anxiety about what we would call propaganda in government. In *The Prince*, Machiavelli advised the ruler about the importance of appearances. Subverting Christian assumptions about the obligations of rulers above all others to speak and act sincerely, according to the dictates of conscience, Machiavelli, by infamously urging the ruler to imitate the lion and the fox, to perform a series of roles, to conceal and to feign, to utter what served his ends rather than express his beliefs, to misrepresent himself, encouraged the prince to use (what we would call positive and negative) propaganda.[69] In the sixteenth and seventeenth centuries, Machiavelli was all but universally condemned as ungodly, even diabolic. But he stalked the imaginations of all, not least by raising doubts that were never thoroughly suppressed about princely sincerity. For all the protestations of Christian kings and queens that, as James I put it, their heart was a crystal through which subjects might see that what they uttered expressed their true self, royal words, all representations, were searched and scrutinized by suspicious fellow rulers – and subjects.[70] The Elizabethan stage even in representing supposedly virtuous rulers, such as Henry V, was preoccupied with Machiavellian stratagems and princely sleights of hand; and if they were not quite valorized, they were (increasingly) accepted as part of statecraft. There was an uncertainty in early modern England about whether government was an act of faith or statecraft that included what we would call propaganda: pronouncements for cynical interest's sake as well as out of sincerely held belief.

As the experience of world wars and Cold War recedes, historians appear to be less uneasy about the phenomenon of propaganda, and again willing to use the word non-pejoratively in discussions of the representation of authority. A. K. McHardy, taking his reign as an important development in the use of public relations and image-making, analyses Edward III's 'use of propaganda'.[71] Sidney Anglo, more recently a sceptic about the success of Tudor representations, discusses Henry VII's printing of a papal dispensation for his marriage as propaganda; Carole Levin deploys the word in her study of Reformation representations of King John, and Lois Schwoerer claims without hesitation that in 1688, 'Englishmen and Dutchmen together mounted the most sophisticated and extensive propaganda campaign in the history of Western Europe'.[72] The idea of propaganda, even when the word is not used pejoratively, evokes systematic orchestration directed to the end of controlling the image projected; and several scholars who shy away from using the word clearly discern such systems in the past. Students of the Wilton Diptych, for example, have described Richard II's patronage of the arts and placement of a series of statues in Westminster Hall as aspects of a 'coherent ... ideology of kingship'.[73] Writing on Henry VII's first progress to his northern capital, a scholar identifies the 'carefully orchestrated appearances' devised by a 'public relations machine'.[74] The language of our modern experience can here be both helpful and misleading. Today, as we know, huge efforts and budgets go into attempts to direct public opinion and consumer choice. Yet, leaving aside for the moment the issue of their success, such campaigns involve sometimes delicate negotiations and differences over how best to present a product or manifesto. In early modern Europe we can trace how particular monarchs, personally involved in their representation in speech, on canvas and coin, in stone and spectacle, endeavoured to direct a programme of representation. Henry VIII and Charles I may stand as English cases: Louis XIV of France as a paradigm.[75] However, though he is right to interpret the French academies of painting, letters, sculpture, science, music and architecture as institutions of royal direction, I think Tim Blanning is wrong to conclude that 'there was no branch of high culture not subject to state control'.[76]

For one, the mechanics and practicalities of representing authority at least complicate the notion of totalizing control or indeed of an umediated relationship between royal representations and subjects and citizens. Like scribes and secretaries, printers, even royal printers, introduced, as historians of the book have shown, errors, slippages and differences.[77] Many painters were powerful and wealthy figures who could not easily be directed, who sometimes had their own clear ideas and agenda, and whose experience and advice were invaluable, especially to patrons (including royal patrons) in an early modern England that was far behind Europe in sophisticated appreciation of the arts and devoid of native portrait painters of international standing. As for ritual and spectacle, the stage management of these, like the orchestration of any theatrical performance, involved many hands and assistants. The image of the monarch in procession or on progress was an image not just of one man or woman but of an entourage, a troupe all of whom needed to perform their part in order to effect the spectacle. And, rather like the modern relationship between public relations companies and politicians, in many cases the staging of the ruler was largely scripted and arranged by others. A recent historian of Elizabeth's progresses and state entries writes of those 'commissioned' to prepare accounts of them.[78] However, coronation entries and civic pageants were usually devised, and paid for, by the metropolitan and civic authorities respectively. While, in most cases, the intention was to please and flatter the sovereign, and it is quite likely that discreet soundings were taken at court on how to do so, in the end it was the corporations and livery companies who paid pageant makers, from poets to carpenters and scene painters, to represent the ruler. And themselves. For the arrival of a king or queen into the capital or any other city presented an opportunity for a dialogue with, an address to, as well as a display of the monarch; and in myriad instances London and provincial towns used the occasion to bring royal attention to local difficulties, needs and grievances, even to counsel and admonish the ruler. A vocabulary of propaganda and control should not be outlawed; but nor should it pass over the many interme- diaries, hands and agents involved in presenting and representing majesty nor the various purposes intended in acts of representation. Whatever the talk of direct and immediate access to the royal person, on the street or on the page, acts of representation were mediated and multiple, rather than the work of a sovereign author – or authority.

Describing Queen Victoria's progresses, Margaret Homans argued that 'seeming, appearing or being represented are instances of the Queen's agency regardless of whether self-representation can be said to have been chosen or actively undertaken'.[79] At an extreme level, that is, the queen, whatever the desire of others to flatter her, performed scripts and roles devised by others; to use a different language, she was not the author of herself. It is interesting in this respect that in early modern England several stage soliloquies of kings, and the poetry of some Tudor and Stuart kings and queens, meditated on the paradox of sovereign authority and the subordination of self to public performance as well as duty.[80] If early monarchs did not always feel in control of the performances of the state theatre and spectacle, they were certainly not able to determine what they meant or how they were received. Though many witnessed a coronation entry, most subjects experienced royal representations through report. Though a figure like Richard Mulcaster may have been, as William Leahy puts it, 'on a commission' to prepare an official record of Elizabeth's entry, his official narration vied with dozens of cheaper, more popular broadsides and ballads that related, and thereby interpreted, the occa- sion.[81] Readers, illiterate spectators or auditors of such texts, then, read and heard and 'saw' Queen Elizabeth through the representations by other subjects of her representation by the city corporation and companies of London. When we add to that, as we shall see, the fact that the market – the consuming public – determined which accounts of occasions like this circulated most widely, we return to the problematics of a language of propaganda and control in study of royal representation. What has been said about the nineteenth-century images of monarchy applies as much to the sixteenth and seventeenth centuries: 'there was by no means a simple top down aesthetic'.[82] Rather than positing a model of royal control or a binary relationship between sovereign authority and subjectivity, we should recognize that kings, courtiers, corporations and companies negotiated over the image of the monarch; and, while they did not have the sophisticated focus groups of modern pollsters or advertisers, all appreciated that, as well as them all, it was audiences – subjects – who had agency in the making, still more in determining the meaning, of royal pronouncements and display.

One of the most important developments in the study of the humanities over the last two decades has been a move from exclusive concentration on the authors to study of the readers of texts. Such a move probably emerged from the decentring of authority that followed the late twentieth-century critique of modernity and gave birth to a new field of enquiry, now known as the history of the book. The history of the book and the history of reading that it has incorporated insists not only on the multiple and unstable authorship of texts but on the recognition and authority of readers as interpreters and exegetes.[83] Some scholars have argued that because the reader is imagined – sometimes anxiously imagined – by writers in the very act of authoring, readers helped to fashion texts in ways that make the binary model of authors (who, of course create out of their own readings) and readers too simple.[84] Whatever their role in the authorship of texts, readers were (and are) certainly agents in the interpretation of texts, that is in the construction of meaning. Contemporary and successive readers performed a variety of readings which may have been different to any the author intended. The history of the book is a twentieth-century approach that has greatly illuminated the pre-modern age, not least our understanding of the Renaissance and early modern period. For, as literary scholars have for long instructed us, authorship was not a fully formed idea in early modern England. The author was often taken to be the authorizer of a work and, in some cases, Spenser's *Shepherd's Calendar* for example, it is the name of the aristocratic dedicatee (in this case Sir Philip Sidney) rather than the author which appears on the title page.[85] Moreover, humanist rhetorical theory, as we shall see, necessarily drew attention to the uncertainties of reception: to alternative arguments and readings and hence to potentially resistant readers. As I have argued elsewhere, the epistles to readers and other paratextual devices which increasingly introduce sixteenth- and seventeenth-century books bear witness to authors' sense, and sometimes fear, of the power of readers and to their efforts to direct interpretation.[86] Not surprisingly, as much as authors, it was authorities that sought to delimit or police the freedom of readers: by censoring books, prescribing who might read the Bible, or by discouraging, as Ann Clifford's husband appears to have done, private readings not directed by the head of the household or another reliable, male, pillar of the community.[87] If, as Terry Eagleton argued, ideology is as much about the fixing of meaning, 'of making a meaning *stick*', as its creation, the freedom of a reader was (and as modern examples show is) a political space and enfranchisement that, as I have demonstrated extensively for one case, enabled highly individual and radical readings and values far removed from official orthodoxies.[88]

Though it has become a fashionable field in its own right, the history of reading, with its emphasis on the reception and audiences of texts, needs to be brought, as in a few studies it is beginning to be, into the mainstream of histories, including – perhaps especially – political histories. As Mark Knights wrote of political petitions and addresses in later seventeenth-century England, the meanings of them were 'conferred by readers or listeners as well as authors'.[89] How we recover readers making meanings is a challenge that scholars have tried to meet through theory, notions of an 'implied reader' or 'interpretive community', or through case studies of individuals – Gabriel Harvey, John Dee or William Drake.[90] We need also always to remember that, as well as an individual practice, reading, of proclamations or sermons for example, often took place in communities – communities of illiterate as well as literate auditors – and so helped to forge social identities and ideologies through a dialogue between the codes and values of such communities and the texts of authority. Our concern here is to recognize that the authors of official representations – authorities – were in a rhetorical culture acutely aware both of the importance of tuning their representations to different audiences and of the need to control, and the difficulty in controlling, the reception and interpretation of their own texts: declarations and proclamations, statutes and decrees. The exercise of authority in early modern England was (as it still is) a textual process; and whatever the wishes of royal authors, as Renaissance rhetorical theory fully recognized, all texts and locutions were open to interpretation by readers and subjects who brought to the texts of authority their own experiences of other texts and locutions. The rhetoric of power, like all rhetoric, assumed readers who needed to be persuaded, and acknowledged resistant as well as complaisant readers.[91] The turn from authors to readers in critical studies has been central to my approach, as I shall show, to the representation and publicization of monarchy in all forms of speech, writing and print.

What I also wish to urge here is the applicability of this turn to the reader for our understanding of other genres, forms and media of representation, especially the visual and performative. The latter, more obvious case has attracted scholarly attention. Anthropologists and students of spectacle and ceremony have appreciated that audiences are essential to the meaning and purpose of public displays, even if they have not adequately pursued the ways in which participants and observers constructed and performed meaning. Sociologists and historians of other periods and countries have also investigated the role of the crowd in public rituals, public executions in particular.[92] Such studies, though they risk making 'the crowd' a collective and underplay divisions, conflict and individual agency, have provided excellent examples of how audiences can interpret, act and bestow legitimacy in ways quite contrary to that intended by governments. Audible or symbolic public support for a traitor or felon, even if demonstrated by pulling on a hanging victim's legs to hasten death and spare him the full horrors of disembowelling alive, challenged both authority and a principal theatre of authority – the scaffold. We need to extend this focus on audience, as we shall see some scholars are beginning to do, from executions and grand state occasions to more quotidian royal performances as well as progresses, Garter processions and public prayers.

What has been much slower in emerging, especially in the historiography of early modern England, has been a similar audience and reception-led approach to visual materials in all their forms. Historians, nervous about interpreting images, tend to concentrate on trying to elucidate what the commissioner or artist intended rather than showing interest in how images performed or were received. Access to the responses to, say, portraits, poses many difficulties: there are happily no marginalia to be found on Van Dyck canvases. But, as with the history of the book, questions of reception and performance could be tackled by consideration of the material form and genre, the commerce and distribution, the productions and reproductions of the visual text and the evidence of perceptions and receptions revealed in sale, copy, circulation, imitation and contestation. Starting by asking, say, who was the author of Holbein's Privy Chamber portrait of Henry VII and Henry VIII and their wives, historians might, more than they have, investigate the geography or placement of such a portrait, who commissioned copies, the distribution of engravings, why and how it became an iconic image of the second Tudor, how owners of reproduced forms (whether painted copies, prints or medals) collected, catalogued or displayed them, and so on. As I shall develop and document, owners of images, no less than owners of books, could control their meaning for themselves and how they performed in their communities. We must also keep in mind that even elite images displayed in privileged and political spaces needed, in order to represent the majesty they displayed, an audience – or, since the topography of rooms and politics of access were elaborate, different audiences. And, as early modern commentators were themselves fully and often anxiously aware, viewing and interpreting do not result in fixed, unchanging responses; they depend on positions and circumstances; and, whatever the intention of the patron or artist, meanings cannot be fixed or controlled. At the most obvious level, what in a Catholic observer aroused devotion, a strict Protestant conceived as idolatrous; the equestrian portrait in a gallery of such portraits, which some viewed as a symbol of imperial glory, another might take as a sign of delusions of grandeur or see as evocation of a foreign and popish regimen. In changed circumstances either viewer (after acts of violent iconoclasm or civil war, for example) might change his mind. As with the complex materiality of the book, the subject, arrangement, size, use of space and line, placement, and, as much, the perspective of the viewer of a painting (or woodcut, or medal) all influenced interpretation, as did, of course, the conditions of sex and status.

In the case of written works, Terence Cave powerfully argued that a (in some cases) reluctant acknowledgement of the interpretative power of readers (and, we might add, auditors and observers) led some Renaissance authors (Rabelais and Montaigne, for example) to build in multiple meanings and not only to draw attention to the problem of how they should be read but also to 'give licence to an interpretative approach'.[93] Readers and observers produced their own meanings whether they were licensed to do so or not. And they could undermine the power of representation by a variety of responses ranging from indifference, through appropriation to quite different purposes, to opposition or destruction. As Andrew Bell observes of the role of statues in ancient Rome, citizens could venerate them or simply refuse to accept them as part of the fabric of the city; their public performance, that is, depended not just on their erection and placement but on a community's acceptance of them as part of their community.[94] How images were received and treated and by whom both responded to and transformed their performance of meaning. It would seem that it was during the seventeenth century that those who purchased prints began, instead of keeping them in drawers, to frame and display them on walls.[95] Though the reason remains unclear – woodcuts had long been pasted on tavern walls – such a change in the habit of consumers changed and increased the audiences for this visual medium and, of course, the ways in which prints performed commercially, socially and politically. Changing audiences and shifting patterns of reception, collecting and arrangement, of sale and exchange, were inseparable from performances of meaning. Consequently, the texts and images of representation, rather than simply proclaiming or displaying authority, were sites of dialogues about, negotiation over, authority. As Helen Hackett noted, and anyone with a memory of student poster art will endorse, 'the use of an image need not indicate agreement with the ideology which produced it'.[96] As scholars of several different periods are beginning to argue, the rhetorics of authority and of opposition are interdependent: 'such', in Paul Binski's words, 'is the history of power and the appropriation of its value systems'.[97] Readers and viewers of our early modern period indeed appropriated official images for reinterpretations critical of government. 'While Tudor iconographers came to present Henry VIII after the break from Rome as a divinely chosen ruler akin to the biblical David, the king's subjects frequently adopt the role and language of David, the beleaguered but righteous psalmist, in order to sustain themselves through periods of royal disfavour'.[98] Airing his frustration at how the 1688 image of Jove throwing the thunderbolts at a Phaeton meant to figure James II was interpreted by some as God's wrath against William and Mary's usurpation of the throne, one Whig sympathizer proclaimed: 'I wish the author had either consulted books or men for a more significant and unexceptional emblem'.[99] If his quest was indeed for a book or emblem closed to any other than official interpretation, it was doomed. All the texts and emblems of power were, and are, open to interpretation and exposed to criticism.

Yet, just as we should not commit the idealizing (or Foucauldian) error of assuming authority's control of meaning, in other words ideological hegemony, nor should we conceive of opposition as necessarily destructive of, or even free of, official scripts and emblems. The most potent critiques of state were often those that appropriated or re-presented authorized representations. In such cases, while the authority of official representations armed opponents with a discourse of legitimacy, such vocabularies, texts and icons also limited the destructive force of opposition. Binski insists that in Henry III's reign, the rhetoric of power was in step with that of opposition; a scholar of Elizabethan England reminds us that 'portraits and panegyrics co-exist with gossip and rumour'.[100] The historian of Queen Victoria's image argued subtly that just as her official regal image depended upon and was appropriated by subjects, no less the proponents of 'antimonarchism responded to, negotiated with and [were] *compromised* by the media making of Queen Victoria'.[101] Authority and its representations existed throughout our story in an interdependent relationship with the multiple audiences and receptions, interpretations and critiques of regality. The changing relationship among them and the points of crisis that turned interdependency into violence or revolution are the subject of this study.

Important to the representations and perceptions of authority, to the relationships between sovereigns and subjects, in the early modern period was the condition of the market and the emergence of a consumer culture. In our own time the relationship of a market and consumer culture to the presentation and perception of government is clear in many obvious ways. Not only do governments package and sell themselves using the language and techniques of advanced capitalism (not least the advertisers' manipulation of desire and anxiety), as importantly subjects 'buy into' political as well as commercial brand images and the lifestyle they conjure and promise. As pollsters know, there is a vital link between voters' political moods and affiliations and the objects – house, car, clothes, newspapers – they buy. Just as twentieth-century people construct an identity from wearing a designer logo – that is through becoming part of the advertising culture of modern capitalism – so many of us adorn houses or cars with political posters or stickers, wear a red rose of New ('newer, better') Labour, or perhaps a red nose of publicized compassion and commitment. And though the ubiquitous tourist shops in central London selling souvenirs of the royal family may seem to be targeting only visitors (who by consuming them buy into a certain sort of vicarious British identity), there is no shortage of British customers for the regal memorabilia advertised in the middle and lowbrow Sundays – whether coins, plates, figurines or other objects commemorating a royal marriage or the memory of a member of the royal family. National and political, like class and age, identities are manifested and solidified, even formed, in patterns of consumption. Indeed, in the West such patterns may be said to form the essential bond between governments and subjects, an ideological affinity that, whatever its internal tensions, serves to cohere and unite Western societies against other, less or anti-consumerist, polities.

Though it has been advanced beyond measure by the (related) processes of industrialization, democratization and mass media and mass culture, the link between the consumption of goods and the representation and experience of authority is not new. Plunkett used an appropriately capitalist lexicon when he described Queen Victoria's jubilee during which 'an excess of reproduction [of souvenirs] was officially sanctioned'.[102] And he made a direct connection between a new medium of representation and object of consumption with a changing politics: 'the democracy of the celebrity carte . . . stems from the power they gave to individual consumers'.[103] In recent years, scholars have traced a connection between goods, consumption and political change back to the dawn of the Enlightenment. Neil McKendrick, John Brewer and others, for example, have argued for a link between the decline of the court at the beginning of the eighteenth century and the shift to a market-driven culture, in which the authority of patronage was transferred to the consumer and ultimately that of the monarchy to the middle classes.[104] Tim Blanning discerned a similar pattern of change throughout Old Regime Europe in which, he argued, the feudal social relationships were dissolved by the exchange of goods and the culture of Louis XIV's Versailles was replaced by the rise of a paying public.[105] We should not lightly challenge such a historiographical consensus that offers an interesting new refinement to an old Marxist history or to the story of the rise of modernity. However, Blanning and Brewer too readily characterize earlier societies as feudal or pre-market, pre-consumption economies and polities, as a number of scholars working on other periods have begun to demonstrate. Writing of ancient Greece and Rome, Andrew Bell argued that, even in antiquity, 'the value of many commodities of empire was established by the dispositions of popular political taste', and so not only connected consumption to politics but identified in antiquity a political freedom for consumers to participate in the establishment of value, that is in the 'political economy', as well as the commercial economy.[106] The leading historian of fifteenth-century visual culture, who did not shrink from using the word 'market' to describe the culture in which works of art and objects circulated, defined it as 'a relation in which two groups of people are free to make choices'.[107] Michael Baxandall's recognition that consumer choices are also political choices (as we are only too well aware) is confirmed by the study of prints as 'objects of consumption' in early modern Europe. Prints which often circulated religious scenes or portraits of princes, that illustrated ballads and broadsides and cartooned figures of authority, became fashionable commodities that stimulated a market economy. But they did not create it; 'the evolution of the print and of print collecting . . . trailed the larger commercial developments of the culture'.[108]

In England, the rise of a market economy and an affective political economy were both – and interconnected – developments of the sixteenth and seventeenth centuries. The consumption of goods, that is, was related to the consumption and the representation of authority. The most obvious manifestation of this relationship, and of the 'choices' involved in it, was, of course, early modern theatre.[109] Not coincidentally did the first leisure industry focus on the representations, the display, and interrogation of monarchy. It is not the only example. During the course of the sixteenth century, a demand developed and was met, particularly by Elizabeth's reign, for copies of royal speeches, for accounts of royal progresses, and, as a number of Elizabethan proclamations attest, for portraits of rulers.[110] During the 1590s, not only did the aristocratic fashion for building long galleries reflect, and further stimulate, a demand for portraits of kings and queens to accompany those of ancestors, but books of woodcuts and engravings of past English monarchs began to be published and sold to buyers beyond the narrow ranks of the elite.[111] We also see in late Elizabethan England the beginnings of the collecting of royal souvenirs: a ceramic plate in the Museum of London adorned with a simple verse praising the queen and dated 1600 would seem to be designed for a broad market; medals and playing cards bearing Elizabeth's image reached a broader public still.[112] By the end of the sixteenth century, not least in response to the insistent representation of authority since the Reformation, subjects developed a desire to own some material emblem of authority. Such desire for ownership evidences the power of representation in creating the affective political economy that was the psychological underpinning of the idea of the commonweal in Tudor England: the consuming subject sought an emblem of the king or queen's person as well as power.[113] But as the images and objects, the materials of royal representation, proliferated, consumers were increasingly, to return to Baxandall's phrase, 'free to make choices'. And such choices enfranchised subjects as well as consumers. At a simple level, even ordinary subjects could (and indeed needed to) decide which play to attend, which image or object to buy, linking, in Elizabethan England as in antiquity, the value of commodities to popular political taste. More importantly, the ownership of such goods, such emblems of authority, not only fostered subjects' investment in authority (as was probably intended) but also developed their own participation in power. An artefact or object once owned could be venerated and displayed or derided and spurned; it could be 'valued' or held at little worth. A marketplace for royal souvenirs and memorabilia commodified not just the culture but authority – monarchy – itself.

 Not only an emerging but a changing marketplace and consumer culture forms an under-studied aspect of our account of the representations and perceptions of regality. In so many ways, the market altered the media of representation: it changed coterie printing into an industry of publication; it reproduced mysterious icons of majesty as cheap woodcuts, objects in porcelain and images in popular games of chance; it influenced spectacles to ensure that they impressed, through elaborate firework displays for example, the people to whom were sold the souvenir accounts of spectacular state occasions.[114] Most of all, the changing market demanded different strategies and forms of representation. Whatever her fantasies of controlling her image, or reservations about publicization, Elizabeth I undoubtedly participated in the commodification of herself, intuiting a public desire for an affective connection to her. James I sought, for all the difficulties he faced, to write his authority into the minds of the purchasers and readers of his works. As Harold Weber has suggested, Charles II skilfully adapted his representation to a new and different marketplace as well as a post-revolutionary political culture.[115] Where the magnificent illustrated souvenir folio of his coronation entry, produced and sold by John Ogilby, sold, as it were, shares to the elite in the new restored monarchy, the various popular accounts of Charles's adventures, disguises and narrow escapes as he fled from Cromwell's Ironsides after the Battle of Worcester followed the taste for romances as well as meeting the desire for a more human face to majesty.[116] Elsewhere I have suggested that even Charles II's public sexual dalliances and priapic self-display followed a fashion for bawdy verse that signalled a widespread reaction to the puritan restraint of the republican Commonwealth.[117] The new leisure services of the coffee-houses, with their supply of pamphlets, news and political chatter and gossip, prompted the first official government newspapers; and by the 1680s consumer culture as well as political culture was being shaped by partisan allegiances and loyalties, as publishers and artists increasingly identified themselves with party programmes and positions.[118] Such a late seventeenth-century world may seem, and in many respects was, far removed from the early Tudor England where our story will begin. Yet it was the Tudors' wish – and need – to publicize themselves, to make themselves the objects of attention and desire, that immersed monarchy in an emerging commodity culture which in turn influenced and complicated the politics of representation. The New Labour rose has not been the first brand image – or rose for that matter – that has been promoted and then been tarnished, as the people's consumer and political choices have changed. Publicity has always carried risks.

Discussion of a bourgeois consumer culture leads us to a subject at present very *au courant* in early modern studies, the rise of a public sphere. Though first posited as a sociological model for understanding the rise of modernity four decades ago, Jürgen Habermas's *The Structural Transformation of the Public Sphere* was not translated into English until 1989 and has only yet more recently captured the interest of early modern historians.[119] In his original formulation, Habermas described a public sphere as created when private citizens came together to debate public matters rationally and freely. He identified its historical origins in later seventeenth-century Britain with the emergence of a fully fledged mercantile economy, the coffee-house and public press and the frequent parliaments and elections that followed wars. Habermas, as the title of his book indicated, was more concerned with the disintegration of this (idealized) arena of rational critical debate through the change to a mass consumer culture which, he believed, surrendered political participation for passive consumption of goods. Most scholars, however, have concentrated on his account of the emergence of the public sphere, and, as much, on the chronology he provided of it. In particular, several scholars of early modern England have argued that the conditions for the emergence of a rational public debate prevailed in earlier periods: for David Zaret the Civil War, for Joad Raymond the 1620s, for Peter Lake the succession crises of Elizabeth's reign.[120] In my own case, as we shall see, I argue for the Henrician Reformation as the period of the birth of a public sphere in England.[121]

Here, I wish to suggest that, as well as a questionable chronology, there are other problems with Habermas's model, stimulating though it has been. First, Habermas posited the public sphere as emerging in opposition to the 'representative state', which he characterized as one of passive subjectivity as opposed to active citizenship. By contrast, as I have begun to suggest, we should rather see a public sphere as emerging from, and as part of, the representational state which (even though it may not have been intended) fostered debate and critical discussion of politics and power.[122] The constituents of Habermas's public sphere – market capitalism, media and spaces of public discussion, frequent parliaments and party politics – may have developed together in late Stuart Britain, but each, and all, existed earlier; and they were fostered by the insistent and ubiquitous representations of early modern monarchs. Habermas paid attention to print and the coffee-houses but these had their Tudor equivalents in the alehouse, the fair, the marketplace and theatre, and in rumour, oral and printed. Habermas underestimated the importance of an oral culture that, as scholars have begun to document, fed into and was further stimulated and circulated by print.[123] When we read endless Tudor proclamations anxiously endeavouring to check rumours about royal policies or plans, we can be in no doubt that Henry VIII and his successors discerned a public sphere which was far removed from the passive subjects discussed by Habermas.[124] Secondly, by concentrating on the bourgeois public sphere, Habermas diverted attention from a broader popular arena of public debate and participation that in some ways declined in the late seventeenth and early eighteenth centuries. The gossip that pilloried Anne Boleyn as a whore, the widely circulating stories about Elizabeth I's sex life, the vast outpouring of crude ballads and pornographic squibs during the Overbury scandal in James I's reign witness a broad public discussion of, and involvement in, politics that should not be subordinated to notions of a superior bourgeois 'rationality'.[125] Again, monarchs who fanned popular anticlericalism or anti-Spanish hysteria could find that the public, far from passive, redeployed them to critique later royal policies. In some respects, there was a popular public sphere in sixteenth- and seventeenth-century England that did not re-emerge until Wilkes, Paine and the Chartists. Thirdly, far from being destroyed by popular consumer capitalism, England's early modern popular public sphere developed, as I have suggested, alongside and out of a consumer culture. When a draft Elizabethan proclamation referred to the 'natural desires all sorts of subjects and people have, *both noble and mean*, to procure the portrait and picture of the queen's majesty', it acknowledged a link between popular consumption and politics.[126] Because in late twentieth-century capitalism 'rational political debate' has been 'replaced by consumption', we should not conclude that such was, or is, the necessary consequence of consumerism.[127] Throughout the period of nearly two centuries covered by my volumes, we discern that representations of kings and queens promoted, performed in, and were interpreted and interrogated by, a public sphere of subjects and citizens whose consumption of those representations permitted and included rational critique as well as commodity acquisition. Like monarchy, that public sphere did not speak with one voice; like the representations of rulers, it changed with the economic, social and political changes that it helped to fashion. But an appreciation of its presence, not least because early modern rulers were themselves always aware of it, is essential to our understanding of the texts, images and rituals of power in Tudor and Stuart England.

Important to any figuration of the public sphere are the modes of communication and the changing media and technology of communication. In the short half-century since the mid-twentieth, we have witnessed political as well as cultural revolutions which have followed in the wake of the invention and (as important) mass ownership of TV, video, the internet, mobile phones and wireless digital communications that have enabled the transference of vast amounts of data, news and images which consumers can store, compare, review, edit and redistribute as they choose. If McLuhan's axiom that the medium is the message still remains provocative, it seems to be daily more realized in a communications culture in which the medium and technology as much drive use and content as demand and content stimulate invention.[128] While, however, the speed and intensity of our technological changes may not be matched in past societies, the perception of rapid technological change has been; and for other periods we need to reimagine the relationship between media technology and perceptions of politics. John Plunkett captures well the impact of Victorian photographs that consciously imitated Gainsborough and Reynolds in offering 'a court portrait for every hearth'.[129] And he points to the techniques of retouching photographs (now of course the norm for celebrity images) used to erase the signs of an ageing Queen and to sustain the myth of monarchy into which subjects happily bought – as today they buy into the myth of celebrity by purchasing endorsed products. Such technological inventions in the media of representation have not received much attention from students of early modern politics but merit consideration in a study of representation. For example, better minting, casting and later machine-striking techniques enabled important changes in the representation of monarchs on coins, from a generalized figure of regality to the likeness of a particular crowned individual. Similarly the development of screw presses and the shift from striking to casting greatly improved the detail on coins and medals, which formed the most widely distributed images of power.[130] Where woodcut blocks enabled cheap illustration of popular books and broadsides, engravings and later mezzotints transferred to visual reproductions the complex lines and shadowing of paintings and especially portraits. It is no coincidence that the greatly improved quality of prints in the seventeenth century coincided with the rise of businesses and shops that specialized in the design, execution, publication and sale of prints and with new habits of collecting and displaying them as objects of aesthetic worth and political interest.[131]

New technologies often led monarchs to recruit from abroad the cutting-edge artists and craftsmen who were best able to represent their authority. Like Henry VIII before him, Charles I, in the absence of indigenous artists skilled in the baroque arts of illusion, attracted to London one of the leading European painters, while Inigo Jones was sent abroad to learn the techniques of Palladian architecture and stage perspective which enabled him to refashion the *mise-en-scène* for the new Stuart dynasty. In the seventeenth century it was German engineers who were most adept at orchestrating the magnificent firework displays that were increasingly popular at state spectacles.[132] James II had cause to rue the dominance since the sixteenth century of the engraving business by Dutchmen who in 1688 largely served the Prince of Orange and the Whig cause. New technologies, as nations and political parties are now obsessively aware, cannot be left to or be monopolized by rivals. The arts of successful representation necessitated a quick response and adept deployment of the technologies of communication and of those expert in the new media. Van Dyck's knighthood, no less than Lord Saatchi's peerage, acknowledged a government's dependency on highly skilled media men who had mastered the arts and technologies of representation.

Early modernity's principal media revolution was, of course, print. Though the recent scholarship of Adrian Johns, Adam Fox and others has rightly moderated the messianic claims made by Elizabeth Eisenstein for print as the single most important agent of change and revolution, it remains the case that print was perceived in ways not very different to reactions in our own time to cinema, television or the internet.[133] Despite some predictions, the internet has not killed the printed book; and print, we must always recognize, did not signal the end of manuscript or oral culture. What it did, as well as adding a vital new medium of communication, was transform other media, just as terrestrial TV has been transformed by digital broadcasting and recording. Using language that recalls early reactions to the internet, Brian Cummings wrote of print in early Tudor England that 'the medium . . . induced in officialdom a state bordering on paranoia'.[134] The reaction was understandable given the virulent printed exchanges that had followed Luther's attack on the Catholic church: the history of European print was not just synchronic with, but interdependent with, denominational controversy and religious war. On the other hand, the potential power of the new technology to reach a wide international and domestic audience made it attractive and indispensable; and made the risk of surrendering it to others unthinkable. As we shall see, from Henry VIII onwards, several rulers, some indulging the fantasy that they could control it, made print the principal medium of their communication and representation. Like other authors, they developed strategies to attempt to influence readers – the display (or concealment) of authorship, an authoritative voice or familiar, intimate tone, octavo availability or folio authority, typographies (usually black letter for the words of kings), indices and margin notes, all of which merit closer attention as acts of authority than they have received. What concerns us now is how the new medium refashioned both the representation and perception of authority, how, one might say, print textualized regality in early modern England. Through the anonymity of print the royal voice moved from person and hand to page, and the recipient of royal declarations became a reader. The medium of print, then, both universalized and depersonalized the word of a king and rendered it, too, an object of scrutiny, a commodity owned by subjects. Some critics have gone too far in describing the ruler as a text or 'effect of discourse'; but print unquestionably made texts the principal mode of experiencing regality and in turn fostered a textual dialogue with, and about, authority.[135] Through representing authority, print also gained authority – an authority that was then available for others to use to question kings and queens. Given the inequalities of access and resources, it would be simplistic today to think of the internet as technology open to use by all. Similarly, with official presses, royal printers, wealth, power and some mechanisms of censorship, rulers, governments and elites enjoyed clear advantages with the new medium of communication. But from the beginning, they were unable to monopolize it, control it, or prevent contestation. As has been the case with other technologies of communication, the political history of print has been one both of official representations and contests for representation, of struggles for authority in which, as contemporaries were fond of saying, the pen was no less potent a weapon than the pike.

II

During the fifteen years since I began work on this project, scholars have taken new approaches to and revised our understanding of key concepts such as authority and power, propaganda and legitimation. And we have seen a shift from the authors of royal representations to the audiences, consumers and interpreters of them: to how they performed in a public sphere. Much of the new work has directed us to different premises and methodologies which have hitherto attracted few historians of early modern England. Where, for example, several scholars working in other fields and periods seem comfortable with applying modern perspectives to study of the past, most historians of early modern England – perhaps an enduring legacy of revisionism – remain anxious about the risk of anachronism. Suzanne Lewis found film theory a valuable tool for understanding a medieval artefact, for example; and literary scholars, brushing aside the almost universal scepticism of historians concerning it, assert that 'images of monarchs seem to crave [*sic*] some sort of psychological approach'.[136] What has most influenced recent critical studies has been an emphasis on surfaces and appearances which most historians, if they consider them at all, subordinate to what they regard as substantial and real. In particular the idea of societies, polities or selves as 'constructed' has made a new history of power and politics more a cultural than an institutional history. As Roger Chartier wrote, 'the history of the construction of social identities . . . becomes a history of relations of symbolic force'.[137] Very much in the spirit of that manifesto, discussing Henry III's promotion of the cult of Edward the Confessor as a 'narrative self-construction', Paul Binski insists that 'art represents a form and not an exemplification of power'.[138] Not only, such an approach implies, are the images and artefacts of a culture the primary texts in a symbolic system that constituted (rather than simply reflected) power; the history of authority and politics is the history of such constructions – of the processes of the formations, presentations, deconstructions and reconstitutions of signs. Though the language here may be more familiar to the anthropologist and critic, an attention to the constructions of authority promises rich insights for historians of early modernity when, as we have learned, notions of 'fashioning' preoccupied contemporaries.[139] As much as about the images themselves, this study is concerned with the construction and fashioning of the representations of rulers through verbal, visual and spectacular signs.

Emphasis on the constructed nature of symbolic systems has brought with it a greater awareness of their artifice and vulnerability. Arguably it is the function of all ideological systems to present and represent as 'natural', stable and uncontestable what is artificial, open and partisan – to make the contentious and contingent normal and timeless. But it is the historian's as well as the critic's role to return ideology to history and to the circumstances and processes from which it emerged. This reading against the grain results in a revealing unravelling of a wide variety of historical texts. Writing from a belief that art 'can indicate the vulnerability as well as strength of any political system', Binski discerned in Richard II's devotion to Westminster Abbey and his portrait there not mere proclamations of his power but the 'peculiar anxieties of an insecure, fastidious and hypersensitive young king'.[140] Using a similar psychological language of anxiety, Plunkett identified 'the fissures and instabilities of Victoria's representation'.[141] Such language has not much featured in the historiography of early modern England. Indeed, an earlier generation of scholars, led by Lovejoy and Tillyard, has been accused of simply accepting (one might say being seduced by) the representations the Tudors (interestingly, not the Stuarts) gave of themselves.[142] While more recent work has undoubtedly complicated the image of, say, the mighty Henry VIII or the deft and confident Elizabeth, few historians have read below or between the lines to consider the uncertainties and anxieties that Tudor images, in words or on canvas, were endeavouring to overcome.[143] It is time to consider the vulnerabilities as well as strengths of early modern polities and the processes deployed to manage that vulnerability.

The new address to the constructed nature of ideological performances invites a new approach to representations in another respect. If what is constructed is partial and meant to conceal anxieties, part of the process of ideological construction and representation is occlusion and silence. Historian colleagues will be quick to claim that a consideration of what is not said, as well as what is, has always been an aspect of the best historical study of documents. However, the critic's engagement with silences, spaces and occlusions goes beyond the historical concern with 'bias'. A rhetorical approach to texts takes silences and spaces not – or not only – as the suppressed counter-narratives to, but as part of the articulations of, authority. Indeed, some scholars have advanced the subtle argument that, especially in divided political cultures, some forms of propaganda, rather than even claiming a univocal coherence that eclipses other voices, acknowledge them and admit the instabilities and incompleteness of their own performances. Identifying the apparently contra-dictory classical and Christian symbols on Saxon coins, Anna Gannon, rather than trying to explain them away, suggested that 'the charged ambiguity between temporal and celestial symbols and attributes may be intentional and thought provoking'.[144] Such approaches that bring ambiguities and silences to the surface of texts of power may again offer rich possibilities for the study of early modern England. Central to a humanist training in rhetoric was the daily school and university practice of arguing *in utramque partem*, that is on both sides of an argument. Such an education (perhaps until the second half of the twentieth century still the essence of grammar school and university educa-tion) led all students instinctively to imagine, hear or conjure the opposite argument to whatever was articulated.[145] Together with the dialogic form of much Renaissance writing and argument, a training in rhetoric fashioned readers and writers who could not but conceive, along with what was said, what was not said, or said differently. Among those Renaissance readers, writers and speakers were kings, queens and princes who knew that, like them, educated subjects could and would always imagine other arguments. The skilful rhetori-cian, therefore, did not repress other positions but aired them, in the hope of controlling alternative arguments by ventriloquizing or authoring them them-selves. This was the common tactic of the dialogue; as we shall see, Henry VIII himself used the form to persuade his subjects of the legitimacy of his divorce and Queen Elizabeth translated dialogues to assert her authority.[146] In some genres, such as proclamations or statutes, other, alternative arguments may appear less obvious than in dialogues or speeches. But they are always there below the surface, and monarchs always knew that they were there. As we turn to examine Tudor and Stuart royal representations we must consider, as well as statements and objects, silences, spaces and alternatives that, whether highlighted or not, were part of the construction and representation of authority. In some cases, Peter Lely's portraits of Charles II's mistresses, for instance, we may even suggest that space, absence, constituted the most powerful representation of presence, that, like the empty throne in the Presence Chamber, the king was powerfully and mystically present though he was not there.[147]

Our discussion of recent work on authority and propaganda and of new methodological approaches has been illustrated with examples of the writings not only of historians of other periods and countries but also of art historians, numismatists, classicists and literary critics. Recent scholarship on representation, in other words, has been interdisciplinary. Interdisciplinarity has for some years now been a buzz word, too often used by university administrators as a code for amalgamating and reducing the numbers of departments and lecturers, especially in the supposedly less relevant humanities. Even when genuinely new intellectual agenda lay behind plans, many scholars – and most historians – have reacted to interdisciplinary moves by highlighting the risks involved in undervaluing disciplinary training and rigour, or the danger, as the most hostile see it, of dissolving solid scholarship into present-driven, unempirical and empty 'trendiness'. Though in the case of many historians, the objections disclose a protective fear for the survival and nature of the discipline, such criticisms should not be dismissed. Much of that interdisciplinary programme called Cultural Studies has seemed to fade into the banal and obvious or the obscure and impenetrable and has, through insufficient respect for historical circumstances, failed to illuminate past cultures or societies.[148] Yet most university teachers regret that, as students pursue one subject, they all but lay aside what they have learned by studying related disciplines and all too often separate their leisure reading of a wide variety of books from their studies. To be specific, most university students of history will have studied novels and poems and probably been trained to pay some attention to language, metaphor, syntax and so on. Few – and few academic historians – however apply such skills to reading historical sources. Perhaps more surprising is how a modern scholar or student, used to unpacking a political speech by Bush or Blair, identifying rhetoric and strategy, reads pronouncements of previous ages uncritically or naïvely. Or how few with highly developed exegetical skills shaped by experience of modern movies or advertisements apply them to pre-modern visual texts. In part this failure to make connections, to transfer critical skills, has been a casualty of a modern tendency to specialization which an industrial world seemed to require. If our post-industrial circumstance might suggest a different emphasis, the same must be said of the early modern past. Scholarly disciplines, it is worth reminding ourselves, were not given or natural; they were (and are) constructions, and constructions made to serve ideologies as well as to facilitate intellectual enquiry. In some respects, any study of past cultures or mentalities in which perception and understanding were not structured by or through disciplines is limited by our disciplinary specialization. A historical rigour that denies a place for myth, fable or romance will not take us far towards understanding the early modern past.

Though much more might be said in general, my particular point here is that the study of the image and representations of regality and the culture of authority *must* be interdisciplinary. This is no less true of specialized studies than of a broad review such as this. So, for example, a recent work on the iconography of Saxon coins has identified 'the eclectic use of a great variety of sources beyond those of purely numismatic derivation'.[149] As well as other coins, Dr Gannon showed, Saxon coins drew on Greek political theory, classical symbols, Christian signs, literary tropes and Germanic and Celtic legends, the investigation of all of which is necessary to an appreciation of Saxon iconography and state-building. Similarly, a historian of coronations has observed how, specific though his investigation is, the study of coronations has to embrace, as well as other rituals, sermons, panegyrics, plays, paintings and portents, all of which have tended to be studied in different disciplines and institutions.[150] For any period a *cultural* history of politics must break out of disciplinary specialism. As a historian of Edward III has argued, to understand that king's representation we need to examine how conventional hagiographical tropes and Edward's murals combined with divine services in St Stephen's Chapel.[151] Increasingly, too, a number of scholars have urged, against the traditions of intellectual history and connoisseurship, the need to consider 'the interaction between ... representation and the technical and material', between, that is, conception and execution.[152] One of the signs of a new interdisciplinarity has been a sense of the limitations of the languages of any one discipline. Accordingly, Helen Hacket wrote: 'somewhere between and among psychoanalysis, political history and aesthetic criticism there must be a language to talk about images of monarchy'.[153] Certainly, though historians have not been prominent in so doing, scholars have begun to borrow the vocabularies and concepts of other disciplines for their own. Following the pioneering work of Michael Baxandall, for example, several historians of art and architecture use terms such as 'imaged discourse' or study a building as 'a representation of certain discursive practices', with reference to discourse theories that have transformed the study of words.[154]

The interdisciplinarity which I have found most helpful is not simply that which leads us from the Bayeux Tapestry to French epic or from a poem to a medal, but that which sees in others' working methods an approach or tool to help interrogate, or even sometimes recognize, a new question. As I have indicated, I have found the history of the book's address to materiality and commerce and the history of reading's attention to audience and reception invaluable in thinking about other than written texts: paintings and woodcuts, medals and coins. For me, far from threatening, the critic's insistence on the textuality, the rhetoricity of all locutions, declarations and representations has enriched an understanding of early modern authority. As one scholar put it succinctly, 'in the gap between history and textuality' we have 'the rhetoric of power'.[155] An investment in such interdisciplinary approaches comes with what a distinguished practitioner calls dangers. Most young scholars, and no few older ones, are rightly worried about their insufficient expertise in more than one discipline. We must indeed acknowledge that we cannot read a coin in the same way that we read a proclamation and that a true understanding of a Van Dyck portrait requires knowledge of Titian and Rubens, of classical and Christian art and iconography, and of technique and form. Yet, I would insist, simply placing a Holbein next to a sermon, or viewing a medal alongside a spectacle, or attempting a thick description of an engraving are themselves informative and worthwhile. In the end, each scholar has an objective; in pursuing it, it is worth at times using the tools of another craft. The questions the historian of royal representation asks of a portrait are not the same (or at least not necessarily the same) as those posed by an art historian, but the questions and approaches of the art historian, or, as likely, the anthropologist or literary critic, may usefully assist the enquiry.

As I shall later more freely confess, this study is a work of amateurism as well as interdisciplinarity because it had to be. One cannot understand regal representations in early modern England by separating words from images, woodcuts and coins from portraits, rituals from sermons, or any of them from the histories of production, circulation and reception that were all stages in their ideological performances. The world of the Renaissance, early modern England, was an intertextual world which we can only begin to comprehend, as contemporaries comprehended it, from multidisciplinary as well as interdisciplinary perspectives. If, however, our attempt to understand regality and authority necessitates not only multidisciplinarity with all its risks but also a rejection of the traditional historical distinction between events and representations, what we must retain is the historian's (perhaps unique) concern with exact moments, particular circumstances, and change. Whatever, then, my use of others' tools and crafts, what follows is a historian's study of politics and power in the sixteenth- and seventeenth-century past.

Because my purpose is not only to illuminate each reign but to enable comparisons and contrasts, to identify developments and changes, for each of the monarchs studied I will investigate representations in words (familiar and neglected), images, in several forms, and various rituals of state. Though this remit is broad, and prevents monographic treatment, only examination of all enables us to discern the extent to which there may – or indeed may not – have been a royal or governmental programme of representation for which different writers, artists and impresarios working in different media were recruited; how significant it was that some rulers, or the same monarch at different times, favoured (or succeeded with) one genre rather than another; and how study of each medium helps us to interpret another and recreate the multi-media presentation of authority that contemporaries experienced. For each reign, also, a chapter or section, necessarily if regrettably a brief sample of the evidence, attempts to assess reactions to, and opposition to, official representations, in order to illuminate the success of official scripts and images and the dialogue with subjects.

Though in each section an effort will be made to distinguish what we know to have been royally authored or officially commissioned representations from those created and distributed by others, in the spirit of John Plunkett's point that regal representations circulate as such 'regardless of whether [they] can be said to have been chosen', we will include texts and forms intended to promote majesty whether they were officially patronized or not.[156] Whatever their own (varying) interests and efforts in crafting their own image, rulers depended upon courtiers, preachers, poets and painters to represent and mediate their authority, even though such mediations involved the authors' own interpretations and preferences. As we have seen, any concept of 'control' is something of an illusion and, in early modern England, authoring was not confined to acts of individual creation. What matters – and the various volumes of Elizabeth's prayers or the *Eikon Basilike* provide good examples – was not so much whether Elizabeth I or Charles I wrote them but that they were received as regal pronouncements, just as portrait copies were taken as images of the ruler whether or not they emerged from the studios of court artists. The contests for the royal image did not follow officially authored representations but were always part of them: part of court, elite and popular politics and social and political relations that other historians have studied from different perspectives. While this is a study of kings and queens, it is hoped that it has something broader to contribute to our understanding of the culture of authority and the politics of early modern England, to the history of the people as well as rulers and elites.

'In the beginning was the Word' – so let us start with a few words of explanation about the approach taken here to verbal representations. Traditional historical study of royal words has left large bodies of royal texts completely unexplored. To be specific, royal statutes, declarations and proclamations are used as evidence in most royal biographies and histories. Some other types of writing also make it into the realm of accepted evidence if they are obviously 'political', such as, say, James VI of Scotland's *Basilikon Doron*. Yet whole tranches of other texts have been ignored, presumably because historians have considered them to be 'unreliable' or irrelevant to the history of politics and public affairs. To take an obvious example, the standard edition of James I's 'political works' omitted all the king's biblical exegeses and commentaries as well as his poems; and most subsequent editors, and all those who are historians, have continued to exclude them.[157] That James himself, when he gathered in 1616 his own *Works*, placed two biblical commentaries at the front of the volume surely suggests that editors may have misrepresented a king whose principal self-presentation was as a mediator and interpreter of God's word.[158] Moreover, in his lifetime James published as well as wrote poems and a treatise on poetry and probably planned a collection of his verse. His self-image as a poet was recognized by several contemporary panegyrists, notably Ben Jonson who flattered the king by describing him as 'best of poets' as well as monarchs.[159] *All* of James's writings – treatises on tobacco, translations of psalms and amorous verse – were, as critics have begun to demonstrate, as much advertisements of and apologias for royal authority as were his *The Trewe Law of Free Monarchies* or his directions to preachers.[160] Royal authorship in early modern England made what we categorize as the personal, the interior, the intimate or the fictional, texts of state. Perhaps the best-known text of James's reign in England was the King James Bible or Authorized Version as it is still known. That Bible nicely illustrates a point I have made: that, though it was largely the work of others, the king was very much seen as the author (authorizer); and, not least on its engraved title page, it symbolized and represented his royal authority and his person.[161] As we shall discuss, the King James Bible had material affinities to the king's *Works* and we will not appreciate the performance or importance to contemporaries of any of these texts unless we consider them in relation to each other. To divide James's writings into those that are of historical and political significance and those that are not misses the opportunity to interrogate more 'private' genres of writing (itself a complicated term, given that many were published) and to hear the different voices of a ruler who had a very keen sense of genre and whose private and public bodies were often in tension. Now the subject of a monograph as well as a stimulating volume of essays, James's writings have begun to disclose the rich materials that historians have for so long ignored.[162]

James VI and I is the paradigmatic but by no means the only example of an early modern ruler whose representation in words awaits a study. Critics have begun to take an interest in Henry VIII's lyrics and songs as self-representation as lover and warrior; Elizabeth I's verses, recently re-edited, are being re-read as devices that deployed female coterie genres to make public pronouncements and as a medium of the queen's clever manipulation of privacy and publicity.[163] Her verse translations, of Boethius, Horace and Plutarch, have not yet attracted modern editors or commentators, perhaps because translation is not fully accepted as the work of the writing self; but it is, we will show, a revealing form of self-construction and publicization.[164] If, even in Elizabeth's case, there is much more to do, the writings of other Tudor sovereigns, Edward VI and Mary, have hardly been noticed as texts of self-presentation. The neglect is greater still for the later Stuarts, especially James II. Only recently has a historian begun to see the importance of Charles II's own narrative of his escape after the Battle of Worcester and only James II's latest biographer begins to consider the king's memoirs and devotions as materials of self-presentation, as polemic as well as biography.[165] James's military memoirs, meanwhile, though edited now for nearly fifty years, have yet to be read as an image of the king.[166] I hope that my brief discussions in the chapters that follow of some of these writings will encourage others to more systematic analysis. For what these neglected texts often do is cast a new light on the better-known, political writings. To hear Queen Elizabeth in verse musing on her divided self as sovereign and woman and on the agonies of reconciling affairs of state and the heart compels us to read her speeches, perhaps the whole politics of her reign, differently.[167] No less to read James II's conversations with his God as well as his military memoirs is to observe a king constructing his own identities, identities that have been subsequently overwritten by Whig polemics.

Vital though they are, a simple recovery and a reading of such royal writings are not all that is required. Their material forms, distribution and reception histories are important. Henry VIII's lyrics, for example, remained in manuscript, despite his use of print for polemical justification. But, especially where verse is concerned, manuscript cannot be simply equated with privacy: some of them set to music, Henry's poems circulated, were known and (it has been argued), directed at critics of his behaviour, 'constituted public performances'.[168] A similar case has been made that some of Elizabeth's apparently most personal verses were widely circulated in manuscript, leading us to suspect that they may have been distributed with her approval.[169] Interestingly, though they were not published in her lifetime, neat copies of some of the queen's translations are found in scribal hands in the state papers, suggesting public rather than private performance. In the case of printed works, some of the volumes received as the queen's prayers do not carry her name on the title page. Several of James VI and I's manuscripts show signs of revision and we know that he reworked and glossed one poem to dispel any sense of sympathy for Catholicism.[170] And, of course, which of his Scottish writings he reissued in English and how he re-rendered the original tells us much about the image he desired to present to different audiences in particular circumstances.[171] The copying of all, or any, of these royal writings into commonplace books, their placement and arrangement with other extracts or verses, both underlines the importance for contemporaries of royal authors and figures and opens insights into the textual relations of kings and queens with other writers, readers and subjects. As Milton was to acknowledge, the words, the fictions, of royal authors carried great authority with subjects and needed to be systematically discredited if regal authority itself was to be successfully challenged.[172]

In *Eikonoklastes* Milton devoted hundreds of pages to identifying and exposing the rhetorical artifice and stratagems of what passed as a royal text. As we have remarked, such adversarial and rhetorical readings have not been much practised by historians of early modern England. Though there is no excuse for this where speeches are concerned, it may seem on a superficial reading that, say, proclamations do little more than issue a straightforward royal order. However, as we shall see, proclamations justified and explained as well as proclaimed royal wishes; for all their closing threats of condign punishment for non-compliance, they were texts of persuasion. (And not only texts: often read aloud before a noisy crowd, proclamations at the market cross were performances of royal authority and at times became scenes of performed responses to it.) When we read the most obviously political and public genres of royal writing alongside other, sometimes more obviously literary, royal texts, we may better sense the rhetorical techniques a royal writer favoured or best deployed. Certainly, at least to this reader, Elizabeth's complex manipulation of gender and affect in speeches and letters is illuminated by reading her poems and prayers. Differently, in different genres, the use of first or third person pronouns, the shift from active to passive verbs, the language of self-assertion or self-abnegation, a tone of distance or familiarity, the figuring of community or party, formed vital constituents of the rhetoric of self-presentation and authority. Occasionally, as with James's treatise on poetry, we are gifted with direct royal reflections on the arts of rhetoric, the poetics of power itself.[173] But to appreciate how all monarchs and rulers represented themselves in words, we must treat all their locutions and writings as texts artfully composed with the aim of persuading. Whether they bore his or her portrait or arms as a frontispiece, the royal name on the title page as author, or the imprimatur of the royal printer, all texts that circulated as royal represented regality and – whatever royal wishes to the contrary – initiated a textual dialogue about kingship.

Our second concern for each reign is the visual representation of the ruler. Though most historians appear more comfortable or confident with words and tend, rather than analysing them as texts, to use pictures as illustration,[174] many would concur with the art historian Jonathan Brown's statement that 'since antiquity, portraits of rulers have reflected the aspirations, ideals and pretensions of those in power. Because these images epitomise a ruler's self-concept, they are valuable sources for understanding the personalities and programmes of the sitters.'[175] As I shall discuss, the Tudor and Stuart centuries did not simply coincidentally see a revolution in the art of portraiture as well as revolutions in the state; and it is no accident that the portrait images of Henry VIII, Elizabeth I and Charles I are so well known to the educated public. Scholars of Tudor and early Stuart England have been fortunate in the art historians who worked on this period with a full sense of the importance of the portraits as historical objects. Not only did the former Keeper of the Queen's Pictures, Sir Oliver Millar, bring an unrivalled learning to some of the most important canvases of kings and queens; leading scholars from the Warburg School applied their broad interdisciplinary training to the interpretation of allegorical paintings. The name of Sir Roy Strong is inseparable from any discussion of Tudor and Stuart art or of the visual culture of early modern England: his recently published collected essays stand as a monument to his pioneering research.[176] Yet, perhaps typical of the great scholars who ask more questions than they can find answers to, Strong brilliantly identified the many areas of little knowledge or understanding in studies of sixteenth- and seventeenth-century British art. Over forty years ago, Strong lamented the gap between art historical and historical studies that had left much archival evidence neglected; in particular, he commented, there was a 'strong prejudice among connoisseurs and art historians against source material which is not factual' (diaries for example), while, on the other side, historians regarded inventories as the business of the art historian.[177] Turning to artists, Strong and those gathered with him at a conference to assess the state of the art in British art history, noted that there was no good study of Holbein, no *catalogue raisonné* of the work of Van Dyck, and no book on Michael Wright, not to mention more minor figures urgently in need of study – Hans Eworth, Marcus Gheeraerts the Younger and William Dobson or the miniaturists Isaac Oliver and John Hoskins. Almost in passing, Strong urged further research on engravings, stressing their 'enormous value for the historian', and woodcuts – 'another sorely neglected field'.

Finally, in a meeting to discuss art and ideas, Strong observed that 'the study of British art ... has suffered because of isolation from the general currents of political, religious, cultural and social history and is handicapped by a continuing tradition of connoisseurship in which a genteel attitude towards pictures keeps the viewer from asking what they are about'. By corollary, he also criticized political historians who, he insisted, 'should study portraits, seals and other visual material'. Introducing the last subject, art and monarchical propaganda, Strong called for an approach that 'would cut across the history of art into that of political, literary and ideological history' and posited Charles II and William III as figures much in need of just such interdisciplinary attention.

It may seem otiose to reprise a discussion that took place over forty years ago, especially as, since then, as well as Strong's own work, we have fine studies of Holbein and Van Dyck, an excellent monograph on the propaganda of William III and so on.[178] However, what is striking is how many of the gaps and problems Strong identified remain. Indeed, the approach he most criticized, that of genteel connoisseurship, if anything became more dominant in art historical scholarship on painting in subsequent years and the broad interdisciplinary and historical programme he advocated found fewer champions.[179] Strong was – and in some circles remains – a controversial figure among art historians, while few historians, with the notable exception of scholars like Robert Scribner and Tessa Watt, pursued his suggestions into less elite visual forms such as woodcuts.[180] After the 1960s and '70s, as far as early modern England was concerned, art historians and historians, far from pursuing the dialogue Strong had urged, went off in different directions, leaving the visual culture of the period an unexplored terrain.

Very much in Strong's spirit, however, a scholar of an earlier continental period began to publish some of the most important and influential manifestos for the exploration of visual culture that continue to inform the approach I take in this study. In major studies of *Painting and Experience in Fifteenth Century Italy*, or *The Limewood Sculptors of Renaissance Germany* and in books and essays outlining a methodology for the historical interpretation of pictures, Michael Baxandall laid out a manifesto which challenged the existing historical and art historical communities and practices.[181] Criticizing the typical analytical naïvety of historians when discussing visual materials – what he rightly dismissed as 'the philistine level of the illustrated social history' – Baxandall, against the connoisseurs, insisted that 'social history and art history are continuous' and that, not merely aesthetic objects, 'paintings are, among other things, fossils of economic life'.[182] Baxandall urged art historians to move away from a preoccupation with 'influence', to relate paintings to other visual practices and, beyond, to 'the experience of such activities as preaching, dancing' – in fact all 'social experience'.[183] To historians Baxandall issued a challenge and promised an opportunity: to discern in what ways 'a pictorial style gives access to the visual skills and habits and, through these, to the distinctive social experience' of any period in the past.[184] In a wonderfully suggestive phrase that resonates with any student of literature,

Baxandall declared that 'a picture may profitably be construed as a piece of problem solving' and so read as a rich text of an individual and society's grappling with its tensions and problems.[185]

Baxandall's description of pictures as 'material and visible deposits left behind by earlier peoples' activity', has been influential in a shift of approach from connoisseurship to an interest in visual and material culture, to a historical anthropology of the painting as visual artefact and of other material objects in which (as Jules Prown and others have argued) cultural values are embedded and represented: be they clothes, furniture or musical or scientific instruments,[186] Along with semiotic and gender theory, Baxandall's studies and the turn to material culture have been the most important influences on scholars of visual culture of many periods. Paul Binski, drawing attention to materials and forms, has insisted on 'the potential of any artefact not only to shape our understanding of a culture but actually substantially to form that culture'.[187] A study of Saxon coins reads from their materiality and forms ideological tensions in the broader culture which the author found other artefacts and literary remains helped to explicate.[188] In works such as these, the aesthetic value judgements of an older art history were replaced by an interdisciplinary study of visual and material culture, concerned as much to illuminate the culture as the object, and ideology as much as (a supposedly trans-ideological) aesthetic. get on w it!

In the chapters that follow, I will examine visual representations of monarchy alongside verbal and ritual representations. Our emphasis will be placed on endeavouring to elucidate what the portrait, painting or object discloses about cultural values and political programmes and how it seeks to present and represent authority. As well as paying attention to words written on or in paintings, we will read courtly canvases alongside other visual materials close to regality, such as seals, medals and coins; and study more broadly circulating reproductions of regal images in engravings, woodcuts and, in some cases, souvenir objects. Medals and coins, both because they were regal forms and because they usually combined an image with a legend and were struck and issued to mark a particular event or occasion, offer especially rich insights into how a ruler intended his or her image to perform.[189] By identifying and explicating the source of the legend, we may open the literary or mythological context and culture and reconstitute the interpretative environment in which these representations were read and circulated. Engravings and woodcuts resituate visuals in a world – and war – of words in other ways. Published as separates, in various states and forms, they were often accompanied with words, from simple descriptions to elaborate exegeses, from classical verse to doggerel ballads.[190] Whether large and expensive fine copperplate or small cheap block, engravings and woodcuts performed in quite different communities of consumers, collectors and observers. In the case of the portraits of rulers as illustrations to books, royal images might be seen, depending on the text, as simply illustrating a chronicle of events, as a sign of authority, or as part of a moral narrative of good and bad princes which fashioned popular memory and popular politics. In the case of all visual materials, portrait or coin, we will consider genre, form and materiality – the size of a canvas or print, whether a medal was issued in gold or copper – as well as content. Most of all, we will treat all visual materials not as illustrative of, but as constructing, a social and political culture – as attempts to transform as much as reflect values. When we consider the portraits that emerged in moments of political and representational crisis, such as the Reformation or regicide, we will reconsider Baxandall's suggestion that 'a picture may profitably be construed as a piece of problem solving'. For to think of Hans Holbein's authoritative portraits of Henry VIII, Oliver Cromwell's appropriation of the courtly forms of Van Dyck, or Godfrey Kneller's equestrian portrait of William III as attempts to address problems of legitimacy opens rich new perspectives; not least it invites us to read pictures, like other texts, as responses to crisis or as sites of anxiety about alternative imaginings and representations that authority was concerned to paint over. Because regal images were not the outward signs of an established and secure authority but part of the anxious and contentious process of constructing and sustaining that authority in the face of animadversion and contest, new styles and forms in art were often responses to new difficulties in the state. From Richard II onwards, we have learned, the growth in the display of royal badges testified to dynastic insecurity;[191] while, in the case of James I, the royal adoption of the imperial laureate bust on medals and coins signified, along with the hopes of empire, the difficulties in fashioning a British imperium.

In other words, part of the problem that any visual representation sought to solve was the potential persuasiveness of other representations, visual or verbal. Writing on the German Reformation, Jules Koerner observed that it is not only images that 'never go away'; it is also 'iconoclasm itself that never goes away'.[192] 'Images ... persist and function by being perpetually destroyed.'[193] Such a dialectic may be as applicable to secular as to religious art. In all ages political opposition has often been first expressed in acts of iconoclasm. Yet acts of iconoclasm acknowledge the power of visual forms to symbolize and even reify authority. The same may be said of cartoons, which began to emerge in our period. Evidently a satirical image of him circulating on the London streets led Richard Cromwell, Oliver's son and successor as Protector, to confine himself to his chamber.[194] But sixteenth- and seventeenth-century cartoons not only drew on and from official images; directed at ministers rather than monarchs, they yet signalled a respect to the end of our period (the Hanoverians were the first to suffer direct visual satire at the hands of English subjects) for the sanctity of the mystical royal body.[195] Just like written texts, that is, the visual forms of the royal image were conceived, circulated and contested within a culture of icon and iconoclasm, a condition of struggle for cultural and political authority as well as religious dominance. We must endeavour to return visual texts to those circumstances.

The third aspect of our study of each reign focuses on forms that combine verbal and visual representations: state spectacles and rituals. Spectacles are events as well as representations and have probably received more historical attention as the former. Few histories or royal biographies, that is, will fail to relate the fact of a coronation, funeral or even a royal progress; but full descriptions of the triumphal arches, pageant shows, verses, speeches or interludes that constituted the theatre of these occasions have often been left to other scholars, especially literary scholars, to explore. Indeed, most of our modern editions of texts of triumphs and pageants have been published by critics and are usually classified in libraries (the persistent guardians of disciplinary boundaries) as literature. Significantly, it was scholars from the Warburg Institute (where famously the library is not arranged by conventional classification or disciplines) who developed and transformed study of Renaissance spectacles. Devoted to the classical tradition, Warburg scholars, rather than passing over these pageants as simple entertainments, identified through close research complex webs of allusion to classical texts, Neoplatonic philosophy and the hermetic and cabbalistic traditions. Surveying a broadly European classical inheritance, they showed how the state pageants of various countries drew on a common stock of ideas and were often in dialogue, as rulers vied to surpass each other in magnificent display and learning. While vitally important for taking pageants and spectacles seriously, as often articulating large philosophical statements, Warburg scholarship on spectacle risked detaching pageants from the local, historical circumstances that gave them their particular meaning. Emphasis on the shared philosophical traditions and common European vocabularies, not least because it understates the ways in which iconographical and symbolic traditions can do new work in new circumstances, has tended to subordinate the specific politics of spectacle. Such emphasis has also often left aside questions about audiences. Though state spectacles were displays of princely power and aristocratic wealth and privilege, they were, in several senses, popular: they were staged before the people; they required popular attendance and participation; and the people flocked to them. The more philosophically complex the pageants were shown to be – the more their 'meaning' depended upon knowledge of the classics – the more the question arose of how effective they could be in communicating to the people. It was just this concern that led the leading scholar of sixteenth-century English spectacles to doubt the point of his own life's scholarly work. In 1992,

Sydney Anglo revisited, in *Images of Tudor Kingship*, subjects he had explored for two decades and doubted whether, along with paintings and poems, spectacles should be treated with 'deadly seriousness'.[196] Ordinary people, he now observed, did not comprehend complex iconographical programmes or emblems: 'esoteric and complex ideas were likely to lose the audience'.[197] And progresses, he added, should better be seen as motivated by desire to flee a plague-ridden capital than as intended to communicate spectacular display to the provinces.[198] Though here and there he sounds a salutary note of caution against the heights of Warburg interpretative extravagance, Anglo misjudges the reach and appeal of spectacles and, crucially, their capacity to function at different levels. As we shall see, devisers of pageants often went to lengths, including the incorporation of informative labels and keys, to identify mythological or classical pageant figures for the less learned; and, along with learned speeches and poems, pageants often included simple verses and popular songs delivered by folk heroes or popular figures from history, memory or myth who spoke for the common man. Moreover, Anglo underestimates a popular acquaintance with emblems and their significations not least because, along with other Warburg scholars, he subordinated the religious to the classical themes of spectacles. Appearing as woodcuts in or on the borders of devotional books, or woven into cloths, religious and moral emblems, never far removed from popular proverbs and fables, were part of the fabric and household of those below the level of the learned gentry, even of the illiterate.[199] A language of signs in early modern England was by no means the monopoly of the elite.

Since Anglo's early work and that of the Warburg School in general, the study of festival and ritual, indeed of early modern culture, has taken a more popular and anthropological direction. Left-leaning historians in particular, shifting the scholarly focus from a history dominated by elites to what has been called 'history from below', began to study popular festivals and rituals – especially charivari, rough music and village shaming rituals which underpinned community norms and constructed and sustained social codes.[200] However, largely because research in this field was carried out by social historians who, from the 1970s, were becoming more detached from an increasingly narrowly conceived political history, few explored the political dialogue that was being conducted between elite and popular ritual forms. Just as in royal and metropolitan pageants popular figures were staged, so, it often seemed, popular festivity aped, appropriated, and at times mocked, elite ritual tropes in ways which might be revealing of popular attitudes to authority and its representations.

More theoretical and anthropological approaches held out the promise of a more nuanced understanding of how spectacles constructed and represented a system of signs which helped to cement social and political communities. In that respect it is regrettable that few historians of early modern rituals, elite or popular, paid any serious attention to Michel Foucault's discussion of the epistemes that determined what it was possible to think, or to the figure who was to emerge as the most influential anthropologist of his generation, Clifford Geertz.[201] In *The Interpretation of Cultures* (1973), Geertz posited a new method for approaching ritual and spectacle as a symbolic system and for the analysis of politics and power as the interplay of rituals and signs. Yet, though they did not ignore the people, neither Foucault nor Geertz left much room for popular agency in their models of the performances of symbolic systems. Where Foucault regarded them, even when they appeared to license dissent, as hegemonic systems in the service of totalizing power, Geertz tended to assume the success of symbolic actions, leaving it unclear how his model of cultures as control mechanisms for the regulation of behaviour might explain subversion.[202] In the field of anthropological enquiry, it has been James C. Scott who, studying Malaysian peasant society, has formulated a model of the scope and spaces for resistance within structures of domination and argued that even the weakest wield weapons – often symbolic weapons – that enable them to question and contest authority.[203] It has been a shift of emphasis from authorities to subjects, authors to audiences, and from models of hegemony to instability, that has begun to reorient historical work on spectacle and political culture more generally. In Janos M. Bak's study of medieval and early modern monarchical ritual, as well as the obvious influence of Geertz on analysis of coronations as 'part of a whole world of symbolic action, gesture and behaviour', we encounter a new need to ask how rituals were 'perceived by those present'.[204] Recent studies have brought this dimension to the fore. In his brilliant study of *Spectacular Power in the Greek and Roman City*, Andrew Bell, while acknowledging that spectacle may (and was probably intended to) confirm subjects in a position of 'passive subjecthood', critiques earlier assumptions of hegemony and control.[205] Arguing that 'charisma generally requires sustained engagement with the sensibilities of consumers of political celebrity', Bell showed how Caesar incorporated communal rites into his spectacles and suggested that spectacles constituted 'a web of interactions, mutualities and reciprocities' which were designed for aesthetic and political 'complicity' but which left spaces for difference and resistance – even for what a recent scholar of Tudor progresses insisted was 'the potential for resistance on the part of the common people'.[206]

That 'potential for resistance' could be realized in many different ways in early modern England, from the silence or hisses of the crowd on Anne Boleyn's entry, to the mob murder of an officer on a royal progress in 1592.[207] Once again, they include acts of appropriation. As Ian Gentles and John Adamson have shown, during the course of the Civil War, the Long Parliament appropriated royal precedents and forms for the state funerals of its leaders John Pym and the Earl of Essex.[208] 'By imitating the extravagance and pomp of the traditional royal ... funeral, the Long Parliament was attempting to proclaim the greatness of its leaders.'[209] Such an appropriation, as well as evidence of a shared heraldic and symbolic culture, signified a division within an aristocratic and gentry culture. More interesting perhaps is the appropriation of these ritual forms by the Levellers Thomas Rainborough and Robert Lockyer whose funerals were attended by thousands wearing, as if in mockery of heraldic symbols, the green ribbon of the Levellers, outlawed by Oliver Cromwell.[210] If here, as often, opposition drew something of its force from official rituals, we cannot but be led to ponder the extent to which rituals and spectacles, as well as representing authority, enabled subjects to figure and represent themselves not as 'passive subjects' but as political actors.[211]

In this study, reminded as we are by occasions when official programmes did not go to plan, we shall endeavour to bear in mind the complexities and dialogues involved in state spectacles such as coronations, civic entries, funerals, Garter festivals and progresses. Though we will identify common themes and vocabularies that rulers borrowed or appropriated from predecessors (the figure of Truth, as we saw, appeared in both Mary and Elizabeth's coronation pageants), we will need to consider how each ruler adapted ritual forms for his or her very different personal (as well as political) circumstances – of age, sex or marital status, for example. We must also keep in mind the various elements that made up any ritual occasion: a coronation, for instance, usually involved a formal entry, a religious service, a sermon, a feast and other ceremonies, such as the creation of Knights of the Bath, as well as the anointing and investing themselves; a progress involved a large procession which displayed the royal household, often pageants along the way, civic entries and addresses, church attendances, the giving of gifts and the knighting of mayors or hosts. As always in writing the history of the England of the long Reformation period, we must recall that, just as the word 'ritual' itself has its origin in acts of worship, so state spectacles were religious occasions and inseparable from the liturgies, and from the debates about liturgy and ceremony, of the church. If, as has been argued, the Tudors emphasized the secular over the religious aspects of coronations, arguably they did so by appropriating the sacred for state rituals, the role in which of Christian and distinctly Protestant symbols has received surprisingly less attention than the classical or philosophical motifs.[212] Finally we should not forget that, though for many spectacles and rituals were experienced as occasions or events, our only access to them is through texts – an entirely different medium of experience.[213] Charisma, for example, is far harder to communicate on the page than in person; the dazzling of the sense by rich jewels, clothes and colours, lofty arches or extravagant firework displays is impossible to render in words as it was experienced; most of all the affective, emotional and communal bonds formed through shared participation are less easily felt or formed alone in the study, or even perhaps reported in a tavern. Whatever the power of modern media, those who attended Princess Diana's funeral evidently became caught up in a cathartic release of shared emotion, a communal experience which was very different from that of those who watched the occasion on television in a domestic environment, with other affective relations more obviously to the fore.[214] Though, however, we must recognize that our own understanding of ritual and spectacle is limited by being mediated through texts, we are thereby led to consider the performances of those textual accounts of spectacles which served as souvenirs for those who had been present and, doubtless, as a form of inclusion for those who had not. As we noted, from Elizabeth's reign there was a market for accounts of royal rituals and progresses that witnesses a broad desire to participate in processes of representation, in a monarchical commonwealth. But as the differences between and omissions in some accounts make clear (none include the Spanish envoy's 1578 report that Elizabeth told Norwich: 'I know you do not love me here'), such textual representations did not simply reflect, but themselves endeavoured to construct, affective bonds.[215]

In the last chapter of each study of a reign, we will briefly glance at other representations of the ruler: the more negative, oppositional images that circulated in the ruler's lifetime or, when enough is known, the contested memory and posthumous representations of the sovereign. A proper study of the appropriations of the royal image of any one ruler in life and death and of the counter-images of all rulers, because it opens on to the full social, political and cultural history of the sixteenth and seventeenth centuries, cannot, it hardly need be said, be attempted here. My aim is more modest: a brief glance at other representations and memories is intended to further illustrate the openness of official scripts and images to contest, and ultimately the inability of monarchs to control, their representation. However that may generally be the case, though, the forms counter-representations took, and the extent to which they overrode or were contained by authorized images, are highly revealing of the success a ruler enjoyed. Though, for example, Henry VIII suffered from rumours about his unsuitable liaisons with Anne Boleyn, and Elizabeth was bruited to have given birth to several bastards, overall it was their own self-representation as strong, determined rulers that won through and bequeathed an image of strength to memory and history. Interestingly, at the end of the seventeenth century each was respectively hero and heroine of romance fictions; and both, like Charles II later, have been handled with some affection in popular biographies or histories.[216] Queen Mary, James I and James II, by contrast, suffered the fate of having their critics and opponents override their own self-presentations and determine, even to our own day, their historical reputations. While Mary and James II's Catholicism may offer some explanation in their cases (though it risks being too simple an explanation), James I, who was a committed Protestant and who assiduously authored his own image in words, would seem to demand other explanations. Moreover, in assessing why or how counter-images of a ruler overtook their own representations, we must recognize that it is inadequate to think in terms of an entire reign. James VI and I, after all, was greeted with widespread relief and rejoicing which really only turned sour after the Overbury scandal and the crisis in the Palatinate. Elizabeth's image after forty years on the throne was unquestionably tarnished, yet, as she neared death, the spell she had earlier cast over her subjects was again manifested in widespread affection and nostalgia. As we shall see in detail, Charles I was a ruler whose most brilliant act of self-representation was his death; his posthumous iconic life as martyr bears witness to how the seeming victory of enemies can in a moment be turned into defeat.[217] In a not dissimilar way, James II, though expelled from his throne in 1688, crafted in exile an image of wronged rectitude which destabilized British government for more than half a century.[218]

How far then, we might ask, was it the character and skills of individual monarchs and their impresarios and supporters and how far events and circumstances that determined their representation and reputation? How adroitly did rulers shape their languages and rhetoric to changing circumstances or refigure their image through periods of religious turmoil or popular unrest? Were visual representations more effective in a largely illiterate culture and how did expanding literacy, print and news, transform modes of representation? What, in fine, do changes in the genres and forms of representation tell us about larger shifts in the culture and politics of the period, in the nature of royal authority and perceptions of royal authority?

Such large questions have themselves dictated the unusually broad chronological reach of these volumes. But, aside from my perennial interest in the period, there are other reasons why the sixteenth and seventeenth centuries demand a study of royal images and the politics of representation. When I first conceived this project, I began by testing a hunch. I showed a variety of friends and acquaintances (a few ex-undergraduate historians, most not) photos of the kings and queens of England. Few failed to identify most of the Tudors and Stuarts; few were able to recognize rulers before or after – with obvious exceptions such as Queen Victoria. Nearly all failed to differentiate the three Georges or identify medieval monarchs other than, in a couple of cases, Richard II who was, of course, recognized from the Wilton Diptych. One explanation for this – it was indeed ventured by one of my focus group – was the quality of artists who depicted Tudor and Stuart monarchs. Yet, as we have observed, Holbein, Gheeraerts, Van Dyck, Lely and Kneller, to name only a few, were not native artists; they were recruited by English sovereigns (and subjects) who evidently discerned the need for their talents. From Henry VIII to William III, English sovereigns showed a new concern with art and their portrait image and endeavoured to commission and authorize official portrait types which presented them as sovereigns but also, unlike earlier generic royal images, as distinct, recognizable individuals who wore the crown. Early modern English royal portraits, like European Renaissance portraits, suggest a new preoccupation with personal identity and its relation to public authority. By the turn of the eighteenth century, if it is not so much regal portraits that strike us but a new vogue for 'conversation pieces' and scenes of leisured aristocratic life, the change in taste was surely related to social and political changes that a study of such representations helps to illuminate.[219]

The second feature which makes the sixteenth and seventeenth centuries such a fruitful period for this approach is a new preoccupation with spectacle and display. Coronations and royal progresses, of course, were not new in early modern England. But it was during that period that English rulers first showed a keen interest in the theatricalization of power that had long been a characteristic of the representations of continental Renaissance princes. Henry VII, as we shall see, grasped the importance of royal progresses in establishing the authority of a new dynasty with a questionable title; but it was Henry VIII who, most famously at the Field of the Cloth of Gold, deployed display as a weapon in the diplomatic struggle for power abroad and who, at home, staged jousts, festivals and state entries as advertisements of his supremacy.[220] By the end of our long period, the age of the theatricalization of regality had come to a close. The historian of English coronations, for example, described those after 1688 as 'shadows of the great ceremonies of earlier periods'.[221] Queen Anne continued the ceremony of touching but was the last monarch to do so. The court of George I showed little interest in display and George II seldom appeared in the capital or went on progress round the country.[222] In 1734, Defoe described the court at St James's as 'the contempt of foreign nations and the disgrace of our own'.[223] The role of magnificent display in constructing and sustaining royal authority had all but died out and it was arguably not until Victoria's reign that a (different) tradition of spectacular rule was reinvented.

As well as the age of the most visible and charismatic rulers, the sixteenth and seventeenth centuries were centuries of cataclysmic events and crises that were also reflected, enacted and disputed in the modes and media of representation. The crises of Henry VIII's divorce, Mary's succession, Elizabeth's marriage, civil war, regicide, Restoration and the 1688 Revolution were both causes and consequences of crises of representation and need to be, as they have not been, studied as such.[224] The early modern state as it developed under the Tudors and Stuarts was a representational state in which political crises were inevitably bound up with crises of representation. Indeed, it was the first crisis of state in this period, Reformation, that necessitated a new emphasis on the arts of royal representation and cast a long shadow over the whole period that we will review. From the 1530s when Henry VIII broke from Rome and so became, in the eyes of orthodox Catholics, a heretic, the representational state was also a state confessionally divided. While division was not new in English history, a profound ideological fissure was; and it transformed the style of kingship. Deprived of the legitimacy that was endowed by religious orthodoxy (of which his father had made such skilful use), Henry VIII sought to appropriate papal authority for himself – to sacralize his secular authority in order to represent himself as the only divinely ordained authority in the realm. From the Reformation onwards (with the exception of Mary who sought to reinstate papal authority), English sovereigns in different ways struggled to persuade their subjects of their sacred power and position as God's chosen lieutenant, with authority to determine matters of faith as well as state. Struggled that is against others who doubted their orthodoxy and favoured other faiths. Not until the toleration that followed soon after 1688 was religion, in some degree, as Tim Blanning put it, translated from the public to the private sphere.[225] Certainly when the long struggle between Protestantism and Catholicism was over, there was less need to emphasize the sanctity of the sovereign. George I stopped touching to cure the king's evil and even advised those who approached him for a cure that they had better ask the Pretender.[226] Jonathan Clark has been right to warn historians of the rise of modernity that they should not neglect the continuing importance of religion in the *ancien régime*.[227] Yet it remains the case that matters of conscience were no longer in England the causes of public crises and that the representation as sacred was no longer, as Henry VIII had made it, the foundation of regal authority. Again that is not to argue the complete separation of religion from politics – which has still, of course, not taken place. As Durkheim sagely observed, 'society never stops creating new sacred things'; and at times throughout history, as in our own time, the people have chosen to sacralize figures of authority.[228] In 1844, the *Penny Satirist* predicted that, if Victoria published a journal of her travels, the people 'would study it like a prayer book, a book of Queen Elizabeth's homilies'.[229] A tendency to worship and deify, as our celebrity culture makes apparent, is not absent from a secular society. What is important is that it is an impulse that has come from below. That is, the shift from a representational state to a public sphere effected a change to a state in which the mystification of majesty became less the programme of rulers and governments and more the election and desire of subjects and citizens.

At the heart of the large historical thesis expounded in the three volumes that constitute this study are the processes of publicizing monarchy as sacred, contesting the divinity of individual kings and monarchy itself, and re-endowing rulers with the aura of the sacred: processes of mystification, demystification and re-sacralization. These processes, I shall argue, were interdependent and synchronic. Indeed, for all their devotion to sacralizing their regality, dynasty and persons, the Tudors, by publicizing themselves, contributed to a process through which the royal person and body became more familiar and less mystical. While, in quite different ways, the Stuarts endeavoured to claim sacred kingship, acts of publicization, of representation, had compromised the claim. Charles I's martyrdom, as he intuited, checked a trend towards a rationalization of power; but, for all Milton's worries, it did not stop it. Charles II did not attempt to represent his body as mystical – rather the opposite; and by Anne's reign the royal body had become desacralized, making way for the cartoons that grotesqued her successors. Just as the programme of sacralization had been enacted in words, images and spectacle, so all the media of representation, by the end of the period, were subject to change. By 1714, A. S. Williams has argued, 'the unabashed mythologizing of earlier political verse had been thoroughly and explicitly discredited'.[230] A gradually developing belief that things mysterious could be explained began to forge a more rational aesthetic in which the numinous aspects of ceremony began to lose their spiritual underpinning.[231] Anne's attempt to revive ritual did not translate into sacred authority. Indeed, in an arresting phrase that sums up a revolutionary change in sensibility, Sir John Clark, seeing the queen bandaged and in pain, asked (albeit in the private space of his journal): 'what are you, poor mean like mortal, thought I, who talks in the style of a sovereign?'[232]

Personal monarchy survived the 1688 Revolution but perhaps sacred kingship did not. Significantly there was little interest in prints or other images of the Hanoverians, who also renounced any claim to cultural leadership or authority in matters of taste.[233] Yet if Tudor modes of publicizing monarchy had begun a process of demythologizing regality, Henry VIII and still more Elizabeth 'established the terms through which a popular fascination with monarchs as celebrities could flourish'.[234] And on popularity, as the shrewd Charles II understood, a new foundation of power could be built which included elements of the sacred. 'The numenal sense indeed dies hard' among subjects; and even to our own day there have been rulers who have succeeded in turning popularity into iconicity.[235]

'Much', Charles II once declared, 'may be done by the personal intervention of kings.'[236] Though, therefore, our purpose is to illuminate cultural and political developments across the period, in the end, the royal image-making was for each ruler 'contingent and personal'.[237] Certain vocabularies – of scripture and law; certain images – such as the figure of Justice with her scales; particular spectacles (most obviously coronations and state openings of parliament) themselves carried authority and needed to be appropriated and reprised, just as older and newer media of representation had to be harnessed and used. But how, when and with what success each ruler did so requires the particular study of each monarch, each reign – or each regime.

Finally, it seems appropriate to close a long prologue discussing the terms and concepts which underlie this study and a review of approaches that have influenced it with a frank acknowledgement of the random and serendipitous. In the spirit of Blanning's broad anthropological definition of culture as 'knowledge, belief, art, morals, law, custom and any other . . . habits acquired by man' in society, I have cast my research net far wider than the kinds of text normally studied as political sources.[238] Because the material for this study has been hard to delimit, my reading of prayers and sermons, histories and plays, translations and travel books, poems and treatises on art, alongside royal proclamations or portraits has perforce been selective and, no doubt, here and there, specialists will complain, insensitive to generic context. But as well as attempting different contextualizations, I am encouraged by Michael Baxandall's recommendation of a seemingly unsystematic noting of 'bits of social practice' that give insights into a culture.[239] For all the theoretical and methodological influences I have identified, this study is founded on a reading of thousands of texts that, often classified into different disciplines, are here brought together to explicate each other. Present experience of spin and media manipulation posed the questions that initiated this work; but it is study of a broad range of past texts, fictions as well as facts, that informs us how politics and power have never been a matter simply of institutions but are part of a complex culture formed through representations and negotiations.

PART II

TUDOR FOUNDATIONS

CHAPTER 2

FOUNDING A DYNASTY,
FORGING AN IMAGE

Almost every school pupil knows that the Tudor dynasty was founded when, after a bitter battle against Richard III at Bosworth, Henry Tudor became king after retrieving, at least in Shakespeare's dramatized account, the crown from a hawthorn bush. The Battle of Bosworth Field, fought on 22 August 1485, effectively ended the thirty-year civil war known as the Wars of the Roses, between the Yorkists and Lancastrians, in favour of the latter, as well as replacing the Plantagenet family with the Tudors.

Such is the certainty of hindsight. In reality, though Henry slayed the Yorkist Richard, it was far from certain in 1485 that Bosworth would mark a final conclusion to civil war: Henry was under attainder; his claim to the throne was tenuous and disputed; he faced a nobility and a country bitterly divided into camps; and further Yorkist challengers rose up against him almost to the end of his reign. Historians who have sought to explain how Henry overcame opposition and obstacles to remain on his throne and so found a new dynasty that ruled for more than a century used to write of the first Tudor building a 'new monarchy' – a more centralized and authoritarian mode of rule. Some even ventured to suggest that his reign and new style marked the end of a medieval and the beginning of the modern England. While later, more subtle researches have shown that, rather than innovating, Henry developed the institutions and practices of late medieval monarchy, biographies still focus on his financial administration, his use of the Council, Star Chamber and other legal instruments and his relations with parliaments.[1] Interestingly, Francis Bacon, the first historian of the first Tudor, in his *History of the Reign of Henry VII* highlighted other aspects of the king and reign. Bacon noted, for example, how immediately after his victory at Bosworth, Henry 'caused Te Deum Laudamus to be solemnly sung in the presence of the whole army'.[2] He similarly observed how, on entering London, 'he went first into St Paul's church' to make 'offertory of his standards' and how on progress he made ostentatious pilgrimages and organized thanksgivings.[3] Bacon's Henry VII was a king who paid attention to rituals of state and church: he prepared carefully the coronation of his queen, Elizabeth of York, to display Lancaster and York united under his rule;[4] he sponsored jousts and tournaments to entertain the nobility;[5] he graced the sergeants of the law with his attendance at their feasts;[6] on progress in the west he combined majesty with a common touch when he 'gave the citizens great commendations and thanks'.[7] Far from the bureaucrat of much twentieth-century historiography, Bacon's Henry VII was a ruler who, 'being sensible that majesty maketh the people bow', 'kept state and majesty to the height'.[8]

It may be revealing that, writing in 1616, after a half-century of what we shall characterize as the Tudor theatricalization of monarchy, Bacon identified these ceremonial aspects of Henry VII's kingship. If so, it is surely not coincidental that more recent scholarship in our own media age has also addressed the symbolic rather than the institutional and administrative aspects of the first Tudor's rule. Such a perspective, of course, can be traced back to Gordon Kipling's *The Triumph of Honour,* in which he argued for a 'distinctly Tudor style of royal magnificence' that was borrowed from Burgundy and initiated in England by Henry VII who built a new palace, filled it with portraits of kings, attracted Flemish artists and commissioned tapestries and pageants to celebrate the marriage of his son, Prince Arthur, to Catherine of Aragon.[9] But it was not until later that royal cultural borrowings and patronage were interpreted as arts of securing the compliance necessary to retain the throne. It was (significantly, I would suggest) from the early 1990s that historians of politics turned to the ceremonies and symbols of power in the reign of the first Tudor. Writing in 1991, for example, Steve Gunn asserted that 'the early Tudor court was designed to impress and it succeeded', even if it was, in his revealingly contemporary words, 'a confidence trick'.[10] Dismissing the prevailing view of Henry as but a 'grim bureaucrat', Gunn drew attention to the thirteen tournaments held in the last seven and a half years of his reign and to the gilded armour, bejewelled trappings and outfits festooned with red and white roses that displayed (Gunn was not ready in 1991 to say 'constructed') Tudor dynasty and authority. Two years later, an important volume of essays following a symposium on the reign of Henry VII at Harlaxton emphasized the rule of the first Tudor as 'a reign to which public display was integral'.[11] Ranging over buildings and books, chapel glazing and music, contributors to the volume traced the ways in which Henry endeavoured to overcome the insecurities, the sense of temporariness, that he faced on taking the throne, by stamping façades, artefacts and books with Lancastrian and Tudor royal badges: roses, portcullises, greyhounds and dragons.[12] Henry determined 'to dress his residences and the buildings of state in his own livery' and endeavoured to 'outstrip all previous standards of princely magnificence'.[13] As well as building on the site of Sheen the new Richmond Palace, Henry constructed a royal chapel at Westminster Abbey which was intended to represent his kingship as well as piety.[14] In this chapel, decorated with dynastic badges and glazed with the scenes of the history of his family, Henry VII was figured in prayers and represented in sermons delivered there as another David or Solomon.[15] Here in what, as well as a principal site of worship, was a 'theatre of power', at the heart of the royal administration, Henry reinstituted public crown-wearings on the holy feast days of Christmas, Epiphany, Easter, Whitsun and All Saints, on which occasions he blended Christic with Tudor majesty.[16] Having appropriated for his rule Edward IV's Windsor chapel and Henry VI's Sheen and promoted Henry VI's canonization, Henry willed that for his monument his image be set in the midst of a crest on the shrine of St Edward. Aware to the end 'even after twenty years as king of the tenuous nature of his claim to the throne', Henry sensed that his kneeling, votive figure in Edward the Confessor's shrine might endow him and his heirs with legitimacy and sanctity.[17]

In addition the first Tudor instituted the special service that formed the rite for the ceremony of touching to cure the king's evil.[18] He also commissioned for Richmond sculptures of past British kings going back to the mythical Brutus; and in emulation of the *real d'or*, struck in the Netherlands by Maximilian, king of the Romans, he issued in 1489 the heaviest gold coin ever known in England – importantly the first currency to depict the king wearing a closed imperial crown.[19]

Recent work has demonstrated how this new concern with the politics of display and symbol was not confined to the court or the capital. We have for long had accounts of Henry's first royal progress to York in the spring of 1486, a few weeks after his marriage. Relations of the entertainment and the pageants that greeted him describe six Henries and a Solomon welcoming the 'most prudent prince' of them all; a figure of David emerging from a castle to offer the king the sword of victory; and Our Lady from heaven promising to mediate with her son to bestow his grace on the new sovereign.[20] Hall's chronicle makes clear that, far from a simple entertainment or victory parade, Henry had gone on progress to 'purge the contagious smoke of dissention' and, in particular, to attempt to secure the obedience of parts of the country that had been Yorkist strongholds.[21] Henry's progress to York therefore was 'necessarily a reciprocal display', in which the new king and former attendants of his defeated rival had to negotiate authority and allegiance.[22] While York flattered Henry with praise and pageants of subjection, Viscount Lovel was plotting an uprising against him and Henry was acutely aware of the need to win the sympathies of the local people. Accordingly, as well as paying careful attention to clothing and spending lavishly on jewels, Henry appeared at York on the Eve of St George crowned and the next day, amid mounting rumours of revolt, celebrated the feast of the Garter with all solemnity. If, as a recent study observes, 'Henry Tudor needed to court the affection of the northern capital as much as the city itself needed the royal will', that was true also of other cities and towns – Worcester, Hereford and Bristol – which not only similarly atoned for past disloyalty by staging entertainments commemorating the king's victory, but also deployed praise and petition as the 'delicate tactics' of counsel and instruction.[23] Henry himself devised a 'stately and carefully planned tour' with the aid of a 'public relations machine' and monitored every move in the quest to highlight the reciprocal obligations of king and subjects.[24] Far from the remote bureaucrat, the Henry VII who emerges from such studies was one who fully grasped the 'power of personal intervention in influencing public opinion' and the centrality of both regal magnificence and personal piety in public ceremonies.[25] 'Carefully orchestrated appearances at divine service, the staging of crown-wearing at York, his observance of tradition, and sacred customs, the magnificence of his attire and that of his henchmen on all public occasions, and even the military and political might of his entourage as it drew near ... must have served to reassure the people of their new sovereign's piety, generosity and princely dignity'.[26]

If an interest in political culture and a sense of the reciprocity of display and representation has begun to influence historical appreciation of Henry VII, it has not yet much influenced any new biography. Though it discusses the large expenditure on the coronation and marriage of Prince Arthur, on the chapel at Westminster and on jewels, the latest short biography of the first Tudor offers little analysis of the programme of panegyric in poetry and paint to which the recent *Oxford Dictionary of National Biography* entry points.[27] In Steve Gunn's words, published in 2004, Henry, be it in buildings, plate or hunting, 'knew the advantages of visible greatness' and exploited them.[28]

And yet – readers will have noted that his name does not head this chapter – it is not with Henry VII that this study really begins, so I must pause to explain why. Let us begin by returning to Bacon. For though he identified the first Tudor's deployment of ceremony as a means of securing his precarious dynasty, Bacon, from the standpoint of having experienced Henry's successors, did not regard him as a master of these arts of majesty. Henry VII did not, he concluded, perform on the stage of power: 'in so much as in triumphs of jousts and tourneys, and balls, and masques, which they then called disguises, he was rather a princely and gentle spectator, then seemed much delighted'.[29] For all his building, the king dwelt 'more richly dead in the monument of his tomb than he did alive in Richmond, or any of his palaces'.[30] And if the purpose of pageant and progress was to win the people by love rather than fear or reverence, Bacon could only conclude that he failed, having 'the last in height, the second in good measure, and so little of the first [that is love]'.[31] As for 'visible greatness', whatever his patronage of artists, Henry VII was the Tudor who failed my postcard recognition test. He has not imprinted himself on the nation's imagination or in its memory: as a recent web discussion put it, 'Henry VII is not a king we remember well in terms of innovation or splendour'.[32] Two other popular websites concur: Henry VII, his Wikipedia entry closes, 'was succeeded by his second, more famous son'; 'he is not', the website of world royalty judges, 'the Tudor king best remembered today. That honour belongs to his infamous successor.'[33]

Infamy was not the only reason why Henry VIII, with his six wives, has been better remembered than his less colourful father. The truth is that his father was, in the most literal sense, less colourful, that is less spectacularly represented than Henry VIII or Elizabeth who, to quote the History Learning Site, both 'over-shadow ... Henry VII's reign'.[34] Whatever Henry's interest in ceremony and spectacle, it palls beside the later Tudors' magnificent displays abroad, as at the Field of the Cloth of Gold, or at home, as with Elizabeth's coronation entry or progresses. Henry VII may have, in Bacon's report, used 'strange sweetness and blandishments of words', but his rhetoric did not come near the skills of the later Tudors.[35] Unlike Elizabeth, Edward VI and Henry VIII, Henry VII did not write or circulate verses, songs or translations that publicized his policies and regal power. Though his publication of the papal dispensation for his marriage to Elizabeth of York has been described as 'one of the earliest and most striking examples of the use in England of the printing press as an instrument for the dissemination of propaganda', Henry VII was, in the words of one biographer, 'somewhat slow in grasping the full potential of printing': he did not even appoint the first official royal printer, William Facques, until 1504.[36] Henry was a patron of poets such as Bernard André and John Skelton, of historians like Polydore Vergil, and of new humanist scholars such as John Colet and Thomas Linacre; and he was a keen collector of books.[37] Yet, even though he had spent fourteen years abroad and his court was cosmopolitan, 'English styles in painting, architecture and literature lagged behind those of the continent', leaving the court of the first Tudor with the reputation of having been 'a backward and barren place'.[38] The Tudors may be, in Sidney Anglo's words, 'the most recognised royal house' and two of them were indeed voted into the top fifty in the BBC's poll of the Greatest Britons of all time; but it is not Henry VII who has left his mark on the nation's memory, except as the first of a dynasty of better known and regarded successors.[39]

The purpose of this book is to try to explain why and to trace the processes through which Henry VII's successors became more visible, that is more ubiquitously represented and more broadly recognized (in both senses), than the first Tudor. Part of the explanation (and so a part of our story) relates to developments in the media of distribution and the market for texts and images of authority. The rapid rise from first tentative beginnings in the fifteenth century of a commercial printing business in England is the most obvious media development, cheap print bringing with it, as well as words, a flood of new images in the form of woodblock illustrations to books and broadsides. Economic and social change, not least the increasing wealth of classes below the gentry, clearly lay behind the emergence of a market for books and objects, including, by Elizabeth's reign, souvenirs of monarchs. Technological developments and commercial changes are vital to our story of the increasing publicization of regality.[40] However, our contention is that these large historical developments were not just the causes but the consequences of a revolution in the nature of royal representation: that is that royal actions and representations stimulated the growth of print and a consumer culture which the Tudor rulers needed to secure their dynastic survival and regal authority.

It has rightly been argued that Henry VII's concern with public display was in direct relation to his dynastic insecurity. As far as the Yorkists were concerned, Bosworth Field was just another battle in the long series we call the Wars of the Roses and Henry was still an outlaw under attainder. As Bacon analysed them, there were three claims to the English throne: that of Elizabeth of York, the house of Lancaster, and the claim of conquest.[41] Since 'the first of these was the fairest and most likely to give contentment to the people', the Lancastrian claim 'condemned by parliament' and the argument from conquest dangerous and of dubious legality, Henry's position was virtually unsustainable before his marriage to Elizabeth and precarious even thereafter.[42] Henry therefore emphasized his Tudor more than his Lancastrian pedigree and endeavoured to present a 'distinctly Tudor style of magnificence' to mute old divisions and to form a new allegiance no longer dependent on divided loyalties to the white or red rose.[43] From the outset, Henry faced challenges from Yorkist pretenders such as Perkin Warbeck, who claimed to be Richard, the younger of the princes incarcerated in the Tower, and Lambert Simnel, a protégé of Richard III's designated heir, John de la Pole, Earl of Lincoln. Much of his foreign policy and diplomacy was necessarily determined by the need to discourage foreign powers, especially France, aiding claimants to the English throne. And, if time itself began to promise some greater security, the deaths in 1502 of his queen, on whom many thought his title really depended, and his elder son, Arthur, on whom the future security of the dynasty and country rested, exposed the vulnerability of the Tudors.[44] It may have been the gravity of the situation where now only an unmarried son stood between the survival and demise of the Tudors that led Henry, just weeks after Arthur's death, to propose a marriage between the now widowed Catherine of Aragon and the king's second son.[45] That marriage, because it breached scriptural and church rules about affinity, required papal dispensation which did not arrive for over two years, by which time a major change in Anglo-Spanish relations bedevilled the union. Thereafter, despite frantic efforts to find himself a new wife and heir, as well as a bride for his son, Henry VII failed to remarry. Though his son succeeded him, Henry VII remained to the end rightly anxious and insecure about the long-term future of Tudor rule.

And, though his son succeeded without challenge, that instability and insecurity were exacerbated during the reign of Henry VIII and beyond through the rest of the century. As is famously known, Henry VIII had great difficulty in siring a male heir. Daughters who would inevitably be married to foreign princes (since any English husband would have reopened renewed dynastic and civil war among the nobles) could not secure the Tudor line. Henry reigned nearly thirty years before Edward VI was born – three decades during which he faced threats of foreign invasion and domestic rebellions. With the mortality rate of sixteenth-century England, one frail boy scarcely guaranteed the Tudor line, especially when Henry was nearing the advanced age of fifty and his only queen to have borne him a son died days after giving birth. As his father had frantically sought another wife, so Henry married three more times during the last decade of his life, in the desperate hope of siring another son. As he became ill and approached death, the king's desperation can only have mounted as he faced what every early modern prince dreaded: leaving a sickly minor as his heir in a country still riven by contending noble families. And worse: a country beset by the new problem of fundamental ideological and religious divisions.

It is one of the many ironies of Tudor history that the course Henry VIII took as a desperate measure to safeguard the succession had the consequence of exposing his person, his family and the nation to the greatest danger it had faced since the Norman Conquest. In divorcing Catherine of Aragon, Henry alienated her mighty Habsburg nephew, Charles V, Holy Roman Emperor and head of the most powerful family and state in Europe. Moreover, he surrendered what his father had used as a central plank of his legitimacy: the support of the papacy, which had provided the first Tudor with two invaluable dispensations to marry that had probably secured him his throne. Henry VIII surrendered more than that. As we have seen, a claim to orthodox Catholic piety was a central motif of the representation of Henry VII who appropriated and advanced the cult of the saintly Henry VI and who sought, in his new chapel at Westminster, to associate Tudor kingship with that of the holy Edward the Confessor. After his divorce from Catherine, by contrast, Henry VIII appeared to many, perhaps most, of his subjects as a man who had breached the laws of the church and scriptural injunctions. That rumour bruited that he had done so out of lust for a new mistress only exacerbated the royal sin. From May 1533, when Thomas Cranmer annulled the royal marriage, Henry was no longer a true son of the church; after the passing of the Act of Supremacy the next year, he claimed an authority over matters spiritual as well as temporal that defied centuries of history and alienated loyal Catholics.

Not least by his marriage to Elizabeth, Henry VII had sought, as well as an heir, to reconcile warring families and to begin to heal divisions. When he rejected papal authority and divorced Catherine, Henry VIII opened new divisions between noble families and factions at court and in the country. The fissures that opened in the English state in the 1530s were not just replays of the baronial rivalries that had bedevilled the realm for decades; they were different in kind – fundamental, ideological and permanent. Not least because Henry's pregnant mistress Anne Boleyn's family favoured the cause of religious reform, Lutheranism, Henry's rejection of his Catholic wife for his lover opened doubts about the king's own faith.[46] Habsburg Catholic hostility also made continental Protestant powers the more likely allies for England in the event of any papally led crusade against the English king. Whatever his own faith, which George Bernard has characterized as determined more by his conscience than by *realpolitik*, Henry's actions divided the realm and discredited a vital traditional discourse and image of kingship: the representation of the monarch as a figure of piety and orthodoxy and as a protector of the Catholic church and defender of the faith.[47]

As well as other crises, the English Reformation brought about a crisis of representation. By creating the greatest ideological division in the state and detaching the monarchy from the papacy and Catholic church that had added sacred to secular authority, Henry was faced with a dreadful challenge: not just of restructuring and redefining his royal position but of re-presenting his authority, of rewriting and refiguring his kingship, and kingship itself. His desperate concern to secure his dynasty with an heir, the problems brought about by Reformation and Henry's endeavours to re-script and re-present kingship were his legacies to his successors and are the subject of this book.

Roy Strong once described Henry VIII's construction and dissemination of his royal image as the first propaganda campaign in English history.[48] Though, as we have seen, several scholars would make that claim for earlier periods and rulers, Strong's assessment remains persuasive. Because he had to, Henry VIII systematized what a scholar has recently called the 'governmental arts' into a programme of representation that was novel in intensity and kind. To quote Mary Polito, 'The reign of Henry VIII saw the emergence of a new form of secular government designed to strengthen the state . . . through innovative legislation, the dissemination of propaganda, the appropriation of ecclesiastical and pastoral modes of rule and new and sometimes spectacular rituals of statecraft'.[49] Polito interestingly and properly does not make a rigid distinction between legislation and propaganda as spectacles of state or between government acts and arts. For Henry, assisted by councillors and impresarios, made governmental actions – statutes, for example – into rhetorical performances and spectacles into principal acts of government. Because he recognized that the new style of rule and of representation necessitated by Reformation depended upon each other, Henry once warned; 'I shall look on any injury offered to the painter [he was referring to Holbein] as [an injury] to myself'.[50]

Though he desired to stress dynastic continuity, Henry VIII had perforce to distance himself from his father – and not just by sacrificing Henry VII's rapacious and unpopular ministers, Empson and Dudley. Where his father had publicized his proximity to Rome, Henry was to construct himself as the head of an English church and the head of a nation, as God's lieutenant in matters spiritual as well as secular. Brian Cummings is right to argue that the process of effecting those changes was, in various respects, a textual process.[51] As we will see in detail, Henry wrote treatises arguing for his divorce and making his claim to determine doctrine; he commissioned poets, theologians and historians to laud and justify his actions and newly claimed powers; his ministers encouraged playwrights to 'set forth and declare lively before the people's eyes the abomination and wickedness of the bishop of Rome . . . and to declare and open to them the obedience that . . . subjects by God's and men's laws owe[d]' to the king.[52] In addition, Henry endeavoured to control the press through systematic use of a king's printer and licensing; his minister Thomas Cromwell had the word 'papa' excised from prayers and, as the imperial envoy Chapuys complained, none were permitted to preach at Paul's Cross except those who favoured the king's cause and preached openly against the pope.[53] The process of effecting the Reformation, however, was not simply textual if by that, as his examples suggest, Cummings means verbal. In the Catholic culture of sixteenth-century Europe and England, the process of transferring authority from the pope to the crown, the process of sacralizing monarchy, had also to be a visual process. Revealingly and significantly, it was after the break from Rome that Henry devoted new attention to his visual image. Henry had not even bothered to change the portrait bust of his father on his coins until nearly twenty years after he succeeded to the throne.[54] Though he employed artists such as Lucas Horenbout, Vincent Volpe and Antonio Toto, he showed little interest in the great Hans Holbein on his first visit to London from about 1526 to 1528; the first surviving payments to the artist in the royal accounts date from 1538.[55] Indeed it seems likely, as we shall see, that Holbein's first portrait for Henry was designed to justify and celebrate the 1534 Act of Supremacy that proclaimed Henry's imperial power and headship of the church. The miniature of Solomon receiving the Queen of

Sheba (figures who in Christian iconography represented Christ and the church), with Solomon depicted with Henry's features, sacralized Henry as the miniature form itself iconicized him.[56] Though Holbein had painted some portraits before coming to England and many since his sojourn in London, it seems likely that this revolution in the portrayal of monarchy, coming as it did some years after Holbein's arrival, was more at the king's than the artist's direction. As well as further images advertising Henry's divine authority and supremacy, Holbein transformed the royal dynastic portrait with his Privy Chamber mural of Henry with his father, mother and third wife, which can be dated to 1536–7.[57] The only wife who bore him a son, Jane Seymour was also the only consort whom Holbein was commissioned to paint as queen. Most importantly, the new full frontal image of Henry himself became the prototype for a new kind of royal portrait which became 'highly successful in establishing the monarch in a consistently recognisable way'.[58] It was a portrayal that not only radiated majesty and personal authority but one that inspired awe, even 'fear', in those who viewed it.[59]

The portrait and the fear it evoked in at least one observer point to a larger change that Henry effected in royal representation and the perception of monarchy: a change that affected subsequent Tudor representations and refashioned the psychological relationship between sovereign and subjects. Henry, I shall argue, made the matter of his divorce a matter of personal conscience. In order to justify his divorce he publicized, indeed published his own conscience and, in Polito's words, 'worked on the intimate territory of conscience' of his subjects.[60] Having renounced papal authority, Henry, in order to exercise supremacy and wield authority in matters of faith, had to make his conscience the conscience of the realm. The Reformation, that is, impelled the reach of royal authority into the realms of interiority, the forging of a spiritual connection between king and people. The strategies of Henry's – and his successors' – representation were directed at effecting that connection and extending authority into the arena of conscience, of the imaginings of English men and women. Henry's own writings, images of the king as Christic, the appearance of royal arms on rood screens all contributed to a process whereby 'under the Tudors, the royal presence acquired some of the awesome sanctity of Christ's real presence in the eucharist', so 'binding ruler and ruled together in a communion.'[61] But the extension of royal authority into the interiority of subjects was not simply about its reach into personal conscience. It involved too an eroticization of power and a manipulation of desire.

In arguing his case for a divorce from Catherine, Henry VIII exposed to print not only his conscience but the royal sexual body, as the question of whether Catherine had consummated her marriage with Prince Arthur became a central issue.[62] Even before that, amorous songs and verses by the king were circulating at court and beyond, publicizing his wooing of, and obvious sexual desire for, his mistress Anne Boleyn. The rumours that circulated about the lovers may have contained more lurid details than Henry could tolerate but they too were a direct consequence of his own publicization of the royal body in print. And perhaps too in paint. Holbein's Privy Chamber portrait of the king who had recently sired his first son is, of course, a dynastic image. It is also an image of sexual prowess and accomplishment. The individual portraits of Henry VIII taken from it, the famous image of the king full-frontal, elbows akimbo, with legs apart and a large codpiece, focus on the royal genitals as generative and sexual. If one of the challenges of early modern kingship was that of reconciling the royal bodies personal and public, Henry VIII here presented his private, sexual body as a public representation of his rule, indeed as the body not just of a man and dynasty but of a nation. Henry's authority, I shall argue, as represented and performed, was inseparable from his masculine, sexual body.[63] In publicizing, indeed emblematizing, his sexual body, Henry, as Polito begins to discern, 'worked on the intimate territory of . . . desire', as well as conscience.[64] Again because he needed to, Henry, through acts of representation, formed a new relationship with his subjects – one that developed the chivalric connection between the erotic and the political. Not for nothing did one of the monarchy's principal spin doctors, Richard Morison, speak of the 'lovely bond' between king and people.[65] Faced with a rupture in the church and nation, Henry needed to form new affective bonds, to generate a nation we might say, recalling the etymology of that word in birth, in order to survive.

In order to overcome the problem of dynastic insecurity, still more the novel problems of religious division and a rupture of the bonds of faith, Henry fostered new conscientious and affective relations with his subjects through new modes of representing himself. Though these strategies ensured his survival and (uniquely in countries divided by religion) even appeared to enhance his authority, they also had unforeseen consequences. In some respects, in advertising his personal body, Henry VIII demystified it. While he earned popular affection, even later being figured as an 'ordinary guy', public access to, familiarity with, the king's body rendered it public property as well as public representation. Secondly, the extension of royal authority and representation into the imaginings of subjects effected, at least in the long run, important psychological and political changes. A historian of Henry VII's extension of royal power astutely comments that 'a centralising trend in the constitution did actively mean a constitutionalising trend at the centre'.[66] Similarly we may suggest that, in projecting his authority into the consciences and imaginings of subjects, Henry VIII made them self-conscious, that is aware of themselves as actors as well as subjects. While the 'lovely bond' identified by Morison undoubtedly helped secure Henry VIII, loving relationships were (and are) founded on reciprocity, even perhaps a measure of equality. If, as well as demonstrating that 'English subjects engaged vibrantly with the governmental arts', 'Tudor history shows that power depends on the complicity of subjects', it may have been Henry who – unwittingly – fostered a complicity that could and would lead subjects to question as well as support regal power.[67]

Certainly, in the ways in which he constructed and represented his authority, Henry VIII helped to shape the discourses, symbols and strategies of opposition to that authority. Just as in 'a culture founded on division', he sought to appropriate sacred texts and signs, and deploy affective languages of state, so critics and opponents of royal policies aped the king.[68] Where, for example, Henry was presented as Solomon, the captains in the Pilgrimage of Grace took names from the holy virtues of Charity and Faith to make their case polemically as well as militarily.[69] Elizabeth Barton, the Nun of Kent, was by no means the only one to vie with the king in claiming the sacred.[70] Meanwhile, the amorous, even priapic, representations of regality were subverted not only by Henry's suspicions of adulterous wives and incestuous liaisons but by widely circulating rumours and gossip about relationships – that is polities – founded on lust rather than love.

For better and worse, Henry bequeathed to his successors and subjects a new set of challenges to authority and representational strategies that influenced the exercise and image of monarchy for the rest of the century and beyond. Henry's successors continued to practise the governmental arts that he had made his own: to represent themselves through the printed word, visual images in various media, and theatrical performances and spectacles, as they sought to preserve their authority in a country increasingly divided over religion and allegiance. Because he had authorized such modes and media of representation and had claimed the sacred and amorous as discourses of state, Henry's successors could not easily abandon them. Dynasty required the generative fertile royal body; supremacy the claim to be the nation's conscience; affective languages and symbols helped bind a commonweal. Who is not struck by little Edward VI's virtual replication of his father's priapic stance in the portrait by Scrots?[71] Or who doubts that Queen Elizabeth's volumes of prayers, with the engraving of her at her devotions, did not owe a debt to Henry's great bible? Scripts, languages, symbols and signs fashioned by Henry VIII perforce conditioned the representation of his Tudor heirs.

Yet because they had been responses to his very particular and personal circumstances, Henry's modes of representing himself also posed serious problems for his successors. The king's self-presentation as the priapic dynast and object of desire was – it hardly needs saying – premised on Henry's sex and age. In early modern England, no woman, let alone a queen, could safely advertise her sexual body; and, as the ten-year-old Edward's portrait illustrates, the pose of fertile procreator was not an easy one for a minor. His portrait apart, there is no evidence that Edward endeavoured to eroticize his authority; and the reason may not simply lie in his Protestant asceticism (which has, anyway, as we shall see, been exaggerated). Queen Mary, once married, made much display of her fertile and (as she believed at one stage) pregnant body; but, of course, being female and married to an unpopular Habsburg prince, she could not derive from such representation the affective benefits that Henry had enjoyed. As for Elizabeth, the territories of the generative and sexual presented her with the greatest difficulties of her reign. Unmarried, she stood as a public sign not of the strength but of the fragility of dynasty; as a single woman, she was not culturally licensed to have any sexual life or presence. Elizabeth tempered such insurmountable difficulties by transferring the actualities of marriage and motherhood into metaphors of community and congress with her subjects; and by combining the erasure of her public sexual body with amorous and flirtatious words. However, the Tudor dynasty ended with her; and she failed, for all her genius, to control the public representation of her body personal, and so surrendered authority to others.[72]

No less than his public image as fertile patriarch, Henry's sacralization of himself posed endless difficulties, though very different difficulties, to his successors. Beyond the Solomonic and Davidic, Henry was presented as Christic, as a Caesaro-papist with spiritual powers. Such claims, such images could not be proffered by either a boy or, not least since women could not be priests, by women. Since the claim to exercise the clerical office, to have sway in matters spiritual, was a vital foundation of Henry's post-Reformation kingship, that rendered the position of his successors extremely vulnerable. Edward endeavoured by prodigious learning and piety to show himself fit in future for spiritual leadership and supremacy. Mary, who did not of course wish to exercise the pope's authority, struggled to restore England's subjection to Rome. Elizabeth, while cautious not to transgress the codes of gender by claiming the title Supreme Head, sought to exercise that authority in reality and through others. None succeeded. Not until the first Stuart could and did an adult male monarch take up the verbal and visual significations used by Henry VIII to figure himself as God's lieutenant on earth. By 1603, for all James's efforts to revive the royal spiritual supremacy, much had happened to vitiate the claims Henry had made seventy years earlier.

Though they could not for reasons of age, sex or circumstance easily replicate the representations of Henry VIII as procreator and priest, his successors understood and emulated his efforts to extend the reach of royal authority into the imaginations of subjects: to make themselves the psychological centre of the nation. After Henry, Tudor monarchs made, if anything, increasing use of the printing press to publish artfully rhetorical declarations and speeches; and Edward and Elizabeth followed their father in writing their own authority in a variety of genres: diary and prayers, poems and translations. Though, for the rest of the century, no artist who matched Holbein's genius was brought to England or enjoyed royal patronage, Henry's successors took pains over their image; famously Elizabeth even tried to censor portraits of herself and to license an official prototype portrait and to control its reproduction. Mary, as we shall demonstrate, used innovative double portraits on her seal and coins to proclaim her marriage and authority.[73] And state ceremonies and rituals, initiated on a grand scale by Henry VIII, remained extravagant to the end of the century, with costumes and pageant devices growing ever more elaborate. By the close of the sixteenth century, the last Tudor ruler was even more deeply impressed in the minds of her subjects than her father had been. To adapt Julia Walker's phrase, Elizabeth I came to rule, as Henry had sought to, 'within the minds of her subjects'.[74]

In representing and publicizing themselves, Henry's successors enjoyed the advantages and also faced the problems of some of the technological and media developments and the social changes we have touched on above. By the late sixteenth century, there was a significant growth in literacy, especially in London and other cities, a greatly expanded print industry and a market for books that distributed royal speeches and relations of royal progresses and pageants more broadly than Henry could have foreseen. A growing interest in the arts, albeit slow, began to see more copies of royal portraits hung in aristocratic and gentry houses and town halls; woodcut images of kings and queens began to be sold and bought along with other souvenirs of monarchs.[75] Elizabeth I was in consequence almost certainly better known to her subjects, and not just elite subjects, than her father or any of her predecessors.

But as Henry's modes of publicizing himself helped to fashion the languages through which his authority was critiqued as well as represented, and even to begin to form citizens whose participation in the process of representation enfranchised them as political actors, so the history of subsequent Tudor representations was a story also of mounting opposition and increasing self-consciousness of subjects as political agents in the commonweal. Indeed, changing circumstances after the 1530s accelerated some of the developments that were the unintended consequences of Henry's representation. The most obvious is confessional division. Albeit with limited success, Henry had tried to make his a 'king's reformation', not a Protestant reformation. Whatever his apparent wavering, his apparent openness at first to some reformist agendas, then subsequently strict insistence on Catholic orthodoxy, Henry to the last strove for religious unity and obedience to the supremacy. After 1547, by contrast, England was ruled by a boy king and advisers who were unequivocally and actively Protestant and a woman who was devoutly Roman Catholic. New prayer books and persecutions radicalized confessional allegiances and sharpened the divisions opened by Henry VIII's divorce, leading to bitter divisions within royal counsels, to polemical, and episodically to armed, conflict. Such divisions and conflicts in turn intensified opposition to Henry's successors and undermined the first Tudor's self-presentation as the conscience of the commonweal, as the head of a united church in England and as the much-loved head of the nation. As religious wars intensified in Europe, Calvinist and Counter-Reformation pamphlets advocating tyrannicide circulated in Scotland and England.[76] And as the strategic importance of the British Isles in the grand confessional struggles became ever more evident, it appeared all but inevitable that England too would be plunged into religious war. In contrast to Henry who, having divorced to secure the succession, could still represent himself as the embodiment of one nation, Edward and Mary could expect only the loyalty of their own co-religionists and faced rebellions from opponents who, it was feared, might seek foreign aid and invasion.

It has often been remarked that, in not publicly espousing such a clear confessional position as her predecessors, Elizabeth I reverted to the policy of her father. That is only half true, because changed conditions meant that she could not exercise the supremacy as had Henry; but it is not our main point here. What requires our attention is how Elizabeth returned to the representational strategies of her father; and, importantly, how she adapted them to her own very different personal and political circumstances and difficulties. We have observed that as a woman Elizabeth could not publicize, as had her father, her body as sexual. That said, while presenting herself as the Virgin Queen, Elizabeth was subtly eroticized in early portraits; and, it has been suggested, her decision from the mid-1580s no longer to be painted from life may have been motivated by a desire to hold on to an image of youth that sustained the fiction of generative possibility and power.[77] As a range of writing from Spenser to pornographic verse evidences, Elizabeth's body, like her father's, was an erotic site and central to her representation and her relationship with subjects. If there is any truth in the story of her appearing in armour at Tilbury, it would seem that Elizabeth even overrode the proscriptions of gender to present her body as masculine and military, in a manner that no other successor of Henry's did before the Civil War.

The sexual royal body was a potent symbol, especially after decades of failed heirs and disputed successions, because it promised dynastic continuity and national security. Elizabeth did not fulfil that promise and her single, childless condition was responsible for the greatest threats and political tensions of her reign. However, as well as holding on to the fiction of her possible marriage and motherhood, Elizabeth effectively appropriated them as metaphor, representing herself as the bride and mother of her people. In favouring metaphoric over actual marriage and motherhood, Elizabeth fell short of satisfying her councillors and people. But, as the collecting of her painted, engraved and woodcut portraits suggests, her represented body helped forge affective bonds with subjects that lasted long after her death.

Henry VIII had publicized his conscience as a principal strategy of his representation. By 1558, however, far from being the public conscience of the commonweal, that of Elizabeth's immediate predecessor had led to persecution, exile and bitter division. In the face of religious conflict, it is understandable that Elizabeth did not follow her father in penning and printing treatises on doctrine and religious orthodoxy. Yet, though famous for her promise not to make windows into men's souls, Elizabeth provided at least glimpses into her own that were meant to manifest her piety. The various volumes of prayers published as the queen's, or bearing her portrait image, advertised her relationship with God, while cleverly avoiding language that too rigidly identified her with a confession or that offended Catholic subjects.[78] While, that is, she did not in the same way disclose her conscience, Elizabeth emulated her father in publicizing private devotion in order to promote religious unity and order. While the goal of unity eluded her (and all her successors), that England escaped religious civil war in the late sixteenth century owed much not only to her policies but – perhaps more – to her image and representation.

Elizabeth skilfully adapted Henrician forms of representation to her sex and to new circumstances brought about by religious conflict. Differently, but even more successfully than her father, she made herself the centre of the people's interest and gaze: the emblem and embodiment of the nation. And she did so, from the beginning, by an artful courting of popularity. From her coronation entry into London, Elizabeth displayed a common touch and a skill in combining majesty with a familiarity that won the love of subjects. Elizabeth was the first monarch whose accession day became a calendrical day of celebration; the first whose speeches on public occasions not only won over auditors but sold in many copies; the first whose progresses and travels drew thousands of spectators and an even larger audience for the printed accounts that reported them. By the time of the Armada, she had made the nation and the Tudor dynasty not merely inseparable but, in the public perception, one and the same. Shakespeare's history plays, though neither her name nor character appears explicitly in any, are all about Elizabeth and could not have been performed without her achievement in making the Tudor dynasty the focus of national and popular attention.

However, in developing Henry's position as the psychological as well as political centre of an emerging nationalism and nation, Elizabeth also exacerbated the problems that followed as a consequence. I have suggested, and will explore at length, how through projecting his person and power, Henry VIII began a process of demystifying kingship and enfranchising subjects. Both developments were far more marked in the second half of the Tudor century. Perhaps not least on account of the highly charged religious situation at the time of her succession, there was more attention paid to Elizabeth's coronation entry into the capital than to the coronation rituals themselves.[79] To this day scholars remain uncertain whether the elements of the mass were elevated during what was an essentially Catholic service, or indeed whether Elizabeth signalled Protestant sympathies by withdrawing from part of the ritual.[80] Whatever actually happened, the details were not published. By contrast there were several, as well as the official, accounts of the queen's famous procession through the city to Westminster. Elizabeth and her advisers, it appears, emphasized the queen's interaction with her people over the sacred ceremony; and in some respects that shift of emphasis became a hallmark of the reign. Though progress pageants and entertainments did stage religious subjects, the more common themes were classical and pastoral. Interestingly, the Elizabethan theatre dealt little, at least overtly, with religious controversies, or matters which, as well as being dangerous subjects, were not perceived to represent monarchy as it had emerged. To return to David Kastan's point, the theatricalization of monarchy in Elizabeth's reign, both on the stage and on the streets, may have contributed to the tendency to desacralize regality.[81] Theatre represented kingship and government not as mysteries but as arts. Even the most pious and heroic rulers, such as Henry V, were portrayed as adept at manipulating the rhetorics and symbols of power and we cannot divorce such representations from the contemporary experience of Elizabeth's rule and representation. As Malcolm Smuts and others have argued, and as we shall examine, by the late years of Elizabeth's reign there was an extensive literature of statecraft that marked an important recognition of styles of government and politics far removed from traditional notions of Christian kingship.[82] Near-contemporary historians of the queen, such as William Camden and Robert Naunton, reflected such changes in their highly Tacitean analyses of power, which were to become the common themes of the stage by the end of the century. Thomas Heywood's famous play about Elizabeth, *If You Know Not Me*, captured the change by suggesting that 'monarchical identity might derive more from the performance of royal acts than from a sacred anointing'.[83]

Theatre – and theatricalization – did not just expose power as performance to the investigative gaze of an audience, it made it contingent upon spectators. All governments had depended upon the obedience and co-operation of the people, but in breaking from Rome Henry had fuelled popular anticlericalism and harnessed and fostered popular nationalism to buttress royal authority against the papacy. During Elizabeth's reign, faced with the dangers from Spain, at a time of religious tensions at home, the queen projected herself as the people's princess and protector, and they responded by taking her to their bosom. In the process, John Watkins suggests, Elizabeth became a different kind of sovereign – one not mystically set apart from mortals but one who epitomized the experience of the people.[84] One might say that in epitomizing their experience, Elizabeth began to represent the people, rather than simply represent herself to them. Here the vogue for souvenirs and mementoes of the queen is pertinent to both. For while, on the one hand they evidenced the power of the queen's representation, they were objects bought and owned by subjects – subjects who in some measure had begun to 'own' the queen herself. As we remarked, during her life and long after, many appropriated Elizabeth's name and authority for a variety of causes she had not supported. Her subjects, that is, like the spectators at a play, interpreted her as they chose. And the more the queen appeared in performance, or on the page, the more available she was to be seen and read, scrutinized and interpreted. 'In her forty five years on the throne,' writes Julia Walker, 'Elizabeth changed the image of monarchy for ever'; 'her most profound change was worked within the minds of her subjects'.[85] Elizabeth long remained, and remains, an iconic figure. But by 1603 her iconicity, we might suggest, owed less to a sanctity proclaimed by official scripts and images and more to a celebrity status granted by subjects. More than any of her predecessors, Elizabeth's power and authority depended upon the will of her subjects, who were soon to show that what they granted they might also withhold or take back.

To close this chapter with a queen who was both iconic and yet demystified, who exercised authority for nearly half a century yet ended up more than ever dependent on the complicity of her people and subject to their own representations of her, takes us far beyond the point where our story has properly to begin. However, the ambiguities, the paradoxes that Elizabeth epitomizes are not just paradoxes endemic to the social psychology of power and subjectivity. They emerged from particular modes and styles of representing rule which Henry VIII adopted, especially from the 1530s. Tudor royal representations devised to secure survival and enhance authority led authority itself to be negotiated as well as represented. That is, they helped to form a strong dynasty and monarchy *and also* a public sphere of active citizens.

How each individual ruler negotiated those dichotomies and adjusted their representation to their circumstances goes far towards explaining the success and reputation of those early modern monarchs who, until a much later and reluctant acceptance of religious toleration, lived with the legacy of Henry VIII's Reformation. It is to him, his Tudor successors and their representations that we now turn.

PART III

REPRESENTATIONS AND REFORMATIONS

CHAPTER 3

WRITING REFORMATION

More perhaps than any other monarch, Henry VIII has imprinted himself on our history – or rather our histories, scholarly and popular, of royalty, religion and state. In part the explanation for this lies in the momentous events of his reign: the second Tudor established a dynasty, waged war against France, gained international renown and effected a break from Rome which revolutionized church–state relations and ultimately led England to Protestantism. On the domestic stage, as is popularly known, the king married six wives and executed two. But the momentous events of the reign cannot be separated from the man. Whatever the importance of his ministers such as Thomas Wolsey and Thomas Cromwell, for all the influence at times of noblemen or factions, Henry was, as has recently been powerfully demonstrated, a king who ruled: who confronted problems, initiated policies and made decisions.[1] This is not to argue that he did not consult or weigh the views of others, or even modify an action as a consequence of counsel. The exercise of monarchy in early modern England was personal but not autocratic; it involved the advice and co-operation of confidants and ministers at court and of nobles and gentry in the localities.[2] But in the end it was the person of the king who was sovereign, and Henry came to assert his personal authority to a degree that some, perhaps many, considered tyrannical.[3]

As sovereign, Henry possessed the legal authority to determine actions, to lead armies and to punish recalcitrants. However, in an England in which communications were poor, and the monarch had neither a standing army nor paid local bureaucracy, the execution of royal orders depended on gaining compliance and consent. Whatever the will of the ruler, the enforcement of his will involved a series of dialogues and negotiations – within the royal family, at court and council with ministers and nobles, in the localities with leading aristocrats and gentry. And ultimately it involved a relationship with ordinary subjects which was, in some sense, reciprocal: a relationship, that is, in which the king merited the obedience and love of his people through his protection of justice and provision of good government for all. The image and perception of the monarch were essential to the exercise of royal authority.[4]

While recent scholarship has given us a more subtle understanding of the processes of royal decision-making and enforcement, studies of royal representation, of the image of the king, for long tended to emphasize ideas of hegemonic direction and control implicit in what is described as Henrician 'propaganda'. Henry VIII was depicted as the author and orchestrator of texts and images which were disseminated to subjects in order to effect obedience to royal policy and the royal will. In his pioneering essay, Sir Roy Strong boldly characterized the reign of Henry VIII as that which saw 'the earliest deliberate propaganda campaign in English history'.[5] More recently, Sidney Anglo and Greg Walker have challenged any model of systematic propaganda and questioned the effectiveness of Tudor representations in securing compliance.[6] While their cautions have been salutary, it is hard not to agree with Strong that we discern a new and different emphasis on projecting the royal image in the reign of Henry VIII. But what is persuasive as a general argument needs refining in a number of particular respects. In the first place, as we have observed, the word propaganda, though again in use, can be misleading.[7] Originally coined in the sixteenth century to describe the Committee of Cardinals responsible for overseeing foreign missions, since the early twentieth century the term has implied the systematic and tendentious propagation of information that is false or intended to mislead.[8] We will not begin to understand Henrician England, by contrast, unless we appreciate that the texts and images constructed and disseminated by the king and his advisers were what he passionately believed to be the truth, rather than the cynical pleadings of a party or cause. Public representations of Henry VIII were not at variance with his private conscience; they were texts of his conscience disseminated to disclose the integrity of the king's private as well as public body.[9] Secondly, for all the proper emphasis on Henry's dominance, we need to recognize that the 'king's image' was the construction of many pens and brushes rather than a figure of the king's sole devising. As we shall discover, at various stages, ministers and counsellors, poets and pamphleteers, painters and sculptors and architects and engravers spoke for and figured the king, sometimes with little or no royal direction. Thirdly, as circumstances changed – from the vicissitudes of age to revolutions in policy – new representations of the monarch were called for and new impresarios and artists emerged to re-present the king in and for a changed world. If the military, chivalric hero of Henry's youth gave way to the king as Supreme Head, the change was necessitated as much by the break from Rome as by Henry's increasing age and girth. The royal image, in other words, was not stable or static; royal *images* in the plural were endlessly constructed and reconstituted by various agents who, through changing circumstances over the course of the reign, forged quite different, even contrasting, representations of the ruler.

Another consideration I want to introduce is genre. Strong was right to draw attention to all the various media and the 'small army of painters, sculptors, architects and craftsmen' as well as writers engaged in presenting the king.[10] Certainly we need to consider the ways in which proclamations and pamphlets, paintings and pageants, which modern disciplines separate, were all deployed together at times to present a case – for the king's divorce, for example, or for claims to Supreme Headship. But we also need to recognize that different genres and media spoke to different audiences and also signified differently. Royal speeches and coins, portraits and processions were freighted with generic codes, memories and expectations that made each a different act of representation as well as part of 'an interlocking network of ideas'.[11] The many texts that presented Henry VIII to his subjects could, that is, be read against each other as well as in concert.

All these considerations – the multiplicity of commissioners, artists and impresarios, the endless flux of circumstances, the varieties of genres and audiences – underlie what will be central to our study: the multiple, variant and contested constructions and performances of the royal image over the four decades of Henry's reign. Whatever the desires of the king and government, the image of the second Tudor was not simply devised at a court (which was itself increasingly confessionally divided) and communicated to subjects. As the king and regime were fully – often anxiously – aware, the auditors of a speech or sermon, the crowd at a procession or execution, the readers of a proclamation or ballad formed their own impressions of the policies and person of the ruler. In the light of that recognition, official texts and representations had to be, and were, couched in the languages and forms that might best appeal to subjects and persuade. The languages of fatherly love for the people and care for the commonweal were discourses designed to forge affective bonds with subjects.[12] Yet such languages and tropes could be appropriated and redeployed by subjects and were contested by other representations and performances: ballad, satire, prophecy, or even rebellion.

Our study, then, of the representations of Henry VIII must sketch and sample all the forms of propagation – letters, pamphlets, panegyrics and histories, poems and songs, canvases and coins, ceremonies and rituals. And it must include not only the king but the many who claimed to, competed to, or were perceived to, represent him and those who represented him quite unsympathetically or unfavourably. 'We be men and not angels,' wrote Sir Thomas Elyot, 'therefore we know nothing but by outward significations.'[13] During the reign of Henry VIII, the religious and political disputes familiar to historians were not only polemical battles, they were contests for and over those 'outward significations' which, we must never forget, were all that most subjects knew of their king. If, for all the resistance he encountered, Henry not only survived the revolutionary changes of his reign but reinforced royal power and imprinted his image indelibly on our history, that is not least because he went to new lengths to make the arts of representation a principal art of securing compliance.[14] Under Henry VIII, representation became not simply the 'outward signification' of regality but the process by which royal authority was sustained and enhanced.

It is a mark of the success of Tudor representations that we often underestimate the fragility of that family's hold on the crown. After decades of disputed succession and civil war, the future of a family that had seized a crown in battle was far from secure. As we have seen, it was not least of the skills of the first Tudor to promote the legitimacy of his rule and to found his claim on the texts by which all authority was validated in early modern Europe: scripture, law and history. By acts of piety and charity, Henry VII presented himself as a devout Christian and loyal son of the pope, who rewarded him with the sword and cap of maintenance and the title of Defender of the Faith. Civic pageants reprised Henry's pious self-presentation in the provinces, the royal entry to York staging King David paying homage to King Henry. For the pageant to welcome Catherine of Aragon in 1501, Henry's court was likened to the court of heaven and he and Prince Arthur were figured as God the Father and Son. Henry VII's claim to divine kingship was inextricably bound into a telling of English history. Henry exploited the cult of St George as the symbol of the Christian knight and commissioned an altarpiece depicting him and his family kneeling in prayer beside the saint. And during Henry's reign, systematic efforts were made to secure the canonization of the Lancastrian King Henry VI and to portray the first Tudor as the rightful successor to his saintly virtues and piety. While Henry's continuation of the building of King's College, Cambridge manifested in stone the Tudors' piety and lineage on which Henry's tenuous authority rested, the work of denigrating rivals, notably the Yorkist Richard III, famous to us as an evil and deformed Machiavellian impostor, was furthered by chroniclers and historians.[15]

The carefully devised image of Henry VII unquestionably contributed much to the peaceful succession – the first for over a century – of his second son, Henry, in 1509. Henry inherited from his father not only a throne but also a royal script, or rather series of scripts, for the representation of Tudor kingship. But from his succession the new king's circumstances were different and, during the course of his reign, were to be revolutionized. Piety and history were to remain templates of Tudor representation; but at various times Henry VIII, his ministers and subjects, were to modify, revise, reconstitute and contest the languages and idioms of the royal image in a process that fundamentally transformed the culture of authority and the monarchy itself.

From the outset, Henry VIII's self-presentation revised as well as reprised the representational legacy of his father. As an athletic, confident young man who succeeded without challenge, Henry was ambitious to leave behind the cautious, pacific diplomacy of his father's reign and to make his reputation on the battlefields of Europe. Along with military campaigns and public displays of strength, Henry also entered the lists as a champion of the new humanist learning that was making it increasingly important for a ruler to be, as well as a soldier, a man of learning and letters. The traditional royal virtues of justice, piety, bravery and lordship remained vital to the royal image; but changing circumstances also stressed new qualities and characteristics. As we review Henry's representations in print, visual images and performances, we shall trace the challenges that shifting circumstances posed to the royal image and the ways in which Henry and others negotiated the problems of presenting revolutionary changes in the colours of custom and tradition and of devising new texts of regality acceptable to subjects. Scholars may question whether there was a Tudor revolution in royal representation any more than in the administration or institutions of government in Henrician England. But in his focus on and co-ordination of the arts of representation and by new styles of self-projection and publicization, I shall argue, Henry created a new monarchy that was to reach into the imagination of the people and ultimately be transformed by them.

I

'In the beginning was the Word.' Scripture figures divine authority as logos.[16] God's uttered commands in Genesis – 'and God said' – are acts of creation and his Son is represented as the gospel, as God's word embodied to renew life after the Fall separated sinful man from God's voice. In the Christian state, the holy city that St Augustine had posited as the means to bring humanity closer to God, authority also resided in discourse – in the word uttered and writ. Like God's, the word of a king created, made and unmade, determined and judged; the royal word was a sacred bond.[17] Shakespeare brilliantly evokes for us, in so many famous royal soliloquies, the interdependence in early modern England of royal authority and acts of speaking and writing. And he does so at a time when, the authority of the word having been fixed by a gradual shift from memory to written record, print was transmitting the word to every corner of the realm.[18] Print made all authority, especially royal authority, ever more textual. And it made the proclamations and declarations indispensable media of royal authority and royal representation.[19]

From the beginning of his reign Henry VIII displayed a recognition of the power of the word and of print and a determination to deploy publication as a medium of sovereign utterance. The second Tudor was preoccupied with books and print. Henry was learned, read several languages, and read and annotated books carefully. Knowing his love of them, courtiers often presented him with books as New Year's gifts. And Henry developed the royal collection which he inherited from his father and Edward IV to create what was effectively the first royal library in England, and one that by the end of his reign was dominated by printed books rather than manuscripts. Henry built libraries at Greenwich and in his new palaces at Hampton Court, and a 'new library' at Westminster which he developed, having acquired York House from Wolsey.[20] The recently edited inventories of the king's goods list hundreds of books and manifest the relationship in Henry's kingship of books to authority and policy. As well as bibles, editions of the Fathers and scriptural commentaries, works of ancient philosophy and texts of the new humanism, Henry owned, and often had bound with his arms, books on royal and ecclesiastical authority, on the power of the pope and the emperor, works almost certainly consulted and in many cases acquired as part of the argument for his divorce from Catherine of Aragon.[21] The several writing-tables inventoried amid the catalogues of books and manuscripts underpin a sense of texts acquired for use, for their translation into royal argument and utterance.[22] The listing of the 'king's [own] book in English', almost certainly Henry's *Necessary Doctrine* in a 'removing coffer' (or box for valuables) among works of Aquinas, St Anselm and Peter Longbard not only indicates, as do the references to 'spectacles', the relationship of books to royal writing, but also suggests that the royal library moved with the king as a necessary daily prop to his authority.[23]

And not just a prop but also a representation. Henry's concern with books was not only demonstrated in the materials and chests of books packed and unpacked as an itinerant court moved between royal residences or on progress. The royal library was a synecdoche of the royal learning, itself a representation of a new humanist prince, opened to the public view in the preface to Thomas Elyot's Latin–English dictionary published in 1538. Elyot, who borrowed books from the royal library and who had dedicated *The Book Named The Governor* to Henry in 1531, and who was published by the king's printer, Thomas Berthelet, aptly publicized the relationship between kingship and books that the royal library represented. It was, Elyot wrote, access to the king's books, the support of his library and of the king himself that had enabled a revision of his labours and given his own book its authority; and he gave 'your majesty most hearty thanks as to the chief author' of his book.[24] The royal library and royal learning were essential foundations of royal authority. In turn, throughout his reign, Henry deployed his regal authority to establish authorized texts of learning and pedagogy, such as an official Latin grammar and common primer; and beyond that, he endeavoured to prescribe and proscribe not only which books might be printed or owned, but by whom and how they were to be read.[25]

Indeed, as his divorce fuelled polemical dispute in rumour and print at home and abroad, Henry became ever more insistent on his control of print and the authority of his own word. In 1536 a statute made it treason to forge 'the king's sign manual and privy seal', in a manner that, as Seth Lerer has put it, made 'royal writ take on an almost spiritual quality'.[26] The sacred quality of the royal word was, as we shall see, graphically displayed in the engraved title page of the Coverdale Bible, on which the king as patriarch and logos hands the word as regal and divine gift and command to his kneeling bishops and nobles.[27] In Henry's kingship, the royal word – in speech, letter, proclamation or pamphlet – was not only a device of kingship; it was also a *devise*, a blazon: a representation and sign of royal authority.

To urge the centrality of the royal word in the representation of Henry VIII's kingship is to confront a problem. In the case of several of the king's own writings, whether theological works, proclamations or polemics, there is a suggestion of more than one hand involved in the composition; royal speeches to parliament were often delivered by others, usually the Lord Chancellor; and not even all letters sent out under the sign manual were the authorial script of the king.[28] However, if this problem is not removed by our own age of spin doctors in which we are familiar with politicians being only nominally the authors of their own representations, it is one that looks very different when viewed from a sixteenth-century perspective. For while in the twentieth century, despite the existence of speech-writers, we are invested in notions of personal authorship and ownership, in early modern England authorship was, and was seen to be, a process of several hands. In a world before the development of copyright, books were regarded as the products and property of publishers and printers (who freely amended manuscripts deliberately and by error) as much as writers.[29] Moreover, patrons and dedicatees were described at the time as the true authors of books, those who gave them life and authorized (the two terms 'author' and 'authorize' were freely interchanged) their appearance.[30] It was in recognition of such social conventions that Elyot described the king as the 'chief author' of his dictionary.[31] In the realm of politics, on the other hand, the statutes and proclamations that bore the king's name, along with his regnal year, privilege and later the royal arms, were texts that emerged from several drafts and contributions after deliberation (and doubtless often dispute) in Council.[32] That is to say, although the 'king' was the author of texts, he was also an authority which others sought to appropriate for their own purposes and agendas. The history of Henry's reign was in part a history of the endeavours of various ministers, counsellors and confidants who sought to secure the royal authority for their own designs. But the question of royal authorship also needs to be seen from the perspective of sixteenth-century readers who may not have been aware of the complex negotiations that underlay royal utterance or script. Those who saw the king's name at the head of a proclamation posted on a market square or his arms engraved as a frontispiece to a book, those who read on title page or colophon a declaration that a work was published 'cum privilegio', read the words contained in it as authorized, that is authored, by the king – as the royal voice and will. Like the king's voice and hand, the printed page that bore his arms or vaunted royal privilege was seen to be a representation of the monarch, a symbol that expressed and signified his authority and command.

Though the first royal texts we shall examine were unquestionably Henry's own personal voice and script, at first sight they may appear to have no place in a study of the politics of the royal image and until recently they have been all but ignored. Henry's songs, musical compositions and love letters to Catherine of Aragon and Anne Boleyn belong to what we have defined as genres of leisure, privacy and intimacy. At the court of Henry VIII, by contrast, leisure was the privilege of the political classes and intimacy, as David Starkey has demonstrated, the essence of political influence and power.[33] Henry VIII was an accomplished musician who, as well as playing the lute, virginal and flute (his psalter is illustrated with a miniature of the king playing a lyre, a symbol of the prophet David and of virtuous and gentle regimen), composed masses and anthems.[34] A manuscript song book in the British Library contains thirteen instrumental pieces and twenty-one songs all datable to the king's twenties; and there may well have been more.[35] If the composition of masses and anthems publicized Henry's personal piety, his songs, though they conjoined 'God and my right and duty', were distinctly more secular in tone. As a young man, Henry was concerned with the traditional noble pastimes of youth and love but his rendition of these themes in song and verse cannot be dismissed as merely conventional.[36] For by the very act of composing as a king, Henry transformed convention into a personal voice; and his reworking of standard tropes also exhibited 'strong individual elements' which modified stereotypes.[37] Quite simply, in his songs, Henry advertised his virtues and values as a ruler. 'God and my right and duty from them I shall never vary,' Henry proclaimed in song, linking his descent, his obligation and his divinity in a couplet.[38] As a virtuous Christian king, Henry's songs not only denounced the sinfulness of idleness and asserted the importance of 'company with honesty', but also announced the king's own self-admonition and promise:

My mind shall be;
Virtue to use,
Vice to refuse[39]

In implied answer to those who might criticize his youthful pastimes, and critics of the king and his minions there were, Henry sang of feats of arms, his love of jousts, as activities 'pleasant to God and man', as the antidotes to sin.[40] In Henry's verse, love too is defended and elevated both as the proper pursuit of the virtuous young nobleman and as a social bond that cemented aristocratic society, representing the king as the figure who sustained its codes. Describing love as 'a thing given by ... God' and gesturing to the familiar Christian symbol, the holly that never changed its colours, Henry sang of his fidelity to his lady.[41] 'Love,' he continued, 'maintaineth all noble courage, / Who love disdaineth is of the village' – that is, outside the realms of noble society and virtue.[42] Henry figures right love as both a personal bond and a symbol of the trust that cemented feudal relations:

Who so that will all fealty obtain,
In love he must be without disdain;
For love enforceth all noble kind.[43]

The love of a virtuous noble for his lady was a bond of allegiance; and as he sang of love, Henry, as king, revalidated and revitalized the bonds of fealty that sustained aristocratic society – and monarchy itself. Played and sung within courtly circles and perhaps circulated in manuscript, or reprised by aristocratic hearths, Henry's songs were representations of his kingship and proclamations of his authority.

They were not, however, uncomplicated assertions of royal authority. In and between the lines of Henry's songs, we can hear a new young monarch urging a position that he suspects is not shared and celebrating values which he fears are in decline. As Peter Herman has rightly observed, there is a defensive tone to Henry's justification of his pastimes, a counter-argument to

They [who] would have him his liberty restrain
And all merry company to disdain.[44]

The king's insistence, against his critics, 'I will not so whatever they say', the repetition of the first person pronoun in the fourth line of his song, 'This life will I', sounds a note of defiance rather than confidence – a reading supported, I believe, by Henry's ambiguous deployment of the first person plural pronoun in the lines:

But I will not so, whatever they say
But follow his mind in all that we may[45]

That 'we' stands for the youth of the song and the king; but in shifting from first person singular to plural, Henry seeks to write himself into a community of men and values as well as to shape it. Perhaps too in his insistent underscoring of the values of chivalry, fealty and love, Henry discloses some anxiety that love no longer – and here the political language is arresting – 'reigned as it hath been'.[46] Change had rendered the trust of a noble age suspect and affective social bonds fragile. Knowing that his own authority rested on, as well as validated, those codes, but recognizing too that, in the end, 'everyman hath his free-will', Henry wrote songs that, for all their assertions, were part of a political dialogue and negotiation: songs, we might say, of persuasion.[47]

As well as meditations on love in the abstract, several of Henry's songs are addressed to Queen Catherine, with whom Henry had initially lived in a loving marriage. His surviving love letters, however, were sent to a mistress rather than a wife, indeed the mistress who brought about the end of the Aragonese marriage and whose relations with Henry initiated what became a religious and political revolution. Henry's love letters to Anne Boleyn were implicated in the politics of court faction, of church and state, and of international diplomacy. But in claiming their place in our study of Henrician representations we must argue what may appear a paradox: that while seeming the most personal of scripts, love letters were a genre familiar to writers and readers and were written from the tropes of other literatures that circulated publicly – the romance, for example. In his De conscribendis epistolis, Erasmus positioned all letters, as well as his own correspondence, on the borders of private and public, individual and communal, the erotic and the political.[48] In Henry VIII's case, his letters to Anne Boleyn were at once secret and public. As Seth Lerer observes, the texts 'are fraught with fears of interception' and it may be that they circulated in court and diplomatic circles before ending up in the Vatican Library, quite possibly because they were stolen by a papal ambassador.[49]

The style and language of Henry's missives support a reading of royal letters as social and political advocacy as well as personal suit. Indeed, for all the at times graphic personal intimacy (the expression of his desire to kiss his mistress's 'dukkeys' or breasts), Henry frequently intermingled references to business and mentions his lack of time to write at greater length.[50] A suggestion that Henry's letters to Anne are indeed a representation of the king's two bodies – both his private and public self – gains warrant from Henry's own words. Separated from his mistress, Henry sends Anne 'the nearest thing' to his person: 'my picture set in bracelets'.[51] Though a personal, even intimate, gift, the picture representing the king signals his royal status as one who is so represented. In another letter Henry yet more graphically couples the royal body personal with his public body as king. 'Seeing my darling is absent,'

Henry writes, 'I can do no less than to send her some flesh representing my name, which is hart flesh for Henry, prognosticating that hereafter, God willing, you may enjoy some of mine' – that is his flesh and his heart and the sexual intimacy with his person and proximity to his public authority represented in the hart, his blazon.[52] As here in a series of clever puns and correspondences, throughout Henry's letters intimacy is written in the vocabulary of politics and power. 'Absence' is the warrior king's 'enemy'; the physician of the body politic, he sends a trusted doctor to cure his lover's illness, 'to have you healed'.[53] And Henry, while following the literary convention of writing as the servant of his mistress, as king advises, instructs and cajoles.[54] It is not, he tells Anne, wise to 'struggle against fate' or against the royal will which is equated with it.[55] The king invokes and defines Anne's conscience as well as his own in rejecting her candidate for Wilton Abbey and insists on her subordination of all familial considerations to his honour. Having at last persuaded her, Henry, as the rational head of the commonweal, writes of his joy 'to understand of your conformableness with reason and of your suppressing of your inutile [useless] and vain thoughts with the bridle of reason'.[56] Full of clever conceits and wordplay, and drawing on chivalric tropes, Henry's love letters were displays of gendered literary authority. In that they were also expressions of royal authority – of the authority of a king instructive, paternal, commanding and even threatening.

Yet perhaps again also insecure. For in a very immediate and personal as well as rhetorical sense, Henry, whatever his royal status, was a suitor; and for some agonizing months Anne was a non-compliant mistress and subject. Henry's letters seem to me, *pace* recent claims that Henry himself refrained from sexual relations with Anne, to voice the frustrations of a lover and king unable to command or persuade.[57] Henry writes of the 'great elongeness' (perhaps loneliness as well as ennui) felt by the ruler as well as the suitor.[58] For all his authority and endeavours, Henry finds himself in an uncomfortable place of flux and uncertainty, at the mercy of another's whim: 'not yet sure whether I shall fail or find a place in your heart and affection'.[59] Reading Anne's letters, 'debating with myself' and 'turning [them] over in his thoughts' and sleep, Henry clearly found himself in 'a great distress', not knowing 'how to interpret them'.[60] Sometimes Anne does not even respond and the royal pen and heart pour out into silence.[61] As suitor, servant and 'secretary' in his relationship with Anne, Henry had to woo and persuade, to negotiate, and ultimately to offer her his hand not only on paper but in marriage.[62] Permeated with topical references and freighted with political language, Henry's letters suggest that the compliance of subjects too could not simply be commanded but needed to be won through acts of speaking, writing and 'representing': that the relations between king and subjects, like that between king and mistress, involved reciprocity as well as command.[63]

Henry, as the editor of his letters argues, carefully supervised correspondence, even though he disliked writing and wrote to few with his own hand.[64] Whatever his disinclination, he grasped the place of royal letters as not only a representation of his kingship but a performance of rule. Royal letters functioned, sometimes simultaneously, as command, admonition, licence, grant, gift and intimate gesture. Intimating violence and love they were texts of a royal government that, as writers were to complain, rested on fear as well as affection.

In the arena of diplomacy, Henry's letters should be viewed, rather like the extravagant pageantry of the Field of the Cloth of Gold, as displays of power and strength. Accordingly Henry wrote to the Duke of Milan of glorious victory over the Scots granted by God; to Margaret of Savoy he wrote of his succession to a kingdom 'in good obedience, peace and tranquillity'; to Cardinal Bainbridge he boasted of 'our fleet of six thousand men . . . now at sea'; to the king of Scots he sent threats of retribution for his invasion during Henry's absence in France.[65] As Henry knew, in letters as on the pageant field, displays of authority were also part of the processes of diplomacy and negotiation. To offset the danger presented by the Duke of Albany's return to Scotland in 1515, Henry had to mix insistence with imprecation in letters to Francis I and affection and command in letters to James V.[66] In the case of Pope Clement VII, in 1528, Henry combined a pressing of his suit, 'as urgent as it is upright', with the promise of eternal support and the voice of a 'suppliant' who did 'strenuously implore . . . the favour of the Apostolic See . . . that it deign to show itself compliant . . . in conceding our just and sacred cause': a favour which 'ought not, cannot justly be denied to our piety'.[67]

In letters to princes and popes we might expect supplication as well as command. But even in letters to subjects, Henry, for all his insistence on his will, deployed a language of request and reciprocity as well as a voice of command. To his minister Thomas Wolsey, the king sent thanks for his 'great pains' in 'our business', and announced his appreciation that 'service cannot be by a kind master forgotten'; to the Dukes of Norfolk and Suffolk, whom he appointed to suppress the Pilgrimage of Grace, Henry reciprocated their assurance of loyal service with his oath to, in the event of their deaths, 'remember your children . . . with our princely favour'.[68] When we recall the real danger that such magnates might have joined the rebels, we are led to read such language as other than simply rhetorical. Indeed, St Clare Byrne argued that Henry owed his success in defeating the rebels not least to his letters: letters that combined appreciation for support, conciliation and 'imaginative terrorism', according to the recipient and moment, in an artful way.[69] For even, as we shall see, in his answers to the rebels' petitions, Henry, whilst disclaiming any need for princes to respond to 'rude and ignorant common people', answered the rebels' charges and fears and justified royal policy, not simply as the royal will but in the name of 'God's law, equity and justice'.[70] If the Pilgrimage of Grace did not ultimately develop into a national uprising that toppled the Tudors, it was not least due to Henry's skilful separating of the 'corrupt members' of Yorkshire and Lincolnshire from 'our whole commons' and the loyalty he was able to secure from nobles, gentry and people through letters.[71]

At times the language and argument of Henry's letters suggest address to a readership far broader than the designated recipient: a circle of courtiers perhaps, a noble family, or a local community. In some cases the king licensed for publication letters written to individuals, as though acknowledging their significance for the wider representation of his kingship. In 1526, for example, Richard Pynson, the king's printer, issued *A Copy of the Letter Wherein The Most Redoubted and Mighty Prince Henry VIII . . . Made Answer to a Certain Letter of Martin Luther*. Similarly, in 1538 *An Epistle of the Most Mighty Prince Henry VIII Written to the Emperor's Majesty* but now 'to all Christian princes and to all those that truly profess Christ's religion' was published 'cum privilegio'. In the first case, the text translated Luther's letter responding to Henry's *Assertio septem sacramentorum* and printed the king's point by point angry reply. Henry's preface to the work indicates that either their exchange or more likely Luther's letter was in circulation and that a false impression had formed that the king favoured his doctrine. Henry accordingly addressed 'all subjects' to set the record straight: to explain his purpose, as the preface continues, to oppose heresy, to demonstrate Luther's errors and 'poisoned points', to save his English subjects from deception and to exhort them 'not [to] descant upon Scripture' but to follow 'the advice of your pastoral fathers'.[72] Clearly the king intended that the publication of the correspondence would not only present his own position but also demonstrate the compelling force of his argument and critique. But as well as being an unusual step in itself, the text exhibits an unease. This is apparent in the lengthy and abusive dispatch that Henry returned in response to Luther's measured missive. It is audible too in the preface where, for all his aim that this might 'further the hearts and minds of his subjects in the right religion', Henry feared that by 'subtle means' Luther might have seduced them to error.[73] While ordering the public burning of the English Bible that Luther had promoted, and commanding conformity, Henry felt the need to proffer the bribe that such obedience might 'encourage well learned men to set forth and translate into our own mother tongue many good things . . . which for fear of wrong taking they dare not yet do'.[74] Moreover, while insisting his subjects not 'descant upon Scripture', Henry's published exchange opened to his subjects the debates that the king had taken as threats to his authority. In publicizing debate, by the acts of speaking and writing (which revealingly the king had initially been disinclined to do), Henry rendered his letter both a performance of authority and a negotiation for authority.[75]

The circumstances were very different in the case of the publication of the royal epistle to the emperor written in April 1538. By 1538 England had broken from Rome, Henry was Supreme Head and divisions over religious change had sparked a rebellion that rocked the throne. The printed letter, therefore, was addressed as much to Henry's divided subjects as to the princes of Europe who were themselves torn by religious wars and troubles. The letter states firmly Henry's reasons for not attending the Council at Venice while reiterating his support for Councils (to which at an earlier stage of negotiations for a divorce he had appealed) in general.[76] England, Henry proclaimed in his letter, had banished all popish superstitions from the realm. Yet, for all its insistent and uncompromising tone, Henry evidently did not feel that the letter spoke for itself – at least to his English subjects. The preface to the published text explained how General Councils were not properly constituted, being dominated by agents of the pope. The Bishop of Rome, Henry continued, desired nothing less than the destruction of the nation and so, he asked his people in an artfully posed rhetorical question: 'do we not violate the judgement of nature if we give him power and authority to be our judge?'[77] Rather than being founded on scripture, the papacy had risen from superstition, gained power through violence and claimed an authority directly contrary to Christ's. 'Read ... O Christian reader,' the epistle urged, 'truth is coming home.'[78] The English reader was exhorted to 'step forth and meet her', the king not doubting 'but a reader not partial will soon approve such things as we write'.[79]

For all the pose of confidence and the gloss, this is a royal letter that Henry recognized could no longer speak to a whole commonwealth – only to those readers 'not partial' to Rome. Years after the break from Rome and all the polemics justifying the divorce and royal supremacy, there were many not persuaded, many who did not step forth to embrace the 'truth' as expounded by the king. Royal letters, in representing the king, then, also revealed the complex realities behind the languages of love, obedience and harmony, the fictions of state. Moreover, letters in writing, performing and publishing an act of power also exposed power as script, performance and publication. As we shall see, they were not the only genre of representation to expose as well as advertise authority.

From the tongue, Henry wrote in *A Necessary Doctrine*, 'cometh exceeding great benefits ... if it be well and wisely governed'.[80] The king quoted the famous passage from Ecclesiastes – 'where the word of a king is there is power' – and urged the duty of subjects not only to revere kings but to have 'a regard to their words'.[81] Given the importance he attributed to royal words, it may seem odd that there are not numerous examples of Henry's oratory. As a student of the new humanist learning and especially rhetoric, Henry was well trained in oratorical skills and could and did speak effectively. But in early modern England it was quite common for others to speak on behalf of the ruler, to represent his speaking, as customarily the Lord Chancellor or Lord Keeper did in parliament. In Henry's case, in April 1530, after the new Speaker, as was again customary, ritually declined the post or 'disabled himself . . . for lack of wit', the 'king . . . answered', 'by the mouth of the Lord Chancellor', Thomas More.[82] It was not uncommon for others to speak on the king's behalf. In January 1512, for example, the Archbishop of Canterbury, William Warham, addressed parliament on the themes of justice and peace, explaining how the injustice of the French king necessitated Henry going to war.[83] A decade later, in the parliament of April 1523, it was Cuthbert Tunstall, Bishop of London, who addressed the assembly on the office of king, the virtues of Henry as a ruler of judgement and learning and the 'mischiefs' that required remedy by statute.[84] In 1530, More, pointing up the deficiencies of existing laws and the 'new enormities sprung amongst the people', presented the king to his auditors as the 'shepherd, ruler and governor of his realm' who 'forseeth and provideth for all things which either may be hurtful or noisome to his flock'.[85]

Parliament was not the only forum where others spoke what was heard and received as the words of the king. On 13 February 1528, Wolsey summoned the Justices of the Peace 'and other honest personages to a great number' to Star Chamber, where he announced that 'his grace's pleasure is that I should declare to you'. Wolsey, as the king's ventriloquist, then spoke to explain and defend Henry's decision again to go to war against the Emperor Charles V. The cardinal catalogued in detail the misdeeds and deceptions of the emperor and closed with a rhetorical flourish: 'I am sure that I could show you twenty articles of promises which he hath broken with the king . . . which I am sure the great Turk would not do', and urged his audience to report back to their 'countries', or localities.[86]

On occasion, however, Henry did speak for himself and, not least because they were uttered sparingly, the royal words were delivered as if a royal gift. At the coronation of Anne Boleyn, as crowds accompanied the king and his new queen to Tower wharf, Henry 'gave great thanks and praises to all the citizens for their great kindness and loving labour and pains in that behalf' – to, we are told, 'the great joy and comfort of all the citizens'.[87] Earlier in a personal speech to papal legates in the Great Hall at Blackfriars, Henry had aired to them and the bishops and 'great company of ladies and gentlemen present' his 'troubled . . . spirits' and the vexed conscience his marriage to Catherine now caused him, so that he could 'scantly study anything which should be profitable for my realm and people'.[88] And at greater length in an oration to nobles, judges, councillors and 'diverse other persons' at Bridewell, Henry, prefacing his speech with a reminder that his reign had brought wealth and peace, related his doubts about his marriage to Catherine and his fears for the 'mischief and trouble' that would ensue 'if our true heir be not known at the time of our death'. In a powerful appeal to recent memory, he continued: 'some of you have seen after the death of our noble grandfather King Edward IV and some have heard about what mischief and manslaughter continue[d] in this realm between the houses of York and Lancaster by the which dissention the realm was like to have been destroyed'. It was 'for this only cause' that Henry had requested a Council of Christendom to review his marriage, not for any personal disaffection towards a queen 'without comparison', let alone any inclination to another mistress. Indeed, were his conscience settled, Henry claimed, and 'were I to marry again, if the marriage might be good, I would surely choose her above all other women'. It was these concerns that Henry ordered his auditors to 'declare to our subjects' as our 'mind and intent', 'according to our true meaning'.[89] It was an intensely personal speech rendered all the more forceful for being delivered by the king personally. In speaking in person about such personal matters (normally *arcana imperii*), Henry skilfully tied his conscience (a sceptic might say his desire) to the anxieties about succession and to the very survival of the realm. As well as ordering his words to be published to the country, Henry's speeches on his divorce were fully reported in the chronicle Edward Hall was commissioned to write of the reign.[90]

Perhaps the most remarkable oratorical performance by Henry of which we have a record was his speech to his last parliament on Christmas Eve 1545. The king opened by drawing attention to his unusual personal response to the Speaker's address and his reason: his desire to 'set forth my mind and meaning and the secrets of my heart' in a way that even his Chancellor could not do. What followed was nothing less than a rehearsal of the virtues of his kingship. Where the Speaker had praised the monarch, Henry underlined his encomium by (seemingly modestly) thanking him 'that you have put me in remembrance of my duty . . . to obtain and get such . . . virtues as a prince or governor should . . . have'. For the subsidy granted, the king expressed gratitude 'regarding more your kindness than the profit thereof' and the common trust in 'my good doings with the profits of the chantries'. Rising from particulars to general statements, Henry, passing over recent strains and tensions, exclaimed that 'no prince in the world more favoureth his subjects than I do you nor no subjects or commons more love and obey their sovereign lord than I perceive you do me'. 'Only one thing', Henry paused, and the rhetorical caesura is still audible, tarnished this 'perfect love and concord': that the same charity and love between king and people were not given by his subjects to each other. Castigating the clergy for fomenting divisions and the laity for their contempt of priests and religion, Henry, reminding them that he spoke 'as your Supreme Head and sovereign lord', exhorted and commanded that they serve God as 'brother and brother'.[91] It was a remarkable performance. Speaking for the first as well as the last time, Henry endeavoured to remove the bitter divisions bequeathed by his break from Rome and to reconstitute through royal utterance a harmonious commonweal, united and obedient to the sovereign.

As modern readers and historians, we cannot but ask what impact such rhetorical performances had. In the case of Wolsey's speech in Star Chamber, even the loyal Edward Hall reported that 'when the cardinal had said [spoken] some knocked other on the elbow, and said softly he lieth . . . other said that the French crowns made him speak evil of the emperor'.[92] When Henry spoke to his nobility, judges and 'beloved subjects' about his concerns for the legitimacy of his marriage and anxieties about the succession, reactions seem to have differed, 'for some sighed and said nothing, others were sorry to hear the king so troubled'.[93] Such responses should remind us that, especially before audiences also trained in the arts of rhetoric, let alone divided in opinion, even accomplished oratorical performances might fail to persuade. Indeed, both in their delivery and content, royal speeches (speeches both by the king and on his behalf) appear to have recognized the potential freedom of auditors or readers to form their own opinions, to follow or reject the king's 'mind'. Henry spoke of love and concord because he knew that without them he could not exercise rule. But he knew too that, whatever his injunctions, his word had a limited power of command. For in the end, as Thomas More put it in a speech on behalf of the king, in a remarkable rendering of a familiar royal metaphor, 'his people maketh him a prince, as of the multitude of sheep cometh the name of a shepherd'.[94]

While letters often circulated widely and speeches were communicated by nobles and magistrates to the localities, for most Englishmen and women the royal word was experienced, read, heard and seen in the form of a proclamation nailed on the market cross, read aloud by a sheriff or other local official, or circulated and reported in village or alehouse. Though in most cases we do not know whose minds first conceived or whose hands first drafted the text of a proclamation, the document that was transmitted to subjects was marked with the signs of, and received in the localities as the command of, 'our sovereign lord the king'.[95] Royal proclamations bore the king's sign manual, the authenticating symbol of the royal will and (increasingly) the royal arms. Yet, as the editors of *Tudor Royal Proclamations* point out, for all their calling attention to the royal prerogative, 'the introductory element of an early Tudor proclamation frequently appeals to some source of civil authority other than the king's': that is to the Privy Council, to the advice of parliament or to the laws – of God and the realm.[96] Moreover, many proclamations contain a 'rationalization', we might say a justification, of the order 'to ensure broad popular acceptance'.[97] The form of a proclamation, then, incorporated both the assertion of royal authority and argument for royal authority that we have identified in other genres of royal discourse. Too much of the scholarship on Tudor proclamations has been preoccupied with their constitutional status or particular injunctions to the neglect of the rhetorical forms and tropes by means of which they rationalized specific policies and, implicitly, justified the authority that enjoined them.[98] It is as the complex representations of a monarchy that had to write authority that we must re-read them for, in the new age of print, proclamations published the royal word and rendered royal decrees texts to be read and debated.

Proclamations commonly threatened the 'king's displeasure' or, in less affective language, the 'utmost peril' to those who disobeyed royal injunctions. Punishments threatened in order to discourage disobedience ranged from loss of office,[99] or forfeiture,[100] to imprisonment,[101] the whip,[102] 'grievous pain',[103] 'extreme punishment'[104] or 'fire and sword' 'to the dreadful example of other like offenders'.[105] But proclamations combined with threats of harsh punishments a language of grace and mercy. The king's 'gentle heart', a proclamation of 1536 explained, 'more desireth the reformation of his loving subjects by gentle warnings and monitions than by rigour and extremity of laws';[106] or, as another put it, 'reconciliation by merciful means [rather] than by the order and rigour of justice'.[107] Henry VIII presented himself in proclamations as, like God, a king of both dreadful justice and mercy. It was by reading and obeying the royal word, as the sacred word of God, that men escaped the punishment of sin and enjoyed the fruits of mercy.

Proclamations underpinned Henry's regal authority by asserting the legitimacy of the king and his power under God as Supreme Head and by figuring him as the embodiment of royal virtues: as just, open to counsel and petition, and as the protector of the body politic against the enemy and the rebel. In proclamations, military victories were presented as signs of God's favour to king and commonweal and, a declaration of 1544 urged, 'for the continuance of God's favour towards us, let us pray for the prosperous estate of our noble good and virtuous lord governor and king'.[108] From the beginning of the reign proclamations praised the king's 'most godly disposition' and his 'tender zeal for the honour of almighty God'.[109] The title Defender of the Faith conferred by Clement VII in 1521 was quickly announced in proclamations that presented Henry, in the tradition of his most devout predecessors, as the protector of the church against heresy.[110] Though the break from Rome posed serious problems of representation for a king who had so conspicuously advertised himself as a champion of the church, proclamations endeavoured to minimize the difficulty by a skilful combination of simple statement and careful justification. It was 'not only upon good, just and virtuous grounds', the proclamation of June 1535 stated, but 'upon the laws of God and Holy Scripture' and 'by due consultation, deliberate advisement and consent of parliament' that the king had extirpated the abuses of Rome from his kingdom.[111] And it was, too, not for personal ends but 'for the public weal of this our own realm' and 'by one assent' that the 'dignity and style of Supreme Head' was – the passive voice confirms it as a communal act – 'united to the crown imperial'.[112] We might here sense that, as the reign progressed, the claim to consensus was increasingly made to counter charges of arbitrary action. At a time of great uncertainty, proclamations were also used to reassure subjects that the king still intended 'to defend and maintain the faith of Christ and sacraments of Holy Church'.[113] For God, a proclamation of November 1538 ran, creating a new church in a casual phrase, had committed 'to his Majesty over all the congregation of the ... church of England' a 'great cure and charge' which Henry promised to exercise for the protection of a national church and commonweal.[114]

Increasingly during the 1530s, proclamations link the Supreme Headship to developing ideas not only of a national church but a nation state. From the beginning of the reign, proclamations had rehearsed the familiar tropes of the king's 'entire love' for his people and 'tender zeal' for 'the increase of the commonwealth of this realm'.[115] However, after the break from Rome, we discern a more insistent use of the term 'commonweal', emphasis on the church of England as synonymous with that commonweal, and a language that sought to connect the king as head to the members of both.[116] To erase the authority of the pope and to write the new supremacy of the monarch, proclamation after proclamation described the king as 'sovereign, chief and supreme head', and presented Henry literally as the embodiment of spiritual as well as secular authority.

Historians usually interpret the Supreme Headship as an enhancement of Tudor royal power; and in many respects so it turned out to be. But to read back into the 1530s the longevity and triumph of the Tudor dynasty is to risk remaining deaf to the undertones of anxiety in proclamations that tried to dispel deep concerns. Again we should note how often the new authority claimed for the king is validated as the will and work of others – of the Council, parliament and ultimately of subjects themselves. It was, proclamations claimed, by 'common assent' and 'by authority of parliament as also by the assent and determination of the whole [sic] clergy' that the legitimacy of the king's marriage to Anne Boleyn was determined;[117] and 'by one whole assent' that the Supreme Headship was knit to the crown.[118] It was, a proclamation announced in June 1530, only after consulting the primates 'and also a sufficient number of discreet, virtuous and well learned personages in divinity' that Henry decided to ban the Tyndale New Testament;[119] when 'divers' requested a vernacular Bible and insisted his highness was 'bounden to suffer them to have it', Henry again 'consulted' and, while rejecting their suit, held out the promise of scripture in English if the people forsook all 'erroneous and seditious opinions'.[120] The justification and exercise of the Supreme Headship produced in proclamations a rhetoric of consultation as well as the language of sovereign authority – both to counter the reality of widespread dismay and disaffection.[121]

On occasions proclamations themselves acknowledged the difficulties of justification and representation. The many proclamations for the 're-valuing' – that is the debasement – of the coinage are brief, unspecific and cite as reasons only vague 'divers and great urgent considerations', doubtless because it was all but impossible to present measures that hurt so many people as for the good of the commonweal.[122] When other social ills persisted, the engrossing of grain for example, and repeated proclamations showed little sign of having reformed behaviour, blame was transferred from the crown to the 'negligent oversight' of justices, mayors and sheriffs so as not to tarnish the image of the king as protector of all.[123]

As England divided over matters of faith and Henry perceived that his authority was inseparable from his determination of orthodoxy, a series of royal proclamations was issued to prescribe worship and belief. The proclamation ordering the new Great Bible bearing Henry's image to be placed in every parish church decreed that it was 'to the only intent that every of the king's majesty's loving subjects . . . might by occasion thereof not only perceive the great . . . omnipotent power of almighty God, but also to learn to obey . . . their sovereign lord'.[124] When, however, as another proclamation acknowledged, the reading of scripture proved, as Henry's own amendment put it, 'much contrary to his highness's expectation', the king confronted the intractable problem of how to limit or control reading and interpretation.[125] Successive proclamations, recognizing that the problem for authority was not simply the prescribing (or proscribing) of books, endeavoured to promote the 'right use and understanding' of them.[126] The irony was, of course, that the freedom of interpretation taken with holy writ could be, and was, taken also with royal writ. Like all the texts and symbols of royal authority, proclamations, as the exasperated language of those repeating injunctions and warnings testifies, met with resistance as well as compliance.

Although not the most common, the most dangerous resistance to royal authority came from rebels who, as well as the military threat they might pose, obviously fractured the fictions of love and harmony so carefully scripted in official discourses. Rebellion exposed the regal language of 'true faithful and loving subjects' as a (false) rhetoric and so challenged the hegemony of the royal word.[127] Moreover, by action and petition backed with arms, rebels demanded a hearing and response, so making the king himself, in a reversal of the discursive hierarchy, a respondent. When he faced rebels during his reign, Henry, as well as arming against them, answered them and addressed subjects concerning them, in his own voice and in a remarkable series of proclamations and declarations that deserve our attention as discursive representations of the king at moments of greatest crisis. The Pilgrimage of Grace undoubtedly marked the high point of crisis in Henry's reign. As the rebels of first Lincolnshire and then Yorkshire opposed royal commands and appealed to defenders of the old religion to rally behind the banner of the five wounds of Christ, they gathered in arms what amounted to 30,000 men and began to attack the houses of those officers involved in the dissolution of local monasteries.[128] On 10 October 1536, though castigating the rebels for their presumption, Henry, as one tactic in his response to the Lincolnshire rebellion, answered their petition with care and skill. In a clever attempt to contain the resistance, Henry isolated the Lincolnshire men as the 'rude and ignorant' of 'one of the most brute and beastly' counties of the kingdom. Casting them as acting and speaking 'contrary to God's law' as well as England's, the king yet took up their concerns in detail.[129] The monasteries, the king explained, that served God were not suppressed; only those which, rather than dispensing charity, nourished vice. While describing the Act of Uses, against which the propertied had loudly protested, as something that did not concern them, Henry explained the legal basis for his action.[130] As for first fruits, the king observed that he had been granted them not for personal gain but for the protection and maintenance of his subjects. In general, reasserting his devotion to his people, and so making critics of his policies enemies of the people, Henry played the patriotic card by urging them not to shame their country or 'undoubted king' with treasonous acts. In the conclusion to his response, he held out an olive branch of leniency in exchange for immediate return to obedience: 'We, and our nobles, can nor will suffer this injury at your hand, unrevenged if ye give not place to us of sovereignty and show yourselves as bounded and obedient subjects'.[131]

Muriel St Clare Byrne describes Henry's address as a 'vigorous document'.[132] But it was also one which recognized that, at least until the king had assembled a large army, and perhaps even then, power needed to be reinforced by acts of persuasion.[133] And it was not least the royal words that checked the rebels from marching on London before any troops reached the north to prevent them. The next month Henry took up his pen again to answer the rebels in Yorkshire who, if anything, presented a greater threat. Again denouncing ignorance, false report and the audacity of subjects who presumed to instruct their king, Henry tried to quell rumours and calm fears about his devotion to orthodox religion, the maintenance of the church and his commitment to law and justice. As with his reply to the Lincolnshire rebels, though without this time resorting to slurs on a proud and important county, Henry tried to divide and rule: to separate 'shameful' and 'unnatural' insurgents from 'the rest of our whole commons' who, it was implied, were no less wounded than the king.[134] And, in a language of authority that endeavoured to preserve the illusion of power, he offered the Yorkshire rebels a deal:

> Our princely heart rather embraceth ... pity and compassion ... than will to be revenged ... we are contented if we may see and perceive in you all sorrowfulness for your offences ... to grant unto you our letters patents of pardon.[135]

If the language, not by coincidence, echoes that of the clerical remission of sins, Henry, also in insisting on the surrender of 'ringleaders' to condign punishment, announced his intention to symbolically display his power over the bodies of his subjects. For the rest of them, the choice, as with salvation, was theirs: 'ye may have pardon ... if ye list'.[136]

In his answer to the rebels, Henry manifested his conviction concerning the power of the word and handled the difficult problem of representing what was in fact a negotiation with rebels as an act of sovereign grace and authority. He appropriated the language of grace and pardon to render insecurity as a priestly and traditional royal virtue; by renaming rebellion and opposition as 'lightness', 'ignorance' and 'false report', he not only sustained a fiction of love and concord, he again took control of language.[137] Henry used words skilfully to conceal his weakness and to present himself as in control; and the rebels trusted his words rather than called his bluff. Even as he faced his greatest challenge, Henry represented his authority in carefully chosen words that helped to secure it. Though the legacy of the Pilgrimage was a more than ever 'acutely polarised' church and nation, Henry had survived by denying it.[138]

Read carefully, the proclamations and declarations of Henry VIII both disclose the anxieties about authority and demonstrate the importance the king attached to the word as an instrument and representation of his rule in the first age of print. As we have seen, Henry VII had been the first monarch to see the potential value of the new medium of communication when he authorized the publication of the papal dispensation for his marriage to Elizabeth of York.[139] By that act, the king had hitched his regality to papal authority. His son was to face very different circumstances; and the second Tudor was to make a much greater and different use of print. Henry used the press to construct, defend and sustain an authority that was his own and, in the process, to fashion a mode of kingship that was to be highly textual and discursive.

Henry VIII was one of the few monarchs in English history to write treatises and tracts and the first to use print and establish a royal printer to disseminate texts of royal authorship. The king himself drew attention to the unusual act of royal authorship when he stated that the pope might well be surprised to find a king who studied the martial arts and affairs of commonwealth writing and publishing.[140] Henry's first authorial performance in print was his Latin rebuttal of Luther's attack on the sacraments in *The Babylonian Captivity of the Church*. Henry's *Assertio septem sacramentorum* was published in 1521 and dedicated to Clement VII, to whom the king sent no fewer than thirty copies.[141] Almost from the day of publication, doubts were raised about whether Henry wrote it. Luther himself questioned the king's authorship, though of course it was in his interest to do so.[142] Thomas More later referred to the 'makers' of the book.[143] But there is no reason to doubt that in essence the *Assertio* was Henry's text, whatever help he may have received in writing it.[144] There is evidence that Henry had begun to draft a response to Luther in 1518; in 1521 he was reported to be 'writing against Luther'.[145] And when, at a ceremony on 12 May that year, Luther's books were publicly burned, Wolsey, according to the Venetian ambassador, held the king's book in his hands.[146]

Whatever the exact contribution from the king's hand, what was important, as we have remarked of other texts, was that the *Assertio* was presented, received by the pope and read across Europe, as well as in England, as the work and words of Henry VIII. Because it was the words of a king it became, in Scarisbrick's words, 'something of a best seller', with over twenty editions published before the end of the century, and an international reputation.[147] Modern critics and theologians have not been impressed by Henry's polemic: there is little original or sophisticated in its arguments and the frequently deployed device of *reductio ad absurdum*, not to mention personal abuse of the 'little man' Luther, detracts, at least for the modern reader, from its effectiveness. Yet the *Assertio* deserves to be reconsidered less as a theological treatise than as a defence of authority in general and a representation of Henry's authority in particular. The foundation of Henry's argument was that Luther flew in the face of tradition, received learning and established authorities, and that it was 'forbidden to change or move the things which have been for long time immoveable'.[148] The doctrine of transubstantiation, Henry observed, was taught by the Fathers; confession was commended by the saints; the sacrament of marriage was consecrated by God himself. Luther, Henry claimed not entirely unfairly, not only disregarded the authorities of Scripture, the Fathers and the church, he denied that of the pope, to whom even the savage Indians submitted, and of bishops and priests for whom he expressed scant regard. Luther, the *Assertio* protests, asserted his own 'opinion' and placed it above the tradition, law and officers of the Catholic church.[149]

That challenge concerned Henry as a Christian: mindful of his duty to God, 'we will not', he vowed, 'decline from thy judgements because thou hast appointed us a law'.[150] But Luther's attack concerned him also and particularly as a king. Henry confessed to some unease about the interjection of his own interest into a work of theology: 'I forbear to speak of kings lest I should seem to plead my own case'.[151] But plead his own case is what he did. In challenging the authority of the church and pope, Luther, he charged using a phrase that makes a significant connection, 'robs princes as prelates of all authority'.[152] What was, he asked, the power of a prince if he could make no laws? Where in Luther did one read 'be obedient to your governors'?[153] Henry had come to see the threat that Luther's teaching presented to royal as well as papal authority and he wrote to counter it and to underpin his own position by urging 'all Christians' to support the pope.[154] In the short term, there can be no doubt that the *Assertio* was an effective defence of traditional authority and a representation of Henry as a pious and dutiful son of the church. Henry gained some reputation in Europe as a scholar as well as soldier king; and the reward from Clement VII, the title Defender of the Faith, strengthened his claim to be a fitting descendant of pious and Christian kings. The *Assertio*, however, reveals an unease amidst its bombast; indeed, the abuse of Luther as a 'sophist', as a 'blockish' trifler who endlessly contradicted himself, suggests an anxiety that Henry himself aired in his conclusion 'to the reader'.[155] 'What avails it,' the king asked, 'to dispute against one who disagrees with everyone . . .?'[156] Clearly Henry hoped that by disputing against Luther he might at least persuade others, if not his protagonist. In contrast to the harsh words against his opponent, Henry wooed the 'gentle reader' with rhetorical seduction and inclusive pronouns and, far from declaiming, invited readers into a dialogue.[157] Where against Luther he insists and asserts, the king now 'advises', 'beseeches' and, in fine, 'begs' readers 'to shut their ears against his impious words'.[158] Whatever his hopes, Henry did not shut down dispute or prevent the spread of Luther's teachings. Luther in fact responded in pugilistic style, dismissing Henry as a fool, a pig, a drunkard and a monster.[159] The polemical battle that followed – this time with Fisher and More as the king's aids and champions – was not the only difficulty that this first act of royal authorship presented Henry in representing his kingship. His passionate defence of tradition and papal authority was to become a text that, republished, re-read and reinvoked, served to compromise the king in his later claims for his own authority in matters spiritual.[160] The *Assertio* is a reminder to historians, as it was uncomfortably to Henry VIII, how, in changed circumstances, a royal text could perform quite otherwise than was intended or it had at first; indeed that texts of royal representation could in others' hands become texts of counter-representation, of opposition to rather than validation of royal authority.

Certainly by the time Henry next ventured into print, though the reassertion of his authority had never been more vital, the strategies for arguing his case had been transformed by events. *A Glass of the Truth* was published by the royal printer in 1532 amid Henry's endeavours to persuade the pope, the learned of Christendom and his own subjects that his marriage to Catherine of Aragon was unlawful and invalid. If a letter to Anne Boleyn in which Henry refers to the satisfactory progress with his book on which 'I have spent above four hours a day' can reliably be dated to August 1528, then it may be that *A Glass* had been a long time in the drafting.[161] But in its title as well as final form, the book owed much to the publication in Antwerp in 1530 of William Tyndale's *The Practice of Prelates: Whether the King's Grace May Be Separated from his Queen Because She Was his Brother's Wife.* The intervention against the king of Tyndale, who had translated the New Testament into English and who had been a virulent critic of the papacy, was a serious blow to Henry's cause. In particular, Tyndale's taunt that Henry remained silent from fear not only of the emperor but 'of his commons and subjects' required a response.[162] The difficulty for the king was entering the polemical fray while still presenting himself as the dutiful son of the church awaiting the resolutions of its learned doctors and divines. One way Henry evidently tried to square the circle was by publishing *A Glass* without his name. If the erasure of the authorial name from the title page was intended to enable denial of authorship, the evidence that Henry wrote it, or had the largest part in its scripting, is strong. On 23 September 1532, Richard Croke, envoy to Italy to promote the king's case for a divorce, wrote to Thomas Cromwell to report that 'many . . . cannot believe it is the king's writing and though they admit his wit, thinks that he lacks the leisure'.[163] Croke knew otherwise and knew too that this was anything but a work of leisure. *A Glass* was printed by Thomas Berthelet, the king's printer, and was taken throughout England to be the king's own statement of his cause.

Statement, however, it was not – at least not in any formal or simple sense. *A Glass of the Truth* took the form not of a univocal argument, as had the *Assertio*, but of a humanist dialogue between a lawyer and a divine. As well as owing its title to Tyndale (who described his own tract as a glass), Henry seemed to invite the reader to view, to inspect and reflect, while artfully arranging what he wanted them to see.[164] The anonymous preface to the readers introduced the work as a 'dialogue' 'declaring the pure truth alone *that you shall be right sure to find*'.[165] That truth, lest any fail to find it or read aright, was 'the plain truth of our most noble and loving prince's cause'. And that cause, the epistle makes clear, was 'ours' as well as 'his': the need for a legitimate male heir and the danger from the prolonged delay in making it possible to sire one. The argument from necessity and security is reiterated insistently, nervously insistently, as truth: 'without colouring, dissembling, pretence and all outward painting ye shall find here the mere truth'.[166] And, connecting the king's cause not only to the nation's but to God's will, the preface closes by urging readers 'to imprint well in your hearts this mere and sincere truth and so to follow it that you may do a thing acceptable to the pleasure of almighty God and the contentation of our sovereign and prince'.[167] Here was a text of two voices which if read rightly, the preface instructs, could only lead to one conclusion: support for a cause that was the divine and national, as much as royal, will.

For all its dialogic form, A Glass is a text in which dialogue is a rhetorical vehicle not to air difference but to arrive at a consensus after a display of deliberation. Both the lawyer and divine marvel that any should think the matter of the divorce 'disputable'. While the divine emphasizes the weight of scriptural arguments, ancient authors and Councils and the 'opinion accepted by the whole church' on the king's side, the lawyer invokes Henry's 'pains for this his commonwealth', the 'unnatural[ness]' of failing to do one's duty to him and the need for 'the greatest union between the head and the body that ever was seen or heard of'.[168] The speakers unite to assert the jurisdiction of Councils, to deny the authority of the pope and to proclaim as fact that the marriage between Catherine and Prince Arthur had, contrary to the queen's protestations, been consummated. Reiterating how 'the truth favoureth our prince's cause', the lawyer and divine concur in insisting that king and parliament, not 'foreigners', should resolve the issue and 'press the metropolitan of the realm . . . to set on . . . and to take a greater regard to the quieting of his grace's conscience and this realm than to the ceremonies of the pope's law'.[169]

Though the dialogue stages the representatives of religious and secular learning, the intended audience for A Glass is clearly broader than professional elites. The language is straightforward, the theology unsophisticated, the nationalistic appeal downright jingoistic and, in the report of Arthur's alleged remarks about being in and out of Spain all night, the wit ribald.[170] Most importantly, A Glass of the Truth conducts in print what Henry desperately desired in reality: a deliberation that led to a clear vindication of his cause. And in the process of argument towards consensus, it cleverly conjoins the king's conscience, the nation's good and will, and God's decree. Though it was no less an assertion than the Assertio, Henry endeavoured in this text to distance himself from the polemic not only by the dialogue form but by a prefatory voice that talked of him in the third person. How was it received? Croke was certain of its success: as he wrote to Cromwell, 'the book has done more for the king's cause than all that ever has been written, and many have altered their stubborn minds to the contrary'.[171] Yet, as his closing as well as prefatory address make apparent, Henry knew that his cause was part of a wider conversation, abroad and at home, that was less consensual than that of the lawyer and divine; that 'malicious reports' might 'hinder the accepting of this our treatise'.[172] In less than a year after its publication, Friar Peto published, with documentation damaging to Henry, a 44-page introduction to a planned answer to *A Glasse*.[173] At home, Henry's subjects, far from moving like the lawyer and divine to a consensus, were even more sharply dividing, not only over the divorce but over the fundamentals of doctrine and belief.

By the time that Henry published the last of his treatises, England was rent by doctrinal disputes and, it is not too much to say, was divided into Catholic and Protestant parties vying to establish, or re-establish, their faith as the religion of the nation. As events had unfolded and wives, ministers, bishops and nobles had jockeyed to exercise varying influences on the direction of royal policy, Henry's own position appears to have wavered. A recent case has been made for Henry's personal direction and consistent belief, but the fact remains that the king supported a vernacular Bible but was swift to try to control its readership; ordered the dissolution of the monasteries and an attack on superstitious rites but insisted on adherence to prescribed cere-monies; and followed the Ten Articles of 1536 that went some way to endorsing tenets of Lutheran theology, not least on justification, with the Six Articles of 1539 that seemed to arrest any move towards reform.[174] Though his orders may have appeared wavering or inconsistent to others, it has been suggested that Henry was working out his own beliefs and was, in his biog-rapher's words, 'his own theologian'.[175] In 1543 he not only made a clear public statement of his position, he published, with a title that announced both royal authorship and royal authority, *A Necessary Doctrine and Erudition for any Christian Man Set Forth by the King's Majesty of England*, which came to be known simply as 'The King's Book'.

A Necessary Doctrine was a statement of personal belief that the king as Supreme Head sought to prescribe as the faith of the newly created Church of England. Henry defined faith, glossed the creed, reinstated, prescribed and interpreted the sacraments, explained the commandments, 'expounded' the Lord's Prayer and deliberated on the bitter controversy concerning free will and justification.[176] Though it has recently been re-examined as a treatise that balanced reformist with traditional positions, the text deserves a fuller expli-cation as a work of theology. Our interest, however, lies more in *A Necessary Doctrine* as a representation of royal authority: as a statement in itself of that authority and as a masterly attempt to underwrite it.[177]

On this occasion, unlike *A Glass of the Truth*, the text was written, very insistently, in the king's own personal voice – that is the voice of a king who was Supreme Head and the voice of Henry Tudor. The title page bore verses from Psalms 19 and 20, placing Henry in the line of kings descended from David: 'Lord preserve the king'; 'Lord in thy strength the king shall rejoice'. In the preface Henry announced his purpose. Though with the aid of God he had cleansed the realm of superstition, evil spirits threatened to re-enter and corrupt a house purified. Accordingly, 'we set forth a doctrine and declaration of the true knowledge of God and his word, so all may learn what is necessary for every Christian to know'.[178] The book was intended for a wide circulation and consumption: even bound in leather with clasps it was not to be sold for more than 12 pence.[179] To attract a wide readership it was written, Henry explained, 'with simplicity and plainness as the capacities and understandings of the multitude of people may easily conceive and comprehend the same'.[180] As Supreme Head, and in realization of the image on the title page of the Great Bible, Henry was conveying the word – his word – to all his people.

Not only did A Necessary Doctrine endeavour to determine doctrine and belief, it was throughout a reaffirmation of royal authority against the challenges of both papal claims and domestic critics. A full decade after the break from Rome, Henry went to some lengths to deny the pope's claim to be Christ's vicar on earth. The Bishop of Rome's pretended power, the text asserts, was 'utterly feigned and untrue and was neither given to him by God ... nor allowed by the Holy Fathers'.[181] Under Christ, Henry maintains, Christians were to follow the teachings of 'the particular church' of the region where they were born and were bound 'to honour and obey ... Christian kings and princes which be the head governors ... in the particular churches'; for God himself, the king continues, 'ordained the authority of Christian kings and princes to be the most high and supreme above all other powers'.[182] True Christians loved unity, and that unity, A Necessary Doctrine argues, was to be found in particular national churches – the Church of England was worthily called a Catholic church – and in obedience to Christian kings.[183]

The necessity of obedience is perhaps the doctrine most insistently prescribed in the king's book. God commanded princes to defend the faith and true doctrine of Christ, eradicate heresy, uphold justice and protect the public peace and common good; and he mandated bishops, priests and laity to obey kings, out of conscience as well as from fear of punishment. As he glossed the fifth commandment, Henry instructed that, as well as the natural father and mother, it embraced 'also princes and other governors' who were nursing fathers to the church.[184] It was God's law, 'the very law of nature', that everyone should 'employ himself to preserve and defend the head'; and God punished those who rebelled against princes, having 'assigned no judges over [kings] in this world'.[185]

As he moved from commandments and sacraments to creed and prayer, Henry unrelentingly pressed the need for authority and obedience in general and, in places almost casually, argued his own case and cause. While reaffirming, for example, the sanctity of the sacrament of marriage, he was swift to point out that a man should never marry within the forbidden degrees, especially his brother's wife; and that, if a marriage were found to be unlawful, 'the church may and ought to divorce the same persons', for a marriage 'within the degrees forbidden' breached the seventh commandment against adultery.[186] The commandment, 'Thou shalt not steal', Henry reads, conjoining divine with regal proclamation, as a pronouncement against the ills of oppression, bribery, usury, false weights and engrossing of goods that undermined the ideals of the commonweal and social justice.[187] Commenting on the Lord's Prayer, he paused to observe that the 'forgiveness . . . spoken of is not so meant in Scripture that by it . . . laws of princes should be broken, condemned or not executed'.[188]

A Necessary Doctrine was a brilliant rhetorical performance that deserves a closer formal analysis than can be offered here. By skilfully and apparently artlessly weaving the particular with the general, by almost seamlessly moving, often via syntactical slippage, from God's to king's injunctions, by placing the most polemical and contentious passages in the midst of exegesis of the sacraments, by a direct appeal to national sentiment and through use of homely idioms (he compares the rejection of papal authority to the dismissal of a royal officer!),[189] Henry sought to reconstitute, along with his authority, unity, harmony and obedience. His final pages on the articles of free will and predestination skilfully attempt a synthesis of words that he hoped might resolve a controversy over which much of European Christendom was now at war.[190] The king was all too aware of the sharp differences among his subjects. He knew that, in large part, those divisions arose from different interpretations of the central texts and tenets of Christian faith. Texts such as the commandments and Lord's Prayer had authority because Christ was known to be their author. Henry hoped that as Supreme Head, exegete of Christ's word and royal author his word too would be heeded: that subjects would honour princes 'with a regard to their words'.[191] Accordingly, in language that melded discourse, authority and faith, Henry 'exhorted' 'our people of all degrees willingly and earnestly to read and print in their hearts the doctrine of this book.'

II

Reviewing the king's writings as representations of his kingship, we have seen how texts published in the king's name were often not the script of his hand alone. In a variety of ways, the representation of regality, like the exercise of monarchical government, involved many others – ministers, advisers, editors, secretaries and printers. What we must now appreciate is that the representation of the king, especially in print, was not confined to words of his own devising. Other voices and hands spoke and wrote for Henry, whether they were commissioned to do so by the king or his ministers, whether they took it upon themselves, or whether texts were, or were not, received as 'royal' or officially sanctioned. Representing the king in print was, as J. Christopher Warner has described it, a 'business', presided over by the king's printer who saw it as his role to 'represent properly – not only accurately but ornately – the king'.[192] When readers saw the royal arms or name of the king's printer, or the advertisement that a book was published 'cum privilegio', whatever the complexities of authorship, 'they would have understood that the text was doing official service: stating the king's views, representing the king as he wanted others to see him'.[193] Emanating from court circles and circulating in manuscript, or printed by Richard Pynson or Thomas Berthelet with privilege, many texts claimed to present Henry VIII to his subjects. They could be panegyrical or offer advice – or both; but, along with Henry's own writings, they constructed images of the king and government that helped shape the course of the reign.

Literary and political tradition dictated that, from the hour of the death of his predecessor, a new monarch was heralded in verse panegyrics, a genre of succession poems that still awaits full research. Typical of the genre, a funeral elegy for Henry VII lamenting the loss of so noble a governor consoles the nation with the presence of a son, an adult male heir, 'in beaut force and lust', a fitting heir to Hector, Julius Caesar and Solomon.[194] The celebration of Henry's 'lust', that is both his sexual prowess and his youthful strength, was, understandably given he was the first young prince to succeed in nine decades, to be a motif of succession panegyrics. The coronation on 23 June 1509 provided the occasion for exuberant verses in praise of the vigorous young king and queen from a nation that showed joyous relief at the smooth succession and looked forward to an era of peace and stability.[195] Immediately on the first Tudor's death, his former tutor John Skelton wrote and dispatched to Henry VIII 'A Lawde and Prayse Made For Our Sovereigne Lord The Kyng' subscribed 'by me, laureate poet of the Britons'.[196] Skelton's themes were Henry's rightful descent and succession, the end of conflict and chaos, and the joyful hopes of peace and prosperity in a new era and reign. Skelton celebrated the fact that 'The rose both white and red' was united in Henry whose succession, by God's grace, banished the 'dolours' of the last century.[197] Now, as in a golden age, the poet promised, distancing the new ruler from the unpopular rapacity of his predecessor, justice would be restored, the law would rule and the commons could be free from extortion. Skelton represented Henry not only as the best of English kings but as one who belonged in the ranks of classical and mythical heroes, a second Alexander, an Astraea (the goddess of justice), a Priam (who reigned forty years and sired nineteen children) and an Adonis. Adonis was a figure associated with spring and regeneration and in that spirit Skelton presents Henry, 'our king, our emperor' as 'of fresh colour', 'of youthe', 'the godely flour [flower]'.[198] If the wolf and bear which in the poem had brought woe to England alluded to Empson and Dudley, the rapacious ministers of Henry VII's reign whom Henry soon after his succession sent to the scaffold, the poem may be read as exhortation and counsel as well as praise.[199] Skelton's final line – 'God save him in his right' – may be read as a hope as well as celebration, the hope indeed of a poet who had experienced the rise and fall of fortune and dislocation as well as triumph. Skelton's 'Lawde and Prayse' represented England's new king as 'Martis lusty knight', as the symbol of vigorous renewal and as a champion of his people.[200]

Stephen Hawes's *A Joyful Meditation . . . of the Coronation of our Most Natural Sovereign Lord King Henry VIII*, as well as also being presented to the new king in manuscript, was printed by Wynkyn de Worde (who worked closely with Pynson and printed several texts with royal privilege) and was published in 1509 'to all England'.[201] Hawes, a former groom of the chamber to Henry VII, acknowledging that some had charged him too with 'avaryce', did not echo implied criticisms of the first Tudor but praised 'our late soverayne his fader excellent'.[202] Yet, as well as figuring the new king as a fitting heir to his father, Hawes presents Henry as a rightful successor to Henry V, the heroic victor of Agincourt, whom he describes (paying an even greater compliment to his new king) as 'your worthy predecessor'.[203] Together with his queen, Catherine – and a woodcut images the pair crowned with a Tudor rose and thistle – the 'yonge king' Henry promises the end of 'our trouble', a stable, fertile dynasty:

> This ryall tree was planted as I knowe
> By God above the rancour to downe throwe[204]

Yet, for all the celebration, Hawes cannot quite dispel the memory of past rancour. Having praised Henry VIII (not least for his swift 'iustyse' in dealing with oppressors), Hawes calls on the gods to protect and serve him and to bestow on him their divine gifts: on Jupiter to send the light of truth, Mars power, Venus love and Mercury eloquence. In each case, Hawes also invokes their aid in cementing love between the king, the nobles and the people: 'to make our hertes mekely to enclyne to serve our soverayne', to excite 'love and honoure/Amonge the lordes', to 'suberte our soveraynes enemyes', and to steer the 'kynges counsayll' to just courses.[205] In fine, Hawes implores God:

> So save our soverayne from all manner wo
> And this his realme from mortall warre also[206]

Loyalty and love, though clearly celebrated, appear here as fragile, ever in need of divine support, the assiduous attention of subjects and the constant care of rulers. The poem calls upon all Englishmen to 'be true and love well eche other' as well as to 'Obey your soverayne'.[207] But while lauding Henry, Hawes also counsels, perhaps admonishes, him: to follow God as the best defence against 'murmurynge' enemies; to reward the loyal with 'largesse'; and to punish extortion as the means to retain the people's service and affection.[208] The relationship between service and reward, sovereign and subjects, is presented in this poem, like that between Henry and Catherine themselves, as a union, from which sprang the hope of rich fruits. Hawes's poem was a prayer as well as panegyric, advice as well as praise. Far from simple propaganda, coronation verse voiced the threats and problems that faced new rulers, aired the flaws as well as virtues of princes, and posited the reciprocity of obedience and good government, royal justice and the subjects' love.

Another literary genre which both addressed the monarch often in person and also represented him to his subjects was the sermon. In recent years, the early modern court sermon has begun to attract more scholarly attention as a text of theology and as a rhetorical performance.[209] What we need still to address more closely is the court sermon as a voice of the king and government as well as that of the preacher. Invitations to give sermons were, of course, opportunities to address the king. But, published with authority, sermons delivered to a king at his coronation or in his royal chapels at Whitehall or Greenwich also became public texts of policy as well as piety and representations of the monarch.[210] Moreover, in Tudor England the sermons regularly preached publicly at Paul's Cross were regarded as official occasions and the preachers appointed by the Bishop of London to deliver them were heard as 'the mouthpiece of the administration'.[211] Indeed, it is hardly surprising that, delivered at the site at which royal proclamations were routinely read aloud and public penance was performed, these sermons were seen as part of the texts and performances of authority. The audiences that attended were large, mixed and, if sermon notes may be a guide, often attentive. By no means all the sermons were published, but we have contemporary reports of several that appear to have been closely tied to royal policy: sermons against marriage with a brother's widow, against the papacy, in defence of royal supremacy, on the Church of England as the true church, and against rebels.[212] Preached by archbishops, bishops and clients of Thomas Cromwell and Thomas Cranmer, the sermons presented and justified royal actions and programmes in the language of scripture and providence.[213] But by their very form, sermons were seldom straightforward panegyrics. Even when addressed to the king himself, they exhorted him to recall his duties to his Lord as much as they reminded subjects of their obligations to their ruler. And, while praising the sovereign, preachers did not draw back from cataloguing and criticizing the ills of the commonweal – the vices of extravagance, greed and fashion, of moral abominations and lack of charity – and pressing the king to remedy them; some, as we shall see, used sermons to contest royal policy.

The sermon also offers interesting cases of how forms of royal representation could be received quite otherwise than they had been intended and indeed of their availability to those with agendas quite opposed to the king or government. When, for example, at Easter 1533, Dr George Browne prayed for Queen Anne Boleyn at Paul's Cross, the congregation walked away in protest; another preaching the king's case against Catherine of Aragon was interrupted in the pulpit by a friar; and it was reported of Dr Edward Crome's preaching that there was 'variety of opinions and contentions among the people of London' following his sermons.[214] Sermons denouncing the preachers of others served, of course, to make Paul's Cross and the published texts emanating from its pulpit sites of dialogue and dispute rather than official declaration. Over the decades of the 1530s and 1540s, as theological and clerical disputes heightened, Thomas Cranmer and Hugh Latimer, John Hilsey, Bishop of Rochester, and Alexander Seton denounced the Paul's Cross preachers and in some cases charge and counter-charge were exchanged from the pulpit for weeks.[215] There were dramatic moments, too, that exposed the fragility of any planned programme of sermon propaganda. In April 1540 a fray broke out during a sermon, and the next month Bishop Sampson of Chichester was arrested as he was about to preach, as was Robert Wisdom the following July.[216] Moreover, for all the careful vetting and selection of preachers, by no means all, once standing in the pulpit, toed the official line. On three successive Sundays in the Lent of 1540, the preachers Robert Barnes, William Jerome and Thomas Gerard railed and 'raged' against the bishops; in August 1536 a chaplain to the king was accused by one of Cromwell's agents of preaching sedition, though he had evidently been appointed in place of Dr George Browne who, it was feared, might 'excite sedition'.[217] Amid the revolutionary and sudden turns and changes of the 1530s and 1540s, even those who had once been unimpeachably orthodox could no longer be relied upon to ventriloquize government views. Different patrons with their own faiths and preferences promoted their own candidates as preachers and, once standing in the pulpit, many used it to proclaim their own. The sermon in early modern England was regarded as having a vital role to play in instructing the people in what to believe and in inculcating habits of obedience and a horror of rebellion. But, as its historian concluded, especially for the post-Reformation years, 'the use of the Paul's Cross pulpit as an organ of public persuasion . . . had more than one result'.[218]

As an expanding culture of print stimulated not only increasing literacy but also a market for a variety of genres of text, the Henrician government discerned the value of diverse literary forms as potential vehicles for disseminating both specific policies and the royal image.[219] Given the centrality of the issues of dynasty and succession, heightened by Henry's difficulty in producing a male heir, it is not surprising that a keen official interest was taken in chronicles and histories. But as well as the English past, the new humanism directed attention also to the histories of Greece and Rome which were held to offer exemplary texts and lives of vice, virtue and political wisdom. In the words of Thomas Elyot, 'there is no doctrine be it either divine or human that is not either well expressed in history, or at the least mixed with history'.[220] The chronicle, not least because it remained the most popular form of historical writing, clearly came under the government's eye. In 1530 and 1532, for example, as Henry entertained a national solution to his marriage crisis, editions of *The Chronycle Beginning at the VII Ages of the World with the Comynge of Brute* were published with the royal arms, the emblem of the Garter, the Tudor rose and the portcullis, another badge of the Tudor dynasty; and John Rastell's chronicle was published with royal privilege.[221] Beginning with God the creator, and moving swiftly thence to 'Brute who came after the making of the world to this land', the chronicle plotted a history of the English Christian kings that led to, as the frontispiece displays, King Henry.[222] The next year, the full title of a new edition of *Fabyan's Chronicle*, published 'cum privilegio' by William Rastell, an associate of Lord Chancellor Thomas More, made explicit the connection between past and present and the ideological value to the crown of historical texts. Fabyan's chronicle was 'newly printed with the . . . acts and deeds done in the time of the reign of prince Henry VII, father of our most dread sovereign lord King Henry VIII unto whom all honour, reverence and joyful countenance of his prosperous reign, to the pleasure of God and weal of his realm' was due.[223] The chronicle, in fact, was a seven-part paean to 'this fertile yle' and to its kings from Brutus to Henry, and, literally given its two volumes, a weighty foundation for the second Tudor's rule.[224] As Jürgen Beer has argued, 'the chronicles have a great theoretical and emotional bias towards the crowned king of England'.[225] They both placed Henry in a dynastic and providential narrative that made his kingship the triumphant end-point of the nation's destiny and God's divine plan and figured him as an object of the people's affection and love.

The reign of Henry VIII saw the birth of other forms of historical writing which had already begun to transform both the study of the past and political discourse on the continent. Thomas More's *History of King Richard III*, uncompleted but incorporated into Hardyng's chronicle (published in 1543), invented and portrayed, as overt Lancastrian polemic, a crippled hunchback Richard whose cruel, tyrannical regimen, symbolized by his deformed body, the Tudors succeeded to dispel.[226] More's was to be a pattern for what became the later, fashionable 'politic histories' of the second half of the sixteenth century.[227] During the first half, it was chronicles which remained the dominant form and the business of officially representing Henry in history was undertaken by Edward Hall, who was a lawyer and under-sheriff of London and a loyal supporter of the king entrusted with acting as commissioner to inquire into transgressions of the Act of Six Articles. Hall's was almost certainly a commission and the first edition of his chronicle was printed by the royal printer Thomas Berthelet in 1542. No complete copy of that edition survives. The revised chronicle was published by Richard Grafton, whom Cromwell had consulted over an English Bible, a year after both Hall's and Henry's death; and this and its later editions became, as had surely been intended, the principal source for the history of the reign.[228]

Edward Hall's chronicle was an apologia for, and a celebration of, the person and reign of the second Tudor. A forceful argument for the importance of the royal prerogative and supremacy, the chronicle depicts Henry as, in Anglo's words, 'the flawless hero of a huge historical drama'.[229] Hall traces the history of the union of Lancaster and York from the 'first author of their division' to the 'reign of the high and prudent prince King Henry the Eight, the indubitate flower and very heir of both the said lineages' as though it were inevitable, natural and providentially determined, rather than contingent and contested.[230] In turning to the 'triumphant' reign of Henry itself, Hall wrote his chronicle, as it were, from the king's perspective, so that the reader sees as the king directs. Skilfully he lays emphasis on the first two decades of the reign and presents the king, as Henry had sought to present himself, as the embodiment of martial prowess and magnificence.[231] Hall conveys in lavish detail, as we shall see, the rich apparel, costly jewels and elaborate pageants through which the second Tudor impressed contemporaries with his wealth and power. Obscuring the less than glorious outcomes of campaigns, Hall devotes pages to the king's triumphs in France and Scotland, highlighting Henry's role in what reads as 'a personal adventure story'.[232] Hall interspersed his narrative of martial glory abroad with accounts of brave jousts at home, but also with vignettes that depict Henry as the ideal monarch, the just yet merciful prince who, in 1517, dramatically pardoned at the eleventh hour riotous apprentices who stood in halters awaiting their execution.[233]

The divorce and break from Rome might have presented difficulties to a historian committed to representing Henry's reign as harmonious and happy and the king as an ideal ruler. Hall, however, cleverly negotiated that difficulty. In the first place, while retaining the impression of straightforward, hindsight-free chronology, Hall inserts into his narrative at the time of reporting his wedding to Queen Catherine the king's doubts about his marriage, thereby implying that neither later events nor Anne Boleyn turned the king's conscience. Hall describes Henry as an innocent, 'not understanding the law of God', implicitly blames the pope for granting an unlawful dispensation (against, he claims, the advice of the cardinals) and, probably to discredit Catherine's later popularity, reports the 'detestable marriage' as 'much murmured against in the beginning' as 'plain contrary to God's law'.[234] By such devices, the chronicle cleverly sets up the 'scruple' which troubled the king's conscience twenty years later.[235] Even at this point, Henry's role and motives are discreetly handled. The usually dominant Henry is placed in the background of the story as Hall relates in passive verbs how 'divers divines well learned secretly informed him that he lived in adultery' and his 'counsellors advised him to know the truth'.[236] With the emphasis on the king's conscience, Hall says little of either the dynastic or personal reasons for the divorce.[237] Henry is described as having loved Catherine 'as well as any prince might love his wife'.[238] As for the rumours that it was Anne Boleyn who broke up the marriage, this, Hall writes, was but the 'foolish communication of the people'.[239] If the narrative was constructed to smooth over the controversies and to validate the divorce, Hall also interrupted his account – quite uncharacteristically – to insert documentation that supported Henry's case. The determinations of the universities of Orleans, Paris, Anjou, Bruges, Padua and Toulouse took up ten pages in the 1548 edition and so served to add weighty European support to the early misgivings that, despite the papal dispensation, the marriage to Catherine was illegitimate because against God's command in Leviticus.[240] The massive citation serves both to validate Henry and the divorce and to undermine the authority of the pope by isolating him from those truer Catholics who upheld God's law and the teachings of the church. Accordingly, by the time he comes to the actual divorce and Catherine's appeal, Hall's reader is led – almost seduced – into concurring that 'every man that had wit and was determined to follow the truth . . . might plainly see that all appeals made to Rome were clearly void'.[241] The delegitimization of the papacy and the emphasis on Henry's conscience as the purer custodian of God's law serve in Hall's narrative to render the break from Rome and the assumption of the supremacy actions not contingent and contentious but rooted in scripture and history.

Hall in fact initiated a Whig historiographical tradition of writing about the Reformation which until relatively recently marginalized critics and opponents of the break from Rome as backward, un-English and ungodly.[242] Though he acknowledged opposition to the divorce and break from Rome and could even admire opponents' integrity, he presented the king's critics as misguided or worse. Thomas More, who stood as a martyr for his beliefs against Henry, is described as going to his death 'with a mock' rather than a sincere profession of his faith, while Fisher's protest and martyrdom are summarily dismissed: 'wonderful it is that a man being learned should be so blind in the Scripture of God that proves the supreme authority of princes'.[243] And, as his last pages return Henry to the battlefield, making the Reformation seem all but a minor interlude in the normal affairs of kingship, Hall also emphasized Henry's attentive concern for the good of his church and nation: 'the king's highness . . . never ceased to study and take pain for the advancement of the commonwealth of this his realm of England, of the which he was only supreme governor' and for 'the defence of the same' against the 'cruel serpent, the bishop of Rome' and his agents who sought 'utterly to destroy the whole nation'.[244] Edward Hall, the son of parents who 'seem to have been important ... among the more advanced reformers', made the break from Rome, the nation's safety and well-being and Henry himself inseparable.[245] His chronicle not only echoes Henry's own words, it essentially worked out a narrative from the historical claims made in Reformation statutes that asserted England to be, and to have been, an empire governed by one supreme head and king.[246]

Hall does not quite succeed in silencing all other voices or erasing any doubters from the commonweal of Henry's England. There are frequent references in the chronicle to rumours and 'murmurings' of 'gentlewomen and servants', even the populace at large.[247] Coming to the year 1525, he reports the protests against the levy known to historians as the Amicable Grant which, he admits, resulted in bills 'set up in all places', accusing the king of not having paid back what he had borrowed and denying any good reason to pay more.[248] Under the next year, he relates how the tax was denied and 'the commons in every place was so moved that it was like to have grown to rebellion'.[249] But in the main, resistance and opposition are made light of and dismissed as foolish or worse, evil. The Lincolnshire rebels, 'wicked and foolish', 'ignorant and rude' were, Hall claims, misled by priests who 'deceived' them.[250] As for the Pilgrimage of Grace in Yorkshire, Hall castigated the Pilgrims as this 'rebellious garrison of Satan' which might have led a deluded people to slaughter, had not a miracle of God (a rising ford) and the king's mercy spared them.[251]

Hall's recent biographer for the *Oxford Dictionary of National Biography* argues for a strong measure of independence and even hints of criticism in the chronicle. This should not be exaggerated. In the main, Hall's chronicle represents Henry from the king's own perspective and, at key points, in his own words. His work demonstrates that, while others may have had a hand in writings published under the king's name, other writers acted virtually as the king's voice and pen to represent him as he would have wished himself. Hall's chronicle powerfully illustrates the degree to which Henry and his ministers recruited, patronized or encouraged writers to orchestrate official views and to present the king in a favourable light to contemporaries and to posterity.

The evidence for official direction, even in Hall's case, is tenuous and circumstantial rather than direct. But a pattern of mounting official control and influence over what was written is clear – both from the trend of publications and from, as Greg Walker has brilliantly demonstrated, the complaints of those (including many former supporters of the king, such as Thomas Elyot) who felt an unacceptable pressure on their freedom as authors.[252] Cyndia Clegg has noted that of 2,233 titles published during the reign of Henry VIII, only 302 were printed 'cum privilegio'; but that there was a marked increase in the proportion of such officially sanctioned works after the break from Rome.[253] Moreover, after a period of some laxity in the use of royal privilege that, for example, permitted 'annotations and additions' to a work after it was granted, increasingly from the mid-1530s, there were moves to greater control, with more of the books published 'cum privilegio' also being printed by the king's printer, Thomas Berthelet.[254] Berthelet (who succeeded Richard Pynson in his office in 1530), though he faced competition, evidently took even more seriously his role as the representer as much as publisher of the monarch and sought to assert his own as well as the king's supremacy and authority.[255] Yet even though before the troubles over his divorce Henry's public image in print 'allowed . . . a space for multiple voices', the publication of a book by the royal printer inclined readers to interpret it as a text that was 'doing official service'.[256]

Early in the reign, the official imprimatur was granted to the publication of a variety of books in the traditional 'advice to princes' genre, as Henry sought to publicize his learning and claim to be an ideal philosopher king. John Lydgate's *The Governance of Kings and Princes*, for example, was reprinted by Pynson in 1511, at, the title page announces, the command of Charles Somerset, Lord Herbert, Lord Chamberlain to the king.[257] Frontispieces bearing the royal arms held aloft by angels and a crowned Tudor rose reinforced the clear impression of this as a representation of the monarch as well as a treatise of advice on monarchy. Lydgate's fifteenth-century text called upon the good king to follow God, to be schooled in philosophy, to be governed by reason and counsel and to be pious, temperate, liberal, righteous, magnificent and virtuous. The injunctions were conventional and the book not new; yet, printed by the king's printer at the command of his senior household officer, Lydgate's work became a text by which the young Henry presented himself to his new subjects as a king who respected learning and advice, who was fully cognizant of the duties and responsibilities of royal office and who sought to attain the ideals outlined by Lydgate. In a similar vein the translation published in 1533, 'cum privilegio a rege indubto' of Agepetus's advice to the Emperor Justinian, *The Precepts Teaching a Prince or a Noble Estate his Dutie*, very much announced its origins in official circles and hence its representation of Tudor rule.[258] The translator, Thomas Paynell, a diplomat (who was sent as envoy to the German Protestant princes) and royal chaplain to Henry, dedicated his translation from the Greek to Lord Montjoy, Lord Chamberlain to the queen, observing that, in this little book, 'not only a prince but all other estates may learn to do justice, may learn by humanity and gentleness to order their subjects . . .'.[259] Counselling humility, constancy, liberality and piety, *The*

Precepts described the best kings as philosophers and, in granting royal privilege to such a work, Henry presented himself as, no less than Justinian, a philosopher king who was also God's servant.[260]

The most famous author and translator of advice-to-princes literature in the reign of Henry VIII was Sir Thomas Elyot. The son of a judge, scholar, diplomat and, as we have seen, author of a Latin–English dictionary with privileged access to the royal library, Elyot is one of those figures who belies any separation of the literary culture and politics of Henry's reign.[261] He is also one who complicates simple ideas of propaganda and official representation. For, though a client of Wolsey and Cromwell, Elyot was also a friend of Thomas More, the most vocal opponent of the supremacy, showed mounting concern about the oppressive nature of Henry's government, and ultimately fell from royal favour. During the 1530s, however, through Cromwell, he was close to the intimate circles of the court and several of his books, though they contained implicit criticism as well as compliment, were published by Thomas Berthelet. Elyot's 1534 translation of Isocrates's *The Doctrinal of Princes* has recently been persuasively re-read as an attempt by Elyot to counsel Henry, at a difficult time of change, to moderation.[262] But, printed by Berthelet, possibly with royal direction,[263] Isocrates's oration to King Mirocles, rehearsing (as well as the need to heed counsel) the royal virtues of bravery, learning, magnificence and liberality, would almost certainly have been read as a celebration of a Henry who, like Mirocles, 'knewest [these things] before' and might even be a 'prince equal to gods'.[264]

As well as translating, Elyot authored his own contribution to the genre of advice to princes in the book for which he is most remembered and one of the most famous works of the sixteenth century: *The Book Named The Governor*. Published in 1531, Elyot's text, written as he explains to outline 'the form of a just public weal', was dedicated to Henry VIII who is compared, in the introduction, to Alexander.[265] Elyot asserts the importance of order and of monarchical government as its best security, being proven by scripture, nature and history. English history since the Saxons, Elyot argued, had manifested the need for 'one capital and sovereign governor' as the best for the people.[266] *The Governor* prescribes the ideal education and training and virtues of the perfect prince. While again much is conventional, throughout this treatise the local, topical and personal are also prominent. Elyot specifically praises the arts in which Henry so visibly excelled – riding the great horse, hunting and hawking, shooting with the longbow (Henry was a legendary marksman).[267] Specifically praising the 'worthy renown' of King Henry VII and his circumspection, justice, diplomacy and good governance, Elyot underlines how such 'praise, with the honour thereunto, as inheritance descendeth by right unto his most noble son, our most dear sovereign lord that now presently reigneth'.[268] Elyot's *Governor* was not unalloyed panegyric.[269] Even the passage quoted hints that while praise descends by 'right', it must also be deserved and earned. Elyot's praise of modest diet and his proscription of 'ostentation and vainglory' might well have been read as veiled criticism of Henry's extravagance.[270] And the emphasis on how subjects' obedience and love had to be earned is insistent and striking: 'the benevolent mind of a governor not only bindeth the hearts of the people unto him . . . much stronger than any material bonds, but also guardeth more safely his person than any tower or garrison'.[271] Such language, as well as hinting that Henry may have pursued military glory more than nurtured his people's love, supports Walker's argument that *The Governor* is by no means an apologia for 'unchecked sovereignty' and seriously questions Stanford Lehmberg's description of Elyot as an advocate of royal absolutism and a Cromwellian propagandist.[272] However, Elyot's emphasis on duty need not be – and was probably not intended to be – criticism, or at least not criticism without compliment. Describing in a treatise published with royal privilege by the king's printer the need for a king to regard advice, parliaments and the laws both counselled Henry and represented him as a king willing to listen to such counsel: as a king open to advice, even implied criticism, rather than a despot in thrall to flatterers.[273] At least until the Reformation, royal representations freely proclaimed the duties as well as rights of the king and, in reminding him of his duties as much as in praising him, writers could still serve to represent Henry as he wished to be seen.[274]

Elyot came to be deeply disappointed not only by his own failure to secure high office and favour but also by Henry's growing tendency to follow his own will arbitrarily. When, after the decade of the 1530s, his disillusionment reached its height, he returned to advice, Elyot again concealed his own voice behind a supposed translation of a life of Alexander Severus to present criticisms of royal policy and the style of government. Even at this point, with his patron Cromwell having fallen a victim to royal violence, Elyot folds criticism into praise of a Henry whom he presents as learned, noble and potentially worthy of 'immortal renown' like Severus.[275] From the beginning of his writing career to the end, though hope gave way to disenchantment, Elyot combined counsel, criticism and encomium in representing the king, leaving readers (among them the royal reader) to determine the meaning and message for themselves. It was that obliqueness, as much as any perceived disloyalty, that ill equipped him to be the spokesman for the king's cause in the 1530s. Though he participated in the pageant to celebrate the coronation of Anne Boleyn, Elyot remained conservative in matters of religion; more importantly he never ventured into print in support of the king's supremacy.[276] During the years of his divorce and break from Rome, however, Henry demanded just such defences: justifications of his actions that were unequivocal and directed to ordinary, as well as his most learned, subjects. The Reformation, as Elyot discovered to his discomfort, not only led to a new style of government but required a different kind of representation of the monarch, a more directed programme of propaganda, and a new breed of writers ready unquestioningly to support specific royal acts and the authority the king claimed in enacting changes.[277] It was that shift that was orchestrated by Thomas Cromwell who paid no less attention to the skilful representation and justification of the royal supremacy than he did to enacting it; and who looked to new, skilful spin doctors, less hedged in their support for the king's great matter, to serve that end.

Cromwell appears to have been responsible for, or for encouraging, the return to England from Italy of two figures who were to become the powerful pens in rewriting Henry VIII as Supreme Head of the English church and nation. Thomas Starkey, a humanist scholar studying in Padua, returned in late 1534 and almost immediately was appointed a royal chaplain.[278] His rapid promotion is now more easily explained by the work of Thomas Mayer who has shown that Starkey had already written *The Dialogue between Pole and Lupsett* in which, in arguing it fitting for a philosopher king to seize an opportunity to improve his position and that of his realm, he advertised himself as the perfect scriptwriter for new circumstances and a new representation of kingship.[279] Richard Morison followed Starkey from Pole's household in Padua to England at the invitation of Cromwell in May 1536 and was set to work to answer the German humanist Johan Dobneck (Cochnaeus) who had written against the king.[280] In the altered circumstances of the 1530s, Starkey and Morison were to represent Henry VIII to his subjects and to refashion, if not fashion, the art of royal representation itself.

Starkey's major contribution to the promotion and justification of the king's cause, his *Exhortation to the People Instructing them to Unity and Obedience*, was begun probably in the summer of 1535 amidst discontent at the executions of More and Fisher and was published by Berthelet in 1536 at the time of the risings in Lincolnshire and Yorkshire.[281] In a prefatory address to the king, which itself foregrounds royal authority, Starkey praised Henry's 'high judgement' in affairs of religion and government and his efforts to settle the nation in unity, founded on 'a wholesome, quiet and just reformation'.[282] Turning to readers, Starkey pointed up the divine injunction to obedience and concord. Skilfully invoking the horrible consequences of discord, sedition and war in Germany (news of which had excited alarm in England), he led readers to draw the inevitable lesson that unity and peace should not be jeopardized for the sake of a few disputed ceremonies.[283] 'Things indifferent', Starkey argued, audaciously but cleverly including papal authority among them, were not themselves important; 'yet when they be set out with authority . . . then the people are to them bound, yea by the virtue of God's own word'.[284] Obedience, Starkey's address to the reader concluded, was due not to the pope or even to General Councils, but to the authority within the nation, in England 'princely authority'.[285]

As he entered into the main body of his work, Starkey acknowledged the divisions, 'pestilent and devilish division of spirit', that fractured the realm and threatened 'the ruin of good order and of the just common policy'.[286] For this ill, the best and only remedy, he asserted, lay with the prince. Dismissing the papacy as irrelevant to salvation and its claims to authority as 'madness', Starkey argued that spiritual unity was found only in a kingdom where there was 'one head to govern'.[287] Echoing Henry's own language, he promised that, under the Supreme Headship of the king, England might see the restitution of Christ's glory, the reform of abuses and corrupt ceremonies, indeed 'the reformation of all such things as pertain to religion'.[288] However, the effective reforms that were desired required obedience 'to all such things as by common authority either are or shall be received', 'on pain of damnation'.[289] As he descended to details and his vision of the future, the reform of the monasteries but the retention of ceremonies, images and the worship of saints, as he called for a mean between superstition and impiety, Starkey presented Henry's preferences and prescriptions as the best course not just for him but, and the nationalistic appeal is evident throughout, for England. The realm had, Starkey told readers, a prince who 'by his clear judgement seeth what is best'; the 'head' he wrote with repeated and inclusive pronouns, 'of our church and our nation' could be trusted to sustain 'public order and good Christian civility'.[290] It remained only for subjects to 'be obedient to all such things as shall be thought by our politic head to the common quietness convenient'.[291]

Starkey's treatise subtly and deftly erased the papacy from the scripts of salvation and church government to present the break from Rome and the Supreme Headship not as contingencies but as rational and natural developments, for all they seemed to some 'strange'.[292] His language of things indifferent itself neutralizes, or seeks to neutralize, the sharp and violent division over ceremonies and doctrine that significantly receives almost no discussion. Rather than dwelling on the international conflicts over the mass or solifidianism, *An Exhortation* appeals to national sentiment, emphasizes more secular priorities and uses a language of unity and 'civility'. Indeed, the thrust of the argument is utilitarian. For all the promise of reformation, the individual's struggles over faith are subordinated to the interests of peace and the common good, which are guaranteed only by the king. Starkey's text is not crude propaganda for unfettered royal authority. Starkey writes in his *Exhortation* of a nation electing a head of its church.[293] He is willing to consider other sovereign authorities than monarchy – indeed any 'laws, constitutions and ordinances' which secured unity.[294] But his treatise is both a powerful summons to the nation to unite under the king's spiritual leadership and a skilful re-presentation of Henry VIII not as warrior prince or philosopher king but as head of a harmonious and self-sufficient church, nation and commonweal.

Though it appeared in 1536, Starkey began writing his *Exhortation* before opposition to royal policies broke out into open rebellion. Richard Morison's first publications on behalf of the government, also published in 1536, by contrast were clearly written as a direct response to the uprisings that threatened to topple the regime. *A Lamentation in which is Showed what Ruin and Destruction Cometh of Sedition*, written against the Lincolnshire rebels, and *A Remedy for Sedition*, written at the time of the Pilgrimage of Grace, were both published by Berthelet without Morison's name or any identifying marks of authorship. They rehearse many of the same arguments as Starkey for royal authority as the guarantee of order, in the circumstances of popular rebellion; yet they seemed to address common as well as noble readers, or at least to address the concerns that led them to revolt. Morison acknowledges in *A Remedy* that the poor might question their lot and the social hierarchy that placed nobles over them but tells them that a whole 'commonwealth is . . . wealthy and worthy the name' only 'when every one is content with his degree'.[295] It was, he assured them, the duty of governors to 'look to the commons profit' but governors not the people who 'must rule'.[296] In their case, God had appointed Henry to rule them so, he asked, 'will we take upon us to know who ought to govern us better than God?'[297] The rhetorical question having answered itself, Morison expounded the need for all to obey a king who cared for the souls as well as weal of his subjects, to reject any siren voices that urged otherwise and to 'abhor sedition and rebellion'.[298] True to its name, *A Remedy* offers a palliative for both the religious and social discontents that had fuelled rebellion. Assuring them that the king had secured for them the word of God and that their lot was far better in a fecund country than that of foreigners reduced to eating frogs and snails, Morison endeavoured to persuade his readers to obedience and 'contented poverty'.[299] Most of all, he represented to them Henry as a king who well knew that 'the chief honour that a Christian prince should seek is the saving of his people', as, that is, himself the remedy for, not the cause of, their discontents.[300] If Henry survived the rebellions because the Pilgrims were ready to petition him for remedy rather than march on London to topple him, he may have owed much to treatises like Morison's which seem to be written to the commons as well as about them and to recognize the need to represent Henry and his 'benefits towards all his subjects'.[301]

By 1539 when Richard Morison published his second *Exhortation*, this time *An Exhortation to Stir All Englishmen to the Defence of Their Country*, the break from Rome and dissolution of the monasteries which had caused the 1536 rebellions were accomplished; but the heat of the conflict over doctrine had intensified and a heretic king and divided nation faced a serious threat of a Catholic crusade led by the Habsburgs and France. Morison's treatise was a call to arms but, as vitally, an appeal to unity behind the king. For all the anti-papal invective of the last seven years, including his own, Morison recognized that Rome might find supporters within England as well as in Europe and wrote primarily to undermine domestic resistance and to underpin loyalty to the king. Rome, he argued, using a language that signalled the affective relationship that Henry had tried to forge with his subjects, threatened 'that lovely bond . . . observance of the members to the head, of the subjects to their sovereign'.[302] He continued in almost lyrical vein to press the notion of a commonweal, a national community, that during Henry's reign had also become an important discourse of state: 'what thing,' he asked, again posing a question which connected political obedience to public welfare, 'is more bene-ficial to man's life than politic order, the mutual society of men . . . one to help and comfort each other in all things?'[303] Morison placed the king at the head of the godly community of Englishmen, observing that 'God ordained kings' and obedience to them 'is the knot of all commonweals'.[304] If then the pope were, as was threatened, to turn from war against the infidel Turk to an assault on this Christian prince and state, England had never had a better cause to fight for. And Morison brilliantly appealed to the proud English fighting spirit. Did not, he asked, the chronicles tell of the bravery of the English and their success in battle? Did not Scripture yield examples of those who with small numbers vanquished the mighty? If God were with them, Morison asked, what did numbers matter?[305] And, he assured readers, God was with those who fought for their true faith and with Henry VIII whom God had advanced to his throne as the scourge of superstition.[306] Turning the recent insurrections to his purpose, Morison even argued that the late rebellions in the north had better equipped Englishmen to fight and made northerners in particular eager to atone for their faults and display their loyalty: 'as we be one realm,' he wrote glossing over deep divisions, 'so our enemies shall find us of one heart, one fidelity, one allegiance.'[307] *An Exhortation* closed with a prophecy from Esdras and a final, messianic peroration. The eagle, Esdras had prophesied, would be destroyed by the lion; and Morison, gesturing to the lion in the royal arms, 'conjectured' that Henry would be triumphant over Rome.[308] 'See ye not,' he ended, 'to what honour God calleth our nation?'[309] God had chosen King Henry to fulfil biblical prophecy and his divine plan, so, he urged, 'let us fight this fight . . . with English hands and English hearts'.[310]

Such language sounds almost familiar to any of us acquainted with Second World War or Cold War propaganda. But in 1539, Morison could not simply appeal to national sentiment against Rome; he had still to construct it and to portray Henry as the embodiment of national destiny as well as God's providence. In the representation of Henry, therefore, Morison shifts emphasis from the portrayal of a chivalric prince and figure of European humanist learning to the divinely appointed head of a chosen nation.

Morison was very much Cromwell's man. After the fall of Thomas Cromwell in 1540, Sidney Anglo has argued, the campaign of propaganda against the papacy was relaxed; and with the return to hostilities between France and the Habsburgs in 1542 the immediate threat of a joint assault on England faded.[311] But with alliances fragile and the Scots in league with France, England was far from secure during the last years of Henry's reign. Treatises representing Henry, therefore, continued to stir a sense of nationalism as well as to urge the need for subjects to obey and support their prince and the just and righteous cause for which king and nation had to prepare to fight. In 1545, for example, Edward Walshe dedicated to the Lord Deputy of Ireland a treatise on *The Office and Duty in Fighting for Our Country* in which, linking classical and biblical examples of devotion to country, he urged all to fight for their native land under the exemplary leadership of Henry, 'who most tenderly desireth the wealth of his loyal subjects and painfully studieth the same'.[312] The next year John Beckinsau dedicated to Henry a tract, *De supremo et absoluto regis imperio*, intended, as he informed the king, to demonstrate to all that God had appointed Henry to rescue the people from the servitude of a Babylonish papacy and to exercise 'imperium' over church as well as state.[313] Beckinsau's defence of royal supremacy and imperium was to be issued during the reign of James I who, half a century later, also claimed title to an 'empire of Great Britain'.[314] John Bale, however, accused Beckinsau, a scholar of New College Oxford, of writing only for lucre.[315] Whether he wrote out of conviction or was paid, Beckinsau offers an example of the greater planning and direction in the presentation of Henry's case and evidence of a recruitment drive, following the arrival of Starkey and Morison, of writers able effectively to represent the king as head of a national empire.

In several of these treatises, we discern address to a broader audience and a popular, not to say populist, rhetoric and jingoistic appeal to national sentiment and interest, as well as to history and Scripture. Other genres of writing and other writers explicitly targeted popular audiences. John Foxe was to claim that Cromwell retained 'fresh and quick wits . . . by whose industry and ingenious labours both ballads and books were set abroad concerning the suppression of the pope'.[316] And William Gray of Reading composed antipapal ballads which, in the evocative words of his biographer, 'trounced the followers of Rome with a thorough-paced vigour'.[317] As well as scorning Catholic superstitions, Gray, in his verses against 'malicious slanderers', prayed that 'God preserve and kepe the kynges noble grace':[318] a king who, he praised, 'uniformly to knit us hath traveyled full sore' and whom it behoved all to serve in 'love and concord'.[319] As Gray's biographer argues, 'the ballad as an instrument of propaganda seems not to have been extensively used before the early part of the sixteenth century'; and, if Gray can justly claim a place as the first balladist to serve a government in that capacity, the explanation surely lies in the regime's new concern with representing the king not only to the common people but in their own genres and terms.[320]

While the politics of these ballads awaits fuller exploration, the politics of another popular genre has recently been the subject of renewed scholarly attention. Typically it was Richard Morison who advised Thomas Cromwell that plays might effectively present 'lively before the people's eyes the abominations and wickedness of the bishop of Rome . . . and to declare and open to them the obedience that your subjects by God's and man's laws owe unto your majesty'.[321] Cromwell was so persuaded by the advice that a scholar of Tudor drama writes of an 'energetic dramatic campaign' conducted under government sponsorship and spearheaded by Cromwell's own troupe of players.[322] Few of these plays survive. But Bale's *King John*, the subject of excellent historical readings by David Kastan and Greg Walker, conveys something of the flavour of a drama that denigrated the papal claims to supremacy and advocated obedience to the monarch in matters spiritual as Supreme Head of the church. In the final scene of Bale's drama, the figure of Imperial Majesty outlines the divine origin and authority of kingship and the dependence of true religion on the power of kings, in support of John's own claim that 'the powr of princys, is gevyn fro[m] god above'.[323] Bale's *King John* can be read as a statement in dramatic form of the arguments of several of the treatises we have examined that represented Henry as Supreme Head of church and nation. Critics, however, have identified problems in any simple reading of the play as propaganda. In the first place, in the dramatic story, King John is excommunicated and poisoned and in one text of the play the action ends with his dying speech.[324] Whatever the assertions of his divine mandate, the similar risks to Henry and England in 1538, following the king's excommunication, cannot be expunged from the imagination. Nor, of course, was King John in other respects an unproblematic figure. Though Bale seeks to downplay his reputation as a despotic ruler, the chronicle histories of the reign depicting John as the enemy of English freedoms had already established bad King John in memory and myth.[325] As David Kastan argues, in several ways, with regard to Scripture and history, the play nervously acknowledges a hermeneutic indeterminacy – an openness of text to various readings and the difficulty, for all Bale's efforts, of fixing meaning. In consequence the play 'admits what it wants to deny': that the supremacy itself is not after all a truth but an argument, a claim that can and will be contested.[326] Secondly, in any reading of *King John* as a representation of King Henry, we confront the distance between the playwright's own agenda in 1538 and that of the king himself. Bale's John is not only a protector of the Church of England against Rome, he is, in Walker's words, 'a thorough zealot in the Protestant mode'.[327] As Bale was well aware, even if further Protestantization of the church was part of Thomas Cromwell's programme in the late 1530s, it was not in that of the king who was acting by this time to check the pace of reform.[328] Like much of the drama of the medieval and early modern periods, *King John* was a 'play of persuasion' – an attempt not simply to represent or praise Henry but to move him in a particular direction. It may be these unstable elements in the drama, its uncontrollability, its dialogic form and openness, as well as Cromwell's fall from favour, that led to legislation and proclamations in 1543 and 1544 limiting the places and subjects of dramatic performances and interludes.[329] A king who had allegedly himself drafted a tragedy about the misdeeds of Anne Boleyn and who had presented to his imperial visitor a dramatic performance which staged the alliances and alignments of Europe may have come to see that others might use or interpret the drama for purposes at odds with his own and that theatre was too unsure a site of representation.[330]

The drama by its very form stages many voices, leaving the dominant voice or meaning to be determined by the audiences or readers. What we need to appreciate is that, though in a less obvious manner, the same was the case with all the literary representations of the king, whether his own compositions or those of others representing him. In his 'own' songs, letters, speeches and proclamations, and treatises defending his authority and courses, there was a multiplicity of hands at work, some with agendas different from the king's. Beyond that, there were even more readers who might, whether innocently or maliciously, receive the king's words differently from his intent. Henry himself was reported as giving the same book to two readers of opposite views and asking them to interpret it; so he wrote from a recognition of the difficulty of controlling meaning, the difficulty, that is, of exercising authority.[331] The essence of power, as, we recall, Stephen Greenblatt states in *Renaissance Self Fashioning*, is 'the ability to impose one's fictions on the world'.[332] As well as acts of speaking and writing, attempts to impose those fictions also involved, especially from the 1530s, measures to suppress others. In the most obvious ways, the Henrician regime endeavoured to erase other accounts: to rewrite Richard III as deformed, to re-present Thomas Becket as a traitor and rebel, to castigate the pope merely as a corrupt usurper or enemy of the nation.[333] Each of the texts that presented and re-presented Henry might be read again for the other voices that it seeks to suppress, not least because, in a sophisticated rhetorical culture and increasingly in a divided nation, contemporaries discerned and recovered those other voices and resistant readers again turned them back against the regime. As his image shifted from that of a martial figure on the European stage to the head of an English church and nation, and from loyal champion of the papacy to excommunicant or Supreme Head and priest-king, representations of Henry VIII could be, and were, played off against each other in the private imaginations of English men and women as well as in the public sphere of discourse and debate. Yet, though his reign was marked by newly sharp polemical battles, a vicious contest in print more bitter than any England had witnessed, Henry hung on to power. And he did so not least because he and those others who represented him, if they did not 'impose his fiction on the world', made it the dominant story of a newly emerging nation. Their success in doing so lay in their skilful polemic and powerful oratory. Yet, as even that accomplished wordsmith and brilliant polemicist Morison had advised, for many, and especially the common people, they needed to reach, 'things sooner enter by the eyes' and men remembered 'more better that they see' rather than read or hear.[334] The fiction of Henrician power was, as we must now turn to examine, written on canvas and stone as well as on the page.

CHAPTER 4

IMAGES OF ROYAL SUPREMACY

In our modern world, brand image and brand recognition are held to be the key to commercial success and cultural and political authority. The need to be 'seen' and identified has become essential to many people's sense of self and recognition has become a vital attribute of self-assurance. In some ways these concerns separate us from a pre-modern world in which authority rested more on signs of social rank and worth than on personal visual identity. But *if* that is the case (and since the visual has always been a primary medium of signification, it is an if), the early modern period marked a transition to a greater concern with identity and display. And that concern was manifested not least in portraiture: in greater interest in visual representation generally and in a new concern with capturing on canvas likeness, feature and character.

It may be no coincidence that the *OED* traces to the sixteenth century the first uses of the words 'recognition' and 'recognize' meaning 'having existence' or 'entitled to consideration', although it may have been another century before our sense of 'knowing by means of some distinctive feature' became common usage.[1] And it is revealing that the first recorded use of 'recognition' in relation to a royal title was in the statute 1 Elizabeth Act 1, cap 3.[2] For it appears that changes in attitudes to identity and to its visual representation were related to changes in attitudes to authority and its exercise and representation. The Europe of the Renaissance, early modern England, ubiquitously deployed a lexicon of sight and looking – of view, perspective, mirror, glass, regard, eye, portrayal and even gaze (Skelton is the first recorded user) – because men and women were beginning to look at their world and themselves afresh and to be preoccupied with seeing and the arts of being seen. That several of these terms also entered the language of politics and texts about kings and (in mirrors and glasses) *for* kings, who presented themselves as the privileged eye on the world, underpins the connection between the specular and political realms.[3]

In the Europe of the Renaissance, princes and rulers began to become patrons of the arts and to take a keen interest in their own visual representation.[4] Portraits in particular began to be essential to the representation and negotiation of power on the European stage, as canvases were sent from one ruler to another as diplomatic 'gifts', and as newly constructed long galleries displayed paintings of princely families and dynastic pedigrees.[5] As rulers strove to enhance their standing abroad, and at home sought to fashion themselves as the heads of the newly emerging nation states, the depiction of their rule, their dynasty and their person took on great import. The relationship between political, social and aesthetic developments, between a greater princely patronage and the new technologies of representation – in portraiture and perspective, engraving and woodcut, the striking of medals or the pressing of coin – is difficult to determine; but it is indisputable.[6] Lavish princely courts provided new employment, new prestige and new markets for artists and craftsmen who won favour and renown for their techniques and skills; in turn a new breed of artists with international reputations attracted the attention of rulers in what soon became the highly competitive world of image and display that was a characteristic of early modernity.

In English history, no ruler has better established visual recognition – his brand – than Henry VIII. His image is unforgettable and he is the first ruler whom most English people, and many outside England, recognize. This is largely due to the images of Henry created by Hans Holbein. To an England which still favoured late Gothic art, Holbein's portrait of Henry for the (now lost) Whitehall fresco must have appeared a revolution in the portrayal of regality. Before we turn to it, however, we must note that Holbein was not initially brought to England by Henry VIII and came to work for the king later on a second visit to London. Holbein, who had executed relatively few portraits before he arrived in England in 1526, though doubtless attracted by what he had heard of Henry's dazzling court, worked principally for others than the king: for Sir Henry Guildford, acting Master of the Revels, for Sir Thomas More and for the merchants of the Hanseatic League at the *Stalhof*, or Steelyard, in London.[7] It was when he returned to London in 1532 (by which time his patron More was out of favour) that Holbein came to the notice of Thomas Cromwell whose magnificent portrait, now in the Frick Gallery in New York, he painted that year.[8] About the same time, the artist also drew the portrait of Anne Boleyn, it has been suggested to commemorate her royal entry as new queen into London.[9] Holbein, that is, established important court connections at the time England was embroiled in the revolutionary events of the break from Rome and the royal assumption of the Supreme Headship. But it was not until Lady Day 1538 that Holbein's name appears in the royal accounts as the recipient of a salary, which suggests that the Whitehall mural may have been the artist's first major commission for the king.[10]

It was not, however, by any means Henry's first act of patronage of portraiture. By the time of Holbein's visit, the king was collecting canvases of his European royal rivals and employing Gerard Horenbout, Vincent Volpe and Antonio Toto to paint him and Catherine of Aragon.[11] While some of these are now missing, in an inventory of Henry's goods made in 1542 we find listed a picture of the king 'being young wearing his hair with a flower of silver'.[12] Certainly from early in his reign, Henry appreciated the role of art in proclaiming his dynasty and authority. Henry commissioned, probably from a Flemish artist about 1513, a painting that recorded his campaign in France which ended in the taking of Tournai.[13] The canvas depicts the meeting between Henry and the Emperor Maximilian I, with the English and imperial guard, soldiers, pavilions and cannon, and with Tournai visible in the left background. It has rightly been observed that the placing of the rulers and their entourage visually claims an 'equality of power' somewhat removed from the reality of the respective Habsburg and Tudor positions. But what we should note is that here, as in the depiction of the Field of the Cloth of Gold, the focus is more on Henry's martial prowess and England's military might than on a figuring of his person.[14] Henry also patronized a miniaturist, Lucas Horenbout, to enable him to send portraits to Francis I and his sister who had presented the Tudor with lockets containing pictures of the French king and his sons.[15] At home, too, Henry paid increasing attention to his representation in miniature on plea rolls. As Erna Auerbach's careful study demonstrated, the number of portraits on the plea rolls increased from 1515, the time that the royal image also began to appear in colour and full face.[16] Still, however, the emphasis in these images was on the regalia rather than on accurate likeness: Henry was shown without a beard although he his known by then to have worn one.[17] It was the mid-1520s that saw a shift in the king's depiction on plea rolls, and it may be significant that this coincides with the royal patronage of Horenbout. On the plea roll of 1526 'for the first time ... the king's portrait is conceived with the self assurance and dignified greatness of the Renaissance figure'.[18] Classical influences and Italian style had begun to reshape the royal image, and the miniatures, on letters patent as well as plea rolls, became lifelike representations of Henry VIII.

Well before Holbein was recruited to paint him, Henry appreciated the politics of his image as advertisement of martial prowess, as diplomatic token, and as a symbol of his personal authority painted on to the records of the law. Yet for much of the first twenty years of his reign, rather than signalling the revolution in royal portraiture for which he is famous, Henry's painted image drew heavily on the precedents of his father. A portrait, in the National Portrait Gallery, by an unknown artist, of Henry VIII about 1520 very much recalls images of his father, as Henry looks out sideways, his hands clasped together in front of him obscuring his body. Miniatures were probably based on this portrait, but no other pre-Reformation portraits of the king survive.[19] By contrast there are many for the period after 1532. It seems that, as with the representation of the king in pamphlets and panegyrics, it was the divorce and the break from Rome that dictated a change in the image of the king and indeed new, more polemical and personal modes of his visual representation. In an inventory of Henry's goods, item 10632 is listed as 'a table [that is tablet] with the picture of King Henry VIII standing upon a mitre with three crowns, having a serpent with three heads coming out of it and having a sword in his hand wherein is written Verbum Dei'.[20] The picture has not survived but it is obvious that it figures the overthrow of the papacy and Henry's claim as Supreme Head to present and mediate God's word to his subjects. The image probably dates to the time of the Coverdale Bible, on the title page of which, as we shall see, Henry hands the book of God's word to his bishops and nobles.[21]

It was probably about that time, too, that another portrait of Henry was painted by the Antwerp artist Joos van Cleve. In this canvas, Henry holds, as though having just unfurled it, a scroll which bears the Vulgate version of the text of St Mark 16 verse 15: in English, 'Go your way into all the world and preach the gospel.' The use of the Vulgate Bible is significant; as John King has argued, as well as alluding to the Coverdale Bible, the painting shows Henry appropriating a text used by the Roman church to uphold the papal claim to apostolic succession from Christ.[22] In this canvas, Henry becomes the pope in England and is represented as disseminating Scripture. Though we do not know who commissioned this portrait, and while it may express the hopes of those with more radical reforming ideas, these paintings and their place in the royal collection suggest that Henry himself authorized images of his royal supremacy and a new, imperial kingship.

When we view the Van Cleve, for all the clarity of the royal features, as well as details of dress and jewellery, we cannot but again be struck by the revolution effected by Holbein only about three years later. But it may be that Holbein was brought to the king's attention by the same circumstances that had given rise to Van Cleve's portrait as well as by Cromwell, for whom the artist was already working and who had championed the cause of reform. For in about 1535 or 1536, Holbein painted a miniature that was evidently designed as a gift to the king. The miniature on vellum portrays the biblical story of Solomon receiving the gifts of the Queen of Sheba, but with Solomon having the distinct and bearded features of Henry. Not only did this flatter Henry by figuring him as another Solomon, the embodiment of divine wisdom, it painted Henry, in the church's eyes a heretic king, into biblical history and as the descendant of biblical kings. The painting has been persuasively interpreted as an allegory of the

1 Henry VIII by an unknown artist.

2 Miniature of Solomon (with features of Henry VIII) and the Queen of Sheba.

church's new subservience to the crown.[23] The royal supremacy is announced as divine ordinance in the inscription on the canopy behind the king: 'Blessed be the Lord your God who delighteth to set you on his throne that you might reign as king for the Lord your God.'[24] It is not certain who commissioned this miniature; and it has been suggested that it may have been intended to lobby Henry as much as to praise him – to urge him to use the supremacy to fulfil God's will to the end of full evangelical reform.[25] Cromwell may have suggested it to a Holbein who was doubtless keen to receive royal patronage. Whatever its origin, what is important politically is how the miniature presented the king as the agent of divine authority (the architecture melds the features of a palace and temple), and as the recipient of divine wisdom and virtue. Aesthetically, too, the miniature marks a change in being the first image we have that placed an enthroned Henry at the centre, raised on a dais above his supplicant subjects. All the compositional lines lead our gaze to the king who, alone of all the figures, looks directly at us.[26] The composition effects, in fact, what years of polemic had endeavoured to argue: it centres the monarch as the beholder of all and as the one whom all behold and to whom we are all beholden.

It may well have been *Solomon and the Queen of Sheba* that elevated Holbein to the position of king's painter and which led to the Whitehall mural to which all discussions of the image of Henry VIII must return. For all the iconic centrality of this image, we confront the problem of discussing what no longer exists. The original fresco was destroyed in 1698 in a fire at Whitehall and we are left with only a seventeenth-century copy on canvas by Remigius Leemput and with Holbein's drawn cartoon for the left section, fortunately that containing the figure of Henry VIII.[27] There has also been controversy over where the painting was located. It is described in a later inventory as in the Privy Chamber; but, it has been suggested, the designation of rooms at Whitehall had altered since Henry's reign and the likelihood is that the

3 Henry VII, Elizabeth of York, Henry VIII and Jane Seymour by Remigius Leemput.

painting was displayed in a more public space, perhaps the Presence Chamber.[28] Wherever it was displayed, we should not, as too many have, forget that this was a fresco. The painting, that is, of Henry and his wife and forebears, was not hung in, but was part of the fabric of, the new Palace of Westminster (later Whitehall). And it became part of the environment in which diplomats and dignitaries, courtiers and common servants, conducted their business.

The theme of the fresco was dynasty. It depicted Henry VII and Elizabeth of York and Henry VIII and Jane Seymour, the mother of his only male heir, Prince Edward. The four figures, with the first Tudor and Elizabeth placed behind Henry and Jane, are grouped around an altar, with the two kings on our left. They stand in a palatial setting on a rich turkey carpet which, pulled back to give prominence to the altar, displays the opulence of Renaissance kingship, while the altar itself gestures to the spiritual authority claimed by the dynasty and especially now by Henry VIII. A Latin inscription on the altar debates whether father or son was the greater victor. It continues:

> both indeed are supreme. The former often overcame his enemies and the fires of his country and finally gave peace to its citizens. The son, born indeed for greater tasks, from the altar removed the unworthy, and put worthy men in their place. To unerring virtue, the presumption [*audacia*, the Latin word, is more negative] of the Popes has yielded. And so long as Henry the Eighth carries the sceptre in his hand, Religion is renewed, and during his reign the doctrines of God have begun to be held in his honour.[29]

Like the painting, the inscription links dynasty to true faith. Henry and Jane have continued the Tudor line, peacefully agree, and their son is a pledge of security to all citizens. The word, centred, solid and eternal, is Henry's bequest as godly prince to his people. Though it is the inscribed altar that fills the centre foreground of the canvas and causes the carpet, the symbol of secular wealth, to be drawn back, it is the figure of Henry VIII standing to the right (our left) that has struck all since as powerful and imposing. Where his father, like the two women whose gender dictated subordination, draws his arms into his person and looks slightly aside, Henry stands legs wide part, his prominent codpiece drawing attention to dynasty, masculinity and fertility.[30] With his hands on his hips, he dominates his space and looks straight ahead at the viewer. Henry stands at the right hand of God as represented by the altar. Henry's fashionable clothes and his glove and dagger symbolize the military and refined virtues of this truly Renaissance prince. But the dagger that points to the altar, connecting the king's body to the claims made on its inscription, to the word and the faith, reminds us of the sword and book with which Henry was represented on the Coverdale Bible. In the wake of threats from abroad and rebellion at home, and years of insecurity about the succession, the Whitehall fresco represents Henry as both heir to his father and yet as founder of a new church and polity, a new monarchy.

As John Rowlands has suggested, this was a portrait to be seen, 'so placed that all important people would have been subjected to its potent influence before entering the royal presence'.[31] A near-contemporary visitor even hinted at the fear evoked by the image. Writing in 1604, Karel Van Mander reported that 'the king as he stood there, majestic in his splendour, was so lifelike that the spectator felt abashed, annihilated in his presence'.[32] Describing the painted figure as not an image of the ruler but 'the king', Van Mander nicely captures for us the relationship between the authority of Henry and the authority of his representation and of the interdependence of the two. Henry's image after the Privy Chamber mural, atypically combining full face and full-length portrayal, was repeated in many copies by Holbein, his studio and followers throughout the sixteenth century and engraved, 'suggesting that it was highly successful in establishing the monarch in a consistently recognisable way'.[33] As Henry's own writings endeavoured to do, Holbein's portrait makes the personal body of the king, physical, commanding, fertile, also the synecdoche of the body politic, of an emerging nation. Nor should the priapic features of the image pass without comment. In his letters to Anne Boleyn, Henry, as we saw, conjoined his royal with his sexual power in ways that Seth Lerer characterized as dominating, even threatening.[34] In Holbein's cartoon for the fresco, where Henry VII folds his robes over his body, Henry's arms gesture to and frame his prominent codpiece and the royal penis; the viewer is presented with a king who engenders and who is desired as well as desiring, whose relation with his subjects is itself rendered, as it was in royal language, in amorous, eroticized terms.

Henry was evidently pleased enough with Holbein's work to use the artist in an important dynastic role: to paint the European princesses who might become a suitable bride for the king after the death of Jane Seymour in child-birth in October 1537. Holbein was sent to France, Burgundy and the Netherlands and was rewarded handsomely on his return.[35] As is well known, it was the flattering portrait of one potential bride who became the king's fourth queen that ended his work for the king, as Henry manifested his disappointment in the appearance of his new wife, Anne of Cleves, whom he considered not as fair as she was represented.[36] But one of Holbein's last major commissions, albeit not for the king, was a portrait of him, enthroned and granting a charter to the company of Barber Surgeons. The canvas, damaged and probably the work of studio assistants as well as the master, has not been the subject of critical acclaim. It is interesting for our purposes, however, as a representation

4 *Henry VIII and the Barber Surgeons* by Hans Holbein.

of Henry and a deployment of his court painter for the company's purposes. In this portrait, in a manner that evokes the *Solomon and the Queen of Sheba*, Henry sits enthroned, surrounded by members of the company on his left and right. All look directly towards the king, the focus of all authority, who looks straight out of the canvas, commanding the viewer. In what is a direct gesture to the earlier image, Henry holds a sword in his right hand and with his left proffers to one of the company (as he did on the frontispiece to the Coverdale Bible) the charter, which is also displayed on the wall. The king, who grants by his authority is figured, in relation to the members of the company, larger than life. Greg Walker is right, therefore, to argue the company's desire 'to proclaim by association the gravity and dignity of its own members', but wrong, I think, to deny the force of this image as a representation of the power of the crown and of Henry personally who grants the charter which, as the wall display underlines, gives the company its existence.[37] By commissioning the king's painter, by reference to other representations of the king, and in the composition of the painting, the Barber Surgeons, in their very act of appropriating royal authority and the royal image, re-presented that image to other subjects as a display of dependence as well as privilege.

Another, anonymous portrait, painted towards the end of the reign, probably about 1545, also owes something to Holbein. *The Family of Henry VIII* depicts Henry enthroned between four columns and beneath a canopy of state emblazoned with the royal arms and badges. Beneath the canopy, which again recalls *Solomon and the Queen of Sheba*, Jane Seymour stands, as she had in the Privy Chamber mural, on the king's left. On his right, with Henry's right arm

5 *The Family of Henry VIII.*

around him, stands Prince Edward in dress and a pose reminiscent of Henry's in portraits after Holbein's mural. Outside the columns, on our left and right respectively, are the figures of Princesses Mary and Elizabeth, behind each of whom arches open on to other figures (the king's jester and a maidservant) and royal lodgings and gardens. While the queen and princesses are depicted in half-profile, Henry, and significantly in this canvas his son – the only figure in bodily contact with the king – gaze straight at us.[38] As well as marking and helping to make the succession, the portrait subtly depicts the hierarchy of the royal descent. Though they stand within the royal palace, the figures of Mary, on her father's right as the elder daughter, and Elizabeth open out on to other worlds – other households, lives and future marriages. Enclosed within the columns and canopy, it is Henry, Jane and Edward who continue the dynasty and, as the royal arm and touch signify, Edward who is the undisputed heir to the royal body. Though a minor, whose legitimacy was disputed by Catholics and threatened by rival claimants, Edward's succession is asserted and proclaimed. And it is a divine as well as dynastic succession. Roy Strong long ago observed that the composition 'derives ultimately from that of a Virgin and Child enthroned flanked by standing saints'; and we have suggested an evocation of the depiction of Henry as Solomon.[39] The family of Henry VIII, then, is a portrait of a holy family, of a king who, as on the Privy Chamber mural to which this again gestures, has defended the word and faith and of a son who will continue to secure them. Continuity is marked in this canvas in another important respect. In the anonymous portrait executed only a couple of years before the king's death, Henry appears still a figure of imposing physique and sexual prowess (the codpiece is again prominent even in the seated image) not as the bloated, ulcerated and ailing figure we read of and even see in one unflattering engaving. And Edward, rather than the child he is, is presented as another Henry, as ready to take up rule as he has his father's demeanour.

The reign of Henry VIII witnessed major shifts in the representation both of monarchy and of the person of the king. As well as proclaiming dynasty and regality in general, we discern, from the late 1520s on and especially in Holbein's magnificent portraits, a new emphasis on capturing on canvas the features and physiognomy of the man. We are far from paintings which 'might look like anyone or no one provided that the arms and badges were correct'.[40] Portraits of Henry seldom figure him with the regalia which feature prominently in earlier images of kings; the emphasis is on the person and personal authority of the man and sovereign.[41] The person of the ruler, and his royal and sexual body, are inseparable from his regal authority, as from his dynasty. And the royal body, enthroned as a Solomon or Christ figure and surrounded by subjects, is presented as not only the protector but the literal embodiment of the new church, state and commonweal. Henrician portraiture, in seeking to erase the tensions between the king's two bodies, seeks to remove the tensions – not least between conscience and allegiance – created by religious innovations and divisions.

As with the discourses we have examined, it is important to read these images of Henry as texts: to consider the many hands involved in their commission or composition, the concerns which they address, the audiences they may have sought to reach and their performance and reception in the broad political culture, one increasingly marked at court and in the whole country by division and contest. Recently some scholars have questioned whether such images had any public reach beyond the court where, it is argued, they preached to the converted.[42] On several counts, this is simplistic. In the first place, it was the nobles and leading figures in a divided political nation, where unquestioning allegiance could not be assumed, who were the most important audience, those the king first needed to persuade of his right and newly assumed authority. Secondly, there is evidence that many, including those below the levels of nobility, had access to the court or royal palaces. Visitors and servants, of course, attended the king and courtiers; and we recall that Henry opened his banqueting house at Greenwich to 'all honest persons' for a few days to display his opulent tapestries and silverware.[43] And importantly it would appear that, as there was a desire to see the king, there was a growing interest in obtaining an image of the king whether as a display of loyalty or of a nobleman's own proximity to power. While the exact extent is hard to measure, we know from inventories that there were copies of royal portraits, often studio work, hung in many noble and some gentry houses.[44]

There were, for example, copies of Henry's portrait after Holbein's fresco in East Knoyle, Cambridge and London (as well as Rome); and of a portrait of Henry holding a staff, which owes a debt to Holbein, copies are found at Castle Howard, Warwick Castle, Knole, home of the Sackvilles, and Seaton Delavel, Northumberland, the seat of Lord Hastings.[45] Those with access to such noble houses, whether local gentry, servants or tenants, were increasingly likely to see some image of the king.

That image was disseminated more broadly still in other media and forms. Woodcuts and book illustrations became increasingly important media of representation in the reign of Henry VIII as England attracted foreign artists, especially Flemish engravers. Illustrated books were evidently valued by the king. In 1542 the French courtier Jean Mallard presented him with a psalter which, illustrated with miniatures of Henry as King David playing the lyre and studying his books, not only flattered Henry's learning; it was the images that made the Psalms the king's own and Henry a biblical king.[46] The most famous engravings of Henry during his reign were the Holbein title pages for the Coverdale Bible (1535) and the Great Bible of 1539. In the first case, surrounded by biblical scenes of God's gift of his laws and the dissemination of the gospel (one of them citing Mark 16, verse 15, the text on the scroll in the Van Cleve portrait), Henry sits enthroned beneath the tetragrammaton and the title entablature. 'This,' declares the verse from Matthew 17, 'is my dear son in whom I delight, hear him.' Flanked by the figures of the Old and New laws, King David on his right and St Paul on his left, and with a large royal arms at his feet, Henry with a sword in his right hand, with his left presents the bible to attendant bishops. The figure of David replaces that of Peter which is typically paired with St Paul but who, as the basis of papal claims, has no place in this validation of the royal supremacy.[47] Holbein's title page is a visual proclamation of the supremacy, of Henry's claims to mediate the law and the gospel, almost to be the word again made flesh.

In the second case, the title page to *The Bible in English*, Henry sits enthroned, this time above the title entablature and directly beneath the figure of Christ. Scrolls from the king's mouth mingle with those of the Lord. While Christ presents the word of his own mouth, asks that it be revered and praises all who follow his will, Henry, presenting the book of the word, *verbum dei*, with both hands, as a second Christ urges all to 'precipe et doce', receive and teach, for, as a scroll proclaims, 'by the king it was decreed that throughout the kingdom all would tremble before the living God'.[48] Beneath Henry, on left and right, the clergy and now also the laity pass the word down to preachers and magistrates who call upon all to seek peace and obey rulers. Below them, small figures of the people, of soldiers, citizens and the poor, even some in jail, cry out 'vivat rex' and, in English, 'God save the king'. The engraving, unlike

6 Henry VIII as David with lyre.

the title page to the Coverdale Bible, depicts a hierarchical community, a commonweal. And it figures the king as God's lieutenant on earth, ensuring the spiritual well-being of all subjects who, happy and loyal, pray for the king. In the light of the rebellions that had erupted in 1536, it was no simple statement of the real situation of a nation increasingly divided over faith. Greg Walker has argued that the illustrated title pages of both the Coverdale Bible and the Great Bible, as it was known, may evidence the tensions between evangelical urgency and royal caution and represent partisan attempts to hijack the royal image to advance Protestant reform; and his suggestion is supported by the identification among the bishops on the Coverdale Bible title page of the figure of Thomas Cromwell.[49] Yet there can be no doubt that

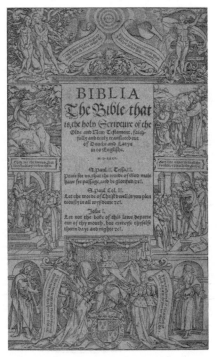

7 Coverdale Bible title page, 1535.

8 Great Bible title page, 1539.

Henry authorized these images, in the case of the Great Bible not only once but twice, for the 1541 edition describes it as appointed by the command of the king, 'supreme head of this his church and realm of England'.[50] Whatever the influences at work on them or their undoubted multiple agendas, Holbein's title pages represented Henry VIII to subjects and proclaimed visually what much Reformation propaganda had argued at length: the divinity and supremacy of the king.

Several other woodcuts represented Henry as legitimate monarch to his subjects. An illustration to Stephen Hawes's meditation on the coronation depicts Henry and Catherine of Aragon beneath a Tudor rose with imperial crowns held by prelates above their heads.[51] An account of the coronation of Anne Boleyn is illustrated by a woodcut of Henry and his second queen enthroned, hand in hand, the touch affirming her legitimacy against detractors who had accused her of seducing the king from his first wife.[52] In 1548, the title page to Richard Grafton's edition of Hall's chronicle displayed Henry above two columns, seated in Council as the good ruler taking advice; the second edition figured Henry with sword and sceptre atop two genealogical trees showing his descent from both the houses of Lancaster and York.[53]

Not all woodcut images, however, flattered Henry or served his ends. Like print, the medium was used by critics of the monarch as well as supporters. One image, for example, which may be contemporary, depicts Cardinal Wolsey with a scroll that reads 'Ego, meus et rex' – me, mine and then the king. Satirizing Wolsey's arrogance and suggesting his domination of the king, the woodcut probably emerged from the circles of the cardinal's enemies at court and was likely intended to discredit him with the king and perhaps the people.[54] We have also the curious caricature of Henry late in life executed by Cornelis Matsys, a contemporary of Dürer. As David Starkey and others have observed, the grotesque fat face suggesting a bloated and decaying royal body is far removed from the portrait of Henry VIII and his family painted about the same time.[55] We know neither who, if anyone, commissioned this engraving nor Matsys's purpose in executing it. The royal arms are displayed on the left and the king is dressed in a rich coat of ermine, so the image may be simply an accurate portrayal of the king by a foreign artist, unaffected by official patronage or representations. Alternatively, it may offer an early example of how woodcuts and engravings might appropriate and caricature official images in a medium that could be produced quickly and circulated widely. Whatever the explanation, the Matsys reminds us that, as with words, neither the king nor the government controlled the media and that there were variant texts representing the king to his subjects.

If traditional art history and connoisseurship have consigned woodcuts and engravings to an obscurity from which scholars are only just beginning to

9 *The Noble Tryumphant Coronacyon of Queene Anne*, 1533, title page.

rescue them, the performance of the royal image in the broader material culture of early modern England is a subject still in its infancy. There have been excellent studies of silver focusing on fine technique and execution.[56] But listed among the inventories of Henry's goods, recently helpfully printed, we find a myriad objects, many of everyday use, that featured a picture of the king: a box, for example, with Henry's picture in clay, jewels with the king's picture, or a 'coffer covered with black velvet containing the physiognomy of King Henry VIII cut in wood in a case of metal'.[57] Such and other objects handled daily by diners and servants, in various royal palaces and on progresses, communicated

10 Henry VIII by Cornelis Matsys.

the royal image in ways that our modern fascination with celebrity objects might lead us to appreciate as powerful. Evidently Henry attached great importance to objects that bore his likeness. He took the Emperor Charles V to Winchester to view what was claimed to be King Arthur's Round Table, on which the figure of the robed, crowned and bearded King Arthur bore a close likeness to Henry himself.[58] Whilst a concern with exact likeness was a new emphasis in Henry's reign, the king also continued to be ubiquitously visually represented on objects by his arms and devices. The king attributed great importance to such signs. Henry ordered the royal arms set up in churches and in *A Necessary Doctrine* wrote of the importance of such images in churches as books of instruction in virtue.[59] On his first visit to England, Holbein was employed in decorating the Banqueting House with royal insignia and the king's sergeant painters, Andrew Wright, John Brown and others, were principally employed in painting and gilding 'escutcheons of the king's arms'.[60] Soon after taking over Hampton Court from Wolsey, Henry ordered that 'his arms and badges should be affixed to every part of the palace', outside and in, in stone and wood.[61] Payments for decorating the royal barges with the king's arms appear in the accounts of the Privy Purse and Henry added the name 'imperial' as well as royal arms to new ships in 1523 and 1524.[62]

Badges and arms of Henry Tudor were, for any who attended a royal palace or lodge, literally part of the fabric of daily life: the rose and portcullis, the greyhound and dragon were woven into tapestries and carpets, as well as carved on wainscot and walls. Along with the actual portraits of Henry, these devices announced his authority to an aristocracy and gentry who, in the sixteenth century, were becoming increasingly sophisticated in their appreciation of the arts of heraldry and the significations of escutcheons and emblems. Indeed, a growing literature was beginning to school Englishmen in reading the histories and mysteries behind the beasts and symbols of the arms.[63] In his *Governor*, for example, Elyot stresses the importance for young gentlemen of an education in the visual arts, which included both learning to interpret and to practise the skills of painting, carving, engraving and embroidering.[64] Images, Elyot posited, communicated virtues and should be devised so that 'other men in beholding may be instructed or . . . persuaded'.[65] The ubiquitous display of the royal and Tudor arms, on buildings and furniture, in churches and books, was intended to do just that – to instruct and persuade, to engrave the signs of the king's legitimacy, virtue and authority on the consciousness as well as material environment of his subjects.

Henry VIII's buildings themselves blazoned the king's identity and authority. Like other Renaissance princes, Henry regarded his palaces as a display of the virtue of magnificence but also as a representation in stone of the solidity and durability of the Tudor dynasty. In the words of Simon Thurley, 'Henry VIII was certainly the most prolific, talented and provocative builder to sit on the English throne'; and he was one actively engaged in the details of design.[66] Throughout his reign, Henry purchased properties, exchanged properties (on terms very favourable to the crown) and seized properties by attainder: no fewer than five major buildings, including York House and Hampton Court, passed to the king on Wolsey's fall from favour and death.[67] As Edward Hall reports, Henry immediately oversaw the development of these acquisitions into palaces worthy of a king which impressed visiting envoys with the scale of their grandeur.[68] Stables and tiltyards were added to Greenwich, tennis courts and bowling alleys to Hampton Court, chapels to Eltham and Beaulieu and libraries, studies and galleries to many royal residences.[69] While these additions and conversions themselves advertised Henry's piety, martial prowess and learning, decorations proclaimed him a true Renaissance prince devoted to the cult of antiquity. At the palace of Nonsuch in 1508, the walls were decorated with images of the seven liberal arts, the virtues and the fable of Hercules, along with portrayals of Henry and Prince Edward who were thus placed in a line of heroes as well as being presented as patrons of the new learning.[70] Statues of the Roman emperors similarly lined up to gesture to the Tudors' imperial descent, while the statue of Henry trampling on a lion was a familiar anti-papal image.[71] New buildings and additions provided a further opportunity for incorporating into the structure – as at Hampton Court on the outer gatehouse, hall roof, windows and ceilings – royal and Tudor insignia.[72] Henrician royal palaces were the advertising hoardings for, as well as monuments to, the virtues and powers of the new Tudor brand.

When we think of new buildings we should not confine ourselves to surviving edifices in brick and stone. The reign of Henry VIII also saw a proliferation of temporary structures erected for a pageant or a joust, or the reception of a visiting monarch or envoy. Yet it remains almost as true now as when Professor Anglo wrote forty years ago that 'temporary palaces and banquet halls have received less attention from scholars than their importance in the history of court festivals merits'.[73] Temporary structures such as that built to entertain the French ambassador in 1527 were decorated all over with roses, pomegranates, royal beasts and cosmological symbols, as well as tapestries depicting the history of King David with whom Henry was often paralleled.[74] Not least, these temporary erections may have helped resolve one of the problems of architectural representation identified by Simon Thurley: the fact that in the case of a king like Henry who married several times, there could be embarrassing reminders set in stone of past liaisons, proclamations of love, political as well as amorous alliances.[75] Where temporary structures could be designed to signify topically in specific circumstances, buildings, like texts published at one moment and read in another, could signify quite otherwise than had originally been intended. Buildings too, though erected to impress, could be viewed in different ways: as signs of extravagance rather than magnificence, as monuments to greed rather than piety, and as reminders of events and people that disclosed the human and contingent in royal regimen. Especially in the eyes of many Catholics, Henry's lavish palaces represented not the magnificence of a glorious monarch but the plunder of a heretic who had despoiled the monasteries to fund temples to Mammon. Yet that was also the point. Tudor palaces were erected to be the temples of a new monarch who ruled over church as well as state; and they undoubtedly have their place in any story of Henry's success in overcoming opposition and carrying most of his people with him.

'In spite of all the splendour of ceilings and carved woodwork,' Roy Strong wrote, 'the ultimate *coup de théâtre* was achieved through movables.'[76] Henry VIII introduced what one scholar has described as 'a new politics of ornament'.[77] And it is significant that the new status of those craftsmen who created that ornament found recognition in portraiture – in Holbein's portrait of Mr Mornet, the king's jeweller, for example.[78] The sheer scale and political importance of these movables have become more than ever apparent to us thanks to the recent edition of the inventories of the king's goods. While the full riches of the edition await the forthcoming volumes of annotation and analysis, the lists themselves are sufficient to indicate how thousands of objects proclaimed Henry's dynasty, virtue, piety and power.

For whilst many items in the royal collection were inherited and timeless – the regalia, crowns and sceptres, and 'King Arthur's cope', for example – what is immediately striking from reading the inventories is the number of artefacts that were made for, and indeed made to represent, Henry VIII.[79] The royal arms of Henry Tudor were displayed on cups, pots, spoons, salts, monstrances, censers, assay cups, lanterns, musical instruments, furnishings, coverings, bedclothes and warming pans. The Tudor rose is similarly found on cups, spoons and linens as well as furniture and Henry's badges and heraldic beasts appear on new jugs and salts and the like. In some cases the inventory refers specifically to a salt 'with the king's word about the cover', a jug cover with 'the king's word thereon crowned holden by his majesty's beasts', or a toasting cup with the king's arms displayed on the bottom, visible to others as it was raised to drink his health.[80] The king's arms and badges are also displayed with other symbols of royalty – with the sun, for example, on a basin or on a lantern associating the king with light, the heavens and Christ himself who was, as he said, the way, the truth and the light.[81] Clearly the arms, mottoes and devices on all these objects in general represented the new Tudor dynasty; but in some cases they signified more specifically. One item, 'a piece of arras', according to the inventory, depicted 'the coming into England of King Henry VII, taking with the one hand the crown from Richard III, usurper of the same, and with the other hand holding a rose crowned'.[82] Objects presenting the king's arms held aloft by an 'antique boy' or (as on the cover of a cup) by Lucretia in the act of suicide connected the Tudors to classical themes and legends which displayed a fashionable acquaintance with the new learning.[83]

The display of arms and dynasty is in many cases explicitly associated with religious objects and scenes and scriptural stories and verses. Alas, because in most cases we are not able to date the artefacts, we cannot know whether or how such objects, beyond a conventional display of piety, relate to the break from Rome and the claim to supremacy; but some items are suggestive. As we have seen, the king's arms were on a large number of religious objects – censers, frankincenses, monstrances, vessels for holy waters – even an altar cloth 'with the Assumption of Our Lady' and the king's badge.[84] Salts and monstrances engraved with biblical scenes (of Adam and Eve or the woman of Samaria), cloths and tapestries depicting the story of David and Goliath, chairs with 'Spes Mea Deus' all represented Henry as a king of piety as well as prowess: a king who surrounded himself with the lessons of Scripture and a king the very fabric of whose daily life manifested his proximity to the divine.[85] A basin with a shield of the king's arms held aloft by angels, proclaiming 'Dieu et Mon Droit', making a clear connection between regal and holy regimen was, we know, made in the time of Jane Seymour.[86] Henry's attention to the cult of St George, the emblem of spiritual valour and Christian virtue, was also manifested in objects. Along with sculptures and jewels representing St George, the figure of the Christian knight slaying the dragon of sin was displayed on tableware, cloths and tapestries.[87] Whatever the vicissitudes of divorce, break from Rome, theological wrangles or religious protest, Henry's daily accoutrements advertised him as a Christian king, heir of Old Testament kings, St George and the Confessor, a ruler who, as the cramp rings reminded all, could use the sacred royal touch to cure the king's evil.[88]

A holy king, a martial prince, a man of learning surrounded by books, musical instruments, charts, maps (with the royal arms) and scientific equipment, a sovereign whose cushion was embroidered with the symbols of equity and justice, Henry's very belongings represented him as the ideal ruler outlined in the *speculum principis* literature.[89] Indeed, there may have been a deliberate allusion to the genre in one object inventoried: a mirror of Henry's with 'about it the physiognomy of the King's majesty Henry VIII and his wives and children', self-examination and reflection being a principal virtue of the philosopher king.[90]

Yet, for all the ideals they advertised, the daily objects that surrounded Henry, his courtiers and visitors to court also presented graphic and often unhappy reminders of unfortunate events – former queens, failed marriages, ex-ministers and treacherous nobles, all symbols of the turmoils of factional strife and dynastic struggle, of bitter divisions, and of the humanity and vulnerability of the king and monarchy. We find in the inventories dozens of everyday objects with 'the late cardinal's arms', even a chair which, with the king's arms topped by a cardinal's hat, evoked not only Wolsey's former intimacy with the king but his audacious pretensions.[91] Similarly, goods formerly Thomas Cromwell's and bearing his arms as Earl of Essex, the mark of royal favour, were listed as received at Westminster and Hampton Court after his execution.[92] Were these objects still in daily use? While we know that one of Cromwell's gilt flagons was received out of the 'secret' jewel house and a chair with Wolsey's arms was inventoried as 'unserviceable', the listing of these objects alongside scores of others, formerly the property of the two royal ministers, suggests that most were still used.[93] If so, what did it mean for courtiers or visitors to drink from the cup of an ex-servant executed for treason, or indeed to sup with the spoon of the attainted Lord Stafford or pour from a jug with the arms of the late Marquis of Exeter, beheaded in 1538?[94]

Such questions about the evocation by objects of incidents of betrayal and treason come into sharper focus as we peruse the hundreds of items which commemorated Henry's past passions and marriages. Gilt bowls with 'the late Queen Katherine her arms enamelled', a box with the initials H and K, cups with their monograms 'knit together on the cover', salts and cups with both their arms, seemed almost to refute the king's claims about an illegitimate union with his first wife.[95] And the countless objects – spoons, plates, cups, bowls, cushions, more intimately bedsteads and valances, carved and embroidered with H and A, or Henry's and Anne Boleyn's arms, survived to recall past scandal as well as passion, an adulterous queen for the love of whom a deceived king had ventured his realm. Was the chair 'covered all over . . . with silk and gold with the late queen's [that is Anne's] cypher' and the king's arms a love seat they had shared?[96] Again we cannot but wonder whether such items of painful memory and potentially dangerous signification were locked away, out of sight; but there are reasons for thinking they may not have been. Item 9365 in the inventory lists as at Greenwich a bedstead with accompanying bedclothes. The base is described as of cloth of silver 'embroidered with Venice gold with the king's arms and Queen Anne's cypher', while the corners of the bedstead itself were listed as 'painted with the king's arms and Queen Jane's cypher'.[97] Evidently here Anne Boleyn's bed continued in use, suggesting that even in the intimate places and spaces, the signs of a past wife, a past life, remained visible – and with them all the protestations, declarations and controversies that Henry and many (but not all) others might have preferred to forget. With so many signs of past promises and unions broken, even the intertwined initials of Henry and Jane Seymour on hangings, cups and musical instruments might have appeared to signal a less enduring or successful marriage than it turned out to be.[98]

At Whitehall and Hampton Court, at Greenwich and Nonsuch, at Windsor and Woodstock, in the Tower, the Robe House and Jewel House, in the Office of the Revels and royal chapels, in garderobes and removing coffers, thousands of objects – clothes and jewels as well as tableware and furniture – displayed Henry VIII's kingship and, in so many ways, the history of his reign. We should not fall into the error of concluding that such items of everyday court life were seen only by a few. The courtiers, nobles and gentlemen, ambassadors, visitors and servants who used and saw these artefacts and objects were by no means an insignificant few. As the large number of portable coffers indicates, many of these furnishings travelled with the king and his queens on progress; and of course the most movable goods, jewels, clothes and suchlike were seen wherever the king or his consort, with his liveried retinue, appeared. Henry wanted his magnificence to be seen and opened his tapestries and cupboards of plate to public view.[99] He accumulated possessions 'as a matter of public policy'; the items in his inventory of goods were 'essential props of the theatre of magnificence'.[100] And in some cases they made very specific arguments to advance the king's cause. The painting, for instance, listed as in the Long Gallery at Hampton Court, of the four evangelists stoning the Bishop of Rome, we might reasonably conjecture was acquired in very different circumstances to the picture of St Peter with the keys.[101] Other artefacts, not only former queens' and ministers' goods but a hanging of David and Absalom, might have opened observers' minds to different reflections on the drama of state than those the king would have wished.[102] But that they were intended to reinforce Henry's authority as well as display his wealth and virtue seems indisputable. Writing in *The Book Named the Governor* of plate and vessels engraved with scenes from history, fables or proverbs, Sir Thomas Elyot observed:

> one of these commodities may happen: either that they which do eat or drink having these wisdoms ever in sight, shall happen to receive some of them or by purposing them at the table may suscitate [stimulate] some disputation or reasoning.[103]

Doubtless Henry's precious and quotidian goods drew disputation as well as admiration. But they ensured that it was the king who stood in the spotlight and who drew the gaze of all towards him.

For all that paintings, images and arms of Henry were seen by more than an elite few, most subjects viewed the king's image in other forms – on seals and medals and, most of all for common folk, on coins. In all these cases, Henry's reign marked important developments in the arts of representation. Henry's first seal was the same as that of his father and what has been described as 'the Gothic Great Seal' was still in use in the 1520s.[104] A major shift in the seal took place in 1527 with the golden bulla that sealed the treaty with France in September. The seal with a throne flanked by pillars and putti, with a large Tudor rose, 'represents the first example of an ostentatious Renaissance seal' in England.[105] As with the image on the plea rolls about this time, the portrait of Henry is more lifelike, with a confidence visible in the pose and expression. On the third Great Seal, produced in 1542, the king is portrayed enthroned with his royal arms on either side, with the badge of the Garter and with an inscription announcing him to be King of England, France, Ireland and Supreme Head of the Church. The new seal, in the Italian style, with a Palladian throne, further develops the portrait likeness of the king to assert his personal as well as regal authority, indeed to render the two bodies of the king one.[106]

Contrary to Sydney Anglo's assertion, Henry also issued medals and, it has been argued, 'the medallic history of England really opens with the reign of Henry VIII'.[107] As well as a portrait medal of Anne Boleyn, which was almost certainly cast for her coronation, to promote her legitimate accession as queen, medals of Henry were issued from the 1520s and then later, after portraits by

11 Medal commemorating the Supreme Headship, 1545.

Holbein.[108] Medals were an important medium of royal representation because they commemorated specific events. In 1542 Henry issued a medal to celebrate his title of king of Ireland; gold and silver medals struck in 1545 commemorated the recognition of Henry as Supreme Head (as well as Defender of the Faith) and repeated on the reverse the inscription announcing his titles in Greek and Hebrew, the language of Scripture.[109] Among medals of uncertain date, one with Henry's portrait and badge on the reverse carries the legend 'Securitas altera', another security, signalling the king's protection of his people.[110]

Seals and medals we may think of still as of limited importance in the broader dissemination of the royal image. However, in an extraordinary passage, Bishop Stephen Gardiner suggested a far wider audience and significance for these forms. Writing to the captain of the Portsmouth garrison in 1547, Gardiner observed: 'He that cannot read the scripture [*sic*] written about the King's Great Seal, either because he cannot read at all, or because the wax doth not express it, yet he can read St George on horseback on the one side and the king sitting in his majesty on the other side and readeth so much written in those images as, if he be an honest man, he will put off his cap.'[111] Gardiner may have himself made a slip and, as Somerset gleefully observed, misread, as the figure of St George, a portrait of the king.[112] But his letter provides powerful testament that such images were seen by common people as well as nobles and gentry and that, for the illiterate as well as the learned, the image was seen to represent the king. Those honest men who removed

12 'Securitas altera' medal of Henry VIII.

their caps (and we note the recognition that some did not) read seals and medals as signs of the king's personal authorization and authority.

In the case of coins, a significant shift had occurred, as we have seen, in the reign of Henry VII, whose currency was 'the first to bear an artistic likeness of an English monarch'.[113] Indeed, the first Tudor emulated the imperial crown used by Maximilian I for his coin struck at Bruges, and issued it perhaps to commemorate the match made for Prince Arthur with Spain, as well as to claim imperial status for the new Tudor dynasty.[114] Henry VIII minted coins to advertise his martial inclinations and victories, such as that at Tournai, some bearing his portrait and some, rubbing salt in the wound, resembling the French *gros a bleu*.[115] While the French crown of the sun again influenced Henry's crown of the rose, minted in August 1526, the issue the same year of the George noble bore an archetypically English, indeed nationalistic icon.[116] Over the early years of Henry's reign, prior to the infamous debasements, silver coinage took on a new aspect as Henry increasingly added his badges, the crowned double rose in 1526, the portcullis to the farthing in 1523, and a new profile portrait.[117]

Coins of course cannot simply be assumed to be the product of the king's sole direction. As the historian of the Tudor coinage reminds us, 'engravers had minds of their own and a will to fashion the detail of agreed design to their own

13 Henry VIII George Noble, 1526.

liking'.[118] Moreover some of the various mints were accountable, at least in the
first place, to others than the king. During the 1520s, for example, the mint at
York issued groats and the Durham mint pennies with Cardinal Wolsey's hat
stamped under the king's arms.[119] But overall, coining was seen to be a prerogative intrinsic to the crown and coins were received as royal currency, with the
image and signs of the king establishing their authenticity and value.[120]

The relationship of image and value, however, was a delicate one that
worked in both directions: if the royal portrait was what guaranteed the coin's
value or worth, decline in the market value of a coin might well also debase
the royal brand and image, the signs of royal authority. In *The Governor*, Elyot
illustrates a discussion of the nature of nobility by reference to the coin, the
noble, in what is a revealing passage: 'We have in this realm coins which be
called nobles; as long as they be seen to be gold, they be so called. But if they
be counterfeited, and made in brass, copper or other vile metal, who for the
print only calleth them nobles? Whereby it appeareth that the estimation is in
the metal and not in the print or figure.'[121] *The Governor* was published in
1531. Within five years Henry VIII had embarked on a debasement of the
coinage, beginning with the Irish currency but moving on to English coins in
the early 1540s.[122] Both debasements were necessary to fund the costs of war:

as the 1540 proclamation put it, Henry sustained 'great costs and expenses' because he 'keepeth a great army in his land of Ireland'; and in the 1540s he embarked again on continental campaigns.[123] Whatever foreign wars did to reinforce his power abroad, there can be little doubt that debasement tarnished the royal image at home. In the proclamations of the 1540s one can hear the government struggling to justify its policy, to advertise the debasements as for the public good: to avert a shortage of coin or for 'the wealth and enriching of [the] people'.[124] The reality was, as the proclamation itself acknowledged, that subjects tried to use debased Irish coin in England, or later to send devalued English coin overseas; while both a rise in prices and the reluctance of producers to bring their goods to market for fear of payment in debased currency added further social to economic problems.

Historians have studied the economic consequences of the great debasement; however, our interest here, following Elyot, is its consequences for the perception of a royal authority which depended on intrinsic value as well as script. Yet, as the costs of war mounted, more and more debased coin was minted in a hurry and another issue was 'badly executed and clearly reveals the inferiority of the metal from which it was struck'.[125] As Henry looks out full-face from a silver groat, with his arms on the reverse, his image is debased along with the metal and value of the coin. If my, indeed Elyot's, suggestion that debasement affected the signification of coin is persuasive, then the sheer output of new coin under Henry VIII takes on a new significance. For the new coins minted during the 1530s and 1540s, which looked very different from those they replaced, drove most of the existing coin out of circulation.[126] As Dr Challis has written, although it is not easy to find evidence to assess 'with what concern this change was viewed by the general public', the fact of resistance and opposition is clear. And there is evidence that the government was not only sensitive to it but responded with concessions. The withdrawal in 1548 of the testoon or shilling issued only four years earlier acknowledged the strength of feeling, as did the new government's decision to issue a new gold coinage in 1549.[127] Much of this new coin, at least initially, was no better in intrinsic value or quality than what it replaced. Change was felt necessary 'for psychological reasons'.[128] The story of Henry VIII's coin offers us a microcosm of our larger history of royal representation. It demonstrates the delicate relationship between image, spin and public perception; and it manifests both a concern with projecting image and a sense of the need not only to persuade subjects but to respond to public reaction and concern.

CHAPTER 5

PERFORMING SUPREMACY

The Tudor debasement revealed the danger of too great a disjuncture between the face value and intrinsic worth of coin. Similarly the representation of monarchy, for all that it idealized the king, only functioned effectively when such idealized images were not perceived to be obviously at odds with the experiences of subjects. The most important presentation of kingship was the king himself, and his most important representation of his kingship was his appearances and performances in the habit and role of a king, as scripted by himself, by custom and by the expectations of nobles, gentry and commoners. The king's daily life was a representation of his rule and his court was the principal stage on which he performed the part of a king. In the largest sense, if (that is) we include as we should all those who resided, attended on or visited the king or his wives, ministers and courtiers, in all of his palaces and on remove, the court was by no means a small community. Thousands more gentlemen and citizens observed the king in one of the formal state pageants, in processions or at jousts, or on progress. As we shall see, Henry spent a considerable time on progress and visited many of the counties of his kingdom.[1] For those dwelling in the south, there must have been frequent opportunities to see the king and court on the move between royal residences or on the routes between London and Greenwich or the ports. Beyond those subjects who actually saw their monarch, however, a larger community of the nation was, thanks to print's stimulus to news and report, beginning to know much about their king. And what was reported, from first-hand witnesses or from 'reputation', was as significant in shaping perceptions of the king as the representations we have been discussing. For most subjects the Henry VIII they knew (part officially disseminated, part hearsay and anecdote) was a figure of many facets. But, as over a century of civil war had shown, if he were to reign in peace and exercise authority, Henry had to make the Tudor brand, his person and the institution of monarchy inseparable in the minds of his subjects.

Henry started off with what no one today would question was the greatest
asset in public life – good looks; or to use terms more pertinent to the
sixteenth century, strong physique, youth and vigour. Henry VIII was the jock
who wanted to be the international sporting celebrity in an age when that
meant renown in acts of chivalry, the tournament and the joust. As Lydgate's
Governance of Kings and Princes, re-published in 1511, put it: 'chivalry
conserveth the memory', and in such martial deeds it became a king to shine
like Phoebus in the aristocratic firmament.[2] In this Henry needed no teaching.
In the chronicler Edward Hall's words, 'the king being lusty, young and
couragous, greatly delighted in feats of chivalry'.[3] As well as being active in all
vigorous sports, Henry loved to issue challenges to jousts, shrugging off the
doubts of 'ancient fathers' who urged caution, 'considering the tender youth
of the king, and divers chances of horses and armour: in so much that it
was openly spoken that steel was not so strong, but it might be broken'.[4]
Henry, in other words, took big risks. Indeed, until 1527, when he was thirty-
six, he fought as chief challenger in every major English tournament.[5] And in
a famous episode in March 1524, when a lance splintered against his open
helmet to the horror of all observers, the king, in Hollywood hero style,
remounted and took the victory in the ensuing contests.[6]

Tournaments and jousts constituted much of the court entertainment of
the reign and were put on for ambassadors and envoys who were obviously
impressed by Henry's personal valour and skill. The Venetian ambassador
described him in 1515 as 'expert in arms' and it was this reputation that spread
throughout Europe.[7] Henry displayed his martial skills on the international
stage as part of the intricate game of diplomacy. When he led his army to
France in 1513, he was already renowned for his martial accomplishments;
when he went over to Boulogne he personally ordered that his tilting equipment go with him.[8] Much of the intricate pageantry at the Field of the Cloth
of Gold consisted of tilts and barriers in which both Francis I and Henry took
a leading part.[9] It was such displays of personal courage and skill, as much as
the splendid entourage of nobles, that advertised the might of the monarchy
and nation. It was Henry's personal prowess that endowed with his charisma
the signs of his dynasty, the roses on his tents and pavilions. It was Henry
himself who gave England a ruler ready and able to fight. And the rulers of
Christendom acknowledged Henry's reputation for valour in the gifts they
sent him of harnesses 'for the field and tilt'.[10]

At home, Henry's youth, physical agility and triumphs in the tiltyard established a dynasty which might with a different (a female, aged or infant)
successor to Henry VII have looked like another temporary occupant of the
throne. Until the Reformation, the theme of Henry's self-presentation and of
perceptions of the king was that of the martial prince, 'ever desirous to serve

Mars'.[11] Tournaments were, we should recall, theatre as well as military tattoo. When he fought well, Henry effectively became what the figures in the pageants which were part of the tournaments represented: Fame, Renown, Gallant.[12] And while the obvious audiences for such spectacles were the other participants, the queen and noblemen and women, they were not limited to a courtly entourage. At Greenwich, where Henry first built a permanent structure for jousting, his incorporation of a viewing gallery and two observation towers (fenestrated with 'castellar overtones') suggests a large number of spectators; and the tiltyards could certainly have accommodated them, that at Hampton Court, for example, measuring 1,000 by 450 feet.[13] Numerous workmen engaged in the construction of these towers and yards (over a quarter of a million bricks were used on that at Hampton Court) and on their regular maintenance, such as raking, almost certainly witnessed the events there. And as well as the privileged in their seats, 'the common people simply leant against the rails'.[14] Along with jousts, the king's (real) tennis playing (he built courts at several palaces), his archery (he practised with his guard at butts constructed at royal houses) and hawking and hunting all publicized Henry as a man of action, who lived out the scenes of the chase depicted on so many of the tapestries listed in his inventories.[15] For a wider audience than those who saw him in tiltyard or field, Hall's chronicle followed the king – from joust to hunt to foreign encampment – reporting deeds of daring and presenting Henry, from his very first triumph incognito at a Christmas joust at Richmond, as the most accomplished of all knights in arms, as the king who 'ever ... brake most spears'.[16]

Along with its focus on matters military and martial, Hall's chronicle devotes what conventional historians of politics might consider disproportionate space to entertainments, pageants and rituals. Yet not only were these integral features of jousts and tournaments, they were for Hall, as for Henry himself, no less significant in the representation of kingship. As Alastair Fox puts it, reading Hall, 'Henry's reign seems like one endless sequence of tourneys, disguisings, entertainments and pageants'; and other long contemporary descriptions of entertainments on the visit of Charles V, Henry's entry into Calais and Boulogne and at the coronation of Anne Boleyn only add to that impression.[17] If Fox's observation hints at the distance we might feel from an appreciation of such preoccupations, Muriel St Clare Byrne, writing of the Field of the Cloth of Gold, is more explicitly anachronistic in condemning 'elaborate and *useless* pageantry'.[18] Our own time has given us a different perspective from 1936 when one can appreciate that there were other priorities than pageantry and even a desire to downplay its importance; writing half a century later and from a background in literary criticism, Bill Readings described the same occasions, in the language of Cold War capitalism, as 'the first modern example of combat by conspicuous consumption'.[19] To a large extent, Henry's whole government rested its authority on conspicuous consumption and display: on the paramount 'visibility of the political' (and vice versa).[20] As Henry himself wrote of religious rituals, so he hoped that rituals of state might 'enter to excite or stir up men's devotion and to cause them to have more reverence'.[21] It was a hope partially fulfilled.

Where Lydgate had written that it '[be]longeth to a king once in a year to show him in his state royal and best array', Henry's year was pricked out with routine as well as extraordinary entertainments.[22] The traditional court pageants of the Christmas and New Year season became increasingly elaborate, albeit they for long continued to enact conventional heraldic themes. On his third New Year, for example, the king and his knights assaulted a castle erected in the hall at Greenwich to hold the court ladies, who yielded to their assailants in a spectacle which, both medieval and Petrarchan, linked martial and amorous pursuits befitting a 'lusty' young king and his bachelors.[23] Three years later, on Twelfth Night, the court staged a pageant of wild men who fought with noble knights until they were expelled and the court noblemen and women, representing order triumphant over chaos, emerged from a tent to serve a banquet to the king and queen, the symbols of virtue and order.[24] Months later, Henry and Catherine were themselves involved in the spectacle as they rode with their attendants to Shooters Hill where they encountered 200 yeomen 'clothed all in green' and led by Robin Hood. At a pre-arranged signal, the yeomen (in fact the king's own guard in disguise) fired a volley of arrows in such skilful unison that 'the noise was strange and great', before entertaining the royal couple in an arbour with a feast of venison.[25] Beyond the obvious compliment to a king who was an excellent archer, this entertainment interestingly combined pastoral elements (becoming fashionable with renewed interest in the classics) with popular historical legend, evidently to represent the king as, not only the source of order, but an object of love and allegiance. In some cases the message of an entertainment or disguising appears to be more explicit and topical. The Garden of Experience, for example, set up for a Twelfth Night pageant in 1517, featured at its centre a gold pillar topped with an arch crowned with gold in which was placed one bush with red and white roses and another of pomegranates, the badge of both Queen Catherine and King Solomon.[26] In the garden beneath the pillar (a garden, the fruits of which stood as promises of the fertility of the royal couple), six knights and six ladies walked, symbolizing the union of the dynasties of Habsburg and Tudor.

One annual pageant that took on renewed importance under the Tudors was the festival of the Garter. Henry VII had resuscitated the Order and his son revised the statutes and assiduously kept the Garter feasts.[27] In 1520, for instance, Henry led a procession of all the English knights of the Order from Colebrook to Windsor 'in gorgeous apparel' and there dined at what, to Hall,

resembled 'the feast of a coronation'.[28] Annually thereafter the feast was celebrated 'with great solemnity', at Windsor, Richmond or Greenwich where in
1534 the lords, knights, ladies and gentlemen assembled 'to a great number'.[29]
Henry's Garter festivals and processions were watched by many more. Indeed
the different locations enabled large numbers to observe the spectacle and
such may even have been a consideration. Certainly visitors and observers
appear to have been welcomed. In 1520 it was reported that at the feast 'all
things were plenteous to strangers that resorted thither'.[30] An occasion of
spectacle and hospitality which combined martial and spiritual meaning, the
Garter festivals represented Henry VIII as himself a fitting heir to St George
whose image appeared, as we have seen, on so many everyday royal objects.

A pageant that grew in importance in Henry's reign is one little studied by
historians of the early modern period: the royal procession to parliament.[31]
The procession, though less spectacular than great state occasions such as royal
coronations and funerals, became an increasingly common sight as Henry
called more parliaments than his predecessors to enact the legislation required
by the break from Rome. In 1529, Eustace Chapuys, the imperial ambassador,
described to the emperor the ritual of the 'first day of the convocation of the
estates', with the king in his ermine and crimson, all his bishops and nobles in
scarlet proceeding by barge to Westminster, observed by a public which, he
noted, was devoted to such rituals.[32] David Dean, the first scholar to investigate
this subject, argues the importance of these rituals: 'a parliamentary procession
emphasised the royal authority particularly through the representation of
the legal, political and religious elites'; the procession symbolized too the 'all
encompassing power of crown in parliament' and, as well as advertising the
king as a ruler who sought counsel, may have 'evoked expectations of problem
solving among the spectators'.[33] In processions to parliament, then, the king
was represented both as virtuous sovereign and as part of a larger public body
in which power was shared with the representatives of the king's subjects. As we
shall see, other representations themselves manifested that ambiguity, themselves proclaimed authority as royal sovereignty and yet as a partnership with
the public. For rituals of state required not simply the compliance of the people
but their participation – a participation which rendered ceremonies dialogues
with, rather than simple proclamations of, sovereign power.

The first great state pageant staged by any new ruler in early modern England
was the funeral of his predecessor. Our account from Hall of the 'funeral pomp'
of Henry VII's obsequies demonstrated how the ritual of death served also
to mark the succession of the new king. Henry VII's body was brought, in a
symbolic reversal of the king's normal passage (from public rooms to private
retreat), from the private to the public rooms of state; from the Privy Chamber
to the Great Chamber 'where he rested three days and every day had the dirge

and mass sung'.[34] The corpse was then conveyed into the hall, the most public room of ceremony, for a further three days, where mourners attended 'all the service time', replicating their attendance on the former king in his lifetime.[35] Finally, the body was placed on a hearse emblazoned with the king's arms and badges and accompanied by all his household servants from Richmond, Henry VII's favoured residence, to London Bridge, and then to St Paul's. The next day a procession conducted the hearse to Westminster where Garter King at Arms cried out for the soul of Henry VII, 'late king of this our realm'.[36] The following day, masses were sung and the king's banner and courser, the symbols of his honour, were offered up and all the household officers broke their staves and threw them into the grave as Garter called out 'Vive le Roy Henri le Huitienne, Roi D'Angleterre et de France'.[37]

What we need to appreciate from this brief description is the ways in which the funeral interred not only the physical but the representational body of the king. The king's arms and badges were ceremonially removed from the world, as was his image.[38] On the chariot hearse that carried his corpse 'was an image or representation of the late king laid on cushions of fine gold and the said image was apparelled in the king's rich robes of state with a crown on the head and a ball and sceptre in the hands'.[39] As the king's soul passed to the attention of priests and to the hereafter, his 'representation', an effigy, was also removed from the present to the realm of memory, making way for his successor and a new image of majesty. The moment of interment was the occasion of the first proclamation of the new king, by Garter King at Arms; it also instigated the preparations for the first representation of the new monarch. In Hall's words, 'when the funerals of the late king were thus honourably finished, great preparation was made for the coronation of this new king' – and made with 'pain, labour and diligence', for 'decking, trapping and adorning', so that 'more rich, nor more strange, nor more curious works hath not been seen'.[40] Henry VIII and his queen left the Tower to process through the city, the streets of which were hung with tapestry and cloth of gold, with the members of the guilds ranked in order. The king, in a jacket embroidered with diamonds and rubies, was conducted under a canopy of state and accompanied by all the office-holders of his household, two of whom wore the robes of the duchies of Guyenne and Normandy to represent his suzerainty over those kingdoms. Following the household, nine children of honour were mounted on horses with trappings displaying all the king's titles – as monarch of England, France, Gascony, Guyenne and Normandy, Aragon, Cornwall, Wales and Ireland.[41] At the feast after the coronation service, where the new king was served, as a sign of their allegiance, by lords, the king's champion, Robert Dimmock made a ceremonial entrance to challenge any who denied Henry's title or inheritance. Later jousts were staged in the Palace of Westminster, in one case involving a device of a turret, from which Lady Pallas presented her knights who were challenged by those of Diana. The knights of Pallas, the goddess of war and patroness of the arts (who also symbolized justice) and those of the moon goddess Diana, worshipped for her fertility, had the equal in the contest, representing the equal and mutually reinforcing virtues of the king and queen who sat in an enclosure gilded with their initials and arms.[42] Here, then, was presented a martial, chivalrous, prince, a just, learned ruler and, interestingly in the light of the issue of Catherine's marriage to Arthur and later controversy over her virginity, a chaste bride (Diana was the goddess of maidens) – in other words what all hoped would be a harmonious and fruitful marriage. The day he was crowned, Henry VIII was represented as rightful heir, martial, just prince and future father of a fertile line.

As the new prince of a new dynasty, Henry regarded a display of arms and his strength abroad as a vital part of his standing – at home and in Europe. The rhetoric of his early campaigns in France evoked the glorious memory of Henry V and rhetoric appeared to become reality in the siege of Tournai in September 1512, a triumph the like of which had not been seen since the victories of the Hundred Years War.[43] Unquestionably, Henry would have wished to push ahead with a full-scale war but when shifts in European diplomatic alignments, not to mention papal pressure for a European peace, dictated a rapprochement, it was vital that Henry be seen to make peace, as he had war, from strength.[44] The occasion on which Henry and Francis I met to seal their uneasy accord or truce was the site of perhaps the most famous pageant of the reign: the Field of the Cloth of Gold. Some may think it inappropriate to consider that pageant in a chapter primarily concerned with the representation of Henry's kingship in England. But, as Hall, indeed Henry himself, was right to discern, the Field of the Cloth of Gold was a display of strength to English nobles as well as foreign princes, a presentation of a new-style warrior king who could cut a figure in Europe and who might again lead a proud nobility and nation to victories as had Henry V at Agincourt.[45]

The pageant, of course, also began and ended in England, with the remove of all the court with the king and queen to Canterbury where news was received that the Emperor Charles V would land at Dover, on his way to Germany.[46] Henry VIII rode to meet him and escort him back, with a torchlight procession, to Canterbury where the two celebrated the feast of Pentecost, a symbol of their union and shared Christian piety. As Charles departed for Flanders, Henry and his entourage sailed to Calais whence they proceeded to Guisnes, to a sumptuous royal palace constructed for the occasion. Thence, on 7 June, the royal party set off for the meeting place in the valley 'le Valdora'. Henry, with the sword of state borne before him, was followed by 500 guardsmen and 2,000 foot, the Archbishop of Canterbury, dukes, nobles and knights. Hall devotes twenty pages to the details of the meeting, to the sumptuous clothes and jewels, lavish feasts, extravagant architecture and rich pageants which provided the *mis-en-scène* for this diplomatic meeting and show of strength.[47] Once again both kings were concerned to display their chivalry, symbolized by the Tree of Honour, festooned with silk flowers and symbols of the two kings, on which also their armorial shields were hung. Banquets hosted by each side (themselves a competition to impress) provided regular occasions for a full procession from the field to the French encampment at Ardres and the English at Guisnes; and masques, such as that on the last day which presented the English as worthies led by Hercules, proclaimed the persons of the rivals as heroes and gods.[48] All was carefully stage-managed to veil the uneasy accommodation and competitiveness with an etiquette of strict equality and mutual respect. The Field of the Cloth of Gold enabled both rulers to preserve their honour with each other and to enhance it in the eyes of spectators: to stage peace as victory and to display national military might and personal bravery (they both entered the lists) while concluding hostilities.

Crucially for Henry VIII, the occasion provided another opportunity to present his dynasty and himself as the heir to King Arthur and Charlemagne, Hercules and Hector, Alexander and Caesar. Nor, important and numerous though those in attendance were, was this show staged merely for the audience of two courts. 'During the triumph,' Hall tells us, 'so much people of Picardy and west Flanders drew to Guisnes to see the king of England and his honour.'[49] When the royal entourage finally moved off back towards Calais, accompanied by Francis I and Charles V, there were more days of festivities and festivals before the English party took ship. Through all these weeks, news of the spectacle had attracted many more to come and observe them. The sheer magnificence of the plate, vessels, jewels, clothes, and the delicacy of exotic dishes ensured that the feasts, no less than the feats of arms, were 'far in realms proclaimed, which caused most people of noble courage thither to resort'.[50] To compare, as one is tempted to do, the Field of the Cloth of Gold with a Hollywood extravaganza is to underline not diminish its global cultural significance and authority. Henry VIII had achieved what his father would not have dared to imagine: he had secured – at least the impression of – equal standing with one of the most powerful nations and princes in Europe. No wonder his chronicler was determined to publicize it.

An opportunity to perform the role of a power player on the international stage was, in the most literal sense, spectacularly seized with the occasion of the Emperor Charles V's second, more formal visit in 1522. Charles V, accompanied by nobles from Spain, Flanders and Germany, landed at Dover on 26 May, whence the next day he was escorted by Henry to Canterbury. The party having travelled to Gravesend, they there embarked on thirty state barges to Greenwich where the emperor was lodged in royal apartments that even 'the Spaniards wondered at'.[51] After days of jousts, tournaments (in which Henry again took part), feasts and masques, on 6 June the emperor and king commenced their march into London for an elaborate triumphal procession which the city had been preparing since March.[52] As they processed, two swords borne before the emperor and Henry, behind them 'an Englishman and a stranger rode ever together, matched according to their degrees', to symbolize the rulers' union and alliance.[53] In an oration, Thomas More praised the 'peace and love between the princes' and said 'what comfort it was to their subjects to see them in such amity'.[54]

As they approached the drawbridge at Southwark, the procession was presented with the first of many pageants: of giants representing Hercules and Samson with the emperor's arms on an escutcheon. On the bridge, a representation of Jason's victory over the dragon staged a compliment to Charles who was head of the Order of the Golden Fleece, while verses compared his entry into London to the greatest triumphs of Scipio. At the conduit at Gracechurch Street, flanked by towers inscribed with verses celebrating their lineage and virtues, pageant figures representing the emperor and Henry were presented by 'Charlemagne' with the swords of justice and victory. As the procession moved on to Leaden Hall, they encountered a magnificent pageant (no less than 80 feet in length) of John of Gaunt at the root of a genealogical tree, on the branches of which were set the images of fifty-five kings and queens, topped with those of the emperor, Henry VIII and Catherine of Aragon, to signify the rulers' descent from one family. At Cornhill, a figure of King Arthur, attended by kings, greeted them, while a poet compared the two princes to Cato and Alexander, to Caesar and King Arthur himself, a pantheon of classical and British heroes. At the Great Conduit at Cheapside, along with a pageant of the four virtues, on a large tower flew the arms of Spain and England, at the foot of which a figure representing King Alphonso of Spain, with other kings and queens attending, addressed the two kings as heirs with a common ancestry. The final pageant raised praise to celestial heights. At the Little Conduit at Cheapside, a heaven containing the Virgin, the apostles and saints (including St George and Henry VI), bestowed a blessing on Charles and Henry, just as they moved off to be received by the Archbishop of Canterbury at the west end of St Paul's.[55]

The procession though the city, then, also took a symbolic route through classical triumph, medieval Spanish and English history, to apotheosis. It was, of course, intended to pay a compliment to the first emperor to visit England since Sigismund in 1416. But it was, too, every bit as much propaganda for Henry VIII. What strikes us, reading the description of every pageant, or the verses spoken or displayed, is the emphasis on the equality as well as unity of the two sovereigns. Charles and Henry were presented as heirs of a common stock, as brothers, and Henry was represented as the equal of emperors and 'of kings the great glory'.[56] Indeed, in the last pageant Henry claimed the higher place symbolically as it is St George and Edward the Confessor who are shown flanking the figure of the Virgin.[57]

Though 'a classic instance of the use of public spectacle as an instrument of policy', the reception of Charles V was not solely, or principally, devised by the government.[58] As was customary, it was the corporation of London and the livery companies, the Hanseatic merchants and the Italian merchants, who planned, constructed and paid for the scenes and ceremonies. However, from the beginning the court of aldermen oversaw the plans and it is unlikely that they acted without consultation with the royal court or ministers. Indeed, an official account of *The Triumph and the Verses that Charles the Emperor and the Most Mighty Redouted King of England Henry VIII Were Saluted With, Passing Through London* was printed and published by the king's printer, Richard Pynson, the same year.[59] *The Triumph* does not recount the pageants – as we shall see, the author assumes readers have seen them – but his text translates the Latin verses inscribed and prints those spoken (and sometimes not heard or understood) both to publicize broadly and to memorialize the occasion.[60] The printed account manifests that, whatever its vital role in cementing an accord between Charles V and Henry VIII to contain France (a purpose made clear in the play performed before the emperor at Windsor), the triumph was intended to speak to an English audience: of nobles, city dignitaries and, we should note, of common people.[61]

The next great state entry of Henry's reign could hardly have taken place in more altered circumstances. It was a decade later when Henry once again rode in triumphal procession through his capital, but this time with a new queen who had supplanted the emperor's aunt in the royal bed; and Henry was now at war with Charles V. As importantly, England was fundamentally divided over the divorce and remarriage and there were, on the one part, doubts about the legitimacy of the marriage to Catherine and, on the other, hostility towards Anne Boleyn who some thought had seduced Henry from his wife.[62] In such circumstances ritual can fulfil its most important role. The coronation entry, therefore, was intended as an official and public affirmation of what had taken place, as a presentation of the pregnant Anne as rightful and fertile queen, as reassurance of the security of dynasty and realm, and proclamation of Henry as a righteous ruler who had followed his conscience and God's will and who was careful for the welfare of his subjects. On this occasion we know that the initiative behind the spectacle came directly and personally from the king himself who, Hall informs us, 'addressed his gracious letters to the mayor . . . signifying that his pleasure was to solemnize and celebrate the coronation'.[63]

On 29 May 1533, the mayor and aldermen led a flotilla of barges, behind a large pageant dragon figuring the legend of St George, towards Greenwich. The barges flew ensigns fore and aft, with the king's and new queen's arms atop sail, and, together with the barges of the livery companies, they each bore a large metal escutcheon with Henry's and Anne's arms on their side. From Greenwich the queen, with dukes, marquesses and lords, was rowed to the Tower where, to the sound of shot, she was greeted by the king with a kiss.[64] It was nearly two weeks later, on 9 June, that Anne was conducted into London under a canopy of cloth of gold to be welcomed by a series of spectacular pageants. At Gracechurch Corner, the cavalcade was halted by a 'marvellous cunning pageant' figuring Mount Parnassus (the home of the Muses) and the fount of Helicon atop which sat Apollo (the sun god) and Calliope (Muse of poetry), with the Muses praising the queen for her virtue, beauty and fertility.[65] At Leaden Hall, Virgilian motifs gave way to British themes as here, under a heavenly canopy, on a 'root' or tree on top of a mountain, surrounded with red and white roses, perched a falcon (the badge of Anne Boleyn) which was being crowned by an angel. Beneath the tree, the figure of St Anne with her issue linked Anne to her holy namesake, mother of the Virgin, as well as to the future of the English nation, while a child 'made a goodly oration to the queen of the fruitfulness of St Anne and of her generation, trusting that the like fruit should come of her'.[66] As the queen and her procession moved on to Cheapside, she was presented with a device of the Graces, handmaidens of Venus, each of whom spoke in praise of Anne as wine flowed (the Graces symbolized generosity) expressing bounty and abundance. After the presentation of a purse at the Strand, a seventh pageant at the Little Conduit staged the story of the Judgment of Paris, at which Mercury presented her with all – and represented her as the embodiment of all – the gifts of wisdom, riches and felicity.[67] As she came to St Paul's Gate, three virgins who were seated on a throne bore the message that Henry so desperately hoped the nation would echo: 'Regina Anna: Prospere, procede et regna'. Each maiden bore a tablet inscribed respectively: 'Come friend you will be crowned' (an allusion to Christ's words on the cross), 'Lord direct my way' (I am the way, said the Lord) and 'Trust in God'. Beneath their feet, an inscription proclaimed in words that echo the annunciation: 'Queen Anne you shall bear a new son of the king's blood, there shall be a golden age unto thy people'.[68] Finally, after a pageant at Fleet Street, the procession entered Westminster Hall where the next day the coronation took place 'with all . . . ceremonies'.[69]

The coronation procession and pageantry presented Anne Boleyn as a classical heroine, saint and fertile mother who heralded for England a golden age, an age, as the many references to music make clear, of harmony. The official account of *The Noble Triumphant Coronation of Queen Anne Wife unto the*

Most Noble King Henry VIII represented the deeply controversial, divisive and unpopular marriage as a symbol of the great concord and love between the ruler and his subjects. The woodcut frontispiece depicts, unusually, the royal couple enthroned and touching hands, a visual proclamation of their physical union and perhaps another gesture to fertility.[70] Throughout the text references are made to the 'sweet harmony' of instruments and singers, the order of the procession and the accord between king and people, the 'loving labour and pains' (the language perhaps puns on Anne's pregnancy) they had taken and the 'great joy and comfort' they took from the event.[71] Just as pamphlets of the 1530s endeavoured to naturalize the supremacy and erase the papacy, so here ritual attempts to neuter the opposition to the revolutionary act of divorce and the fact of dispute: to re-present the king's desire as the will of God and the people. It might well be that, at a time when the king's councillors and courtiers were themselves divided, Henry was more than ever concerned to claim popular support.

After the coronation ritual for Anne Boleyn, there were no major state pageants for several years. One scholar has suggested that, with the Reformation, the arts of pageantry took second place to cruder mechanisms of persuasion and enforcement. In the words of Professor Anglo, 'the pageanteer, court reveller and scenic artist were succeeded by the political pamphleteer, preacher and public executioner'.[72] The break from Rome undoubtedly saw cruder forms of propaganda and more brutal measures to enforce the royal will. But such an explanation underestimates both the value of ceremony and ritual as forms of persuasion and Henry's own appreciation of the politics of spectacle. It was plague in London that caused Henry to defer a public coronation of his next queen and Jane Seymour's tragically brief life and death in childbirth in 1537 that prevented ritual public celebration of another royal marriage or the birth of the prince.[73] Though it was less spectacular than earlier celebrations, Henry certainly planned a state reception for his fourth queen, Anne of Cleves in 1540. For her arrival a ceremonial route was laid out from rich pavilions on Blackheath to Greenwich Park where the aldermen, knights and merchants of London were aligned, 'apparelled in velvet and chains of gold', to greet her.[74] Henry set out to meet her, accompanied by earls, visiting ambassadors and bishops, on a horse trapped in cloth of gold. The king and queen's trains being united, they rode between the ranks of assembled nobles, while the citizens rowed up and down the Thames, their barges decorated with Henry and Anne's arms. Some days after the marriage ceremony at Greenwich, the royal couple made their way to Westminster by river 'accompanied with many nobles and prelates in barges', and attended by the mayor and city companies.[75] Though on this occasion there was no official state entry, Anne was ritually and publicly presented as queen. A month later the marriage was annulled.

Whether it was the reception of an emperor or the coronation of a queen, the pageants of state were, in a number of ways, truly public spectacles. Not only did they, as the events and vicissitudes of the reign unfolded, present and re-present the king to the people – as legitimate heir, classical hero, or god-like prince; they represented Henry as a ruler loved by his subjects. All the accounts of processions make much of the crowds who gathered to see the king and the official accounts go to some lengths to point out the large numbers present. 'Many commoners', as well as nobles and dignitaries, attended Henry VII's funeral cortège to St Paul's, 'rude and common people' followed Henry and Catherine of Aragon's coronation procession to Westminster Abbey; at Charles V's entry, the citizens were penned within rails while 'in every house almost' people were crowded to watch and sing; at Anne's coronation, the press of people was such that constables were needed to keep order.[76] These were occasions intended to be public and remembered, and large audiences (as today) enhanced the authority of the performers and the impression the day left. Official accounts also inform us that verses attached to pageants, which being in Latin have often been assumed to be directed only at elites, were translated: 'to the ende that to eache state/ lerned and unlerned they should be celebrate'.[77] Speeches not heard in the mêlée were printed so they could be savoured later; pageant constructions, like those at Fleet Street, were left up for weeks or even months after the spectacle of the day as monuments to great events; and explanations of the classical themes and iconography of allegorical tableaux were offered in print to those who needed or wanted them.[78]

Not merely an audience, the public were – and importantly were seen to be and reported as being – very much participants in the spectacle. It was their presence that validated the occasion and demonstrated what Morison had called the 'lovely bond' between king and subjects.[79] The orderly behaviour of the spectators replicated and realized the ideals played out in the pageants which were presented; their cries of joy and shouts of 'God save the king' (printed, we recall, on the Great Bible) affirmed the loyalty and love they felt for Henry. 'You must not forget,' Hall advised his readers, 'for all the pageants, how the citizens well apparelled stood within the rails.'[80] Moreover the audience was essential to the royal performance: the representation of the king as loving father of his people. Though some were to play it with infinitely more skill than others, the role of rulers in state rituals was to acknowledge the applause of the citizens and to respond with thanks and warm words. When Anne of Cleves and Henry VIII processed through Greenwich while the barges rowed up and down the Thames, the 'sight and noise they much praised'.[81] At the coronation of Anne Boleyn, when 'the wonderful number of people that ever was seen . . . stood on both sides of the river', Henry stopped and 'gave great thanks and praises to all the citizens for their great kindness to the great joy and comfort of all the citizens'.[82] Rather than simple propaganda, pageant and festival, as well as proclaiming royal sovereignty and reaffirming royal policies, acknowledged some element of reciprocity in the relationship between monarch and subjects; at least an obligation on the monarch to embody and demonstrate the virtues which pageant celebrated.

On these occasions by no means everything ran according to the script. It was, as we shall have further occasion to consider, not unheard of for either the organizers of such events or the people observing to express, in various ways, their dissatisfaction with royal policy or the government. More than one state ceremony was the occasion of disorder and unruliness. On the very day of Henry and Catherine of Aragon's coronation, after the couple were escorted into Westminster Abbey under a canopy of cloth of ray, 'the cloth was cut and spoiled by the rude and common people' – an unfortunate intrusion of Mammon into divine ritual.[83] The next year, a pageant structure erected to receive the lords and ladies after a dance was destroyed in an unseemly fracas: 'suddenly the rude people came to the pageant and rent, tore and spoiled the pageant so that the Lord Steward [principal officer of the king's household] nor the head officers could not cause them to abstain'.[84] Such signs of disorder clearly threatened to puncture the ideals of harmony expressed in verse and song. But as well as general unruliness, politics too, in the form of uncomfortable memories, other loyalties of clientage or faith, differences and disputes, could undermine the illusion of power. We are told that Christmas festivities at Greenwich in 1529 were less joyous, for all the 'great plenty of viandes [meats]', because Catherine, anxious about the fate of her marriage, 'showed them no manner of countenance and made no great joy of nothing, her mind was so troubled'.[85] In 1532, for all the 'great solemnity' with which the king kept up Christmas, 'all men said that there was no mirth in that Christmas because the queen and the ladies were absent'.[86] The next year Thomas More's conspicuous absence from Anne Boleyn's coronation was noted and seen to 'damage Henry's image' and popular dissatisfaction was clearly expressed in ways that showed how ritual could easily be subverted.[87] According to one account, rather different in tone to the official report, nobody greeted the king and his new queen with the customary cry of 'Dieu gard le roi'. When one of the queen's servants required the mayor to order the people to give the usual welcome, he retorted that he could not command the hearts of the people, (adding, for good measure) any more than could the king himself.[88] The French observer adds that some wags, observing the interwoven initials of Henry and Anne, made of them 'ha ha ha' and mocked the queen's appearance as 'monstreuse'.[89] While the reporter may have had his own agenda, his observations graphically illustrate how easily all aspects of state spectacle could be turned into carnival, how, for all their preparation and magnificence, the ultimate meaning of these occasions was in the eye of the beholder – indeed the common beholder.[90]

As well as large state spectacles and jousts and tournaments, Henry introduced to the English court a new genre of royal entertainment and representation which was to be a dominant courtly form for the next century – the masque. The early history of masque in England remains obscure, not least because for some time contemporaries were apt to use the terms 'masque', 'mumming' and 'disguising' interchangeably.[91] However, Edward Hall appears not to have doubted that something new was introduced to Henry's court. 'On the day of Epiphany at night,' in 1512 he informs us, 'the king with eleven others were disguised after the manner of Italy, a thing not seen afore in England.'[92] In his very brief description which dwelt principally on the apparel 'wrought all in gold', Hall suggested that the entertainment consisted of disguise and dance, the constituents of a masque. Thenceforth, though the details and conceits of these new entertainments remain lost to us, there is plentiful evidence that masques became a regular feature of the court year, as well as being performed on special occasions. The inventories of Henry's goods list masquing costumes, which included buskins; if these suggest classical themes, the 'garments for moors' and 'frocks for Egyptians' point to themes and disguisings that long pre-date Ben Jonson's famous Jacobean *Masque of Blackness*.[93] Henry staged masques at Christmas at Greenwich and, in the 1520s, at Wolsey's palace to entertain envoys and to celebrate triumphs such as the victory at Tournai; in one, we know, the king performed the part of the prince of Castile, 'in a masque all richly apparelled'.[94] Along with Henry, his queens and children performed in these entertainments, Princess Mary, for example, dancing before her father at Greenwich in May 1527.[95] This is the occasion which the historian of the masque takes as the true beginning of the masque genre: dialogue, dance and revels were all part of the entertainment, the subject of which was a contest between love and riches.[96] Alas, lacking detail about the relationship of the representation to the occasion, a visit of the French ambassadors, the politics of this masque, as of all Henrician masques, eludes us. Yet it is quite apparent that the masque was seen to be political as well as recreational. For one, the essential elements, dance and music, were widely held to be intrinsic to a humanist education in virtue: Elyot devotes a chapter of his *Governor* to 'how dancing may be an introduction unto the first moral virtue called Prudence', in which he explains how various steps and moves signified particular virtues of industry and circumspection.[97] More particularly, the participation of the monarch as a performer (as well as observer) made masques political acts, and acts that might announce policy as well as dance 'moves'. Henry's 'great chamber of disguisings', as such language indicates, was perceived by ambassadors and courtiers as a chamber of state: indeed, the imperial envoy Chapuys interpreted the king's

preoccupation with masques in 1538 ('he cannot be one single moment without masques') as 'a sign that he proposes to marry again'.[98] For all that the texts are now lost to us, such comments leave no doubt that contemporaries regarded the masques introduced from Italy by Henry as representations of the king and indications of his inclinations in matters of state.

What we have begun to learn in recent years is that the daily life of the court was itself a performance and representation of kingship which was scrutinized by visitors and subjects alike. Indeed, if dialogue, movement, music and performance space are the defining characteristics of a masque, they were also aspects of the quotidian life of the early modern court. In a pioneering piece of research, David Starkey long ago explicated the major changes effected by Henry in the court, especially the king's remove from the Great Hall and Presence of the medieval court into a newly constituted Privy Chamber and even more private apartments.[99] Such changes expressed architecturally the idea of the king's two bodies; and they effected a complex semiotics and politics of space in representations and perceptions of the monarchy.[100] As the king retreated into more intimate spaces with access confined to a few trusted attendants, influence and politics became bound up with spaces and places. Moreover, even more than before, at the Henrician court, royal movements and the translations of courtiers and personal servants plotted political, as well as architectural and geographic, trajectories. As Simon Thurley has observed, with Henry spending less time dining or being seen in public at court, 'a formal daily procession to the chapel gave the king a chance to proceed through the outer rooms of his palace showing himself to his court'.[101] Envoys and courtiers were quick to perceive the significance of moves and places: the denial of a room to Wolsey on his arrival at court was interpreted to signal his fall; by contrast the fine lodging provided in 1528 for Anne Boleyn at Greenwich was widely read as a sign of her imminent elevation.[102] But the most closely observed moves were those made by Henry himself.

Not least then as a consequence of Henry's changes, the court was viewed as a complex site of royal favour and intention. It was, of course, conventionally held that the court was a representation of the king. Lydgate had counselled monarchs 'of thy courts loke thou be dylygent' and a new humanist literature of advice to princes, notably Castigliano's *Il Cortegiano* (translated into English as *The Book of the Courtier* in 1561) described court life as an elaborate theatre of roles and performances, gestures and movements, in which the king was not only impresario but principal actor.[103] Henry's own sense of the politics of spaces and places may well have extended to representations, as well as to an exact codification of who went where. We recall that the king opened the Banqueting House at Greenwich so that 'all honest persons' might view both the magnificent plate and the tapestries depicting the story of King David: a licensed peep, as it were, into the mysteries of monarchy which was carefully stage-managed. More careful analysis of the inventories, when research on them is completed, may confirm a sense that Henry paid attention to the relationship of objects and rooms as important to the image of his rule. For the inventory of pictures is suggestive. At the Palace of St James's, for example, which Henry built for the royal children as an architectural expression of Tudor succession, the king displayed a large collection of dynastic portraits of European rulers and English kings from the age of King Arthur.[104] The politics of entertainments and interludes at the court of Henry VIII was bound up with not only moments and circumstances but places and spaces; and the shifts in royal representation were geographic no less than temporal.

The court too was ever in motion, traversing not just the symbolic sites of the realm – parliament, lawcourts and cathedrals – but the wider geographies of royal palaces and hunting lodges and, ultimately, the realm. Because he was a king who acquired and built new residences, Henry VIII was a king often on the move, seen by servants, nobles, gentlemen and commoners, as his vast entourage of over 800, with their baggage train, slowly made their way by water and land from one residence to another. Simon Thurley estimates that over the course of his reign Henry made about 1,150 moves with his court, 830 to his own houses and the rest to those of abbots, bishops, courtiers and noblemen: an average, that is, of over thirty moves a year.[105] Neil Samman has shown that, as well as frequent, Henry's royal progresses traversed much of his kingdom – the midlands and York as well as the southern moves – culminating in that of 1526 when Henry was away a third of the whole year.[106] Such progresses in a very literal sense took the royal show on the road. Hall describes Henry's first progress in 1510 as an active time, with the king 'exercising himself daily in shooting, singing . . . wrestling, casting of the bar . . . hunting, hawking and shooting'.[107] The king who appears to have regarded himself as on a tour to publicize his talents was also on a fact-finding mission. For it was 'in his progress [that he] heard every day more and more complaints of Empson and Dudley' and responded by sending writs out for their execution.[108] If Hall can be taken as a guide, Henry appears to have appreciated that, like state pageants, progresses performed in two directions: that they served to represent the monarchy to subjects but also as an opportunity for the king to observe and listen to the people's concerns, in order to ensure their loyalty. Such progresses were all the more important in time of crisis. We recall Henry VII, soon after the victory that brought him the crown, resolving to progress to York to ascertain the mood and reinforce the allegiance of subjects, many of whom had supported his Yorkist rival.[109] In the same spirit, his son, in the wake of the risings in Lincolnshire and the Pilgrimage of Grace, planned a progress to York as part of a larger effort to justify the government to the people.[110] The progress was not finally undertaken until 1541 when, with his throne secure, Henry travelled to York, to receive, in the presence of the public, the formal submissions of the magistrates of Lincolnshire and Yorkshire who presented the king with thanks for his gracious pardon and the present of a purse.[111] Whether in displaying his athletic skills or virtues of clemency and concern for his people, progresses reaffirmed the king's authority and re-established the natural love between king and people. As the purse they presented was a gift to the king, so his presence was a gift to his people, a visible presence that made the words and signs of his majesty flesh.

As we have begun to see, subjects, vulgar as well as noble, had expectations of a monarch, the more so as print circulated more broadly a literature of advice to princes that listed the virtues traditionally associated with good lordship and virtuous rule. Chief among them were justice, mercy and liberality.

Though he has gone down in history as a brutal ruler and was accused of being a tyrant in his own time, Henry VIII endeavoured to use the stages of justice, the courts and the scaffold, to present himself as a virtuous ruler who combined mercy with justice. On the one hand, therefore, John Jones and other crown servants were hanged wearing the prince's livery; while, though he rebuked his servant at a Star Chamber trial for riot, Henry spared Sir William Bulmer and, condemning only Lord Ogle for having committed murder, pardoned other rioters, proclaiming to his servant: 'one we will favour now and another at such time as we shall like; and therefore Sir William if you serve us heartily you shall not be forgotten'.[112] What indelibly tarnished the reputation of a king who had early won plaudits for royal justice executed against oppressors were the actions taken to enforce the Reformation and to suppress opposition to the royal supremacy. Former admirers of Henry, such as Elyot, Wyatt and Surrey, increasingly came to perceive Henry as a tyrant who ran roughshod over legal processes.[113] And, of course, as religious divisions hardened, any shared idea of justice gave way to highly partisan attitudes to what were harsh, as opposed to godly, courses of action against heretics. Just as he endeavoured to plot a middle way in matters of doctrine, Henry evidently took pains to represent royal justice as free of confessional allegiances. On one occasion, for example, Henry ordered three Catholics and three Protestants burned at the stake in a spectacle of grisly symmetry.[114] But, as religious divisions became ever more bitter, both Catholic and Protestant martyrs showed their readiness not only to die for their faith but to denounce a ruler who had departed from truth and justice. In large measure, the king's reputation for justice and mercy was consumed with them.

Second only to justice in the virtues catalogued as essential in a good prince was liberality, which was, as much as an ethical desideratum, a political necessity for medieval and early modern kingship. What has been well described as the cynosure of early modern monarchy was the bestowal of patronage and favour in return for loyal service.[115] In his coronation poem Stephen Hawes neatly expounded the relationship between reward and service, urging the lords and 'noble knights':

Vnto our sovereigne be meke and tendable
Wiche wyll rewarde you well and nobly[116]

The coronation was customarily an occasion for conferring honours, creating Knights of the Bath, for example, and a moment, in Jennifer Loach's words, for 'distributing largesse to the upper ranks of society'.[117] At his coronation, Henry richly rewarded his champion, Sir Robert Dimmock, with a gold cup and cover and rich harness of the trapping on which he was mounted, the second best, according to Hall, in the royal armoury.[118] On that occasion, the king also dubbed the mayor of London a knight as the wine that flowed from the pageant castle constructed for a joust symbolized the king's virtue of liberality.[119] Henry VIII was especially careful to display the virtues expected of a king in acts of charity and generosity. As part of the coronation celebrations, Henry sought to distance himself from his father's reputation for rapacity and 'made restitution of great sums of money to many persons taken against good conscience', perhaps by agents of Empson and Dudley.[120] Two years later at Christmas at Greenwich, Hall reports a free abundance of food 'to all comers of any honest behaviour' in a traditional gesture of seasonal piety and charity that emulated Christ.[121] As well as general acts of charity, Henry seems to have had that distinctive mark of the most charismatic leaders – the ability to remember a favour done for him and the good deeds of even the lowliest servant; and a generosity in rewarding them all. So, in the records of the Privy Purse, we find, as well as endless bequests of charitable alms donated to the poor and blind, thoughtful gifts of nightcaps to the royal stable boys, a wedding gift to John Holland of his guard, and rewards to servants who found a lost ring or brought home Bull, the king's beloved dog, lost in Waltham Forest.[122]

Such personal incidents lead us at last to consider the person of Henry VIII as his own representation. Curiously the traditional histories and biographies of monarchs have little considered their self-presentation or image. But over the last twenty years or more, scholars from other disciplines have explored the close exchange between theatre and politics, and the importance of the performative dimension in the exercise of authority.[123] Nor is such attention anachronistic. Already by Henry's reign, and still more as the century developed (as we shall see), contemporaries used theatrical language to describe government, and monarchs compared themselves to actors on a stage. In Greg Walker's phrase, we may view Henry's exercise of kingship as a 'donning and shedding of roles', and we must see that donning and shedding as inseparable from the business of power and survival.[124]

Following the scripts that described the ideal ruler, Henry enacted the roles of warrior, chivalrous lover, theologian, man of piety and conscience, imperial prince, abused husband, and 'bluff King Hal'. Accordingly, when he led his army to France, he donned, as if on a crusade, the badge of St George and a robe with a red cross; when he presided over the trial of John Lambert for heresy, he dressed all in white to symbolize the purity of his judgment.[125] Knocked unconscious by the Duke of Suffolk in a joust, the king rose and, brushing himself down, delivered the matinée hero's line that 'none was to blame but himself'.[126] After a riot in the city, when prisoners were brought before him in halters, he pardoned them, as we saw, with perfect dramatic timing.[127] By his hesitancy and deliberation in the early stages of his divorce, he acted the part of the man of conscience and circumspect philosopher king, seeking a right and just outcome; when his patience failed, he turned in a powerful performance as patriotic defender of the nation against foreign powers.

Blessed by nature with a 'princely countenance' and muscular physique, Henry played all these parts on the stage of the court, the realm and Christendom.[128] To raise the question of his sincerity is to miss the point: an early modern king was expected to perform roles as well as to be 'himself'. His 'self', in fact, like his body, was a public as well as a personal thing. And much of the art of royal representation was concerned with reconciling the two: performing the roles that subjects expected of a king and retaining, indeed affirming, his identity as Henry Tudor. As we have seen, in many of the forms and occasions of representation, some reciprocity between king and subjects was tacitly acknowledged. It was acknowledged because the very performance of the kingly office was increasingly seen as that – as performance; and as an exchange with, as well as presentation to, an audience in what men were beginning to describe as the theatre of state.

CHAPTER 6

CONTESTING SUPREMACY

On the stage of state the king's was by no means the only voice heard. Indeed, as the king and government took advantage of the new medium of print to represent their authority and to argue a case, they publicized what had been *arcana imperii* and so cast the king's business, even the intimate matters of marriage and conscience, into the arena of public debate. Though we must be wary of anachronism and cautious about applying a concept to a period nearly two centuries before its Habermasian moment, something that we can begin to describe as a public sphere came into being with the Henrician Reformation.[1] With the emergence of a public sphere of debate and division, others with different agenda to the king's used the public stage and new media of publication to present their case. In myriad ways, Henry VIII found that his representation of his policies and kingship was countered by other representations – and countered by commoners as well as counsellors, prophets as well as playwrights, and rumour as well as riot.[2]

Sixteenth-century England witnessed both a growing identity of the people with the Tudor dynasty and the nation on the one hand, and a mounting sense of local community on the other. While Henry patronized John Bale and others to gather materials for an English history, local topographers and antiquaries were beginning to trace the histories of their counties and towns.[3] After the break from Rome, while the royal arms replaced the trinity in parish churches, in towns like Norwich it was the city's arms that were displayed in places of worship.[4] In other words, while the sixteenth century gradually saw the decline of the over-mighty nobles who had in the previous century vied with the crown, while the power of the monarchy was unquestionably enhanced, other bodies, be they parliaments or local communities, indeed subjects, were developing a greater sense of their identity, a consciousness of themselves as participants in the public arena – in the exercise of authority. The events of the divorce, the break from Rome and the debates on the nature and extent of religious reform were not only the agents of new identity formations; the representation of those changes and official appeals for public support encouraged a dialogue about policy and authority which transformed the exercise of rule.

As we have observed, the official representation of Henry VIII was often the business of others than the king: others who had beliefs and desires of their own. Along with disaffected ministers or counsellors determined to promote a policy, others outside as well as inside the court used drama, print, prophecy and rumour to represent and advance a very different commonwealth to that published by the king. Scholars of early modern drama have debated the extent to which theatre allowed for criticism as well as compliment; in the case of Henrician England, Greg Walker has argued persuasively for a drama of 'persuasion', as one facet of a discourse of counsel, more recently for plays as texts of opposition to both royal courses and the king's tyrannical rule.[5] Moreover, publication in changed circumstances could transform the most loyal of performances into critical texts. It seems likely, for example, that John Skelton's *Magnificence* was, when performed in 1519, intended as praise of a king who had expelled his young favourites; when it was published in 1530, many readers might have read it instead as a critique, since most of the 'minions' had returned to court and were joined by new intimates who were advising on the king's divorce. As J. Christopher Warner has argued, in 1530 references to lust and debauchery risked being taken as dangerous allusions to Henry's affair with Anne, while passages about false counsel took on a more specific and contentious resonance amid the divisions over the divorce.[6] In the case of John Heywood's *The Play of the Weather*, the use of drama as a counter-representation appears to be deliberate and undeniable. A member of Thomas More's circle, Heywood remained a staunch Catholic who, in the 1540s, was accused of implication in a plot against Archbishop Cranmer. Though its date remains uncertain, the play has been tentatively dated to 1529–33 and read as an intervention in the debate on anticlericalism in the Reformation Parliament, which Henry and his ministers hoped to use to pressure the pope. By 1533, when it was printed, the play clearly condemned the king's assault on the church, his enhancement of his powers and his sheltering of his own ambitions for aggrandizement behind the veil of parliament's request that he assume the supremacy. As Warner argues, Heywood not only offers a different account of Henry's motives and actions, but the play mocks the king's representation as one who acts only after taking counsel.[7] What might once have been innocent or gentle advice had become what reads as satire. And that even loyal contemporaries were quick to read plays in this way is evidenced by no less an authority than Edward Hall himself. The chronicler describing a 'disguising' performed at Gray's Inn at Christmas 1526 but written twenty years earlier notes:

The effect of the play was that Lord Governance was ruled by dissipation and negligence, by whose misgovernance and evil order, Lady Public Weal was put from governance: which caused Rumour Populi, Inward Grudge and disdain of wanton sovereignty to rise with a great multitude.[8]

The morality play was praised by most, 'saving of the cardinal [Wolsey] who imagined that the play had been devised of him' and who claimed too that 'the king was highly displeased with it'.[9] If a disguising performed within the Inns of Court could so easily arouse the ire of king and minister at what they read as criticism, we might consider more than we have what other readers of Henrician drama made of a variety of plays in the changing circumstances and dramas of state of the 1530s and '40s.

Hall's reference to 'Rumour Populi', however, directs us to that wider arena in which the king performed: the theatre of public opinion. Rumour was not, of course, a new phenomenon of the early modern age. But, as the work of Adam Fox and others has demonstrated, print infiltrated and fostered oral culture, rendering published texts swiftly the hot gossip of parish, inn and alehouse, which was recycled as (sometimes printed) ballad and verse.[10] Hall is again an interesting witness who frequently refers to 'rumour' and 'fame' as disseminating and influencing views of Henry and his government. In the late spring of 1529, for example, a 'rumour sprang so much' that Henry was advised that his marriage was illegitimate; in 1530 the 'foolish communication of people' began to spread the news that it was Anne Boleyn who 'enticed' the king from his wife.[11] In 1532, when Thomas Abell preached and wrote a book affirming the royal marriage, news of it spread quickly and 'caused many simple men to believe his opinion'.[12] Though on all occasions Hall is at pains to support the king's position, he offers plentiful testimony that rumour often presented Henry quite unfavourably and fuelled dissent and opposition. When war was declared in 1527, 'the common people much lamented that war should arise between the king and emperor' whose dominions had supplied them with grain, and the rumour spread that more grain-ships to relieve the starving had been stayed by Henry's orders.[13] 'Common rumour' condemned the arrival of Cardinal Campegius to, as it was believed, arrange the king's divorce (which was 'of the common people abhorred'); and Anne Boleyn was pilloried in tavern talk as well as popular ballads and squibs.[14] Even the determinations of the universities, printed and circulated to support the king's case, could not, according to Hall, 'satisfy their wilful minds'.[15] Rumour, and what Elyot listed as its accompanying vices – detraction and calumny – were the basis of alternative and unflattering representations of the king which, as a proclamation of October 1536 worded it, could 'alienate the true and loyal heart of our people' and even 'stir up division, strife, commotion, contention and sedition'.[16]

As Hall observed, rumours were often stirred by 'divers preachings in the realm', by prophets and visionaries who, increasingly from the 1530s, communicated very different messages to those of government polemic.[17] Prophets, timeless witnesses to the freedom of the spirit to conjure its own world, were, of course, not new to the early Tudor age. Yet, once again, with the new publicity of print and amid the fevered debates of the Reformation, prophecy became a more public discourse and a prevalent form of political protest. The historian of Henrician prophecy, Sharon Jansen, documents those such as William Neville who foretold from his reading of other prophecies that Henry would not reign 'the full xxiiii year' and those like Mistress Amadus, possibly the wife of the Keeper of the King's Jewels, who proclaimed that 'the king's grace . . . is cursed with God's own mouth' and would be banished.[18] Interestingly, at the height of the northern rebellion in 1536, there appear to have been several prophecies of Henry's death – which Cromwell and his agents took seriously; they punished the perpetrators severely, especially when they were known to have spread abroad their prognostications.[19] For whilst prophecy might be 'a kind of desperate attack against authority', its broad circulation to ordinary men and women could make it a dangerous force undermining the king and government.[20] Prophecies often drew on traditional and familiar texts, legends and beliefs as did, for example, 'The Prophecies of Rhymer, Bede and Merlin' which invoked St George and Thomas of Erceldoune as well as Bede and Merlin.[21] As Jansen argues, 'the prophecy worked by using methods that had been valid for centuries and by relying on the authority of men traditionally regarded as prophets'.[22] But in predicting the coming of a new king who would return England to Rome, it turned tradition into revolution.[23] Similarly, the mid-fifteenth-century prophecy known as 'the cock of the north', was recirculated in the 1530s with Henry now identified as the accursed mole from which the realm needed to be saved. So much concern did this excite in official circles that counter-interpretations were published demonstrating how the king could not be the mole in the prophecy.[24]

As well as many examinations pursued by nervous government agents of those who spread or read prophecies, there is other evidence of their popularity and influence.[25] In some cases the medium of either print or manuscript offers clues to the intended audience: 'The Sayings of the Prophets', for instance, was copied on to sheets folded for the pocket, probably to be read and shared along the highways of the realm.[26] The writing and reading of prophecy could also appropriate the form of a popular game like dice to predict the fall of the prince and rise of the people.[27] Whatever the form in which they were communicated and distributed, the records of the government reveal large numbers of ordinary men and women, 'those who were more commonly voiceless', who found in prophecy a voice and mode of articulating protest.[28] The importance of prophecy is apparent also in the government's response. Though local courts were instructed to investigate such 'tale tellers', the regime itself deployed prophecy as an instrument of representation. The printer Thomas Gibson, who was part of Cromwell's circle, assembled a collection of prophecies 'that sheweth of a king that shall win the holy cross' and government propagandists, such as Morison, interpreted prophecy to reveal the destiny of England as tied to an assault on papal tyranny.[29] But for all these efforts, prophecy remained too dangerous when the trances of Elizabeth Barton could be used by others for 'false, malicious and traitorous intents' before an audience of 'two thousand persons', not to mention the larger audience of print.[30] Accordingly in 1542, an Act was passed 'touching prophecies' which endeavoured to outlaw the telling of fortunes founded on 'names, arms [and] badges'.[31] The statute, which we should study as part of the legislation enacted to enforce the Reformation, ordered that 'if any person or persons print or write, or else speak, sing or declare to any other person of the king or of any other person . . . upon occasion of any arms, fields, beasts, fowls or other such like things . . . or by reasons of letters of the name of the king . . . to the intent to set further such prophecies', they should be subject to the penalties of felony – that is death and forfeiture.

Though the penalty was draconian, the statute all but acknowledges the impossibility of its endeavour: the regulation not just of oral culture but of interpretation. Prophecy threatened royal policy and programmes and under-mined the royal image and official representations. In the 1530s prophecy became counter-representation, 'its poetry . . . a persuasive popular discourse that challenged the official language of proclamation and statute'.[32]

The historian of Henrician representation is faced with the questions that we shall need to ask of each reign: how successful was it, to what extent was the 'royal image' under Henry's personal control and how far did others undermine the image that Henry and his advisers went to such pains to construct and reconstruct over the course of his reign? Like many of the most interesting historical questions, this is, in large measure, an intractable problem. Even today with all the mechanisms of information technology and focus groups, govern-ments cannot attain completely reliable information about their popularity or unpopularity; not least, silence is hard to measure. We can be certain that in Henry's reign a new attention was paid to making a public case and to presenting a public image; and that the Reformation rendered the arts of repre-sentation ever more essential to government. And the fact of Henry's survival is a striking testimony to his success that should not be underestimated. Henry ruled for nearly forty years through the threats of dynastic challenge, excommu-nication, foreign invasion, religious opposition and aristocratic and popular rebellion. Through those decades, since he had no independent military force of his own, he evidently convinced most subjects, nobles, gentry and commoners, of the legitimacy of his authority and the rectitude of his courses. He led his people to tolerate a break from Rome, divorce from a popular queen, religious uncertainty and liturgical change, foreign wars and the assumption of new powers over church and state. Henry defeated opposition and rebellion by a combination of ruthless force against a few and a fostering of loyalty in most; even the Pilgrims of Grace retained a perception of him as a pious and merciful king; it was not least their faith in him that enabled Henry to crush them.

Though by no means universally so, Henry was a popular king who enhanced the power of the crown as the symbol of the nation. As he divided opinion in his lifetime, so he continued to do after his death. But Henry VIII remained throughout English history a figure, indeed today we would say a brand, whom the champions of various causes felt the need to appropriate or denigrate. Whatever the view of him, Henry remained always in view – painted on the canvases of history, memory and myth.

A *Lamentation of the Death of the Most Victorious Prince Henry the Eight* was published immediately on the king's death. 'Such is the losse,' the anonymous author began, 'that a publycke weale hath' and went on to depict the realm as left now like a child without a father.[33] Henry, the *Lamentation* continues, had been a king of 'martial prowes and civile policie'. He had overcome the superstition and 'devilish doctrine' of the papacy, to advance the truth, had provided livings and built colleges. Despite his opponents and assailants, the Lord had protected him. The author, however, recognized that the multitude would be hard to govern and that the realm was sharply divided. Urging all to live in obedience to the noble Edward, as they had to his father, the verse pleaded almost in Henry's words to his last parliament:

Set contencion apart as a thyng vayne
That you may embrace concord and unitie[34]

Indeed, published with privilege, the *Lamentation* may have been an official panegyric as well as exhortation to obedience. The divisions it acknowledged were starkly focused on Henry himself in another memoir written by an Englishman and published in Italy soon after his death: William Thomas's *The Pilgrim: A Dialogue of the Life and Action of King Henry VIII*. Thomas's choice of a dialogue enabled an airing of the very different perceptions of Henry VIII that were the legacy of his reign and representation. In what is allegedly a report of a conversation in Bologna, Thomas reports the charges levelled against Henry by the Italians who accused him of tyranny and cruelty. Cataloguing his faults, the spokesman listed Henry's abuse of Catherine of Aragon, his cruel treatment of More and Fisher, his plunder of the church and overthrow of the monasteries, his deceit in not honouring the pardon offered to the Pilgrims, his illegal conquest of Ireland, his indefensible wars in Europe and his unjust execution of Norfolk and others. Thomas's other speaker undertook to answer all such charges in great detail.[35] What is of most interest for our purposes is that he answered them in terms and language close to that of Henry's own arguments and declarations. He based his defence of the dissolutions on the reports of the investigators into the monasteries; and in his defence of the break from Rome he 'repeats the most important arguments Henry VIII and his propaganda apparatus employed'.[36] In great detail he rehearsed the evidence of Anne Boleyn and Catherine Howard's adultery and treason to demonstrate the justice of Henry's actions. Henry, the *Dialogue* concluded, was not a cruel Nero but 'one of the goodliest men that lived in his time'.[37] Thomas, a future secretary to the Privy Council of Edward VI, had left England in 1544 on account of his strong Protestant convictions. His *Dialogue* not only ventriloquizes the very different perceptions of Henry that were held in England as well as on the continent, but also suggests how rapidly Protestants would seek to appropriate him as their monarch.

The ensuing reigns of a minor and a woman married to a foreign prince served only to increase in the nation's memory the standing and popularity of good King Hal. At Queen Elizabeth's coronation, a bystander called out from the crowd: 'Remember old King Henry VIII.'[38] Poets appealed to the queen to emulate her father, than whom 'no greater king ever ruled in our shores'.[39] For Shakespeare, Henry fulfilled and embodied the providential destiny of the Tudor dynasty and the nation as a king of majesty and splendour.[40] During Elizabeth's reign and that of her successor, Thomas Deloney and Thomas Nashe set their novels, *Jack of Newbury* and *The Unfortunate Traveller*, in the good old days of Henry's reign; and in 1613 Samuel Rowley's *When You See Me You Know Me* brought on to the popular stage a Henry who was a roisterer and adventurer – one of the boys, as well as king. That depiction of a popular, indeed populist, Henry VIII had a long life throughout the seventeenth century. From the 1670s and 1680s, for example, *The History of the King and the Cobbler*, a romance describing Henry's intimate friendship with a shoemaker, became something of a bestseller with over twenty-five editions.[41] The Henry who, in this work, against the advice of Wolsey, became an intimate and admirer of the common man established the myth of bluff King Hal.

If the place of Henry VIII in the politics of early modern popular literature, myth and memory is worthy of further investigation, the shifting representations and deployments of the images of the king in a variety of overtly political texts still await a full study.[42] For the polemicist of the Reformation, John Foxe, Henry had to be turned into the staunch Protestant whom the reformers required him to be; it was Gardiner rather than the king who became the scapegoat blamed for the persecutions of the godly.[43] For critics of absolutism, such as Walter Ralegh, Henry served as a warning against monarchical tyranny: 'If all the pictures and patterns of a merciless prince were lost in the world,' Ralegh wrote, 'they might all again be painted to the life' in King Henry VIII.[44] Richard Perrinchief, the Royalist author of a *Conference . . . Between the Ghost of Henry VIII and Charles the First* used the figure of Henry as a foil against which to point up the piety and virtues of Charles I who, unlike his Tudor predecessor, never committed adultery, engaged in acts of pillage and cruelty, nor exercised arbitrary power.[45]

Interestingly, Perrinchief dwells on a piece of advice that the ghost of Henry gave to the spectre of Charles: 'Could you,' it asked, 'by no printed papers insinuate into the minds of your subjects how much you stood devoted to their safety and prosperity?' The passage continues: 'When I was resolved to use my arbitrary power, that I might appear unto the world to undertake nothing by force, I caused books to be dictated according to my own pleasure . . . as if they came from the monks themselves'.[46] Perrinchief explicitly contrasts Henry's dissimulation with Charles's sincerity and implicitly the Tudor's artful representation with the Stuart's failure to argue his case.

If Perrinchief paid attention to verbal propaganda, it was the image of Henry and the spectacle of his reign that were the focus of Shakespeare's play. As Bill Readings writes, 'a concern with spectacle and display distinguishes *Henry VIII* from all Shakespeare's other history plays; and the play itself proceeds via visual tableaux rather than strict historical sequence'.[47] With its emphasis on masque, procession and public rituals, the play presents political power as 'an order that is given to the eye'. It is no accident that Shakespeare chose Henry VIII for his dramatic meditation on 'the acute visibility of political power in the Renaissance'. Just as he had taken in new directions the arts of spin, so Henry was – and was perceived to be – the architect of a new spectacular politics. In Henry VIII as in *Henry VIII* 'political power is a matter of vision . . . of representability' and 'nothing but representability'.[48]

As is so often the case, Shakespeare intuited what an unfolding history has since explored. Henry VIII has been remembered and re-presented largely because his own representation was so powerful, as well as an instrument of his power. Though he bequeathed a legacy of divided opinions, the figure, the person and the kingship of Henry VIII have been etched into the nation's imagination, more than any other ruler. When Charles Laughton played Henry VIII in Alexander Korda's 1933 film *The Private Life of Henry VIII*, the actor posed in a manner that replicated Holbein's famous portrait and was immediately a Henry for the twentieth century.[49] There may be more we can appreciate about the memory and image of Henry from Korda's film. As Greg Walker has demonstrated in a rich new study, Henry was used at a critical moment in European power politics and domestic tensions to project an image of Englishness – because he had made himself in his own age the figurehead of an emerging national sentiment which he had fostered in his campaign against Rome. But, as the title indicates, Korda's film focuses on the private life, on the man as well as the king. Walker writes suggestively about the film's relation to contemporary changing gender politics, but we need to ponder further the portrayal of facets of Henry's character and intimate relationships. Korda's Henry is presented as both majestic and ordinary – 'just like you and me'.[50] The king expresses his readiness to swap his majesty for the place of 'a groom who sleeps above the stable with a wife who loves him'. [51] And the erotic *frisson* of the film derives from this ambiguity and the voyeuristic insight into the private part of public life. Korda not only focuses on Henry's desirable body, he films scenes in which the camera enters into the king's bedchamber where servant girls gossip about his sex life, slide their hands down the sheets and imagine his penis – 'what he looks like in bed'. Such characterizations and titillations are, of course, Korda's creation. But I would suggest that they worked so effectively because they corresponded with the audience's imaginings of Henry and the king's own self-presentation.[52] In Korda's film, cinematic representation drew on Henrician self-presentation: that of a ruler who novelly exposed himself to, and eroticized his relationship with, his subjects who to this day remain fascinated with the man as much as the monarch, with the relationship, in his life and reign, between sex and power.

Academic historians continue to debate the measure of Henry's personal control, the influence of ministers and factions, the place of conscience or *realpolitik* in his policy, his arbitrary exercise of rule, and the nature of his personal faith. But, as Korda's film so obviously demonstrates, Henry VIII can hardly be imagined except in terms of the representations that he, and others, constructed and authorized. Over four hundred and fifty years after his death, Henry remains a powerful presence today; in the words of one panegyrist, he still reigns in 'the court of memory'.[53]

PART IV

REPRESENTING GODLY KINGSHIP

CHAPTER 7

REPRESENTATIONS OF EDWARD VI

If by his birth Prince Edward fulfilled all the hopes of Henry VIII for the Tudor dynasty, he was also, on his succession, a focus of anxiety and fear. Edward was male, but a minor; and the history of minority rule in England had not been a happy one – the last being the victims of a violent coup and murder. Many feared that the reign of a minor might see the revival of noble factions, even civil war; in 1547 a heretic England was especially vulnerable to a crusade by the Catholic rulers of Europe; and the Scots were ready to seize an opportunity to avenge their crushing defeat at Solway Moss in 1542.

The young Edward VI presented, too, a problem for the image of Tudor monarchy. While he had done much to strengthen (as well as weaken) the crown – by institutional reform, the acquisition of land, magnificent foreign appearances and the assumption of the Supreme Headship – Henry's authority had very much rested on his person. He began his reign as a young, athletic man of exceptional martial prowess and accomplishment, as married and imminently expected to produce an heir. Even as he aged, the memory of the intrepid youngster remained to add strength to the formidable will that Henry had displayed. Whatever the role of his ministers, much that was effected in his reign – the divorces, the rejection of the papacy and assumption of supremacy, the campaigns abroad and the shifting fortunes and fates of families and individuals at home – were Henry's decisions and actions: and they were seen to be his. Henry VIII, perhaps more than any other ruler, appeared to personify personal monarchy – adult, male, strong, brave, decisive, authoritarian.

From the time of the birth of Edward in 1537, it must have become apparent that he would probably succeed as a minor. It may well be for this reason, as well as the emerging fashion for humanist education, that Edward was embarked on a rigorous programme of study, under the direction of Richard Cox and Sir John Cheke, Regius Professor of Greek at Cambridge.[1] If,

PARVVLE PATRISSA, PATRIÆ VIRTVTIS ET HÆRES
ESTO, NIHIL MAIVS MAXIMVS ORBIS HABET.
GNATVM VIX POSSVNT COELVM ET NATVRA DEDISSE,
HVIVS QVEM PATRIS, VICTVS HONORET HONOS.
ÆQVATO TANTVM, TANTI TV FACTA PARENTIS,
VOTA HOMINVM, VIX QVO PROGREDIANTVR, HABENT
VINCITO, VICISTI, QVOT REGES PRISCVS ADORAT
ORBIS, NEC TE QVI VINCERE POSSIT, ERIT.

14 Edward, Prince of Wales.

as W.K. Jordan writes, 'Few monarchs . . . have been as well equipped for their task as was Edward VI', it was not least because he had to be equipped quickly.[2] Indeed, as a leading authority on Holbein has observed, the earliest portrait of the prince is one in which 'the maturity of the royal baby has quite naturally been overstated'.[3] The Holbein of Edward aged two or three (now in the National Gallery in Washington) depicts the prince with none of the reticence or uncertainty of infancy. Dressed like his father, the little boy has raised his right hand as if to declaim, while the rattle in his left appears almost like a small sceptre. The verse accompanying the painting by Thomas Cromwell's

15 Edward VI.

spin doctor, Richard Morison, presents Edward as the heir to his father's virtue, who will emulate all his accomplishments of honour. Profile portraits of the prince, aged six, like that in the Metropolitan Museum in New York, also reveal a confident, adult figure, clad in the ermine of the regality he is to assume.[4] A portrait of Edward in the Royal Collection, datable to the last year of Henry's life, depicts Edward beside a column – a symbol of authority – in the pose of his father, with his legs slightly apart and his right hand on a dagger, wearing a jewel with Prince of Wales feathers, ready to assume the mantle of kingship, as well as manhood.[5] It may even have been just a year

16 Edward VI.

before Henry's death that a version of Holbein's Privy Chamber mural added the figure of Edward to the Tudor family first painted a decade before.[6] Such a suggestion gains in probability when we recall the portrait of the family of Henry VIII in which Edward is figured, at his father's right side, beneath a canopy of state, with his left hand on the hilt of his sword.[7] While Karen Hearn rightly argues that the portraits of Edward as prince bear witness to 'intense contemporary interest in the male heir to the throne', we might add that they insistently proclaim his legitimate succession; and, masking his childhood, his readiness to assume his father's throne.[8]

As with so much of Tudor royal representation, there was a fundamental ambiguity in the representation of Edward, when he succeeded as king on 3 January 1547. On the one hand, as a boy of less than ten, he could not exercise rule, as was recognized in Henry's will which provided for the prince's uncle, Edward Seymour, to be Protector. On the other, after his proclamation and escort by the nobility from Enfield to the Tower, where he was sat in state to await his coronation, Edward *was* king.[9] Edward's biographer unwittingly but nicely captures the ambiguity, describing the 'Edwardian interim' as a period 'free of the immense personal authority of the crown', yet writing of royal proclamations as 'weighted with the full authority of the king in Council'.[10] The representations of Edward VI, after or before his succession, endeavoured to limit, if not resolve, that contradiction: to present the person and personal body of the boy Edward not as infant or in tutelage but as the site of authority and regality. As Edward grew older, across the crucial teenage years of his brief reign, the disjuncture between the image and the realities of the exercise of power was diminished. Unquestionably the last two years of his reign saw Edward, in his biographer's words, 'emerging into regal competence'.[11] But the process of presenting Edward as ready for rule and ruling is evident from the beginning. And, in this sense, it was a process in which the young king himself played a, perhaps the, key role.

I Writing Regal Authority

Edward clearly threw himself into his studies with enthusiasm. Martin Bucer, the Strasbourg preacher in England from the spring of 1549, described the prince as 'learned to a miracle'. He is, Bucer continued, 'well acquainted with Latin and has a fair knowledge of Greek. He speaks Italian and is learning French. He is now studying moral philosophy from Cicero and Aristotle, but no study delights him more than that of the Holy Scriptures.'[12] Edward, in other words, followed the ideal course for the education in classical and religious learning that the new humanism and Protestantism outlined as the training for a godly ruler. What was less well known until recently was that

Edward did not neglect physical activities and martial sports.[13] Although he was too young to follow his father in the jousts, the prince took 'great delight . . . in representations of battles, skirmishes, assaults and all kinds of military exercises'.[14] He enjoyed challenges, and, it seems, later participated in them.[15] From childhood he rode and shot and evidently showed great interest in fortifications. Later, though he 'never neglected his studies', according to the Venetian ambassador, he loved exercise, 'tilting, managing horses . . . drawing the long bow, playing rackets, hunting and so forth indefatigably'.[16] Edward's programme of education was, of course, managed by others – his Protector Somerset and the Duke of Northumberland, as well as tutors. But what is quite apparent is Edward's own eagerness to equip himself to rule – and to be seen to be ready for rule. In particular, his writings bear testimony to his self-education and increasing involvement in public business and the use to which he put his training in debate and textual studies in weighing positions and affairs of state.

Edward's writings, I wish to argue, were, far more than a mere school exercise, a principal agent of his claim to rule and an essential act of self-representation. Even before his succession, Edward had in correspondence, not least with his stepmother, laid out his own values and not hesitated to admonish and instruct.[17] To his father and to Archbishop Cranmer, he proclaimed his full understanding of the importance of study and humility; letters, he informed his stepmother, foster good conduct.[18] In a letter to Queen Catherine (Parr) of May 1546, thanking her for her love for him and his sister, Edward did not hesitate to remind his stepmother that 'the only real love is the love of God' and exhorted her to 'preserve . . . my dear sister Mary from all the wiles and enchantments of the evil one, and beseech her to attend no longer to foreign dances and merriments which do not become a Christian princess'.[19] He similarly counselled and admonished his close friend Barnaby Fitzpatrick to remember, while travelling, 'your learning, chiefly reading of the scripture' and 'for women, as far as you may, avoid their company'.[20]

Before he succeeded to the throne, Edward was a prince with a strong sense of values and a propensity to present himself as the embodiment and tutor of these values. And his reading instilled in him personal convictions, as well as commonplaces about kingship which he committed to paper, doubtless to show to his tutors. Glossing Isocrates on the obligations of kings to rule with mildness and clemency, Edward described those attributes as the outstanding virtues of a monarch; by contrast 'feroces reges sunt impii'.[21] And he observed, as self-education and self-representation, that the multitude of men are wont to imitate the behaviour of rulers who thereby had a special obligation to stand as an example of virtue.[22] The tone of these reflections suggests that they were no mere pedagogical exercise: only months after succeeding to the throne, Edward was writing to his uncle urging him to ensure that he sustain equity, justice and true religion; for, as Protector, Somerset represented the king who saw himself to be, and wished to present himself as, protector of these virtues.[23] While a minor and still in tutelage, but an anointed king, Edward deployed his writing to represent his power, to construct and publish his identity and to attain, and validate his claim to, rule.[24]

Edward VI's 'Chronicle' is an extraordinary document that has not received the close attention that it deserves.[25] Although the document, a hybrid form of personal journal and political memoir, may have been started as a pedagogical exercise, it was evidently from the beginning a text that the young king saw as representing himself and his rule.[26] The neat italic hand, as well as the style, suggest an audience other than the self, and the royal arms indicate that this was seen at the time as a testimonial to be preserved rather than ephemera to be discarded. The chronicle is, as its editor has argued, 'in part private diary . . . and in part considered notes on policy and administration'.[27] What it also suggests is that the process by which the boy under tutelage became the ruler was through writing, observing and recording: that the chronicle presented Edward as a boy fit to reign as king.

The chronicle begins (though of course this must have been an introduction he made later) with Edward's birth and education. The third person – 'was a prince born to King Harry' – modally recognizes the baby's and infant's lack of agency.[28] At six, it continues within a few lines, he was brought up 'in learning of tongues, of the Scriptures, of philosophy, and all liberal sciences'. These accomplishments, it is implied, led to Edward's creation as Prince of Wales; but no sooner had this elevation taken place than Henry died, to 'great lamentation and weeping', and 'suddenly he [Edward] [was] proclaimed king'.[29] For much of the early years of his reign, the passive voice continues as events are chronicled: 'Gardiner, Bishop of Winchester was . . . committed'; 'a parliament was called'.[30] But by the time of the third year of the reign, the first person pronoun, and the possessive personal pronoun, begin to be used in ways that disclose Edward's growing sense of himself and his authority. 'Because,' he writes, with typically chilling lack of emotion, 'there was a rumour that I was dead, I passed through London.'[31] By the summer of 1550, Edward is recording that 'the books of my proceedings was sent to the Bishop of Winchester'.[32] That Edward was acquiring a full appreciation of his kingly authority is suggested by one of the few amended entries made to the chronicle in March 1551. After some disputes over her right to practise her Catholic faith, Mary was called before the Council and the king. The report begins with a passive but swiftly moves to a boldly reiterated personal pronoun: 'She was called with my Council into a chamber where was declared how long I had suffered her mass ["against my will" crossed out] in hope of her reconciliation and how now, being no hope, which I perceived by her letters, except I saw some short amendment I could not bear it.'[33]

The entry evidences not only Edward's personal concern and direction in this matter, fully congruent with positions he took in other writings; it also manifests his new concern that nothing be recorded as having happened 'against my will'. Edward's clemency, not his opposition to it, was proclaimed, and his insistence now on compliance was asserted. A few lines later he adds to the report of an injunction to the princess to obey as a subject that she act 'not as a king to rule'.[34] There was one king and, by 1551, Edward was concerned that everyone, including his sister, recognized and acknowledged it; and the chronicle itself asserted it. After 1551, the chronicle indicates Edward's growing involvement in public affairs – which, as we shall see, is confirmed by his other writings – and his assumption of some command. While the entry for 22 January 1552 – 'the duke of Somerset had his head cut off' – is passive as well as chillingly clipped, that may well be due to Edward's desire to distance himself emotionally from a decision which had been taken 'almost certainly with the king's full knowledge and consent'.[35] The efforts made by Northumberland and others to divert the king's mind from the impending death of his uncle support rather than undermine the impression that Edward had been complicit in the judgment – and might change his mind and exercise his royal mercy.[36] Edward had been attending Council meetings since the previous summer, receiving envoys and entertaining in state.[37] In negotiations with the German princes, he had insisted that 'I would have the matter of religion made more plain'; and he closely examined in his study, as he points out, the articles of a proposed league with them.[38] On 28 March 1552, the entry boldly presents the king exercising that traditional prerogative of kings – control of foreign affairs: 'I did deny,' Edward writes, 'the request to enter into war, as appeareth by the copy of my answer in the study.'[39]

If this entry announces both Edward's new authority and its relation to the construction and representation of this authority in writings, it was rapidly and tragically followed by a personal record that rapidly brought the chronicle back to the frailty of the royal body personal. On 2 April, Edward notes 'I fell sick of the measles and the smallpox.'[40] Two weeks later the young king was too ill to preside over the dissolution of the parliament.[41] Yet Edward continued to keep abreast of foreign affairs, noted the reform of the Order of the Garter (along lines that he had proposed), and in the summer went on a magnificent progress.[42] But in the autumn the sickness returned and with it the journal comes to an end, at the end of November. Edward died on 6 July 1553. While sickness must remain the most likely explanation for the termination of the chronicle, we should not discount another possibility: that it had served its purpose. Edward's chronicle had been part of the process of a training for rule, and a document of his claim to rule: by the time of his illness he was unquestionably ruling. As he points out, even though he was too ill to attend the parliament, 'I signed a bill containing the names of the acts which I would have pass, which bill was read in the house'.[43] It was Edward's will that was now the command that effected action. Though several of the events of 1552 – financial disbursements, promotions to office and rank, inspections of fortifications – were described in the passive voice, it was Edward himself who 'received advertisement' of foreign developments abroad and Edward himself to whom all now made account.[44] Did the termination of the chronicle announce a shift from ruling to acting – to being closely involved in the business of rule? Though it might have, had time permitted, in the end the answer to that question must be no. Edward's brief exercise of rule seems to have ended more or less when his journal ends, and this underlines the symbiosis of governing and ruling, rule and representation of rule in his brief life.

Towards the end of his journal, Edward notes discussions about England joining with the emperor in a crusade against the Turks. 'The reasonings,' he reminded himself, 'be in my desk.'[45] Edward did not only record events and observations in his chronicle and weigh reasons filed in his desk, he wrote papers for himself and his Council which evaluated arguments, suggested courses and mandated reforms. In this series of position papers, it has been suggested, Edward was 'seeking to lay down the lines of policy for his reign, quite independently and often in decided contrast to that of the Duke of Northumberland and the majority of the Privy Council'.[46] Once again, as a young prince, it was through writing that Edward found a mode of self-expression and self-assertion, ensuring that his views, like his take on events, claimed a record and response.

The earliest of Edward's 'state papers and political essays', as the editor of the king's literary remains describes them, is datable to April 1551, about the time when changes in the style and content of the chronicle indicate his growing personal involvement in affairs. Though the manuscript is untidy and probably unfinished, the minor alterations suggest that this memorandum was intended for broader than personal use, as does the declamatory tone.[47] In this untitled paper, Edward posits a view of church and state and a vision of reforms that owed much to the commonwealthsmen of the 1530s and '40s who had influenced the prince's education.[48] Even more than his chronicle, it advertised the values and programmes that Edward wished to pursue; and it is as self-proclamation, one perhaps even directed beyond the narrow confines of the ruling clique, that it should be read. Edward's outline of the ecclesiastical part of government clearly affirmed his Protestant commitment as Supreme Head to the teaching of the word, to the new Prayer Book, and to moral discipline. 'The temporal regiment,' he writes rehearsing a familiar conceit, 'consists in well ordering, enriching and defending the whole body politic of the commonwealth and every part of the whole . . .'.[49] Edward employed the familiar trope of the body politic to expand in detail the role of each part or social group and to emphasize the need for proportion and for consideration of the poor – unlike in France where, he observed, 'the peasantry is of no value'.[50] In a pithy formulation Edward reiterated the ideal of the Tudor commonweal and the foundation of his own rule:

> The gentleman ought to labour in service in his country . . . the artificer ought to labour in his work, the husbandman in tilling the ground . . . but the vagabonds ought clearly to be banished as is the superfluous humour in the body . . .. This is the true ordering of the state of a well-fashioned commonwealth: that every part do obey one head, one governor, one law, as all parts of the body obey the head . . ..[51]

'This is most of all to be had in a commonweal well ordered,' he repeats, 'that the laws and ordinance be well executed, duly obeyed and ministered without corruption.'[52]

Edward reiterated the ideal, not least because his own act of utterance adds royal authority to a familiar theme. But as a representation of authority, as well as intervention in government, the second half of the paper is more interesting still. Having 'seen how things ought to be', Edward shifts gear to describe how they are in reality – and describes a very different world in which gentlemen rack rents high, merchants and tradesmen cozen, and none rest content with their allotted place but aspire to 'call themselves gentlemen'.[53] The paper presents the king as the means to reform, to make the commonwealth ideal real, and in the process to re-establish that social order on which government depended. The royal medicines are good education, good laws, good examples and encouragement as well as punishment. Displaying his own good education, Edward cites Horace on the vital importance of upbringing.[54] Turning to laws, Edward reminded readers (and readers he obviously foresaw) that 'I have showed my opinion heretofore what statutes I think most necessary to be enacted this session', but added a wish that legislation be simplified and modified to make it more effective.[55] In fine, the paper urges that the nobles attend to their duties in seeing these statutes executed, as the king has in seeing them passed. 'No man,' he concludes, 'that is in fault himself can punish another.'[56] The king had given the lead and example, as rulers were to do, and it was now for magistrates to imitate that example in their own counties. In his first policy paper, Edward took a traditional conceit but reconstituted it in language and time, rather different from his father's, and very much as his own. The structure of this paper (it is common to many) – the crisp summary of the ideal, the problem, and the solutions – connects the king's claim to be the ruler, the reason of the commonweal, to his personal attainment as a scholar and to his rhetorical skills of exposition. This was no exercise for 'private use', nor merely a paper for discussion, but a manifesto of kingship and a proclamation that England already had an ideal king.[57]

The second paper we shall consider is a memorandum that Edward prepared for a Privy Council meeting on 9 March 1552, on reasons for establishing a mart in England. Our interest here is not principally in the arguments of the paper but in its function as another representation of the young king – a statement of his full participation in the business of a council, to which he had been admitted only a few months before, and in the business of kingship.[58] The holograph, with minor additions and alterations to syntax, bears all the marks of a paper to be presented, rather than delivered orally. Once again it is notable for its clarity of logic and organization. Edward lists and numbers (to ease assimilation and debate) the reasons why it is 'now most necessary to have a mart in England'; the causes why the time was most commodious to establish one (with enumerated subheadings); the means to institute a mart at Southampton (also with subheadings); the 'discommodities', or arguments against – with a point by point rebuttal; and a list of 'the remedies and answers'.[59] As the editor of Edward VI's papers has argued, this memo provided an 'elaborate and detailed blueprint' for an English mart at Southampton which might replace an Antwerp now beset by European war as an entrepot for trade.[60] Though he may have miscalculated England's readiness to succeed to this position, Edward's analysis is intelligent and well informed. And that may have been its most important function: to display the young king's knowledge of European, as well as English, affairs; and to take a lead in Council as a proposer of policy, not only as a passive auditor. Other, less finished, papers support that suggestion: that in the second half of 1551 and 1552 Edward wished to lead, and – as importantly – to be recognized as a leader of the discussion of affairs and the making of policy.

His next surviving document is brief and unfinished; but, rather than the 'jottings' described by Jordan, the complete sentences suggest that this was intended, in fuller form, for presentation.[61] Edward presents basic tables of the crown and government's financial position in the summer of 1552 – perhaps again for a Council meeting on the desperate state of England's credit. The brief document is notable for the use of personal pronouns and a confident, even assertive, tone. Edward writes, as if fully out of protectorship, of 'my debts owing me', 'the treasure I have' and is clear that his recommendations ('I think this last') will be effective ('do much good') and should be followed.[62] Argument is still supported by reason – the need, for example to procure lead and bullion – but the reader of this text hears an Edward who expected to be heard because he was king and because the commonweal and church (including 'church plate superfluous') were in his charge.

Taking charge as king meant that Edward had personally to direct meetings of the Privy Council, and two papers in his hand provide full evidence of how the king, in the closing months of his reign, moved to assume that authority. Endorsed by William Cecil as 'the king's majesty's memorial, 13 October 1552', a paper headed 'A Summary of matters to be included' was evidently written as a memorandum to be laid before the Council.[63] Indeed, it set an agenda for discussion and courses of action to deal with fiscal problems, religious issues and arrangements for the defence of the realm. Again, the paper is clearly set out with each section ('for religion') containing proposals numbered – and carefully renumbered when one is deleted. Interestingly, in a paper that asserts the king's views, the alterations erase the personal pronoun – 'my money' becomes simply 'money', 'my defence' 'defence' and so on. Possibly as in effect now a ruling king, Edward felt no need to assert his person; at fifteen his person and office, his private and public bodies, had become one. Other corrections – the numbers of the men to be discharged in Ireland – reveal Edward's usual care to get things right and again, together with the full sentences, indicate that this was a public document, not merely notes for the king's own use.[64] But the style of this memorandum is also different: Edward simply lists what he wants discussed and dealt with and there is no, not even brief, argument or justification for the proposals: 'for religion: 1. a catechism to be set forth to be taught in all grammar schools' . . . 8. The making of more homilies'.[65] Moreover, Edward commands particular actions, as well as general injunctions: '7. The placing of Harley into the bishopric of Hereford'.[66] And he returns to what had once been a suggestion now as one of a list of straightforward desiderata or commands: 'the device of two marts, one at Hull, another at [South]ampton'.[67] Edward's memo ranged across all the key areas of government and indicates a long-term vision, as well as a tackling of the immediate problems. Doubtless he was briefed. But in his October proposals, Edward sought to stamp his personal authority as a policy-maker, with now not only clear views on the duties and rights of kings, but a detailed blueprint for the church and commonweal.

Three months later, a final memorandum in Edward's hand which we can date with certainty fully manifests that, despite the termination of his chronicle in November 1552, the king's illness had not yet removed him from affairs. In this case, rather than discussion of, or instruction for, policy, Edward addressed reform of the central organ of government, the – what he now calls His Majesty's – Privy Council. Pressure of business had led to recent reforms, and Edward himself may well have been influential in advancing them. His chronicle entry for 3 March 1552 gives unusual space to a decision that 'for the better dispatch of things', commissions of the Council would take responsibility to oversee the execution of penal laws, revenues, suits and petitions – perhaps because he had himself been instrumental in it.[68] The paper presented on 15 January 1553, 'Certain Articles Devised and Delivered by the King's Majesty for the Quicker, Better and More Orderly Despatch of Causes by His Majesty's Privy Council' clearly belongs to the history of reform of the central administration.[69] But Edward's tone here suggests more immediate and personal objectives; for, as well as sensible general instructions about determining particular days and times for business (suits were to be considered on Monday mornings and answered on Saturday afternoons, for example), or referring cases to the relevant court and tightening procedures for fiscal warrants, Edward's memorandum was directed at instituting measures to secure greater royal direction and control. Edward required that on Sunday nights the Secretary should deliver to him a schedule of Council business from which he would appoint an order of discussions. Presumably for meetings that he did not attend, he required a report of how they had conducted business, and also of – what the official register of the Council does not include – 'the principal reasons that moved them to conclude on such matters as seem doubtful'.[70] After they had delivered this, the secretaries were to attend on Edward and 'know his pleasure upon such things as they have concluded'.[71] The king imposes not only his preferred methodological style of considering business, requesting that even unfinished discussions be minuted according to 'what point the matter is brought and which have been the principal reasons on each side', but he also stamps his authority on a body which, as he here makes explicit, is advisory to the king.[72] Edward, the king, is here written as the focal point of the Council: when 'it shall please the King's Majesty himself to be at the debating ... the warning shall be given, whereby the more may be at the debating of it'.[73] The boy, who for his greater education in affairs of state had been brought to attend meetings of the Council in the summer of 1551, was now making it clear that he was very much in charge of 'His Majesty's Privy Council'.[74] The repetition of 'King's Majesty', and more generally of the possessive pronoun 'his' ('his court', 'his majesty's laws') underscores his point. That copies of his memorandum survive in state papers domestic underlines the increasing authority which the imperial envoy noted Edward was exercising.[75]

In this case, Edward's memorandum led to actions: Sir William Petre, principal secretary, drew up an abbreviated version of Edward's articles and the proposals were brought to the Council, though given the defective Council minutes for the last years of the reign we know nothing of their implementation.[76] In the end, the outcome of Edward's paper is not our subject. Edward's memo formalized on paper, and so institutionalized, what had been emerging – not least thanks to his writings – for over a year: royal control. The authority he had written was now itself writ.

Indeed, there is some suggestion that Edward's direction, his ambition as well as intention, was extending to matters foreign and martial as well as domestic. As W. K. Jordan rightly describes them, Edward's notes concerning the occupation of Tournai in the reign of Henry VI constitute a 'puzzling treatise' which yields little clue to the king's purpose.[77] Did Edward, as he approached majority, begin to dream of revived English glory abroad and of the service of patriots like Fastolf who advised his monarch against any deal with the French that would compromise England's claim to the throne? Part of the document looks like personal notes, but the full sentences and odd correction of detail point to intended circulation.[78] What we can say is that the notes evidence extensive research into documents of the period of the Duke of Bedford's regency, into details of how money was raised in the duchy of Normandy and the charges of maintaining the fortresses. If these notes do speak to Edward's dreams of future martial glory, it is fitting that they are focused on fiscal and administrative details, careful research and written memoranda. Edward VI was not the last of the kings we shall study who founded his authority on and represented it through his writing. But he was one of the most successful in making his pen the vital instrument of his power.

Two other documents in Edward's hand deserve our attention in a study of how Edward presented his values and ideals as a young king emerging into the full exercise of regal authority. The first, which is undated, but which the editor of Edward's literary remains assigns to the year 1550–1, were various schemes for the reforms of the Garter, the principal chivalric order which Henry VIII had promoted as the equal of the Habsburg Order of the Golden Fleece.[79] Alterations to the Garter ceremonies and statutes had already been effected early in Edward's reign, removing rituals, such as the churchyard processions and the regular mass, not deemed suitable for a Protestant realm.[80] Such reforms were not sufficient for Edward who, if John Foxe's anecdote can be trusted, was sceptical of the whole story of St George.[81] What is unquestionable is that the young king considered the order too popish and was resolved to reconstitute it as a Protestant as well as chivalric order. The opening of the three drafts of the new statutes that he sketched emphasized the Christian foundations of the order established 'that all Christians, might be bound together with the bound of charity' so as to have 'unity and concord' in God's defence.[82] Since its foundation, Edward continues, the Order has been perverted with 'superstitiousness' and 'almost destroyed with bringing in of popery and naughtiness'. To remedy these 'abusions', Edward proposed that the name of St George be excised as idolatrous and the order renamed 'the Order of the Garter or defence of the faith wholly contained in Scripture'.[83] The knights were evidently no longer to wear a George, the figure of the saint on horseback conspicuous in Henry VIII's portraits, but a brooch of a king holding in one hand a sword inscribed 'Justitia' and in the other a book on which was written 'Verbum Dei'.[84] The seal of the Order with the same image on one side was to carry on the reverse the arms of England with the circumscription 'Verbum Domini manet in aeternum'.[85] Knights elected to the Order were, in Edward's proposed reforms, to take an oath to 'refuse the bishop of Rome's authority and fight in your country's cause against him and his pestilent heresies' and to defend Scripture against 'men's traditions'.[86]

Though some of the original chivalric, and charitable, purposes of the Order remained – it was important not least to a minor that the knights 'show friendship unto the sovereign' and defend him – the reforms proposed by Edward would have transformed the Garter.[87] And his commitment to doing so is confirmed by two other drafts, one in English and one in Latin, the latter perhaps intended for the Catholic European princes who were knights and who were to understand that they were members of what was now a Protestant order. In the second English draft, in which he carefully replaces the word sacrament with 'communion', Edward changed his prescriptions for the Garter ornament to a horseman piercing with a sword inscribed 'Protectio' the book ('Verbum Dei') and holding in the other hand a shield of faith ('Fides').[88] If the image here is less quiescent and more martial, it is one of a more militant Protestantism, armed and ready to fight in the cause of God's faith.[89] As Nichols correctly summarized them, the drafts of Edward's reforms of the Garter endeavoured to transform the Order from one of 'personal distinction' and 'chivalric association' to one that might 'promote the religion, learning, and general improvement of the country'.[90] Given that the Garter was a major representation of English overlordship and kingship, Edward was presenting and representing himself in these proposals as the protector of a new, true faith and as the martial ruler of a Protestant commonweal.

The most polemically Protestant of Edward's writings are those which may appear to present the most problems to modern observers. The verses entitled the 'Instruction of King Edward the Sixth concerning the eucharist' posit a fully Protestant interpretation of Christ's spiritual presence in the sacrament and a denial of a corporeal presence: 'Not with our teeth his flesh to teare, / Nor take blood for our drink: / Too great absurditie it were / So grossely for to think.' 'None other Transubstantiation,' the paper concludes, 'I Defend of the Eucharist.'[91] No holograph survives, and for the attribution to Edward we have to rely on Foxe, compiler of the *Acts and Monuments*, or Book of Martyrs, who may have had his own agenda in promoting Edward as the author. But if, as has been suggested, the verses circulated in print with this title in Edward's time, then they were clearly taken as representing the king's position, whether or not they were the product of his hand.[92]

In the case of Edward's treatise against the supremacy of the pope, the problem is of a different nature. The British Library manuscript is unquestionably Edward's autograph, bound and stamped with the royal arms, but the date, 14 March 1549, raises questions about the extent to which this was Edward's own work at the age of twelve.[93] The manuscript is in French and may well have been an exercise prepared for Edward's education in that language; it is corrected in another hand, probably that of a tutor. However, his French tutor, John Belmaine or Belmayne, states categorically that Edward himself wrote the book; but even here Belmayne's position, and his own Protestant convictions, might have led him to exaggerate the king's role in the treatise.[94] The treatise clearly owed a debt to others' writings, notably to Ponet's translation of Bernardino Ochino's *A Dialogue of the Unjust Usurped Primacy of the Bishop of Rome*, dedicated to Edward in 1549; but it redeploys rather than simply rehearses Ochino's arguments.[95] What is significant is not only that Edward clearly had some major role in making the text but that he was perceived to have written it and that he dedicated it to his uncle, Protector Somerset, as a statement of his religious views and of his kingship.[96] Edward's purpose, he tells his uncle, is to answer the charges of papists who call those who follow the light of Scripture heretics when they are, in fact, heretics themselves. In the present age, he argues, the devil had perverted England through the agency of his minister, the pope.[97] Edward then continues with the traditional Protestant argument that the keys to heaven which the Catholics claimed as the symbol of authority given to Peter were given to all the apostles, and that, rather than any potentate, only God's gospel and the text of Scripture opened the gate to heaven. Rather than God's lieutenant, the pope was 'in everything opposite to God'.[98] Reasserting the supremacy assumed by his father, Edward insists that God 'by his sovereignty hath placed kings to be his lieutenants over the earth'.[99]

But Edward's purpose and position were not those of Henry. Rather, the conservative measures of Henry's later years Edward described as the diabolic work of Rome: 'during the reign of my late father, the king, when the pope's name was blotted out of our books, he stopped the mouths of Christians with his six articles . . .'.[100] And in an explicit shift of tone from, if not complete break with, the rhetoric of Henry's reign, Edward even embraces the rejection of tradition and history. Against the charge that the Protestants defied the ancients, Edward, with forceful use of the personal pronoun, rebuts: 'I know very well that our religion consists not of old customs or the usage of our fathers but in the Holy Scripture and divine word . . . which is older than the world . . . our religion ought not be governed by our forefathers ['pères' in the French better suggests an explicit, perhaps psychologically revealing, distance between Henry and Edward], for as Ezekiel says *Walk ye not in the statutes of your father for they were polluted.*'[101] The only authority Edward recognized was Christ, and, as his lieutenant, it was his duty, first and foremost, to protect

Christ's word: in the original French 'nous nous devons efforcer que l'evangile soit preschée par tout le monde'.[102]

If Edward's treatise had its origins in an exercise, it is clear that the exercise was no simple pedagogic piece. The text was evidently written to be read by Edward's uncle, the Lord Protector (who is exhorted at the same time as he is flattered as one with a great love for 'sincere religion') and beyond.[103] The corrections, in his tutor's hand, suggest that this was being prepared for revision, and some form of publication – a suggestion strengthened by the binding with royal arms, and the existence of a second copy now in Cambridge.[104] Edward's treatise was intended, I suggest, as a public statement, and as a representation of the young king himself. There can be no better testimony to corroborate that suggestion than the words and metaphor that Belmayne deployed in describing it: 'Tout ainsi qu'un bon Paintre peut representer le visage, regard, contenance et corpulence d'un Prince: ainsi par les ecrits, parolles et actions d'un Prince, on peut facilement entendre quel esprit est en lui et a quoi il est ordonné . . .'.[105]

Like a picture, Edward's treatise, all his writings, represented his learning, character, his soul, his inclinations and values.

'The root concern in all [Edward's] writings,' wrote W.K. Jordan, 'is with the maintenance of the structure of royal power.'[106] Though I would qualify that assessment, to argue that many of the young king's writings were concerned with the *acquisition* of royal power, there can be no question about Jordan's statement when we turn to the *Message Sent by the King's Majesty to Certain of His People Assembled in Devonshire*.[107] In June 1549 an uprising broke out in Devon, at Sampford Courtenay, a village near to the Launceston–Crediton road. Having heard their priest William Harper use the new Prayer Book for the first time on that Sunday, a riotous assembly prevented him from using it again the next day, Whit Monday, and forced him to celebrate the old mass, in full vestments and in Latin. The uprising spread rapidly to Crediton, where the Devonshire rebels joined with rioters from Cornwall. By the end of the month, the rebels were a large and organized band and, having refused to negotiate with Sir Peter Carew unless the old religion were restored, they went on to besiege Exeter with 2,000 men.[108] The government response was, as was commonly the case with Tudor rebellions, a combination of conciliation and offers of clemency with threat, military force and brutal suppression and punishment. It was on 8 July that the government responded with both proclamations against rumours and enclosure and 'The King's Answer'.[109] The document has been the subject of some uncertainty and confusion, but surprisingly little close attention. In the *Calendar of State Papers*, it was attributed to Cranmer, but it now appears that this mistook the 'king's answer' for another response, unquestionably written by the archbishop.[110] Similarly the assertion, made by Tytler and others, that the text was Somerset's answer is corroborated by no holograph copy – none of the copies in state papers is in the Protector's hand.[111] The other larger doubt arises, again, from the fact that Edward was only twelve years old. However, what we have seen of his writings suggests that he would not have been incapable of drafting such a text, and would most likely have seen and approved what was sent out in his name. Though Edward's chronicle does not mention the answer – or *Message* (the king refers to none of his own writings), it contains a full entry on the rebellion in Devon.[112] And the Council, as a postscript to its letter to Russell, described the document as 'the King's Majesty's answer'.[113] As we shall see, the question of whether the young king was, or was not, in control was a matter taken up by the response itself. And, in the spirit of the rebels' insistence on hearing the king's own authority, the *Message* was issued – and probably received – as expressing that.

The *Message* was a skilful rhetorical document which was remarkably moderate in tone. Suggesting that the rebels had been seduced to act against their own interests, it predicted with confidence that most would return to loyalty on hearing the command of their prince – especially a prince who used his authority like a father to admonish, rather than a judge to punish. How, the prince asks, could rebels answer to God who commanded obedience to a king chosen by his ordinance as well as lineage? It was for the king to protect the people and see the laws well administered, Edward insisted, and in terms that underline his preoccupation with his authority and script he protested: 'You use our name in your writings to abuse the same against ourself.'[114] After general injunctions to obedience, the *Message* turns to the fears and rumours which had sparked the uprisings. Those who spread stories that under the new ordinance christenings would take place only on holy days, or that the sacrament was despised as 'common bread' were, Edward explained, papists and traitors who sought only to mislead the people to bring about their destruction.[115] The new service, the *Message* attempted to assure readers, was essentially the old service, but Englished to facilitate understanding.[116] Shifting from reassurance to admonition, the *Message* reminded subjects that the Prayer Book had been revised by the clergy and established by parliament, and that it was therefore right and necessary for subjects to obey.[117] Would any dare stand against the 'law of the whole realm' as well as their ordained king?[118] For those rebels who had requested that any implementation of change should await the king's coming of age, Edward's answer had a definitive retort: 'Be we of less authority for our age?'[119] Was the king not now a king, and they not subjects? The *Message* answers its own rhetorical question: 'as a king we have no difference of year, no time', albeit 'as a natural man . . . we have youth'.[120] Moreover, with the Council of 'our' uncle, the king's answer continued, he had kept up state, maintained the defence of the realm, and reigned nobly with no loss of honour to the nation. It was the rebels of Devon who inflicted the first assault on the nation's honour and safety, at a time when foreign enemies menaced them.[121] The paper ends with the threat of the 'power of . . . God in our sword' but also with the promise of mercy on submission and repentance.[122] This printed and published *Message* skilfully cut the ground from under one of the rebels' principal platforms: that the changes were not the will of the king himself. Whoever was its author, it presented Edward, for all his youth, as knowledgeable, understanding of, and in charge of, policy. The king's body public experienced no minority and the youth of the 'natural man', as the text demonstrates as well as claims, was no impediment to his rule.

In what appears to have been a separate and later declaration, 'The King's Answer to the Supplication of his Subjects of Devon and Cornwall', reference is directly made to 'an anointed king who rules by counsel'.[123] This paper urges the people to return to their harvest, reminding them that parliament was the proper place for reform. Referring to the earlier printed message to the people of Devon, this later answer adds to reassurances about the sacrament of baptism, assurance that the order of confirmation will be still readily learned by children.[124] And repeating the reasons for abolition of the Six Articles ('which all our whole parliament almost on their knees required us to abolish'), this second answer dismisses as self-destructive folly the request for the revival of the statute making words treasonable: 'when we are content to rule like a father . . . do you call for the bridle and whip?'[125] Most importantly, the document again goes to lengths to assert Edward's personal charge of events. 'You object unto us as though these things were done us not knowing. But we do declare unto you that there was nothing but at our consent and knowledge, nor nothing passeth in parliament but our consent is at it.'[126] As for the Prayer Book, 'we know nothing is in it but according to the Scripture and the word of God and that we ourself in person, although as yet young in age, are able to justify and prove'.[127]

In this second response, 'Edward' also moves on to more secular grievances, including taxes and other social problems. The 'Answer' gives a detailed justification of the real costs of armies and garrisons, the debts inherited by the crown, and the need for levies on sheep and cloth, to enable the government to protect the people – adding that the rebellion itself increased costs, as the French and Scots armed to take advantage of England's problems. Echoing the philosophy of the commonwealthsmen, the 'Answer' assures subjects: 'we esteem our wealth to consist in the wealth of our subjects and our loss in their loss'.[128] As for dearth of victuals, 'Is this the way,' Edward asks, 'think you to make plenty?'[129] In conclusion, the rebels of the west are exhorted to emulate others who have returned to obedience and received mercy, rather than tarry for the sword of justice. God, the fount of obedience, would see disobedience chastised, and even 'in our tender age' the king might be constrained to act as the agent of God's punishment: 'to teach you how great a mischief it is to subjects against their prince to make an insurrection'.[130]

Though drafts of a reply to the rebels are found in the Public Record Office in Somerset's handwriting, when the Protector and Council wrote to the Lord Privy Seal, Lord Russell, on 27 July they informed him in a postscript that they had 'sent you the King's Majesty's answer to the rebels of Cornwall's supplication' along with other 'proclamations'.[131] Whoever wrote the 'Answer', even among councillors it was held to be the king's and so represented his position and his authority.

The reference in the letter to Russell to proclamations returns us to that written form of royal representation which reached into all the towns and parishes of England: the proclamation, typically printed in black letter, with established forms of royal address. Whatever Edward's hesitancy about the use of the first person pronoun in the early entries of his chronicle, in proclamations not only the smooth succession from father to son but the continuity of authority of the crown was manifested in the language and forms of Edward's proclamations from the very first. As that proclaiming the succession begins: 'Edward VI by the grace of God King of England, France and Ireland, Defender of the Faith and of the Church of England and also of Ireland in each the supreme head, to all our most loving, faithful and obedient subjects and to every of them, greeting'.[132] Interestingly that first proclamation, for all that it establishes Edward as king, in fact as well as name, also acknowledges the element of reciprocity in Tudor rule. The king registers that 'like as we for our part shall . . . show ourself a most gracious and benign sovereign lord to all our good subjects . . . so we mistrust not that they and every of them will again . . . show themselves unto us most faithful, loving and obedient subjects'.[133] It was a fitting first statement. For, albeit he was a minor, Edward's proclamations were presentations of his grace and benign kingship and strategies by which subjects were persuaded of, and hopefully tied to, their 'bounden duties and allegiances'.

If, as we have observed and shall further examine, proclamations often disclose some of the nervousness about the reality of a governmental authority that ultimately rested on co-operation and consent, those of Edward's reign faced the problem of royal authority itself: of presenting the king as governing but recognizing the realities of a protectorate, at a dangerous time of social and economic instability and religious change. While it was normal for early Tudor proclamations to mention the advice of Council or parliament, especially on controversial matters, Edward's youth and circumstance led to more specific references to such other authorities. In an early proclamation establishing injunctions for religious reform, as in the book of homilies appointed to be read in churches, the orders 'by the king's most royal majesty' were given 'by the advice of his most dear uncle, the Duke of Somerset, Lord Protector of all his realms, dominions, subjects and governor of his most royal person, and the residue of his most honourable Council'.[134] While similar formulations were used in the early proclamations – regarding the export of grain, or metal[135] – in certain cases (the payment of Henry VIII's debts and the collection of subsidies still owing from his reign, for example), the king's will was presented as the sole source of command.[136] In these cases, it may be that matters close to the king's personal prerogative – finance, for example – were seen to be best presented as acts of the king's will, as were new regulations for pleading in the king's courts, acts of pardon, and encroachment on royal forests.[137] We cannot be sure. But there is no question that, after the fall of Somerset, the language of the proclamations altered to emphasize the king's personal control. Although, as was conventional, the proclamations frequently referred to conciliar advice, it was now very much 'the king's most excellent majesty' who called 'to his princely remembrance' how 'according to the regal power and state to him committed by Almighty God', it was by 'order . . . from his majesty' that actions be effected to reform abuses or right the ills of the realm.[138] Edward's growing authority, which we have seen written on to and into the king's own scripts, was also published in the declarations and proclamations that went out in his name.

To argue that the establishment of the king's authority was necessary to the exercise of that authority is no mere tautology or paradox. While the history, political culture and prevailing disposition of noble and common subjects endowed the crown with considerable strength, each monarch had to re-iterate, revalidate and appropriate for himself (or, as we shall see, still more difficult, herself) the discourses and legitimizing languages on which the crown rested. As the circumstances of each reign were different, and altered across the reign with age and time, so those languages and forms needed to be subtly reconstituted and re-presented – and represented as though they had remained timeless and enduring. That art, difficult for any ruler, required especial finesse in the reign of a woman or a minor who could not so easily present themselves as the warrior, martial prince, or the father of the realm. We have seen how in Henry VIII's reign, in proclamations as well as other representations, Henry, especially from the 1530s, began to present himself as the head of the commonweal and Supreme Head of the church, as well as Renaissance warrior prince. Edward's proclamations deployed the ideology of the commonweal to advertise and to underpin the boy's kingship. Scores of proclamations concerning social ills referred to the king's 'pitiful and tender zeal to his most loving subjects, and especially to the poor' or to his 'being always ready and studying for the benefit in every part of his common-wealth'.[139] By corollary, the ideal of order that these proclamations sought to uphold is presented in the Tudor homilies on obedience as the justification of due subjection to kings. That is, where the idea of the commonweal posited 'every degree of people in their vocation', a world in which 'every one have need of each other', that ideal of community was presented as depending on the authority of the king: 'Take away kings, princes, rulers . . . and such states of God's order [and] no man shall ride or go upon the highway unrobbed, . . . no man shall keep his wife, children and possessions in quietness, all things shall be common and there must needs follow all mischief and utter destruction both of souls, bodies, goods and commonwealths.'[140]

The reference to 'souls' underlines the religious as well as secular components of the commonwealth idea, stated more directly in an Edwardian proclamation enforcing the usual Lent fast: 'his highness hath not only care and charge . . . of his realm and dominions as a king, but also as a Christian king and Supreme Head of the Church of England and Ireland, a desire, will and charge to lead and instruct his people to him committed of God, in such rights, ways and customs as might be acceptable to God, and to the further increase of good living and virtue.'[141] Edwardian proclamations presented the king as Supreme Head, acting, as in other areas of social reform, to eradicate abuses – the 'manifold enormities' which had crept into his realm through the false, usurped power of the Bishop of Rome.[142] It was not least to sustain unity and love that the king proclaimed his desire for, and action that he was taking so that, 'one and a most godly conformity might be had throughout all this realm'.[143] The proclamations, in fact, announced what they desired: co-operation, harmony, unity, order and obedience. When the king acted to correct abuses, proclamations frequently claimed that it had been at the petition, request or 'pitiful complaints' of subjects.[144] Indeed, even the most contentious and divisive of religious changes were presented in royal proclamations as the wishes of the king's subjects – as 'the earnest and fervent desire of his dearly beloved subjects', as the preface to the 1547 *Sermons and Homilies* put it, 'to be delivered from all errors and superstitions'.[145] As if writing over the bitter conflicts of religious factions and divisions, the proclamations represented the Edwardian Reformation as the opposite of what its modern historians have argued it was – as the will of the people.

And, of course, as the will of God. Through all the contentions of Henry VIII's divorce, the breach from Rome and the vicissitudes of religious policy, it had remained essential for the king to claim to act as God's lieutenant on earth. As, under Edward, England shifted at least officially to become a Protestant country, that claim had to be ever more insistently made, not least because for many, whether Catholics or simply traditionalists, it was a claim that seemed no longer self-evident. *The Sermons or Homilies Appointed by the King's Majesty To Be Declared and Read* (1547) went to some lengths to assert that the high authority of kings was the ordinance of God and that 'ye must needs obey not only for fear of vengeance but also because of conscience'.[146] God detected and punished disobedient thoughts as well as deeds, even when against wicked rulers. Therefore, governed as they were by a good and godly ruler, it was 'an intolerable ignorance, madness and wickedness for subjects to make any murmuring, rebellion, resistance, commotion or insurrection against their most dear and dread sovereign lord and king ordained and appointed by God's goodness for their commodities'.[147] Proclamations presented Edward in the same ways: they asserted his rule to be divine and insisted that obedience was natural; and they endeavoured to exclude challenge or resistance from the godly commonweal as mad and sinful acts. As we have seen, even rebellion was re-presented as the fruit of the 'ignorance and ill enticements' of a few against 'God's peace and his [the king's]'; and pardon was granted, in religious as well as regal language, for penitents who submitted 'for the benefit and grace of his mercy'.[148] When they did not pretend a unity that did not exist, proclamations sought to turn resistance into an attribute and display of royal grace as well as command.

The authority of the young Edward rested, in large measure, on such fictions as the proclamations wrote. That is surely why the Edwardian regime took representations that exposed those fictions as fiction – namely rumour – as one of the greatest threats to its authority. Rumour, as we shall see, emphasized change, division and contention where royal proclamations stressed continuity, unity and peace.[149] From May 1547 to July 1551 no fewer than seven proclamations threatened dire punishment to disseminators of 'vain and false tales' and forewarned subjects who 'hitherto have not felt the peril of these poisoned and evil people' and their rumours, 'dangerous to their sovereign lord and his estate'.[150] One of the longest, a proclamation *Enforcing Statutes against Vagabonds, Rumour Mongers, Players and Unlicensed Printers,* takes us to the heart of Tudor government and the representation of Tudor rule. The proclamation opens, conventionally, by reminding subjects of the king's care for God's word, the faith, the quiet and the welfare of the realm. But, less typically, the text acknowledges and laments the behaviour of 'many of his subjects' who abuse the word of God and the prince 'to dispute of his Majesty's affairs, to sow, spread abroad, and tell . . . rumours'.[151] The proclamation attributes the blame for this to the failure to enforce all those statutes (against alehouses and forestallers, for example) which were at the core of the commonwealth programme, devised for 'each man to have lived in quiet' in his degree. And, though it threatened the 'extremity of correction', the proclamation presented a king who preferred a 'fatherly fashion' of admonition. In the end the proclamation resorted to reiterating the very statutes and earlier proclamations which had failed, and again to 'command[ing]' the cessation of 'rumour' and 'talk', along with plays and print not authorized.[152] Though somewhat exceptionally revealing in its language, the proclamation of 28 April 1551 underlines the extent to which the authority of the government depended on its representation, and the degree to which that authority and its representation depended on the rhetoric of power – on the persuasiveness of the king's' words. In 1551 and 1553, respectively, were published by the king's printer 'cum privilegio ad imprimendum solum' volumes of proclamations and statutes issued in Edward's reign, so that none might pass over them or offend in ignorance.[153] Edwardian government, like the Protestant religion it established, rested on the word of a king.

In the case of Henry VIII, we have seen that the word of a king was not confined to the king's own words: the king was represented discursively by others who, sometimes with official direction and approval, sometimes not, wrote the script of kingship for the reign. As a boy, Edward was – at least for his early years – more dependent than usual on other pens in writing and presenting his authority in sermons, treatises, pamphlets and even ballads.

At the very moment of his coronation, Edward's representation as godly ruler of a Protestant nation was set out in a brief speech by the Archbishop of Canterbury, Thomas Cranmer who had battled throughout Henry's reign for godly Reformation. The coronation oath Edward had taken to forsake evil, Cranmer informed the king and all, was 'not to be taken in the Bishop of Rome's sense'.[154] Subtly revising the meaning of the coronation oath and ritual, Cranmer explained that no English king could subordinate his authority to Rome. Nor, now he was Supreme Head, could any implication of the king's accountability to his bishops be permitted: kings, Cranmer declared, are 'God's anointed, not in respect of the oil which the bishop useth, but in consideration ... of their persons, which are elected by God and endowed with the gifts of his spirit for the better ruling and guiding of his people'. Elaborating the divine source of royal authority and the illegitimacy of any other claims, Cranmer addressed the young king and all in Westminster Abbey: 'Your majesty is God's vicegerent and Christ's vicar within your own dominion.'[155] Edward, he continued, offering counsel as much as praise, was 'a second Josiah sent to reform, to see God truly worshipped, and idolatry destroyed, the tyranny of the bishop of Rome banished from your subjects and images removed'. Cranmer's speech, which substituted for a coronation sermon, concluded with the traditional injunction to the new king to reward virtue and punish vice, to dispense charity and justice and to rule in peace, but qualified even that conventional admonition with a clear statement that, other than to God, the king was accountable to none. Edward was presented – to himself and to his subjects – differently to any of his predecessors: as the sovereign lord of church as well as state, with a mission to emulate Josiah and 'reform the church of God in his days'.[156]

During Edward VI's brief reign, the sermon became a central text of the representation of the new king and reign, as well as an address and counsel to the monarch. From 1550 weekly sermons were ordered at court and care was taken to ensure that nearly all preachers were supporters of evangelical reform.[157] Many of the sermons – all delivered in the royal presence – were published by the king's printer, 'cum privilegio ad imprimendum solum' and often carried the king's arms as an advertisement of official status and approval. In his first sermon to the new prince, delivered at 'his grace's palace at Westminster' in March 1549, Hugh Latimer opened, as had Cranmer, with the proclamation that the two swords, spiritual and temporal, were in the hands of the king who had his authority from, and was answerable to, God alone.[158] The new king before whom he preached, Latimer declaimed, was 'a most precious treasure', given by God to lead the people from bondage.[159] But, unlike Cranmer, Latimer stressed the need for the king to reform the state and, in particular, to implement the programme of the commonwealthmen who advocated action to limit greed, prevent enclosure, and foster employment and wealth. In a series of seven sermons before the king over the course of the next year, Latimer publicly presented Edward as, and sought to make him, the champion of secular and religious reform; and in epistles to readers the king's printer urged the remittance of all ills to the 'Godly wisdom of the high magistrate'.[160] Latimer urged Edward 'to study God's book, to see that there be no unpreaching prelates in his realm, nor bribing judges; to see to all estates; to provide for the poor'; and both in listening and licensing publication of the sermon Edward publicized his heeding of that counsel.[161] For, whatever his praise of Somerset, it was a godly king to whom Latimer appealed, and whom he wanted to seize the reins of power. Indeed, from the time of his second sermon, as early as 15 March 1549, Latimer was asserting Edward's personal authority in words which directly echo those sent to the rebels of Devon in the king's name: 'a king in his childhood is a king, as well as in any other age'.[162] Against those – often papists – who wanted to claim that policies were 'but my lord Protector's and my lord of Canterbury's doing', Latimer retorted: 'have we not a noble king? Was there ever a king so noble; so godly . . . his Majesty hath more godly wit and understanding, more learning and knowledge at this age than twenty of his progenitors . . . had at any time of their life'.[163] It was Edward in whom Latimer laid his hopes for reform of the commonweal and church, him whom he continually called upon to take full charge, and him whom he counselled in words that virtually describe Edward's childhood and devotion to reading and writing: 'he must be a student, he must write God's book himself'; 'he shall see it written, and rather than he shall be without it, write it himself'.[164]

Other preachers took up the same method of appealing to the godly prince and sonneting his authority in the loftiest strains. Thomas Lever, a leader of the most ardent Protestant reformers at Cambridge, rose to be a court preacher and one close to the king and government. In a Lent sermon before Edward and his Council, he, like Latimer, surveyed the religious failings and the social ills that beset the commonwealth – the abuse of preachers, avaricious landlords, deceitful lawyers, and insufficient provision for the poor – and pressed the king to stir his nobles and magistrates to act.[165] Praising the king and his advisers for 'driving away the wild force of papistical superstition', Lever described in lyrical terms the place of a powerful king in the commonwealth programme: 'The wings of God be stretched abroad here in England by the king's grace and his honorary council of mighty power, with ready will to shadow, defend and save all those that with reverend love come humbly creeping under their ordinance, rule and governance, which is the power, the wings and the honour of God.'[166] Lever's is a language which reminds us that, for all its admonition and calling of its royal auditor to duties, the court sermon could be, especially when published, one of the most powerful representations of the authority of divine kingship, of what had started as an expedient claim to royal supremacy.[167]

Though perhaps the most important, sermons were not the only texts in which Edward, even as a minor, was represented as the leader of a godly, Protestant nation. In his epistle dedicatory to the final volume of the 1548 edition of the *Paraphrases* of Erasmus, for example, Nicholas Udall, the Lutheran scholar and headmaster of Eton, skilfully presented the young king as the embodiment of humanist learning and godly piety. Citing Plato on the happiest state being the one where kings were philosophers, 'that is to say such as know and love God', Udall brought the axiom home: 'how happy are we Englishmen of such a king,' he wrote, especially a king who 'will by God's governance far pass your said father.'[168] Like Edward himself, Udall emphasized the mature wisdom of one who, despite his youth, was a 'sapient king and governor'.[169] Though the preface went on to admonish Edward to do his godly duty, Udall presented him as a king appointed by God to carry out his high work, as a king, that is of 'English Israelites'.[170] 'You', Udall urged and praised the king, are, after a father who was a Moses, 'the Joshua who God has appointed to bring us to the land of promission'; after a David, the Solomon to build in England a house for God, another Ezechias or Josias to secure the word.[171] Appropriating Erasmus as an unequivocal enemy to Rome and advocate of Protestant reform, Udall coupled Edward with him, indeed presented him as a superior in advancing God's true religion.[172] In his preface to a work which Edward ordered to be placed in every parish church, Udall represented the young king as holy patriarch and virtuous learned prince. Similarly, Thomas Wilson, the Cambridge Greek scholar, dedicating his *The Rule of Reason Containing the Art of Logic* to Edward in 1551, praised a young ruler to whom God had given all the gifts of power, wisdom, innocence and godliness with which he had endowed biblical kings.[173] Edward was, and would be, *The Rule of Reason* proclaims, not only a model of scholarly attainment and logical reason (the art of logic, the book argues, was the knowledge of God) but 'an example of kingly worthiness and a mirror of princely governance'.[174] Printed by Richard Grafton with the royal privilege, Wilson's treatise brought its author royal favour and a prebend at Windsor.

Other writers endeavoured to appropriate for Edward's kingship the traditional martial qualities and glories which had been central to Henrician representation. In his account of *The Expedition into Scotland . . . of Prince Edward* (1548), William Patten, Teller of the Exchequer, presented Edward, as well as his uncle, as in some way the champion of 'our most valiant victory over our enemies'.[175] For though the focus of Patten's praise is Somerset, the Pompey of England, Patten heralds Edward as 'an image so near representing his father's majesty and virtues'.[176] Moreover, he presents the new England of Edward VI as a country that has freed itself from the 'servile thraldom' of popery and established the royal supremacy: 'we have now the grace to know and serve the one God, so are we subject to but one king; he naturally knoweth his own people and we obediently know him our only sovereign, his highness state brought . . . from perdition and . . . subjection unto the old . . . absolute power again'.[177] With such victory attained 'in this the first year of our king's majesty's dominion and rule', Patten looked to a happy and glorious reign, under a king chosen by God.[178]

Two years later, John Coke, a clerk for the King's Recognizance, vaunted England's claims under Edward, whose preachers did preach the 'pure word of God', to far more greatness than France which maintained hypocrisy, superstition and idolatry.[179] Tracing the English monarchy back to Brutus, as the more honourable of the two, Coke delivered a challenge to Edward's enemies and a plea to the king to emulate his ancestors and undertake the conquest of France, which had been denied his father by the division in the realm. As a godly mission was added to traditional chivalric and martial images, Edward was also presented as the head of a martial Protestant nation, ready to assert its place in the world.

The histories printed during Edward's reign – often by the royal printer or with the royal privilege – selectively and subtly rewrote the history of England, and particularly of Henry VIII, to present Edward as the heir of a Protestant dynasty. Kelton's verse *Chronicle* of 1547, for example, printed by Richard Grafton, 'cum privilegio', traced Edward's genealogy from Brutus.[180] In a preface to the young king who had just ascended the throne, Kelton dismissed the scepticism about the Brutus legend as the efforts of those who rightly feared that such a descent eclipsed even imperial (that is also Catholic) lineage.[181] Edward descended, Kelton proclaimed, from ancient British stock and from a family from Wales, a land with an ancient reputation as a refuge for holy men. From this family came Henry VIII, Edward's father, to become a king beyond comparison with any before him. From him Edward inherited 'a sovereignty passing all other', as 'the supreme head of the Church of England and Ireland'.[182] This popular verse history, written in simple metre, not only underpinned the Tudor dynasty, at the moment of the succession of a minor; it traced the history of Britain as a Protestant history (had not the Welsh rejected the pomp of Italy?) and celebrated how 'The power of Rome so long misused / Our kyng hath now utterly confused'.[183] What Henry VIII had accomplished, Kelton told Edward, was now 'under support of your benign grace' continued, as the new king embodied all the virtues as well as power of his father.[184]

Thomas Lanquet's *Epitome of Chronicles* (continued by Thomas Cowper to the reign of Edward VI) was published in 1549, with a preface to the Duke of Somerset, praising the 'godly and public governance' of the king and Protector.[185] While the original chronicle proceeded conventionally enough, the addition by Cowper, a staunch Protestant and Master of Magdalen School, Oxford, at three times the length, turned the narrative in a distinctly different direction. Cowper weaves the history of Britain from the time of Christ into a larger canvas of the Roman emperors to chronicle, and demonize, the false claims of Boniface to be universal bishop, to the dishonour of God.[186] Moving through the reigns of medieval kings, Cowper pauses to note the conclusion of the Chronicle of Basle decreeing that the Bishop of Rome was a heretic.[187] The *Epitome* reaches the reign of Henry VIII who 'abolished the usurped power of the Bishop of Rome', 'redressed the state of religion, diminished superstition and idolatry ... and greatly advanced and set forth the true knowledge of God's word'.[188] Passing over the details of Henry's affair with Anne Boleyn and divorce, Cowper repeats how it was determined that 'the Bishop of Rome's unlawful tyranny' should be ended 'and that the king should be reported and taken as Supreme Head of the Church of England and have full authority to reform and redress all errors, abuses and heresies in the same'.[189] It was to this inheritance that Edward succeeded aged nine and Cowper ended his chronicle with a note of the orders sent in the king's name to destroy images and to celebrate the eucharist in both kinds and with proclamation of Edward's God-given mission 'to exercise over us that perfection of Christian governance which even now by many tokens showeth itself in his gracious majesty more abundantly than we could wish'.[190] In 1550 *A Breviat Chronicle* similarly presented Edward as the heir of all the kings descended from Brutus and of a father under whose rule 'we his people of England lived a joyful and peaceful life reduced from the error of idolatry to the true knowledge of God and his word'.[191] After detailed description of Edward's coronation and the festivities that surrounded it, *A Breviat Chronicle* moved swiftly to the pulling down of images and the changes to the mass, and urged all to pray for the long life of a king who would advance God's word and triumph over his enemies.[192] The same year *The Three Books of Chronicles* which John Carion gathered was published, with an appendix by John Funke of Nuremberg, covering the years 1532–50 and with a dedication (by Walter Lynne) to Edward VI, the Supreme Head of the church.[193] The addition dwelt on Pope Clement's efforts to eradicate the Lutheran faith and Henry VIII's championing of the rightful resistance to his 'usurped authority'.[194] Under Edward, the text continues, Englishmen were at last brought to the 'true and unfeigned worshipping of God ... with due obedience to their prince'.[195] Under the new king and Protector, chantries were dissolved, popish processions ended, idolatrous practices put down and godly preachers, such as Latimer, were free to propagate the gospel. Comparing Edward to biblical predecessors who had enacted religious reforms – 'Josias and other godly and virtuous princes' – Funke saw in the first three years of the reign 'manifest tokens of the promises of ... this jubilee of grace'.[196] Similar to Moses' proclamation to the children of Israel, Edward 'proclaimed a godly Christian freedom to the long captived consciences of his natural and obedient subjects'.[197]

The chronicles and histories published in Edward's reign, then, took a very selective and partisan view of England's past to represent Edward as another Josiah (the pious king of Judah who ascended the throne aged eight and so even younger than the Tudor) who would lead the realm into a godly future. Already we see laid down the foundations of a historiography that, when fashioned into a bestseller by John Foxe, enshrined the inevitable triumph of Protestantism as the nation's story and dismissed opposition to the Reformation as superstitious and outmoded.

When the chronicles refer to the resistance to the new religion they dismiss it as 'a great conjunction of rustics in Cornwall by popish priests'.[198] And other pens were swift to join the *Message* sent out in Edward's name to counter the articles and arguments of the rebels and to underwrite royal authority and the supremacy. John Cheke's *The Hurt of Sedition*, published in 1549 with its title page framed by a large royal arms, could hardly have come from circles closer to the king.[199] Cheke was, as well as Professor of Greek at Cambridge, Edward's tutor and may well have overseen some of his own writings. In *The Hurt of Sedition*, Cheke emphasized the duty of obedience and the offence given to God, as well as the sovereign and the commonweal, by rebels. Asserting that 'the magistrate is the ordinance of God', Cheke informed the rebels that what was done against God's agents was also a sin committed against Him.[200] Moreover, since 'there can be no just execution of laws' nor 'reformation of faults' but from the king, the 'mad' rebels were nothing but 'murderers of your selves' in opposing order and authority.[201] Besides the need for some sovereign authority if the country was to 'well stand ... and the people grow to wealth', in Edward VI, the realm, Cheke argued, had a godly and virtuous king who could be trusted to rule and reform.[202] 'The King's Majesty', Cheke reminded them, giving the full credit for making policy to Edward himself, 'hath reformed an unclean part of religion and hath brought it to the true form of the first church that followed Christ.'[203] Echoing Edward's own words, Cheke presented him as one who preferred to rule as a loving father over loving children, but as a monarch with the power to execute sharp justice.[204] 'God is angry with you for your rebellion,' Cheke concluded his address: 'leave off with repentance and return to your duties' and allegiance to a king 'in whose mind God hath poured so much hope'.[205] Like Edward's own writings, Cheke's text occasionally betrays fear of an outcome that he elsewhere claims to be impossible ('if', he writes to the rebels, 'you do overcome'); and he acknowledges that some remain who prefer 'superstition' to true faith; but his careful appeal to homage, national sentiment, reason and self-interest helped to constitute true subjects: 'we live under a king to serve him at all times when he shall need our strength'.[206]

Robert Crowley, a printer of Holborn, appears to have been a more independent spokesman for royal authority.[207] In *The Way to Wealth Wherein is Plainly Taught a Most Present Remedy for Sedition*, as well as addressing the causes of social uprising, Crowley went to some lengths to argue that the office of a king was 'God's office', and that there would be no justification for a breach of God's ordinance mandating obedience to his chosen rulers.[208] Rebels against Edward's government threatened 'the great peril and danger of their anointed king in his tender age', and so threatened their own safety and welfare.[209] Such defences of Edward's kingship and royal authority in general were not only expounded in such carefully argued works, they are also reprised in ballads which vilified the rebels as papists and celebrated their overthrow by a godly prince: 'God,' the refrain of one ballad repeats 'hath given our king the victory.'[210]

This literal underwriting of Edward's power and policies in all the literary genres of sermons and histories, epistles dedicatory and songs, continued to the last days of the young monarch's brief life. Indeed, John Hayward, the first proper historian of the reign, informs us that during the king's illness, the Earl of Northumberland, evidently an early practitioner of the distillation of false news, 'caused speeches to be spread abroad that the king was well recovered in health' – which, as he adds, 'was readily believed, as most desired it to be true'.[211] Northumberland's misinformation, and its successful fulfilment of its purpose, nicely manifest the importance of the image of King Edward and the modes and strategies of its presentation in texts, both those issued under Edward's name and others.

The last textual representations of Edward were prayers devised by others and spoken by the king in his last days.[212] *A Prayer Said in The King's Chapel in the Time of His Grace's Sickness* presents Edward as 'possessing the word and holy name', as a second Ezechias safeguarding the Israelites and as one who had begun the 'rooting out of error, idolatry and superstition and the planting of true religion'.[213] Printed with the royal arms, on a single sheet, the *Prayer* may have been intended not only to bind in prayer a wider audience (the text was available at 'the sign of the Rose Garland' in Fleet Street) but for display on a wall and for public recital. Weeks later, Edward's own last 'private' prayer was published to the nation.[214] Edward asked his Lord only to deliver him into the ranks of the chosen and to bless his people: 'O Lord God save thy chosen people of England: O my Lord God defend this realm from papistry and maintain thy true religion . . .'. Printed and published, the prayer was claimed to be Edward's dying words, 'his eyes being closed and thinking none had heard him'. No more than with the earliest words presented as Edward's, can we be sure that these last were his own. But we can be certain that, like all his words, 'the prayer of King Edward VI' proclaimed the king's virtues and godliness and enshrined him for ever as what his many advocates had claimed him to be: not only England's Ezechias but the nation's Josias.

II Rituals and Reform

This ubiquitous image of Edward as the sickly but pious boy king whose principal achievement was to make England a Protestant nation threatens to mask other realities and other representations of the reign which were vital for both the young king and his advisers. As we have seen, Edward's own chronicle was by no means dominated by religious matters;[215] and the king's papers describe his own effort to establish identity and authority by participation in a wide variety of secular affairs – domestic and foreign.

Central to the representation of monarchy was the image of the king as chivalrous knight and warrior prince. Whilst Edward's boyhood posed some difficulties in so presenting him, we should not underplay the place of tournaments and jousts in the king's life and reign. Edward's chronicle documents not only the frequent tilts and tourneys which were staged but, too, the king's personal interest in them. Edward records, for example, how at the wedding of John Lord Lisle and his Lady Anne, daughter of the Duke of Somerset, he saw 'six gentlemen of one side and six of another run the course of the field twice over'; others – he left the names blank to fill in – ran four courses apiece, the 'last of all came the count of Rangone with three Italians who ran with all the gentlemen four courses and afterward fought at tourney'.[216] Similarly, at the end of the Christmas celebrations of 1551, Edward described the 'tourney', named the defendants and expressed his appreciation that the participants 'fought right well, and so the challenge was accomplished'.[217] His obvious joy in this occasion led to a letter to his close friend, Barnaby Fitzpatrick, for whom Edward described the Twelfth Night barriers in detail.[218] Moreover, Edward was no mere spectator. For 31 March 1551, his chronicle entry records 'A challenge made by me that I, with sixteen of my chamber should run at base, shoot and run at ring with any sixteen of my servants, gentlemen at court'.[219] The next day, 'the first day of the challenge at base, or running, the king won'.[220] The next month, on 3 May, Edward records the loss by his side after a vigorous '120 courses': 'the challenge at the running at ring performed, at which first came the king, sixteen footmen and ten horsemen, in black silk coats pulled out with white silk taffeta'.[221] Contrary to Jordan's assertion, then, it would appear that Edward did 'personally incur the danger of . . . contact sports'.[222]

As his first biographer, John Hayward, reports of Edward: 'His courage did appear in the great delight he took in representations of battles, skirmishes, assaults and of all kinds of military exercises; his judgement was great either for errors or fine contrivances in the field. And no actions of men were executed in his time but he would perfectly understand by which advantage on the one side or oversights on the other event succeeded.'[223] Hayward went on to list the other 'exercises or activity' in which Edward 'took great pleasure': 'wrestling, leaping, running, riding, shooting at roves and at rounds and such like games, and at riding and shooting [he] would sometimes be one of the sides.'[224] Edward wrote to Barnaby of his pleasure in hunting; and records of payments for improvements to archery butts, tiltyards and tennis courts, as well as gifts of bowstrings and hunting dogs, suggest a young boy with a love of vigorous activity.[225] What is as important as the fact for our study of the royal image is that it was this Edward who made an impression on contemporaries and visiting envoys. Towards the end of the king's life, an Italian visitor reported how Edward 'delights in hunting and he does it so as to have an excuse to ride'.[226] Soranzo, the Venetian envoy, observed that after Somerset's fall Northumberland encouraged these exercises and reports Edward 'arming and tilting, managing horses and delighting in every sort of exercise, drawing the bow, playing rackets, hunting and so forth indefatigably . . .'.[227] The imperial agent Jehan Scheyve made a similar observation when he reported that 'The king of England is beginning to exercise himself in the use of arms and enjoys it heartily'; his prowess, he noted, earned the admiration of the French ambassador.[228] The envoys' interest and observations were no mere casual comment. An involvement and interest in matters chivalric and martial were intimately associated with war; and it was the business of envoys to gauge the inclinations of the young king and to foresee the course his foreign policy might take. And what would have been apparent was Edward's fascination with matters military, and especially with fortifications. Scattered throughout the young king's chronicle are comments on the state of defences and fortifications – at Calais and Guisnes, for example, in detail that suggests knowledge and understanding; and Edward wrote a careful and critical assessment of the fortifications at Portsmouth where, he told Barnaby Fitzpatrick, 'we find the bulwarks changeable, massive well rampured, but ill fashioned, ill flanked and set in unmeet places'.[229] In his memorandum for the Council of October 1552, Edward included, as a list of business to be addressed, the fortifying of Portsmouth, Berwick and Dover and noted Fastolf's recommendations concerning fortifications in his notes on the occupation of France.[230] Edward was – and importantly was seen to be – a king interested in matters martial and military, one who was perhaps on the point of emerging, before his fatal illness, as a warrior prince on the European stage.

The perception of Edward as a young king devoted to chivalry, exercise and martial affairs was strengthened by the attention he paid to the Order of the Garter. Edward notes in his chronicle elections to the Order and the details of ceremonies that accompanied investiture, recording, for example, Henry II's gift and the orations delivered to mark his election.[231] And he was no less concerned with the role of the Order in the representation of his kingship; from the start of his reign Edward wore his George and Garter and was portrayed wearing them; he stipulated that his image on coin's should depict him wearing his Garter chain.[232] When Monsieur de la Tremoille and Monsieur Humandaye came to court in April 1550, to his first chapter as sovereign, they 'saw the Order of the Garter and the Knights with the sovereign receive the communion'.[233] As we have seen, Edward penned various drafts for reform of the Order, which underline its importance to him, for all his desire to rid the rituals of their Catholic association. Whilst those suggested alterations undoubtedly reflect Edward's aversion to popery and his Protestantism, they depict the Order very much as one of service, of knights ready 'to die in his countries and master's service, and against his enemies or the commonwealth's cause'.[234] The young king was similarly proud of his investiture into the French Order of St Michael and, the Council reported, 'caused his arms, surrounded with the order of St Michael, to be set up in Hampton Court each Michaelmas Day'.[235]

If the image of Edward as Josiah has overshadowed the chivalric prince, Protestant historiography has paid little attention to the court entertainments and pageants of the reign – perhaps on account of later, Puritan distaste for revels. Certainly, the Edward who kept Christmas with 'banqueting, mummers, plays and much variety of mirth' did not accord with the most godly sensibilities of Elizabethan and early Stuart England.[236] Many of the 'tourneys' in which Edward took such pleasure were clearly accompanied by allegorical entertainments and masques, about which we have only tantaliz-ingly brief snippets of information. Shortly after his coronation, Edward was presented with an 'interlude' of 'the story of Orpheus, right cunningly composed'.[237] In January 1552, we learn from Edward's chronicle that along with a barriers (or martial exercise) at court, there was a play and 'after this followed two masques, one of men, another of women'.[238] Documents from the Revels Office provide abundant evidence of Edward's interest in such entertainments. Payment records document tailors working day and night on masquing costumes, elaborate masques featuring Greeks, Irishmen, Moors and Jews, and, most importantly Edward's own performances from early in his reign.[239] Edward's delight in masques was such that, while his uncle languished in jail, Northumberland arranged them to distract the king from his sadness; and a letter from the Spanish envoy reports him rewarding the entertainers with pensions.[240] Indeed, for that entertainment Edward revived the office of Lord of Misrule, which had not been filled for fifteen years and the figure appointed (George Ferrers) outlined to the Master of the Revels elaborate plans for the entertainment he would stage and the entourage which would accompany him.[241] His mention of a serpent with seven heads, together with references in Revels Office Accounts to costumes for friars and 'crowns and cross for the pope', indicate that much Edwardian court festival was anti-papal and anti-Catholic; indeed the imperial ambassador Scheyve was horri-fied at a procession that ridiculed the Catholic mass.[242] Though a later Protestantism was to reject revelry, Edward's image as a godly monarch in no sense dulled the glitter of court entertainment or the image of the king as a beacon of magnificence.

Nor was the display of magnificence confined to the court. The pageantry of state which had once been an extravagant feature of Henry VIII's reign, and an important contribution to his power, was a characteristic of Edward's reign from the very beginning. The day after Henry VIII died (after midnight on 28 January), Seymour and other nobles with knights, squires and gentry rode to the prince at Hertford where he was lodged. On the following Monday, the new king was escorted to Enfield and thence to London where all the nobility waited to receive him and a shot of ordnance greeted his arrival.[243] Over the following days, while elaborate arrangements were made for Henry's funeral, preparations were begun for Edward's coronation, which commenced on 19 February. With the streets railed, and, within them, all the city companies and crafts ranked in their order, and with cloth of gold and tapestry hanging from all the windows, the procession made its entry into London to present the new monarch to his people. Behind trumpets, squires of the body, dukes, earls, marquises, bishops and all the officers of his household, heralds and, in fine, a little before him, his uncle, Somerset, came the nine-year-old 'the king's majesty walking a little before his canopy because the people might the better see his grace'.[244] As a small boy, Edward needed to be seen – and, in his rich gown of cloth of silver embroidered with gold and precious stones, seen to be a king. Ordnance sounded from the Tower as the cavalcade entered Mark Lane and then Fenchurch Street where the king was regaled by men and children singing.[245] The party progressed to the conduit at Cornhill where sweet wine flowed freely to symbolize royal liberality and there 'was ordained a goodly pageant'.[246] Two children addressed the boy king, in the imagery of spring as well as the emblematic language of the Tudor dynasty: 'Hayle redolent rose . . .'. Edward was heralded as a 'flourishing flower' who brought 'earthely joy'. But he was an earthly joy who was the gift of God:

> whom God hath provided for our great comfort
> to reigne in this realme of excellent fame,
> the only cause of unity and concord,
> thanks be therefore unto our heavenly Lord.

A song praised the Lord for Edward 'whom we sought to honour; bothe love and to drede/as our most noble kyng/and sovereigne lorde; / next under God, of Englande /and Irelande the Supreme hede'.[247] Tudor, divine ruler, Supreme Head, hopeful youth: in the very first pageant that greeted him, Edward was presented as all – to himself and to his people.

As the entourage made its way to Cheapside, it was welcomed at the Great Conduit by a second pageant, opened by two figures: one representing Valentine, a knight of Romance, the other 'wild Urson', clothed in moss with a club. Urson, for all his native garb 'an emperor's son' reared in the forest, promises to defend Edward 'of all rebels', as does Valentine, brought up in 'martial cunning'. Behind them, by a rock 'garnished with roses' and a fountain topped with an imperial crown of gold, stood children garbed as Grace, Nature, Fortune and Charity, who addressed the royal procession in turn, bestowing their gifts: 'moral cunning', strength, prudence and faith, health and fertility.[248] Slightly further on, seven other figures, 'representing Sapience and the other seven Sciences' (grammar, rhetoric, logic, arithmetic, music, geometry and astronomy) offered their services to preserve a king who had already displayed as a prince his aptitude for humanist learning. While, the last, Astronomy, was praising Edward as 'descended lynally through God's provision and his divine poure', on a double stage hung with cloth of gold, a phoenix descended from a cloud to spread red and white roses, gillyflowers and hawthorn boughs.[249] A crowned lion appeared and, after its 'making semblance of amity with the bird', a young lion came forth which was crowned by two angels. The phoenix, famous later in the century as the emblem of Queen Elizabeth, was the crest of Jane Seymour whose marriage to Henry had produced the young lion about to be crowned – a symbol of rebirth. On the lower storey of the stage, a child seated on a throne (representing Edward) gave the allegory specific explication: Regality, with a sceptre, Justice with a sword, Mercy with a curtana, and Truth with a book prepared to crown the king with all the attributes of kingship; while, behind the throne, a golden fleece protected by two bulls 'according to the story of Jason' associated Edward's coronation with imperial order and grandeur (the Golden Fleece was a theme of Charles V's entry to London in 1522).[250] Edward, that is, was represented to the public, many of whom might have viewed that earlier entry, as of imperial descent, a prince born of a father who had entertained emperors as well as won victories in France. As if the display of Edward's descent and lineage were not enough, at the procession's next stop, the Standard at Cheapside, a speech by the figure representing England reiterated what the pageant had played out. Edward was enjoined to follow in the steps of his father who had freed the realm from vice and foreign powers.[251]

By the Cheapside cross, the mayor and aldermen assembled to welcome the king into the city with a gift, before the procession moved on to the next pageant at the Little Conduit, where was set a scene, decorated with a shield of St George and the king's arms, with an enthroned figure of St Edward the Confessor. Below, mounted on horseback, St George prepared to deliver a speech honouring the king and promising to protect him from 'hurt, damage, or any danger'.[252] Though 'lack of time' impeded its delivery, a popular ballad, to the tune of 'Down a Down', sang the joys of Edward's succession and youthful promise:

when he waxeth wight, and to manhood doth sprynge
he shalbe streight of iiii realmes the Kynge.[253]

Tied by his name to England's saintly king and patron saint, Edward was presented as the inheritor of both piety and bravery, a father's son 'of such might that all the world may him feare'.[254] After a comic interlude, possibly designed to provide light relief for the boy, in which an acrobat performed tricks on a rope from St Gregory's to St Paul's, the king and his entourage progressed to the Great Conduit in Fleet Street, where three children emblazoned with the names of Truth, Faith and Justice and in rich apparel saluted the king. Truth delivered an overtly topical speech for any who might have wondered about the religious course that the new government might take:

I auncyent Trewth, which long time was suppressed
with hethen rites and detestable idolatrye,

have in thy realme been in great part refreshed
by God's servant my defender king Henry.[255]

Edward is then exhorted in the strongest terms:

Wherefore if you wyll me lykewise embrace,
as did your father, most loving kynge Edward,
then shall the God of Truth give you his grace.[256]

Edward was not just being celebrated as heir to his father but looked to as 'a
yonge kynge Solomon' after 'old David' – as the godly ruler of a new Israel who
would not only rout England's enemies but build a new temple in the chosen
land. Fittingly it was the last pageant or speech before Edward returned to
Westminster to await his coronation and solemn oath before God and his
people.

The historian of Tudor pageantry found little impressive in 'this totally undistinguished royal entry', much of which appeared to be put together and
borrowed from an earlier pageant for Henry VI in 1432.[257] Such a verdict may
miss the point. Given the traditional anxieties about minority rule, what was
important in 1547 was the portrayal of business as usual, of the smooth
continuity of English history, the succession of the crown, and the Tudor
dynasty. Whatever his later reputation, in 1432 Henry VI had appeared the true
heir to his victorious father Henry V; after being crowned in Paris, he
re-entered London to a magnificent welcome, aged only a year or two older than
Edward whose own father had re-established a foothold in France. Moreover,
Edward's coronation pageants not only evoked Lancastrian and Tudor glories,
they folded into history and presented in the language of patriotism religious
changes that had threatened to tear the realm apart. Henry VI, after all, was held
to be a saint; to appropriate him for godly rule was something of a coup. In
Edward's coronation pageantry, Protestantism *is* patriotism: Henry is simply
presented as bearing the banner of the true word, as his son is called upon to
take it up and found the holy commonweal. Hints of the fear surrounding
minority kingship, and more particularly the turbulence and violence of the
1530s, surface in the references to the dangers of 'enemies' and 'rebels'.[258] But in
the pageant such opposition is figured as other, as foreign, and is dispelled by
the protectors of England, indeed by England itself. 'The strengthe of a realme
is in a ryghtous kyng.'[259] As 'Christ's champion' Edward was safe, and the nation
was safe 'in Goddes hand'.

Edward's brief reign was not lacking in ceremony and, in the words of his
biographer, the king 'loved pageantry'.[260] His chronicle describes, in unusual
detail, a water pageant after a dinner held at Lord Admiral Clinton's. There at

Deptford, 'after supper was a fort made upon a great lighter on the Thames which had three walls and a watch tower . . .' which was assaulted and taken by the admiral of the navy.[261] Whether the entertainment, as so often sieges of castles were, was symbolic on this occasion we cannot know; but in the factional rivalries of Edward's reign, Clinton's advertisement of his capacities was certainly a political bid. And Edward clearly had a sense of the importance of pageantry in his own representation and bid for power. Increasingly he refers to visits of envoys to him and his own place as the centrepiece of court spectacle.[262]

We may detect the first signs of this in Edward's recording his importance and role in the visit of the Seigneur de St André, marshal of France, who in July 1551 led an embassy to present the order of St Michael to the king. Edward stresses the proximity and intimacy of the visit – he 'supped with me . . . and after came and made me ready'.[263] The next day, he recorded, 'he came to see my arraying and saw my bedchamber . . . and saw me shoot. He dined with me, heard me play instruments, ride, came to me in my study . . .'.[264] In November 1551, the Queen Dowager of Scotland came to court and, Edward reports, 'In the hall I met her with all the rest of the lords of my Council . . . the court, the hall and the stairs were full of serving men, the presence chamber, great chamber and her presence chamber of gentlemen . . . I went to her to dinner. She dined under the same cloth of estate, at my left hand. . . . After dinner when she had heard some music, I brought her to the hall.'[265] Anglo explains the greater interest in pageantry, and an increase in expenditure on revels, in terms of the succession of Northumberland as royal Protector after 1549.[266] But we sense here rather the king's sense of pageant as an advertisement of his own place at the centre of spectacle and power. The construction of a special banqueting house for the marshal's visit and the expensive and pleasing gifts presented to the French certainly made an impression – and doubtless not only on Edward's foreign guests.[267] Seeing the king in discussion and state with envoys, or attended (even by his own family) kneeling presented Edward as increasingly what he was: a monarch in fact as well as name, one who would shape foreign policy as well as affairs at home.

And the presentation and representation of Edward as king were not restricted to the courtly entourage at Whitehall or Hampton Court. Albeit his journeys were largely confined to the south, Edward maintained an annual progress and himself appears to have grasped the political function and importance of royal progresses. In his chronicle of the summer of 1549, as we have seen, Edward records, 'In the mean season, because there was a rumour that I was dead, I passed through London.'[268] Behind that spare sentence lies Edward's own recognition of the importance of a monarch being seen, and especially a minor who had no heirs and on whom the dynasty and realm rested. Accordingly, the chronicle marks every summer progress: in May 1552, for example, Edward notes plans for a journey to Portsmouth and Poole, Salisbury and Windsor; and it is evident that he regarded these journeys as both the display of, and further preparation for, his kingship.[269] In July, Edward removed to Guildford, then Petworth, and thence on to Waltham before arriving at Portsmouth on 4 August. Here he spent time viewing the town's storehouse and the forts at the entry to the harbour before progressing to Southampton via a sojourn at the Earl of Southampton's manor at Titchfield. At Southampton, it seems, Edward received the French ambassador, before moving to Beaulieu in the New Forest, presumably to hunt. The progress then continued through Christchurch to the house of Sir Edward Willoughby at Woodlands, where Edward recorded news of a peace between Duke Maurice and the emperor and the advance of the Turks, suggesting that business very much followed him on his journey. The rest of August was then taken up by a journey from Salisbury to Wilton, Mottisfont and Winchester. Edward stayed with the Earl of Winchester at Basing and the Duke of Suffolk at Dunnington Castle, before returning to Windsor, via Reading, in mid-September.[270]

Hayward claimed that this progress had very specific political import: 'Edward', he wrote, having been sick of the measles that spring, 'rode his progress with greater magnificence than ever before . . . whether it were to maintain his majesty or to manifest the fear which had formerly been impressed, he carried with him a band of 320 men, which made up his whole train above the number of 4000 horse.'[271] We have direct evidence of the young Edward's recognition of the purpose of the progress in his letter to Barnaby Fitzpatrick in which he provided details of the houses in which he had lodged, the hunting, and the opportunity travel had afforded him of 'viewing of fair counties'.[272] Edward noted the country's freedom from plague and delighted in the good cheer the citizens afforded him and the 'costly tables' they kept. He was also aware of the role of the progress as a public relations exercise, for, in July, Edward observed that because the number of bands with him (as Hayward had observed) was great, it was decided 'they should be sent home . . . this was because the train was thought to be over 4000 horse which were enough to eat up the county; for there was little meadow nor hay . . .'.[273] To effectively represent him as the just ruler of the commonweal, Edward's progresses, as he had appreciated, had to combine magnificent display with a minimal burden on the country through which the court travelled. The maintenance of the authority of monarchy depended on an acute grasp of circumstance and mood, and on the performances and actions, as well as image, of the king.

III Figuring Godly Rule

It may come as a surprise, given the modern familiarity with the images of
Henry VIII and Elizabeth, to learn that 'of all the Tudors, [Edward] seems to be
the most fully represented in drawings and pictures'.[274] And while many of the
nearly one hundred portraits of the boy king were posthumous representations, there are more than a few of him as king, as well as prince. We have
observed the anonymous portrait of Edward, attributed to the eve of his
succession, depicting him in white satin doublet and russet satin gown, with his
right hand on his dagger, and in a stance that echoes Holbein's Whitehall
portrait of Henry VIII.[275] This painting, most probably by Scrots, became the
prototype for the image of Edward as king: a copy at Petworth, Sussex is dated
1547 and the absence of the Prince of Wales feathers confirms that in this
version we encounter an image of a king, one that was copied for dozens of
country houses and for princes or envoys overseas.[276] A mural of Edward's
coronation was commissioned by Sir Anthony Brown, Master of the Horse,
presumably to commemorate his role in the procession; but – though we have
an eighteenth-century drawing of the image which was destroyed in a fire –
there is no evidence of contemporary copies or engravings.[277] Edward's
Household Accounts evidence that artists in the employ of Henry VIII were
retained in the service of his son, including 'Gillam Scrottes Dutchman, the
King's Painter', who was confirmed in office in 1545. Payments to Scrots for two
'pictures of his highness' are recorded in March 1552 and these were evidently
sent to ambassadors who, of course, were scouting Europe for a suitable bride
for the young king, and who may have been sent the portraits as part of
marriage negotiations.[278] Edward himself evidently took a personal interest in
portraits and requested one of his sister, Elizabeth, which is now lost.[279]

A miniature of Edward enthroned in the House of Lords in 1553, with
Garter and other attendants bearing the regalia of state at his feet, is found in
Gilbert Dethick's register of the Order of the Garter at Windsor – but there is
no evidence of any other copy of the image.[280] Unlike those of Henry VIII, the
miniatures of Edward decorating plea rolls are largely undistinguished as
high-quality executions or likenesses. However, the early images of Edward
enthroned beneath a large crown, or with the motto 'Vivat Rex', certainly
present the new monarch as the new ruler, as well as a minor, as did similar
images on letters patent of the reign.[281] Moreover, some of the later illustrations gain in quality as obvious representations of Edward. A fine miniature of
Edward enthroned and crowned, beneath a dove and a scroll inscribed with a
verse beginning 'O mercyfull God,/ do us not forsake', may speak to the hopes
for religious reform placed in Edward, as well as of the importance of the
Tusser family, members of whom attend on the king in the picture.[282] The

17 Edward VI with figures, Easter 1549 plea roll.

illustration to letters patent granted to Gerard Harmond would certainly seem
to speak to the representation of Edward as Supreme Head and conveyor of
the word to his people.[283] Next to the initial letter of the document, Edward is
depicted in ermine, enthroned in his palace, in a style and pose reminiscent of
Holbein's miniature of Henry as Solomon. Edward, attended by his councillors Somerset and Warwick, holds in his right hand a sword, while with his left
he proffers a book to kneeling clergy. On the ground by the king's left foot lies
a mitre. The miniature, also reminiscent of the engraved picture of Henry on
the Coverdale Bible, presents Edward as the conqueror of papal superstition,
as Supreme Head and conveyor of the word to his people. The image suggests
that, as well as dynastic heir, Edward was represented as the leader of reform,
and as authority for the further reformation of the church.

For all the difficulties they present, the engraved portraits of King Edward VI
are important texts of royal representation. While the majority of these post-
date Edward's reign and were used by Foxe and others to advance the cause of
Protestant reform under Elizabeth, some are unquestionably contemporary. A
print of Edward VI seated in Council illustrated Hall's *Chronicle* in 1548 and
was placed at the head of the title page of Richard Grafton's edition of the
statutes of the first year of the reign – perhaps to convey reassurance about the

18   Edward VI with clergy and noblemen, from the letters patent to Gerard Harmond.

continuity of royal authority in a minority.[284] And in Archbishop Cranmer's 1548 catechism there is a frontispiece engraving of Edward distributing bibles to his people which publicizes the young king as, like his father, divine agent and dispenser of the word of God.[285] The portrait depicts Edward seated on an elaborate colonnaded throne with the sword in his right hand, presenting with his left the sceptre to kneeling bishops and nobles who surround the throne, beneath which a large royal arms is encircled by the Garter motto 'Honi soit qui mal y pense'. At the top and foot of the portrait, verses from Proverbs 20 and Joshua I connect the king and the book. 'The King ought to be feared as the roaring of a lion'; 'let not the book of this law depart out of your mouths'. The epistle dedicatory to Edward explains: the king is 'most desirous perfectly to finish . . . that your father did most godly begin'.[286]

Other engravings representing Edward as learned prince, custodian of the word and leader of reform certainly circulated in England and Europe: John Bale's 1547 edition of his *Illustrium maioris Britanniae scriptorum summarium*, published in England the next year, was illustrated with a portrait of Edward enthroned with crown and sceptre receiving from the author his catalogue of British writers.[287] Though the image here is of authorial presentation to the king, it too echoes the representations of Edward as a conveyor of the word

¶ The kyng ought to be feared as the roaryng of a Lyō, ꝩ puoketh him unto anger, offēdeth agaiſt his owne ſoule. p͛o

· E · C · R ·

HONI · SOIT · QVI · MALY · PENSE

¶ Let not the booke of this law depart out of your mouthe recorde there in dape and nyghte, that you maye do accoꝛdꝥ all that is wꝛytten therin.   Joſua, i, ꝟ.   Deut. xvii, ꝟ.

19 Frontispiece to Thomas Cranmer's *Catechismus*.

giving Bibles

and as 'instigator of a new age of reformed religion'.[288] As Stephen Alford rightly observes, such 'representations of the king in books and pamphlets served to underpin the principle that he was personally ... involved in Reformation'.[289]

Any discussion of the representation of Edward as godly reforming prince leads us to the famous image of Edward VI and the pope.[290] The painting, of which there are also engravings, depicts a weak Henry VIII propped up on what is his deathbed, gesturing with his left hand to Edward who sits enthroned beneath a cloth of state displaying royal arms. At Edward's feet lies

20 *King Edward VI and the Pope.*

the body of the pope, bearing the blazon 'All flesh is grass' and a book – the Bible – here open at 'The word of the Lord endureth for ever.' On Edward's left councillors stand and sit beneath a scene of iconoclasm and the destruction of a cross. Traditionally the image has been dated to 1549, and interpreted as the representation of Edward as the heir to his father's supremacy and advocate of religious reform, and as counsel to the new king to further the assault on popery and superstition. In 1993, however, Margaret Aston powerfully argued that the group portrait belongs to the 1560s and to a campaign to persuade Queen Elizabeth to more godly courses of action.²⁹¹ Though Aston's argument has almost become orthodoxy, Jennifer Loach cast doubts upon the redating and suggested that 'the possibility remains that the picture (or some earlier version of it) was painted, as we have always supposed, early in Edward's reign'.²⁹² The uncertainty about the portrait is, for our purpose, instructive. The visual image of Edward in his own reign is hard to separate from the myriad later representations of him as the hope and champion of godly reformation – not least because these later representations, if not the only image of the king, had contemporary warrant.

The medals, seals and coins of Edward's reign, which await full study, are important documents of the representation of Edward as dynast and godly prince. Edward's coronation medal, though it was the first coronation medal struck in gold and silver, 'entirely corresponded with a medal of Henry VIII which was struck on his assuming the title of Supreme Head of the Church'.[293] The gold and some silver versions bore a profile portrait of Edward with sword and orb, with inscriptions in Latin, Hebrew and Greek, commemorating the coronation; other silver versions carried a different, profile image of Edward in ermine. The survival of a lead cast, 'possibly for a medallion of silver which may have formed the centre of a dish or plate', and of counters or medalets indicates the extent to which this coronation was celebrated and commemorated in physical mementoes.[294] A silver gilt piece, probably intended for a locket commemorating the coronation, was issued two years later in 1549, perhaps when, at twelve, Edward was thought to be coming of age.[295] All the medals of course announce the young king as Supreme Head; one bears the inscription 'Scutum fidei proteget eum' – may the shield of faith safeguard him.[296] Edward's Great Seal figured the king seated between the shields of England and France, quartered within the Garter, with a badge of roses and fleurs-de-lis, and on the reverse, the king on horseback in armour.[297] The seal Edward himself proposed for the reformed Order of the Garter added to the arms of England the portrait of the king and the Garter motto ('Honi soit') the religious injunction: 'Verbum domini manet in aeternam'.[298] While the Henrician forms of representation were retained and reprised in Edward's seal and medals, there was, as we might expect, a greater advertisement of regality as supremacy and of the king as custodian and champion of God's word and faith.

The coronation medal and the seal provided only occasional opportunities for revising visual representations of the sovereign. In Edward's reign, the frequent reissue, debasement and then gradual reform of the coinage offered many more. Very early in the reign, the new gold and silver coin ordered by Somerset was abandoned, as government expenses necessitated debasement.[299] In January and April 1549 new coins were again authorized and a new mint had to be opened to cope with the production.[300] Moves to restore

21 Gold medal of Edward VI.

22 Great Seal of Edward VI.

the coin to its earlier worth began in 1550, with the peace with France, and
from early the next year, new coins were minted which, for all the continued
circulation of outdated currency, began the process of reform.[301] Many of the
proclamations of Edward's reign are concerned with the calling in and reissue
of coin: the announcing in January 1549 of the half-sovereign or Edward
Royal, and the crown, or the new angels and half-angels of 1552 with double
roses and portcullises.[302] Edward himself took an interest in the coinage,
recording in his chronicle for September 1551 that it was 'agreed that the
stamp of the shilling and the sixpence should be of one side a king painted

to the shoulder, in parliament robes, with a chain of the order; five shillings of silver and half five shillings should be a king on horseback armed, with a naked sword to his breast'.[303] As this entry indicates, coins took up the representations on medals and the Great Seal to circulate them to a wider public. Gold coins repeated the image of Edward enthroned and in profile and the medallic inscription 'Scutum fidei proteget eum'.[304] Coins, however, also suggest shifts and developments in the royal representation: as well as images of the king and royal arms, gold pieces figure the ship of state, emblazoned with the royal arms and inside the inscription 'Xpe red & per crucem tuam salve nos', with on the reverse a St Michael slaying the monster of superstition.[305] The silver coins more commonly depict Edward crowned, full face, in profile or armed and mounted, with the inscriptions 'Timor domini fons vitae' ('The fear of the Lord is the wellspring of life'), or with a cross over the reverse 'Posui deum adiutorem meum' – 'I have placed myself in God my helper' or 'Induam confusionem inimicos eius' – 'May I ever throw into confusion the enemies of the Lord'.[306] The allusions to Scripture and the use of the personal pronoun, together with the images of England and Edward, present this coin as that not only of a godly prince but of the ruler of an elect nation.

As Jennifer Loach valuably underlined, the image of Edward's court 'maintained all his father's magnificence'.[307] Edward not only lived among the lavish

23 Edward VI gold coin.

artefacts of his father's acquisitions; he bought rich jewels to supplement the collection.[308] The boy loved lavish clothes, garnished with precious stones, and appreciated the importance of conspicuous display for his standing in the theatre of international diplomacy, as well as on the home stage. But for all the relative silence of his chronicle on matters of faith, on medals and coins and in engraved portraits, Edward, as well as publicizing his Tudor lineage, appears to have desired to be presented as the godly reformer, that Josias whom Cranmer had addressed at the coronation in 1547.

IV The Contest for Representation

The presentation of Edward as champion of a godly commonwealth was neither straightforward nor uncontested. The legacy of Henry VIII was still one of uncertainty about the direction of religious affairs and bishops like Gardiner and Bonner still hoped to arrest any further reform: not until 1550 did the balance of power on the episcopal bench move decisively in favour of the reformers; and not until the end of the reign were they able to abandon ambiguous pronouncements for clear Protestant doctrine.[309] As historians of politics have shown, as well as factional rivals vying for power at court and disagreements about the nature and pace of reform, debt, fiscal problems and social dislocation brought Edward's reign close to crisis.[310] Behind one story of the creation of a Protestant nation are, as well as outright rebellions, other accounts of people staying away from church or disrupting the new services.[311] Not the least part of the troubles the government faced, though it has been little studied, were the many false accounts (as the regimes saw them), misrepresentations and rumours that countered the image of a harmonious commonweal and godly nation and threatened widespread popular unrest. From the outset to the death of the young king, Edward's reign was marked by, and by a conspicuous government fear of, rumours and libels – indeed of any alternative representation of events, whether in ballad, play or gossip.

Within a few months of Edward's succession, a royal proclamation referred to the 'divers lewd and light tales told, whispered and secretly spread abroad by uncertain authors, in markets, fairs and alehouses . . . of innovations and changes in religion and ceremonies of the church . . .'.[312] 'Pondering', the proclamation continued, 'the great hurt, damage, loss and disquietness among his grace's subjects which might ensue' and clearly nervous about its inability to control news, the government strictly charged magistrates to pursue not only the authors of such tales but all 'hearing, reading, knowing, or witting' (that is learning of) them until they revealed the name of their source.

Both the change towards a Protestant liturgy and the uncertainty about the course of the new regime were evidently the circumstances in which rumours were ignited and spread like a brush fire through the nation. But in some cases we know that the flames were ignited and fanned by clergy unsympathetic to the new courses and quick to present them in the most unfavourable light. By the spring of 1548, the government identified 'unlearned and indiscreet preachers and other priests' of a 'devilish mind and intent' who were inciting the people to 'disobedience and stubbornness against his majesty's godly proceedings' and who, in particular, were spreading false rumours that new exactions were to be levied for marriages, christenings and burials.[313] The remedy of banning all but licensed preachers failed to stem the tide of rumour. By September, it had become apparent that even licensed preachers had 'abused the said authority of preaching and behaved themselves ... without good order ... whereby much contention and disorder might ensue'.[314]

False rumours reached their height in 1549 and began to pose a real threat to the stability of the regime. The false reports of 'great overthrows, losses and dangers' in the war against the Scots not only undermined the government at home – victory against the old enemy was essential for the legitimacy of early modern monarchy – but exposed it to foreign invasion as strangers took occasion 'to write into distant countries such tales [of defeat] for news'.[315] The authors of these false reports were threatened with slavery in the galleys but, as proclamations urging JPs 'to do their best endeavour' all but acknowledge, finding them was a near-impossible task.[316] Both the economic dislocations and the wars exacerbated the problems of the 'lewd, idle, seditious ... and disordered persons' wandering the realm and 'posting from place to place ... to stir up rumours, [or] raise up tales'.[317] In overtly political language, a proclamation of July 1549 described such 'lewd ruffians, taletellers' becoming 'ringleaders, and masters of the king's people and leading them by deceit and pretence of reforming to uproars and tumults'.[318] So serious had the government loss of the control of news become that magistrates and subjects apprehending and reporting 'rumour runners' were offered full costs and a reward for performing what was, in reality, their legal duty.[319] The fragility of Tudor governments when they could not manage the representation of their policies is nowhere more apparent: effective government meant the winning of hearts and minds.

But neither the promise of reward nor the threat of condign punishment silenced the many counter-representations that challenged Edward's government, his ministers and councillors, its policies and religious reforms. Players, in Henry VIII's reign sometimes (as we have seen) recruited by ministers as instruments of government, were banned by the government of his son for 'interludes as contain matter tending to sedition and contemning of sundry good order and laws'; but they evidently continued to perform – and then publish – entertainments devised by 'light and fantastical heads' throughout the realm.[320] And with the commitment of the Duke of Somerset, rumours rapidly spread 'that the good laws made for religion should now be altered and abolished, and the old Romish service, mass and ceremonies aftsoons renewed and revived'.[321] A popular perception, fuelled by such rumours, that the setting forth of the new service book 'had been the only act of the aforementioned Duke' struck directly at the authority of Edward and his Council, underlining one of the fundamental weaknesses of a minority.[322] A rumour that the king himself had not authorized the religious changes ran directly counter to the government's, indeed Edward's, strenuous efforts to present the king as in charge. Indeed, it was the freedom taken by many to 'speak their pleasure without regard of his highness or his honourable Council' that the regime, rightly, feared was 'tending to rebellion'.[323] When so much of the king's power was vested in the royal word, the devising of 'rumour or talk touching his majesty, his council ... or ministers' and 'the telling of it' were indeed rebellious acts.[324] This was especially the case when those with a different agenda to the government took advantage of the relatively new medium of print to spread tales or present a case. Several proclamations referred to 'divers printers [and] booksellers' who would publish 'whatsoever any light and fantastical head listeth to invent', making it clear that, for all its benefit to government, print was very much an ambiguous medium – one as open to opponents as to defenders of the regime.[325] Attempts to ban the printing or sale of any text in English not authorized by the Council were frustrated by market demand as much as by the practical difficulties of enforcing censorship. Indeed, rumour fed the market for print which, in turn, publicized what began as local stories to the whole nation, in the process politicizing the literate, and the many more illiterate subjects who heard pamphlets or libels read.[326] A proclamation of May 1551 describes in despairing language the reach of opposition texts and the devastating effects they had had on popular consciousness and behaviour: divers 'lewd and seditious persons', it stated, have 'made many slanderous and wicked bills, as well against the king's majesty's most honourable council as against other noble personages within this realm, and the same bills have spread and cast abroad in streets and in divers other places, and have fastened the same to such privy corners where they thought they might best publish their conceived malice'.[327] Not only, it was confessed, would the authors not 'easily be found out to be punished', the citizens, rather than destroying the libels, had consumed and distributed them 'to the maintenance and encouragement of such malefactors'.[328] Print and rumour had helped to forge not only a public sphere of debates about *arcana imperii*, but a citizenry ready to criticize government exactions, debasements and policies.

The power of informed public opinion is hard to measure, but the best evidence of its force are the government's approach to it and obvious anxiety about it.[329] As we have seen, official representations appealed to subjects with a new emphasis on the 'commonweal'; bishops and councillors routinely condemned the greed of avaricious or enclosing landlords; Protector Somerset presented himself as (and was charged with being) an advocate of the people.[330] Though essential – especially in a minority – those appeals to and for popular support exacerbated difficulties in a nation confused and divided about the direction of affairs. Writing with hindsight and an obvious dislike of the Protector, the historian John Hayward viewed Somerset's 'abusing' of Henry VIII's will as a Machiavellian plot 'to extinguish the love of the people to the young king' and to enhance his own power.[331] We do not have to accept his analysis to see that Somerset's personal appeal to the people created complications for Edward's government, especially when the Protector fell from favour. When at his trial, for example, Somerset was acquitted of treason, albeit found guilty of felony, the people, supposing that he was altogether acquit, shouted half a dozen times so loud that they were heard beyond Charing Cross.[332] The execution of the popular Protector had to be carefully stage-managed by a nervous government, and even then popular feeling made itself heard: 'Albeit straight charge had been given the day before to every householder in the city, not to permit any to depart out of their houses before ten of the clock that day, yet the people . . . swarmed to the place . . . and all the chambers which opened towards the scaffold were taken up.'[333] Though Somerset urged obedience to the king, he asserted too his commitment to the public benefit and common good, and hinted at the 'great persons' who had brought him down.[334] Clearly the atmosphere was tense: the late arrival of a group commissioned to appear by the Lieutenant of the Tower sparked a tumult which held up proceedings; and the entry of Sir Anthony Browne on horseback gave hope of a pardon, 'Whereupon a great shout was raised, a pardon, a pardon, God Save the King.'[335] When the reprieve failed to materialize, the people were left to dip their handkerchiefs in the blood of the Protector and to nurture their hatred against Northumberland who had brought about his fall.

In Hayward's later account of these events, the people are presented as a powerful force who nearly checked Northumberland's coup against Somerset and finally brought about his demise. Of those tried with Somerset, Sir Thomas Arundel was only with some difficulty condemned after harassment of the jury; and 'the remembrance of Somerset much moved the people to fall from Northumberland . . . and to leave him to his fatal fall'.[336] Indeed, Hayward claims, in the discussions about the succession, it was even argued that, if either Princess Mary or Elizabeth were to succeed and marry a foreigner so subordinating the realm to another power, 'the people were not unlike to elect [sic] a king of some private stock, a popular and seditious man . . .'.[337] Allowing for the rhetoric of such arguments, the suggestion in 1553 that the people might determine the succession and elect a private man as king remains remarkable testament to the power, or perceived power, of public opinion in the reign of Edward VI. For all the lengths the king himself and his ministers went to to argue their authority and to promote their policies, minority rule, a divided Council and a polarized nation politicized by rumour and print rendered all the representations of authority a negotiation and struggle. At Edward's coronation, a popular ballad, with the refrain 'down a down' had welcomed the new king; as, aged fifteen, he lay on his deathbed, rumours spread that a schoolmistress, brought to attend the king, 'was but an instrument of mischief' to poison him.[338] Rumour accompanied Edward VI to the grave.

I have argued that from soon after his succession, Edward, whose youth threatened to reduce him to 'a symbol of policies determined by the adults around him', endeavoured to forge his own image and to claim for his young person the authority of the crown.[339] In many respects which have been underestimated, he emulated the martial, vigorous image of his father, but in important ways, manifest in his writings, and on his medals and coins, Edward also distanced himself from Henry VIII – at least the Henry VIII of the Six Articles. Even more than his father he deployed the language of social reform; and though religion by no means dominated his self-presentation, in position papers and on medallic inscriptions he made clear his commitment to godly rule. As we have seen, many aided Edward in his construction and maintenance of royal authority. But others, from his uncle the Lord Protector down, had their own agenda which could at times vie with or overwrite the personal representations of the king. Cranmer and Latimer were only the leading advisers who presented the young Edward as what they wanted him to be: England's Josiah, the champion of full Protestant reformation of theology and liturgy and of an iconoclastic campaign against all the vestiges of popery. Even the official image of Edward VI was no single representation: the two protectors, nobles and divines, as well as Edward himself, all contributed to a representation of monarchy which also drew on the needs and grievances of the people. The rhetoric of authority, unity and harmony, which was central to that representation, was itself challenged: by Catholics, Anabaptists and sects, by rebels and popular insurgents who, in diffuse ways, countered official accounts, artefacts and images. Mary's open celebration of the mass,[340] Catholic libels against the Edwardian religious settlement, like the ballad of Little John Nobody,[341] the Anabaptist who interrupted Hooper's sermons,[342] the bare arse turned to the king's herald when he came with a pardon to the Norfolk rebels, all directly confronted the signs of royal authority, as well as authority itself.[343] Edward's reign was the story of a young ruler's struggle to establish his identity, the force of his word and image as the foundation of personal authority and to effect godly reformation in a realm still uncertain that it wanted it.

In many ways he failed. In traditional historiography, the young prince who sought to emulate his father's martial prowess has been depicted as frail and sickly. The Edward who, despite his youth, strove to establish his own position is often presented as a mere child or puppet manipulated by his uncle and the Duke of Northumberland.[344] Most of all, the Edward who had asserted his royal supremacy was depicted by Catholics as simply led into error by Somerset and taken up by various Protestant groups as a symbol of *their* godly reformation.[345] In particular, John Foxe, from the first edition of his *Acts and Monuments* – more commonly known as the Book of Martyrs – singled out Edward as the young Josiah who might be the model for the desired Protestant reform under Elizabeth. For all the reformers' disappointment that reformation did not go further, during and after the reign of Mary, Edward was made the champion of religious causes and parties and his portrait was used to illustrate texts, which there is no evidence that he supported or would have endorsed.[346] Indeed, John Knox and John Ponet were to develop Edwardian ideas about royal responsibility into a radical critique of royal authority when it was not accompanied with godly rule.[347]

The afterlife of Edward's image undoubtedly testifies to the vulnerability of royal representations to myriad appropriations, and indeed reflects the contemporary reality of the reign in which many claimed the king's support for a variety of purposes. But what it also evidences is how Edward himself, not his ministers, had become the image and symbol – that is the authority – that needed to be appropriated. In this respect at least Edward had succeeded: though only fifteen when he died, he had established himself as the symbol of the new church and commonweal. Indeed, in his panegyrical *Funerals of King Edward the Sixth*, William Baldwin depicted Edward as taking the sins of the nation upon himself and, as Christ-like, dying to expiate them and save his chosen people.[348] The oval woodcut frontispiece of Edward VI, repeated at the end, literally makes his image frame the account.[349] Ruling often avaricious nobles, corrupt officers, rack-renters and superstitious prelates, Edward stood as the symbol of virtue and 'constant zeal for truth'.[350]

Until quite recently historians regarded Edward's reign as an inglorious interlude between that of two great Tudors, Henry VIII and Elizabeth. Writing after the reign of Gloriana, Edward's first historian could not defend him as 'equal in either spirit or power' to the strongest Tudors.[351] John Hayward catalogued the many mistakes and misjudgements, noble wranglings and tumults of a 'troublesome' reign.[352] At times, he depicts Edward 'scarce at his own liberty' amid the divisions among his councillors and nobles.[353] But Hayward also recognized the qualities that Edward himself had valued: his 'glory, courtesy and liberality'; his openness to petition, but his insistence on his authority.[354] In Hayward's history, though he faced disorder and rebellion, Edward appears as a young man of understanding 'famous in all places by reason of his foresight and judgement in affairs'.[355] As Edward's sickness heralded his death, some even began to compare him 'with greatest persons that had been, both for war and peace, because in the like pitch of years, none of them attained to the like perfections'.[356] His death, the preface to Hayward's history concluded, was 'premature'. We cannot know whether, had Edward lived, he would have had 'the fortune and fame of Caesar' which his biographer foresaw.[357] But we can be confident that the boy who had striven to establish his personal identity as ruler would have fully deployed the arts of representation as the foundation of his sovereignty.

PART V

REPRESENTATIONS AND REACTIONS

CHAPTER 8

IMAGES OF MARY TUDOR

I Success and Succession *Catholic Queen –*

Where Henry VIII stamped his image on his time and on the nation's memory and the young Edward VI strove to establish his identity and was heralded as the godly Josiah, Mary's reputation has been all but entirely determined by others. And not only others but opponents who characterized her as the secular agent of Antichrist. In large part, Mary's fate was that of all those on history's losing side: the historians of what became a Protestant nation successively wrote her as the obstacle to England's historical destiny.[1] Needless to say, this is not how Mary perceived or represented herself. Nor, as revisionist historians have argued, was it in any simple way how she was perceived by her people during her reign. Assessments of Mary's qualities as a monarch, as of her reign, have shifted with larger historiographical re-evaluations of the hold of the old religion and the strength of Protestant commitments in the 1550s.[2] Our purpose is to review the images that Mary and her ministers – and after her marriage the queen and her husband Philip II of Spain – presented to her subjects; how her rule was represented in proclamation, portrait and pageant. We will examine the *nice* ways in which the first female monarch since Matilda deployed the traditional modes and tropes of royal representation.[3] And we shall seek to evaluate the responses of subjects to Mary's representation and the counter-presentations of her rule by critics and religious opponents. Throughout we shall consider whether Mary lost the contest over representation even during her own reign: whether her failure was a contemporary failure of image as well as of policy, rather than simply the later judgement of a Protestant nation.

At the outset of Mary's reign the genres and forms of royal representation were not the monopoly of any one faith. As Henry VIII had shown, through various shifts in matters liturgical and theological, and as Edward and his ministers had underlined in enacting a Protestant settlement, a supremacy established on rhetoric as much as action had enabled the first Tudors to effect sometimes unpopular religious changes without (at least manifestly) undermining royal authority. Mary's Catholicism, therefore, need not have presented fundamental difficulties to her rule or representation – especially if, as the consensus now is, the realm was by no means a Protestant commonweal by 1553. Yet by 1558, Roman Catholic kingship had perhaps become so discredited that thereafter the texts and discourses of royal representation could be successfully deployed only for Protestant rule. The story of the dramatic shift is as much a story of Mary's (neglected) royal image as of her policies – a story of the first, and only, Tudor who entirely lost the competition for representation, and in the process tainted her faith as well as her memory.

Ironically, Mary's reign began in a contest for representation which she triumphantly won. Having altered Henry VIII's will so as to secure a Protestant succession, Edward VI and his minister John Dudley, Duke of Northumberland, had arranged for Northumberland's daughter-in-law, Lady Jane Grey, to ascend the throne in Mary's stead.[4] When Edward died towards night on 6 July 1553, his death was kept secret while the Tower was fortified and plans were devised to secure Mary in her palace in Norfolk. On the 9th, the guard and officers of the household swore allegiance to Jane, who the next day was received into the Tower 'with a great company of lords and nobles' with a salute of a 'shot of guns'.[5] At six in the evening, the new queen was proclaimed by a herald and trumpet from Cheapside to Fleet Street. The proclamation made claims for Jane's legitimacy and pointed up the danger to the realm had Mary or Elizabeth succeeded and married a foreigner, to the 'total subversion of the public weal'.[6]

Mary received the news of Edward's death on 8 July. The next day she returned to her main residence at Kenninghall and there proclaimed herself queen 'by divine and human law'. The same day she wrote to the Privy Council in London to order them to 'cause our right and title for the crown and government of the realm to be proclaimed in our city of London and other places'.[8] Over the next week, as armed support was canvassed and gathered on both sides, two queens were proclaiming themselves the rightful and divinely appointed rulers of the nation.

Interestingly, neither's claim was made without opposition. On the very day that Jane was brought in triumph to the Tower, Gianfrancesco Commendone, secretary to the Cardinal of Imola, reported that 'although the number of people assisting to the ceremony was very high, no cheering was heard'.[9] Commendone judged that the people favoured Mary and were 'discontented with the election of Jane'. When the latter was hurriedly proclaimed, 'the people heard it with remarkable discontent as hateful to everybody', to the point that 'it could be read on the faces of the heralds themselves how uneasy they felt'.[10] Another observer, the Spanish merchant Antonio de Guaras, noting the surprise and astonishment of the people, reported how a nervous regime took swift and brutal measures in an effort to shore up Jane's authority: 'they cut off at the root the ears of one who demanded why the lady Mary should not be queen, and made great show of heralds who intimidated the people'.[11]

Meanwhile in Norfolk not everything went smoothly for Mary. When, on hearing corroboration of the news of Edward's death, she proclaimed herself queen in her residence at Kenninghall 'and in all the country round about', there were 'some places' (according to Guaras) where 'the inhabitants would not receive her proclamation, being ignorant of the certainty of the King's death and also seeing that all the nobles of the kingdom had bound them-selves to live and die in the cause of the aforesaid Lady Jane'.[12] Over the five or six days that followed Mary's proclamation, Guaras reported, despite her writing to all the nobility on pain of treason to come and pay her homage, not many came over to her side.[13]

For a few days both queens proclaimed their legitimacy, while endeav-ouring to gather support. 'In many parts of the kingdom,' Guaras was informed, 'Jane was proclaimed two or three times over inasmuch as the friends of her highness came to these places and proclaimed her Queen, and as soon as they were departed, the inhabitants, for fear of the Council, proclaimed Jane anew and all were in arms in the greatest confusion.'[14]

Mary, meanwhile, was proclaimed queen in Buckinghamshire by Sir Edward Peckham, Sir Edward Hastings and Lord Windsor, and, after some hesitation, in Norwich.[15] Slowly Mary's support began to come in.[16] Guarras reports fifteen or twenty knights going to Mary, each with the armed support that he could muster, and describes a band of 20,000 assembling 'with the peasants of the two counties' of Norfolk and Suffolk.[17] As this band began to augment and organize, Mary 'inspected the whole camp, which was about a mile long, on foot with her nobles and ladies, thanking the soldiers who had cried out "Long live our good Queen Mary" for their good will'.[18] As she gathered her troops, the queen received a vital bonus. Northumberland had stationed ships off the Norfolk coast to contain Mary's movements and to deprive her of possible foreign aid. However, the ordinary seamen aboard these 'six or seven ships', perhaps local recruits from 'her highness's neighbourhood', 'from their natural love towards her, rose against their captains in favour of the Queen and put into a neighbouring port which was loyal to her highness'.[19]

Faced with Mary's growing support and strength, Northumberland resolved to act. Leaving Lady Jane in the care of her father, the Duke of Suffolk, at the Tower, Dudley left London with four of his sons to seize the Tudor claimant to the throne. Northumberland marched a band of 8,000 infantry and 2,500 horse to Cambridge.[20] But, even as he left London, the troops 'started to disband as unwilling to march against my Lady Mary, being deeply rooted in their minds, in spite of these seditions, a kind of remorse, knowing her to be . . . the daughter of their King Henry VIII'.[21]

Northumberland and Jane Grey's troubles did not end with the deserters from the army sent out to support her cause. Northumberland's absence from London left the Council no longer under his personal direction. The duke had foreseen the problem: he was 'concerned', according to Commendone, 'about some mutiny that might occur during his absence, which he would not be able to quell'.[22] Since he had these misgivings, Northumberland might have taken as an ominous portent the refusal of Suffolk to command the troops; but, perhaps trusting that, as Jane Grey's father, his allegiance was secure, Dudley appointed him his deputy in charge of the Council and affairs.[23] It took no time for Northumberland's suspicions to be borne out. 'After the departure of the Duke from London,' the cardinal's secretary informs us, 'several lords of the Council, freely discussing this matter, reached the conclusion that it was iniquitous and contrary to their duty to permit that the legitimate heir, by law of God and of the country, be robbed of the crown . . .'.[24] Most of the Council left the Tower to assemble at the Earl of Pembroke's seat, Barnard Castle, where Arundel, fresh out of imprisonment, declared against Northumberland's 'ambition to rule' and disregard for the welfare of the realm. 'This crown', he asserted, 'belongs rightfully, by direct succession, to my Lady Mary, lawful and natural daughter of our King Henry VIII' – a queen, he added, 'endowed with all the best gifts' from whom the realm could expect 'real justice, perpetual peace, lasting merciful rule, unfounded clemency and excellent government'.[25] Support for Mary, he reassured the waverers, was not only right but practicable: even if the duke had an army – and that was fragmenting as he spoke – the Council would be formidable 'if we all concur together in opinion'. Raising the spectre – one that still haunted the Tudor century – of civil war and foreign invasion, Arundel urged unity behind Mary. Backed by Pembroke, Arundel's speech persuaded the Council to sign a proclamation declaring Mary queen and sending to the Duke of Suffolk to yield the Tower. Suffolk concurred. 'But', we are told, before leaving to sign the proclamation, he performed an extraordinary symbolic act: 'he entered the room where his daughter was sitting in state, and, removing a baldachin from over her head, as clear demonstration of what had to follow, he told her to do homage to my Lady Mary as to her Queen, as she had been already proclaimed . . .'.[26]

On 19 July, about four in the afternoon, ten days after the proclamation of Queen Jane, a proclamation in Mary's name, announcing her 'direct and legitimate' succession to Edward, was read in London by members of the Council who 'came with their macebearers' to the square.[27] The crowd reacted as soon as the name of Mary was heard. 'The general rejoicing was such that the Earl of Pembroke who was doing the reading was unable to conclude owing to the shouts of people cheering the queen.'[28] 'The content and joy of all,' another account informs us, 'were such that almost all cast up their caps into the air without caring to recover them, and all who had money in their purses threw it to the people. Others being men of authority and in years would not refrain from casting away their garments, leaping and dancing as though beside themselves.'[29] Bonfires were lit and all over the city 'people supped in the streets with great rejoicing and music'.[30] Guaras's account that 'so great were the cries and acclamations when they drank for love of the queen' is echoed by the anonymous diarist who described 'bonfires without number . . . banquetings and singing in the streets for joy'.[31] Whether they had always desired it, or had come to do so over the preceding days, the popular joy at Mary's succession was genuine and effusive.

Hearing the news as he was about to engage Mary's stronghold in Norfolk, Northumberland immediately succumbed without any battle being fought. Again, his capitulation was public and symbolic. According to Guaras's source, he 'took down and tore with his own hands the proclamation of Jane which ten days before he had caused to be published and posted at the corners of streets . . . and waving . . . a white truncheon . . . being the ensign of a Captain General, he cried "Long Live Queen Mary" – and cast away his weapons'.[32] Early in August Mary entered London, with a triumphal entourage of 10,000 or more, to a popular welcome.[33]

I retell the events of these days because, in so many ways, they offer important insights into the politics of symbol and representation as well as of conciliar faction and personal manoeuvre; and into the power of popular opinion as well as regal and governmental authority. For what is in the first place remarkable about these days is that, for all the fortifying of the Tower and gathering of troops, the outcome was not decided by force or violence: as the contemporary historian Robert Wingfield put it, 'a very fierce enemy [was] defeated without bloodshed or a fight'.[34] The absence of violence had not favoured only Mary. The married Queen Jane was proclaimed in a document that appealed to anxieties about unwed queens and foreign husbands; and, whatever their misgivings, subjects had accepted her succession. There were no riots in London, or anywhere else in the country. Mary had to garner support and do so by her own rhetorical appeal to her rightful descent from her father. For a week or more, claims to authority founded on lineage and Henry VIII's will vied with counter-claims resting on the dying wishes of Edward VI, as stated in the Device to alter the succession, and on the expressed support of 'all the nobles of the kingdom' for that course.[35] In the end, if their own statements are to be trusted, the name, memory and will of Henry VIII carried weight with all – even some who had supported or accepted the succession of Jane.[36] The second Tudor, who had so carefully built an image of his own authority, successfully determined the succession from the grave. Secondly, we should note that, during those uncertain days, it does not appear to have been the nobility – or at least not primarily the nobility – that set the agenda after Jane's proclamation. Mary's support came initially from local gentlemen, from sailors, and even 'peasants'.[37] And it was this display of popular support, like the earlier-recognized popular unease at Jane's succession, which may have swayed the elites. Certainly it was the haemorrhaging of men from Northumberland's army that Arundel used as a means of persuading councillors to abandon Lady Jane Grey's cause: as he put it, opinion (and in this case public opinion) would be mightier than arms.[38] Nor should the capitulations of both Suffolk and Northumberland simply pass without comment. While civil war would have been as personally risky as the memory of the Wars of the Roses made it anathema, both nobles must have expected to face a trial for treason and yet they surrendered to Mary's authority. And in both cases they marked their capitulation in symbolic form – Suffolk by removing the canopy of state from over his daughter's head and Dudley by casting away his weapons as he proclaimed Queen Mary.[39]

The most important issue in early modern politics – the succession to the throne – had been decided, then, as much by popular opinion as by noble manoeuvre and as much by the power of memory, image and symbol as by force of arms. Interestingly, whatever its role in the struggles within their consciences or the decisions men made in their minds, religion did not feature prominently in the public rhetoric or language of those days.[40] For sure, the Device to place Jane on the throne reflected Edward's deep Protestant commitments, but it is not clear of how many others this was true; and Jane's succession was not explicitly proclaimed in the name of the new religion.[41] Nor was Mary, despite the support she enjoyed from Arundel and other conservative peers, heralded as the champion of the old faith – but as the rightful heir and daughter of Henry VIII. Unquestionably there were religious divisions in the realm, but the whole realm was not divided over religion: many who cheered so loudly for Mary cheered for a Tudor rather than a Roman Catholic.

What this meant for the new queen, of course, was that she began her reign with a peaceful triumph and an enormous swell of popular support. But what the events of the first days of July had demonstrated was that such support was neither universal – a man was pilloried for contesting Mary's claim on 29 July – nor necessarily a mandate for anything other than lawful succession.[42] In large part, Mary owed her throne to her father's skill in identifying the cause of the nation with the Tudor dynasty – an identification that survived Dudley's efforts to paint the unwed Mary as a threat to the nation. In her heartland in Norfolk, moving among her troops with familiar ease, thanking ordinary men for their loyalty and support, Mary powerfully reinforced that identification and her cause.[43] The art of Tudor government was, as Penry Williams so succinctly put it, the art of winning compliance – the compliance, we now see more clearly, of the people, as well as of the noble elites.[44] In her spectacular triumph over Jane Grey, Mary demonstrated that she had secured compliance. But there was perhaps an ominous indication from the outset that, having won the game in July 1553, she had not learned all the lessons it taught. As she entered London in triumph with 340 attendants in velvet before her and over 200 behind, at Aldgate Street some poor children stood to praise their new queen with a congratulatory oration. 'But,' in the words of an eyewitness who chronicled those days, 'she said nothing to them.'[45]

A few days before her entry into the capital, Mary had met the imperial envoy, Simon Renard.[46] Though her victory was of no less importance to him than to her and his commitment to the Catholic and papal cause absolute, Renard, having observed carefully the past days' events and perceiving that 'the queen is as yet inexperienced in the conduct of public affairs', offered her frank advice.[47] Renard's advice, following instructions from the emperor, was that the queen's 'chief care should be the repose and tranquillity of her kingdom' and that she should 'endeavour to satisfy her subjects of all classes'.[48] Specifically he counselled that she should fix on a 'suitable match as soon as possible' to alleviate the problems of female government, but otherwise to do nothing swiftly or rashly: especially 'not to hurry where religion was concerned nor to make innovations nor adopt unpopular policies but rather to recommend herself by winning her subjects' hearts, showing herself to be a good English woman wholly bent on the kingdom's welfare'.[49] Renard's shrewd advice was, significantly, more concerned with Mary's style and image as leader of a nation than with the details of policy or religion. And Mary's answer is as revealing as it was different: she felt 'so strongly' on the matter of religion and was determined to publicize her faith.[50] The funeral of Edward VI, she announced, was to be conducted with a full Catholic mass to mark the change of rule: 'She had force on her side and would not disband the troops until after the funeral had taken place.'[51] The queen, who had attracted widespread support as rightful Tudor successor, intended to use her authority, indeed force if necessary, to re-establish her faith. In a memoir he enclosed with his report, the ambassador repeated his reservation: 'It is impossible not to be apprehensive of the consequences if it were attempted to make the funeral an opportunity for reintroducing a religion of which the most important features are the mass and other royal traditions, the reappearance of which might cause her Majesty's subjects to waver in their affection', even lead others to 'rebellion'.[52] Renard thought that the queen might be wise to be tactfully absent from the public funeral and hold her own service in private. Mary saw things otherwise. Yet, for all their differences, what united the envoy and the new queen was a sense that image, public display, ritual would be all-important in establishing (or destabilizing) the new reign.

II Words and Silences

Henry VIII, as we have seen, had a keen sense of the importance of the royal word as a foundation of his authority, and had directly intervened in print in the debate over issues vital to his rule. Edward, the first English king fully educated in a humanist pedagogic programme, used his rhetorical skills as a means of exercising more influence and attaining personal rule. Here, Mary began life at a disadvantage: she was a woman. For though leading humanists, from Erasmus on, allowed for female education and Juan Luis Vives dedicated his treatise on the education of women to Mary's mother, the traditional female virtues of chastity, purity and obedience were held in higher regard than great learning. Mary's greatest childhood accomplishment was in playing the harpsichord.[53] Whether led by cultural proscriptions or temperament, Mary wrote (and spoke) less than her Tudor predecessors – and indeed far less than her successor, Elizabeth. We know that, aged eleven, Mary translated a prayer of Aquinas, probably as part of her education in piety as well as in Latin.[54] And while still a princess she commenced, at the request of Catherine Parr, a translation of Erasmus's *Paraphrase of St John's Gospel* into English, and composed three prayers: against adversity, denouncing vice, and for the hour of death.[55] But during her reign, other than her will and correspondence, Mary wrote no text or treatise setting out her views or arguing her case.

Nor, unlike her father or her sister, was Mary given to oratorical performances either on state occasions, such as the opening of parliament, or in a public forum. Here the important exception is a speech given by Mary at the Guildhall in London, at the time when Thomas Wyatt was leading a band of Kentish rebels to the city, to protest in arms about the queen's marriage to Philip of Spain. The moment in January 1554 was critical. For, on the last of the month, soldiers in the Duke of Norfolk's army, reunited to engage the rebels on Rochester bridge, deserted and went over to Wyatt.[56] The duke himself was taken, along with the artillery, and the road to London lay open. The next day, Mary went, with trumpets and an entourage, to the Guildhall to address a crowd, tipped off to be present.[57] Skilfully she opened with a reminder to the Londoners that she was queen by their 'unanimous suffrage', 'since the day you chose me as your queen'; and not only their queen and mistress, she assured them, but a 'mother', full of love for her subjects and for the public weal.[58] Having deployed the language of unity and commonweal, and adroitly defused the issue of her gender with the image of the nurturing mother, Mary set out to deal with Wyatt. Against the rebel's claim that he rose only to rescue England from the slavery of a Spanish match, Mary countered with the charge (and an appeal to chivalric notions of protection as well as loyalty) that he was motivated by his ambition 'to dispose at his will of my own body and of the kingdom which has been entrusted to me with your consent'.[59] Cleverly connecting her own person and cause with the interests of subjects, Mary went on to argue that Wyatt coveted not only the treasure of the realm but 'your own private property'.[60] Having identified her very person with the well-being of the commonweal and appealed to her auditors' self-interest, Mary reminded them of the obedience owed to divinely appointed sovereigns 'on account of the holy unction' and the obligation which lay on all subjects 'confirmed by your unanimous acclamation and votes'.[61] Coming to the marriage, the queen assured her subjects that her first concern was their preservation, peace and tranquillity. No course, she made it plain, was determined before her councillors, 'outstanding for their prudence and expertise', had resolved 'that it would be of advantage and improvement for this realm and to the good of you all . . .'.[62] But, she added, should she now 'notice that it may displease you', she would again refer the matter for judgement.[63] Having powerfully demonstrated her commitment to good counsel, and even her responsiveness to popular concerns, Mary exhibited the first virtue of the ideal ruler: the subordination of personal desire to the public good. 'I should prefer,' she told them, 'to renounce for ever to marriage, than to permit that you, provoked to raise in arms by the displeasure of my wedding, would fight one another for my cause.'[64] 'I am already married to this commonweal,' another account of her speech adds, 'and ye faithful members of the same, the spousal ring whereof I have on my finger which never hitherto was nor shall be left off.'[65] The speech ended with an appeal and a clever move to force men's hands: 'I earnestly beg you, my beloved subjects, to openly state if I may expect from you loyalty and obedience, or if you will join the party of the nefarious traitor against me, your Queen.'[66]

At a moment of crisis in February 1554, as in July 1553, Mary displayed a brilliant capacity to present herself as the rightful queen concerned for the welfare of her subjects and realm and to blend assertions of her authority with appeals to a people whose 'suffrages' had chosen her queen – and against whom, no less than her majesty, Wyatt was in rebellion. It was a speech worthy of Queen Elizabeth, and two accounts evidence its effect.[67] A Spanish observer noted that 'her words were uttered with such firmness and grace that the whole audience was overwhelmed with admiration'.[68] John Proctor, the Somerset divine and contemporary chronicler of Wyatt's rebellion, claimed that the speech 'did so wonderfully enamour the hearts of the hearers as it was a brave world to hear with what shouts they exalted the honour and magnanimity of Queen Mary'; he described the streets lined with cheering crowds as the queen processed back to Whitehall.[69] Though written by a sympathizer, there is no reason to doubt the account. Wyatt was denied entry into the Temple Bar, not least by the London citizens who rallied to Mary. Though she spoke little, Mary could clearly inspire and enhance the love and loyalty of her people on which her authority, as she discerned, rested.

Indeed, the power of this oration suggests that Mary might have taken advantage of other occasions to proclaim and explain her views to the people. Where most subjects were concerned, of course, the closest they got to the royal word, as the representation of majesty, was the proclamation, read to the crowd in the towns and villages of England. We have a nice insight into the authority and the reception of royal proclamations in Mary's reign during the crisis of Wyatt's rebellion, when Sheriff Martin Southwell read an exhortation to the people at Malling in Kent. 'The sheriff reading this exhortation caused one Barrham . . . a servant to the Lord Abergevenny, to pronounce it as he read it, so loud and so distinctly as the people assembled round about him to a very great number in manner of a ring might easy hear and understand every word proceeding from Barrham who of his own head cried out with them: you may not so much as lift up your finger against your king and queen.'[70] Indeed the chronicler of Wyatt's rebellion suggests that it was Wyatt's irreverence, his refusal to allow the reading of a proclamation by the queen's messenger, that turned many against him and to support Mary.[71] Proclamations were both a vital medium in the pronouncements of royal authority and an occasion for the construction and reinforcement of royal authority. As we have seen, Henrician proclamations, while asserting royal orders and power, often usefully explained and justified royal policy, especially at times of uncertainty and change.

Mary's early proclamations skilfully negotiated the difficult circumstances of her coming to the throne. In her first proclamation announcing her succession, for example, as well as insisting on 'the duties of allegiance' and her 'lawful possession' of her 'right and title', Mary spoke warmly of her (Protestant) brother, 'the most excellent prince of most worthy memory', and promised her subjects that, in giving their allegiance, 'they shall find us their benign and gracious sovereign lady'.[72] Her earliest pronouncement on religion continued this ameliorating style and appeal to all. The queen, remembering the 'danger' that had grown 'through the diversity of opinions in questions of religion', and hearing of untrue reports that might mislead her people, informed them of her commitment to her faith, but also her resolution 'not to compel any . . . thereunto until such time as further order by *common assent* may be taken'.[73] Appealing for unity, the queen commanded 'all her said loving subjects to live together in quiet sort and Christian charity, leaving those new-found devilish terms of papist or heretic, and such like'.[74] Royal proclamations announced other popular reforms and conciliatory gestures: Mary announced in August a new reformed coinage to replace the base alloy that had imposed 'great and intolerable charges' on her loving subjects.[75] And, regarding her subjects more than her debts, and 'accounting their loving hearts and property as her own weal and the chiefest treasure that she desireth', the queen, 'considering the good wills' manifested towards her, remitted the subsidy granted in the last parliament of King Edward VI.[76]

During the opening months of her reign, Mary's proclamations, then, presented her as a loving monarch, assiduous in tending to her subjects, as moderate, and, as the first woman ruler, one who continued the norms of government: the arrangements for the coronation, the traditional pardon extended by a new monarch and the ordering of her royal household according to 'the godly and honourable statutes and ordinaries of household of her noble progenitors . . .'.[77] It may be significant that the longest royal proclamation of the reign was Mary's announcement of articles of marriage with Philip of Spain in January 1554. Though royal marriages were, strictly speaking, *arcana imperii*, Mary's proclamation laid out in detail the terms of the marriage: the dowry, the descent through children, and the rights of the king and queen.[78] More particularly, the proclamation reassured subjects that Philip would admit to his service Englishmen, that he would not against her will remove the queen or her goods from England, and that 'the said noble Prince should do nothing whereby anything be innovate in the state and right, public or private, and in the laws and customs of the said realm of England . . . but contrariwise . . . shall inform and keep to all estates and order their rights and privileges'.[79]

When, despite these efforts at forestalling anxiety and opposition, the marriage excited Wyatt's rebellion, Mary, as well as her vital speech at the Guildhall, made use of proclamations to counter Wyatt's claims, representing them as 'sinister motions' 'under the pretence of the benefit of the commonwealth of the realm'.[80] As at her succession, Mary reiterated her devotion to 'the conservation of her subjects from all perils and dangers' and her trust in the aid of her loving people in resisting the revolt.[81] And she even offered and proclaimed the extraordinary concession of sending two councillors to assure Wyatt of her good intention in the marriage and to confer with him 'upon his device and meaning'.[82] Only when they found Wyatt 'contrary to his pretence, a most arrogant, horrible and vile traitor', did Mary issue a proclamation denouncing him and his co-rebels for a treason aimed at 'the only destruction of the Queen's majesty's most royal person (whom almighty God long preserve)'.[83]

Mary's proclamations, then, carefully represented her as loving, gracious and conciliatory. Indeed, we might say that Mary almost opened a discussion with her subjects, making the injunction to obedience an act of their will as well as her command. This is not the image of Queen Mary that has come down to us. And here it is significant that very few Marian proclamations were concerned directly with religion. The first of those, dated 4 March 1554, announced new injunctions for religion which required the execution of all canons and ecclesiastical laws in force 'in the time of King Henry VIII', the end of clerical marriage and the revival of holy days and fast days, processions and ceremonies.[84] Though the injunctions revised the enactments of the Edwardian Reformation, Mary's proclamation carefully distanced 'our most dearest brother King Edward VI' from the heresies and disorder of the time and ordered, in most matters, a return to the 'time of King Henry VIII'.[85] In one respect, however, they radically departed from Henry. The injunctions also insisted that none be required to take the Supremacy Oath – an early notice that Mary intended once again to return England to obeisance to Rome, which she announced, along with Cardinal Pole's legation to effect it, by proclamation in November, as the 'authority in . . . spiritual jurisdiction . . . in the time of the . . . 20th year of the reign of our said father King Henry VIII' – that is before the king's divorce crisis.[86]

Though two outlawed 'seditious and heretical books', no other royal proclamations enjoined religious changes or prescribed harsh penalties for heresy or non-compliance.[87] It is important to remember that the Marian Counter-Reformation, like the Henrician and Edwardian Reformations, was enacted, with the consent of the realm in parliament, by statute, not by royal fiat.[88] Whatever our later view of Mary as dictatorial, bigoted, harsh and cruel, the queen was presented and represented to her subjects in royal speeches and proclamations as 'a gracious sovereign lady . . . more inclined to mercy and leniency than to severity and compulsion': a ruler at one with her 'loving subjects'.[89]

Such was not just the queen's self-presentation. Mary's succession was greeted with popular cheers, as well as with an outpouring of panegyrical verses, elite and popular, which presented the accession of the new queen as the dawn of a golden age. In some cases, unquestionably, praise for the new queen went hand in hand with commitment to Roman Catholicism. In 1553, the fellow of St John's College Cambridge and later Canon of Westminster, John Seton, published a volume of Latin panegyric on Queen Mary, together with a song celebrating the holy eucharist.[90] Seton looked to Mary as one chosen by God to root out heresy and error, to the glory of Christ, and to return the realm to unity in, and with, the church. But as well as praising her as the hope of the church, Seton's volume presents Mary as heiress to an English empire and as the people's joy:

Nam Regina potens, ex Regibus aedita magnis
Anglorum applause suscipit imperium[91]

Mary, he repeats, assumed the mantle of purple and gold, with 'the applause of the people' and as

Quanta plebi gaudia, quae voluptas,
Quanta spes . . .[92]

Lauding the coronation day – 'O diem festum, celebrem, serenum' – Seton described the magnificent procession halting and pausing to hear the congratulations of the nation.[93] And presenting Mary now as the Virgin her namesake, now the woman who won her throne by love, now as a queen of truly masculine spirit ('Principe digne vero'), Seton dispelled the potential difficulty of Mary's sex to compare her coronation triumphs to those of Greece and Rome.[94]

But panegyrics on Mary in 1553 were by no means predominantly Catholic. Indeed, *A Godly Psalm of Mary*, 'which I wryte to Comfort all', published in 1553, even appears to see her as the last hope for the continuance of the 'true religion' of her brother.[95] The psalm opens with celebration that Mary has caused her foes' downfall and was established by God on the throne:

The lawful, just and rightuouse
Of England, head and Queene:
To bee the true enheritoure
As hathe her brother beene.[96]

The poem emphasized Mary's right by birth, descent 'from her godly father straight', and relation to a brother who had been a 'kind of Jesse's stock and root'.[97] Rather than overturning the Edwardian edifice, *A Godly Psalm* sees Mary building on her brother's foundation:

The ground worke he hathe layde him selfe,
And she is left a lon
To buyld the house, and fortresse up
Of trew religion.[98]

Praying the Lord to save Mary and Elizabeth, the verse looks to a time of 'peace and quietnesse' under the new queen.[99] It is not clear whether the author of

A Godly Psalm was urging Mary to follow her brother's work or anxious to suppress the difference between them in the name of 'peace and quietness': the author Richard Beeard was admitted to a living at St Mary Hill in 1560 and wrote a tract on justification dedicated to Queen Elizabeth.[100] Clearly he had Protestant sympathies. But, as well as counsel, the publication of his *Godly Psalm* may suggest that not all in 1553 viewed Mary as a ruler about to champion ultramontane Catholicism.[101] Just as important, *A Godly Psalm* portrayed Mary, as many others saw her, as the rightful heir, God's 'chosen and elect', whose succession had saved a realm threatened by division and invasion from insurrection and war.[102] In 1553, after the prospect of renewed civil war, 'death and ruines rife', praise of Mary as the protectress of 'peace and quietness' and of the queen 'that seeks our preservation' is not hard to comprehend.[103]

Two metrical broadsides also heralded Mary's succession and may have been published to be displayed on a wall, and to be read and sung aloud. The first, *Ave Maria*, printed at Paternoster Row by Richard Lant (about whom we know little), was written by Leonard Stopes, probably while he was still a young scholar. *An Ave Maria in Commendation of Our Most Victorious Queen* structured twenty-four verses under the initial words of the prayer: 'Hail Mary Full of Grace Our Lord is With Thee; Blessed Art Thou Among Women And Blessed Is The Fruite of Thy Wombe Jesus'.[104] As well as making the obvious parallel between England's godly queen and the Virgin, Stopes praised Mary as another Hester pitched against 'the envious Hamon' and as a second Judith, victor over Holofernes.[105] Having vanquished her foes, Mary, the verse argued, will extirpate not only errors and heresies but 'all strife and debate'. In this woman Stopes saw an example of all of her sex, 'in womanly wisdome to leade well their lives'. In Mary, meek, merciful and virtuous, he saw the hope for the nation to 'walke in one way/ In unitie of faith' and of progeny that would rule 'in peace and in rest'. 'Long over us,' the last line prayed, 'she may reigne in peace.' It would be too easy, if not wrong, to dismiss Stopes's popular broadside as the tract of a Catholic party or as utterly naïve in its hopes. Rather, it may have spoken powerfully to a realm that had been dislocated by years of religious division and uncertainty and threatened by Northumberland's coup with the resurgence of civil war over the royal succession. Stopes could not suppress his own anxiety concerning those disposed

> to whisper, to whimper, with traitorous tene
> to mutter, to murmur, with mischevous myn
> Against thy so loving, and gracious a Quene

But, he saw, armed with faith, hope and love, Mary 'our jewel, our joy', the token of God's mercy on the land, would 'as his chosen . . . have heere her ende'. From the fruit of the Virgin, he believed, might come the nation's redemption: 'All Englande is blessed, for this woman's sake.'

A New Ballad of the Marigold, also printed, this time at 'Aldersgate Street', by Richard Lant, was written by the Catholic priest William Forrest who was nominated soon after Mary's succession to be one of her chaplains.[106] But before we read him as the voice of a bigoted Counter-Reformation resurgency, it is worth noting that he had dedicated works, notably a treatise De regemine principium, to Protector Somerset and had shown some capacity to 'accommodate his faith to the reigning powers'.[107] Though he was a Catholic, Forrest was no supporter of the papacy, but a champion of the national church's right of self-governance. Priest though he was, Forrest may have represented a conservatism which was English as well as Catholic and which could without difficulty herald Mary as the 'treasure' to be cherished. The Ballad of the Marigold presents Mary as a special flower of God, a sign for the nation to follow God's word. Praising her education, her patience, her meekness and her conversation, Forrest presented Mary as the gift of the Lord, the token of his grace. In Mary, 'poor and rich', 'the high, the lowe', Forrest informed them, had a gift they should cherish. Forrest prayed that she might 'long endure' in her high estate, and that 'wee all (as one)' might 'love her Grace' and the peace planted with her 'here among us'.

Mary's self-presentation as rightful heir, aided by providence to victory over her enemies, was, then, supported by panegyrics which appear to have been directed at a broad audience. And whatever their Catholic sympathies, panegyrists (at least early in the reign) stressed unity over narrow denominational interest. Though there is plentiful evidence that it aroused concern and discontent, even Mary's marriage to Philip of Spain may not have been universally unpopular, and certainly did not pass without celebratory verse. Alexander Junius's Latin panegyric Philippeis, seu, In nuptias diui Philippi . . . & heroinae Mariae was dedicated to Philip and Mary in terms which suggested that the whole world was in joyous celebration at their nuptials.[108] Junius praised both monarchs as king and queen of peace who saved their nations from savage foes – the Turk and the French, Dudley and the enemies of divine, hereditary kingship.[109] The poem gave thanks for Mary's fortitude and victory and the peace and justice which the marriage, the worthiest marriage in the world, now brought as its dowry to England.[110] The union of Philip and Mary, the poem posited, joined not only the stock of two crowns 'et populos stabili coniunget foedere binos'.[111] Rather than foreign and alien, Philip was the son and hope of Albion and Ireland, as much as of Spain and Belgium.[112] From panegyric Junius moved to description of the pomp of the marriage procession to close with congratulation.[113] The poem ended with an address to the reader explaining the brief reference to Philip's descent from the

Lancastrian line. The marriage of Philip and Mary was, in fine, lauded as truly a union not only of victory and nations, but of branches of the English royal family.[114]

John Heywood's ballad 'Specifying Partly the Manner, Partly the Matter In the Most Excellent Meeting ... and Like Marriage Between Our Sovereign Lord, and ... Lady' was an altogether different text, directed towards a popular audience.[115] A broadsheet published as well as printed by the commercial bookseller William Riddell, it was the work of a man who had been a musician at Henry's court and who, though he got into trouble for denying the royal supremacy, survived to be 'well benefitted by the king' in the reign of Edward VI.[116] Heywood, a Catholic, delivered an oration during the pageants for Mary's coronation and is said to have devised entertainments to amuse her in her Privy Chamber. Heywood's ballad, very much in the tradition of his lyrics for Princess Mary's household, presented the marriage of Philip and Mary as the union of the eagle and the lion, the heraldic beasts respectively of Spain and England.[117] The lion, England under Mary, the verse ran, is 'No rampant lion masculyne' but 'the lamblike lion feminyne' which allures the bird to alight, so that 'this lamblike lyon and lamblike burde' 'lamblike be concurde'. Here was 'So meete a matche in patronage/ So meete a matche in benignite'. And in the loving gentle union of Philip and Mary, Heywood hoped all their subjects might 'lyke lambs' give their 'acordes' and thanks:

> And that all we, their subjects may
> Them and their lawes, love and obay

Like the language of Mary's speech and proclamations, the panegyrics on her reign and descriptions of her union with Philip II dwelt not primarily on religion but on the queen's lineage, right, virtue and – most of all – the peace and unity secured and promised by her succession.

Whatever the refrains in panegyrics of unity and peace, the events of Mary's reign witnessed division and rebellion, from the moment of Jane Grey's coup, through Wyatt's rebellion and contention over the course of religious and foreign policy. Those writers who were close to Mary, and defended and publicized her authority, were fully cognizant of the challenges and threats that she faced; and where verse panegyrists preferred to subsume anxieties about disorder in celebration, others, in championing the queen's rights, directly engaged with the real world of contest and division. James Cancellar's 1556 *The Path of Obedience* even announced in its full title that it was 'right necessary for all ... the King's and Queen's majesties loving subjects to read, learn and use ... due obedience to the high powers'.[118] In his dedication to Mary, Cancellar, one of the queen's chapel, as he described himself, freely acknowledged the hurt disobedience had caused and the danger that the 'ugly monster' still presented.[119] Cancellar coupled the disobedience to the queen with that to 'our mother church', and insisted: 'as long therefore as we were within the goodly fold of obedience to our mother the Catholic church, we like obedient subjects quietly obeyed the laws and ordinances of our princes'.[120] God, the treatise continued, gave the whole body of the people a king to be their head and commanded their obedience.[121] To resist the prince, therefore, was to go against God's will. No wonder, then, he argued, that it was heretics and sects who disobeyed scripture who also challenged princes.[122] Queen Mary's virtues shone as a light to the world: obedience to her and to the Catholic church was obedience to the power ordained by God and to his truth and will.[123]

Another treatise arguing the duty of obedience was written by John Christopherson, another of the queen's chaplains, printed by John Cawood, printer to the queen, and bore a prefatory address to Mary, along with prayers of thanks for her preservation. Christopherson's treatise was entitled *An Exhortation to All Men to Take Heed and Beware of Rebellion*, and his title certainly announced his purpose.[124] While there were many antidotes to the disease of rebellion, Christopherson argued – arms being one – 'yet in mine opinion no more fitter remedy can there be found than that seditious men's hearts by gentle exhortation may be thoroughly persuaded'.[125] Christopherson, in other words, publicly voiced what other of his contemporaries discerned and what goes to the core of our argument: that authority was an act of exhortation, be it in words, images or examples. Christopherson pointed to wise orators in antiquity who had won over rebels – Marcus Valerius and Publius Scipio, for example – and urged the need for their like to counter the sugared voices of sirens who claimed, in rebelling, to be doing the public good.[126] Rebellion, the *Exhortation* argued, had its roots in misrepresentation – in 'murmur and grudge of mind'; sometimes 'by reason that the prince is a person of no good qualities'; most often 'diversity of minds touching religion'.[127] The people therefore needed to be persuaded that rebellion not only breached the commandment of God but led to the destruction of their lives and goods.[128] 'Princes are anointed by God,' he asserted, and all should 'plainly perceive that all those that seek for honour by rebellion come at length to a miserable and wretched end'.[129] As for religion, Christopherson urged that faith should never be a justification for resistance when one 'is commended by the holy word of God to be obedient'; and he thought it important that the people be educated to see that 'such men as pretend such holiness are most of all other to be taken heed of': not all who went to the fire were martyrs.[130] Those of true faith submitted to the prince – and to the Catholic church; heresy, the vice of private wills, bred disobedience.[131] Turning to the late rebellion against the queen, Christopherson identified the rebels' professed aims as the deliverance of the realm from foreign oppression and the restoration of the Lutheran religion. Both claims, he argued, had been published to deceive the people.[132] Mary had entered into marriage in pursuance of God's will in order to bring benefit to her subjects and to preserve her commonweal.[133] Rather than a foreigner, Philip II, a descendant of Edward III, was of the English blood royal and was so wise, gentle and beloved of his subjects at home that they grieved to see his departure.[134] The royal marriage then, he argued, rather than undermining, strengthened England. Rebellion was irrational and against the people's interest. As for those who rebelled to restore heresy, God had already extended his protection to Mary: how then, Christopherson asked, playing on the queen's name, would any draw swords to shed a virgin's blood?[135] Skilfully deploying gender and language that we are more familiar with in representations of Queen Elizabeth, Christopherson figured Mary not only as virgin but as the tender 'mother of a whole realm' and urged subjects to venture their lives for her 'as the child is bound to tender the mother'.[136] For Nature taught all to love their prince, as their mother, and especially a 'loving mother' such as Mary who sought justice, wealth and a prosperous, happy life for all her subjects.[137] It was those of the new religion, 'bringers in of all confused disorder', who were 'sowers of sedition'.[138] Christopherson excoriated them as carnal, promiscuous hypocrites who subverted the order of families as well as the state, and who sought the overthrow of Christ as well as the prince. Appealing to the traditional affection for images and ceremonies, with homely comparisons between religious icons and domestic portraits, Christopherson portrayed the reformers as despoilers of all religion, and as the very destroyers of England, as they had been of Germany.[139] It was, he asserted, not they, but the prince who was the 'safeguard of all ... subjects', of their souls as well as of their bodies and goods.[140] 'Refrain from discord', Christopherson exhorted in his peroration, 'and begin one to love another', and tenderly love the queen 'as she loveth us all'.[141] The treatise ended with a prayer: that Mary might be safeguarded to, like Sarah, in age produce a son who would be the hope of long peace; and that she might long reign 'to deliver this realm' and to advance true religion.[142] The royal chaplain led the readers in a closing prayer to God – for amity, concord and peace, with all joined in one church and in obedience to the anointed queen.

Christopherson's *Exhortation* was a skilful and effective manifestation of the conviction that effective authority rested on persuasion and representation. There is little mention of force or threat of secular punishments in the treatise. Rather, Christopherson appealed to people's self-interest and conscience, innate conservatism and suspicion of innovation; and he redeployed the discourses of Nature and God to reinforce obedience. Artfully constructing

Mary as the Virgin and Mother, and as God's handmaid, he rendered opponents as a 'rabble' outside the family of the realm as well as the fellowship of the church.[143]

Another treatise written to represent Mary in the wake of resistance was John Proctor's *The History of Wyatt's Rebellion ... Whereunto is Added an Earnest Conference with the Degenerate and Seditious Rebels for the Search of the Cause of their Daily Disorder.*[144] Proctor was not, like Christopherson, close to Mary's court or the centres of power. A former scholar of Corpus Christi, Oxford, he was Master of Tonbridge School, where he wrote the treatise in 1554; but his history was published 'cum privilegio' in London by the printer Robert Caly who had migrated from Rouen to London in 1553, and in Canterbury by John Michel. In a dedicatory preface to Queen Mary, Proctor explained how he had originally kept notes on the rebellion for his own information but had decided to write a full history, so that 'both the good may be encouraged in the execution of perfect obedience and unspotted loyalty and [the] wicked restrained'.[145] In a preface to the reader, he restated that purpose: that the book was published to expose the hateful visage of rebellion and to offer an example of, and admonition to, loyalty, to ensure that no insurrection occurred again.[146] Like Christopherson, Proctor from the outset coupled rebellion and heresy, and exposed the religious motives that lay beneath Wyatt's opposition to a foreign marriage. And he took pains to make two observations: that Mary's cause was favoured by God, and that the people, once disabused of the pretences of Wyatt, would return to loyalty to the queen, and 'did so much abhor ... their treason'.[147] In Proctor's account, Wyatt was defeated by providence ('overthrown spiritu Dei' not 'vanquished') and by the loyalty of the people.[148] Drawing attention to the queen's reluctance to use force, Proctor described Wyatt's rebellion as a contest of hearts and minds – that is, a contest to control the representation of authority. As Wyatt advised his followers of the need 'to continue good opinion in the heads of the multitude', Mary and her magistrates addressed the people, assuring them of her assiduous care for their well-being.[149] But whatever its course, the outcome of the contest was presented as determined 'chiefly by the mighty hand of God', who acted 'to defend his chosen and elect virgin'.[150] At his arraignment, Proctor argued, Wyatt learned the lesson of the event: 'rebellion never from the beginning prospered'.[151]

And those were the lessons which Proctor wished to impart to his readers: 'God always defends his chosen' and 'the inevitable end of rebellion is certain confusion to the rebel'.[152] In a closing 'Conference with the Degenerates', Proctor had the figure of England herself address the rebels and praise the queen. Could, he asked, there be greater evidence of love than a ruler who had tempered the rigour of the laws, repaired noble houses and remitted subsidies? 'What fault find you in her whom the whole world judges to be most perfect?'[153] Was not to quarrel with her to contest with God and Nature? If the rebels' creed were 'contempt of magistrates, licentious and dissolute living, oppression of the poor . . . breach of godly order', could such men be endured in any Christian nation?[154] It was Mary, England declaims, who restored us unto 'that ancient and blissful state'.[155] And it behoved all to love and obey 'this noble princess'.[156]

In the wake of rebellion, supporters – both at court and in the provinces – wrote to represent Mary as God's chosen and as the custodian of commonweal and nation. In these representations, theological controversy was hardly mentioned, the rebels' claims were exposed as pretences, and their religion caricatured as licentious and anarchic. And far from her enduring image as a relentless and cruel persecutor of the saints, Queen Mary was figured as a queen of 'singular clemency and benignity'.[157] In prose, as in verse, in pamphlets and histories as in panegyrics, Mary Tudor did not want for advocates who presented her not as the curse, but as the blessing of the nation.

III Depicting Mary and Marriage

Mary Tudor was the daughter of the ruler who transformed the nature and art of royal portraiture – the heir to a visual revolution in the representation of monarchy. That representation had, in Henry's case, and to a measure in that of his son, been predominantly dynastic, chivalric, martial, patriarchal – and priapic. For all the difficulties Edward faced as a minor, Mary faced a greater challenge with regard to her visual representation. How was a woman to depict her authority in a world of masculine regimen? Time and change presented other questions. The break from Rome, the royal supremacy and the commissioning of the King's Bible had featured other representations of Henry, then Edward, as champion of the word – of the vernacular Bible. And in Edward VI's case, full Protestant Reformation, with an accompanying assault on the icons of worship and a suspicion of imagery as idolatrous, had unquestionably changed the culture in which images performed and were read. If, in 1553, Mary faced the challenge of how to present herself visually as England's first queen in four centuries and as a Catholic successor to what was now formally a Protestant nation, her marriage the next year posed other questions of representation. Were Mary and Philip to be painted together – and as equals? Would Mary be the dominant figure as natural queen, or take the subordinate place that a woman and wife often did – on canvas, as in society?

Certainly, care had been taken over the portraits of Mary as a princess, not least on account of their importance for potential marriage negotiations.[158] As well as in the Tudor family groups, there are paintings of Mary as princess by Holbein and Holbein's studio, in several noble collections, as well as the Holbein drawing at St James's Palace.[159] As a young woman, Mary had something of a reputation as a beauty, with ambassadors sent as marriage agents and courtiers all extolling her charms. Drawing especial attention to her eyes ('those lamps of joye'), which the Spanish envoy described as 'sparkling', John Heywood versed:

Her beutye twinkleth like a starre
within the frostye night.

Her couler comes and gose
with such a goodly grace,
More ruddye then the rose
within her lively face.

I think nature hath lost her moulde,
wher shee her forme dyd take
Or ells I doubt yt nature coulde
so faire a creature make.[160]

As well as being a looker, Mary was renowned for lavish and fashionable dress and for bringing back to court the extravagance associated with female presence.[161] However, as she aged, Mary evidently began to look older than her years and to take on what the Venetian ambassador called a 'grave and sedate cast'.[162] But, even then, he felt that the queen's appearance commanded awe, and was certain that as 'a well looking lady' she would never 'be spoken ill of for want of sufficient beauty'.[163]

Not least on account of her beauty, age and suitability for marriage, numerous portraits of Mary were painted. And those, too, were widely disseminated, as copies in the Escorial and a myriad noble households (Lumley Castle, Berkeley Castle, Castle Howard, Hatfield, Knole and Penshurst, to name but some) testify.[164] Mary's principal painter was the artist who succeeded Holbein at the English court from the early 1550s. Hans Eworth painted his English subjects in the style of Holbein, though, from a family linked with the goldsmith's trade, he paid particular attention to jewellery. His relationship to Mary appears to have been close, for he was given access to her jewels and he may have become an official court painter, though, in the absence of surviving records, we cannot be certain.[165] Certainly Eworth painted several portraits of the queen in different formats and sizes from half-length miniatures to three-quarter-length portraits on panels of medium

24 Mary I by Hans Eworth.

size.[166] An early signed portrait, dated 1554 (now in the Society of Antiquaries) is a 40″ × 30″ panel which depicts Mary in a gold embroidered and jewelled robe with pearl and sable trimming, wearing a pearl necklace and locket with pendant pearl, and with jewelled rings on both hands.[167] Not only is Mary represented in costly dress and jewellery, the geometry of the panel serves to underline royal authority by centring the queen down the vertical axis of the portrait. Against the backdrop of a red curtain with perfectly squared folds, Mary stands, with her dress skirting outwards symmetrically to the edges of the portrait and with her hands folded at the waist, in a pose that recalls that of Jane Seymour in Holbein's Privy Chamber mural. This appears to have been the model for other portraits of the queen, both by Eworth and his studio. Another portrait, now at the Fitzwilliam Museum in Cambridge, highlights the elaborately worked jewellery and lace against a plain gown but in the angle of the head, the position of the hands and the pomander hanging from the waist, the canvas clearly echoes the Society of Antiquaries portrait.[168] Other images, such as that at Charlecote Park of *Maria dei gracia Angliae regina aetatis 41, 1556* cannot be attributed with any certainty, but this evidently follows Eworth, not least in the attention given to the pearl necklace, the locket, the rings and the jewelled head-dress.[169] Mary's fondness for extravagant clothes and jewellery was as conspicuously displayed on canvas as on her person – perhaps as a statement of female regality and authority. In some of these canvases, Mary wears a cross at her necklace, and in the Charlecote Park portrait the large locket even resembles a small reliquary.

Mary was also painted, seated in three quarter length, by the Utrecht-trained artist Antonio Mor. Although this image survives in variants, it has been persuasively argued that Mary had little control over it, that its format 'remained alien to English painting' and that the work was commissioned to commemorate Mary's marriage to Philip II in July 1554.[170] Philip took Mor into his service at the end of the year, and it may be that the portrait of Mary was his first commission for the king. As Karen Hearn wrote, 'The reconciliation of the English and Catholic churches on 29th November and the belief that Mary was pregnant make this an exceptionally propitious moment from a Habsburg perspective'.[171] Indeed, Mary herself is almost marked as a Habsburg, her diamond ring and pendant jewel representing betrothal gifts from Charles V and Philip. Mary's seated position, untypical of English royal portraits, echoes that of other Habsburg brides, and (it has been suggested) the rose that Mary proffers with her right hand may be read as a tender of her love to her husband, as well as a family emblem and sign of her (and her holy namesake's) virginity.[172]

If copies of this portrait or heads taken from it were disseminated widely – and it was said that Mor gave copies 'to great men' – we must wonder how they were received.[173] In the queen's own case, though she did not commission the canvas, it has been persuasively argued that she had a copy.[174] More generally, as Joanne Woodall has argued, for all the conspicuous Habsburg motifs, the portrait makes some attempt to marry Habsburg and English traditions, just as did the pageantry devised to celebrate the wedding.[175] Moreover, in the portrait busts which were the most widely distributed form of the image, the departures from a native English style were least in evidence. Mor's Mary, then, could have been viewed as a compliment to an English queen, enthroned before a pillar of authority in rich costume and jewellery. But the display of her betrothal jewel unquestionably made this an image which announced

25 Mary I by Antonis Mor.

Mary's marriage to the Spanish Philip II, with all the ambivalent or outright hostile reactions that espousal provoked.

Mor's portrait may have been intended to be paired with one of Philip. And in a later portrait, dated 1558, once ascribed to Eworth, Mor's image of Mary forms the model for a joint portrait with Philip, now in the collection of the Duke of Bedford at Woburn Abbey.[176] In this canvas, Philip and Mary sit on the left and right, she enthroned, each side of a doorway, beneath the Habsburg and English arms displayed on the walls. The queen holds a red rose, while Philip wears the Garter round his left knee and the Golden Fleece

26 Philip II and Mary I.

about his neck, heraldic symbols of their dynastic union. Two dogs lying peacefully together at Mary's feet may symbolize their union and fidelity. The window in the upper part of the door looks out on to the Thames and St Paul's; and an inscription above gives the dates and years which Philip and Mary had ruled as monarchs of England, Spain, France, Sicily and Ireland, as Archduke and Duchess of Austria, Burgundy and Brabant, and as Defenders of the Faith. Whatever the views of some of her subjects, Mary advertised and visually represented herself as a loving wife of a Habsburg prince, who, the double portraits imply, ruled as her equal over England.

27 Engraving of Mary I by Frans Huys.

Contemporary engraved portraits of Mary are few in number, the notable ones published in her lifetime being a pair of prints ascribed to Frans Hogenberg, the Flemish engraver. The first is of Mary in her usual position and dress, with her pearl necklace and diamond jewel and jewelled head-dress. With the date 1555, each side of a Tudor rose, the engraving (which may have been later) is inscribed in the oval 'Maria Henr. VIII F. Dei gratia regina Angliae et Franciae et Hiberniae fidei defensatrix', and carries at the foot Mary's adopted motto, 'Veritas temporis filia'.[177] A second is inscribed in an oval 'Illa ego cui superare suos Deus optimus hostes iustitiaque dedit gentem frenare Britanniam anno aetat suae XXXIX'.[178] In both cases, the inscriptions make assertions, not only of Mary's authority, but also of her convictions. As John King explains, in her motto Mary reappropriated the female figure of Truth to make the iconography of Veritas temporis filia into praise of herself and of the Catholic faith: 'when Mary adopted the phrase as her motto, she converted it into an argument for the validity of Catholic tradition, rescued by time from oppression' – an argument repeated, with the motto as we shall see, in seals, coins and pageants.[179] In the second case, the claim to be God's chosen agent to fight his enemies and, as Justice, to bridle and order the British people, publicized the queen's mission as well as authority. In this case, there is evidence that at least one contemporary read the engraving as a provocative production. The author of *The Lamentation of England* (1558) castigated Mary for her willingness to subordinate England to a foreigner and to claim falsely a pregnancy so as to 'give the crown of this noble realm to the prince of Spain to the intent that he, with his proud Spaniards, might bridle this Britannish nation according as it is set out in print about the fisnamy [physiognomy] or picture of the queen in these words Illa ego, cui superare suos Deus optimus hostes/ Iustitiaque dedit gentem frenare Britanniam'.[180]

Such a reading was not inappropriate. Indeed, in her visual presentation more than her discourse, Mary presented herself not only as the wife of a Habsburg prince but as the restorer of a Catholic church. This was true both in what Mary did not, as well as in what she did, represent. Hostile to the English Bible, Mary ceased to depict herself, as had Henry VIII and Edward VI (and as Elizabeth was to), as the deliverer of the word to her people. Her reconciliation with Rome also muted the nationalist stance of the queen's supremacy, a nationalism which had been figured, in John King's words, as the crown opposed to the tiara.[181] But there were also more positive depictions of Mary as Counter-Reformation prince. A miniature of Mary in a manuscript volume of prayers to be used 'by the queen's highness in the consecration of the cramp rings' depicts Mary kneeling before a book and an altar.[182] On the wall behind her, a statue of the Virgin and Child announces the reversal of the

28 Mary I as Catholic Queen.

Edwardian programme of iconoclasm and the revived role of saints and images in worship. On the altar, an image of Christ and the accoutrements of the mass are portrayed as sacred mysteries; the queen turns to them in adoration, her book apparently a missal, rather than Scripture. In the borders of the miniature, as well as the Tudor rose and foliage, a woman with a severed head almost certainly gestures to the story of Judith, the saviour of the Jews with whom Mary was frequently compared.[183] If, here, Mary appropriates for the Catholic cause the conceit of the prince as leader of the elect nation, the lower border image of St George, mounted with his spear, not only restores an icon banished by Edward but associates Mary with the saint protector of England. Mary's image fused national now with Catholic images, to represent her as protectress of her people, martial Christian prince, and successor of the holy Virgin.

Though seen and used by her court and household, the volume of prayers in which this representation is found was neither published nor public. But Mary is figured as God's handmaid in John Heywood's *The Spider and the Fly*, an allegory of the Reformation published in 1556.[184] Here Mary was presented not as the warrior for Christ but, in gendered terms that Elizabeth was again to adopt, as the meek servant of God who does the Lord's will; at the same time she destroys the Protestant spider and 'with her foot presseth him to death'.[185] The image of a queen as God's handmaid, historians must recognize, pre-dates Elizabeth I. In the copy I have seen, Richard Beeard's *Godly Psalm of Mary Queen* was followed by a service book of Latin psalms and prayers richly illustrated. In this volume, biblical scenes of the annunciation, the nativity, the circumcision and the crucifixion are engraved in vivid detail, along with a portrait of Mary being crowned by angels and presented with the orb.[186] Not only did the images announce, in the very first year of the new reign, a more visual spiritual culture, they visually enfolded Mary into a scriptural narrative, as though the second Mary reigned to fulfil the promise announced to the first. Here again, the Mary 'which brought us comfort' was figured as the servant of God to bring 'his people England' to him.[187]

The queen's portraits on documents repeat several of these themes. As early as the 1553 Michaelmas plea roll, a miniature within the initial letter depicted two angels leading Mary, as God's chosen, to her throne – on which she sits with a sword in her right hand beneath a cloth of estate decorated with the royal arms.[188] Above, a dove represents both the peace of Marian rule and, perhaps, the blessing of the Holy Spirit. On the left, a scene of hills and trees shows a land at peace, in contrast to the scene on our right (the queen's left) of arms laid down, and, in the background, of a large force – here probably being surrendered. Altogether, the image appears to celebrate Mary's victory over the rebels, her succession and the divine blessing on her rule. Other

AND THE FLIE.

The maide being at poinct to treade the spider to death: the spider praieth her to here him speake ere he die: and then to adiudge him iustice. the maide graunting to vse him (as he dyd vse the flie) as male best stand with reason, law, custum, and conscience. She at his request (for the time) withdrawing hyr foote, they fall to reasoning of the case.   Cap. 90.

29   Woodcut of Mary I in Heywood's *The Spider and the Flie.*

miniatures depicting the holy dove, in colours reminiscent of religious illuminations, support the impression that Mary sought to present herself on legal documents, as on canvas, as a Catholic, as well as a Tudor, queen. Indeed, one limning in the Augmentation Office Book of Mary enthroned has the motto 'Dieu et mon droit' and on the canopy the inscription 'D[omin]e salvam ac regina'.[189]

After her marriage, illustrations to documents bear portraits of Mary and Philip jointly enthroned, she with the sceptre of rule, he with the sword signifying his titular authority. In the initial letters of the documents, under a large

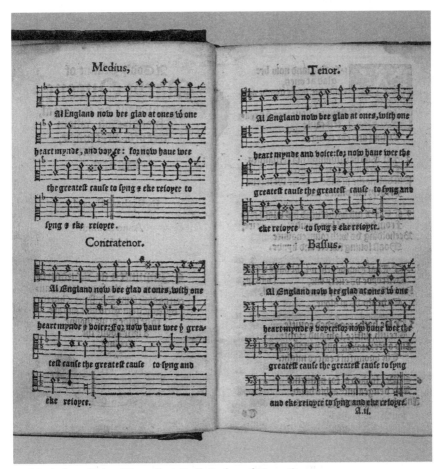

30 Music from Richard Beeard's *A Godly Psalme of Marye Queene.*

crown that stands above both figures and with background cloths and canopy embroidered with their initials and the script 'Vivant rex et regina', Philip and Mary look towards each other, as their sceptre and sword gesture to the crown they now share.[190] On this Easter roll for 1556, the Tudor rose and pomegranate (the emblem of Catherine of Aragon, adopted by Mary) frame the pair, who also wear a mixture of English and Spanish costume. Interestingly, in images after Michaelmas 1556 the position of the king and queen were transposed and Mary sits on the right, the normal focus of the observer's view, with Philip at her right hand.[191] The perpetuation of this arrangement suggests deliberation; but whether or not the shift was intended to highlight

31 Mary with figures in a landscape, Michaelmas 1553 plea roll.

Mary in the face of criticism of Habsburg influence we cannot say. What is apparent in the later images is a greater attention to likeness, to representing the two rulers not just as monarchs, but as the Philip and Mary regnant whose initials PR and MR adorn the canopy over their heads.[192]

Mary's Great Seal, medals and coins rehearse some of these same themes and motifs. Evidently, it took some time to produce a new seal for the queen, which does not appear to have been ready until the end of 1553: a pardon granted to Francis, second Earl of Huntingdon, dated 14 November that year bears the seal of Edward VI.[193] When it was ready, the new seal had on one side Mary enthroned with a sceptre, between the royal arms and a large Tudor rose and, on the other, the queen mounted. On both sides the border inscription proclaiming the queen's titles, including 'Defensor fidei', was accompanied by a subscript of her motto 'Veritas temporis filia' – a motto which, we have seen, Mary appropriated for a Catholic representation.[194] The seal did not have a long life: shortly after her marriage, Mary commissioned a new Great Seal with a rich and complex re-presentation of her role. On the obverse, Philip and Mary are seated, enthroned, left and right respectively of a plinth on which a crowned inscription bears their intertwined initials, P and M. Each bears a sword, Philip in his

32 Mary and Philip, Easter 1556 plea roll.

right hand, Mary in her left, and with the other hand each reaches towards the other to touch a large orb bearing a cross, which sits on the plinth. Above the orb, the arms of England are crowned and enclosed in an oval bearing the motto of the Garter: 'Honi soit qui mal y pense.' Round the border the inscription proclaims the joint titles of the rulers as monarchs of England, Spain and their territories. The canopy that covers them, like the initials and hands joined on the orb, symbolizes the joint and equal rule of a king and queen who half turn to each other as well as to the viewer. On the reverse, both figures are mounted, with Philip again bearing a sword in his right hand, Mary in her left. In this case, the queen, riding side-saddle beside him, looks directly to her husband whose elaborately decorated mount dominates the image. And here the inscription marks out what were essentially Philip's titles as Archduke of Austria, Duke of Burgundy, Brabant and Flanders. From 1555 onwards the Great Seal cannot have comforted those who feared that Mary's marriage to Philip might dissolve her, and England's, authority in a large Habsburg empire.[195]

Medals of the reign also publicized and celebrated Mary's marriage, even those that represent her alone. An early medal of Mary enthroned in 1553 with crown, orb and sceptre with, on the reverse, her arms in a Tudor rose, was presumably issued to mark the coronation.[196] A medallic tribute to Mary

33 Philip and Mary with figure, Hilary, 1557–8 plea roll.

presenting her as Peace destroying the arms of the turbulent rebels was commissioned by Philip II and another drew on a medal issued for the marriage of Archduke Maximilian of Austria to Charles V's daughter.[197] Other medals depicted Philip, alone, with Habsburg emblems (such as the eagle) or celebrated the marriage of the two monarchs and the union of nations that it signified. One medal, with on the reverse 'Pro lege, rege et grege', described Philip as 'Hispaniarum et Angliae rex'; a second depicted him, in defiance of popular opinion, as 'Securitas populorum'.[198] On another, the images of Philip and Mary appear to have been on opposite sides; while a fourth, conjoining their arms and promising a political as well as personal union, bore the inscription 'Amicitia servat concordia'.[199] A medal of Mary with a nuptial torch between olive branches may have signified not only the unity of the nations but the reunification with the Catholic church.[200]

Some of these medals were struck abroad, and we cannot be sure about the extent of their circulation in England. In any study of the royal visual representation in England, the coins deserve a larger place. As we have seen, the Marian government took care to re-establish the intrinsic value of the coinage and to reissue pieces that would reaffirm confidence in English money and monarchy. Though real reform did not come until later, as early as August 1553 orders were

34 Seal of Mary I and Philip.

35 Medal of Philip II and Mary I.

issued for the production of gold and silver coins – sovereigns, royals, angels and angelets; and shillings and sixpences were added by December of the same year.[201] Mary's first sovereign issue carefully depicted the queen enthroned and crowned with a sceptre in her right hand and an orb in her left, between two small columns or pedestals, above the portcullis, a Tudor blazon taken from the Beaufort badge adopted by Henry VII.[202] The reverse, with the royal arms set inside a large Tudor rose and inscribed 'God brought this about and it is marvellous', underlined Mary's succession to the Tudor dynasty and throne and perhaps attempted to marginalize the queen's sex.[203] Another gold coin certainly depicted her in masculine and martial pose steering the ship of state, which bears the emblem of the Tudor rose and a standard and ensign emblazoned with the letter 'M'. Silver coins, playing on her being named after the Virgin and on the Tudor emblem, bore the inscription around the image of Mary 'Rosa sine spina' – the rose without thorns – or carried Mary's motto 'Veritas temporis filia'.

After her marriage, Mary's coins again showed her and Philip as joint rulers – commonly as two profile figures who look affectionately towards each other under one shared crown, or on opposite sides of coins, the inscriptions to which describe each as ruler of their combined kingdoms. From the time of the marriage, the ship of state on the gold coin bore, as well as the royal arms,

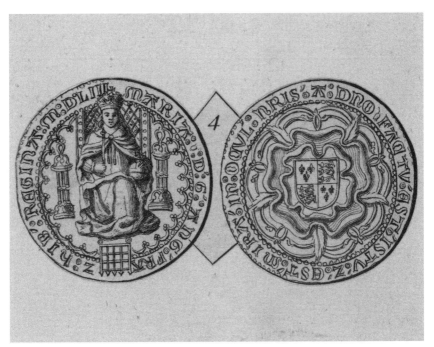

36 Sovereign of Queen Mary.

the initials of both Philip and Mary and a cross. If the marriage ceremony had not sufficiently announced it, the coinage publicized a husband and wife united in faith: as some pieces, appropriating a legend from Edward's coins were inscribed, 'Posuimus deum adiutorem nostrum'.[204] Like her claim inscribed on her first sovereign to be ruler by God's divine intervention, in their marriage piece Mary represented herself with Philip as two rulers protected by the Lord and as divine agents of his will.

In her visual representation, Mary faced difficulties which the devisers of her image attempted to redeem. First, Mary was presented as her father's daughter, as a Tudor, and as the heir to his authority, enthroned with the insignia of regality. In so far as her sex was concerned, the Marian images skilfully utilized Mary's femininity in the obvious conspicuous display of wealth and extravagance in clothes and jewels; and in associating the queen both with masculine authorities and with biblical heroines, as well as with emblems of Tudor sovereignty – notably the rose, also a traditional Christian symbol of the Virgin. Mary also authorized visual statements of her appointment to rule by divine decree: the references to God's deeds to be wondered at by men doubtless were intended to recall the victory of Mary over Lady Jane Grey's challenge to her rule, as well as that over the Wyatt rebellion.

37 Gold coin of Mary I.

When it came to her marriage, Mary appears to have been happy to publicize her status as a married woman, wife of the heir to the Habsburg empire; and in dynastic terms it made perfect sense for her to do so. In portraits and on medals and coins, the royal couple were depicted as equal rulers, and Mary was credited with the titles to Philip's lands as much as he is presented as king of England. Whatever the unpopularity of this match – and we must here recall that Wyatt's failure stemmed in part from overestimating that unpopularity – this representation of Philip and Mary as joint custodians of the realm was effectively the only choice available to her.

With regard to her faith, Mary (as the virulence of the opposition testifies) succeeded in no small measure in reappropriating authorized (and in some cases what had become Protestant) symbols for Catholicism and Catholic kingship. Portrayed as God's chosen, God's handmaid, as the Virgin and as one who, having been chosen by God, took him as her guide and protector, Mary appropriated traditional conceits (such as that Truth was the Daughter of Time) for both her church and her rule.

Mary, in other words, established an image and an identity as a godly queen of a true church, who, in union with her husband and with Spain, would bring peace and harmony to her people. History has decreed that this image and

38 Coin of Philip and Mary, 1554.

identity were a failure: that Mary failed, in every sense, in the arts of rule. Before we so conclude, we should recall that Mary was a monarch who paid particular attention to visual representation, having, it is said, been led to fall in love with her future husband by seeing his portrait by Titian.[205] Her chaplain and apologist argued the importance of images in the state no less than the church. Did not, he asked rhetorically, men remember more a ruler when they came into a house and found his (or her) image? 'It was wont to be said,' he continued, 'that such as were the king's very friends would have the king's image in their houses both to make them remember their duties towards him and also to declare their good will that they bore him.'[206] 'Lively images,' whether of the monarch or of Christ, 'make folks remember the man that is represented.'[207] In Mary's case, history has not remembered the person as she was represented – the Tudor daughter of Henry VIII who sought the peace and prosperity of the nation. Few popular portraits of her survive: interestingly (might it have been strategically?) no woodcuts depicted Mary in Foxe's Book of Martyrs.[208] Instead Foxe's powerful visual text emblematized her reign with endless illustrations of martyrs and persecutions, and roundly condemned her along with her faith.

IV Reviving Catholic Rituals

Henry VIII strengthened the regal power that rested on an initially shaky foundation by a display of authority and magnificence, not least by the development of a court that drew the mighty subjects to Whitehall and became a focus of Tudor rule. We have seen the degree to which, even as a minor, Edward's reign preserved the court and how Edward, for all his different circumstances and sensibility, attempted to uphold the majesty and state of his father. The image, and authority, of the monarchy, as a body of English literature written in the wake of Castiglione's *Courtier* proclaimed, were bound up with the splendour of the royal court. But what of the court of a woman? How would the court of a queen regnant (as opposed to consort) represent the martial glory, humanist learning and dynastic prowess of the Tudors?[209] Moreover, Henry had organized his court to remove himself into a newly created bedchamber which he had staffed with his confidants as well as companions. Clearly men could not perform body service in the bedchamber of a woman and female attendants would not be permitted to wield the influence of men like Sir Anthony Denny, Henry's Groom of the Stole, and others. A feminine court presented as great a problem for the representation of authority as did a female sovereign for the exercise of authority.[210]

Mary, of course, had had a court as princess before she ascended the throne as queen, and was frequently in attendance at the royal court of her father, and subsequently her brother. Many of the personnel – her confessor, the Vice-Chamberlain, and her Master of the Horse, for example – transferred to the queen's royal court and as trusted servants guarded access to her person. Mary's court as princess also had a distinct identity. Mary loved and patronized music; she favoured rich clothes and jewels and enjoyed recreations, games (such as cards, dice and dancing) and the vigorous exercise of coursing and the chase.[211] She was fond of entertainments and revived traditional festivities such as May games which her brother's court had banned.[212] And, of course, her court was known for the queen's Catholic piety. Even those who did not share her faith praised Mary's charity and liberality towards churchmen.[213] More infamously, as princess, she clashed with her brother over the right to exercise publicly the rites of Catholic worship in her court, in relation to which right she appealed to the emperor for support.[214] When, in December 1550, orders were issued to arrest her household chaplains for saying mass, Mary defiantly informed her brother that 'her soul was God's and her faith she would not change, nor dissemble her opinions ...'.[215] Mary continued to hear mass in her household, albeit less publicly, and the Edwardian regime left her undisturbed.

When she succeeded to the throne, Mary added to the women who had served her as princess a number of female relatives of her leading councillors;

but, it has been argued, these formed no centre of power or influence.[216] Rather Mary gathered, apart from the Council, a small circle of male advisers and confidants, and increasingly relied on the service and counsel of her Lord Chancellor, Bishop Stephen Gardiner.

The court of Queen Mary, strictly speaking, had a short life as, after July 1554, barely a year after her proclamation as queen, the royal court, for all her husband's absences, became the court of Philip and Mary. And whatever the verdict of her critics or later historians, a husband was a distinct advantage to the royal court. For when Philip was present, the jousts and tournaments which had been so important to the image of the first two Tudor monarchs, but which her sex meant the queen could not participate in, were again frequently staged – evidently before a wide audience. The merchant Henry Machyn, for example, recorded in December 1554, 'the great triumph at the court gate by the King and divers lords both Englishmen and Spaniards . . . they ran as fast with spears and swords at the tournay'.[217] The next month, there was 'great running at the tilt at Westminster with spears' and on 19 March, 'in the morning the King's grace ran at the tilt . . . and broke four staffs by 8 o'clock of the morning'.[218] The next week, 'the 25th day of March the which was our lady day there was', Machyn reported, 'as great jousts as you have ever seen at the tilt at Westminster; the challenger was a Spaniard and Sir George Howard, and all their men and their horse trimmed in white and then came the king and a great menee [retinue] all in blue and trimmed with yellow, and their helmets with great tufts of blue and yellow feather and all their [forerunners] and their footmen . . . and a company like Turks rode in crimson satin gowns and capes . . . and there was broken two hundred staffs and above'.[219] A London edition of Gawin Douglas's *The Palace of Honour*, dedicated to Queen Mary, underlined the powerful importance of the chivalric ideal and, in a compliment to the queen, gestured to the court of Venus, at which the Muses were in attendance.[220] Though we know little about the queen's attendance at these occasions, it would appear that Mary may have been a lady of the tournament before her more famous sister. Certainly we need to qualify Alan Young's assessment that Mary was 'not particularly interested in feats of arms and the political benefit that she could derive from them'.[221] The Mary who, when Wyatt approached, 'with undaunted spirit' refused to withdraw and 'even asked to go and fight herself', was no less concerned than Elizabeth to manifest that her sex did not preclude a martial spirit or representation.[222]

Nor did female governance inhibit the round of entertainment and rituals that marked the household calendar and publicized the court and queen to her entourage, visiting ambassadors, the nobility and gentry, and others attendant on, or visitors to, Whitehall, Hampton Court and such royal palaces. Thanks to the surviving Revels Accounts, edited from the Loseley Manuscripts, we have quite detailed information about the nature and frequency of court festivals and entertainments in Mary's reign.[223] Weeks after ascending the throne, Mary signed a signet warrant for the delivery out of the Revels Office of the French costumes and props for a play by the 'gentlemen of the chapel to be shown and played before the Queen's majesty at her highness's coronation', 'as in times past hath accustomed to be done'.[224] Court plays and masques appear to have been regular diversions, and the brief accounts in the Revels suggest increasingly elaborate themes and costumes. Payment for 'mariners that were masquers', lion masks and headpieces, and masks for Greek worthies, as well as for drums, pipes, bows, arrows, rich 'gowns of crimson cloth of gold', and clothes embroidered with crowns and roses hint at the scale of the spectacles and their role in celebrating the Tudor dynasty.[225] Masques were frequently organized around the themes of the Greek virtues, the story of Hercules and other classical legends.[226] But we have entries also regarding 'a masque of 8 patrons of galleys like Venetian senators with 6 galley slaves for their torch-bearers', 'a masque of Turks magistrates with 6 Turks archers', and 'a great masque of Allemagnes, pilgrims and Irishmen ...' performed on 25 April 1557.[227] Signs that chivalric love may have been a theme appropriate for a female court are found in references to a masque of '6 Venuses or amorous ladies with 6 Cupids and 6 torchbearers to them', the Shrovetide 'masque of women like goddesses huntresses, 8 with 8 Turkey women their torchbearers', and in the description of a cloth 'embroidered with a man of arms of silver riding with a mount and a lady standing in clouds casting darts at him, with hearts and ciphers of gold'.[228]

The deviser of several of these 'dialogues and interludes' and 'certain plays' was Nicholas Udall, who had organized the entertainments for the entry of Anne Boleyn into London in May 1533 and assisted with an English translation of Erasmus's *Paraphrase* of the New Testament. Under Edward VI, Udall had been recruited to answer the rebels of Cornwall and Devon and had reasoned with great force against their Catholic arguments.[229] It may then seem surprising that Mary took him into her employ, as did Bishop Gardiner who appointed him a tutor in his household. There is some evidence that, whatever his earlier Lutheran sympathies, Udall was persuaded to serve the times (he assisted in securing the Protestant exile Thomas Mountain's recantation); but how he served Mary as deviser of entertainments in the three years before his death in 1556 remains unclear. If the attribution, on grounds of style, to Udall of the play *Respublica* can be trusted, the court may have seen performed an attack on the Reformation and an encomium on the restoration of the true Catholic faith.[230]

For the most part, however, the evidence of the Revels Accounts does not support any picture of a campaign to make court entertainments propaganda for Catholicism. Among all the classical costumes, we find only the stray reference to a priest's gown; reference to garments for figures such as Sickness, Deformity, Self Love and Genus Humanum suggest that the opening interlude to mark the coronation was more a traditional morality play than a narrow denominational polemic.[231]

What was different about the revels at Mary's court was that they ended the cycle of anti-papal entertainments that had commenced under Henry VIII and become more virulent in the reign of his successor. Moreover, Marian entertainments were again tied to the traditional Catholic calendar of festivals and saints' days: Candlemas, 'St Martin tide' and 'St Mark's night', as well as the once-again traditional Christmas and Shrovetide.[232] And not only were these interludes and masques now part of a different liturgical calendar, they were also performed in a transformed ritual context. Henry Machyn described what was a popular court ritual, reinstituted by Mary, taking place during Rogation week, on 3 May 1554: 'at the court of St James's, the queen's grace went a procession within St James, with heralds and sergeants at arms, and 4 bishops, mitred, and all three days, they went her chapel about the fields, first day to St Giles and there sang mass; the next day Tuesday to St Martin's in the Fields and there a sermon and sung mass and so they drank there; and the third day to Westminster, and there a sermon and then mass, and made good cheer; and after about the park and so to St James's court . . .'.[233] Court festivals now routinely involved the celebration of the mass and Mary revived the habit of court processions on the holy days of the Catholic calendar. If the processors of Rogation week were the Gentlemen of the Chapel who had performed for Mary's coronation and at Whitehall, the entertainments of Mary and Philip, whatever their content, were those of a Catholic court.

As we have seen, the pageantry of Mary's reign began in unusual circumstances outside her control. It was at 2 p.m. on 1 August, three weeks after her brother's death, that she commenced her entry into London, with an escort of a thousand courtiers and over 10,000 others, to the greeting of 'such a discharge of ordnance that the like has not been heard there these many years', and, at least according to the Spanish merchant De Guaras, 'amid all imaginable joy of the people'.[234] While the city prepared for the usual gesture of compliment, a coronation pageant, arrangements were made for the funeral of Edward which took place a week after Mary's entry, on the 8th. 'At his burying', Machyn recorded, was 'the greatest moan made for him of his death as ever was heard or seen of all sorts of people, weeping and lamenting', as the funeral cortège with all the king's banners and regalia symbolically announced the demise of his public body.[235] Over the next months, Mary resided in the Tower, awaiting the ritual presentation of the queen to her people that the coronation pageant had become. As we have observed, this was no simple act of royal propaganda but a ritual manifestation of that complex symbiosis (and negotiation) between ruler and subjects that constituted royal government in early modern England.[236] Though the city dignitaries doubtless conferred with councillors and royal confidants, the coronation entertainments were paid for and created by city companies with their own desires, hopes and concerns. As such, it was an occasion to send the monarch a message as well as to proclaim him or her. Given the recent history of rapid religious changes, an initially successful revolt against Mary's succession and the concern of some in a London more Protestant than any other part of the realm, the coronation pageant presented complex difficulties – and, as events unfolded, perhaps not unambiguous signals.

On 18 September, Mary went by barge to the Tower to make her coronation entry on the 30th. We have several accounts of the day, by foreign observers ranging from Pole's legatine commissioner Monsignor Commendone to the Spanish merchant Antonio de Guaras and by domestic chroniclers, such as Henry Machyn the London merchant, and the anonymous chronicler of Mary's first two years. The queen and her courtiers prepared themselves with full magnificence. Mary rode under a canopy of gold in an open chariot – 'gorgeously be-seen', according to Machyn, 'in a gown of blue velvet furred with powder and ermine, hanging on her head a caul of cloth of tinsel beset with pearl and stone and . . . upon her head a round circle of gold . . . beset so richly with many precious stones that the value thereof was inestimable'.[237] The queen was followed by her sister Elizabeth and by Anne of Cleves, by two more triumphal chariots and by sixty peeresses and ladies all dressed in crimson velvet. Before them rode nobles, ambassadors and Gentlemen of the Household all 'superbly adorned', then horses decked 'some with gold, some with embroidery which caused great admiration not more by the richness of the substance than by novelty and elegancy of the device'.[238] As the cavalcade proceeded along the one-and-a-half-mile processional route, Guaras tells us that they came to 'many triumphal arches of rich construction with dainty devices'.[239] Machyn similarly listed 'goodly pageants' at Cornhill, Paul's Yard and Fleet Street but tells us nothing of them.[240] Whatever the dainty devices of the others – he mentions in passing those of the English and the Hanseatic merchants – Guaras describes only two. Commendone is more frank and more blunt: 'on the street were several arches but only two of them were worth noticing': those prepared by the German and (unsurprisingly) the Florentine merchants.[241]

The pageant of the Genoese was staged around a triumphal arch which bore an inscription, 'Mariae Reginae inclytae constanter piae coronam infamici imperii et palmam virtutis accipienti Genuenses publica salute iaestantes cultum optatim tribuunt'.[242] On the other side, the text celebrated the triumph of virtue, truth, justice and piety and the restitution of peace and serenity to the commonweal. On a platform above the arch were 'four great giants' and a child who greeted the queen with a 'salutation'. While the theme is not recorded, it seems likely that Mary was hailed, as in the inscription, as the embodiment of virtue, justice, piety and truth – the last perhaps a gesture to her motto – and as the hope of peace after rebellion and conflict. The Florentine pageant consisted of an arch inscribed 'Mariae Britannarum reginae victrici piae augustae gloriae insignia erixerunt'. This arch bore four statues: of Pallas Athena, over the inscription 'Invicta virtus'; of Tomyris, with the inscription 'Libertati ultrici'; of Judith, 'Patriae liberatrici'; and of the queen herself, represented as 'Salus populi'.[243] Here, Mary is compared not only with the Greek goddess both of war and the arts who, born of Zeus, checked the wild fury of Mars, and with the heroine Tomyris, queen of the Massagetae, who defeated Cyrus, the founder of the Persian empire; but also with the biblical leader Judith (with whom we have seen Mary associated in visual representations and panegyrics), who saved her homeland from the Assyrians. As Sidney Anglo has argued, the immediate gesture to a Northumberland who days before had, like Holofernes, been decapitated on the block, underscored Mary's political triumph.[244] But the parallel with a woman who had saved her chosen people, along with the Genoese praise of truth and piety, subtly presented Mary's Catholic faith as the restitution of right as well as peace. As a verse on the silver drapery beneath the statues proclaimed, Justice, Piety and Peace returned with Mary, the virgin who effected what no man could achieve. The Florentines, who took this conceit from their favourite poet, Dante, proclaimed perhaps not only their patriotism but also their Catholicism.

As Mary passed the conduit at Cornhill, three girls dressed as Graces (each with crown and sceptre), Virtue (with a cup) and Nature (with an olive branch) knelt to sing verses of praise; and children sang for her at the schoolhouse in St Paul's Yard where Mary was entertained by an acrobat on the weathercock.[245] As she passed the dean's house, children stood with perfumed tapers to light her way to Fleet Street, where a final pageant 'made like a castle' was presented with songs of rejoicing.[246] As she made her onward journey, 'the multitude was infinite that, greeting her majesty in succession, escorted her to the palace'.[247]

The celebrations were, as such occasions usually were, the product of many heads and minds as well as purses. While the praise of Mary, as legitimate heir who had defeated a rebel, might have united most, the conceit of Truth returned and Piety enthroned doubtless meant different things to different observers, not only Italian and English, but Catholic or reformed. The (ideal) role of ritual and pageant was to gloss these differences by discourses and symbols behind which all would unite. As important, the coronation pageants played out the relationship, the reciprocity, between the monarch and the city, the sovereign and her subjects. As she received the people's acclamation and the city's gift purse, so Mary had taken pains to reveal herself 'in a chariot open on all sides'.[248] As she rode to her coronation in Westminster Abbey the next day, that reciprocity was nicely demonstrated in a gesture which might appear to be something between recognition of the desire for a souvenir and a reciprocal gift of thanks for the crowd: 'The queen reached the Church and the streets through which she passed were all adorned with fine drapes which [were] afterwards distributed to the people'.[249]

If the rituals in the street announced continuity, the service inside the abbey marked an important change. Much, of course, was familiar: Mary was placed in a throne on a dais and on all sides was shown to the people by the Bishop of Winchester who asked if they accepted her, at which the crowd shouted their affirmation.[250] But the queen's often 'prostrating herself' before the altar, the Te Deum Laudamus, the 'magnificent ceremonies' and old customs, most of all the mass, during which (according to Guaras) she knelt 'with grave devotion', publicized a restitution of the sacramental status of the occasion which the Edwardian government had underplayed.[251] Mary's assembly of a clerical procession with crosses, a choir and bishops in mitres with their croziers displayed a priestly status and authority long not seen – 'todos los canonigos y clericia', according to a Spanish account, 'con grande devocion y grandes senales de religion . . .'.[252]

We have no account of any reaction to the coronation ceremony – and so no reason to conclude that it was unpopular. The anonymous chronicler appears wearied by 'so many and sundry ceremonies . . . and other old customs' that made it so long – '4 o'clock before she came out' – and 'noted' that the queen was led several times to the altar; but others expressed no direct antipathy.[253] Machyn recorded more the post-coronation banquet, which Guaras also considered a lavish occasion and great success 'so much as the order and due and timely performance of the ceremonies was concerned'.[254] Rather than foreseeing trouble, the Spaniard believed that, with this magnificent occasion, 'regulated with great prudence and wisdom', 'this kingdom and their magnanimous queen have given ample employment for the authors who may desire to write concerning them'.[255]

The next major pageant of Mary's reign celebrated an event less popular than her accession: her marriage to Philip of Spain. As well as the general xenophobia of an increasingly jingoistic nation, many feared that Mary's marriage to a foreign prince would subordinate the queen and England to the Habsburgs; and committed Protestants were, of course, anxious about Habsburg rule. For Mary, however, and many in the government, the marriage not only linked England to empire, it held out the possibility of an assured succession, a powerful ally in Europe, and the end of major threats to the security of the realm. The pageant expressed both these senses of celebration and unease.

Juan de Barahona related to his uncle Antonio the journey of Philip who set sail from La Coruña on Friday, 12 July 1554. As Philip's flotilla spied English land, an English escort greeted the Spanish with a salute and conducted them to the Isle of Wight, whence they were conveyed by ship to Southampton. Here, the Earl of Arundel presented Philip with the Order of the Garter, while the English Horse Guard stood in attendance on the pier, and the Spanish king was then led to his mansion, which was 'lavishly adorned with brocade and gold fabrics and embroidered canopies'.[256] The following Saturday, while the Spanish and English nobles exchanged compliments, Philip went to mass 'with all his courtiers with him and escorted by the English guard'.[257] After Philip's first encounter with his English subjects at Southampton, his wedding awaited him nearby at Winchester; and on the 23rd the entourage set off 'accompanied by all the Spanish and English noblemen who were there, may be three thousand horses without counting the horse guard . . .', in what must have been one of the most spectacular displays of regal majesty the south coast had witnessed in living memory.[258]

Just outside Winchester, six principal noblemen, each with a company of 200 horse, rode out to lead Philip into the city where, at the cathedral, he was met by Bishop Gardiner and five other bishops who accompanied him to the high altar for mass while a Te Deum Laudamus was sung. Afterwards Philip paid a brief visit to the queen, speaking to her in Spanish (she replied in French) before retiring to his apartment. If, for all that he had donned English dress for the occasion, the 'strangeness' of Philip was now manifest to all – he knew no English – the fact of their union was made public the following Tuesday when, on Philip's entry to court, 'her highness descended and . . . did kiss him in presence of all the people'.[259] After attending a service, Philip was escorted by torchlight back to the dean's house, to prepare for his wedding the next day.

On the 25th, ambassadors and nobles escorted Philip to the cathedral, to await the queen, who entered with the sword borne before her.[260] The two ascended to the raised traverse which, in Barahona's words, 'looked like a theatre'.[261] And appropriately, just as the ceremony was about to commence, in a dramatic moment, Figueroa arrived with letters patent from the emperor of a wedding gift – the kingdom of Naples with Jerusalem. The gift, according to Barahona, 'pleased very much everybody' in attendance, not least because it announced Philip as a king as well as prince.[262] The wedding itself may have been for many their first – certainly the first for some years – display of full Catholic ceremonial. 'The organs used such sweet proportion of music and the like was never before . . . heard.'[263] A mass was said for both Philip and Mary (who publicly took both the bread and the wine), 'the king's highness at the Agnus Dei kissing ye celebrator according to the celebration of marriages used in holy Catholic churches'.[264]

The service over, the king and queen went, 'hand in hand' under a canopy of crimson velvet, to their wedding banquet (at Gardiner's episcopal palace) at which they were again seated, for public view, on a raised platform, under a 'very rich canopy'.[265] A cupboard full of gold and silver vessels stood on one side of the hall to embellish the space with 'beautiful decorations'.[266] All was carefully prepared to display Philip and Mary as a married couple whose wedding represented the union of two kingdoms. Philip wore English-style clothing; Mary wore a gown 'of the same material as the robe of the king with the same embroidery', sported the betrothal diamond given her by her husband, and had her hair dressed after the Spanish fashion.[267] Even the dances were discreetly chosen. The ambassadors of Bohemia were requested to dance an 'allemande' 'because the King was unacquainted with the dances of England and the Queen with those of Spain'; and this enabled them to dance together 'with no little contentment' to the bystanders.[268] For some days after the nuptials, the Scottish cartographer John Elder told his correspondent, there was 'triumphing, banqueting, singing, masquing and dancing as was none in England heretofore . . .'.[269] After ten days at Winchester, the couple journeyed to Windsor and then Richmond, to prepare for their entry into London.[270]

The popular mood in London was not auspicious. When, the previous January, the Spanish ambassador who had come to 'knit up' the marriage had been led through Cheapside to Westminster, 'the people nothing rejoicing' had 'held down their heads sorrowfully' and impudent boys had pelted his entourage with snowballs, 'so hateful was the sight of their coming in to them'.[271] But, in the wake of Wyatt's rebellion, the city also needed to demonstrate its loyalty and affection for the queen, and a Court of Aldermen appointed a committee to devise pageants to welcome the newlyweds into the capital.[272] Interestingly, two of the commissioners were former royal printers – a suggestion perhaps that there may have been plans to publish an account of the event; of them, one Richard Grafton, who had been close to Edward VI, had been deprived of his post for printing the proclamation of Queen Jane.

Philip and Mary entered the city on the 18th, to an elaborate spectacle and series of pageants.[273] The first, at the drawbridge of the Tower, featured two giants, Corineus Britannus and Gogmagog Albionus, who, as Britain and England, welcomed Philip with proclamations of the citizens' love. As they passed the conduit at Gracious Street, 'new painted and gilded' and written over with adages and proverbs, the party encountered a pageant of the Nine Worthies and of King Henry VIII and Edward VI – all with maces, swords and axes, except for the figure of Henry VIII 'which was painted having in one hand a sceptre and in the other hand a book, whereon was written Verbum Dei'.[274] At this point, the anonymous chronicler of Mary's first two years pauses to relate a hitch in the proceedings:

> After the king was passed, the Bishop of Winchester, noting the book in Henry the Eighth's hand, shortly afterwards called the painter before him and with vile words calling him traitor asked why and who bad him describe King Henry with a book in his hand . . . threatening him therefore to go to the Fleet. And the painter made answer that he thought he had done well and that no man bad him do the contrary, 'for (saith he) if I had known the same had been against your lordship's pleasure, I would not so have made him.' 'Nay, (said the bishop), it is against the queen's Catholic proceedings.' And so he painted him shortly after in the stead of the book of Verbum Dei, to have in his hands a new pair of gloves.[275]

If there was any fuss at the time, it was, as is the case with such occasions, glossed over as the party moved on; but the episode was by no means over. The painter's protestations of innocence may have been genuine; but the image of the king with the Bible was familiar from the frontispiece to the Great Bible of 1539 and those who had not bid him to the contrary included printers of the King's Bible, which had, as we have seen, become a symbol of the Reformation and royal supremacy: of events which Queen Mary was dedicated to undoing, and which had robbed Philip's cousin, Catherine, of her throne. In this pageant, only Henry and Edward were ranked with the worthies, and the sword no less than the sceptre was prominently displayed as the badge of true kingship. Gardiner's reaction, his desire to find the author and his threat of harsh punishment suggest that the government interpreted this as an opportunity taken by opponents of the queen to manifest their opposition. We cannot know how many other than Gardiner read the image this way. But the representation of Henry with 'Verbum Dei' was familiar to all; and it seems as though the incident drew further attention. Two reports relate the 'immediate commandment' to alter the image; and the London chronicler, later nervous about how his account of it might be interpreted, crossed out the lines quoted above in his journal.[276]

The remaining scenes did not excite such controversy. At the end of Gracechurch Street, appropriately at the sign of the splayed eagle, a Habsburg emblem, the Steelyard merchants had constructed a pageant of Spain supporting her heraldic symbol, a castle, and of Britannia bearing the arms of England. The pageant, 'garnished [with] many goodly stories with images of the 7 Cardinal virtues', may have represented the qualities the two rulers brought together.[277] On top of the arch, a statue of Philip mounted was ingeniously constructed, so as 'by a pretty device ... to mount and turn round about', as Philip, whom it represented, came by.[278] The image was underwritten with verses in honour of a Philip 'most earnestly wished for', who was urged not to budge from right.[279] Given the threat to their privileges, the Hanseatic League had offered not only an extravagant gesture of praise but perhaps, too, a subtle endorsement of the king's (and queen's) Catholic convictions and it pleased 'their majesties very well'.[280]

The next pageant at the conduit at Cornhill, 'of a great height', was, in Elder's report, 'excellently handled and set out'.[281] Here figures depicted the four Philips of classical and historical fame: Philip, King of Macedonia, Philip the Roman emperor, Philip the Good Duke of Burgundy and Philip the Bold. A verse explained their heroic feats and praised 'Thou Philip' who 'passest those Philips four, alone'.[282] Sidney Anglo points out the reference not only to ancient warriors and Burgundian princes but to the description of Philip the emperor, said by Eusebius to be the first Christian emperor.[283] If, as he argues, this was intended to parallel the resurgence of the Catholic faith in England, the image set 'over [the figures] under a rich cloth of state, in the top of the pageant' of Philip and Mary may have represented another race of Philips, heirs of the union and empire of Britain and Spain.[284]

The device at Cheapside featured a leafy mount, with Orpheus playing his harp, surrounded by the nine Muses playing instruments. Nearby, men and children dressed as wild lions, foxes and bears were pacified by the music. The familiar conceit, often a metaphor for rule, was explained in verse: 'The prince that hath the gift of eloquence/May bend his subiectes to his most behove' – and England joyed to hear Philip's voice, no less than were it Orpheus's and the Muses' sweet melody.[285] We do not know who orchestrated this pageant but we do know that it evoked rather different reactions. While the royal couple were 'satisfied' with it, Foxe was quick to deplore the comparison of Philip's English subjects with brute beasts, led to dance after his pipe; and, though he was *parti pris*, that may not have been merely his own interpretation.[286] There may also be another reading of the scene. As well as being praised, Philip was being warned by the Orpheus pageant: that the compliance of English subjects could not be assumed but had to be won – and by persuasion, not by force. If, as the verse ran, the nation's 'minds afore' – was it before Philip's gracious presence or apprehension of the marriage? – were 'bleke'; it was for the Spaniard to reassure them.[287]

As the royal couple moved on, they passed the cross at Cheapside – newly 'with fine gold richly gilded' – and they paused, in meditation, Philip removing his cap 'very humbly' at the crucifix.[288] Here, doubtless the obeisance to a very public religious image, after a regime of iconoclasm, evoked mixed responses in the crowd, but the record is silent. At the little conduit at Cheap, the royal pair came to the last, and what John Elder considered the 'most excellent', of the pageants which looked forward to the fruits of the marriage and to God's blessing of progeny.[289] The pageant displayed the genealogical descent of both Mary and Philip from Edward III who was represented as an old man with a 'closed crown' and a ball and sceptre, lying under a tree. From the tree on both sides sprang branches on which sat children representing all the royal and noble descendants of Edward, with their names. On top of the tree, a king and queen '[re]presented their majesties; above whose heads was written their new style and title' and their arms 'joined in one under one crown imperial'.[290] Beneath the pageant, a verse hymned Mary and Philip as the offspring of 'ancient men' and heirs to 'glorious acts' and urged subjects:

> With al thy hert to love and to embrace,
> Which both descended of one auncient lyne
> It hath pleased God by mariage to combyne.[291]

As well as reprising the pageant for Catherine of Aragon and Charles V, this device had immediate and local resonance. Here the foreignness of Philip, which worried some, was muted by emphasis on English descent; the marriage was presented as divine plan; and the fruitfulness symbolized by the tree and children gestured to the hope of offspring to continue the dynasty and unite all, subjects and rulers as well as king and queen, in love.

Fittingly, the pageant led Philip and Mary for prayer to St Paul's, where a Latin oration celebrated Philip's English descent, virtuous rule and piety and the marriage effected by God.[292] After a Te Deum sung in the cathedral, the royal couple processed to a last pageant at Fleet Street, depicting a king and queen with Justice and Equity on their right, and Veritas (with a book inscribed 'Verbum Dei') and Misericordia on their left. From aloft Sapientia descended to crown the king and queen, while verses beneath praised Philip as the ideal king, gentle, just and true.[293] Though this time there is no reference to any objection, the image of Veritas with the book perhaps performed as both compliment and counsel. For while it echoed Mary's own motto ('Veritas temporis filia'), it also, again, associated truth with the word and with a motto and image which had been marked as Protestant. Were the artisans of London informing the king and queen that Truth was not theirs but God's? Certainly the praise of Philip also sounds a conditional note:

> When that a man is ientle, iust and true
> With vertuous giftes fulfilled plenteously,

If wisdome then him with hir crowne endue,
He governe shal the whole world prosperously.[294]

As they moved on to Temple Bar, the king and queen read what we might call the credits: a statement 'that such triumphs and pageants . . . were devised and made in the noble city of London by the lord mayor, thereof, his brethren and the citizens for their entries'.[295] While the crowd, Elder tells us, rejoiced and prayed for their long rule, Philip and Mary were reminded, subtly, that their images – and not just the material statues and artefacts – were 'devised and made' by others. It was a statement about monarchy itself.

The wedding pageant had been the work of many with different views and convictions. While it performed its function as celebration (Philip told the Princess Regent 'I was received with universal signs of love and joy'), the pageant ranged from general paeans to virtue and oblique references to revived Catholicism to defiant gestures of Protestantism.[296] Successful royal representations would need to embrace them all.

After the marriage, however, and especially after she believed herself to be pregnant, and a Catholic succession secured, Mary's self-presentation in public pageants increasingly publicized Catholic kingship. On 12 November, for example, when parliament met, Philip and Mary rode to Westminster Abbey. In the account of John Elder, the procession passed magnificently 'with all princely ensigns of honour', but the less sympathetic Henry Machyn referred to 'the mass of the holy ghost', as though marking the novelty of the proceedings.[297] The next week, Cardinal Pole, who had come to effect a reconciliation with Rome, was publicly received as he embarked from Gravesend, and led, with a sword borne before him, to the queen at Whitehall, before he proceeded to take up his lodging in the Archbishop of Canterbury's palace at Lambeth.[298] On 27 November, the three estates were called to parliament to hear Pole explain his commission and to praise the king and queen whom God had appointed, as he put it, 'for the restitution of true religion and extirpation of all errors'.[299] Pole knew his country well enough to flatter the English, commending them as the first nation to receive the light of Christianity. But now, reversing the deployment of nationalism against Rome, he argued the special respect and tenderness the papacy had always shown towards England whose people in turn had always manifested 'fervent devotion' towards Rome, skilfully touching on ('I will not rehearse . . .') the 'manifold benefits' the realm had received from the apostolic see and the 'manifold miseries' of the late separation, the 'tumults' of Germany and the plague of innovation.[300] Pole represented Mary as God's chosen, preserved by Providence against enemies, to restore the faith. As, he told his auditors, it was God's work to join her and Philip in marriage, 'so it is not to be doubted but that he shall send them issue for the comfort and surety of this common-wealth'.[301] In Pole's oration, the power committed to Philip and Mary by God complemented the fiat given to Rome, with whom the nation would now again join to effect the divine plan.

On the first Sunday of the next month, with the bells ringing a Te Deum of thanks for the queen's conceiving, Pole came into the City to be received by an even more public audience at St Paul's – 'such an audience of people', Elder claimed, 'as was never seen in this place before'.[302] Taking the text of Romans 13, Lord Chancellor Bishop Gardiner exhorted his auditors to cast away dark-ness and heresy and to follow the 'king's and queen's majesties' godly proceed-ings'.[303] Elder, who welcomed 'the most holy catholic faith coming home again', described many in the audience 'weeping tears'.[304] But it was likely that not all that did 'change their cheer' wept out of sadness for the last years of Henry and Edward; some were probably weeping at the new turn of events – and the presence of a papal legation once again on English soil.[305]

Mary and Philip's public embrace of Pole firmly tied the representation of their rule not only to the Catholic faith but to the, more unpopular, see of Rome. Throughout the rest of their reign, royal public ceremonial was simultaneously – and predominantly – Roman Catholic ritual, even on occa-sions (such, as we shall see, as the funeral of Anne of Cleves) when it seemed singularly inappropriate. In the case of the Garter festivals, for example, Mary completely reversed the Edwardian changes, reinstating 23 April as a saint's day as much as the festival of a chivalric order. Accordingly, on St George's Day 1555, the king and Garter knights processed 'with three crosses, and clerks and priests and my Lord Chancellor mitred . . . singing salva festa dies as they went about'; and this became the pattern for the reign.[306] Ascension Day (which had not been celebrated under Edward VI) saw the king and queen 'with all the lords and knights' ride into Westminster to process about the cathedral cloister before a ceremonial mass.[307] On St Andrew's Day 1557 the queen rode with Pole from St James to Whitehall to mass, 'all the monks and clerks singing salva festa dies'.[308] And the openings of parliament were heralded with missal processions as well as the pageants of state.[309]

Catholic rituals not only publicized the new world, they were employed to endeavour to erase the old, to gloss over the dark years of Henry VIII and Edward, so as to repair the rent (as Mary, like Pole, saw it) in the fabric of English history. In November 1553, the queen had ordered a goodly hearse for 'the late king' 'hung with cloth of tissue and a cross and a pax, silver candlesticks' with '13 beadmen holding tapers and the dirge sung in Latin'.[310] For the funeral four years later of Anne of Cleves, Henry VIII's fourth wife and sister of the leader of the Lutherans in Germany (whom Henry had married to cement a Protestant alliance against Charles V), full Catholic burial rites were ordained.

The corpse was followed from Chelsea to Westminster by 'many priests and clerks, and then the grey amice [religious orders] of Paul's and 3 crosses, and the monks of Westminster' as well as her servants and gentlemen.[311] Received at the abbey door by the abbot in mitre and cope, the body was laid in state until the next day, when the abbot conducted a requiem mass. The Bishop of London sang the mass while the abbot 'did cense the corpse' – that is bless it with incense – before Anne was laid in her tomb.[312] To those of Protestant conviction, the service must have appeared a violation of, even vengeance against, the royal corpse; to some, perhaps, it was of a piece with the afflictions suffered by the bodies of the living godly in the faggots and flames of Smithfield.

Pageants and festivals were, for the most part, confined to the audiences of London and the ceremonial roads between the city and royal palaces. And in the words of one scholar, Mary 'abolished the expensive custom of progresses'.[313] But this is to simplify. Mary began her reign, or rather her quest to secure her throne, in her home counties of Norfolk and Suffolk, and her wedding took place in Winchester. Throughout her reign she was often on the move: in July 1556, for example, from St James to Eltham, accompanied by a 'great number'; in September to Croydon and back; in March 1558 to Greenwich for Easter; on in the summer to take journeys to hunt.[314] Philip II's travels in and out of the country – to the Netherlands (in 1555) or to Brussels (in 1557), for example – saw not only the king on what was an effective progress to his port of embarkation, but the queen, too, who rode with him in July 1557 to Dover, the two spending the night at Sittingbourne in Kent en route.[315] On such occasions, Mary could display the common touch for which her sister has been better remembered: in August 1555, for instance, as she and Philip were removing to Oatlands, Mary encountered 'a poor man with two crutches, and when that he saw her grace, for joy he threw his staffs away and ran after her grace, and she commanded that one should give him a reward'.[316] The princess who had, it was said, visited the houses of the poor in disguise, the queen who had spoken so effectively in London at the time of Wyatt's rebellion, who was renowned for acts of charity, who had remitted a subsidy as a gesture to her people, and who had earned not only their thanks and 'admiration' but what one observer described as subjects' 'idolatry', cannot be charged with not understanding the rhetorics of power or the arts of representation.[317] It is rather that, after her marriage, representation was for her the projection of herself as the wife of a Spanish Habsburg prince and heir to empire, and as the godly agent of the restitution of the true faith. Because not all her subjects were united in that purpose, and many more remained hostile to foreigners, Mary's pageants and festivals disclose unease, discontent and opposition below the surface of praise and harmony. Such tensions in the texts of royal representation were not new, and in themselves would not have

constructed the image of Mary Tudor that history has remembered. That
derived from very different public displays of antipathy – the scaffold, the
block and the stake.

It is as the religious bigot and cruel persecutor that Mary is best known, so it
may seem perverse that hitherto this image has not been dominant in our
discussion. It is, however, important to appreciate that, like other monarchs
and her Tudor predecessors, Mary was very concerned first with dynasty; as a
woman that meant with marriage and the succession. For the opening weeks,
and months, she had to secure her own succession, then to marry and
conceive, so as to give birth to an heir. Central to that concern with succession,
of course, was that it be Catholic succession, so that she did not face the situation (the prospect of a heretic successor) which Edward had confronted on
his deathbed, and which had led him to take such revolutionary courses.
But it was the throne and the marriage that came first – and came first in
the representation of Mary (and Mary and Philip) as well as in the conduct
of policy.

From the outset, Mary made no secret of her devotion to her faith. As a
princess, she had made frequent charitable payments to displaced friars,
Catholic priests and even to the Society of Jesus; and she quarrelled with her
brother's government over her right to practise Catholic worship in her
household.[318] Guaras informs us that, as soon as Mary heard of her proclamation as queen in London, she had a crucifix put up in her chapel – the first
to be so displayed in years – and a Te Deum sung; a Latin Catholic service for
the dead was held in her chapel before the requiem mass for Edward.[319] Yet,
whatever her own public convictions, Mary initially showed no inclination to
force the faith of her people. One of her first proclamations, we recall, was to
call on her people to live in charity, not disputing or calling each other
heretic.[320] The queen would not 'hide that religion which God and the world
knoweth she hath ever preferred', and she hoped that her subjects too would
embrace it; but she was not minded for compulsion.[321] Mary continued to use
the title 'Supreme Head' and probably hoped that her people would be led
back to the true faith by leadership and ministry.[322]

The sermon had been the principal agent of Protestant evangelism and was
deployed in Mary's reign to present the virtues of the old faith. After the
unhappy start, when at the first Paul's Cross sermon of the reign by the
queen's chaplain 'there was a general uproar and shouting', a series of sermons
there was preached in favour of traditional rites and doctrine.[323] James
Brooks, Master of Balliol, for example, preached on 12 November A Sermon
Very Notable, and doubtless persuasive.[324] His theme was the authority and
embrace of the Catholic church: 'needs must', he told the congregation, 'we

grant to the Catholic Church . . . authority of judgement for the decision of all controversies in our religion', for all who took away this authority sacrificed certainty.[325] Perhaps attending to the sex of the queen, he pressed, 'he can not now have God to his father who will not vouchsafe to acknowledge the church for his mother', but assured them that the church was a tender mother moved with pity for her children led astray by innovation.[326] Brooks, in words that may have brought comfort to many, reaffirmed the rituals of psalms, ashes and holy crosses, images and holy water, and the mass, and he invited the lost home.[327] In 1555 Hugh Glasier, another chaplain to the queen, in a similarly titled, *A Notable and Very Fruitful Sermon*, attacked those who had despoiled the church and who 'lie in beds . . . made of the church stuff'.[328] At court, meanwhile, Gardiner preached free will and the benefit of works in securing salvation, against the heresies of the last years.[329] Other works by priests close to Mary denigrated those who had sought to pull down Christ along with his image and praised the old faith as 'wholesome, substantial and godly'.[330] Even when not published, such sermons drew, as Machyn recorded, large audiences – in one case, 'as great as I ever saw in my life'.[331]

While sermons and polemics traduced Protestant heresies and revalidated Catholic rites and beliefs, works such as *A Uniform and Catholic Primer*, published in Latin and English in 1555, restated and reinstated the Catholic forms of prayer for confession of sins, the matins of the cross, evensong and the like, together with an almanac of all the saints' days and engraved illustrations of biblical women, especially the Virgin Mary at prayer.[332] That such preaching and publishing could be effective is witnessed by the nervous reaction of Protestants. John Old, for example, a convert to Protestantism and former commissioner for the diocese of Peterborough, who fled to exile under Mary, thought the traducement from the pulpit of Edward VI's church was desperately in need of a counter; but he asked himself, 'how should a man leap in to defend the church, seeing such a sort of cruel . . . enemies object so many and so heinous crimes against us'.[333] In particular, he feared the charge that Protestantism flew in the face of antiquity and prompted disorder; and tried to defend his faith against it.[334]

With time, there can be little doubt, Mary's early hope that her subjects would return to the faith would have been realized. But it was time that, at thirty-eight, Mary did not have. As a consequence, the promotion of the Catholic religion, which may not in itself have been unpopular, became embroiled in the business of the queen's marriage and what was an essential precondition of a European marriage – a full reconciliation with Rome. In July 1554, Nicholas Harpsfield, Archdeacon of Canterbury, prayed 'in his beads' for the marriage of Mary and Philip (who had just landed at Southampton) and a Te Deum procession and bell-ringing were ordered in every parish.[335] On

30 September, at Paul's Cross, as well as preaching a sermon on charity, Gardiner condemned heresy and 'praised the king and his dominions and riches'.[336] That November, a royal proclamation ordered obedience to Pole on his mission from 'the pope's holiness' and, as we have seen, it was Pole who stood at Paul's Cross, with Philip II, and all the queen's Council, while Gardiner preached the old faith.[337] By the end of 1554, Catholicism in England was not only again English, it was ultramontane – and Spanish. To celebrate the conception of the Virgin, the Spanish went in procession at the Savoy, 'the priest carrying the sacrament royally', with friars and priests bearing tapers.[338] The next St Paul's Day (25 January) was celebrated by a procession from Westminster to Temple Bar, with Philip and Cardinal Pole in attendance.[339] The following April, 1555, the Bishop of London ordered bells to be rung for Pope Julius III; in December Pole was led by the Bishop of York in a procession around Westminster Abbey.[340] In June 1556, the Spaniards conducted the sacrament, under a royal canopy, on a procession through Whitehall.[341] Public penances were again regularly staged at St Paul's.[342] As we shall see, the opposition of what appears to have been initially a minority grew, as the old faith began to be associated with the foreign, papal exactions, Habsburg priorities – and simply with hated foreigners and despised clerics. In response, Queen Mary, who had gained her throne through the love of her people and who had initially trusted to God and time, began, especially after her 'fake' pregnancy and failure to conceive, to grow desperate. Desperation prompted firmer measures to ensure the truth – such as proclamations outlawing all heretical books and enforcing statutes against heresy.[343] When they too failed, Mary, recalling perhaps Gardiner's sermon in her chapel, came to conclude that her 'lenity and gentleness' had only fostered contempt; and that the time had come when, to ensure a godly commonwealth, 'the rotten and hurtful members' had to be 'cut off and consumed'.[344]

In early modern England, the scaffold was one of the most important sites of authority. And in Mary's case, at the start of her reign, the processes of justice and punishment were skilfully used to validate both the queen's legitimacy and her faith. Coming to the throne after defeating a coup to replace her, one of Mary's first acts was the arraignment and trial of the perpetrators, notably Dudley, Duke of Northumberland. Though the anonymous chronicler attended a dinner at which a possible pardon had been discussed, there could have been little doubt about Dudley's fate.[345] His trial was conducted with the full theatre of justice, the commissioners seated on rich cushions on a stage 'richly tapestried'.[346] With the Duke of Norfolk presiding as Lord Marshal, all was, in the words of the Spanish merchant Guaras (who appears to have been present), 'conducted with great dignity'.[347] To the three capital charges of treason, Northumberland pleaded guilty in full court and expected swift execution. However, in his last hours, he renounced his Protestant faith in audience with Bishop Heath, and Mary's government moved to postpone the execution in order to extract maximum propaganda benefit from the duke's apostasy.[348] The next day, that set for the execution, a crowd of 10,000 gathered at Tower Hill but were dismissed. Instead, another ritual was played out in the Tower chapel, to which 'there was sent for into London for divers of the best commoners and Common Council of the City' to stand as witnesses.[349] Here, in the chapel, a solemn mass was said, 'with elevation over the head, the pax giving, blessing and crossing on the crown', in which Northumberland participated, taking the sacrament and saying the *confiteor*.[350] In what one chronicler clearly suspected was a staged event, Northumberland 'turned himself to the people and said . . . "My masters, I let you all to understand that I do most faithfully believe this is the very right and true way out of the which true religion you and I have been seduced these sixteen years past, by the false and erroneous preaching of the new preachers, the which is the only cause of the great plagues and vapours which hath light upon the whole realm of England" ' – after which he knelt.[351] The small gathering was almost a dress rehearsal for the large public theatre of the next day, as, belatedly, Northumberland was led to execution before 'the whole town of London [that] concurred to attend the spectacle'.[352] Many had gathered, Guaras thought, 'full of curiosity' about what the duke, and co-conspirators, 'would say especially on matters of religion' – perhaps in the hope of some drama beyond the usual, grisly spectacle.[353]

We have several accounts of the occasion, at which Northumberland evidently asked to speak to the people; Guaras was one who 'heard' it 'from being very near him'.[354] His death day though it was, Northumberland worked the crowd, and asked them to implore God for his forgiveness. He thanked the queen for her grace in commuting the traitors' sentence, of hanging, drawing and quartering, to a beheading; and then launched into a speech about the evils that had befallen the realm since it lapsed from the true Catholic faith.[355] It was false prophets, the duke proclaimed, who had brought him to his fate, but now he had come to 'die a true Catholic Christian' and confess his faith. In what was a dream scenario for the regime, if it was not scripted by them, Northumberland assured the doubters 'that none should believe that this new conscience arises from being urged upon me by any [especially "the queen's doing"] or that any have persuaded me in this . . . I tell you what I feel at the bottom of my heart . . .'. Pointing to a Germany ruined by heresy, the duke encouraged others to 'have no let or shame in returning to God' and embracing the church; and he ended with an exhortation to obedience, before he knelt to pray, making the sign of the cross.[356] Clearly some in the crowd were taken aback – Commendone thought many 'baffled at the speech', having 'expected from him anything but that'; some took 'great offence'.[357] But, overall, Guaras's belief that 'the Duke's confession has edified the people more than if all the Catholics in the land had preached for ten years' was not excessive hyperbole, but close to the truth.[358] Certainly that was the official perception – as a copy of the speech was sent to the queen's printer for swift publication. Translations were soon published from the presses at Cologne, Louvain and Vienna: in all, nineteen editions appeared by the end of the century.[359] The first public execution of Mary's reign had been an unparalleled propaganda triumph for church and state.

Almost as the axe fell on Northumberland, the scene was being set for other executions. The view, during the winter of 1553, that Mary was set on the Habsburg match was to fire rebellions led by Courtenay (who had himself hoped for Mary's hand) in London, Lady Jane's father Suffolk in Leicestershire, and Sir Thomas Wyatt in Kent. The risings were taking place the very week of Northumberland's trial and by the end of the first week of February were over – but for the processes of justice against noble and common rebels.[360] Again, many of the leading offenders acted the parts of confession and atonement that the theatre of the scaffold scripted for them. Brought to Westminster for his trial on 17 February, Suffolk was deemed to have 'confessed himself guilty of treason'. The next week, on the scaffold at Tower Hill, Suffolk duly informed the 'good people' assembled there that he was 'one whom the law hath justly condemned and one who hath no less deserved for my disobedience against the queen's highness of whom I do most humbly ask forgiveness . . .'.[361] Assured that it was granted, Suffolk continued: 'I beseech you all, good people, to let me be an example to you all for obedience to the queen and the magistrates'.[362] Then, declaiming his faith, he knelt for a final psalm. His daughter, Lady Jane Grey, however, gave a more equivocal performance. Though acknowledging her guilt in consenting to treason, she denied any role in instigating the conspiracy. Moreover Jane, rather than emulating her father-in-law's conversion, subtly reaffirmed her Protestant faith in her last moments. Holding 'her book' – most likely a bible or possibly a devotional manual – Jane asked the assembled to 'bear me witness that I die a free Christian woman, and that I look to be saved by none other means but only by the mercy of God in the merits of the blood of his only son Jesus Christ'.[363] The silence on the subject of the Catholic church, the denial of mediation, the implicit reference to justification by faith alone, all made Jane's a death that later apologists could present as a martyrdom.[364]

The arraignment and execution of Wyatt himself clearly caused the authorities a problem. First, at his trial in March Wyatt declared himself 'guiltless' of the charge of conspiring to cause the queen's death.[365] Before an audience of observers hostile to the match, playing to their prejudices, he declared his 'whole intent and stir was against the coming in of strangers and Spaniards, and to abolish them out of this realm'.[366] When he went to his execution on 12 April, Wyatt also carried 'a book in his hand' – was this a symbol that the reformed had agreed to adopt?[367] As he passed Secretary Sir John Bourne, Wyatt implied that he might have been pardoned, and gone on to do good service, had he been spared, which discomfited the Secretary.[368] There was to be further discomfort. On the scaffold Wyatt spoke, stating that he had been 'lawfully condemned' and then, in language which appears equivocal, said 'Let every man beware how he taketh anything in hand against the higher powers. Unless God be prosperable to his purpose, it will never take good effects.'[369] Wyatt then embarrassed a government that had others in mind for punishment by publicly exonerating Lord Courtenay and Princess Elizabeth from the charge that they were privy to his rising. The Dean of Westminster, Hugh Weston, Wyatt's appointed confessor, interrupted him and tried to turn his words around: 'he saith that that which he hath showed to the Council . . . of my lady Elizabeth and Courtenay is true'.[370] Wyatt was reported to be 'amazed at the interruption' and might have countered, one account suggests, had others not 'plucked him by the gown back'.[371] Machyn reported a 'skirmish' between the guard and Wyatt's followers.[372] Controversy did not end with his death. In the official account of the rebellion, John Proctor relates that Wyatt deplored all rebellion and announced his conversion to support of the Spanish marriage, which he had come to see as a benefit and honour to the realm.[373] Nervous at what had happened, and at public reaction, the government, it appears, printed what it had wanted to happen. Meanwhile, rather than Wyatt's execution providing the awful example of the consequences of the sin of treason, the crowd, according to the French ambassador, dipped their handkerchiefs in his blood – and within days removed his head from the stake, perhaps with a view to treating it as a Protestant relic.[374] In less than a year on the throne, Queen Mary had lost control of the theatre of justice and punishment and of a crucial stage for the representation of majesty.

Early the next year, on 28 January 1555, the first trial began that led to the burning of John Rogers for heresy. Over the next three years another 300 victims went to the flames. Yet as we know, far from suppressing heresy and reinforcing authority, the executions strengthened the resolve of hard-core Protestants and, more broadly, tainted Mary's government with the (foreign) vices of cruelty and severity. Contemporary observers, even Catholics, did not doubt that 'such sudden severity is odious to many people'.[375] Revealingly, the imperial envoy Renard advocated 'secret executions'; Edmund Bonner, the Bishop of London, three years later suggested the same.[376] The Mary who had succeeded on a wave of popular support which she had skilfully cultivated had, by presenting her rule as Spanish and papist, narrowed her support; and had handed to heretics and enemies an opportunity to present themselves as true subjects, true Christians, and true Englishmen and women. After 1555, Mary lived amid fear of conspiracy and rebellion, while others won the contest for popular opinion and support. Early in her reign, the image of Mary and her government was slipping from her control to be painted by others, often with little regard to accuracy, in bloody hues.

V Opposition Images

Historians remain uncertain and divided about the extent to which Protestantism had taken hold across the nation by 1553, but there is no doubt that from the beginning there was a small caucus of committed opponents to Mary's succession and rule. Though it was overturned by the tide of support for legitimate succession, there had been support for Lady Jane Grey – whose death on the scaffold stirred 'deep compassion' in the bystanders.[377] Wyatt, too, had gathered a large body of followers and come within yards of entering the city. Whilst he was defeated, not least by the unwillingness of Londoners to fall in with him, even an official report on the rebellion admitted that 'doubtful were the hearts of the people and marvellously bent to favour Wyatt'.[378] Commendone even questioned the loyalty of some of the queen's men, reporting that, at the defeat and securing of Wyatt, many present thought that 'their encounter should be called a tragedy rather than a battle because it is said that many of the new soldiers of the Queen were shooting their arrows into the air instead than at their enemies, showing their attachment to the party of the enemies'.[379] The Spanish match was, and remained, unpopular; and with the arrival and residence of Philip, it became still more so. But Mary, who had before skilfully contained her people's anxieties, after 1554, as we have seen, persistently proclaimed her joint rule with Philip. Increasingly, therefore, after 1554, official representations were countered by rumour, squib, polemic or direct challenge to royal rule.

In his invocation to obedience, Mary's staunch supporter John Christopherson had detected the origins of rebellion in 'murmur and grudge of mind, malicious and slanderous words'.[380] In the *Path of Obedience*, John Cancellar concurred: disobedience sprang from 'murmuring, grudgery, canting and evil speaking'.[381] Rumour undermined the regime, in large part by countering the official representations and by exciting the fears that official scripts were written to calm. From early 'rash discoursing' on the queen's 'weighty affairs', the waves of rumour swelled into what by the end of the reign were described as 'horrible, false and seditious tales, rumours and lies', intended to 'disquiet, trouble and molest . . . the hearts and minds of their graces' good and loving subjects'.[382] From early on these rumours were disseminated widely by those with a religious agenda and were rushed into print by stationers who had a keen eye for the market. Some, the government complained, were by 'playing of interludes and printing of false fond books, ballads, rhymes and other lewd treatises' discussing 'doctrine in matters now in question and controversy touching the high points and mysteries of Christian religion; which books, ballads, rhymes and treatises are chiefly by the printers and stationers set out to sale ... of an evil zeal for lucre'.[383] General rumours spawned direct attacks and vicious squibs against the king, queen and the government, which were circulated orally and in print at home and abroad.[384] The opposition appears to have been well organized. In the spring of 1554, a proclamation denounced seditious bills and those who 'do in the night time ... secretly spread and set abroad their seditious bills and writings'.[385] And, from then on, Machyn recorded a regular appearance of miscreants in the pillory, some with their ears nailed, for 'spreading lies and seditious words', 'horrible lies and seditious words against the queen's majesty and her Council', 'words touching the queen's proceedings' and the like.[386] So little success, however, did they have in stemming the tide of rumour and squib that even at the end of her reign Mary was reduced to asking her subjects not to 'give any manner of faith or credit' to such attacks, but to dismiss them as untrue.[387]

In most cases, we do not know the details of the seditious words spoken or the squibs circulated, though the chronology and general report suggest that a good deal of the libels were directed against Spaniards and the Spanish marriage. But in 1555, *A Warning for England Containing the Horrible Practices of the King of Spain in the Kingdom of Naples* directly countered official celebrations by cautioning readers not to be taken in by honeyed words.[388] In Naples, the *Warning* advised, Spain had reneged on all its assurances, had ousted the nation's ruler to take over sovereignty, had levied punitive taxes and seized the people's lands.[389] As if it were not clear enough, the lesson for England was explicitly spelled out. A similar plague would soon fall on the English, for the emperor, knowing that Mary would not conceive a child, had plotted for Philip to seize the English throne and then all the lands taken from the Catholic church.[390] While the pulpits were to be used to deceive the people, it was said, the priests, acting as the agents of the Habsburgs and the papacy, moved to suppress all opponents. 'The faggots,' he concluded – if written before February it was prophetic – 'are being prepared.'[391]

What these last charges dangerously signalled was the way in which opposition to Spain diffused into a wider antagonism towards Catholicism, which had simply not been in evidence at Mary's succession. The pamphlet *A True Mirror or Glass* (1556) appears to have endeavoured to separate the hostility to Spain from Catholicism.[392] In a dialogue between Eusebius, a moderate Catholic, and Theophilus, a moderate Protestant, both respectfully debate their religious differences but unite to condemn the Spanish marriage as the 'utter desolation of English blood', which will subject the nation to military governance and bondage.[393] Both speeches, too, in recognition of a strong national anticlericalism, are critical of priests whose ambition leads them to serve Spanish interests.[394] Moreover, Eusebius assures his companion that he dislikes 'this cruelty' towards those of another faith: 'If the matter were in my hands there should none be put to death except he [who] would obstinately rebel'.[395] The evangelical preacher and later martyr John Bradford, recognizing that 'heretics' had been able to use the hostility to Spain to gain support, made clear his devotion to his Catholic faith and yet abomination of Spaniards.[396] Bradford wrote, he claimed, 'not . . . because any man should think evil or despise god's most holy service', but so that the dissimulations of the Spaniards might be exposed and 'all may know that the very nation of Spaniards is abominable'.[397] Cataloguing them as whores and whoremongers, Bradford predicted that by bringing in Habsburg troops, they would 'suppress the country and keep us in [greater] subjection than once the Danes did . . .'.[398] Having lived among them, the author claimed to know their qualities and colours – and their aims: 'the suppression of the commonwealth, . . . the loss of our liberty, the death of our nobility, the perdition of all . . . lands, goods and children; these things I have found in their letters'.[399] Bradford warned the queen herself to place the country's good before her own will and to be wary that the Spaniard not seize all from her.[400] Though he published a powerful counter-representation of a royal marriage that was central to Mary's image, Bradford at least professed his loyalty to his church and sovereign – of whom, he urged, 'no man can think any evil'.[401]

But, despite such attempts to separate them (which themselves suggest a Catholic opposition to Mary's persecutions deserving of further exploration), Mary's marriage was presented as inextricably bound up with, even the cause of, her religious policy and persecutions. Playing to the nationalism of his native country from which he was now exiled, Wolfgang Musculus, in *The Temporizer*, via his translator Robert Parnell, proclaimed to England: 'Thy faithful natural, native king is changed into a superstitious, unnatural foreign prince' who brought in a 'company of idolaters'.[402] Parnell also wrote and published *An Admonition to the Town of Calais* which warned the subjects of the English monarchy that they were already under another Athaliah (the usurping and bloody queen of the second Book of Kings, slain by the loyal priesthood): 'the utter destroyer of her own kindred, a hater of her own subjects, a lover of strangers and an unnatural step dame both unto them and to thy mother England'.[403] The Spaniard who ruled England sought Calais to bridle France, the *Admonition* continued, and the idolatry that had overrun the English church threatened Calais too.

There can be no doubt that it was widespread hostility to foreign, Spanish influence and to the restoration of papal supremacy that sharpened the invective against, and fostered genuine support for opposition to, the re-establishment of Catholic orthodoxy. John Old, in the *Acquittal,* associated the influence of foreign powers with the preachers set up in St Paul's to spew out the 'abominable poison of antichrist's traditions'; and he proceeded to defend the church establishment under Edward VI as a true Catholic faith founded in Scripture, antiquity and unity.[404] Indeed, growing popular antagonism to Marian Catholicism appears to have run in parallel with more positive portrayals and memories of the Edwardian church, which had not at the time won wide popular support. In 1554, a wag with a full grasp of the symbolism of power, hung on the gallows beside the cross in Cheapside a cat 'habited in a garment like to that the priest wore that said mass; she had a shaven crown, and in her fore feet held a piece of paper made round, representing the wafer'.[405] Recognizing the power of such ritual mockery, the government went to extraordinary lengths to identify the culprit, offering a reward of 20 marks to any informant.[406] The next year it hanged, and left hanging for four days, a poulterer's servant who had railed against the papacy and the mass.[407] The year after that saw a spate of image-breaking that appears to have been anything but indiscriminate and which was carefully targeted to send a message to the government and the public. In February, the head and crozier were taken off a statue of St Thomas of Canterbury; and, after it was repaired, the head and one of the arms were destroyed only two weeks later.[408] This attack on an English saint, who stood for Rome against the English monarchy, symbolized the hostility to ultramontane sovereignty; and the act of iconoclasm gestured to the Edwardian assault on images which had been one of the central platforms of the Reformation. It was doubtless, then, no coincidence that, at the same time as these incidents, Machyn reports men and women claiming that Edward VI was still alive.[409] Government anxiety about such rumours was fully manifested in his accounts of the savage whipping of one who claimed to be Edward VI's messenger, and the hanging, drawing and quartering of a young man named Fetherstone 'who gave himself out to be King Edward VI and whose sayings and pretences had occasioned many men and women to be punished'.[410]

Harsh punishments not only manifested the government's mounting nervousness about opposition to Catholic reformation. Claims that Edward was alive were, of course, challenges to Mary's legitimacy; and, as the government was right to suspect, there was a danger that opposition to Mary's marriage, programmes of re-Catholicization and the burnings of heretics might lead to direct questioning of her right to rule and the nature of her authority – as a monarch, and as a woman. As early as 1553, the re-publication of Gardiner's 1535 treatise in support of the supremacy, *De vera obedientia,* had been issued not only to embarrass the new Lord Chancellor but also to remind readers of Queen Mary's questionable legitimacy as ruler.[411] Gardiner, the translator's preface to the reader points out, now denounced Henry's marriage to Anne Boleyn for which he had once been an advocate, and denied the royal supremacy which he had earlier solidly supported.[412] Though the implications were not made explicit, Mary's right to be queen, and her right as queen to renounce the supremacy (which Gardiner had described as belonging only to God), were questioned just as the new claims for the truth of Roman Catholicism were challenged. Moreover, the vitriol against 'pompous papists and lecherous lubbers of the Devil's larder house' was provocatively gendered in language that came close to a personal attack on the queen.[413] Describing, in a final address to the reader, the Catholic church as 'like . . . Mistress Claire' and Henry VIII's shifts from Rome to God's truth and back as moves from harlot to wife (and back), the treatise came close to calling Mary, as well as the church, a whore – the figure that subverted all the social norms of early modern England.[414] In 1556, there appeared in Edinburgh *A Compendious and Brief Tractate Concerning the Office and Duty of Kings,* a long poem on the nature and qualities of kingship, in the 'advice to princes' genre.[415] The author, William Lauder, who was to join the Protestant cause in Scotland in 1560, stressed the need for kings to appoint and command preachers to teach the word and warned that rulers who did not would be scourged with fire and plague. Kingship, the poem suggested, was a divine duty and trust; authority and allegiance depended upon faith. The engraved title page, a full-length illustration of a king holding the sceptre in his right hand, might have safely distanced the tract from being a comment on Mary's tenure of monarchy. But English subjects, like Scottish subjects, were grappling with questions concerning the obligations as well as powers of kings, of the rights as well as duties of subjects, and with the tensions between allegiance to conscience and to queen.

Such meditations were to produce publications that fundamentally assaulted the theory of divine kingship which had been carefully fostered to represent and strengthen Tudor monarchy. One such treatise was entitled, with deceptive innocence, *Certain Questions Demanded and Asked by the Noble Realm of England.*[416] The very form of the pamphlet, of course, was radical. Subjects did not demand, or ask, questions about *arcana imperii,* and the implied equality of the dialogue form subverted all the official prescriptions of hierarchy and deference. The interrogator of the pamphlet was, too, England, who addresses herself to 'Her True Natural Children', 'English men', as though it was not the queen who was the spokeswoman for, or as she had often claimed the politic mother of, the nation. Indeed, in its opening sentence, the tract posited a radical separation of the royal body personal and public, arguing that the queen could not deliver the realm to another without the consent of his or her heirs and then asked the potentially revolutionary question: 'item: whether a prince can betray his own realm'.[417] The subsequent list of questions constituted a radical critique of Mary's person, legitimacy, policy and power.

Was, the pamphlet asked, Mary worthy to be her father's heir? Could she, having once been declared a bastard, be re-legitimized? Did Deuteronomy chapter 22 forbid a woman to rule?[418] Raising a series of questions about rulers who condemned subjects to death, or seized their goods without the warrant of the laws, the interrogator asked whether an innocent man may be put to death 'because he would not assent . . . in religion'.[419] Perhaps gesturing to Philip as well as Mary, the pamphlet questioned whether a king who before ascending the throne had promised subjects that they might follow their own faith, would renege on the promise[420] Turning to the hated Spanish marriage (which did so much to turn Mary's subjects from her), *Certain Questions* questioned the legitimacy of the match when Philip had been betrothed to another, and then moved to a clear threat of rebellion, asking whether subjects ought to join for their own safety and pull down a prince who sought to deliver them to the hands of the Spaniards, 'who be most justly hated like dogs the world over'.[421] All the fears that Spain would overrun England, make off with the crown jewels, heavily tax the poor and fleece the realm of its commodities were here rearticulated, along with the anxiety that Philip's intent was to take alone the throne of England, 'the last kingdom in all Europe', and to destroy the nobility, as had William the Conqueror.[422] And, as we have seen elsewhere, hostility to the match ignited opposition to Mary's religious policy. The author hinted that the Catholic clergy, and especially Gardiner, would be the agents of Spanish ambition and that the restoration of papal authority was part of the plot to subjugate England to a foreign power.[423] Playing on the anxieties of a landed class which had benefited along with the crown from their sale, the author also suggested that together the pope and Philip II might order the restoration to the church of the dissolved monastic lands.[424] Finally, in an unwitting prophecy of events that were to unfold over a century later in the reign of James II, the pamphlet raised the possibility that the royal couple might substitute another's child as a royal prince, to secure Spanish and Catholic rule – a prospect which, it was implied, presented dangerous choices, with politically revolutionary outcomes.[425] Faced with government repression, the big question was, 'whether all such as in religion follow the commandment of men shall be damned with the man that commandeth if he commandst that is contrary to the law of God?'[426] If the masculine pronoun might seem here to mute or transfer the attack on authority from the queen to her husband, the pamphlet shifted radically to the feminine in the question that proclaimed the rights of the subjects and their conscience over unfit rulers: 'whether the commons may not lawfully by the laws of God and nature stand against such a prince, to depose *her*' who delivered the realm to strangers and who countered God's commands.[427] Did 'the realm of England belong to the queen or her subjects?'[428] Was it, the pamphlet closed, treason to ask such questions? If so (as it manifestly was), then it had become treason 'to say God save the noble realm of England'.[429] The 'true natural children' would have to decide between England and a queen who would deliver them to 'bondage'.[430]

The issues raised by *Certain Questions* are developed into one of the most important early modern treatises of political theory in John Ponet's *A Short Treatise of Politic Power* (1556).[431] Ponet, a reformist preacher, elevated to the bishopric of Winchester by Edward VI, and one of those consulted during his reign about the Princess Mary's worship, was deprived when Mary ascended the throne. He soon fled to Strasbourg, though the chronicler John Stow claims that he remained long enough in England to take part in Wyatt's rebellion.[432] In Ponet's treatment, the novel questions about allegiance to country or queen, God or the secular magistrates, conscience or obedience produced a critique of royal authority never before seen in England, one that echoed the resistance theories that were plunging Europe into religious civil war.[433]

In an opening preface to the reader, as well as proclaiming his fervent love for his country, Ponet asserted that England was a 'mixed state' where the monarch did not have the right to make his (or her) will the law.[434] Laws were made by parliaments which were placed 'in trust' to make laws 'to the advancement of God's glory and conservation of the liberties and commonwealths of this country'.[435] Those who, in obedience to the queen, were again setting up the mass, were therefore in breach of that trust – and, in preferring the judgement of man before God, of God's trust.[436] Ponet then embarked on his discourse on the power of the prince, the subjects' duty of obedience, and the right of resistance to evil governors. Not content with asking questions that subverted all the unquestioned assumptions on which Tudor royal authority had been founded, Ponet posited the subject as a fully empowered political actor, licensed to act according to the dictates of his own conscience and (even) judgement.[437] Commencing with a discussion of whether monarchs had absolute power, Ponet immediately swept aside any pretensions of papal suzerainty – 'his power is worthy to be laughed at'.[438] When it came to kings, the *Treatise* insisted that they are bound by both God's and the nation's law. 'A king may no more commit idolatry than a private man', and 'kings and princes ought both by God's law, the law of nature, man's laws and good reason, to be obedient and subject to the positive laws of their country'.[439] Turning from the obligations of rulers to the duties of subjects, Ponet stressed the importance of obedience to the good order of the commonwealth, but, targeting the papists specifically, he denounced in pointed terms those who 'rack and stretch out obedience too much'.[440] Obedience, he argued, was not a simple act of compliance with the dictates of the magistrate or prelate. The Christian had to weigh the commands of secular authority and refuse them if they opposed the holy injunctions of God.[441] For such refusal they had the warrant of Scripture which offered examples of disobedience to ungodly kings and dictates of conscience which required men not to follow the path to perdition. Moreover, in judging the right course, men were not to consider only God's will; they 'ought to have more respect to their country than to their prince . . .'.[442] For (Ponet continued, with a breathtakingly radical tone), 'the country and commonwealth is a degree above the king'.[443] In a move that overturned one of the recurring metaphors of monarchy, Ponet described princes as 'but members' of commonwealths which could flourish without them – 'where the head is cut off and put on a new head'.[444] Monarchs, then, had responsibilities to subjects and could not diminish the possessions of the realm (such as Calais!), nor take the properties of subjects, nor violate the rights of citizens who were 'freemen' not 'bondmen'.[445]

What recourse, then, did subjects have who were faced with an evil governor who persecuted the people? Ponet did not hedge in answering his own question. God had deposed tyrants, and the course of English history offered examples of kings (Edward II and Richard II) who had been deprived of their thrones.[446] Those who had deposed a pope, he reminded readers, could depose a prince, for 'kings, princes and governors have their authority of the people as all laws do . . . testify'.[447] But the right to rule lay not with every humble man: the people needed to look to good nobles and holy ministers to act, or to tarry in prayer for God's judgment on the wicked ruler.[448]

A Short Treatise of Politic Power owed a debt to John of Salisbury's *Policraticus*. But Ponet's work belongs more to the contemporary school of Calvinist resistance theories that gave rise to Christopher Goodman, John Knox and George Buchanan, as well as to continental treatises such as Philippe Du Plessis Mornay's *Vindiciae contra tyrannos*.[449] Throughout what could have been a philosophical disquisition on the nature of sovereignty, Ponet introduced topical references – describing Bishop Gardiner as another Caligula, Lady Jane's execution as an example of a state that had changed its head, Mary's marriage as mischief covered with 'painted paper'.[450] And the last section of the treatise shifted from philosophical discourse to 'An Exhortation', or rather a warning to the Lords and Commons of England. Here Ponet reminded readers of the plagues prophesied by Edward VI's godly preachers that had come to pass: famine, the 'cursed popish mass', 'butchery and burning of true English Christians', now the Spaniards who, with the friars, were 'all subtle wolves, all viperous generation'.[451] 'Leave your idolatry, and honour and worship God truly as ye were taught in blessed King Edward's time,' Ponet promised, and God would send in place of cruel tyranny godly government.[452]

Whilst it is worthy of fuller study as political theory and polemic, Ponet's *Treatise* was an artful text of counter-representation. In appropriating the metaphor of the head and the body, it seized for opposition an analogue that had long validated and naturalized royal authority; in separating the queen from the nation, it made nationalism serve against government rather than, as had been the case, as royal polemic; in foregrounding the commonwealth as separate from, as entire and self-sufficient without, the prince, it robbed the monarchy of a discourse of unity and harmony which Henry VIII and his pamphleteers had deployed to mute discord and challenge; and, in associating tyrants with 'heretical inquisitors', it recruited nationalist opposition to the Spanish marriage to the side of Protestant polemic against Mary's attempt to enforce Catholic orthodoxy.[453] In all these skilful moves, *A Short Treatise* subverted the discourses and languages in which Tudor monarchy had publicized its authority and represented its legitimacy and divinity. Nor was Ponet unaware of the politics of those representations. In a section on the trust to be placed in rulers, the treatise denounced the 'subtlety of princes (otherwise called policy)' which 'consisteth in this, for a man to appear outwardly that he is not inwardly'.[454] The charge is not only that of being Machiavellian; it is an accusation of misrepresentation. And Ponet brought the charge closely home. The evils of Mary's marriage, we have seen, Ponet described as 'painted over'. That was no casual metaphor, for in his description of the reinstitution of the mass, broken oaths and idolatrous acts, Ponet argued: 'these practices need no painter'.[455] The truth of God's word needed not the embellishment of image and ritual, and true godly rulers needed no 'paint', any more than 'fair words', to adorn themselves. *A Short Treatise of Politic Power* castigated not only Mary's religion and rule, but royal representation itself as ungodly adornment and subtle 'policy'.

While Ponet denounced in words the texts and arts of Marian representation, others acted to challenge the legitimacy as well as the image of the regime. In the spring of 1557 Thomas Stafford – second son of Henry, Lord Stafford and, after Wyatt's rebellion, an exile in France – attempted a raid on England to remove Queen Mary from her throne. Stafford seized the small castle at Scarborough and issued a proclamation in which he announced that the strongholds of England were about to be delivered to 12,000 Spaniards, and that Mary was surrendering the government to foreigners. Stafford called for the restoration of the 'laws, liberties and customs' of the time of Henry

VIII, as well as his own restitution as rightful Duke of Buckingham.[456] As David Loades wrote, 'News of this incursion travelled with incredible speed' and the Venetian ambassador felt certain that the uprising 'revealed the disposition of many persons who could not refrain from showing themselves desirous of a change in the present state of affairs'.[457] Though the support Stafford drew was small and the rising swiftly suppressed by northern forces assembled in readiness for a Scots invasion, the envoy may have been right. The government moved swiftly to suppress his proclamation and to warn subjects to place no trust in it.[458] Certainly Stafford demonstrated that antagonism to Mary's marriage and government might again translate into rebellion. But by 1557, most, perceiving that Mary would now remain childless, preferred to trust to time – and to a Protestant succession.

Princess Elizabeth was herself the most dangerous counter-representation to Mary's government, after the failure of the queen to conceive. She stood as the symbol of all that Mary's person and policies opposed: the marriage to Anne Boleyn, the divorce and break from Rome, marriageable youth and alternative government. Indeed, not only a symbolic counter to Mary, Elizabeth had been throughout suspected of involvement in plots – from Wyatt's rebellion onwards – and she was confined for part of the reign. There were regular plans to marry her off; rumours that Philip himself might marry her if Mary remained barren must have added to the queen's anxiety.[459] At several points, Elizabeth's life was in danger, but, ironically, she enjoyed the very advantage that had brought Mary to the throne: she was the rightful heir and any move to harm or displace her would be met with resistance. So Elizabeth became the focus of the hopes of the discontented and the persecuted, of the opponents of the Spanish marriage and the enforcement of Catholic orthodoxy: her image, that is, had begun to be constructed (in large part by others) well before she succeeded to the throne. Towards the end of Mary's reign, Elizabeth began cleverly to publicize herself as that alternative government in waiting: in November 1556 Elizabeth broke out of virtual house arrest and (in Machyn's report) 'came riding through Smithfield and Old Bailey and through Fleet Street into Somerset Place . . . with a great company of velvet coats and chains, her grace's gentlemen, and after a great company of her men all in red coats . . . and there her grace did lodge at her place [palace] . . .'.[460] Giovanni Michiel, the Venetian envoy, added that Elizabeth's retinue consisted of over 200 horsemen, 'clad in her own livery', and that, though she was not met by any of the lords or gentlemen of the court (some later met her in private), her public procession was 'to the infinite pleasure of this entire population'.[461] Elizabeth was being seen – and seen as a potential queen-in-waiting. In February 1558, she made another public entry into London 'with a great company of lords and noble men', again to lodge at Somerset House.[462] For all Mary's desire to disinherit her sister, Elizabeth, in residence in her palace on the Strand, was the public symbol of a different age, a different faith, a different government – and a very different image.[463]

During Mary's illness in 1557, the Venetian ambassador Michiel Surian reported many flocking to Elizabeth's residence, 'the crowd constantly increasing'.[464] Facing the inevitable, Mary sent to her sister to express her content at her succession and her prayer that she 'maintain the kingdom and the Catholic religion'.[465] The coupling of kingdom and Catholicism spoke much to Mary's self-presentation. Ironically, only hours before her death, Cardinal Pole, her principal adviser, expired his last breath. Even as she conveyed her message, England was buying up 'all the cloths of silk to be found at Antwerp' in readiness for the coronation of a new queen and a new court.[466]

The Bishop of Winchester, John White, preached a panegyrical sermon at Mary's funeral in which he praised an 'innocent and unspotted queen' who had been merciful and charitable, who had returned the country to the church and had 'married herself unto her realm'. Mary, Gardiner claimed, 'had the love, commendation and admiration of the world'.[467] Whatever the force of that claim abroad, at home there were few epitaphs published on Mary's death. But one, 'of the most excellent and our late virtuous queen', printed by Richard Lant at Smithfield, the site of the burnings, deserves notice.[468] The *Epitaph* commemorated Mary as the embodiment of regal virtues: as one liberal to her peers and nobles and open to her subjects' petition. As a 'mirror of all woman-hood', she was 'constant, modest and mild', a 'chaste and chosen wife'. As a Christian, the verse continues, Mary, a 'Mary named right', took God as her shield and her conscience as her guide and could now pass into heaven, 'joy with God to have'. The author praised Mary as a pattern for all princes and all women; and hoped that, now death had set her free from the calumnies of her enemies, 'thy joy shall last, thy virtues live, from fear and all annoys'.

It was not to be. That is not how Mary has been seen. But before we conclude that Mary was inevitably doomed to be recalled as a cruel heretic by a Protestant nation, we should note that the *Epitaph* in her praise went rapidly to a second edition, and that her successor Elizabeth was far from convinced that she ascended the throne of a predominantly Protestant nation.[469] In brief, Mary's Catholicism may not have been the decisive issue. Rather she tainted that faith with the stain of being Spanish, clericist and cruel. And crucially she gave her most committed Protestant enemies, albeit they were a minority, the material with which to construct that image of her – material which Foxe so brilliantly used.

'Unlike her father and her sister,' David Loades observed almost in passing at the end of her biography, '[Mary] seems to have made no attempt to project an image for the benefit of her subjects.'[470] If not entirely inaccurate, that remains too simple a verdict. Mary publicized her marriage and her faith, but without regard to popular sentiments about the one and division over the other. Official pamphlets supporting her policies and rule were far outnumbered by Protestant invectives against her.[471] In Edward Baskerville's words, 'The Protestants ... won their war of words with Mary and Roman Catholicism'.[472] Unlike her father, Mary did not only fail in selling herself as the champion of the English commonweal and nation; she allowed others to present her religion as un-English. That was a legacy that was to shape the representation of her successor as well as a new settlement in church and state.

PART VI

REPRESENTING GLORIANA

PROLOGUE

Perhaps no ruler has left so enduring an impression on the English memory or the collective imagining of the nation's past as Elizabeth Tudor. The queen's words (some probably invented) have been endlessly quoted, her portrait ubiquitously reproduced, and her reign held up as a model of good governance. From the very moment of her death, the name, image and memory of Elizabeth were invoked by various individuals to validate a programme or to criticize her successors.[1] Within two or three decades of her death, nostalgic evocations of the golden days of Good Queen Bess became a familiar refrain of the discourse of politics. In the 1630s, then the 1650s and the 1680s and onwards, Elizabeth was heralded as a godly champion, defender of the nation, founder of English empire and as a virtuous as well as virgin queen.[2] Not only did her female successors – Queen Anne, Victoria, and Margaret Thatcher – draw on her reputation and memory in the representation of their rule; a succession of kings and ministers, from William III and Chatham to Churchill, reprised her words to rally the nation.[3]

The powerful and positive image, the myth, of Elizabeth has been inseparable from the history and historiography of her reign. From her first chronicler, William Camden, to the classic biographer of modern times, Sir John Neale, (largely male) historians have fallen in love with Elizabeth and approached the queen, as she endeavoured to present herself during her life, as an object of desire as well as a focus of impartial study.[4] More recently a generation of feminist scholars has been drawn to Elizabeth as a champion of a woman's rights in a patriarchal world – as 'ever her own mistress'.[5] While more hard-nosed revisionist scholarship has questioned and criticized the queen's handling of religious and foreign affairs, identifying her dangerous procrastinations, equivocations and failure to address the succession, the mystique of the last Tudor lives on.[6] Recently a gay scholar, who has also confessed to falling in love with Elizabeth, has presented a hugely successful TV series on the queen and is currently preparing a second volume to follow his popular biography of Elizabeth as princess.[7] Clearly the appeal of Queen Elizabeth to men and women of the twenty-first century, as well as the 1930s, cannot simply be attributed to that wartime nostalgia for order and harmony which produced Tillyard's *The Elizabethan World Picture*.[8] Elizabeth has remained, even in more cynical times, what she strove to be: the focus and symbol of the nation.

Yet, and this is the principal paradox of Elizabethan representation, for all the power of the queen's image, that image was never entirely stable. Indeed, rather than a paradox, power and instability may have complemented, enabled, each other. Not least because the queen became a validating symbol, someone whose name, image and memory carried authority, many protagonists have invoked her for different, opposing causes. And they invoked her often for causes of which she certainly would not have approved and represented her as she would not have represented herself: as the champion of European Protestantism, for example.

The image of Elizabeth was open to such appropriations and deployments after her death because in her lifetime too that image was not fixed or the product only of the queen's own devising. For all her forceful personality and, in some cases, clear convictions, Elizabeth did not write the script of her reign or draw the template of her image which others followed. Rather she became the subject and site of a 'competition for representation', as various interest groups sought to claim the queen as their patron.[9] Be they councillors or ministers, noblemen or aldermen, Catholics or Puritans, those who sought to influence the queen and to steer her in other directions had also to shift and reshape her representation. Different agendas required different images. And, as well as need, there was opportunity. Not only were her official entries and pageants devised by many hands – courtiers, civic magistrates and merchants – but Elizabeth's very frequent progresses led her into tableaux as well as locales, ideological as well as geographic peregrinations, which were often determined by others and in which even ordinary folk had a vital and powerful role to play.[10] Elizabeth's image, for all its authority, was the product of many agents and was constructed, refined and refashioned in dialogue with contending interests, circumstances and subjects.[11] Indeed, the power of Elizabeth's image, her remarkable success in representing her rule, owed much to her openness and responsiveness to many different voices. Her authority, we might say, was strengthened by an image of responsiveness to the concerns and wishes of her people as much as by the portrayal of the queen as Astraea and Deborah or as divine goddess and God's handmaid.

The success of Elizabeth's self-presentation also owes much to another seeming paradox: the queen's proclamation of her unerring steadfastness, emblematized in her motto taken from her mother – 'Semper eadem' (Always the same), and yet her readiness to adapt to shifting circumstances and change. She was by no means the last lady to boast that she was not for turning while performing deft policy pirouettes as events and time dictated. Elizabeth ruled a very long time: she lived to the advanced age of nearly seventy and reigned for an unprecedented forty-five years. Over the five decades of her rule, the nubile young Elizabeth, with her pretty face, red hair and slender physique, aged into an old woman with wrinkles, a wig to cover her balding hair, and black, rotted teeth. As she aged, for all the rhetoric of constancy, the representation of the queen had to change too; indeed, the image of the unchanging Virgin Queen was emphasized as a counter to the reality of change and decay. Over half a century of rule, Elizabeth faced a variety of challenges: from noble Catholic plotters and puritan critics at home, from France and its old ally Scotland, then Habsburg Spain abroad. Through such changes, the queen had necessarily to temper her reputation for tolerance with harsh justice and exchange the garments of peace for the breastplate of war. If Elizabeth's reign was, and has been remembered as, vital in defining English identity and patriotism, we must recognize that her subjects' shifting perceptions of English interests also helped to shape the queen who knew that she must always endeavour to embody the nation.

One of the most important changes of the Elizabethan era was change itself – and a widespread perception of change. Though all the rhetoric and cultural values of sixteenth-century England emphasized stasis and constancy, contemporary awareness of having lived through, and of living in, an age of flux is everywhere apparent and most obviously manifested in the fashion for histories and antiquities which one scholar has described as a 'historical revolution'.[12] As well as the course of events, of successive reformations, Henrician, Edwardian, Marian and Elizabethan, the social and economic changes of the late sixteenth century gave rise to a new discourse of change and mobility and to new endeavours to arrest or check them. Together with the greatly increased concern with heraldry, the sumptuary laws (regulating which classes could wear which fabrics and clothes) evidence a perception of the loosening of social hierarchies and a greater social mobility, which also became the themes of a new genre of middle-class novels as well as of a new commercial theatre.[13] Especially in a capital that grew beyond all proportion, there emerged, too, a new civic consciousness and with it a new class of urban men and women concerned with their own representation and image, as well as with that of the queen and her government.[14]

Parallel with the growth in the authority and visibility of the monarchy, we discern in the second half of the sixteenth century the emergence of a market society and consumer culture which brought about changes in the modes and forms of, and in the responses to, royal representations. On the one hand, over the course of Elizabeth's reign, a new and widespread fascination with authority as well as personal affection for the queen fostered a desire and demand for portraits and engravings of the monarch along with royal lives, histories and panegyrics. On the other hand, the increase in publication of all genres of print and the huge popularity of the theatres, both beneficiaries of a consumer culture, began to create what scholars have identified as a public sphere, that is an informed community of readers and auditors, hungry for news, information and gossip and quick to receive, embellish and recycle it.[15] Though we have unquestionably underestimated the impact of the Henrician break from Rome on something recognizable as an appetite for news and informed public opinion, the sheer numbers of books and pamphlets emerging from the press in Elizabeth's reign testified to the scale of change. Elizabeth, in other words, was represented to a larger, and increasingly well informed, public than her predecessors and to a larger, we might say today more inclusive, commonweal.

As had been the case since its invention, but now more than ever, print presented the ruler with rich opportunities to communicate to her subjects and to construct and disseminate an image of her rule. But print and publicity offered opportunities also to the disaffected and the enemies of a Protestant queen; even more importantly, they transformed the communities and audiences in which royal representations circulated. As well as overtly political texts, heterodox and orthodox, a proliferation of sermons, histories and classical translations, novels, plays and ballads educated, informed (and misinformed) a public opinion which could and did criticize and contest as well as consume official scripts and representations. The art of royal representation was transformed by the teeming marketplace of print. Just as Elizabethan authors and playwrights acknowledged, and often lamented, the new critical spirit of readers and audiences, so the impresarios of royal representations knew that now, more than ever, they could not assume a quiescent public. Elizabeth I had to perform that most dextrous of moves: to communicate with that public while retaining the aloofness essential to mysterious majesty and to respond to that public while asserting, and exercising as much as was possible, sovereign authority. In her unique success in negotiating these moves lay the key to the power of her image – and perhaps to the endurance of her rule.

If the proliferation of print and information presented Elizabeth with problems as well as opportunities, this is no less true for historians. It is in Elizabeth's reign – another marker, perhaps, of modernity – that the records and archives as well as printed materials expand to more than any scholar could master, even in a working lifetime.[16] Though my purpose here is not to write the history of Elizabeth's reign or government, but to examine her image and representation, the challenge is hardly less daunting. Together with the length of her reign, the changes in the queen's circumstances, and the emergence of a public sphere in which representations circulated and were scrutinized, many new genres of representation, not least a fully fledged commercial theatre, need to be considered. In addition, the secondary literature, historical, biographical and critical, on Elizabeth amounts to an industrial production when compared with the small number of publications on her siblings', even her father's, royal image. The almost unavoidable danger is that any study of Elizabeth dominates that of her predecessors and the length of this discussion threatens to reinscribe that dominance. For all that, in a discussion which is far too brief as much as it is disproportionately long, we will seek to understand who devised and disseminated Elizabeth's representation in words, visuals and performances; how the image of the queen was multiple and often refashioned; the reception of her representations among popular as well as courtly audiences; and the means by which Elizabeth came to be heralded as the icon of the nation, the symbol of a collective public identity – 'a theatre and glass that all the world [did] behold'.[17]

As in our earlier discussions, we will address what Helen Hackett has called the anxieties as well as adulations of Elizabethan representation, what contemporaries themselves called the 'uncertainties' beneath the pose of confident certitude.[18] I shall suggest that, for all its disadvantages, her sex enabled Elizabeth herself to represent both vulnerability and strength and so to ease the tensions implicit in all acts of representation and inherent in the theory of the king's two (immortal and mortal) bodies. Elizabeth certainly was not what she emblematized – always the same; but in advertising herself as she did, she performed as what her subjects needed her to be: an icon of constancy, strength and love in a dangerously uncertain world.

CHAPTER 9

THE WORDS OF A QUEEN

From an early age, Elizabeth's self-presentation was very much as a learned princess, accomplished not merely in the female courtly arts – music, dance and needlework – but in languages ancient and modern. As William Grindal led her through a programme of Greek and Latin, Roger Ascham guided her in Italian and Jean Belmain in French. Elizabeth remained throughout her life, for all her avowed modesty, proud of her linguistic skills, which she evidently associated, in a humanist culture, with authority and power.[1] Unlike feats of arms, they were skills at which a princess, no less than a prince, could excel. Significantly at the young age of twelve, when Elizabeth sought to forge a closer relationship with her new stepmother, Catherine Parr, she presented to the new queen a translation by her own hand of Margaret of Angoulême's devotional work *Le Miroir de l'âme pécheresse*.[2] Not only did the translation display the princess's consummate skill in rendering the original into English idiom, it presented Catherine and Elizabeth as soul sisters 'through the grace of God' and in English gendered the soul as female in a fitting compliment to Catherine's authority as well as an early claim to her own.[3] From her humanist and her Protestant upbringing, Elizabeth learned a clear appreciation of the power of the word and the place of words, speech and script in the construction and exercise of authority.

Throughout her life, Elizabeth continued to read and to cite the classics: at dinner, in audiences with ambassadors and in correspondence. Her virtuoso displays of learning, of history, philosophy and theology, she knew, were vital in surmounting the cultural prejudices against her sex and advertised her capacity to govern. Indeed, amid all the affairs of state, it seems that Elizabeth continued not just to read but to translate classical texts, taking them and appropriating them for a discourse on her own times. According to her first biographer, William Camden, Elizabeth translated Sallust's *De bello Jurgurthino*; she also rendered into English a play of Euripides, dialogues of Xenophon, orations of

Isocrates and epistles of Seneca.[4] Several are lost. But the translations which remain have presented a number of problems to historians of Elizabeth and, along with other Elizabethan writings, have until recently been ignored. Some scholars, puzzled as to why a queen regnant would spend her time on them, appear to have assigned the translations to Elizabeth's youth and described them as though they were pedagogical exercises.[5] Others may have passed over them because translations, which we are too inclined to treat as a faithful reproduction of another's ideas, have seemed to promise little as a source for the queen's own values or inner thoughts. However, as critics have made us aware, the act of translation is always a reconstitution of values as much as language and a reconstruction of meaning as well as words. In the Renaissance, translation was often explicitly intended to reconstitute the original text for use in contemporary circumstances and translations were often, by modern standards, 'free', in order to perform that purpose. All early modern translations offer opportunities for historians to observe contemporaries refashioning ancient texts for early modern use. In the case of a ruler, translation was in itself an unusual authorial act, that is an act by someone in authority. A royal translation proffered an authoritative interpretation; it prescribed the meaning of a text; and the meaning was read as very much the queen's as well as the original author's. In the words to Elizabeth of the great classical scholar, Sir Henry Savile, 'as the great actions of princes are the subject of stories, so stories composed *and amended* by princes are not only the best pattern and rule of great actions, but also the most natural registers thereof, the writers being persons of like degree and of proportionate conceits with the doers'.[6] Savile grasped what was Elizabeth's own sense of the intimate interdependency of writing and authority. It was in that spirit that he wrote 'to incite your majesty to communicate to the world . . . those most rare and excellent translations', translations, he continued, 'if I may call them translations which have so infinitely exceeded the originals'.[7]

Elizabeth's translations were not 'communicated to the world', at least in print, and so may seem of little value in a study of her public presentation. On the contrary, the evidence of the manuscripts which remain suggests that, at least in some cases, Elizabeth intended her translations for circulation and possibly publication. The queen's neat hand, her holograph corrections and the survival of copy texts in the hand of the Clerk of the Signet, and in the official state papers, dispel any idea that these translations were purely 'private' exercises.[8] They suggest that Elizabeth was preparing them for a public readership. Whatever her intention, they were evidently well known and read not only by courtiers (whose hands have annotated and titled some) but by scholars like Camden and Savile who praised them.[9] As with so much of the poetry of the Elizabethan age, manuscript did not equate with privacy, but could be a form of what Harold Love has termed 'scribal publication', that is handwritten but for copying and distribution.[10] Elizabeth's translations were, and were read as, acts of her authorship and authority. As the editor of her works has recently rightly insisted, 'Elizabeth's identity . . . as monarch cannot be separated from her identity as author'.[11]

The queen's translations were many; some have not survived; other manuscripts have probably yet to be identified as hers; and we await a proper edition of the texts we know of.[12] But from those that have been edited we may glean a clear sense of Elizabeth's work as a translator and of her use of translation to deploy classical texts for her own circumstances and her own representation. Her longest known work is the translation she made, in 1593, of Boethius's *Consolation of Philosophy*. The work had attracted an earlier English monarch, King Alfred, and had obvious import for rulers. It was a familiar conceit in the Renaissance, following Plato, to regard philosophers as the best kings. In the theory of correspondences between the cosmos and the natural world, the king in the commonweal was often compared to reason in man, the regulator of unruly passions and appetites. In the 1560s, Elizabeth had sent as a letter to Sir John Harington a translation of Seneca's epistle number 107, on the need to retain a steadfast mind in 'the wandering state of things', to follow God and to 'let equity reign over the mind'.[13] In 1593, Elizabeth may well have felt the need to reiterate that counsel to herself. The news of Henri IV of France's conversion to Catholicism (in his famous words, 'Paris is worth a mass') threatened the delicate balance in Europe and her security; and Camden suggested that it was this shock that led Elizabeth back to Boethius.[14] Certainly her translation was anything but a diversion or private exercise. Elizabeth dictated a large portion of her prose to a Clerk of the Signet, as well as writing the verse sections in her own hand; and she devoted a month full-time to the task.[15] Boethius evidently had something important to say to Elizabeth in 1593. And the queen had something important to say through translating him.

The Consolation addresses the Platonic idea that the happiest commonweal is one where the ruler is constant and wise. In the dialogue Philosophy consoled Boethius that the world was ruled by reason not chance and that therefore obedience to a king, the source of reason, was the 'greatest liberty'.[16] Elizabeth's translation underlined the importance of order and also of faith in harmony and order: 'those that when they disagree be not good, when they are one, must needs be so'; everything shall last when it is one but when it leaves that order it 'must needs perish'.[17] In Nature, the work continued, order was secured by God, in the commonweal by the king and in man by reason. Identifying the good of the individual with the good of the whole ('they that forsake the common end of all things . . . leave themselves to be'), Elizabeth's Boethius reasserted the ideology of the Tudor commonwealth which helped to sustain royal authority.[18] Elizabeth may have turned to Boethius for her own psychological consolation: occasional passages hint at anxieties about kingship and the exercise of power.[19] But in re-authoring the message about the centrality of reason and the necessity and rationality of rule by one, in associating the free will of subjects (passages explicitly reject puritan predestinarianism) with obedience to God and rulers, Elizabeth reaffirmed the ideology which underpinned Tudor kingship.[20] And, in the act of translation, of course, by displaying her learning she advertised herself, despite her gender, as that philosopher king who 'joyeth' in her subjects and guided them to their own happiness and liberty, through their obedience.[21] 'Let persuasion of sweet rhetoric', Philosophy advised Boethius, 'assist thee' to greater understanding and equanimity.[22] Elizabeth's own 'sweet rhetoric' was exercised in her translations no less than her speeches as a principal aid to governance.

Two other translations we shall briefly notice were dated, in a later hand on the manuscript, to November 1598, a time of tension and rivalry at court, following the death of Burleigh and the ambitions of Essex, rumbling discontents in the country and a new spate of satires and squibs lampooning the regime.[23] The first, Elizabeth's translation of Plutarch's essay *De curiositate*, was very pertinent to the times. Plutarch's essay was an attack on those who, over-curious, pried into others' business and especially affairs of state. Using the idiom of early modernity, Elizabeth rendered such impudent curiosity as 'disease', 'palsy' and 'consumption' and admonished readers that 'no man ought permit his sense abroad to range'.[24] Rather than find fault with others, the translation urged, men should examine the 'store of faults' in their own lives; rather than stray to 'court of king', the subject should 'in thy selfe with reasone make abodd / and ther abide not strayinge out of office charg'.[25] Was Elizabeth drawn to Plutarch's sixteenth moral essay as a private rant against the curious and critical in her own time? An endorsement to the holograph indicates that the translation was again 'copied out by her Majesty's order to me' – a suggestion again of intended circulation.[26] To whomever it was addressed, Elizabeth's translation argued the dangers of prying and even, in a clever polemical turn, compares 'curious folk' with the hated informers who were often the agents of tyranny.[27] Boethius's injunctions to avoid assemblies where people gossiped, theatres and public shows were as pertinent to the 1590s, when news and rumour were seen as threats to government, as in Greece or the Rome of Emperor Hadrian.[28]

Elizabeth's other translation of 1598 was an unfinished rendition of Horace's classic treatise of literary criticism, *De arte poetica*. If such a text seems far removed from politics or royal representation, that only re-emphasizes a need to rethink the very nature of early modern politics. For in sixteenth-century England not only were poets, such as Wyatt and Surrey, noblemen at the centre of power, the association between poet and ruler, between good poetry and good government, was claimed by both poets and kings. Where, in his famous *Apology for Poetry*, Philip Sidney made a claim for the power of poetry to inculcate virtue (the purpose of government in a Christian commonweal), in Scotland King James VI penned a manual of *Short Reulis* for the composition of verse which (also influenced by Horace) was as much a treatise on kingship as on poetry and which underlined the interdependence of the two.[29] Similarly, undertaken at a time when satirical verses were attacking her government, Elizabeth's translation of Horace asserted the role of good poetry in imitating and representing the virtuous order of Nature and the power of poetry to re-affirm (through re-presenting) that order. The correct order of words, Horace and Elizabeth wrote, might not merely represent but reorder 'all things . . . as sorteth best their place'.[30] Like a monarch, the poet might, the treatise followed Sidney in arguing, elevate men to virtue and steer them from vice by means of persuasive images. Elizabeth's translation therefore urged the poet:

> Nor Eloquence shal he want, nor ordar cleare
> For Grace and Vertu shal he place, or forbeare.[31]

Elizabeth's translation appropriated the cultural authority of classical philosophy and letters to reaffirm values on which her own regal authority depended: order, deference and eloquent persuasiveness. In authoring these translations, she presented herself as the philosopher prince who embodied order and harmony. The writing of authority, she knew, involved not simply acts of proclaiming it, but the deployment and re-presentation of a variety of genres and texts as arguments for order, obedience and royal government.

As well as translating classical metre, Elizabeth penned her own verse as meditation and discourse on politics. Though the editors of Elizabeth's works point to the efforts the queen made to inhibit broad circulation, the many and variant copies of her poems testify that they spread beyond the confines of the court, into commonplace books and gentlemen's manuscript and printed miscellanies, and were particularly valued as royal texts.[32] As the panegyrist Thomas Churchyard wrote by way of dedication to Elizabeth of his *Handful of Gladsome Verses*, given to the queen at Woodstock in 1592, 'Great Princes have made verse/ And favoured poetrie well', because poets, like kings, 'clime where Gods doe dwell'.[33] Though some of Elizabeth's poems may have their origin in personal reflection, like all her words they also represented her rule, as she surely knew that they did. Only two poems have survived in Elizabeth's own hand and the variant copies of verses raise problems about an unquestionably reliable royal authorial text. But the recent editors of Elizabeth's writings have done much to identify what can reasonably be taken as the queen's and, we must always recall, that which circulated in her name was no less important. In some verses – evidently the genre permitted articulations that official texts could not – Elizabeth disclosed a sense of vulnerability and anxiety about her position: a concern in 1571, for example, that, with Mary, Queen of Scots's arrival in England, 'falsehood now doth flow/ And subjects' faith doth ebb'.[34] Some later poems reflected whimsically on a lost youth when the queen had enjoyed pleasures, not least amorous pursuits.[35] And a remarkable verse, dated to 1582, on the departure of her suitor, Monsieur (the duc d'Alençon), brilliantly encapsulates for us the dilemma that was the queen's two bodies when duty and love pulled in opposite directions:

> I grieve, and dare not show my discontent;
> I love, and yet am forced to seem to hate;
> . . .
> I am, and not; I freeze and yet am burned,
> Since from myself another self I turned.[36]

We should be cautious before concluding from such texts that we have illicitly eavesdropped on the queen's personal anguish. For in these lines Elizabeth also advertised her election to place duty before desire, just as she wrote in a poem to a gentleman of her court, 'to others' will my life is all addressed'.[37] Verse allowed Elizabeth to represent herself personally and publicly, in the modes of both the vulnerable woman and the virtuous queen and powerful monarch. For all her expression of her doubts about future foes, in lines which again play between the personal gendered body of the woman and the public body of the realm, she proclaimed defiantly in verse:

> No foreign banished wight
> Shall anchor in this port.[38]

and added that in the event that any made the attempt, 'My rusty sword . . . shall first his edge employ'.[39] Fortune, the queen told Sir Walter Ralegh in a verse exchange of 1587, did not 'rule my mind', for her virtue triumphed over fate and fear.[40] The next year, in 'a song made by her majesty' on the Armada victory, Elizabeth proclaimed that her strength came from God's protection, from her being his 'handmaid'.[41] As her poem, set to music, was sung before her 'at her coming from Whitehall to Paul's through Fleet St', Elizabeth versed her own public representation. In an exchange of verse with Paul Melissus, Poet Laureate of the Emperor Maximilian II, Elizabeth had used fittingly political language about poetry: 'You are a prince of poets', she flattered him, and 'I [am] a subject'.[42] In reality Elizabeth's poetry, of course, was not that of a subject; it was a medium of her regality and a mode that assisted her to negotiate the doubleness of her majesty, her private and public body, and the disadvantages of her sex.

Thomas Churchyard had reprised Sidney's claim for the divinity of poetry: 'Verse hath a grace the cloudes to pearce /And clime where Gods do dwell'.[43] It was not, however, only in her poetry that Elizabeth presented herself as in conversation with the divine or as the chosen handmaid of the Lord. Throughout her reign a number of prayers were circulated and printed as Elizabeth's own; and recent scholarship has confirmed that many were indeed of her own composition. Today we may be inclined to think that, like amorous verse, prayers are private texts of personal faith, a personal conversation of a believer with God. The title and form of volumes of Elizabeth's prayers, one in Latin *Precationes privatae*, published with frontispiece woodcuts of the queen kneeling in her chapel, create a sense in the reader of eavesdropping on a pious woman performing her private devotions.[44] But in the case of a monarch, piety was not (and is not) a private matter but a business of public import. As early as 1563, collections of Elizabeth's private prayers were published, in Latin, next to verses from Scripture and along with lists of the ecclesiastical and civil offices of the realm.[45] The form of the volume makes claims for the queen even before we begin to read; and as we read, we quickly see that the prayers publicized Elizabeth as a pious princess and godly ruler.

In her private prayers, Elizabeth spoke to God as though in a special relationship with him and as though exercising a trust the Lord had placed in her. 'Thou art my God and King: I am thy handmaid'.[46] 'Thy people', Elizabeth prayed, are 'committed to me' and 'Thou hast made thyself a protector to me' – 'a queen on earth by thy ordinance'.[47] In a prayer that underlined her position, Elizabeth restated what the Tudors had been endeavouring to establish as an axiom: 'under thy sovereignty, princes reign and all the people obey', that they 'may in obedience live together in mutual peace and concord'.[48] As well as affirming her divine right as a monarch to rule, Elizabeth's prayers reveal her concern, perhaps as a woman, to advertise her personal qualities to rule. 'Thou hast destined me', Elizabeth wrote lest any doubted or questioned her descent, 'born of royal parents', and then catalogued her virtues:

> I am unimpaired in body, with a good form, a healthy and substantial wit, prudence even beyond other women and, beyond this, distinguished and superior in the knowledge and use of literature and languages, which is highly esteemed because unusual in my sex. Finally I have been endowed with all royal qualities.[49]

But most of all, Elizabeth's prayers displayed those essential attributes of a good ruler: piety, a sense of duty to her people, and a devotion to their good. In a morning prayer, for example, Elizabeth asked God that she might do nothing which does not please him.[50] In a prayer to be used before consulting about state affairs, she asked God that he might dispose her to follow his will in that 'holy vocation to which thou hast called us'.[51] 'Give me,' the queen prayed, 'the grace to be a true nourisher and nurse of thy people.'[52] Her appointment to rule, she assured God and readers, she recognized as 'a burden and an honour'; and she prayed that she might 'rightly and perpetually use upright governance towards thy people and sound administration of the kingdom and thy commonwealth'.[53] As well as prayers for her own guidance in the exercise of office, the queen prayed, advertising another essential virtue of the good ruler, 'give us also prudent, wise, and virtuous counsellors, drawing far from us all ambitious, malignant, wily, and hypocritical ones' and promised that she would remove from her court all corrupt judges and disloyal ministers.[54] While (perhaps significantly) in a Latin prayer, for the auspicious administration of her kingdom, Elizabeth acknowledged the weakness of her sex – 'I am feminine and feeble' – her private prayers represented her as God's chosen, as a virtuous princess personally equipped to rule and as the handmaid of the Lord, who had restored true doctrine.[55] Rather, then, than simply private, the prayers, the first volume of which was published after Elizabeth's recovery from a near-fatal attack of smallpox, presented the queen to her subjects, some of whom still questioned her legitimacy and the right of her sex to rule, as God's appointed queen, 'placed in dignity . . . to be prayed for'.[56]

Throughout her long reign, several volumes of prayers were published under Elizabeth's name in books illustrated with an image of the queen with a book, at her devotions, in her private chapel, some of which prayers were her own composition and survive in her hand. In all cases the queen's prayers constituted a public as well as personal utterance and were clearly written to take advantage of publication. Elizabeth's prayer at Bristol on the occasion of the signing of a treaty with Spain was probably spoken before an audience (there survives a scribal copy) and perhaps intended for public distribution. Though the immediate context was foreign policy, the recent papal bulls excommunicating the queen, the Ridolfi plot and Norfolk's conspiracy had graphically highlighted Elizabeth's vulnerability to enemies at home. In her prayer, in thanking God, 'for thy mighty protection and defence over me in preserving me', Elizabeth reminded her subjects that, whatever some Catholics might maintain, she had been chosen by God to assure 'a peaceable, quiet and well ordered state and kingdom, as also a perfect reformed church, to the furtherance of thy glory'.[57] As she prayed for 'faithful and obedient hearts' in her subjects, Elizabeth characterized them as 'willing to submit themselves to the obedience of thy word and commandments', as well as her own; and so presented disobedience as a sin as well as treason.[58]

Through the 1570s and early 1580s, the dangers from Habsburg control of the Low Countries and the threat presented by Mary, Queen of Scots, Elizabeth's prayers continued to represent the queen as, 'though a weak woman', 'Thy [God's] instrument', ruler of an England at peace while the rest of Europe was ruined by war.[59] In Latin, French and Italian prayers directed to the learned, Elizabeth reiterated her chosen status, readvertised her virtues of prudence, moderation and equity, and reaffirmed her determination to 'feed thy people with a faithful and a true heart and rule them prudently with power'.[60] Connecting her earthly regimen to God's divine rule, she prayed that in governing she might serve God and make 'Thy grace my strength, Thy favour my life, Thy gospel my kingdom'.[61] This rhetoric of a godly, elect nation became increasingly common and noisy in the wake of the Armada 'victory' in 1588. In prayers after the repulsion of the Spanish fleet, drafted in Elizabeth's hand and found among her Secretary William Cecil's papers (perhaps in preparation for publication), the queen gave thanks to God for the realm's deliverance from 'foe's prey and from sea's danger' and 'not the least for that the weakest sex hath been fortified by thy strongest help'.[62] A sixteenth-century annotation on a manuscript, describing the prayer as 'worthy the Christian Deborah and Theodosia of our days', offers some insight into how these prayers, circulated and published, were read and received and their importance in Elizabeth's self-presentation and construction of her authority.[63] Certainly after 1588 Elizabeth's prayers were increasingly delivered on specific public occasions and often for armies or fleets sent against England's enemies. The queen's prayer for the Cadiz expedition of 1596 has survived in several copies and evidently circulated broadly enough to be copied into commonplace books.[64] At a time when Elizabeth's government and the queen herself were losing some popularity, the prayer justified the campaign as neither personal nor acquisitive but as defensive; and the queen prayed to God for 'surety to the realm, with the least loss of English blood' and for 'the advancement of Thy glory'.[65] Similarly, the next year Elizabeth's prayer for the Azores expedition (also found in many variant copies) repeated in more direct language the claim to a 'just cause, not founded on pride's motion . . . but, as Thou knowest to whom nought is hid, grounded on just defence from wrongs'.[66] Perhaps articulating aloud what she hoped but could not be sure of, Elizabeth again prayed for minimal casualties 'to such a nation as despises their lives for their country's good' and for 'Thy work'.[67]

Elizabeth's prayers complicate any clear distinction between the private and public utterance of rulers. Indeed, the queen constantly moved between the personal and public in her prayers, as a strategy of representation. For even when the tone of a prayer sounds 'private', it offered a glimpse to readers of the person and personal piety that underlay majesty and a comforting demonstration of the queen's humility before God and her trust in him. When composed for a public occasion, audience or readership, royal prayers presented the queen not only as God's handmaid but as the mediator (like the Virgin Mary) between God and her people. Prayers, that is, enabled Elizabeth to reconcile the royal bodies personal and public; and so to temper the problems of sex and gender. By revealing her feminine weakness to God, before whom a stance of powerlessness was apt for any ruler, whilst asserting her public authority as bestowed by him, Elizabeth was able to acknowledge her sex, without accepting the limitations on her authority prescribed by patriarchalism. She was able to figure female rule as the manifestation and agent of a Providence which it was difficult for any to contest. By borrowing from other psalms and prayers, melding her own words with Scripture, and presenting herself as the spokeswoman for the Lord, Elizabeth was also able to represent herself as heir to biblical kings and queens, as Deborah, Judith and 'nurse of thy people according to the word of . . . Isaiah'.[68] As we shall have occasion to remark of other monarchs, prayer, especially after the Reformation, was a vital medium of royal representation and an important discourse of authority.

As we have seen in the case of Henry VIII, letters, like prayers, were a form of public as well as private discourse and, circulated or reported at court and beyond, could become texts of royal representation, even when addressed to only one named recipient. Elizabeth's love letters to Alençon must have been widely known if they found their way into government archives.[69] As with her prayers, Elizabeth was acutely aware of the potentially wider as well as particular audience for her letters and often skilfully used correspondence to negotiate the contradictions of intimacy and familiarity with distance and mystery, at a time when both traditional personal bonds and emerging ideas of a more abstract 'state' made both modes essential to the effective exercise of rule. Trained in rhetoric and ever aware of its force, Elizabeth recognized the importance of letters, dictated many herself, and approved and signed most of those drafted by others. Her correspondence, which deserves a full rhetorical analysis, is too extensive to be treated in a study such as this. But we must glance at some of the queen's letters, not least because until recently they have been neglected as representations of her authority and as strategies for securing and sustaining that authority.[70] In the first place, Elizabeth's letters, especially to leading noblemen, helped to maintain the personal ties and relations with the crown which social changes were beginning to strain. The queen fostered a sense of intimacy by familiar modes of address as well as a style that laid aside the formality of majesty. Accordingly, a letter to Lord Willoughby opened 'my good Peregrine'; one to Lady Drury 'my Bess'. Lady Norris was addressed by an affectionate nickname 'Mine old Crow', while, in a letter to Lord Montjoy in Ireland, Elizabeth, recalling his lament that his lot resembled that of a kitchen wench, wittily began 'Mistress kitchen maid'.[71] Remembering and sharing a jest are the foundations of intimacy, as any modern politician or determined social networker will attest. Concern is another. And Elizabeth was no less assiduous in writing to enquire after the well-being and health of her ministers and nobles, imploring the Earl of Huntington, for example, 'to have care of your health and state of body'.[72] In particular, Elizabeth understood the healing benefits of a royal missive received at a time of difficulty or loss. On the early death of Lord Talbot, the queen, performing the part of preacher as well as physician of the commonweal, consoled the Earl of Shrewsbury that she shared his grief with him because 'we both be interested in the loss' of such a fine young man, which (Elizabeth assured them) afflicted her no less than his parents.[73] To Sir Amyas Paulet, her envoy to France, Elizabeth sent similar commiserations on the decease of his son: 'we knew in him such rare gifts of nature to do us and our realm most especial service'.[74] On the death of her husband, Lady Drury received from Elizabeth, along with words of Christian consolation, practical reassurance that the queen 'leaves not now to protect you . . . and minds not to omit whatever may be best for you and yours'.[75] Lady Drury's reply with thanks for such 'sweet lines of comfort' reads as more heartfelt gratitude than formal compliment.[76] The words of a sovereign, as used by Elizabeth, could, like those of God, be a healing balm and a source of comfort and hope for the future.

Indeed, Elizabeth used her correspondence to manifest her clear appreciation of the relationship between service and reward which was central to the functioning of early modern monarchy. While the queen signed herself as 'your sovereign' to command, she never neglected to express thanks and promise reward to those who rendered services. To the Earl and Countess of Shrewsbury, for example, Elizabeth sent her thanks for entertaining Leicester (her favourite, and possible lover whom she described as 'another self') and taking charge of Mary, Queen of Scots; and assured them that both 'new debts' and the 'old debt' would be acknowledged and remembered.[77] Along with God's reward for his charge, Elizabeth wrote to Paulet, in August 1586, recognizing that even duty was a reciprocal concept, 'how kindly besides dutifully my careful heart accepts your double labours'.[78] In 1600, she reassured the Lord Deputy of Ireland that, despite his fears about critics' reports of him, his sovereign 'esteems' and 'deeply regards you'.[79] With their seals and signatures written with a huge flourish, and yet very personal address and language, Elizabeth's letters to nobles and ministers combined majesty with familiarity in a powerfully affective way that was the hallmark of Elizabeth's royal style.

Elizabeth also knew, however, how, in her correspondence as in her demeanour at court, to deploy distance as well as familiarity and to hold out the threat of disfavour and displeasure as well as the promise of love and reward. In her prolonged correspondence with James VI of Scotland, a ruler whose loyalty was vital to Elizabeth's security but could not be assumed, she played out over two decades a complex psychological game of promise and admonition, of affection and rebuke, of love proffered and withheld.[80] Indeed, it was a language of psychology which Elizabeth herself used when, combining a promise of love with a threat of violence, she wrote to James in 1594: 'affection and kind treatment shall ever prevail, but fear or doubt shall never procure aught from me . . . if you do aught by foreigners . . . it shall . . . make me do more than you will call back in haste'.[81] James took the message and was duly rewarded with Elizabeth's 'unfeigned love'; he remained loyal to a queen who, as well as a loving sister, became a substitute mother (and Elizabeth rhetorically performed both roles) after the execution of Mary, Queen of Scots.[82] Elizabeth's letters to Essex, her favourite, yield another perspective on her use of correspondence as representation. After an intimate, possibly sexual, relationship with the queen, Essex began to aspire to the greatest ambitions and to begin to forget his duties as a subject and royal servant. In a letter to Essex after his failed expedition to the Azores, Elizabeth skilfully combined affection, exoneration of the earl from blame, strong advice that he not renew the attempt, and a clear reminder of where authority lay: 'Kings have the honour,' she wrote with unusual formality to him, using the masculine noun to reinforce her authority, 'to be titled earthly gods.'[83] In a letter sent to Essex in Ireland, whither he had been sent to suppress Tyrone's rebellion, and had acted well outside his orders, the queen's tone changed dramatically. Elizabeth denounced his little success achieved at high cost as a consequence of ignoring her advice and, reverting to her most formal mode of address ('Right trusty . . .') and raising a series of rhetorical questions 'expecting your answer', she sharply underlined her command.[84] Essex's despair is striking evidence of the force of Elizabeth's letters in bestowing and withdrawing favour and of their importance in the exercise of female rule. No longer warmed by epistolary expressions of royal love, Essex embarked on the desperate course that led him to the block.

Whilst royal letters were primarily personal communications to noblemen and royal servants, they were often read and referred to by others. Full of allusions to Scripture and the classics, laced with proverbial wisdom and artfully constructed, Elizabeth's letters read as though they were designed for a larger audience or to be read aloud. In some cases we know that the queen's letters were intended for a public audience and auditory. On 15 August 1586, for instance, Elizabeth wrote to the Lord Mayor of London, in the wake of the defeat of Anthony Babington's plot to murder her and her ministers. The queen wrote to the mayor asking that her letter be read aloud and displayed, with the large royal arms that headed it.[85] In the letter, duly read to a 'great assembly', Elizabeth informed the people that she did not so much rejoice at her escape from death but at the happiness manifested by her subjects at the capture of the conspirators.[86] Then, after subtly reminding subjects of God's protection of her, the queen gave thanks first and foremost for that 'it hath pleased him to incline the hearts of our subjects ... to carry as great love towards us as ever subjects carried towards [their] prince'.[87] In an echo of the language used in letters to nobles, Elizabeth went on to assure the people that their love for her was reciprocated with her care for their safety and welfare and that she desired to live no longer than she 'may not only nourish and continue their love ... but also increase the same'.[88] Though it was read, printed and publicized, the form of a royal letter retained a sense of the personal communication, even while it sustained the authority of the royal word and, at the reading aloud, the theatre of majesty.

Elizabeth also spoke directly to her people and some of her speeches, second only in renown to those of Winston Churchill, may well have inspired Shakespearian royal soliloquies. Elizabeth was not only well trained as an orator; she was proud of her skills, for all her often artfully modest downplaying of them. 'The words of kings,' she told Augustus Gyntzer, secretary to Count Helffenstein, the imperial envoy to England, 'are like the seals of the poor and should be inviolable.'[89] 'The words of superiors', she once quoted Demosthenes as saying, 'are as the books of their inferiors' and had to be no less carefully composed.[90] Though some maintained that in old age Elizabeth's missing teeth made it difficult to understand her, numerous contemporaries testified to the force not only of Elizabeth's words but her style and manner of delivery – which (as Helffenstein observed) was often extempore and 'with many brilliant, choice and felicitous phrases and rare benevolences'.[91] The queen possessed those time-less gifts of the great speaker, which were never more important than in the high age of humanism: sensitivity to audience, a sense of timing and dramatic effect, and a capacity to render the artifice of rhetorical tropes into unstudied, natural speech. We can still almost feel the power of both the metaphor and the theatrical gesture that brought it alive, as we read Elizabeth's speech addressing her Commons on her reasons for not marrying: 'I have already joined myself in marriage to a husband,' the queen told them pausing for effect, 'namely to the kingdom of England and behold, said she', stretching out her hand as if at a wedding ceremony, 'the pledge of this my wedlock and marriage with my kingdom and there with she withdrew the ring from off her finger and showed it, wherewith at her coronation she had ... solemnly given herself in marriage to her kingdom'.[92] In this speech, the familiar conceit of the monarch wedded to the realm is given vital new life, not least by Elizabeth's sex, the coronation ritual is reinvoked and the marriage of Christ to his church recalled in a speech intended to displace criticism and retain control. It is not the only example of a speech in which Elizabeth delivered an answer that was not an answer, but an answer that it was hard for others to answer, or contest, without appearing disloyal to the nation as well as the queen.

Elizabeth's most famous speech is unquestionably the address she delivered at Tilbury, as England faced the awesome power of the Spanish Armada in August 1588. In another psychologically shrewd move, the queen took upon her own female body the anxieties of a small nation threatened by the mighty Habsburg. Elizabeth opened by noting advice she had been given not to present herself among armed multitudes. But, she countered, in a reminder of her virtuous rule, 'Let tyrants fear: I have so behaved myself that under God I have placed my chiefest strength and safeguard in the loyal hearts . . . of my subjects'.[93] Now, the silent implication was, it was for those loyal subjects to display their chiefest strength; and Elizabeth led the way with an example of her own courage, her resolve 'to live and die amongst you'. Personalizing the vulnerability of her realm, Elizabeth acknowledged, 'I know I have the body of a weak and feeble woman'; but, emphasizing the regality as well as the strength of spirit over mere numbers, she continued: 'I have the heart and stomach of a king,' adding for patriotic effect, 'and a king of England too'. Combining nationalism with a chivalric code of honour which required all to protect the virtuous female, Elizabeth articulated her 'scorn that . . . any prince of Europe should dare to invade the borders of my realm'. And, once again, while appealing for resolve in her service, she promised 'rewards and crowns' to the brave, before rallying the troops with a confident prognostication that unity and obedience would deliver 'a famous victory over these enemies of my God and of my kingdom'.[94]

Elizabeth's oration to the troops and people at Tilbury was re-delivered by Lionel Sharpe the next day, circulated in variant copies, and printed in countless histories, becoming quickly the stuff of legend.[95] Some accounts painted a dramatic *mis-en-scène* with Elizabeth riding among her troops in full armour, like Pallas, before delivering her oration, or described a public fast which virtually rendered the speech as a sermon on an occasion of public worship.[96] While we cannot rely on such accounts in detail, there can be no doubting the skill and effectiveness of the Armada speech which, in our parlance, pressed all the right buttons. If this weak woman could find courage, how could her army lack resolve? If she were willing to die for and with them, how could her men not venture their lives for her? If honour did not itself dictate the defence of a helpless woman and virtuous princess, did not national sentiment whet the sword? And if earthly reward were not sufficient recompense for service, did not doing the Lord's work promise rewards in heaven? In a short speech this feeble woman embodied the nation and rallied it for war.

Elizabeth's rousing patriotic oration at Tilbury may be the most famous but it is by no means the only instance of her skilful representation of her authority in speech. As we have seen, Elizabeth attached great importance to her reputation for learning and equated education with power; her addresses to the universities (interestingly still today the locations of major government speeches)[97] before audiences of the scholars, courtiers and citizens of Oxford and Cambridge presented her with occasions to display her learning and opportunities to make other pronouncements. We may take Elizabeth's Latin oration at Cambridge in August 1564 as an early example of her use of such occasions. Highlighting her 'feminine modesty', and her incapacity before learned men, the queen proceeded to a witty, eloquent and important speech, full of classical references and yet of effortless familiarity.[98] In her oration, Elizabeth reaffirmed her commitment to learning – 'the propagation of good letters which I much desire and most ardently hope for' – and held out the promise that in Cambridge she would erect a monument to learning (and, it was implied, her own learning!) 'by which not only may my memory be renowned in the future, but others may be inspired by my example'.[99] Closing with a (completely unnecessary) apology for her 'barbarousness' and a witty suggestion that it were best if they all, like drinkers from the river of Lethe, forgot all she said, Elizabeth did the complete reverse and left a powerful and lasting impression.[100] As she told the university, even without a material monument, the words of princes were books and 'the example of a prince has the force of law'.[101]

Two years later, at Oxford, Elizabeth protested her unease about speaking, being 'uncultivated . . . in letters', yet also reminded them how 'I have applied my effort for some time to good disciplines and even longer in learning'.[102] Praising and thanking the university for all the hospitality and entertainments she had enjoyed and the disputations (that is academic debates) she had witnessed, she yet could not fail to observe that some had been 'imperfect' – 'to which since I am queen, I cannot extend approval'.[103] The judgement was no less than a warning about the dangers of free academic discussion. One of the debates in divinity had tackled the topical and dangerous question of whether a private man might lawfully take up arms against an unjust prince and, despite the university's apologetic prologue to the moot, Elizabeth needed to signal her unequivocal displeasure within an overall speech of warm commendation.[104] Though, she observed, for herself, she was 'worthy of no praise at all', as 'a queen', she had to assert what it was fit and not fit for scholars to dispute. And she ended, with words that underlined her command, 'I have spoken'.[105] Elizabeth returned to Oxford in 1592, and may on that occasion have written a translation of Cicero's *Pro Marcello* and herself participated in the debates staged for her, so enacting her role as philosopher queen.[106] If that was the case, her speech lamenting her poor Latin after years of little use probably carried more rhetorical force. In classical style, Elizabeth praised while claiming not to praise ('your merits are not') the hospitality, declarations and orations she had witnessed, before turning to emphasize their love towards her – a love, she believed, beyond that of parents, friends or suitors. For the love of the most learned men (she flattered them as well as herself) was love of her virtues and her own learning; but, she reminded them in the still tense foreign situation, that she also had a 'special concern, care and watchfulness' so that the country be secured from enemies and tumults and 'not enfeebled under my hand'.[107] As well as advertising her vigilance along with her virtue, the queen proffered advice to the university: that in matters of religion, at a time of increasingly contentious theological dispute, the university should follow the law and her ordinances – 'what the divine law commands and ours compels'.[108] Enjoining the students not to dispute with their masters, the queen closed with an injunction to the scholars, many of whom would become the future parish clergy of her realm: 'be of one mind, for you know that unity is stronger, disunity the weaker'.[109]

In her largely unstudied speeches to the universities, Elizabeth, in both general and particular ways, represented her person and her regal authority and supremacy.[110] Displaying her learning and love of learning, she advertised the virtues of the ideal humanist prince, the philosopher king; by witty rhetoric she strengthened her authority while protesting her incapacity; by reminding the universities of their duties to produce loyal churchmen, she endeavoured to outlaw dissent and foster unity and obedience. Even more than letters, speeches represented a monarch who was very much present – a focus of visual attention as well as an orator. Though Elizabeth came to wonder, as did her successors, whether it was better to speak or maintain silence, her utterances were important devices of her rule and representation.

On no occasion were they more important than in addresses to parliament. From the time of the break from Rome, parliaments had met increasingly frequently as first Henry, then his successor, required new statutes to enact the Reformation, the establishment of the royal supremacy and religious changes. After Mary's Counter-Reformation, Elizabeth again needed statutory legislation to re-establish her supremacy and to lay the foundations of a new church and religious settlement and, later, to enact new treason legislation to counter Catholic threats. In addition, the parlous state of royal finances after Henry's costly continental wars and the need to provide for defence in an unstable Europe meant that parliaments had to be summoned regularly for grants of subsidy. More than her predecessors, Elizabeth had to work with parliaments. Along with the influence exercised by her ministers and placemen in both houses and the promise of patronage and office held out to loyal MPs, the queen's speeches were important weapons in managing parliaments as well as significant occasions for the public representation of the queen, in her highest estate, as Henry VIII had put it, before the representatives of the counties and boroughs.[111] From the outset of Elizabeth's reign, there were tensions in her relations with parliaments which pressed the queen to marry and pressured her to a more overtly Protestant religious settlement than she favoured.

Despite the difficulties and pressures, Elizabeth managed the tricky balancing act of retaining a reputation for heeding counsel while following her own will on most issues; and ended her reign with what was not inappropriately described as a loving relationship with her parliament. In the securing of that achievement, which the next century was to memorialize, the queen's speeches played no small part.[112]

From the first meetings Elizabeth flattered her MPs, took advantage of the weakness of her sex while never failing to assert her authority, and carefully spoke a language of unity and harmony – even in the midst of disagreement. Answering a Commons petition that she marry in 1559, Elizabeth thanked the members for their 'loving care', promised that they would have no cause to be discontented, but gently admonished them that it was not for them to instruct – as that were 'unworthy the majesty of an absolute princess'.[113] While expressing her contentment at the single life, the queen did not close the door on marriage to such a husband 'as shall be no less careful for the common good than myself'.[114] Such warm but noncommital answers continued to be her rhetorical tactic. After a bout of sickness in 1563 revived parliamentary petitions for her to marry, Elizabeth again flattered what was becoming a newly confident Commons that she 'may well term [them] the whole realm'.[115] Yet in the same breath as acknowledging their importance as representatives of the people, she reminded them of her own, higher, calling from God who, through her, had delivered the realm from darkness and who, it was implied, would continue to protect her and them. Skilfully using her sex and gender, promising to be 'mother . . . unto you all', Elizabeth assured them that, but for 'some restless heads', she was not angry with them, and even liked the gist of their petition.[116] Then, with a witty reference to the philosopher who always delayed responding to a hard question, Elizabeth put off answering.[117] It was to be her recurring tactic. To the Lords the queen offered something more: reiterating her belief that virginity was the best state for a private woman, she informed them: 'I strive with myself to think it not meet for a prince'.[118] 'If,' she held out a promise that because it was conditional was still not a commitment, 'I can bend my liking to your need, I will not resist such a mind.'[119]

Delay only purchased the queen time, and the issue of her marriage dominated the difficult parliament of 1566. As the intransigence of the Commons threatened to jeopardize the grant of a subsidy, Elizabeth addressed a delegation of both houses in a speech which was then reported to the full parliament. This time her tone was very different. Excusing the Lords – 'there was no malice in you' – Elizabeth turned her wrath on her Commons.[120] Asking a series of rhetorical questions which invited only the response she wanted, Elizabeth asked how they could doubt her concern for their safety and the good of her people. That her vague answer about a future possibility of marriage had not been 'accepted or credited though spoken by a prince' (again in a difficult situation she preferred the masculine noun) enraged her.[121] Elizabeth tempered her anger with another vague half-promise: 'I will marry as soon as I can conveniently, if God take not him away with whom I have a mind to marry'.[122] Having made this seeming concession, on the matter of her authority she was adamant: it was, she told them, monstrous 'that the foot should direct the head'; 'I am your anointed queen ... I will never be by violence constrained to do anything'.[123] Though sharper in its language, Elizabeth's speech still continued to assure her auditors that, in not determining the succession, she acted for their safety and good, not her own. On this occasion, for all her efforts, the succession issue wrecked the session and on 2 January 1567 the queen spoke to dissolve an acrimonious parliament. Ever aware of the importance of her image as a ruler devoted to her people, Elizabeth expressed her anger at those MPs who had made it appear that, regarding the succession, 'their care was much when mine was none at all'.[124] 'A zealous prince's wisdom', she sharply reminded them, was more to be valued and weighed than 'lip laboured orations out of such subjects' mouths'.[125] (The implied criticism of rhetoric was as audacious as it was hypocritical.) As for the parliament's stand on its liberties, while she assured the house that 'God forbid ... that your lawful liberties should any ways have been infringed', their liberties, she observed, in no way limited her authority to command and correct.[126] However, for all the admonitory tone, Elizabeth still, like a mother scolding a child, excused the 'imperfect dealings' of 'simple men', assured them that she was a 'gentle prince' and did not doubt their basic loyalty.[127] 'The most,' one version of the address concluded, deploying the tactic of isolating the few, 'may assure you to depart in your prince's grace.'[128] Firmly reasserting her prerogative without taking a stand, Elizabeth had been able to take advantage of her sex, and self-appointed role as mother of the nation, to deliver a scolding in the language of love. Rhetoric muted the exchange of angry words and conflict which was to flare up under her male successors.

In her speeches to parliament, Elizabeth underlined her authority by presenting herself as God's chosen queen. Addressing the parliament on 15 March 1576, after a difficult session of quarrels over religious and foreign policy as well as the succession, Elizabeth thanked God (whose 'handmaid' she told MPs she was) for his protection of her from foreign foes.[129] Reminding them that 'these seventeen years God has both prospered and protected you with good success under my direction', she presented herself as the head of a chosen people and rendered the worries of the Commons as doubts about God's, as much as her own, good government.[130] 'I know I am mortal', Elizabeth confessed blunting the criticism that she never considered the possibility of her own death; but, she said, she trusted in God 'who will preserve you safe'.[131] Who could doubt her? By the next parliament, however, the precariousness of her and thus the nation's security had become all too apparent. Plots against the queen's life, almost certainly supported by Mary, Queen of Scots and her Guise French allies, highlighted the vulnerability of the queen and realm and led to the formation of a Bond of Association to defend her. While still not wanting to give way to pressure and determine the succession, Elizabeth expressed her warm thanks for the care her MPs showed and promised reciprocally 'to seek all your best'.[132] But the opportunity the more zealous Protestants had seized to urge further religious reform or a Presbyterian church government, the queen was quick to counter. In a subtle allusion to her own writings and with clever understatement, Elizabeth, uttering her 'hope ... God's book hath not been my seldomest lectures', reproved any who might wrong her by suspecting her of 'coldness' in her faith.[133] Asserting her authority as head of the church ('whose overruler God hath made me'), she condemned those who claimed to interpret God's will themselves, and affirmed that 'mine were the true way of God's will' which she then 'prescribed' to her subjects.[134] Under pressure from puritans whose claim to interpret God's will was, she knew, a direct challenge to the crown, Elizabeth made clear that she would adhere to 'God's holy true rule' and that she alone would be the judge of it.[135]

For much of the 1580s, Elizabeth's authority seemed to rest on her skilful rhetorical manoeuvres to retain the goodwill of her people and parliaments on the one hand and to continue to follow her own preferred courses on the other. The case of Mary, Queen of Scots presented her with particular difficulty. For while a regard for the sanctity of another sovereign led Elizabeth to want to preserve her 'sister', the threat Mary presented and the Commons' insistence on justice against her were hard to ignore. Elizabeth, not untypically, played for time and tried to avoid a direct response to a Commons petition urging Mary's execution. God had protected her, she again told her MPs, against 'manifold dangers'; and as for threats to her life, 'the regard of life which I have', she remarked, 'is in respect of you and the rest of my good subjects', not for her self.[136] Coming to the issue of Mary, Elizabeth confided to her audience her own regret that Mary had spurned her approaches but repeated her reluctance to order her death. In a second reply she opened to the parliament her personal anguish that a 'maiden queen' might cause the 'death of a prince her kinswoman' and her pragmatic worry how foreign potentates might react.[137] Then, acknowledging that 'exceeding care of me ... such as I shall never be able to requite', concurring in general with their judgements, and vowing not 'to draw the matter still into length without cause', Elizabeth yet delivered her 'answer without answer', commanding that 'this answer answerless content you for the present'.[138] Here, the publicizing of her own inner torment and conscience, her concurrence with the Commons, and her hint that 'there must be deeds' as well as words to satisfy their request bought the queen the months she needed and, importantly, the reasonable surety that James VI, Mary's son, would not make his mother's death a cause of war.[139] Elizabeth has rightly been charged by revisionist historians with sometimes dangerous prevarication. But, in the case of her speeches, her skill in buying time was vital to the maintenance and representation of her authority – as a queen who acted not when her Commons pressured her, but when God directed her and she saw fit.

The issues and tensions between Elizabeth and her parliaments were no less, or less contentious, than those of her successors. But more effectively than the Stuarts, Elizabeth used her words and her presence and deployed a language of harmony and love to temper sharp exchanges. Modestly in 1593, refusing, even after the Armada victory, to compare herself in her womanly weakness with princes renowned for their fortitude, Elizabeth yet promised her parliament to vie with any in 'love, care, sincerity and justice' and to use their subsidies only for 'your preservations'.[140] Famously in her so-called Golden Speech to her last parliament, Elizabeth brilliantly defused the mounting criticism of her government, especially of her grants of monopolies and patents which raised prices. Following a by now repeatedly successful device, Elizabeth addressed what had been a querulous Commons with assurances of her devotion to them and her happiness to have 'reigned with your loves'.[141] Having established a warm mood of mutual affection, the queen, theatrically pausing to urge all those kneeling to stand, proceeded to the matter of grievances.[142] Her last thought, she told the assembled, had been to waste or grasp her subjects' goods: rather 'my own properties I account yours to be expended for your good'.[143] So, she explained, she was grateful to those who had brought to her attention the grievance caused by monopolies and so protected her from any 'diminution of our honour and our subjects' love unto us'.[144] The queen had, she told them, never approved a grant of a patent except on the appearance of its benefit to the commonweal; but having now been better informed that some had caused hurt, she 'could give no rest unto my thoughts until I had reformed' them.[145] Those – 'varlets and low persons' – who had deceived her as much as they had oppressed subjects would not escape the judgment of a queen who knew she owed account to the 'great judge' and who was ever willing to venture her life for her people's welfare.[146] Having distanced herself from responsibility and blame and all but represented a major grievance as a course motivated by her care, in an unusually intimate gesture Elizabeth asked that before they departed to their countries, MPs be brought to kiss her hand – as a seal of her love and promise.[147]

Though no other royal speech was more copied or remembered, it was not quite Elizabeth's last to parliament. On 19 December 1601, addressing the members as they prepared to return to their counties and boroughs, she spoke to ensure that they would be spokesmen and representatives now for her rule.[148]

The queen praised the MPs as 'so loving subjects' with whom she had worked in 'sympathy' for the good governance of the realm.[149] Then, reminding them of her own virtues, in a clever and personal metaphor she explained how she had expended her own resources as well as their subsidies in their defence: she had, she put it, 'been content to be a taper of true virgin wax, to waste myself and spend my life that I might give life and comfort to those who live under me'.[150] Through all the dangers that had beset her, she continued, God had made her his instrument to protect her people. Then, after a long rehearsal of her dealings with Spain, endeavours for peace and 'to let you know the grounds and motives of the war to which you contribute', she asked that 'this testimony' the MPs 'carry hence for the world to know', as a public assurance of her care.[151] Not for the first time, Elizabeth's timing had been good: parliament being formally dissolved, the members had not expected a speech and the queen's 'grace of pronunciation . . . her apt and fine words . . . did ravish the sense of the hearers with such admiration', one observer reported, 'as every new sentence made me half forget the precedents'.[152] Clearly the power of Elizabeth's royal addresses owed much to her presence. But we should not underestimate the impact and force of her words: her rhetoric, grammar, use of metaphor, her modest disclaimers and gentle reminders, her tempering of anger with words of affection, her self-presentation as God's handmaid and the people's servant. If the words of princes were, as she had said, like books, Elizabeth's words helped to write the ordered, loving commonweal which she sought and to underwrite the ideals on which her rule depended.

While printed copies of speeches conveyed the queen's words to an increasingly literate nation, proclamations remained the medium through which the royal word was communicated to every marketplace and parish. The form, rhetoric and style of Elizabeth's proclamations, their shifts over the near half-century of her reign, deserve a study. For one, the large royal arms printed at the head of some proclamations appears to have been a new departure; and the shift between the usual third person (her majesty) and first person (we) would repay close analysis.[153] Here, we can only sample some proclamations as representations of authority and compare their language to that of other texts of the queen's representation. Even a cursory reading of Elizabethan proclamations reveals a new rhetoric which was distinctly the queen's and, as well, a nationalism even more pronounced and embodied in the person of the ruler. As with her speeches, Elizabeth's proclamations regularly pointed to the benefits God and her people had 'so largely bestowed upon her', of which 'she would have been loath to have on her own behalf made any mention'.[154] And the rhythms of her prose and familiar metaphors sounded in denunciations of agents of Rome who betrayed not only her but 'their parents, kindred and children, and their religion, country and commonweal to be subjects and slaves to aliens and strangers'.[155] There can be little doubt that many proclamations were the queen's own words and that all issued in her name were approved by her.

Early in her reign, Elizabeth was careful in her proclamations to claim authority at a time when she knew some of her Catholic subjects regarded her as illegitimate. As well as cautious references to 'our dearest sister' and 'the excellent princess Queen Mary, late of famous memory', she often invoked the name of her father, Henry VIII, that 'noble king of famous memory' to whom she made reference throughout her reign.[156] Elizabeth's proclamation of her regal style, interestingly and perhaps diplomatically omitting the supremacy and describing her as 'defender of the true, ancient and Catholic faith', may have been couched to convey to the anxious a sense of continuity, at least until the new regime was established.[157] Certainly, as Elizabeth began to feel settled, her proclamations became more routine and businesslike, were often expressed in the more formal third person, and were free of long explanatory prologues.[158] However, Elizabeth retained a keen sense of when it was politic to explain her actions in order to strengthen support. In 1560, for example, when some suspected appeasement of a Scotland whose queen freely vaunted her claim to the English throne, Elizabeth, 'considering that there may be a diversity of opinions conceived of her proceedings ... hath thought meet briefly and plainly to notify her majesty's certain purpose and intent with the just occasions given thereof' – what was in fact a full argument for her preference for peace.[159] In 1569, she similarly offered a lengthy justification for her ordering reprisals against Spanish shipping to counter circulating Spanish claims and to 'notify to all persons ... testimony of her sincerity'.[160] In the 1580s, a proclamation 'explaining execution of two seminary priests' went to elaborate lengths to underline (to Catholics in particular) the legality of the proceedings and to emphasize that the accused did not die for their religion (the queen explained she desired none should die for their belief) but for proven treason.[161] Explanation and justifications reached their height in Elizabeth's proclamation of the death sentence against Mary, Queen of Scots, in which she took pains to express her reluctance to agree the sentence and her endless efforts to save her sister's honour and life, and to argue the unimpeachable testimonies and examinations which had proved her role in plots and justified her punishment.[162] For all her insistence on her authority, on contentious matters Elizabeth used proclamations to argue, explain and justify her actions.

It was in such cases that, downplaying her own role, she stressed the advice she had received, and sometimes hinted at the pressure councillors had placed her under. Her cancelling of the Maundy ceremony in 1564 at a time of plague, she explained in a proclamation, was against her own inclination to observe such ceremonies and a decision taken 'only by advice and not' (here the third person reinforces the queen's distance from the decision) 'of her own will'.[163] In the case of Mary of Scots's execution, Elizabeth stressed how by 'sundry lords' she was 'earnestly moved and counselled' to examine Mary and how they had then importuned her 'with many reasons of great force' to execute the queen.[164] Despite her own inclination to mercy, then, Elizabeth was, she explained, 'overcome with the earnest requests, declarations and important reasons of all our said subjects' – a claim that, for all its only partial truth, enabled her to distance herself from responsibility for the death of a fellow sovereign, with all its hazardous implications.[165]

On other, less contentious occasions, Elizabeth in proclamations, as in speeches, emphasized her personal authority and implementation of God's charge and courses. 'Her majesty' had 'had the taste', a proclamation informed subjects in 1560, 'of God's singular goodness' who knew 'the justice of her cause'.[166] The queen, her pardon informed the northern rebels in 1569, was 'the minister of Almighty God' against whom, no less than her, they had offended.[167] From the failed rebellion of Lord Dacre in 1570, a proclamation urged 'all persons to take example' and refrain from following any 'against their sovereign lady, being by Almighty God . . . ordained to be the superior and vanquisher of all wicked persons and their attempts'.[168] Increasingly, as she faced and survived domestic conspiracies and foreign threats, the language of Elizabeth's proclamations conjoined God, the queen and the nation. After the Armada, of course, such rhetoric was insistently repeated, so that it might be 'manifestly seen to all the world how it hath pleased Almighty God . . . to have taken this our realm into his special protection . . . with a special preservation of our own person, as next under his almightiness supreme governor of the same'.[169] By presenting her as God's chosen minister and the nation as God's chosen people, Elizabeth's proclamations both advertised her piety and divinely appointed authority and rendered enemies and critics as sinners. Proclamations described attacks on Elizabeth as sinful and pointless opposition to God's divine plan.

Elizabeth presented her claim to be God's minister not just as authority but as a trust which placed deep obligations on her to be merciful, just and careful of her and his people. Repeatedly in proclamations, Elizabeth reiterated her love of peace, her preference for gentle persuasion over harshness and 'the clemency . . . we have ever found our heart possessed towards our subjects of all sorts'.[170] As in her speeches, she emphasized her 'motherly or princely care' and her subordination of her own interests to 'the common good and benefit of all her loving subjects'.[171] Nor did the queen alone determine what was 'the public good'.[172] Many proclamations describe Elizabeth responding to information, complaints and requests from her subjects. It was, for example, 'hearing by report out of sundry counties of the realm' of unreasonable prices that led her to enforce orders for bringing grain to market, as it was 'diverse informations of sundry grievances' which produced the proclamation reforming abuses of patents.[173] Elizabeth represented her rule as rule with, as well as over, her subjects and never ceased to mention the reciprocal love between queen and people which she claimed was a special hallmark of her reign (and perhaps her sex). Denouncing John Stubbs's libel on her, Elizabeth contrasted his bitter invective with the 'universal love, liking and favour of her people'.[174] She 'always esteemed [it] the greatest surety', she explained in 1599, that 'our subjects hearts are assured to us by the bond of love rather than enforced obedience'.[175] Elizabeth, of course, described an ideal more than a reality: the description of her realm in 1570, after the rising in the north, as 'in an universal good peace and . . . constant obedience' glossed the harsh truth of rebellion.[176] But Elizabeth understood that early modern monarchy depended upon the reaffirmation of ideals, even fictions, of peace, harmony and love. And while each ruler endeavoured to revalidate such ideals, Elizabeth, not least by using her gender, made them personal and a support to her person.

Since 1547, successive governments had issued, in the monarch's name, homilies on obedience to be read from the pulpit. Though we cannot know for sure what role Elizabeth had in the drafting of the homilies issued in her reign, publication by the royal printer, with the image of the pelican, her badge, and the motto 'Pro lege, rege et grege' presented the homilies as royal texts and as a statement of royal views. The 1570 *Homily against Disobedience and Wilful Rebellion*, issued in the wake of the rising of the northern earls, repeated the familiar lessons about the necessity of obedience to princes and the sinfulness of resistance to the powers ordained by God.[177] But the Elizabethan homily also referred to the untimely death of England's Josiah (Edward) as an example of God's punishment of a sinful nation and as an admonition to all to pray for the health and safety of his successor who, like him, would establish and protect the true religion.[178] Denouncing the pope and his agents, the homily scorned and cast out of the commonweal the rebels who 'hold with unnatural foreign usurpers against their own sovereign lords and natural country'.[179] Commanding subjects to 'learn obedience both to God and their princes', the homily closed with a thanksgiving for the suppression of the uprising against God and 'thy servant, our queen'.[180] The prayer to preserve 'our church, our realm, our queen' led the congregation in a ritual affirmation of their loyalty to a queen who was presented as the model of prudence and justice.[181] Later homilies rehearsed the same themes and mantras, but increasingly presented Elizabeth as chosen leader of an elect nation who preserved God's truth and chosen people. The homily of 1573, for example, published in the aftermath of Norfolk's rebellion, specifically rejected 'pretences of religion' which 'now of late beginneth to be a colour of rebellion' and proclaimed the wrath of God against any who did 'murmur against their governors', let alone resist them.[182] As we shall further remark, the plots and rebellions against Elizabeth, whatever her earlier desire for a more ecumenical settlement, increasingly reshaped her representation as a Protestant queen of a Protestant nation.

Elizabeth's own writings, speeches, letters, proclamations and declarations were only a part of her representation in words and in print. In fact, no earlier ruler than Elizabeth was so much the subject of all the forms and genres of print, from verse panegyric, epic, romance and histories to sermons, ballads and songs. Along with her own writings, many wrote to present an image of the queen to her subjects. In some cases, even when they lauded her, authors had their own perspectives and agendas which did not accord with hers. So extensive is this material that, for all it has been the subject of several literary (and a few historical) studies, the textual representation of Elizabeth has only begun to be investigated.[183] As we sample just a few of the numerous texts and genres which broadly published the queen to her subjects, we will see how the textual representation of Elizabeth advertised her authority and virtues but also manifested how the expansion of print produced multiple representations and made it ever more impossible to fix or control the royal image.

The second half of the sixteenth century in England saw a wave of literature on the nature of kingship, much of it in support of sovereign authority. Doubtless the religious wars on the continent and the circulation in England of apologias for resistance stimulated both official and unofficial defences of strong government and royal prerogative which, even when arguments were abstract and theoretical, were clearly intended to support Elizabeth. The 1571 translation of Tigurinus Chelidonius's *History of the Institution ... of Christian Princes*, bearing a large royal arms and dedicated to Elizabeth, represented monarchy as the natural order and divine ordination of God.[184] Kings, the treatise asserted, 'represent in themselves (as in a lively image) the example of their Lord'.[185] Nature, the author continued, whether in the form of the sun, in a mineral such as gold, or in the kingdom of the bees displayed 'some show or similitude of royalty' to manifest that royalty was itself natural and to teach that because Nature 'hath given a certain mark . . . of royalty', men should take instruction from the natural world, the best tutor, on 'how to yield obedience'.[186] The beehive, in which those that acted against their queen died, offered an exemplum of Nature's preference for 'unity ... of divers and contrary members'.[187] Appearing shortly after the creation of the world, monarchs were the preservers of that 'harmony, peace and mutual concord' of Nature and so constituted 'the most excellent' government.[188] Though the dedication to the translation of the *History* praised royal marriage, it was clearly an apologia for and representation of Elizabeth's monarchy as well as kingship in general as 'the best approved . . . of all'.[189]

Bishop John Bridges's *The Supremacy of Christian Princes over All Persons throughout their Dominions* (1573) was the first of several defences of Elizabeth's supremacy the bishop penned and was dedicated to the queen and published with a large royal arms.[190] Over almost 800 pages, Bridges countered the arguments against the royal supremacy and pressed unfailing obedience to the queen in matters ecclesiastical. The next year Geoffrey Fenton's translation of *A Form of Christian Policy*, dedicated to Sir William Cecil, demonstrated how kings had been 'raised to a state of divine honour by the which they have the title of Gods'.[191] Though the author had his own agenda – he called for the better provision of preachers and other puritan reforms – the *Form of Christian Policy* powerfully argued for the 'one consent of will and opinion' in the commonweal and the absolute obedience to divine magistrates in terms that echoed Elizabeth herself.[192] In *The Glass of Government*, published with licence in 1575, George Gascoigne made the same case in a play.[193] Announcing in the preface that the plot of his whole tragicomedy centred on the axiom 'obey the king for his authority is from above', Gascoigne's drama taught, through the character of the schoolmaster Gnomaticus, that 'a kingdom is a thing compared to the imitation of God's power' and that the prince was 'to be honoured as the lieutenant of God here upon earth'.[194]

This emphasis on the divinity of kingship escalated in the second half of Elizabeth's reign. *A Brief Discourse of Royal Monarchy as ... the Best Commonweal*, published in 1581 by Charles Merbury, described as 'a defence of absolute government', elevated praise of monarchy to new heights.[195] 'As,' the book opened, 'there is nothing more joyful unto all living creatures than to see the light and shining of the gladsome sun, so there is nothing more joyful unto good subjects than to behold the glory and majesty of their sovereign prince.'[196] Contemning popular forms of government as 'always in confusion', and lauding hereditary kingship as the only sure foundation of order, Merbury rejected any notion that monarchs might be accountable to parliaments as 'prejudicial' to the people and the realm.[197] 'Our prince,' he concluded, 'is the image of God on earth and ... is not to acknowledge any greater than himself.'[198] A licence from the Bishop of London's licenser, a dedication to Elizabeth and a declaration that the work was written 'in dutiful reverence of her majesty's most princely highness', made Merbury's treatise not just an apologia for absolute monarchy but a paean to Elizabeth's rule.[199] Though his was no defence of absolutism (which he regarded as a corruption of monarchy) and though he accorded a far greater role to parliaments, Sir Thomas Smith's famous *De republica anglorum*, an analysis of the English constitution and polity, decreed: 'the prince is the life, the head and the authority of all things that be done in the realm of England' and 'to no prince is done more honour and reverence than to the king and queen of England', and now especially 'the most virtuous and noble Queen Elizabeth'.[200]

The exaltation of monarchy began also to be a theme of the fashionable heraldic and chivalric literature of the second half of the sixteenth century. John Ferne's *Blazon of Gentry* (1586), for example, was an influential instruction manual which placed monarchy at the centre of the whole signifying system of heraldry.[201] 'The king,' he reminded his gentry readers, 'is a person of majesty, a word that signifieth much more than either the terms of honour or dignity can express. For majesty is defined to be a sacred authority on earth . . . next to the supernatural and heavenly power of God.'[202] Accordingly, he continued, 'the king being a sacred and holy function ordained of God for the government of the people in justice and concord and the abandoning of evil from amongst them', he was entitled 'so highly to be honoured in the hearts and voices of all the subjects'.[203] Particularizing his theme, Ferne, who was later appointed deputy secretary to the Council of the North, noted the imperial regimen of England's Elizabeth and proclaimed: 'she is of God . . . her power is from Christ'.[204]

During the closing years of Elizabeth's reign, when the succession was still in doubt, the divinity and authority of kings were confidently asserted by several apologists. In 1600 the Oxford Welshman Thomas Floyd, responding to the republican ideas that were beginning to circulate in the 1590s, in *The Picture of a Perfect Commonwealth* posited that there could be no ordered society without a monarch.[205] Arguing the inconstancy and illegitimacy of any other form of government, Floyd described the prince as 'assigned to us as a perfect calm of permanent festivity'.[206] 'In a monarchy,' he claimed with more idealism than observation of recent experience, 'men are ignorant of quarrels'; accordingly obedience was not a burden but 'true felicity', and that which 'formeth peace [and] establisheth commonwealths'.[207] While, quite conventionally, condemning tyrants and prescribing the qualities of the best princes, Floyd presented the virtuous monarch as the only salvation for the people.[208] In *Reason's Monarchy*, the former law student Robert Mason wrote to render kingship part of the physiology and psychology of Everyman.[209] Instructing readers on the need to suppress the 'rebellious passions' that were the signs of a corrupted nature and which threatened their very humanity, Mason taught them to regulate these passions by that reason with which God had endowed men at creation.[210] Not only did reason teach subjects their duty of obedience, but Mason described it in the gendered language of Elizabethan monarchy. Reason, he instructed, 'as the true princess and queen bears the regal and monarchical place'.[211] 'Reason is the queen,' he added, and passions should be subject.[212] If such language did not make the application to Elizabeth herself clear enough, references to Diana (with whom the queen was frequently compared) surely did.[213] If obedience to reason was the fulfilment of self, then, Mason argued, reason led subjects to obey that embodiment of rationality,

Elizabeth – 'a representation of the majesty . . . of God' – whom all were to follow with a faithful heart.[214]

Such exaltations of monarchy emerged not only from the uncertainties over the succession but also from periods of crisis, uprising and revolt. During Elizabeth's reign, complementing the official homilies on obedience, a host of writers, elite and popular, discoursed on the evils of resistance and the importance of obedience, forming a chorus which may have been more important than historians have appreciated in sustaining Elizabeth's rule. *A Godly Ditty* for the preservation of the queen and country, published by John Awdelay in 1569, to the tune of the 137th psalm, urged all his countrymen to be on guard against 'rebels and traytours' to (and the coupling is important) the nation and 'our queen anointed'.[215] The next year, the rising of the northern earls, the first rebellion against Elizabeth as queen, initiated a flurry of denunciations of resistance and calls to obedience. The reprinting in 1569 of John Cheke's *The Hurt of Sedition: How Grievous it is to a Comonwealth* (first published in 1549) asserted for the new Deborah, who had succeeded to the godly rule of England's Josiah, the need to obey sovereign magistrates appointed by God's ordinance.[216] Thomas Norton published a more local and particular address *To the Queen's Majesty's Poor Deceived Subjects of the North Country*, who had been drawn into rebellion by the earls of Northumberland and Westmorland.[217] Warning the rebels that they had forfeited their right to be Christian Englishmen, Norton counselled them not to be duped by the false claims of men of little credit, but to embrace God and obey 'our most dear mother, nurse and protector', the queen.[218] 'Truth, conscience and zeal for our souls', he added, had led Elizabeth to change the religion of the realm and her care had secured peace, wealth and good government for her people.[219] Norton prayed and urged others to pray that God secure her and confound her enemies.[220] A ballad celebrating the defeat of the rebels popularized the same message. The nobles, the ballad taught, who rose in the name of the Virgin Mary were in fact little more than devourers of the people; they served the pope, not the queen and nation. In simple rhymes which firmly connected Elizabeth to the Protestant cause, the broadside (which was probably intended for display and communal singing) urged trust in God:

> To whom still daily let us praye
> Our noble Queene to sende,
> A prosperous Raigne both night and day,
> From her foes to defende.[221]

Another ballad of the same year 'against rebellious and false rumours' went even futher in condemning resistance.[222] Anticipating Elizabeth's translation of Plutarch's essay on curiosity, Thomas Bette's ballad excoriated rumour-mongers and commanded all 'not to meddle of Princes actes', less 'murmuring spite' foster uprisings. John Barker's *Plagues of Northumberland* denounced the northern counties where ignorance of God's word had led inhabitants to rise against his appointed magistrate. Singing how 'that countre is in full sore plight/ That doth against their prince contend', the ballad, 'to the tune of Appelles', closed:

> Now let us praye as we are bound,
> All for our Queenes hyghe maieste
> That shee her enemies may confound,
> And all that to Rebelles agre.[223]

Thomas Churchyard developed a more nationalistic theme in his *Discourse of Rebellion* which appeared in 1570.[224] Predicting that God would punish all rebels with the scaffold, and divided nations with the plague, his popular verse pamphlet poured shame on any who joined rebels against 'a rightful crown' and God's 'chosen and elect'.[225] And rallying the people 'to serve a mayden quene', he promised them that 'if that you sticke together as you ought/ This lyttle yle, may set the world at nought'.[226] Another song echoed the patriotic strain. It was, the song explained, the example of other realms that had taught England rebellion but such was not the course for 'true subjects' of England to emulate. William Kirkham proclaimed in *Joyful News*:

> . . . that we maye all in this Englysh Nation
> Be true to God, the Queene and the Crowne.[227]

In *A Friendly Larum or Faithful Warning to True Hearted Subjects*, the puritan John Phillips, after surveying the cruel acts of popish wolves, as he described them, in France and Scotland, characterized the late Catholic English rebels as men who sought only the 'ruin and spoil of their natural nurse and country'.[228] 'Where are your English hearts become?' he asked the disaffected: 'regard ye not your nourse,/ your native soyle and land'?[229] If civil war were not to ravage England as it had France, Phillips admonished, all needed to unite in 'obedience to our queene'.[230]

Though these denunciations of rebellion and appeals for loyal obedience voiced powerful support for Elizabeth at a critical juncture and figured her as the leader and embodiment of an elect nation, they deployed a much more virulent anti-papal rhetoric than the queen's own declarations against the rebels, such as that reported by the Recorder in the Guildhall to the citizens of London in October 1571.[231] The outpouring of loyalty in popular songs and pamphlets after the 1569 rising not only represented Elizabeth as queen of a chosen Protestant realm, it virtually represented Catholics as un-English and threatened to banish them to a kind of internal exile. In other words, a decade after she ascended the throne, others, as well as the queen, were directing the representation of Elizabeth and at times were sharpening divisions which she had endeavoured to play down.[232] And events after 1569 served only to accentuate the divisions and to colour the image of the queen more obviously in Protestant hues. The pope's excommunication of Elizabeth in 1570 and the Duke of Norfolk's involvement in a plot to put Mary, Queen of Scots on the English throne further marked Catholicism as treason and, by corollary, rendered loyalty and obedience Protestant virtues. In *The Decay of the Duke*, even the popular ballad writer William Elderton sang a godly refrain, while calling upon all to 'honour and praise' 'our queen and our country'.[233] Renewed plotting against Elizabeth I in the 1580s, notably Babington's conspiracy to assassinate her, stimulated a further wave of works condemning treason and also representing Elizabeth as protected and chosen by a (distinctly Protestant) God. Soon after the execution of the traitors, in September 1586, the printer and ballad writer Thomas Nelson published *A Short Discourse Expressing the Substance of All the Late Pretended Treasons*, with 'a godly prayer to her majesty' that the Lord preserve her from her foes.[234] Uneasily acknowledging the 'wild conspiracies' that seemed to follow one after another, Nelson still assured himself and the nation:

No Rebelles power can her displace, God will defend her still
True subjects all will lose their lives, ere Traytors have their will.[235]

William Kempe's *Dutiful Invective against the Most Heinous Treasons of Ballard and Babington* was offered as a new year's gift to England and the queen in 1587.[236] Cursing those that 'go about to overthrow the living Lord's anointed', and pointing an accusing finger directly at Mary, Queen of Scots, Kempe praised 'our sovereign queen' dear to God and prayed 'that . . . a perfect love and duty may take place towards this peerless prince'.[237] The lawyer Richard Crompton's *Short Declaration of the End of Traitors and False Conspirators*, published after his address to the quarter sessions in Staffordshire, evidenced how closely elite and popular sentiments now ran in connecting queen, nation and godly religious allegiances.[238] God, Crompton told his auditors and readers, had granted the realm both the light of the gospel and a godly queen, 'not a foreigner but one of our nation'.[239] Acting against God's will, rebels could expect only a wretched end, for 'the duty of the subject is always to be obedient'.[240] Celebrating (doubtless more than Elizabeth herself was comfortable about) with the people their 'joy' at the execution of Mary, Crompton hoped for the long and peaceful reign of a queen who took such good care of her subjects.[241]

Crompton got his wish. For all the rumours of conspiracy, after Babington's plot, Elizabeth faced no major Catholic uprising or coup. While the quiescence of her Catholic subjects is a complex story and one disputed by historians, there can be little doubt that the loyalty shown by English subjects owed much to a culture of obedience which had been fashioned, over the Tudor decades, by elite and popular apologias for monarchy. Elizabeth may not always have approved of the stridency with which some heralded her as a champion of godly courses – not least because such rhetoric made appeasement of English Catholics all the more difficult. But those who lauded the benefits of strong monarchical government and praised the rule of a woman specifically also reinforced the queen's own self-presentation and helped to strengthen those lovely bonds of affection which Elizabeth worked so hard to establish with subjects.

More than for any other early modern ruler, the representation of Elizabeth was personal, familiar and even intimate. As she ascended the throne in 1558, the composer (and future Gentleman of the Chapel Royal) William Birch, in a two-part song dialogue between queen and nation, called on 'sweet Bessy' to come over to her lover England who 'am thine both with mind and heart'.[242] For all the cultural proscriptions against female rule, Elizabeth's sex licensed a discourse of friendship and love which, beyond the circles of the court, helped to forge bonds between subjects and sovereign. Aided by her experience of incarceration and narrow escape from death as princess, Elizabeth's sex made her a figure to be protected. And it made her, more than her father, the personification of a sense of belonging (and duty) to nation. The dialogue between two simple soldiers praising Elizabeth which was staged in *The Castle, or Picture of Policy* replicated a voluminous literature of cheap print which circulated representations of Elizabeth as Judith, 'loving prince', the 'star of women'.[243] Reaffirmed by the queen's providential triumph over domestic conspiracies and foreign threats, popular affection for the queen rose to unprecedented heights and ultimately led to the annual commemoration of her coronation which, according to Camden, began about 1570.[244] In *The Blessedness of Britain, or A Celebration of the Queen's Holy Day* (1587), the Denbighshire poet Maurice Kyffin, calling on all to 'adore November's sacred seventeenth day', lauded Elizabeth's thirty years of rule.[245] Praising her justice, temperance and piety, her strengthening of the realm at home and abroad, Kyffin represented her as a second sun which had dispelled the clouds, the 'heir apparent to the Heav'nly Crowne'.[246] His eulogy, if extravagant, was not untypical. After the Armada especially, popular adulation of Elizabeth rose to a crescendo; in Henry Constable's words, 'your praises round about the world is blowne'.[247] Though the disenchantment that followed economic hardship and factional squabbles found some echoes even in panegyrics, they hardly tarnished the representation of Elizabeth as the godly Susannah, the mother of the nation, the object of popular devotion as well as the Petrarchan mistress of courtly verse.[248] Edward Hake's prayer that God would 'Unite both Prince and People's harts/ with love and zeale entire' was, it would seem, granted.[249] The representation of Elizabeth, as well as officially directed and encouraged, was also a new, spontaneous and genuinely popular phenomenon. As we shall see, however, while such popularity endowed Elizabeth herself as well as the Tudor dynasty and the monarchy with enhanced authority, it also signalled and enabled an increased involvement of the people in affairs of state and the business of kings and queens.

The bond between Elizabeth, the nation and the people was also forged by, as well as expressed in, a new fascination with the English past and the histories of kings. From the later sixteenth century antiquarian treatises, popular chronicles and histories, published, staged and sung, represented England as a special country, the Tudors as a chosen dynasty, and Elizabeth as a sacred and glorious queen.[250] As with other texts representing the queen, histories represented the regime very much as a godly rule – as Protestant – and told a story of the nation's emancipation from popish tyranny. As early as 1562, a new edition of Richard Grafton's *Chronicle*, for example, in its dedicatory preface to Robert Dudley, the queen's favourite and a leader of the godly, mapped the history of the nation as a providential narrative, culminating in God's relieving England with 'the most wise and godly government of our most gracious sovereign lady whom he hath through infinite dangers preserved to defend us'.[251] Contrasting Mary Tudor's 'severity and shedding of much innocent blood' with the 'clemency' of Elizabeth, the abridgement of the chronicle closed with a prayer for the queen than whom England had never had 'a more worthy governor'.[252] Later editions of Grafton, published 'cum privilegio regiae maiestatis', affirmed the legitimacy of the Tudor dynasty, lauded Henry VIII, and ended with the death of Mary and her sister Elizabeth's succession which 'made a marvellous alteration in this realm'.[253] By the time of the publication of the 1572 edition, readers of Grafton's *Chronicle* were instructed that Mary's reign was 'condemned almost of all' and were given accounts of the gracious prayers, speeches and actions of the godly Elizabeth who had already 'showed herself a most noble and honourable princess to the people'.[254] In Grafton's *Chronicle*, as in Holinshed's, the British myth of a realm founded by King Brutus and evangelized in the time of Christ by Joseph of Arimathea was joined with a representation of Elizabeth as the chosen ruler and of her reign as the fulfilment of England's historical destiny. Hugh Lloyd's 1584 *History of . . . Wales*, dedicated to Sir Philip Sidney, similarly closed with praise of an Elizabeth who ruled a civilized and peaceful nation.[255] And in 1585, a history of the *Valiant Acts and Victorious Battles of the English Nation* (despite its title) ended with celebration of the 'peaceable and quiet state of England under the blessed government of the most excellent and virtuous princess Elizabeth'.[256] Elizabeth, in other words, had brought about an end to centuries of struggle and fulfilled England's historic destiny. In a dedicatory epistle to the queen, the author, lauding the 'goddess' and 'renowned nymph of Britaine land', prophesied that 'under a mayden Queene/ Renowned England through the world is bright blazed to be seene'.[257]

From the foundation of the Society of Antiquaries, probably about 1586, various antiquarian treatises on English institutions and counties, such as William Lambarde's *Perambulation of Kent*, promoted a strong English nationalism and posited the monarchy as the embodiment of nation and Elizabeth as its personification.[258] The founders of the Society, William Camden and Sir Robert Cotton, planned a full involvement of the queen in establishing a national library and academy of antiquarian and historical studies; and both, throughout their lives, held up Elizabeth as a model of good monarchical government.[259] In a history of Henry VII, the author, perhaps a friend of Cotton, John Hayward, directed his narrative to praise of Elizabeth (Henry's granddaughter), 'the world's diamond'.[260] In a dedicatory preface to the 'phoenix rare', the author praised Elizabeth whom God had 'assigned to be ruler' as a pattern for princes who did 'shine to the commonwealth'.[261] The queen marked the end, the author put it the 'period', of English history – its fulfilment of a providential design.[262]

As well as British chronicles and antiquities, the new humanist histories and lives presented Elizabeth as the personification of the ancient virtues. In his historical compilation of the ancient triumphs of Greece and Rome, for example, Ludovick Lloyd claimed that Elizabeth's succession had been the ultimate triumph that had eclipsed all others: 'what shall we write further of triumphs,' he asked; for 'our day began the seventh of September, the most happy and blessed day of Queen Elizabeth's nativity, of whom we have triumphed 20295 days', outshining those of Xerxes and Alexander.[263] As the personification of virtue, justice and truth, Elizabeth, Lloyd told readers, 'excelled all her predecessors', from antiquity to recent times.[264] In his continuation of Tacitus's history, Henry Savile, for all his critique of corrupt and tyrannous governments, praised Elizabeth and advised readers that, if they contrasted their lot with that of the people of Tacitus's Rome, they could not but 'reverence their own wise, just and excellent prince' and 'thank God for her under whom England enjoys as many benefits as ever Rome did suffer miseries'.[265] While the English edition of Giovanni Botero's *Observations* on the lives of Alexander, Caesar and Scipio placed Elizabeth at the head of a pantheon of classical heroes, Geoffrey Fenton's English translation of *The History of Guicciardini*, dedicated to Elizabeth, compared the queen's rule of peace and clemency to the great age of Augustus.[266] Where chronicles described her as the fulfilment of British destiny, the humanist histories, whatever their exposure of the dark arts of politics in the past, praised the queen and depicted Elizabeth's rule as the height of civilized governance.

The closing years of Elizabeth's reign were beset with problems and anxieties which left their mark on the history books too. John Speed's *Description of the Civil Wars of England*, nervous of even bringing civil conflict back to 'remembrance', took the form of a narrative map of all the civil broils since the Conquest, but carried a large royal arms and paean to Elizabeth.[267] In a different genre, Thomas Deloney's popular ballad collection of *Strange Histories of Kings*, with its emphasis on the vagaries of royal fortunes and the sudden deaths of princes, probably spoke to mounting popular anxieties about the succession.[268] As has been argued and as we shall see, classical histories and historical plays were published, staged and read as critiques of royal government, some would say even as apologias for republics.[269] Yet, in the main, the histories published under Elizabeth, classical and British, elite and popular, represented the queen as godly, virtuous and magnificent, as monarch of a golden age who had steered England to its historical and providential destiny. As such, they fulfilled what the Clerk of the Ordnance, William Painter, emulating Livy, argued was the function of histories:

> For like as the outward show of princes' palaces ... be decked and garnished with sumptuous hangings and costly arras of [re]splendent show, ... even so [in histories] there be at large recorded the princely and glorious gests [of rulers] represented with more ... gorgeous sight than tapestry or arras work.[270]

No less than magnificent structures, histories, and indeed myriad other writings and words (both the queen's own and others') represented Elizabeth to her subjects as Virgin Queen, God's handmaid, model princess and fulfilment of national destiny. More than for any earlier ruler, the expansion of print and a new burgeoning market for books enabled publication and dissemination of the queen as the centre and focus of the commonwealth and the nation. But words were not all. As the fitly named Painter's metaphor (and the large royal arms facing his title page) remind us, a successful ruler had also to be splendidly adorned and displayed as a 'gorgeous sight'. We must turn to the visual representations of Elizabeth which constructed her as the English icon.

CHAPTER 10

'THE PORTRAIT AND PICTURE OF THE QUEEN'S MAJESTY'

I

If a large increase in print publication and the market for print was one major change affecting the representation of authority, another, less heralded development transformed the nature and performance of the royal image. For all the position of the English court at the forefront of humanist learning, in the visual arts sixteenth-century England lagged far behind its continental neighbours. At the beginning of the century there were no native artists of note, so when Henry VIII felt the need to vie with Francis I in publicizing his image on the European stage and, especially after the break from Rome, to his subjects at home, he was forced to attract to royal service a foreign portraitist, Hans Holbein. For most of the century (as we have seen), foreign artists and continental styles dominated English portraiture.

Slowly, however, the situation changed. From the second decade of her reign, despite her continuing employment of foreign artists, Elizabeth patronized, as her principal portraitist, the first English artist to hold such a position – Nicholas Hilliard. Perhaps more importantly, in the later part of the century we discern a slowly developing interest in the visual arts in England, throughout the culture and across the boundaries of class and literacy. This is a development which still awaits exploration and the reasons for it remain unclear. At the level of the court and aristocracy, of course, exposure to the works of great continental artists may have stimulated interest and educated Englishmen, while, at the popular level, the proliferation of woodcuts in imported Lutheran literature appears to have fostered a fashion for illustration of cheap print.[1] For the educated, the classics also provided a stimulus to thinking about the role of the visual arts in society and government, in particular their relation to that other art of representation, poetry.[2] The classical doctrine of 'ut pictura poesis' was a theme of renewed discussion among the Italian humanists and such discussion clearly informed English literary discourse, notably Philip Sidney's *Apology for Poetry* (1595).[3] Rhetorical treatises, the core of the humanist school curriculum, discussed and deployed images as illustrations of the arts of eloquence; and, from the mid-sixteenth century, English rhetorical manuals emphasized pictures as vital means of communication, along with the need for a figurative language which drew on visual as well as verbal forms.[4] It has also been fruitfully suggested that the new Platonism, fashionable in the academies of the late sixteenth century, elevated the status of the artist (hitherto largely regarded as an artisan) as one who could capture the essence or Idea of matter: as a representer, that is, of Nature and the divine.[5]

Drawing on such developments and ideas, what brought them to the centre of English aristocratic and gentry life was heraldry. A response in part to the rise and fall of aristocratic families, the social mobility that was a consequence of the dissolution of the monasteries, and the need of new families to establish pedigree, heraldry became something of an obsession in Elizabethan England and heraldic books among the bestsellers of the age.[6] Heraldry developed from its feudal origins into an elaborate signifying system in which colours, shapes, animals and objects represented virtues and values as well as families. In his detailed treatment, *The Blazon of Gentry*, John Ferne referred his readers to the classical origins of heraldry in the works of Isodore and Pliny and, after discussing the visual arts in relation to oratory, proceeded to explain what he called the 'signification' of heraldry.[7] Beginning with the coronation regalia and jewels, Ferne explained how each of the artefacts and precious stones was intended to remind the ruler of duties and of virtues to be cultivated: sapphire instructing him to continence, or the emerald to justice, for example.[8] Royal arms, Ferne explained, represented royal authority to the extent that 'if the prince should grant to another the bearing of his arms . . . his royal dignity might be deceased'.[9] In the armorial system, identity and authority were constituted through, as well as displayed by, arms: 'the possession of a dignity is proved by having of the ensigns thereunto belonging'.[10] Noblemen and princes, in other words, were what they blazoned. In *The Accedence of Armorie*, the heraldic writer Gerard Legh further explained the meaning of signs and colours and their relationship to rank and authority.[11] Pure gold, he instructed, was reserved to kings in emulation of the sun and because it was a gift presented to Christ; azure similarly because it announced 'the bearer to be of godly disposition'.[12] Entering further into the 'significations', Legh progressed from colours to the figures and partitions on escutcheons, to the meanings conveyed by particular beasts and flowers.[13] Heraldic books such as these developed not just an interest in visual significations, but fashioned an educated interpretative community, fully able to read visual symbols as encodings of values and virtues and of privilege and power.[14]

The (related) late sixteenth-century fashion for emblem books further educated a readership, and a public beyond the gentry, in the significations of visual forms. A combination of motto, picture and epigram, often derived from heraldic devices, emblems were – literally as well as metaphorically – woven and etched into the material culture of the Renaissance: in buildings and tapestries, glass, plate, clothes and jewels.[15] Increasingly, too, printers' devices took the form of emblems and, initially on the continent, books of emblems poured from the presses in hundreds, circulating and explicating these representations of office and craft (as well as gentility) and of moral codes and personal convictions. In Elizabeth's reign, this extensive literature became well known in England and stimulated a fashion for English emblem books such as Geoffrey Whitney's bestselling *A Choice of Emblems*, published in 1586.[16] Drawing on leading continental sources, especially Alciati, Junius and La Perrière, Whitney reproduced and interpreted emblems and was followed by several others in the decades that ensued.[17] Dedicating his work to the Earl of Leicester, Whitney described the 248 emblems he included as published so that 'by the office of the eye and the ear the mind may reap double delight through wholesome precepts'.[18] The frequent reproduction of emblems and the habit of copying them, often with commentary from other texts, into commonplace books, suggests that emblems became texts of English pedagogy and self-fashioning.

Though there has been an understandable tendency to discuss heraldic works and emblem books as elite texts, we should not underestimate their reach into popular culture. Ferne's *Blazon of Gentry*, after all, staged a dialogue among a knight, a lawyer, a divine and a 'ploughman' who keenly enquired after the armorial arts. Similarly Legh's *Accedence*, the work of an apprentice draper, announced itself as an elementary treatise and took the form of an instructional dialogue which appears to have been intended for a broad audience. Emblems also had their popular forms and publications, especially in the growing literature on fables, images of the dance of death and bestial representations of vices and virtues which prolifically illustrated popular pamphlets, broadsides and ballads.[19] Not only was early modern popular culture, as evangelical preachers often complained, steeped in the visual, the populace was not unlearned in the performances of visuals as significations of values, ideology and power.

Whatever, then, the social and cultural developments which stimulated the change, there can be little doubt that late sixteenth-century England was both a more visual culture and one more self-consciously engaged with visual signification and representation. It was no mere coincidence that it was Elizabeth's reign which produced the first English treatises on painting, including Hilliard's *The Art of Limning*, which, along with more theoretical reflections, offered a down-to-earth, pragmatic, 'how-to' guide for what was, we must presume, a growing number of amateur artists.[20] Later in the reign, Richard Haydocke's translation of Pietro Lomazzo's tract *Concerning the Arts of Curious Painting, Carving, Building* commented directly on a new generation of nobles who had excellently furnished their galleries with Italian and German masters, while lamenting a continuing ignorance of the arts.[21] Preceding the technical sections on light and perspective, Lomazzo's treatise opened with a discussion of art as the imitator of the divine order and proportion of uncorrupted Nature and as the representer of figures of authority and 'the decorum which truly belongs to them'.[22] For both Lomazzo and his English translator, the visual arts were concerned not only with moral values and virtues but with 'sacred majesty'.[23]

Lomazzo compared painting with writing, which he described as 'nothing else but a picture of white and black'.[24] In late sixteenth-century England, nothing more evidences the greater prominence of the visual arts, and a belief in the symbiosis of word and image, than the huge growth in illustrations to books. Though England was slow to nurture native engravers, by the second half of Elizabeth's reign, copperplate engravings, as well as woodcuts, introduced and illustrated a wide range of books and were also being published as single sheets.[25] Engraved title pages became increasingly common and elaborate and bibles, histories and travel books began to be illustrated with more maps, tables and pictures. Thomas Hariot's *Brief and True Report of the New Found Land of Virginia* provides a (literally) spectacular example of this trend, with its elaborately engraved title page depicting the Indian god Kivvasa, and extensive copperplates illustrating new world feasts and fashions, ceremonies and cities, which he compared to those of the Picts of ancient Briton.[26] As in our own age of multi-media and the internet graphic, in Elizabethan England the word was read, interpreted and imagined in a visual context and a newly self-conscious visual culture.

The visual culture of Elizabethan England was materially bound up with the forms of authority and power. It was the most expensive and authoritative folio books which bore elaborate engraved illustrations and kings who adorned the title pages or frontispieces of books.[27] Because the arts represented ideas of virtue, order and proportion, they frequently figured princes who, the ideal held, personified those attributes. Yet, while the visual arts were concerned with the representation of authority, we need to appreciate that the reverse was also true. That is, it seems that the new focus on authority and power gave an impetus to, and stimulated a market for, the arts of representation. Study of one of the largest collections of engraved British portraits reveals a large rise towards the end of the sixteenth century in the number of images of monarchs and other figures of prominence and power.[28] Evidently the reproduction of portraits of figures of authority became a viable commercial proposition. In 1601, for example, *A View of All the Right Honourable the Lord Mayors of this*

Honourable City of London published engravings of each of the forty-three mayors of the Elizabethan capital, with brief notes on their lives and tenure of office.[29] Civic pride, a sense of civic history and the increasingly elaborate Lord Mayors' shows, together with a greater interest in visual identity, evidently stimulated a desire to see magisterial authority personified and portrayed. The same was true of the monarchy. The Tudors' emphasis, following the Reformation, on the monarch as God's lieutenant and as the embodiment of the commonweal and nation personalized authority, transmuting the monarch from feudal overlord to national sovereign and forging, I have suggested, a new psychology of power and subjectivity. Moreover, the Tudor emphasis on representation, on the dissemination of the royal image, appears to have stimulated a desire to see, indeed to possess, that image. T.T's *Book Containing the True Portraiture of the Countenances and Attires of the Kings of England*, published in octavo in 1597, was the first book of its kind and marked an important departure.[30] The book consisted of one-page oval engravings, carefully drawn, of all the rulers of England from William the Conqueror to Queen Elizabeth, with only a very brief report of the principal events of each reign. The book, which began something of a trend (several of the images were used again in the printer Henry Holland's influential *Braziliologia*, published in 1618), closed with a homage to Elizabeth, 'a prince adorned with all good literature both holy and humane, a nourisher of peace both at home and abroad'.[31] The image of the queen as well as the monarchy had become a widely published text, and even a commodity.

T.T's – probably the antiquary Thomas Talbot's – collection of royal portraits was an important text of an English culture which, foreign envoys often lamented, was becoming more preoccupied with 'outward appearances' than with substance and was a fitting tribute to a queen who did so much to make the royal image a focus and centre of attention.[32] Though, as ever, parsimonious in her patronage of artists and the arts, Elizabeth had a strong sense of the importance of the visual, especially in relation to princes. In negotiations over her prospective marriage to the duc d'Alençon, the queen placed great importance on seeing his 'visage', as much the outward manifestation of his character as of his attractiveness.[33] In a proclamation of 1560 against the destruction of church monuments, the queen expressed grave concern at the 'extinguishing of the honourable and good memory of sundry virtuous and noble persons', especially kings, and ordered the repair of monuments, statues and glass windows on which they had been represented.[34] Later she ordered pictures of the Babington plotters – early modern 'wanted' posters – to be displayed around London, not only to facilitate their apprehension, but also as images of evil.[35] For Elizabeth held strongly to the view that art should convey the inner qualities: 'it is', she told Alençon, 'for a prince always to resemble himself', and the arts of representation lay in capturing the inner mind as well as the external countenance.[36] As

39 Henry VIII, in T. T.'s *A Booke, Containing the True Portraiture of the Countenances and Attires of the Kings of England.*

she had written to her brother Edward VI, when sending him the portrait of her he had requested, her main wish and hope was that 'the inward good mind . . . might as well be declared as the outward face and countenance'.[37]

We encountered a portrait of Princess Elizabeth as part of the dynastic canvas known as *The Family of Henry VIII*, painted in the 1540s, in which Henry's second daughter, by Anne Boleyn, was placed on the right of the canvas, outside the central group of king, queen and male heir.[38] The canvas accurately represented Elizabeth's position as an unlikely successor, as she was third in line to the throne which was the due inheritance of Edward, the son whom Henry had long awaited and had been divorced twice in order to secure. The picture Elizabeth referred to in her letter to Edward seems likely to be the first individual portrait we know of the princess, aged, judging by the date of the letter, fourteen. The same size as the portrait of Edward attributed to Scrots, the painting of Elizabeth may have been intended as a companion piece.[39] Wearing a dress of crimson cloth of gold with elaborate sleeves, a pendant jewel and a pearl necklace, Elizabeth stands three-quarter length, both hands holding at her waist (where, we recall Edward grasped his dagger) a small book, probably a devotional manual, into which she inserts a slender finger, marking a place.[40] On a table to Elizabeth's right there lies open a folio volume. The princess's pose of serious contemplation bears out the hope she expressed in her letter that her portrait might convey the steadfast mind rather than mere outward appearance. The prominence and arrangement of the books are important. While the octavo held to her lap (conventional in female portraits with books of devotion) signified the princess's sex, gender and piety, the folio on a desk associated her with a more masculine world of learning – indeed, as its are pages open, her engagement with learning. Elizabeth was already renowned as a student of the classics and had already, as

40 Elizabeth I when princess, c. 1546.

an act of learning as well as piety, presented her stepmother with her translation of Margaret of Navarre's *Miroir de l'âme pécheresse*. In her letter to her brother, Elizabeth drew attention to her learning when she quoted an adage of Horace that, she said, she had taken to heart.[41] We do not know who commissioned the portrait of the princess in 1549. But the correspondence suggests that Elizabeth had much to do with it and that it may have represented her as she wished: as studious, pious and contemplative, as one who had, as Horace had taught her, risen above fortune and who, though a girl, was reading and learning to take her part in an active, masculine world.[42]

II

From her accession to the throne in 1558, Elizabeth left little doubt about her grasp of the politics of her portrayal. In the first place, the new queen quickly disposed of the services of Hans Eworth, who had executed a series of portraits for Mary and had succeeded to Scrots's place as semi-official artist to the court. Roy Strong has suggested that, though Eworth's personal religious beliefs are not known, his proximity to powerful Catholic families, such as the Norfolks and Lord Montagu, may have put him out of favour; or it may be that, since Eworth continued to work for the Office of the Revels, Elizabeth simply did not appreciate his style as a portrait artist.[43] Whatever the reasons for it, the initial consequences of parting with Eworth were a series of poor early portraits of the queen, some almost losing her person amid the coronation robes and regalia, others of her looking stiff, awkward and out of proportion.[44] Whatever their quality, however, these 'mechanical workshop productions' were copied and purchased by nobles, gentry families and corporations anxious for an image of the new queen.[45] It was becoming ever more apparent that the visual image of monarchy would be a principal medium of royal representation beyond the narrow confines of court and palace.

Despite their popularity, there is evidence of the queen's discontent with these early portraits. Dated December 1563, a draft proclamation in Secretary William Cecil's hand is entitled 'draft of a proclamation for prohibiting all persons drawing Queen Elizabeth's picture until such time as a pattern for that purpose hath been drawn from the life by some skilled painter by her majesty's order'.[46] Revealingly acknowledging (what we have suggested was emerging) 'the natural desires that all sorts of subjects and people, both noble and mean', had 'to procure the portrait and picture of the Queen's majesty', the proclamation judged it 'evidently seen that hitherto none hath sufficiently expressed the natural representation of her majesty's person, favour or grace, but that most have so far erred therein as thereof daily are heard complaints among her loving subjects'. Implying that the queen had not hitherto sat for her portrait to any appointed artist, the Council proposed as a remedy that 'some special commission painter' might be appointed 'to take the natural representation of her majesty' and that all other portraits and artists be prohibited until an approved template became available. Indeed, until such a satisfactory prototype was prepared, the proclamation banned 'the showing or publication' of existing and corrupt representations. Though we are uncertain about its implementation, the draft proclamation is in so many ways revealing of both the authority and responsiveness of Tudor government and of the role of representation in displays of – and negotiations for – authority. For, while the government planned an official image to be followed, the impetus to it (and there seems to be no reason to doubt the proclamation's claim) came from the desires of the people who took 'great offence with the errors and deformities' of the early portraits. Evidently a concern for likeness and for an attractive representation of the monarch was beginning to be publicly articulated. And, in responding to it, the proclamation offers insight into how the representations of Elizabeth were constructed out of popular concerns and tastes, and circulated and adapted with the sensibilities of subjects in mind. The 1563 draft proclamation offers some evidence, in fact, that the process of representing Elizabeth, like the process of government, was one of negotiation and exchange.

The proclamation, if implemented, did not produce immediate results. A sense that Elizabeth may have been searching for a qualified artist to commission is supported by Catherine de Medici's offer to send her own court portraitist from France in 1564; but evidently no suitable candidate was found.[47] The portraits of Elizabeth which have been tentatively dated to the period 1563–7 continued to appear stiff, awkward and derivative; some are even derivative of portraits of Mary, though a recently discovered oil bust of Elizabeth figures prominently in the lower left corner a small book (perhaps the New Testament) bound in Elizabeth's signature red velvet and half opened by her thumb.[48] Though it is later, lettering (which may have replaced an earlier inscription) announced Elizabeth's understanding of the sacrament as 'what his word did make it' – a Protestant interpretation. In Strong's words, these portraits were unimpressive and 'tentative' ('as tentative as her government'), but at the end of her first decade of rule Elizabeth was certainly being presented as a pious queen who revived and embodied the word.[49]

A portrait which is dated 1569 introduces us to the first of a famous series of allegorical canvases of Elizabeth and reminds us of the extent to which, whatever the queen's desire to control her visual representation, others devised and fashioned her image. *Queen Elizabeth and the Three Goddesses*, attributed to the Flemish artist Joris Hoefnagel, depicts a reworking of the Judgment of Paris.[50] Where in the classical legend Paris had to judge which of

41 *Queen Elizabeth and the Three Goddesses.*

the three goddesses, Juno (queen of heaven), Pallas (goddess of war) and Venus (of love), merited the golden apple, and chose Venus, here all the candidates are found wanting by the queen who, rather than the prize apple, holds an orb and sceptre. As the Latin inscription on the frame explains:

> Pallas was keen of brain, Juno was queen of might,
> The rosy face of Venus was in beauty shining bright,
> Elizabeth then came.
> And, overwhelmed, Queen Juno took to flight;
> Pallas was silenced; Venus blushed for shame.[51]

As a sign that the goddesses bowed to Elizabeth's decision and authority, Pallas's quiver, Juno's sceptre and Venus's roses lay on the ground. On the left of the canvas, raised on three steps, Elizabeth (with Tudor roses on her dress) and her maids stand beside a canopy of state embroidered with the queen's arms, and beneath the Tudor arms on the frieze of the interior, with Windsor Castle visible in the background. The homage to the Tudor dynasty and compliment to a queen who has surmounted all the goddesses and virtues is obvious; and the cast of female characters flatters her sex. Roy Strong, however, rightly drew attention to the composition of the canvas which centres not the queen but Juno, also the goddess of marriage, who, as she turns away from Elizabeth, moves towards the seated Venus, beside whom Pallas also places her banner.[52] Rather than fleeing, she beckons Elizabeth to follow her, to leave her female entourage for Love. The year of the painting, 1569, presented the greatest threat to Elizabeth since her succession – the northern rebellion; rumours of a Catholic crusade against her were already circulating. Cecil and the Council were anxious about national security and pressuring Elizabeth to marry.[53] It may be, as has been hypothesized, that Cecil commissioned the portrait and presented it to Elizabeth as another invocation to the queen to marry.[54] We cannot know. But that the canvas is readable as counsel as well as compliment seems undeniable. From the beginning the image of Elizabeth was not the sole property of the queen.

A second allegorical composition, however, strongly suggests Elizabeth's own involvement in the commissioning of portraits and her keen sense of them as representation and political argument. According to an inscription at the foot, Elizabeth sent to Sir Thomas Walsingham the 'tablet' depicting the family of Henry VIII. The canvas, uncertainly attributed to Lucas de Heere, poet and painter, is often known as *An Allegory of the Tudor Succession.*[55] This group portrait (not to be confused with the earlier one), containing mythological as

42 *An Allegory of the Tudor Succession.*

well as actual figures, centres Henry VIII enthroned on a rich turkey carpet beneath a canopy and the royal arms, with the sceptre in his right hand. On Henry's right, within the colonnaded loggia, Philip II and Mary stand with the armoured figure of War in attendance on them. On our right, Prince Edward kneels to receive from his father the sword, while in front of him, in the foreground of the composition, Elizabeth stands holding the hand of Peace who tramples on a sword and shield, with, behind her, Plenty, bare breasted and carrying a cornucopia. The arrangement as well as the mythological figures point up the contrast staged between war (associated with the Catholic Mary and marriage into a foreign Habsburg dynasty) and the peace that attends Henry's Protestant children, Edward and Elizabeth. The figure of Henry here draws on the miniature of the king as Solomon and his portrayal as the bestower of the word on the title pages of the Coverdale and Great Bible; and (the painting may be intended to suggest) in Edward and Elizabeth, the word is made flesh.[56] Though Henry occupies the centre of the canvas, the left arm which hands the sword to his son and successor follows a diagonal line towards the figure of Elizabeth who dominates the foreground as heir of the best Tudor rule and champion of peace, plenty – and Protestantism.[57]

Strong has persuasively tied the gift of the portrait to the Treaty of Blois, signed by Walsingham in France in April 1572, in recognition of which the envoy was promoted to the position of Secretary of State.[58] However, for the militant Protestant Walsingham, the hope had been that the treaty with France, by the terms of which England was bound to aid her ally in the event of an invasion, might commit Elizabeth to a more active intervention in Europe, particularly in the Netherlands, on the Protestant side. Many in parliament and some in the queen's Privy Council shared his hope and views. In the allegory, by contrast, it is peace that is celebrated as the blessing of Protestant rule and Mary, though relegated to the depths of the composition, is not demonized but described in an accompanying verse as 'a zealous daughter in her kind'. In a gesture that downplays division, Queen Elizabeth (though decentred, the largest figure) is here represented then as embracing and embodying all the Tudor family, male and female, Catholic and Protestant, members. Finally a further message may be intended. Where Philip's right hand gestures to Mary, whose right arm seems nearly joined to his left, Elizabeth points to Peace whose right hand she grasps. Where, that is, Mary married into a European dynasty and brought England to war, Elizabeth is wedded to Peace and Plenty, to the good of her people, with whom she often said she was joined. The queen doubtless had particular things to say in sending this portrait to Walsingham. But the inscription bore the words: 'The Quene to Walsingham This Tablet Sent. Mark of Her Peoples and Her Own Content'. Elizabeth, as she had told her Commons by now on several occasions, was content to be, as the inscription also reiterates, 'a virgin queen'. It was for her subjects to be content with that too – with her love for them and all the abundant fruits which virgin rule and peace had brought in their train.

Shortly after the production of these allegorical canvases, the portraits of Elizabeth took on new forms which are almost certainly related to the entry of Nicholas Hilliard into the queen's service. Hilliard began executing miniatures for Elizabeth in 1572, but it was two full portraits in oils by him, painted just before his journey to France, that began a transformation of the royal image.[59] These are the paintings which are widely known as the Pelican and Phoenix portraits. They have not impressed modern critics: Strong called them 'wooden, stylised', 'awkward in pose', 'flat and two dimensional', as they are.[60] Elizabeth's face in both portraits appears as a mask; other than the delicately painted hand which holds her glove across her stomach, the queen's body is encased in a heavy embroidered gown. It is the jewels which draw our gaze. In both examples, the queen wears at her neck a carcanet, in the Phoenix Portrait also a heavy collar of jewels of a type worn by Henry VIII.[61] In the paintings she wears at her breast, respectively, a pelican and a phoenix jewel which hangs on a vertical line connecting the queen's face and hand. 'Her features just a few bare lines drawn onto a plain flesh colour ground', Elizabeth has, on these canvases, herself become a jewel, an icon.[62]

Such a shift from the drama of allegorical painting (or even from attempts to capture expression and character, as in a portrait attributed to Steven Van der Muelon), obviously reflected Hilliard's own talents as miniaturist and jeweller.[63] But Elizabeth's election of Hilliard as the artist for these half-length oils still requires explanation. As Strong and others have pointed out, the pelican and phoenix jewels *are* the meaning of these canvases and represent Elizabeth and her rule. The pelican, which in Renaissance bestiaries is depicted as sucking blood from its own breast to feed its young, symbolized Christian charity, Christ's sacrifice on the cross and, at times, proof of the possibility of virgin birth.[64] The phoenix had also been a sacred bird among the Egyptians who viewed it as a manifestation of the sun god. Legend had it that when its death drew near, the phoenix made a nest and with the force of the sun's rays burned itself to ashes from which it was reborn. In Christian tradition, it became a symbol of the resurrection and the triumph of immortality over death.[65] In the early 1570s, in the wake of the papal excommunication and Ridolfi plot to assassinate the queen, the symbolic representation of Elizabeth as triumphant over death was obviously a gesture of reassurance and defiance. The phoenix's self-generation may also have been intended to allay fears about the succession. At a time when the pressure on Elizabeth to marry Alençon was mounting, this emblem, which was to become important in her representation, may have been meant to symbolize dynastic continuity.

43 Elizabeth I: the Pelican Portrait by Nicholas Hilliard.

Perhaps, too, Protestant continuity. For the phoenix had been an emblem also of Edward VI, whose mother had died after giving birth to him. The coronation pageant for Edward had featured a phoenix descending from a mount covered with white and red roses and Camden reports that at his funeral the phoenix was displayed with the motto 'Nascitur ut alter' (may he be reborn as another).[66] Both, then, a common Renaissance emblem and a particular symbol of the Tudor dynasty, the phoenix represented hereditary kingship without commitment to marriage. The pelican's association with virgin birth may have hinted at the same idea. While representing Elizabeth as the nursing mother ready, in imitation of Christ, to sacrifice her very blood for her people, the pelican also stood as a symbol of the virginity she preferred. The painting perhaps was another answer to those councillors who pressed her to marry.

The eloquent symbolism of these two portraits may relate to what appears to us to be the virtual effacement of the queen's body. Elizabeth, we recall, had written to Edward of the need for portraits to capture the mind, the inner qualities and virtues, rather than the transient external appearance. In these two portraits, emblematized, the queen becomes attributes – of godliness, maternal care and sacrifice for her people, and constant virtue. The portraits – and surely this is not incidental – divert attention from the queen's sexual and regenerative body in its last days of fertility (Elizabeth was forty at the time of negotiation over the Alençon match) and render her the timeless, eternal mother and virgin. Like her speeches, these portraits, far from 'pedestrian', were highly personal statements at a time of extensive debate and disagreement about the queen's marriage and foreign policy, the succession and the security of the Protestant nation.

Though the iconic effacement of the royal body natural was a mode of representation used later in the reign, it by no means dominated all portraiture from the early 1570s. The so-called Darnley Portrait (named after the Earl of Darnley of Cobham Hall from whose collection it was purchased for the nation) marks another change of style in portraiture of the queen.[67] Strong has attributed the three-quarter-length canvas to Federigo Zuccaro, who was brought to England from Rome in 1574 'to serve her majesty' and her favourite, Robert Dudley, Earl of Leicester, and who certainly made preparatory sketches of them both.[68] While the attribution remains tentative, the portrait, evocative of Titian, suggests a foreign artist and the style of Elizabeth's dress corresponds to the period of Zuccaro's sojourn in England. The impression that this was regarded as a new work of note is confirmed by the portrait becoming a model for several others of the queen over the next few years.[69] On the canvas, Elizabeth stands, turned slightly to the right and wearing a gown of grey silk with fine lace ruff sleeves. At her waist hangs a jewel, with enamelled figures set with rubies and diamonds, from which hangs

44 Elizabeth I: the Darnley Portrait.

a pendant pearl.[70] The queen wears a pearl necklace which is looped to form an oval across her right breast. In her right hand she holds to her body a feather fan, while in the left she grasps, half concealed, a small box – perhaps the casket for a special jewel. On the table to Elizabeth's left, in the half darkness, we see the sceptre and crown, the first depiction of the regalia in a Tudor portrait, emphasizing Elizabeth's status as queen. Little has been written about this painting. Though Strong described the face as mask-like and iconic, others have discerned a naturalism and a pose which shows firmness and strength.[71] What is striking, however, is the prominence – and positions – of the necklace and fan, which, placed at the breast and groin, draw attention to the female sexual body of this woman who is portrayed as a queen. The pearl was regarded as representing, along with power and rank, femininity and the moon (long a symbol associated with Elizabeth) and signifying ideas of purity and virginity.[72] The fan in Babylon, Persia and classical antiquity had been a symbol of sovereignty and, when as here made of ostrich feathers, it signified justice and truth and sometimes represented the goddess of order. The ostrich in Christian iconography was a symbol of Mary's virginal motherhood.[73] In the Darnley Portrait, then, we have a representation of the queen's two bodies: the personal, physical, *sexual* female body of the woman and the royal body public, which we are called to remember by the regalia. Both bodies, and especially the queen's natural body, are pure, perfect, virginal and sacred – indeed the pearl shimmering with light sometimes symbolized Christ. And the face, at the same time both a likeness and a mask, feminine yet determined, is that of a woman and a queen, a virgin and a goddess on earth. If Strong's attribution to Zuccaro is correct, there may be more yet to the canvas. Zuccaro came to England to serve Leicester, the queen's favourite, who was at the height of his intimacy with Elizabeth and, many suspected, her lover. Was the portrait painted for him? And does that box conceal some jewel or token of their love? Leicester commissioned a pair of miniatures of himself and the queen about this time.[74] If the Darnley Portrait suggests intimacy and femininity (as it does), it also presents Elizabeth as a queen – a position which more or less ruled out marriage to an English subject, whatever the affections between them. Elizabeth asserted on canvas her womanhood and her sovereignty, rendering herself desirable yet unattainable. Evidently the painting pleased her, for its composition and face pattern were repeated in portraits into the mid-1580s and no other was so widely disseminated. The queen had found an image she was happy to license.

While the Darnley Portrait became the official pattern for Elizabeth's face, shifting circumstances and the availability of artists saw it repeated in portraits of a quite different composition and performance. The first of the so-called 'sieve' portraits of Elizabeth clearly adopted not only the Darnley face but the small turn of the queen's body to the right and the position of her right hand. Here, while her right hand rests on the arm of a chair, Elizabeth with her left holds against her body a sieve, the inside of which is turned to the viewer. Strong brilliantly explicated the meaning of this symbol.[75] The sieve was the symbol of the vestal virgin Tuccia who carried a sieve filled with water from the Tiber to the Temple, to prove her chastity against charges of incontinence. Though Strong found it 'curious' that Elizabeth's chastity should be proclaimed at the time of the Anjou marriage negotiations, it may be that the painting was meant to counter the rumours about the queen's

45 Elizabeth I: the 'sieve' portrait by George Gower.

sexual relationship with Leicester, with whom she had lodged at Kenilworth in 1575, and by whom she had been entertained with a series of pageants which (it has been argued) hinted at the possibility of their marrying.[76] Moreover, a representation of chastity advertised both virginity (the condition Elizabeth most likely preferred) and opposition to marriage, and her suitability for marriage – as pure and untainted, whatever the loose talk to the contrary.[77] And the sieve conveyed other symbolic meanings. As an implement for separating the wheat from the chaff, the good from the bad, it stood for judgement and discrimination; the motto round the sieve's rim declares: 'The good falls to the ground while the bad remains in the saddle'. In some emblem literature, Whitney for example, the sieve therefore represented the Last Judgment and the separating out of the elect from the damned.[78] In her portrait with the sieve, then, Elizabeth appropriated the humanist virtues of good rule and advertised the essential chastity of the virtuous woman, her virginity and her divine judgment; and she gestured to her Protestant faith. Before we leave this canvas, we should note the globe that stands on the table to our left by Elizabeth's right shoulder; above it is written in Spanish the motto: 'I see everything but much is missing'. As Strong pointed out, the image of England on the globe connects the realm to the chaste body of the queen, in a manner that was (as we shall see) to be repeated on maps and engravings. With the sieve emblematizing judgment and election, it hints too at a chosen nation ruled by a godly queen. England had become Elizabeth and she embodied the realm. And the globe hinted, too, at wider ambitions and the quest for empire.

According to Elizabeth's first biographer, William Camden, the sieve became the favourite device of the queen and other sieve portraits were painted over the next five years.[79] That several different artists reprised the same symbolic image suggests a growing measure of direction in royal portraiture, to which the 1563 draft proclamation had pointed. Later versions, however, added significantly to the symbolism and meaning of the canvas. In one version, dated 1583, not only is Elizabeth reversed to face slightly left, the loop pearl reappears at her right breast, while on the left she wears a large pendant pearl jewel.[80] In the right background we see added a colonnaded arcade with Gentlemen Pensioners and the recognizable figure of Sir Christopher Hatton, identifiable by the white hind badge on his cloak.[81] Hatton was an opponent of the Anjou match and a known supporter of Frobisher's and Drake's voyages of exploration.[82] As he walks from the deep background of the canvas and into our view, Hatton's left foot almost seems to touch the luminescent globe (now placed behind the queen's left shoulder) which figures England in a silvery sea filled with ships about to traverse the oceans. Eliza's England is, under her virgin rule – the compositional line of her left arm connects the globe and sieve – about to extend its sway. On the left of the canvas, Elizabeth's right forearm rests on, and draws our attention to, a richly jewelled column, a symbol of imperial majesty. Indeed, in a roundel at the foot of the column an imperial crown is depicted, while scenes painted in other roundels are taken from the story of Dido and Aeneas; Aeneas having resisted Dido, founded the Roman empire. In fulfilment of Arthurian prophecy, the column suggests, Elizabeth, descendant of Brutus, would revive a great British empire which might vie with Rome. Though the match with France (which many desired) might not be concluded, the virgin Elizabeth, free to labour tirelessly on behalf of her people, might yet found an empire.[83] The jewelled column may convey another message too. For it borrows not only from classical imagery but from the Emperor Charles V's device of the Pillars of Hercules, advertising the reach of the Habsburg empire into the new world.[84] Together with the imperial crowns placed at the foot rather than top of the column, the suggestion is that England's imperial destiny will supplant and eclipse the Habsburgs', just as Sir Francis Drake was beginning raids on Spanish ships and territories. We do not know who commissioned the 'Siena' version of the sieve portrait, though the suggestion that Hatton himself may have done so to urge Elizabeth to support Drake is very plausible.[85] What seems certain is that the repetition and prominence of the sieve signalled the reality now of virgin rule and assured the English

46 Elizabeth I: the 'sieve' portrait by Quentin Metsys the Younger.

people that their safety and destiny were secure under the rule of a virgin queen.

From the early 1580s, when the assassination of William the Silent threatened the collapse of an independent Low Countries and the triumph of

Habsburg arms menaced England, foreign policy dominated government business. Though, with William's death, Elizabeth was at last forced to intervene in the Netherlands, she hoped, right up to 1588, to avoid war with Spain and initiated a whole series of peace negotiations while lending assistance to enemies of Philip II, so as to distract the Habsburgs and remind them of the value of English neutrality.[86] A number of portraits which can be assigned to this period reflect these circumstances and may have been intended for continental as well as English observers. Certainly, abroad campaigns were being waged with the brush and etcher's knife as well as the sword. Canvases and engravings produced in the Low Countries were distributed to draw attention to their plight and to seek assistance, and perhaps in the case of a picture of Queen Elizabeth feeding the Dutch cow, to persuade her to sign a formal alliance to protect them, as she finally did at Nonsuch in August 1585.[87] The only known oil portrait by Marcus Gheeraerts the Elder, his portrait of Elizabeth, belongs to this context. Gheeraerts, a leading Protestant, had fled to England as a religious refugee, so the choice of him as a portraitist was not without significance.[88] His portrait depicted Elizabeth I as Pax with an olive branch in her right hand and with a sheathed sword and small dog (a symbol of faithfulness and motherhood) at her feet.[89] While in the right background male and female courtiers and attendants appear to be in conversation, Elizabeth stands alone embodying (as she had in the allegory of the Tudor succession) the peace she secured for her people and now, it was hoped, would secure for Europe. The theme of Gheeraerts's portrait was taken up in the famous Ermine Portrait of Elizabeth dated 1585 and attributed to the herald William Segar.[90] Though quite different in style – the portrait is flat and lacks drama – the Ermine Portrait rehearses the theme of peace and closely connects it to the queen's chastity and her avoidance of marriage (again we recall the *Allegory of the Tudor Succession*) which might have embroiled her and the country in war. In the Ermine Portrait, Elizabeth's body, clothed in a black gown, merges with the background, so emphasizing the whiteness of her hands and face, centred in a circle formed by her head-dress and a delicate, fine white lace ruff. From her collar hangs a jewel which is known to have belonged to the Dukes of Burgundy – advertising both Elizabeth's descent and the Tudors' claim to new empire.[91] On the table to our right lies a sword, the hilt of which just touches Elizabeth's left arm on which sits, looking up to her face and reflecting back the whiteness of her skin, an ermine with a golden collar which resembles a coronet. In Renaissance emblem literature, the ermine was a symbol of purity and chastity and sometimes, in Christian iconography, of Christ's triumph over evil and sin.[92] Here, purity and chastity are presented as regal – and indeed martial – virtues which Elizabeth embodies and personifies. Triumphant over temptations, the queen is heiress

47 Elizabeth I by Marcus Gheeraerts the Elder.

48 Elizabeth I: the Ermine Portrait.

to the greatest empires and head of a new empire founded on innocence and peace, an empire, as the title of one engraving described it, of 'Eliza triumphans'.[93]

Elizabeth's clear preference for peace by no means won the support of all her Privy Councillors including, we now appreciate, Cecil, to whom the painting may have been presented when Elizabeth visited Theobalds in June 1585.[94] Whatever the merits of her policy, it failed about this time, as from 1585 Philip, frustrated at the queen's undermining of his ambitions, began preparations for an invasion of England. More by luck than anything, England

survived the Armada; but Spain's failure presented Elizabeth with a spectacular opportunity both to press her claim to empire and to boast victory as a
divinely protected queen who had triumphed over enemies abroad and critics
at home.

The very size of the Armada Portrait immediately made claims to imperial
triumph and expansiveness. This unusually large canvas, measuring 50″ ×
43″, is also, untypically, broader than it is high.[95] Physically it represents the
territorial reach of the authority of a queen who stands centred between two
scenes visible over her shoulders. Clothed in a dress decorated with symbols
of the resplendent sun and with a large ruff and jewelled headgear highlighting her face like another sun, Elizabeth holds in her left hand an ostrich-
feather fan of the type we saw in an earlier portrait. Her right hand rests on a
globe with her fingers pointing to America and a line that may plot Drake's
journey to the new world. As we trace another line from the queen's hand up
her forearm, her right elbow aligns with an imperial (closed) crown on a table.
On the right of the portrait, a chair upholstered in the same red velvet with
which the table is covered has, on the end of its arm, the carved figure of a
mermaid 'whose traditional function is to lure seafarers to their doom, just as

49 Elizabeth I: the Armada Portrait.

Spain had been tempted by Elizabeth'.[96] Behind the queen, on either side of her head, are depicted two scenes: on our left English fireships being sent to wreak havoc on the Spanish fleet; on our right, the wrecking of the remnants of the Spanish vessels on the coast of Scotland. The queen's face, placed between struggle and victory, here performs similarly to the monarch's entry in a court masque, transforming chaos and darkness into victory and light. Though complex and crowded, the meaning of this large canvas seems clear: Elizabeth, the sun (her face, as Strong observed, is 'brilliantly lit from the front') defeats the forces of darkness, the enemies of England, and, in securing victory, extends England's imperial sway to the Americas, the treasure-house of Spanish imperialism.[97] Where in the sieve portrait the imperial crown was placed at the foot of the column, here the English crown, with closed arches to delineate it the crown of an emperor not a mere king, is placed directly above the globe over which the chaste queen bears effortless sway, as her chastity also calms the swell of tempestuous appetites.[98] Larger than life – the queen appears to fill this huge canvas – Elizabeth is depicted as what she claimed to be: a conqueror, who, having mastered her own passions, rules as sovereign head of a new empire.

The association of Elizabeth, the imperial crown and the nation was, as we have seen, a ubiquitous conceit of the literature of the 1580s and '90s.[99] But perhaps the most graphic statement of the queen as the literal embodiment of the nation is the so-called Ditchley Portrait, probably commissioned by Sir Henry Lee, Elizabeth's Champion and the deviser of her accession-day tilts, who entertained her at Ditchley Park, Oxfordshire, in 1592. Lee was a patron of Marcus Gheeraerts the Younger and became godfather to his son.[100] Though the canvas seems very much to reflect Lee's own position and concerns – a commemoration of her visit – it adapts and extends icono-graphic themes from other representations, notably the Armada Portrait. One of the few full-lengths of Elizabeth and at nearly eight feet high easily the largest painting of her we have, the Ditchley Portrait depicts Elizabeth in a jewelled, white silk dress, standing on a globe, specifically on a large map of England, with her feet placed in Oxfordshire, at Ditchley. Elizabeth carries in her left hand gloves, in her right a fan, her arms all but spanning the country which lies at her feet. Strong informed us that the original, which has been cut down by some inches, almost certainly extended the map of England to Land's End, the embarkation point for a westward expansion to which the queen gestures with her right hand.[101] While on the horizontal plane of the canvas the arms and skirts of Elizabeth span England, the vertical plane rises from the queen's feet to her narrow waist (the chain of pearls hanging there represents her virginity) and upwards to the pendant pearl at her right breast, to her mask-like face, framed by a laced ruff and wired veil, with two hoops emerging almost like wings at the back. The queen's body, physical and mystical, spans earth and heaven. Elizabeth wears a diamond-encrusted crown with a large red ruby which, Janet Arnold has suggested, may be the Black Prince's ruby – and thus a signifier of long descent.[102] Close to her left ear, Elizabeth wears a jewel in the form of an armillary sphere, a common impresa in the Renaissance and an emblem often associated with Elizabeth and expressing her divine authority.[103] White beneath the rubied crown, Elizabeth's face is centred between two sky scenes, that on her left dark, stormy

50 Elizabeth I: the Ditchley Portrait by Marcus Gheeraerts the Younger.

and raked by lightning, that on her right serene with sun-tinted clouds. Here the suggestion (not dissimilar to the Armada Portrait) that the sun queen herself calms the tempestuous heavens is rendered explicit by a sonnet inscribed on the right side of the painting. Though now incomplete through cropping, the sonnet describes the queen as 'prince of light' and 'the sonne' – a contemporary spelling which may be intended to evoke the Son, that is the Lord (who said 'I am the way, the truth and the light') as well as the sun. The verse explains that thunder is a sign of divine power, but here turned into grace and beneficence by the mediation of the Virgin Queen who, as in her own prayers, is here presented as God's handmaid. Reference in the poem to 'the boundless ocean' extends the promise that England has been chosen, along with 'this yle of such both grace [and] power', for imperial destiny. The fragment of the motto on the left, 'Da [e]xpectat', urges subjects to render Elizabeth the obedience and love to which she has a right as empress and divine queen.

The theme of the queen in control of her own passions and the elements lies behind the famous Rainbow Portrait of Elizabeth which has been attributed to Gheeraerts the Younger.[104] Against a dark background, Elizabeth stands three-quarter length, wearing a mantle of light orange-gold silk, on which all over are embroidered eyes and ears. Her left sleeve is decorated with pieces of jeweller's work: a serpent with a heart-shaped jewel hanging from its mouth and an armillary sphere above its head.[105] As with the Ditchley Portrait, the queen wears a wired veil which protrudes in hoops each side of her head and wears a ruby-jewelled crown with a crescent moon on the top. In her right hand she holds a small rainbow, beside which is inscribed the motto 'Non sine solo iris' – no rainbow without the sun. At a simple level, the signification is clear: Elizabeth is again represented as the sun of the kingdom. Her face is a timeless mask of youth and the flowers embroidered on her jacket gesture to her (even in age) as a symbol of youth and rejuvenation, a gesture emphasized by her half-revealed pure white breasts. The eyes and ears on her mantle have been the subject of much debate but Frances Yates's identification of their debt to the most famous Renaissance emblem book, Caesare Ripa's Iconologia, remains persuasive: for in Ripa, the Art of Government is emblematized with eyes and ears as the means of governing well the commonwealth.[106] If, as seems likely, Robert Cecil commissioned the portrait, his own claim to be the queen's eyes and ears may have been made at a time of jockeying to be the principal minister.[107] In the 1603 English edition of the Iconologia, the figure of Reason of State is shown with eyes and ears, so it may be that, in the changed political circumstances of the 1590s, realpolitik had come to be regarded as a necessary attribute of royal government.[108] Ripa's figure of Intelligence, we may also note, is depicted with a serpent and sphere, the symbols of worldly prudence and divine wisdom, both of which in the Rainbow Portrait appear as attributes of rule.[109] The proximity of the ruby heart to the symbols of prudence alludes again to the idea that Elizabeth had wisely regulated her affections and the crescent moon was a symbol of virgin deities, in Christian art of the Virgin Mary. It is the conjunction of classical and religious signifiers which is striking. For, while the rainbow points to Elizabeth as the sun and gestures to the Greek goddess Iris, it was also the sign of God's covenant with man after the Flood.[110] The rainbow was frequently taken as a symbol of the union between heaven and earth, a reconciliation between heaven and a fallen world effected by the Virgin Mary and, it is implied, here by the Virgin Queen Elizabeth. Christ had been depicted as a rainbow in a 1543 woodcut of *The Last Judgment*, so Elizabeth is also associated with Christ himself, the universal ruler and judge.[111] The eyes and ears, too, bore a religious as well as secular significance. As well as the eye appearing in antiquity as a symbol of the sun god, the eye of the spirit and spiritual hearing were conventional Christian virtues, while the Bible presents the eye as a symbol of God's omniscience and protection of all.[112]

51 Elizabeth I: the Rainbow Portrait.

These dual significations are vital to the meaning and performance of the portrait and should encourage us to resist any simple choice between the secular and religious interpretations proffered by different scholars. Where Yates, taking Ripa and English courtly eulogies as her interpretative guides, has read the canvas as a paean to the queen of a new golden age of peace and prudence, René Graziani has emphasized the religious signification, pointing to the queen's holding the emblem of God's promise to man and the serpent as a symbol of the Redeemer, which represents Elizabeth's faith and trust in Christ.[113] Graziani has suggested that Elizabeth's falling hair figures her as a bride of Christ espoused to his church.[114] Not only are both legitimate readings which can be supported by contemporary iconography and texts, they also remind us of the importance of Elizabeth, towards the end of her reign, asserting both her worldly prudence and powers and her steadfast faith against critics of her government in state and church. A classical goddess and a handmaid of Christ, Elizabeth on this canvas becomes the rainbow which, we note, melds into her dress and body; she becomes, that is, the living symbol of God's promise.

A similar conjunction of the secular and sacred characterizes the portrait painted, about 1602, probably by Robert Peake, of Queen Elizabeth in procession. As in the case of the Rainbow Portrait, it was not the queen herself who commissioned the work but most likely Edward Somerset, Earl of Worcester who was appointed in 1601 Master of the Horse in succession to the Earl of Essex and may have wished both to celebrate his office and express his gratitude to the queen through the painting.[115] Strong has suggested that the view of the castles on the top left may have represented Worcester's seats at Raglan and Chepstow, and the composition of the painting moves our gaze from the queen's face to Worcester's, suggesting proximity and intimacy.[116] The canvas may depict a Garter procession. Certainly Elizabeth is preceded by knights of the Order and followed by ladies, while Gentlemen Pensioners line the route.[117] Four men support an embroidered floral canopy over the queen, who sits on a wheeled chair. Behind the Gentlemen Pensioners and craning for a view of the queen from every window, genteel spectators gaze at Elizabeth as if she were a sacred object. And this is surely the point. While Strong has quite appropriately identified the allusion to a Roman imperial triumph, this scene, perhaps from a progress, also evokes a missal procession.[118] The queen is dressed in white, with her face an iconic mask of youth, and followed by a bride in white who in turn is attended by a woman carrying a rose. If, as has been suggested, the procession commemorated an actual wedding (of Anne Russell, one of Elizabeth's maids), few spectators appear to pay attention to the bride (even though her future husband Lord Herbert gestures with his left hand towards her).[119] They focus instead on the Virgin Queen who is elevated

52 The Procession Portrait.

to a higher plane.[120] The woman who is the focus and object of all desire rules, not as a bride or wife, but as a virgin queen. Carole Levin, discussing the ways in which the cult of Elizabeth as virgin substituted for the worship of the Virgin Mary, argued that 'many of the members of Elizabeth's court believed that having the queen visit on progress was tantamount to having their house blessed'.[121] There could hardly have been a more appropriate courtier than the staunchly Catholic Worcester (Elizabeth called him a 'stiff papist' as well as a good subject) to view the queen as an icon.[122] In its subtle moves between secular and sacred and between the local and topical and larger iconographic gestures, the Procession Portrait represented Elizabeth as an object of worship for all her subjects, Catholic as well as Protestant, and as the (virgin) bride of the kingdom.

This tendency to iconize Elizabeth in portraits, most evident in the two portraits of her in coronation robes probably painted towards the end of her reign,[123] began in the 1580s when the physical reality of Elizabeth's ageing (and infertility) was replaced by a mask of youth – a necessary reassurance of longevity and continuity when there were no heirs to the throne. Interestingly, Gheeraerts's frank portrayal of the queen's wrinkled features did not set a pattern and in later workings of his Ditchley Portrait, 'the features are considerably rejuvenated and softened'.[124] From the later 1580s, and early 1590s, in fact, there appears to have been a renewed concern with controlling the royal image. A Council warrant of July 1596 again referred to the 'abuse committed by divers unskilful artisans in unseemly and improper painting, graving and printing of her majesty's person and visage to her majesty's great offence and disgrace of that beautiful and magnanimous majesty wherewith God hath blessed her'.[125] It ordered all such images 'to be defaced and none to be allowed but such as her majesty's sergeant painter shall first have sight of'.[126] Whatever the Council or queen's concerns, the face of Elizabeth appeared to have been frozen as a timeless mask, leaving the externals of dress, jewels and other attendant figures to locate her image in circumstance and time. The image of Elizabeth, who had taken 'Semper eadem' as her motto, became an emblematic rather than a realist representation and in the process the queen became a sacred icon.

This tendency to represent Elizabeth as an icon was in part related to genre. From the mid-1590s, the artist most patronized by the queen was Nicholas Hilliard who not only evolved 'a formalised mask of the queen that totally ignored reality', but who worked principally as a miniaturist.[127] It was clearly for his miniatures that Elizabeth was drawn to Hilliard. For in a draft patent to her sergeant painter George Glover in 1584, granting him the monopoly of 'all manner of portraits and pictures of our person', she excepted only 'one Nicholas Hilliard . . . to whom it shall be . . . lawful to . . . make portraits . . . in small compass . . . and not otherwise'.[128] Hilliard began in, and was influenced by, the indigenous tradition of manuscript illumination: he illustrated a prayer book of Elizabeth's around 1581. But his illuminations were, with their oval frames, 'conceived in terms of miniature lockets' and it was as a miniaturist that he emerged into a position of royal favour.[129] 'The fashion for portrait miniatures,' Strong informs us in a catalogue to an innovative exhibition of them, 'begins more or less simultaneously with the advent of the Reformation when England . . . went into virtual aesthetic isolation.'[130] The relation of genre to moment was not only aesthetic. A token of intimacy, the miniature, hidden in a lover's boudoir or worn in a locket, was an obviously suitable form for the high age of chivalry in England; but beyond that, miniatures, sometimes kept in small boxes, may also have, in a newly Protestant realm, substituted for reliquaries: a 1570 miniature of an Elizabethan Maundy ceremony certainly lends support to the argument that the form was used for religious as well as secular subjects.[131] Strong has argued that the symbolic role of miniatures developed during the 1580s when the cult of emblems and impresas became most fashionable.[132] But politics and events influenced aesthetic forms too and first the plots against Elizabeth, then the Armada victory, gave further impetus to the fashion among courtiers and nobles for wearing some token of their loyalty and love for the queen, while she in her turn gave miniatures of herself (to Drake, for example) as tokens of affection.[133] Just as the mask-like visage of Elizabeth on portraits was rendering her an icon, so miniatures enabled that icon to be both intimate and distributed.[134]

The repetition late in the reign of the face-pattern of the queen and the scale of production provide evidence of government success, at least in this genre, in establishing an official image. While Elizabeth was unable or unwilling to patronize painters, leaving her courtiers and nobles to commission canvases of her, miniatures could be and were regulated and distributed. The sixteen miniatures Hilliard produced drew on some of the motifs of full-scale portraits, depicting the queen with the mask of youth, her face as a radiant sun: in some she is wearing a crescent moon jewel; one shows her before a throne playing the lute – a familiar symbol of divine harmony; and, another example of a religious theme, one, presented by Elizabeth to Heneage after the Armada, depicts an ark (a symbol of the church and elect nation) tossed on stormy seas.[135]

Ironically, however, the cult of the miniature served rapidly to undermine the world of privacy and intimacy on which the genre depended. From the late 1580s, the miniature, which had been an occasional work, was transformed into an object of mass production and there were consequences for the quality as studio assistants worked to keep pace, using Hilliard's drawings.[136] Mass production was a response to a growing desire, especially after the Armada, to possess some image of the queen. That widespread desire evidenced the success of Elizabeth and her representations in making an impact on the culture of her reign and the imagination of her subjects. On the other hand, the sheer scale of the distribution (to people who could not have afforded a full-scale portrait), together with the increasing deployment of the genre for other sitters, made the miniature no longer a privileged royal form. Indeed, as miniatures of the queen were acquired by citizens' wives, it is not too bold to argue that, though it began as the most intimate of representations, the miniature ultimately 'democratised' the image of Elizabeth, and perhaps, in some measure, the monarchy itself.[137]

III

The distribution of miniatures which were kept in jewelled boxes or worn in lockets served to commodify the royal image and encourage what later became a fashion for portraits of the sovereign on household and personal objects: a plate in the Museum of London bearing Elizabeth's image and a simple motto appears to be the earliest example of royal souvenir porcelain, which remains an industry to this day.[138] Miniatures were often, too, the sources of, as well as inspiration for, the increasing number of engravings and woodcuts of the queen which distributed the royal image more broadly than ever before through the society and culture of late sixteenth-century England. While there are few contemporary engravings and prints of her predecessors, the engraved and woodcut images of Elizabeth are numerous. Moreover, though the engraving industry was still dominated by foreigners, principally Flemish and Dutch, the large circulation testifies to a growing English interest and market, which were in their turn to encourage native artists.[139] By the late 1580s, for example, William Rogers was emerging as the first Englishman to practise copperplate engraving and to make a living from his art.[140] And it is evident that the government also quickly grasped the importance of the medium for representation. The draft proclamation of 1563, we recall, had included 'graving and printing' among the forms it sought to control. However it was twenty years later that, in a more positive move, a patent was granted to George Glover giving him a monopoly right to 'all manner of portraits' of the queen, 'to grave the same in copper or to cut the same in wood'.[141] And it appears that efforts were made to draw foreign engravers into the services of the court. Matthew Parker, Archbishop of Canterbury, for example, recruited the famous engraver Remigius Hogenburg who illustrated

53 Plate in honour of Elizabeth I.

the Bible and who executed portraits of Elizabeth which flattered the queen and rehearsed themes from her own representations.[142]

Many engravings and woodcuts of Elizabeth are undated; however, other portraits, clothing and accompanying verses often enable us to assign a date; and some were obviously intended to commemorate an event. Interestingly, Elizabeth's succession was not marked by a large output of engravings of the new monarch. The genre was still undeveloped in England as opposed to the Low Countries where Frans Hoys etched a portrait of the new queen as part of a series issued by Hans Liefunck.[143] The first engraved image of Elizabeth in England appears to have been the title page of the 1559 edition of Thomas Geminus's *Compendios a totius anatomie delineatio.*[144] Geminus, an émigré from Flanders, had come to England in the reign of Henry VIII and was attached to the court. He had engraved maps and dedicated books to Edward VI, but his 1559 anatomy was his first engraved portrait of an English sovereign.[145] Geminus seems to have taken as his source a portrait of Elizabeth now at Northwick Park.[146] His title page centres the queen, in a dress embossed with flowers and wearing a pearl pendant, with a sceptre, framed between the figures of Justice and Prudence and beneath Victory, with the royal motto 'Dieu et mon droit' below her. Angels hover with the portcullis and rose, emblems of the Tudors, and Victory carries the palm and laurel of peace which Elizabeth has restored and secured and which is also signified by images of abundance and plenty. Geminus engraved another portrait of the queen between 1560 and 1562, which amplified the themes of the first, while perhaps incorporating a recognition of the first steps towards Protestantism taken by the religious settlement. In this case, the size of the image suggests that it may have been intended for wall display, a suggestion supported by the accompanying verses.[147] Beneath a classical arch supported by fluted columns, Elizabeth is figured with her hands enfolding a small book, into which her fingers are inserted, as though marking a passage. To the left of the queen the figure of Faith stands with a book inscribed 'Feare God and Joye in Him'; on the right, Minerva (Wisdom), armed with a sword and spear, suggesting the need to add vigilance to wisdom in a hostile world, may also suggest the need for the Protestant faith to be vigilant or militant. The plinth beneath the queen is inscribed with two legends. That on the left, presenting Elizabeth as virtue and the word embodied, reads: 'From fontaine cleare like springes do flowe, so worde and deed as one. This virtue showeth, uncloked life, and hart sincere alone'. On the right, the motto underlines the need for might to maintain the truth in a land from which the true faith had recently been banished: 'When right from land and countrie cieasithe, then Strength doth banner splaie, Els right by wronge wold sone decay and vice on hie wolde beare his swaye'. Directly below the plinth, Charity, with her children and an inscription commending her fruits in love and good works, associated Elizabeth with virtue and perhaps reassured Catholic subjects concerned about the place of good works in a Protestant country. Above her, atop the royal arms, a crowned figure holding a sword and wreath is flanked by the figures of Hope (with a cross) and Justice. Inscriptions identify hope with 'princely life' and promise 'where justice placed is in the throne, there might is kept at bay'. At the centre of these allegorical figures, Elizabeth, beneath all the books which are stuffed under the arch, represents the word, the truth and the Christian virtues of peace, love and charity in an image which, though Protestant, is also eirenic. Strong has identified the engraving as an adaptation of

54 Engraving of Elizabeth I from Thomas Geminus's *Compendios a totius anatomie delineatio.*

55 Engraving of Elizabeth by Thomas Geminus.

Enea Vico's of the Emperor Charles V which may suggest, along with the two columns, a gesturing to imperial ambitions.[148] We do not know whether Geminus executed the engraving as an official commission. But this early engraved portrait, especially if displayed, made a powerful proclamation of Elizabeth's claims to succession and divine right and of her virtues, faith and imperial destiny.

Evidently soon after the 1563 proclamation efforts were made to recruit engravers who might devise a template for an image of the queen. On the death of Geminus, Matthew Parker patronized two sons of the Munich painter and engraver Nikolaus Hogenberg, Remigius and Franciscus.[149] Franciscus appears to have been employed to etch a series of portraits for the 1568 and 1569 editions of the Bishops' Bible, which was Parker's project. The illustrations were clearly intended to identify the court with Scripture. As well as portraits of Leicester as another Joshua and of Burleigh represented with the Book of Psalms in his hand, Franciscus engraved a portrait of Elizabeth as a frontispiece.[150] In an oval surrounded by strapwork, Elizabeth is figured half-length, crowned with her face turned to the right, with a large orb in her right hand and sceptre in her left. In the decoration to left and right of the royal arms atop the oval, the figures of Charity, with her offspring, and Faith, with cross and book, look down towards the queen. Beneath the oval, a lion and unicorn, the heraldic beasts of England, support a cartouche on which is inscribed the words: 'Let me not be ashamed to be an evangelist of Christ. For the strength of God is security for all believers'. The verse, from Romans 1: 16 presents the queen as the evangelist of Christ and Supreme Head of a faith of works as well as words, just as the Bishops' Bible was intended to address all members of a Church of England, not just the godly readers of the Geneva Bible.[151] Indeed, as well as evoking the memory of her father Henry VIII

56 Francis Hogenberg's engraving of Elizabeth I on the title page of the Bishops' Bible.

whose image had adorned the Great Bible, the engraving implicitly represented Elizabeth (as had Geminus) as defender, and indeed as definer, of truth. Hogenberg's frontispiece, repeated in the 1569 and 1572 editions, was a text of Elizabeth's supremacy which figured her, as she described herself, as head of a church which was independent of Rome and Geneva and which incorporated all her subjects.

An additional woodcut in the 1569 quarto edition of the Bishops' Bible makes the same statement.[152] Situating Elizabeth surrounded by Justice, Mercy, Fortitude and Prudence, above a scene of preaching and the title, it presented the queen as the personification of classical and Christian virtues and as the word made flesh, in an iconographical scheme which, as well as emphasizing Protestant scripturalism, borrowed from medieval Catholic literary traditions. Elizabeth was being represented by her archbishop, who fully shared her wishes, as the unifier of faiths and people, as the head under whom again subjects could unite in worship. Roy Strong has observed that in Hogenberg's engraving of Elizabeth, 'the facial mask is identical with that in the *Three Goddesses* of 1569'.[153] The inference we may draw of an official programme being pursued across various visual media, in the spirit of the 1563 proclamation, is supported by other engravings of the queen, executed by Franciscus's brother, Remigius Hogenberg. A head and shoulders of Elizabeth, signed but not dated by Remigius, appears to be drawn from a series of portraits of the queen of which there are copies at Barington Park, Syon and Burghley House.[154] In the engraved version, however, the image is explicated by Latin verses which praise the beauty of Elizabeth's face and mind, her justice, virtue and piety, all of which bring happiness to her people. On such engravings visual and textual motifs of royal representations were being brought together in what was an increasingly broadly circulating medium to present the queen as the head of a unified church and nation.

Interestingly, Hogenberg also engraved an elaborate allegorical portrait of Elizabeth for the frontispiece of one of the important texts of a developing nationalism, Christopher Saxton's *Atlas of the Counties of England and Wales*.[155] A client of Thomas Seckford, Master of Requests, Saxton undertook his work with the full backing of the Privy Council and his book was published with a dedication to the queen, in 1579. In the engraving, Elizabeth is seated with orb and sceptre (it is worth observing that the regalia which appear seldom in paintings are common in engravings) on a throne inside a colonnaded arch, the whole structure decorated with classical busts and Tudor roses. On the left, the figure of Astronomy in a mixture of classical and Eastern costume, carries an astrolabe; on the right, Geography holds a globe and compass. Above the queen, on the frieze below the royal arms, a medallion contains the figures of Peace (with her olive branch) and Justice (with sword and balance) embracing.

Beneath the enthroned Elizabeth, two smaller figures, again representing Geography and Astronomy (this time left and right respectively) flank two compartments in which are inscribed four elegiac couplets in Latin. The verses laud a merciful, just and pious queen and celebrate the peace and piety England enjoyed under her rule, while other nations experienced the miseries of war and blind error. Here, in a complex image, the queen's learning and faith are represented as triumphant and her preference for peace is vindicated (as we have seen in panegyrics and paintings) as itself a victory; and her policies and virtues are promoted as the means of gaining imperial glory.

57 Engraving by Francis Hogenberg as frontispiece to Saxton's *Atlas of the Counties of England and Wales*.

The theme of Protestant imperialism became a common motif in the 1570s as the struggle in the Low Countries drew attention to England's place in what the godly regarded as an apocalyptic battle between the forces of Christ and Antichrist. Since the 1563 edition of Foxe's *Acts and Monuments*, Elizabeth had been depicted in woodcut illustrations as a Protestant emperor trampling Rome.[156] The early success of Drake's voyages seemed further to signal imperial destiny and increasingly woodcuts figured Elizabeth not merely as queen but as empress. The title page to John Dee's *General and Rare Memorials Pertaining to the Art of Navigation*, for example, depicted an English fleet embarking from a well-defended coast under the protection of an armed St Michael.[157] At the helm of the flagship, bathed in the rays of the sun and under a tetragrammaton, symbol of the godhead, Elizabeth is shown raising her right hand, as if blessing a godly crusade. The name on the ship in Greek, *Europa*, is complemented by the figure of Europa, riding a bull through the waves beside the hull. Atop the mast, the Greek monogram represents Christ as the head of the English ship of state under the command of his lieutenant on earth, the queen. Dee dedicated the *General and Rare Memorials* to Christopher Hatton, Keeper of the Queen's Guard.[158] Though the suggestion here of a call to lead a militant Protestant crusade spoke more to godly than royal agendas, the imperial destiny of dynasty and nation is powerfully advanced and located in the person of the queen.

The imperial theme reached its peak in the wake of the Armada victory, which also fostered a broad popular desire for images of a triumphant and godly monarch. It was from the late 1580s that not only more, but more popular, engravings and woodcuts of Elizabeth were published and at this time that William Rogers began his career, or was commissioned, as the first English engraver of copperplate.[159] Rogers's *Eliza Triumphans* was issued as a single sheet, signed and dated 1589.[160] On the 10″ × 8″ broadside sheet, Elizabeth stands between two obelisks which her skirt flows out to touch at the base. The queen, wearing a crown, large ruff and pearls, holds an orb and the olive branch of peace. On the left obelisk, inscribed 'corono' ('I garland') stands Victory holding a laurel, while on the right column inscribed 'exhilero' ('I bring joy') Plenty, holding an overflowing cornucopia, proffers a garland to the queen. Behind Victory, we see ships on a calm sea, while on the right background is sketched a city amid hills, perhaps an allegory of the church. As Strong has argued, Elizabeth is here represented as Pax; but she is also Victory and it is, in vindication of her long aversion to war, a triumph of peace which is depicted.[161] A second version of the image plays up the religious dimension only hinted at in Rogers's engraving.[162] In a contemporary reworking, the figures of Victory/Peace and Plenty are replaced by astrolabes and the background scenes have become recognizably London (on the left) and a city in flames – Strong suggests Rome but it could equally well stand for a Protestant

58 *Eliza Triumphans* by William Rogers.

city not protected by Elizabeth's sagacity and holiness. The title of this version of the engraving is altered to *Verum decus Christianae reipublicae*, which translates as 'The True Ornament of a Christian Commonwealth'. The word *decus*, however, also means virtue, glory and grace, as indeed *decora* meant both renowned ancestors and victorious exploits in war. Once again image and word were combined to figure Elizabeth as the embodiment of virtue and grace, vigilant Protestantism and empire.

From 1588, the theme of Christian triumph and imperial destiny dominated engraved and woodcut portraits of the queen. Influential portraits by Crispin Van de Passe, produced in the Low Countries, circulated in London as printsellers, responding to a market, published more and more engravings. Van de Passe's half-length of Elizabeth with orb and sceptre, dated 1592, presented her with the motto which, as we have seen, featured on her brother Edward's coins – 'Posui deum adiutorem meum' (I have taken God as my helper) – and described her as the zealous champion of the faith.[163] Accompanying verses, contrasting England's blessed condition with the ignorance and strife of Europe, praised the piety of a princess, chosen by God, who had brought salvation to her people. Another Van de Passe, commissioned and published in 1596 by the bookseller John Woatneel, almost prepared the way for the apotheosis of the queen.[164] In a richly complicated composition, Elizabeth is shown holding an orb topped with a cross and standing between two pillars or columns. The classical columns, identified by Frances Yates as the Pillars of Hercules, the device of Charles V, are decorated with the royal arms and Tudor heraldic symbols and are surmounted by a pelican feeding its young and a phoenix, personal devices associated with Elizabeth (as we have seen) and representing her as nursing mother and eternal virgin. On a table to the queen's right, crossed by her sceptre, an open book, almost certainly representing the Bible, is inscribed (this time in abbreviated form) 'posui deum'. Behind Elizabeth's outstretched arms, England appears with forts, gunnery and ships, as safe and strong. The title describes the queen as 'unicum propugnaculum', as the main, the only reliable, bulwark of the Christian faith; and verses below amplify the description, stating that peace, justice and faith are the blessings brought by a queen who has surpassed all others and for whom God has prepared a heavenly kingdom. Towards the end of her reign, Rogers returned to the same theme. Picturing Elizabeth this time beside a prayer book open at the Psalm 35 ('plead thou my cause ... and stand up to help me'), the engraving printed in a cartouche flanked (again) by a pelican and phoenix a poem which described the queen as 'cannopey'd under pourefull angels wings'.[165] Finally, a Rogers medallion of the queen beside a bible on which is written 'withdraw not thy tender mercy from me' is titled simply 'Rosa electa', the chosen rose – a reference to Tudor dynastic succession, Venus but yet virginity, divine appointment and Protestant faith.[166]

The several states, copies and variants of these images suggest that engravings had become, by the end of the reign, for the first time a principal medium for publishing the royal image. As engraving began to compete with and, over the following years, replace woodcuts in book illustrations, engraved portraits of the queen were routinely published in courtesy books, histories and atlases, so placing the image of Elizabeth at the centre of print culture.[167] Yet, though no longer the preserve of wealthy noblemen, the 1598 edition of Lomazzo's *Art of Curious Painting* still considered that 'pictures cut in copper bear a higher rate of charge than in probability a professed scholar [then as now an impoverished class] can undertake'.[168] The cheaper books and cheap print were still more commonly illustrated with woodcuts which in Elizabeth's reign, importantly, reprised and disseminated for popular readership and the illiterate some of the same themes and iconographic programmes we have identified in engravings. As well as illustrations to the Bible and Foxe's *Acts and Monuments*, the two books ordered to be provided and chained in every parish church, woodcut images of Elizabeth at prayer formed the frontispiece to John Day's popular *Christian Prayers and Meditations* (1569) and *Book of Christian Prayers* (1578).[169] Several

59 Elizabeth I by Crispin Van de Passe.

ballads, like *A Joyful Song of Receiving the Queen at Tilbury*, were illustrated with a portrait of Elizabeth.[170] And Elizabeth was the first monarch to be depicted on a set of playing cards: one of eight introductory cards that preceded the four suits depicting the different regions of England, a portrait card of the queen showed Elizabeth enthroned in coronation robes and with the regalia beneath putti or angels carrying a sword and bible.[171] Verses on the card, celebrating a Deborah who governed with piety and religious zeal and secured peace, popularized the iconography of more elite forms: 'Great warres abroad,

60 Engraving of Elizabeth I in Day's *Christian Prayers and Meditations*.

yet God defends her land'. Such images of the queen were crossing the media and genres of representation and reaching humble as well as elite audiences, making Elizabeth truly the visual focus of the national community and identity.

Nor was the publicization of the royal image confined to portrait likenesses. Another of the introductory playing cards consisted simply of the royal arms of Elizabeth supported by the lion and dragon.[172] Even at the most popular levels and audiences, that is, Elizabeth could be represented and recognized through devices, impresas and symbols, as well as portraits. Though heraldry was still essentially a noble art, there appears to have been a broadening interest in heraldic symbols and even official texts evidently assumed a widespread familiarity with royal devices. The title page to a 1576 form of prayer for a thanksgiving for the queen, for example, published her royal arms above the figures of Faith and Humility, while the 1570 *Homily* on obedience, for example, was printed with an image of a phoenix supported by allegorical figures.[173] By the 1590s, appearing frequently in a variety of texts, phoenixes and pelicans were widely understood to represent the queen and the religious traits they signified as her virtues. Elizabeth had acquired what all her successors would aspire to emulate: brand recognition and an identity that would outlast disillusion and difference and ensure a reputation for greatness and godliness well beyond the grave.

A tendency to greater direction of the royal image is evident not only in portraits and engravings but in royal seals, medals and coins. Elizabeth's first seal of 1559, like the early somewhat faltering portraits, was neither finely executed nor especially innovative; but early on it made a number of statements about the new reign and ruler. On the obverse, the queen sits enthroned under a canopy with the orb and sceptre, beneath the motto 'Pulchrum pro patria mori' – sweet it is to die for one's country.[174] On the reverse, Elizabeth is mounted holding in her left hand a sceptre topped with a fleur-de-lis with behind her a large Tudor rose and another crowned fleur-de-lis. Clearly Elizabeth sought to reassert the right (disputed by Mary's supporters) of the English monarch's claim to the crown of France, especially in the wake of the loss of Calais. The seal also announces Elizabeth on both sides as 'Defensor fidei', the title given to her father by the pope. The legend captures in four words what Elizabeth enunciated in speech after speech: her readiness to serve her people and put their needs and interests before her own. This seal remained in service until 1585 when a very different portrait was designed, and perhaps executed, by Hilliard who had recently been recruited to royal service.[175] Strong argues for 1586 as a turning-point in Hilliard's career, the year in which he painted the face mask or template that was to be replicated in several miniatures and which also marked 'the beginning of a fashion for wearing her image'.[176] A commission issued to Hilliard and the engraver to the Mint, Dericke Anthony, ordered them to 'bring to perfection to be used a new great seal in silver', following a parchment design submitted by the miniaturist and approved.[177] As Strong argued, at a time of mounting danger the second great seal represented 'a radical enhancement of regal divinity coincidental with the cult of Elizabeth reaching its zenith'.[178] To the earlier image of the queen enthroned with coats of arms and Tudor roses, the new seal added two hands issuing from the heavens to hold up Elizabeth's mantle.[179] On the reverse, the harp of Ireland is added to the rose and fleur-de-lis to signify Elizabeth's rule there; and, again, from clouds above her head, celestial rays bear down on her, signifying, as do the hands on the obverse, the divine protection and favour she enjoyed as God's chosen ruler. It has been suggested that, in designing this seal, Hilliard may have drawn from the seal of the Order of the Holy Spirit, a creation of the Counter-Reformation piety of Henri III.[180] If so, the seal audaciously claimed Catholic as well as Protestant spirituality, just as the addition of the harp asserted English and Anglican dominance of a largely Catholic Ireland, which Philip II was planning to make a beachhead for an invasion of England. Elizabeth's second seal, which remained in use until the end of the reign, claimed supremacy, imperial power and a divine mission for queen and country.[181]

61 Second Great Seal of Elizabeth I.

The reign of Elizabeth saw a large increase in the production and distribution of medals which were frequently issued to commemorate particular events and, in response to growing demand, to satisfy a widespread desire for a token of the queen. An accession medal issued in 1558, with Elizabeth's portrait and inscription 'Et gloria Angliae' on one side and a phoenix (with the legend 'Sola Phoenix') on the other immediately established the new queen's personal identity and hinted at rebirth and perhaps religious renewal: the phoenix, we recall, had been a badge of Edward VI.[182] The survival of this early medal in several variants (with different drapery and a larger ruff) suggests that there were several issues in a short time and that, from the very outset, medals were to be important in representing the new monarch.[183] In 1560 a medal was struck to advertise and commemorate the reform of the debased coinage, reform in which, as proclamations of the same year confirm, the queen took great pride.[184] It was, however, the years after 1570 that witnessed a new phase in the history of the medal as a medium of royal representation. Two medals from 1572, one in copper for broad circulation, were apparently struck and issued as tokens of loyalty and thanks for the queen's survival – perhaps her triumph over the rising in the north as well as a life-threatening attack of smallpox. What has come to be known as 'The Defence of the realm' medal figured Elizabeth, head and shoulders profile left, between a portcullis and a rose with the motto 'Quid nos sine te' – what are we without you?[185] The reverse, a castle atop an armillary sphere, an emblem of the queen's divinity, is inscribed: 'What is This Without Arms'? Though the general symbolism is clear enough, the particulars have not been explicated. Strong persuasively argued for the papal excommunication as the immediate context: the medal emphasizes the centrality of Elizabeth to England's survival and the need to defend her, while vaunting her divine authority. The obverse inscription, in the form of an address *to* her (what are we . . .?), also served to make the medal a token of subjects' love, as well perhaps as a plea to her not only to trust in God but to keep her powder dry. The second medal of the year featured Elizabeth, again in profile, with a familiar legend, 'Posui deum adiutorem meum 1572', but one which took on extra resonance in the light of Elizabeth's recovery.[186] On the reverse, a hand from the right edge, casting a serpent into the flames, also symbolized Elizabeth's recovery from illness. But, adapted from a medal of Philip II, and with the inscription 'If God is for us who can be against us', it was almost certainly also a defiance of papal and Habsburg threats and a sign that God protected his queen against rebels at home and enemies abroad. A copy struck in the Netherlands bearing the motto 'Nothing will harm her whom nothing should harm' would seem to confirm such an interpretation.[187]

Reference to a medal struck abroad reminds us that medals were not a genre entirely under royal control. Several struck abroad by leaders with very different agendas to Elizabeth's circulated in England and private subjects commissioned medals, which were evidently not, like coins, regarded as a strict royal prerogative. Indeed the so-called Phoenix medal of 1574 provides a hint that some in England used medals not only to flatter the queen but to counsel her. In one version of this medal, while the queen's portrait and her phoenix topped with the royal arms echoed Elizabeth's own representation, the inscriptions appeared to question the wisdom of her preference for virginity over marriage. That on the obverse, ''Tis sad that such beauty and virtue should be corruptible not eternal' reads as a blunt reminder to

62 The 'Defence of the Realm' medal.

Elizabeth of the passage of time and her vulnerability.[188] And the reverse, featuring the phoenix but bewailing the fate of the English people whose 'only phoenix in death shall be forever lost to the world', ran directly contrary to the idea of eternity and rebirth which Elizabeth had intended the emblem to signify. Strong observed that the first motto had been used by Walter Haddon, an ardent reformer under Edward VI, in his *Poemata* of 1567. Significantly Haddon had in 1566 been a member of the committee of both houses of parliament that petitioned Elizabeth to marry.[189] The phoenix complimented Elizabeth and was worn by those closely attached to her; but here it may have been redeployed as loyal criticism and a warning that, in the wake of the papal excommunication, her advisers and subjects feared for her, and their, safety.

A number of medals struck in the first half of the 1580s, relating to Elizabeth's policy towards the Dutch, seem similarly to blend counsel with compliment. One that we know was struck in Holland during Leicester's expedition to the Low Countries, and probably with his direction, depicted the queen presenting roses to the deputies of the provinces with the inscription 'Macte animi rosa nectare imbuta': literally, 'Honour the rose filled with the

63 The 'Phoenix' medal.

nectar of the spirit'. The historian of British medals interpreted the legend as 'the rose of England is here compared to the nectar of the gods while the Spaniards were reduced to absolute want'.[190] But there may be a hint, too, that, as Leicester along with other councillors believed, Elizabeth was not distributing sufficient favour and taking the Dutch under her protection, as she was only belatedly persuaded to do. Two other medals were issued during the period of Leicester's sojourn in the Netherlands. On one dated 1586, the queen is crowned and seated presenting a sword to the deputies of the provinces while Leicester attends on her left, holding a book, probably Scripture; the inscription in Latin translates: 'Elizabeth feeds he who desires to eat'. On the reverse, a sword piercing a tetragrammaton signified the need for both the word and arms; as the inscription reads, 'The word of God is sharper than any two edged sword'.[191] Here, then, Elizabeth is represented, as she represented herself, as God's agent and a nursing mother, but the people are the Dutch over whom she had refused sovereignty. In 1586, against the queen's orders and in a gesture that greatly angered her, Leicester by his own authority accepted the title of Governor-General of the Low Countries and so involved a reluctant queen in protecting them. The medals appear to have been part of his campaign, as apparently were two others: one depicting Elizabeth's heart as a symbol of hope for the afflicted and a second commemorating his assumption of governorship and describing him as appointed lieutenant by the queen's commission.[192]

Debate about Leicester's actions was conducted in England and the Netherlands, in medals as well as pamphlets, some of which expressed thanks and gratitude, while others criticized his ambition. Where some medals presented Elizabeth as the militant apocalyptic champion defeating the Antichrist, others, almost certainly more in accord with her own view, figured her as Venus restraining Mars, as the mediator of a peace.[193] Peace, however, was not secured; and, as it became clearer that Spain was preparing an enterprise against England, the tensions and differences subsided, as Elizabeth was forced to accept the role of godly warlord which others had tried to impose on her. As we would expect, the defeat of the Armada provided the occasion for striking numerous commemorative medals which presented Elizabeth as the chosen daughter of divine Providence. Where some simply depicted the queen crowned (now with the imperial closed crown of a triumphant empress) and the motto 'No crown richer nor more mighty in the world', others presented finely executed scenes of naval victory with inscriptions referring to new empire and divine aid.[194] The obverse of one medal, inscribed with 'Veni, vide, vive' ('Come, see, live') also condemned the blind folly of those who defied God's will.[195] Another, inscribed 'Post nubila phoebus', like the Armada portrait represented Elizabeth as the sun which dispersed the clouds and symbolized new hope and regeneration.[196] In the case of some of these medals, struck on the continent, we cannot confidently assess their circulation or impact in England. But the badge issued to naval officers to commemorate the victory, found in several copies and minor variant states, amounted to an official memento which, showing Elizabeth with an ark tranquil on a stormy sea, alluded to royal virtues and divine protection.[197] Similarly, a medallion depicting a bay tree (traditionally considered to be immune from lightning) on an island in the midst of a choppy sea, with an inscription 'not even dangers affect it', symbolized the strength of a queen devoted to the faith and the security of an England under her godly regimen.[198] Such medals, as Roy Strong argued, belong to 'the outburst of wild imperialism in the years following the armada'; but, as much as imperial sway, it was godly rule they advertised.[199]

Continuing threats sustained these themes of medallic representations. Towards the end of Elizabeth's life, two medals presented her as the protector of the persecuted and as another Minerva, trampling the forces of evil, as a heavenly crown, held aloft, awaited her.[200] By no means every medal had represented Elizabeth's own policies or preferences. But, especially after 1588, medals, increasingly popular and worn as keepsakes, had disseminated and displayed important representations of a virtuous and godly queen which unquestionably helped to strengthen loyalty and shape perceptions and memories of her person and reign. Thanks to medals, Elizabeth not only was represented as embodying the nation, but her subjects wore her image close to their own bodies – and hearts.[201]

Some of the ideas and images designed for medals influenced coins which, of course, circulated even more widely. Elizabeth, as I suggested, attached importance to coins and regarded the reform of the debased coinage as necessary to the reconstitution of monarchy.[202] In his *De republica anglorum*, Sir Thomas Smith made a connection between the quality of coin, the 'goodness of the metal and weight' and the signifying portrait, 'the prince's image and mask' which, he argued, 'affirmed' the value; and he was not alone in regarding a strong currency as a condition of strong kingship.[203] A treatise on reform insisted that sound money was an essential attribute of royal honour, while in *The Blessedness of Britain*, Maurice Kyffin praised Elizabeth for reforming 'our . . . coin' from 'metal base and mean' to 'perfect gold'.[204] In proclamations Elizabeth herself, using a significantly politicized vocabulary, reiterated her determination to 'deliver this realm from the infamy of all manner of base monies' and, describing it as a 'hideous monster', condemned debased money which, she knew, 'derogat[ed] from our princely honour and royal dignity'.[205] More insistently than her predecessors, Elizabeth identified sound coinage with 'public authority'.[206] Given its importance to her, it is not surprising that she attributed importance also to the image of authority on coins, asking the imperial envoy in 1565 whether his 'gold pennies had any resemblance to his princely highness' – only to be told that 'he was scarcely to be recognised'.[207]

The same charge could not be levelled against Elizabeth's own coins. The Mint was under royal control and a queen who was concerned to control the royal image and who identified coins directly with her authority did not fail to take full advantage of a medium under her direction. The reform of quality proceeded quickly. From 1560 'in a little over a year, the base coin produced under Henry VIII and Edward VI was swept away and replaced by fine ... monies'.[208] And from the beginning of the reign, the images on coins were carefully modelled after portrait patterns of which the queen approved. The full-face portrait of the queen introduced on to sovereigns in 1558 and re-issued from 1584 followed the pattern of the Great Seal, with Elizabeth enthroned, crowned and with the regalia, between columns and above a portcullis.[209] On the reverse, a large Tudor rose and her arms were enclosed within an inscription which paraphrased Scripture: 'By the Lord this is enacted and it is marvellous in our eyes'.[210] Elizabeth's accession was represented on the popular medium of coin not merely as dynastic succession but as divine work. Another succession coin gestured to coins of Edward VI in depicting Elizabeth on a ship of state (decorated with the Tudor rose), with a reverse inscription promising Christ's presence in the land.[211]

Coins figured Elizabeth as her half-brother's heir: about 1561 some silver coins carried the Edwardian legend 'Posui deum adiutorem meum' and Elizabeth adopted the image of St Michael slaying the Devil.[212] But Elizabeth did not hesitate at the same time to issue coins (including pennies and three-farthings) with the inscription 'Rosa sine spina', the rose without thorns, a symbol of the Virgin Mary and a conceit used by Queen Mary.[213] Gender probably played a part here; but the audacious appropriation of Catholic symbols also advertised Elizabeth as the new queen of one church and nation, rather than of a denomination or party. After 1572, government attention appears to have turned to coins of smaller denomination, perhaps in recognition of the importance of reaching ordinary people.[214] If the historian of Tudor coinage is right to describe the silver coins of small denomination as 'the common drudge from man to man', then carefully considered representations of Elizabeth indeed reached far down the social order.[215] Given an estimate, too, that by 1603 the circulating coin 'may have doubled in size compared with eighty years previously', the distribution of Elizabeth's image on currency was wide as well as deep.[216] Indeed, Elizabeth permitted under royal authority coins bearing her legends (such as 'Posui deum') to be struck overseas in the Netherlands and in 1601, to mark the East India Company's voyage, she commissioned a coin in direct imitation of the Spanish *real* – surely

64 Sovereign of Elizabeth I.

as a challenge to Spanish imperial hegemony.[217] The legends and portraits on these coins of Elizabeth wearing a closed crown were those of an imperial sovereign determined to extend godly rule not only to her subjects but throughout Christendom.

The image of Tudor monarchy, as we have seen from the inventories of Henry VIII, was stamped on many of the material artefacts of the court, and on the jewels and clothes worn by courtiers and servants. Henry's claim to imperium and royal supremacy was made not only in pamphlets, proclamations and portraits but on salts, spoons, chairs and cushions.[218] In Elizabeth's case, we have an edited inventory which provides some idea of her household goods and some sense of the changes her succession effected.[219] Elizabeth inherited plate that would have put her in mind of 'almost every turmoil of the sixteenth century': goods which had belonged to Wolsey, Northumberland and Norfolk, jewels of her mother Anne Boleyn, her half-brother and sister, Edward and Mary.[220] The straitened financial circumstances of the crown after Henry's costly wars meant that she could not emulate the expenditure of her father but Elizabeth did acquire precious jewels and plate and was conscious of how goods and possessions might represent her. Her gospel books adorned with the royal badge and a crucifix may have expressed, as well as her private faith, her determination to head a church not narrowly Protestant in worship.[221] Several cups and bowls in Elizabeth's inventories were decorated with the phoenix; a cup known as the Dream of Paris gestured to the portrait of Elizabeth as judge, and the queen added her arms to a host of inherited objects.[222] New plate was commissioned for the Anjou marriage and to commemorate Drake's circumnavigation of the globe;[223] a gold plate was illustrated with a picture of *The Triumph*, which had been prominent in the battle against the Armada.[224] A virginal inscribed 'whoever you are who are asked to sing, I bid you sing "Let Elizabeth live for ever" ' was probably a gift that symbolized the love a courtier or noble felt for his sovereign, which all were invited to chorus.[225]

Whether it were a change of fashion or a reflection of her sex, plate featured less often in inventories and gifts under Elizabeth than jewels.[226] In Elizabeth's reign, jewels became common in the courtly exchange of gifts and, whether worn by the queen or others, often directly took up symbols and conceits which we have traced through other genres and forms of royal representation. In fact jewels presented to her flattered her by closely following her chosen devices and mottoes. Sir Francis Drake, for example, presented the queen with a phoenix jewel and the Admiral, Lord Howard, gave her 'a jewel of gold . . . containing 11 letters, being SEMPER EADEM garnished with sparks of rubies . . . and in the midst a phoenix of gold'.[227] Dozens of jewels in Elizabeth's inventories feature the phoenix and pelican, still more the crescent moon, the sign of Diana or Cynthia, the twin sister of Apollo.[228] Some jewels worn by the queen were designed specifically around known emblems and so advertised the qualities of devotion, wisdom, beauty and chastity lauded by panegyrists. In some cases, even a gifted jewel could signal counsel as well as flattery: one with the device of a crab and a butterfly with an emblem and motto ('Make haste slowly') seems to have been intended to influence her on a particular matter.[229] Certainly several jewels with bows and arrows reminded the queen of the importance of arms as well as peace; and a jewel presented to her in 1587, with two hands holding a sword and a trowel, referring to Nehemiah and the Israelites building Jerusalem after a period of captivity, was most probably intended to encourage the queen to a more active godly programme.[230] While in most cases, when we have no dates, we are left to deduce the message of a jewel or gift, there are instances where we can be clear about the specific intentions. In 1571, for example, the Spanish ambassador reported that Leicester had given Elizabeth a jewel depicting her enthroned with Mary, Queen of Scots prostrate at her feet and France and Spain submerged by waves – a token of support but probably, too, an admonition to act more firmly to counter Catholic threats and enemies.[231] Jewels in the shape of a frog may have been given to Elizabeth by, or presented by her to, her suitor, Alençon, to whom she gave this nickname, the origin of the English calling the French 'frogs' to this day.[232] In 1588 Drake marked his and his monarch's triumph with the gift of a jewel bearing her image and emblem.[233] As Janet Arnold has suggested, the large number of jewels given to the queen in 1587 were almost certainly meant as, and meant to be displayed as, tokens of loyalty at a time of crisis.[234]

As well as those worn by her, it is the jewels that Elizabeth gave to be worn which engage us in our study of her representation. As we have seen, it became fashionable to wear medals depicting Elizabeth and by the mid-1580s even poorer subjects were wearing base metal medallions with her image.[235] At court, the evidence suggests that a similar fashion for wearing cameos of the queen, some in rings, began in the 1570s and grew so that soon 'cameos of the queen probably formed part of the standard stock carried by an Elizabethan jeweller', available to any who could purchase them.[236] One cameo, of Elizabeth clasping a sieve, again illustrates the degree to which iconographic programmes crossed from painting to material objects and into a commodity culture which embraced circles beyond the privileged.[237] At court and beyond, jewels bound queen and subjects and signified their mutual love and intimacy.

In early modern England, clothes were perhaps the most obvious signifier of rank and status; indeed, as social mobility increased, successive Tudor proclamations endeavoured to arrest social change by strict decrees about dress which reserved designated cloths and colours to nobility and, of course, purple and cloth of gold to kings.[238] Not surprisingly, then, clothes were important in the history of Elizabeth's image and representation. Though as a princess she had been noted for her simple dress, by her death Elizabeth had a wardrobe of over 3,000 dresses.[239] 'Increasingly elaborate with the passing years', the dresses asserted her wealth and power, clothed the ageing body in distracting finery and often rehearsed in complex embroidery many of the images and symbols of the representations of the Virgin Queen.[240] Thanks to pioneering research by Janet Arnold (which we lack for other reigns and which has yet to be fully incorporated into studies of Elizabeth), we are able to be quite specific about how clothes performed in representing the queen. Elizabeth, we now learn, actually possessed a gown like that depicted in the Rainbow Portrait, embroidered with eyes and ears; and a similar mantle and slippers embroidered with eyes, which were gifts, suggest that Elizabeth herself became a moving allegorical tableau, whom others were able to read and understand.[241] A fashion for clothes with emblems stitched on to them developed in the reign, probably in emulation of the queen's taste, and most of her

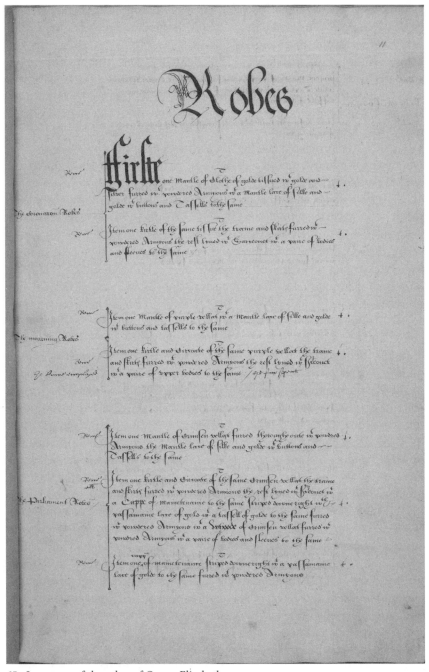

65 Inventory of the robes of Queen Elizabeth.

heraldic and dynastic signs and personal symbols appear time and again on clothes.[242] As well as roses and fleurs-de-lis (the heraldic flowers of the Tudors and of France), the inventory of Elizabeth's wardrobe reveals gowns and mantles embroidered with suns in splendour (a divine symbol and familiar analogue for kings), moons and other planets, and rainbows (as we have seen in the case of the Rainbow Portrait, the sign of God's promise). Clothes were also decorated with serpents (a symbol of wisdom), bees (the natural world's model for the good commonwealth) and pomegranates, a symbol of the Virgin, while embroidered hawthorns, a symbol of purity and prudence, and fountains (of bounty) advertised the royal virtues.[243] The depiction on the queen's petticoat of the nine Muses connected the Elizabeth who was proud of her learning with all the arts and sciences, as the numerous embroidered fruits we encounter symbolized the abundant plenty which she had often boasted she had brought the realm.[244] References in some entries to 'sundry beasts', as well as lions, kingfishers and grasshoppers on the queen's clothes, make it clear that there are still things we do not know about the politics of Elizabeth's clothing.[245] But we can be sure that, as she walked through her court or embarked on progress, Elizabeth's clothes rendered her a moving billboard of advertisement and signification: that is, of the representation of her person and her rule.

Fashion represented the royal wearer to foreign visitors as well as English subjects. We recall that Queen Mary had worn Spanish dress at her wedding, not only as a compliment to her husband Philip but also to signal the importance to her and her rule of a marriage to which many objected: it was, as we might say today of many outfits, a statement.[246] Elizabeth clearly appreciated the signals that clothes could send: it was noted at the Valois court that she wore French dress for the portrait she sent to Catherine de Medici, when the marriage to the duc d'Anjou was being negotiated.[247] We cannot then but wonder whether the Spanish gowns that Elizabeth ordered in the period 1571–7 did not reflect, as well as the imperatives of fashion, her determination to adhere to her own foreign policy, including a possible rapprochement with Spain, at a time when the hotter Protestants pressured her to go to war.[248] Few would doubt that in the Armada Portrait, in which she wore French fashions 'at their most exaggerated English form', Elizabeth was rubbing sartorial salt into the wound of the defeated Spaniard, as well as making a pointedly patriotic statement at a time when England was not renowned on the European stage as a centre of fashion.[249]

The introduction of a masculine style of female dress in the 1570s should perhaps not pass without comment. The first Elizabethan warrant for a doublet was issued in 1575 and it would appear, from subsequent warrants to William Whittell, the tailor, that the trend for wearing a male style of jacket was also started by the queen, as was the wearing of jerkins.[250] Famously, Philip Stubbes, the puritan pamphleteer, in his *Anatomy of Abuses* excoriated this trend of women wearing 'a kind of attire appropriate only to men'.[251] At the beginning of her reign, Elizabeth had faced similar denunciations of the impropriety of female rule. Did she then adopt a masculine style of dress in the 1570s, at a time when the realm was under threat, to assert her authority and to cloak the 'body of a weak and feeble woman' in the raiments of a man? One account has it that she turned up at Tilbury on the eve of the Armada in full armour to reinforce the message of her willingness to fight and die with her people.[252] We know that Elizabeth, especially when she wished to assert herself, used the masculine nouns prince and king: in 1601 she sought, she said, to override her 'sexly weakness' with 'the glorious name of a king'.[253] Did she then use dress to disrupt the signs of gender and to present herself as king and queen? Interestingly, the long-standing and enduring objections to feminine rule resurfaced in the 1570s when a young man named William Cartwright, brother to the Presbyterian leader Thomas, claimed to be the rightful heir to the throne.[254] Carole Levin has argued that the appearance of such male impostors was a feature of female rule in a patriarchal society and a device that opponents could exploit.[255] Under Mary, we recall, rumours abounded that Edward VI was still alive, and some claimed to be the boy king.[256] Similar stories and pretenders (one Emmanuel Plantagenet, for example) re-emerged in late Elizabethan England at a time when the queen's virginity and the succession loomed as increasingly serious problems. In 1591, one William Hacket claimed to be emperor of Europe and caused a great buzz in the city.[257] During subsequent years, a historian has identified 'a generalised sense of dismay at women's rule in the accounts of people arrested for making seditious statements about the queen'.[258] Elizabeth's reaction to such misogyny was increasingly to take on masculine styles and attributes, a direction furthered by a change from peace to a recognition of the unavoidability of war. Several engravings of Elizabeth, late and posthumous, represented her as a warrior and sort of sexual hybrid.[259] In 1587, Elizabeth herself had warned that, though as a woman she preferred peace, should any dare attack her realm, 'they would find that in war she could be better than a man'.[260] It may be that, like her players on the stage, Elizabeth cross-dressed to perform that role: that, like her speeches, her clothes were texts of resistance to traditional limitations on women and represented her authority as that of a mighty and martial king.

In their symbols, colours and designs, then, Elizabeth's clothes, like her portraits, emblem jewels and brooches, connected the intimate private female body to the public body of the realm and resolved the tensions inherent in the queen's two bodies and in the very fact of female rule. Though the fashion of

34   The Fountayne

Let all true Englifh harts,pronounce whyle they haue breath:
God faue and profper in renown,our Queene *Elyzabeth.*
Viuat,vincat,regnat, Elyzabetha.

66 Engraving of Elizabeth I in Munday's *Zelauto.*

courts and nobles, clothes also signified to a broad public as the queen travelled to houses and hunting lodges, on progresses, and to church services. It
was before a large crowd of her meanest subjects that, it is alleged, she
appeared in armour. Clothes were, for the queen no less than her subjects in
an age of theatre and self-fashioning, a public performance, part of the
performance of – and even the maintenance of – regal authority. It is to the
queen's other performances on the stage of state that we now turn.

CHAPTER 11

'VIEWED AND BEHELD OF ALL MEN'
QUEEN ELIZABETH AND THE PERFORMANCE
OF MAJESTY

I

One of the reasons why Queen Elizabeth seems attractive to scholars and the public today is that she was a strong woman, a successful queen in an age which tended to regard that last adjective and noun as a contradiction in terms. The other reason, unquestionably, is that quality democratic politics holds so high: her possession of the common touch. At first, this may seem a curious statement. Sixteenth-century England was a strictly hierarchical society, as well as a kingdom in which the lot of the ordinary man and woman was to obey their betters and their prince; and Elizabeth did not lack any sense of the obeisance due to sovereign monarchs. But she had grown up in an age when the combination of religious division and print had thrust those below the levels of the elite into the world of politics, and in a universe in which ordinary preachers and polemicists had dared to challenge king and church. As princess, Elizabeth would have witnessed the wave of popular support that enabled her sister to overcome Lady Jane Grey and succeed to the throne; she was summoned to court during the days Wyatt's rebels marched on London; and she heard much of the mounting popular disaffection occasioned by Mary's marriage and her rigorous persecution of Protestants. At the height of Mary's unpopularity, we have seen Elizabeth progressing through the city, a visual corporeal reminder of a different queen in waiting. Elizabeth's experience had schooled her in the need for popular support for the exercise of rule as well as in her rights as sovereign. As we have seen, in her speeches, Elizabeth expressed both her especial place as rightful heir and God's chosen handmaid *and* her certainty of the love of her people for a queen who promised that none would care for them more. Though the rhetoric of mutual affection between sovereign and subjects was not new, Elizabeth reiterated and personalized the conceit in hundreds of phrases, gestures and signs, and so made the relation with her people the centrepiece of her representation to princes abroad and to any who sought to challenge her at home.

Essential to that representation was her genius for public performance – for knowing exactly the right moment, word or gesture which would turn spectators into worshippers, subjects into servants who experienced and felt a personal bond of loyalty to their queen, whatever criticisms they might have of her ministers. Public spectacles, royal entries and progresses themselves question any simple idea of sovereign power divorced from popular acclaim. All state rituals – from the coronation to the scaffold – depended upon an audience willing to partake of, and play their part in, the spectacle; in some cases, of course, such as mayor's shows and civic receptions, subjects helped to devise them.[1] From the outset, Elizabeth appears to have had a keen sense of her role *in* state rituals as well as her position as the subject *of* state ritual. She intuited that, at times, it was through responding to (rather than directing) pageants that she could exercise the greatest sway.

In what may seem a paradox, it was Elizabeth's skilful and occasional descent from the heights of mystical majesty that strengthened the monarchy, by exciting the desires of subjects for some sacred figure and divine locus of authority. Not least through her own performances in rituals, often devised by others, Elizabeth rendered herself the object of a cult, so becoming almost a saint whose succession day, 17 November, was the first royal anniversary to be popularly celebrated in England. Through rituals, even more than portraits, Elizabeth became an icon, and Catholic processions that fêted the Virgin Mary were appropriated and transmuted into liturgies and paeans to a Protestant Virgin Queen.[2] For all the uncertainties of events during her rule, the reign of Elizabeth was that which witnessed the greatest sacralization of regality and the deification of the sovereign.

Today, 'rebranding' is a familiar business term and tactic, often used by a new owner or manager of a corporation – often one that has underperformed. Disturbingly to many, the term and concept has become almost as commonplace in politics – perhaps a mark of a world in which tradition has become a pejorative word and novelty is ubiquitously celebrated. This was not the world of early modern England where tradition, custom and history lent authority to actions, and change, often suspected and feared, had to be 'sold' in the language of continuity. As a Tudor woman, succeeding to the throne, Elizabeth's first priority was to establish her lineage and legitimacy which, we must never forget, many Roman Catholics denied.[3] Having witnessed conspiracy and rebellion, she also needed to try to unify her people, and to cool the passions that Mary's Spanish marriage, the loss of Calais, and her religious persecutions had aroused. Others, in her Councils and in the country, had different priorities: the restoration of an unambiguous Protestant religious settlement and, in some cases, further godly Reformation. While it seems likely that Elizabeth was a committed Protestant, she did not, as we shall see, share all the desires of the reformers, and for her, the first principles of any settlement had to be unity and order.[4] Though the hopes and expectations of change of Protestant subjects – not only returning exiles but those who had kept a low profile at home – were high, many had welcomed the return to the old services and ceremonies under Mary (even if they had deplored the burnings); and were doubtless anxious that, once again, all would be swept away. Much therefore was at stake in Elizabeth's first formal appearance before her people as queen. And many – in the court and city, among councillors and nobles, aldermen and citizens – were involved in the elaborate pageants that greeted her as she made her passage through London, on the way to her coronation on 14 January 1559.

An account of *The Passage of our Most Dread Sovereign* was published within days, by Richard Tothill 'cum privilegio'.[5] Tothill was not the queen's printer and, though there was evidently official approval of his account, it was also clearly popular, quickly passing to a second edition. Like his publication, the occasion it describes was evidently a popular success. Elizabeth began her route from the Tower to Westminster, accompanied by her cavalcade and (do we hear the words of a chronicler looking for a good sale?) 'also with a noble train of goodly and beautiful ladies'.[6] As soon as she entered the city, Elizabeth was immediately greeted by 'the assembly, prayers, wishes, welcomings, cries, tender words and all other signs which argue a wonderful earnest love of most obedient subjects towards their sovereign'.[7] As she was to articulate in so many future speeches, Elizabeth appreciated the reciprocity of such love; as did the narrator of her pageant. Having described the outburst of popular affection, he noted that, 'on the other side' (as if of a balance) Elizabeth 'by holding up her hands and merry countenance to such as stood far off and most tender and gentle language to those that stood nigh to her grace did declare herself *no less* thankfully to receive her people's good will'.[8] The account underlines this reciprocity: 'on either side there was nothing but gladness'.[9] And the importance of Elizabeth's very first ritual act – a striking contrast to Mary's silence – can hardly be exaggerated. The people were 'wonderfully ravished with the loving answers and *gestures* of their prince' (she halted her chariot to receive petitions) which was seen to promise 'a wonderful hope . . . touching her worthy governance in the rest of her reign'.[10] Here, in the very words of the chronicler, we discover a clear contemporary appreciation of the power of the sign and indeed of the performance: the city had become the 'stage' of a 'wonderful spectacle', and Elizabeth took pains to play her part.[11]

On a tower at Fenchurch Street, a child welcomed the queen with a speech promising true hearts – which, lest it be lost in the mêlée, was written out in English and Latin and fastened to the scaffold.[12] At Gracious Street Elizabeth faced the first pageant: an elaborate ark which was built across the street with a variety of levels and 'stages', as well as ports and battlements. On the lowest level, the figures of Henry VII and Elizabeth of York, standing clothed resplendently in red and white roses, represented the foundation of the Tudor dynasty. Above them, the figures of Henry VIII (crowned with an imperial crown) and Anne Boleyn effectively erased the king's earlier marriage to Catherine of Aragon, and passed over Mary, to present Elizabeth on the highest level as the Yorkist heir, a second Elizabeth who, like the first, symbolized concord.[13] The pageant scene was in 'all the empty places thereof . . . furnished with sentences concerning unity'.[14] And while music played, the child spoke explaining the whole conceit. Elizabeth, the account tells us, could not hear and so, ordering her chariot to be brought closer, 'required to have the matter opened unto her and what they signified'.[15] Did she need such an explanation of what was hardly a veiled message affirming her descent? It would seem more likely that the queen, as she was to again, went to lengths to demonstrate her interest and involvement – both in the pageant and its message. After the exposition, as it were responding to petition, she promised she would do all for concord, 'as the pageant did impart'.[16]

In what must have been a very visible gesture, Elizabeth sent a servant ahead of her, as she approached the second pageant, to request silence so that she could hear the speeches at the conduit at Cornhill.[17] Here, Worthy Government was figured by a child, representing Elizabeth herself, seated in a throne. Four allegorical figures, with placards explaining who they were, supported the show: Wisdom, Justice, Love of Subjects and Pure Religion. Beneath their feet they trod on Folly, Bribery, Ignorance, Rebellion and Superstition.[18] The verses, posted and read by the child, deployed praise as a vehicle of counsel: subjects 'do trust', they ran, 'these ventures shall maintain up thy throne'.[19] The explanation underlined the conditional nature of the praise: the queen would continue to sit secure in the throne of government 'so long as she embraced virtue and held vice under foot'.[20] One virtue, we note, was Pure Religion and its corresponding vice, Superstition. Elizabeth was being urged swiftly to renounce the religious policy of her predecessor: Protestantism was presented as essential to good government and to secure tenure of the throne. A Mantuan observer, Schifanoya, was surely right to read the scene as 'purporting that hitherto religion had been misunderstood and misdirected, and that now it will proceed on a better footing'.[21] Virtuous rule was presented as Protestant rule, in accordance with the sympathies of the zealous reformer Richard Grafton (who had been deprived of his post of royal printer by Mary) and the committee which devised the pageant.[22] Elizabeth replied with gracious thanks, promising her 'good endeavour' to maintain virtue.[23] Was it an equivocal answer? Certainly it was one that permitted her to bask in the praise proffered without committing herself to a godly religious agenda. It was an art that she perfected.

The third pageant, of the Eight Beatitudes, spanned Soper Lane by the conduit at Cheapside. On a pageant consisting of three gates, eight children represented the beatitudes, 'having the proper name of the blessing that they did represent . . . placed above their heads' (in accordance with Matthew 5).[24] This time – again one suspects as a gesture – Elizabeth had in advance 'required the matter somewhat to be opened' that she 'might the better understand' what was said.[25] As verses celebrated the virtues of meekness, mildness, justice, mercy and peace, she was informed that 'if her grace did continue in her goodness . . . she should hope for the fruits of these promises' which were the 'blessings of almighty God made to his people'.[26] Here again the virtues of good rule were connected with the gospel, which was 'applied to our sovereign lady' and which she was urged to champion: 'Therefore', the verse ran, 'trust thou in God', who, 'as his promise is, so he will make thee strong'.[27]

As she passed the decorated standard and approached the next pageant at the Little Conduit at Cheap, Elizabeth once more 'required to know what it might signify' – presumably to prepare her response.[28] Truth, she was informed, would deliver her the Bible in English. In her eagerness to respond, the queen, assuring them that she would often read it, sent a knight to receive it, only to learn that it was to be delivered in a pageant which lay ahead.[29] This final pageant was an elaborate climax to the series. It consisted of two hills: one craggy and barren, with, beneath a withered tree, a figure 'Ruinosa Respublica', with a tablet listing the causes of the decay of commonwealths; the other, verdant and fertile, with a green tree beneath which sat 'Respublica bene instituta', with the causes of flourishing states. In what reads like a masque, from a cave between the hills emerged the figures of Time and the daughter of Time – Truth, carrying a book on which was written 'Verbum veritatis', the book of truth.[30] As a child addressed Elizabeth, Truth's book, the Bible, was 'delivered unto her grace down by a silken lace' from the pageant.[31] The speech explained that Time had rescued Truth from confinement and that only with Truth restored might a barren commonwealth become a prosperous estate.[32] The causes of a ruinous commonweal were listed as disobedience, rebellion, disagreement among subjects and 'unmercifulness' in rulers; those of a flourishing realm were a wise and learned prince, virtue and the fear of God.[33] Clearly, the general message was, virtuous and prosperous government rested on Truth, and on the word of truth, the scripture in English. But, as we will recall, this moment carried more particular freight: Mary Tudor had taken as her motto 'Veritas temporis filia', and had deployed it as a blazon – on her seal, for example – of her Catholic faith.[34] Moreover, it was a figure of Henry VIII with an English Bible that had caused Gardiner such concern in the marriage pageant of Mary and Philip – which

Gardiner had helped to organize.[35] The Little Conduit pageant, therefore, staged a dramatic reversal of Marian representation and offered to Elizabeth a reappropriation of Truth as a Protestant preserve and figured religious change as the only means by which to transmute a restless and divided commonwealth into an obedient one, as well as a 'merciless' rule into a government of wisdom and love. Its meaning, the narrator informs us, 'depended of them that went before': that is unity, virtue and God's blessings on the queen and the realm depended upon Truth, the word, Protestantism.[36] In this dramatic *mise-en-scène*, Elizabeth received the book, kissed it, and held it aloft to show her assent.[37] In doing so, she literally completed the script of the pageant series and affirmed her identity with the word.

The final device or structure at Fleet Street staged, atop four towers in front of a palm tree, a figure in parliament robes: Deborah the judge and restorer of the House of Israel. On either side of her, nobles, clergy and commonalty sat debating, a tablet explaining that the whole represented 'Deborah with her estates consulting for the good government of Israel'.[38] As Elizabeth ordered silence, a child delivered a final explanation. God had set women to reign among men, like Deborah, but 'it behoveth both men and women so ruling to use advice of good counsel'.[39] Elizabeth's sex was vindicated, her power was exalted by comparison with biblical heroines; but her need to take counsel (and the counsel of the godly) was no less asserted.

As she had progressed, in every word and gesture Elizabeth had shown her openness to advice: to explanation, petition and admonition, as well as praise. She had received the English Bible, no less than the traditional purse of a thousand crowns *from* her people.[40] As historians, we often contrast rule by consultation with absolute power. But in this, her very first year, Elizabeth took the opportunity presented by advice delivered with praise to turn counsel into worship. As she passed by Temple Bar, two giants Gogmagog the Albion and Corineus the Briton, who had, we recall, greeted Philip and Mary at their entrance into the city, now held up a summary of the whole pageant. The verses explained that the first arch had established the queen's descent, the second her virtues, the third and fourth her blessed status as upholder of Truth, and the fifth figured her as another Deborah, sent 'from heaven a long comfort to us, thy subjectes all'.[41] As she stood before them, a child delivered the city's valediction:

> Farewell O worthy Queene, and as our hope is sure,
> That into errours place, thou wilt now trueth restore.[42]

Again, with a brilliant sense of the moment, Elizabeth both responded to the city's counsel and turned it into adulation. Raising her hands, she willed the people to say Amen, as though she were, priest-like, conducting a liturgical service.[43] The queen's performance had been quite remarkable – and it was seen to be so. Indeed, the popular account of her procession took space at the end to recall and note the quite exceptional acts of grace she had performed. Elizabeth had stopped her chariot for ordinary people to speak to her and to hear the poor children of Christ's Hospital; she had treasured simple nosegays given by poor women, and was seen to have kept a humble rosemary sprig, given by a 'poor woman above Fleet', beside her till she reached Westminster.[44] She had received the English Bible with reverence, kissing it, and had lifted her eyes at the cross, praying and comparing herself to Daniel, who had escaped the jaws of death.[45]

As she left the city, one character called out 'Remember old King Henry the Eight'.[46] It was a revealing quip, for the coronation entry had served to all but erase the reign of Mary and to introduce what Helen Hackett calls a 'new Protestant form of state iconography'.[47] As she observed, the 'textual content was more prolific than ever', underlining the centrality of the word and subordinating the image.[48] But whatever the intentions of the designers, Elizabeth also made herself an icon at the centre of a liturgy of public worship. While it may be that the description of the pageant exaggerates the spontaneous outpourings of love of the queen, the coronation entry was etched in the memory of the capital and the nation. Shortly afterwards, Lanquet's and Fabyan's chronicles recalled and memorialized the entry and the 'love showed by subjects to a loving sovereign'.[49] In 1590, reliving antique triumphs, the poet Ludowick Lloyd recalled a coronation which had 'not only exceeded all her predecessors the kings of England, but all other foreign kings as far as heaven surmounteth earth'.[50] Whatever allowance we make for the propaganda element in such accounts, it is clear that Elizabeth from the beginning made a spectacular impression.

It was the personal charisma, and the combination of grandeur and a rare common touch that, perhaps uniquely, characterized her reign. Though it began with the disadvantage of being the court of a queen, Elizabeth's court was widely praised for its order and magnificence and the nobility were drawn to court in ever increasing numbers, as the monarch became the focus of the nation. Foreign envoys and writers described Whitehall as beautifully furnished and noted the 'sumptuous style' of the court.[51] Baron Breuner, in England as agent for Archduke Charles, reported that he had seen no court 'in the world so richly garnished with costly furniture of silk adorned with gold, pearls and precious stones'.[52] Hans Jacob Breuning von Buchenbach told the Duke of Württemberg, 'I have never seen a royal court of such splendour'.[53] Virginio Orsino, Duke of Bracciano claimed not to have seen a court so well ordered.[54] The herald William Segar's boast that under Elizabeth 'the magnificence of her majesty's court' 'exceeded all others' had, then, ample contemporary support.[55] Despite her legendary parsimony, Elizabeth understood the importance of worthy magnificence as a representation of her rule, and exemplified the words of Philibert of Vienne's *The Philosopher of the Court* which was translated in 1575: 'if we be not famous and known, we cannot attain to the perfection of our virtue'.[56]

Elizabeth did not merely maintain the magnificence of the court in the materials of furnishings and fabrics. She elevated courtly ceremonial into rituals of worship of her person. The queen kept state and dined in public only on feast days, when she was served with full ceremony.[57] At Garter dinners and other feasts, however, she commanded 'the same ceremoniousness in her absence as when she is present'.[58] This was the case, a German visitor observed with some awe, 'even when no one sits and dines there'.[59] A 'goodly number' attended in the Presence Chamber at all times and the reverence due to majesty was symbolically displayed in the queen's absence.[60] As Thomas Smith, with the experience of his own monarch in mind, explained in his *De republica anglorum*, 'no man speaketh to the prince nor serveth at the table but in adoration and kneeling, all persons of the realm be bareheaded before him insomuch that in the chamber of presence where the cloth of estate is set, no man dare walk yea though the prince be not there, no man dare tarry there but bareheaded'.[61] When Elizabeth was present, at any court entertainment or occasion, she was surrounded by a large entourage. The Venetian ambassador, reporting on the visit in the first year of her reign of the duc de Montmorency, described the tiltyard 'on all sides beset with lords, ladies and persons of quality, sumptuously apparelled and richly furnished . . . among them . . . stood many of the guard . . . holding an infinite number of torches . . . by which means those that beheld the terrace . . . deemed it rather a theatre celestial than a palace of earthly building'.[62] Such religious language became increasingly common over the course of the reign, as court ceremonies, along with the texts and images we have examined, presented Elizabeth as a goddess. Thomas Platter, another German writer struck by the awe she inspired, reported that 'I am told that they even play cards with the queen in kneeling posture'.[63]

Striking as such testimonies to the grandeur and adulation of the queen are, what makes them all the more remarkable are the countless contemporary references to the humanity, even the familiar intimacy, which this mystical goddess Elizabeth could display. Elizabeth liked to dance, and play the clavichord and lute before an audience; she played the lute in her barge for Baron Breuner.[64] During court balls, she often summoned young and old for conversation – one observer said 'she spoke continuously' and chatted 'most amiably' – and could act with daring coquettishness in the presence of all.[65] The traveller Leopold von Kresszow noted how, at one dance, Elizabeth pointed 'with her finger at the face of one Master or Captain Rall [Raleigh] . . . [and] told him that there was smut on it. She also offered to wipe it off with her handkerchief.'[66] When she proceeded to chapel, preceded by 200 of her bodyguard and lords and councillors, despite the high ceremony, the queen graciously paused to receive petitions.[67] When 'the common people, who formed two rows on either side of her path, fell upon their knees', Elizabeth paused, as she had at her coronation, to speak to them and 'thank you with all my heart'.[68]

Though, as we shall see, it opened spaces for criticism, Elizabeth used this combination of mysterious majesty and common humanity to great effect – with visitors as with her courtiers and councillors. In 1595 Buchenbach paused in his dispatch to the Duke of Württemberg, to report that 'I cannot pass over in silence the fact that at the last audience . . . her majesty came forward a few paces to meet me and that she did not sit down. She stood for longer than a full hour by the clock, conversing with me; which is astounding for a queen of such eminence'; and, he added, 'of such great age'.[69] From youth to old age, Elizabeth, an abundance of literature evidences, combined imperious majesty with intimacy as a device of exercising power as a woman. At one moment, as an ambassador still trembled to recollect, 'the august queen came in with awful majesty and royal bearing into the garden'; at another she would confide and confess to girlish vulnerability.[70] Sir John Harington, her godson, poetically captured her shifts of style and mood as a change from 'a storm . . . a sudden gathering of clouds' to a smile that was 'pure sunshine'.[71]

This combination of majesty and intimacy found its commonest expression at court in the love games played between Elizabeth as Petrarchan mistress and her courtier suitors, and in the sonnets, love poems and plays which these amours inspired. Though for some time scholars have appreciated the seriousness – even the power politics – of these games, their exact role in the representation of Elizabeth to her courtiers and a wider public has yet to be elucidated.[72] The cult of chivalric love, like other discourses deployed by Elizabeth, served to ameliorate the difficulties of representing an (unmarried) queen's two bodies, politic and personal. Chivalric romance enabled Elizabeth to be simultaneously figured as unassailable virgin and eternal object of desire; and, whilst the self-conscious medievalism identified her with pre-Reformation values, the chivalric language of protection gestured towards armed vigilance in the defence of Protestantism. Courtly love also fostered a public and personal allegiance, a combination of religious and political loyalty with an erotic desire which was rendered respectable by its being figured as Platonic love. The historian of Elizabethan chivalry makes further claims: in helping to resolve the tension between honour and obedience, 'through its conventions of feudal loyalty and romantic devotion, Elizabethan chivalry affirmed Tudor sovereignty'.[73] For Richard McCoy, chivalric exercises (and the literature they generated) were symbolic actions which performed like other texts to reconcile contradictions and divisions, personal, religious and social. Chivalry displayed aristocratic honour and privilege and emphasized personal service and allegiance to the monarch – to a queen who was lady, mistress and virgin as well as ruler. Elizabethan chivalry connected the body of the female queen to the masculine public realms of martial prowess, honour and active virtue.

Elizabeth's reign saw not only a self-conscious attention to chivalric rites but also an emphasis on the queen as the personification of these rites. Elizabeth revived Edward III's tilting regulations for tournaments, not least on account of their connection with the story of the Round Table and King Arthur.[74] Several chivalric entertainments took up the Arthurian legend, and Spenser, of course, modelled the Fairy Queen's annual feast on Arthur's.[75] *The Certain Devices . . . Presented to Her Majesty by the Gentlemen of Grays Inn*, at Greenwich in 1581, opened with the banquet held by Arthur to solemnize his conquest of the Saxons and staged a final scene of a pelican feeding its blood to its young, together with poems to a queen who would restore Arthur's golden age: 'that virtuous virgo borne for Britain's blisse'.[76] The tournament prepared in Whitsun week 1587 for the French envoy staged at the Whitehall end of the tiltyard, near the queen's lodgings, a fountain of Perfect Beauty which the children of desire attempted to besiege in vain.[77] As a boy explained to Elizabeth, it was she 'in whom the whole story of virtue is written with the language of beauty'.[78] In this complex device, Elizabeth is represented as the divine sun, which, like Beauty, might restore fallen man to paradise. And here, interestingly, Beauty needs no rescue from assault; from a 'renowned princess . . . nothing can obtain victory but virtue'.[79]

Tilts, tournaments and allegorical devices and shows were annual events from Elizabeth's coronation to virtually her last days.[80] The herald William Segar, in *The Book of Honour and Arms* (1570) and *Honour Military and Civil* (1602), traced the history of combat in England and charted the challenges and tournaments of Elizabeth's reign: 'so many royal and stately triumphs' which, he claimed, exceeded all predecessors.[81] Segar informs us that, at the beginning of the reign, Sir Henry Lee, the queen's champion, vowed to present himself to defend her honour every year on the anniversary of her succession; and certainly on 17 November 1569 there is a record of tournaments that became a regular feature of the Whit celebrations of her succession from the late 1570s and 1580s.[82] At each of these yearly triumphs, motifs of royal representation – the queen as vestal virgin, the triumphs of peace – and badges of Elizabeth (the phoenix and the eglantine) not only figured her as the patroness of honour but represented her as victor, as Hercules, pious princess, and saint.[83] Whatever its origins and role in articulating aristocratic codes and privilege, by the end of Elizabeth's reign chivalry had become another language in the representation of the queen as divine ruler: in Segar's words, 'like as the splendent beams of the sun do spread themselves in giving light, heat and comfort unto all living things ... so from the sacred power ... of emperors, kings and queens all earthly dignities do proceed'.[84]

At the heart of English chivalry was the Order of the Garter, the regulations, rites and majesty of which Elizabeth assiduously upheld. The Order of the Garter, as we have seen, had changed with the liturgical revolutions of the Tudor Reformation.[85] Interestingly, Elizabeth did not immediately change the ceremonial or regulations reconstituted by Mary; and, apart from the removal of the word 'mass' and the use of the English litany for the procession, the Catholic statutes and along with them the restored figure of St George (which had caused such concern to Edward VI) 'survived into a Protestant England'.[86] Elizabeth may have welcomed the ambiguous religious signification of an old Catholic order: in two portraits she is shown holding the George, the badge of the Order, at her breast, as though it were a sacred object; and Gheeraert's engraving of a Garter procession evokes something of a traditional missal procession.[87] The Order, from its inception, took as its emblems the Holy Trinity, St George and the Virgin and thus opened to the Virgin Queen another possibility for the appropriation of Catholic symbolism for Tudor Protestant rule.[88] Granted to Catholic and Protestant princes alike, the Order of the Garter was an ecumenical community which probably represented what the queen hoped for the church and realm.

Elizabeth held the great Garter festivals at Windsor until 1567 when they were moved to Whitehall or Greenwich, from the Chapel of St George to the royal chapel, before the banquet in the Presence Chamber.[89] The procession became increasingly elaborate: by the mid-1580s a canopy was carried over the queen, perhaps like that in the Procession Picture, and the cavalcade made its way three times round the royal courtyard.[90] Von Buchenbach was evidently awestruck by the splendour of the nobles' clothes and 'costly gems and jewels', the rich vestments of the officiating clergy and the elaborate ritual, solemn mass and 'most splendid array of all meats imaginable' at the feast.[91] During the 1590s, the procession of the new knights to Windsor 'developed into a spectacular cavalcade', with some attended by hundreds of men.[92] The Garter represented Elizabeth as sovereign of a chivalric order; as, though female, a martial prince; as head of an order that incorporated the Catholic as well as the Protestant sovereigns of Christendom; as both the Virgin and St George, the guardian of the realm and yet the beloved maiden who needed protection.

Whilst the Elizabethan Garter ceremonies doubtless meant different things to different observers, their importance in representing the queen can hardly be exaggerated. Spenser's *Fairy Queen* is illustrated with a large woodcut of St George and the dragon, and numerous minor panegyrists regarded the Order of the Garter as central to the cult of Gloriana.[93] In his 1593 *The Honour of the Garter*, written to commemorate the installation of the Earl of Northumberland, the chronicler, playwright and poet George Peele, who also contributed to *The Phoenix Nest* his poem 'The Praise of Chastity', identified the Order of the Garter with the sect of Cynthia.[94] In his book bearing a frontispiece of the royal arms and Elizabeth's motto, 'Semper eadem', Peele rewrote in verse the origins of the Order and imagined Edward III addressing Elizabeth as his heir and 'England's great sovereign'.[95] In a dream in which appeared to him Cynthia's castle and a 'host of airie armed men', Peele 'saw a Virgin Queene, attired in white/ leading with her a sort of goodly Knights' – 'the glory of the westerne world'.[96] In *St George for England* (1601), Gerard Malynes explicated the meaning of the Order for its late Elizabethan moment.[97] The dragon he read as 'the chiefest head and cause of all rebellion and variance in countries', and as a lesson in the need for 'concord amongst the members of a commonwealth'.[98] In an epistle dedicatory to Lord Keeper Egerton, he further explained: 'here as under the person of the noble champion St George our Saviour Christ was prefigured . . . so her most excellent majesty by advancing the pure doctrine of Christ Jesus . . . hath been used to perform the part of a valiant champion, delivering an infinite number out of the devil's power'.[99] St George, he added, 'is the king's authority, armed with the right armour of a Christian'.[100] Malynes's St George may offer a barometer of how, for all that the Catholic ceremonial remained unreformed, the Elizabethan Order of the Garter became increasingly a Protestant symbol. But it was also one that validated monarchy, female rule and Elizabeth herself as chosen saint – and at a time when all were facing criticism and challenge.

Traditional historiography has often discussed chivalric and Garter festivities as the idle pastimes of a privileged coterie which sought only to flatter itself.[101] Yet increasingly by the end of the sixteenth century, such rituals were both published and performed before a public which crowded to see them, no less than it hurried to buy woodcuts or prints of the queen. In the words of Jean Wilson, 'The tilts were not merely private court occasions, but public displays.'[102] And though the cost of one shilling (twelve times the entrance to the cheapest standing place in the theatre) was expensive, evidently some townspeople paid it, while still more witnessed the processions to and from the tiltyard, especially on Accession Day when the citizenry were on the streets for the celebrations. In the case of Garter processions, Elizabeth's removal of the festivities from Windsor served to make the occasion more public, as even ordinary Londoners thronged into the court to witness the scene. Von Buchenbach described in 1595 'a great crush in the chapel as many of the common people had thronged together' and observed that the procession around the court was repeated 'so that everyone could have a good view of them'.[103] Deploying her by now famous common touch and acknowledging the Garter festival as a public occasion on the ritual calendar, Elizabeth, the envoy reported, 'spoke most graciously to everyone; even to those who of the vulgar fell upon their knees in homage'.[104]

Along with jousts and Garter feasts, state processions to parliament and entries into London re-presented Elizabeth to subjects eager to see her. Often the texts which relate these events evidence as well as describe the popular audience that attended such civic occasions. So *A Famous Ditty*, to the tune of 'Wigmore's Galliard', related her grace's coming to St James's.[105] And foreign visitors, like Leopold von Wedel, a nobleman from Pomerania, described the 'large crowd of the populace, not only men but also women and girls' who went out to see the queen who processed in a coach 'open to all around'.[106] At the opening of parliament in October 1597, several spectators were crushed 'through the mighty recourse of the people . . . pressing betwixt Whitehall and the College Church to see her majesty and nobility riding in robes'.[107] Such entries into London became a regular fixture of the 17 November festivities where Elizabeth responded to popular desire and became 'the annual celebrity of our voluntary sacrifice of praise and thanksgiving'.[108] The 17 November celebrations, though initially instituted in Oxford University, became not just a spectacle, but what was then called the queen's 'holy day', a ritual of public worship of a monarch who was heralded as a saint.[109]

In a familiar debate between Country and City published in 1579 and 1580 as *Civil and Uncivil Life*, the spokesman for the city derides country bumpkins, who scarcely know the queen.[110] By the middle of Elizabeth's reign, the monarch was clearly familiar, perhaps psychologically as well as visually familiar, to the citizens of the capital. But significantly even the spokesman for the country thought it 'much meet for every gentleman to know the person of his prince' – either, he added, by 'coming to court or places where they resort'.[111] The flocking of provincial gentry, and some below them, to court, a common theme of the complaint literature of the late sixteenth century and of modern social histories of the decay of hospitality and the rural household, has been too little studied as a sign of the mounting desire to see the prince.[112] But in Elizabeth's reign, more than in that of any of her predecessors or successors, the rituals of monarchical representation were not performed only in the capital. Where, not least through the periods of unrest occasioned by religious upheavals, the earlier Tudors had some years confined their travels to houses and lodges close to the capital, the Elizabethan progresses annually took in wider swathes of the country and involved visits to nobles and gentry (as well as royal) houses, with the full panoply of regal magnificence.[113]

¹/₁₀ of time on throne in "progreses"!

II

The sheer scale of Elizabeth's progresses has recently been tabulated in a study which underlines the number and range of her visits.[114] The queen journeyed into twenty-six counties, from London to Somerset, Worcestershire and Rutland, and made over fifty visits each to Essex, Kent, Hampshire and Surrey. She lodged with bishops, Privy Councillors, peers and gentlemen, MPs and JPs, Catholics as well as Protestants, female as well as male hosts.[115] Summer progresses could involve as few as six or over forty stops, and their duration ranged from a short thirteen days in 1602 to over a third of the year, from May to October, in 1575. All in all, Elizabeth spent 1,200 days in progress, or nearly a tenth of her time on the throne. And though she told the French envoy in 1574 that 'we use in the springtime to remove from our standing houses to certain private houses with small companies . . . to avoid great resorts', in truth a progress often involved a large entourage and a huge baggage train of over 300 carts and over 2,000 horses.[116] The journey from house to house along the public highways was a major spectacle – von Wedel described the queen sitting in her coach 'like a goddess such as painters are wont to depict'; and the approach of the cavalcade was often announced by church bells as it passed by.[117] The receptions into the cities and towns of England – Elizabeth visited about fifty – were attended by both citizenry and dignitaries; common folk provided the audiences as well as workforce for the hawking, hunting and walks, as well as pageants, that made up the entertainment at rural seats and lodges.[118] Progresses made Elizabeth's monarchy nationally visible and represented to a wide public both the majesty and humanity of the sovereign.[119]

As with coronation pageants and civic entries, the entertainments devised for the queen on progress – spectacles presented to her which also featured her as the focus of spectacle – often involved conversation and co-operation between queen, courtiers and rural or civic hosts. They also involved negotiation. Just as the capital took the occasion of royal visits to make a case or advise the sovereign as well as praise her, so provincial corporations and individual hosts devised the opportunity to press a suit or advertise a problem, as well as to celebrate a royal visit. And as with her coronation, Elizabeth fully grasped both the reciprocity and theatricality of the progress pageant and performed her role in ways that represented her virtues, manifested her love and strengthened her hold on the affections of her people. The forerunner of the helicopter election-tour, the Elizabethan progress, part a mode of display, part an opportunity to listen, was a vital instrument in that 'securing compliance' which was essential to Tudor rule.[120]

Progress pageants often replicated the motifs and conceits of court entertainments in ways that suggest a common vocabulary and symbolism of representation in Elizabethan England. And whilst each entertainment was, of course, devised for a specific occasion and audience, contemporary printed accounts evidence both the wider audience for these occasions and the broad national circulation of accounts of what had been initially a regional event. The first progress pageant for which we have extensive contemporary report – itself a document of the growing public preoccupation with regality – is that presented at Kenilworth Castle on Elizabeth's progress to Warwickshire in the summer of 1575. The account from Warwickshire by a court attendant written to a merchant friend in London nicely illustrates the exchange of royal news and indeed the passage of the texts of royal representation from city to country and back, a print exchange which served to constitute a public sphere in Elizabethan England.[121] At Kenilworth, Elizabeth's host was also her favourite, Robert Dudley, Earl of Leicester, so this pageant, like several, nicely complicates any simple divide between 'official' and 'private' entertainments. Elizabeth arrived on Saturday, 9 July to the greeting of sibyls clad in white silk, and then, inside the court yard, encountered a porter with a club who, at the sight of such 'heroical sovereignty', laid aside his rough demeanour to open the gates for all.[122] As the queen rode to the inner gate, on an island in a lake, the Lady of the Lake, 'famous', as our narrator reminded readers, 'in King Arthur's book', offered her territory to her.[123] On posts in the grounds, bowls presented various offerings to Elizabeth: the fruits of the gods and goddesses Pomona, Ceres, Neptune and Bacchus, and the accoutrements of Mars and Phoebe.[124] Above, a tablet bearing the queen's arms and initials in gold explained in Latin the gods and their gifts, in verses that, as it was night, were read aloud.[125] As the queen was escorted to her chamber, the last of the gods, Jupiter, delivered his welcome in a spectacular firework display which was seen and heard twenty miles off.[126]

Having been greeted at her entrance by the pagan gods, Elizabeth began the Sunday with divine service before music and dancing in the afternoon – perhaps a calculated rejection of the strict sabbatarian observance already being advocated by the godly.[127] The next day, Elizabeth was taken out to hunt and on her way back, under torchlight escort, was greeted by a savage who, on seeing the queen, broke his oak plant and laid it down as an act of submission. By mistake, the branch almost landed on the queen's horse and all looked on dismayed. However, with her brilliant capacity to turn a tense moment into a joyous one, Elizabeth urged them to go on, assuring the savage 'no hurt, no hurt' – which words the onlookers, significantly blurring real and staged events, 'took to be the best part of the play'.[128]

Over the ensuing days the queen was entertained with walks and hunts, dog and bear fights, music, acrobats and fireworks, and, on St Kenelm's Day, feats of arms and a rural marriage, with spice cakes and Morris dances.[129] A civic play, traditionally performed yearly, but condemned by puritan preachers, was now staged before the queen, in the hope that she might re-authorize the entertainment. Distracted by dancing in the chamber, Elizabeth diplomatically requested it be restaged, on which occasion she rewarded the players as a manifest sign of her 'good acceptance', and perhaps as a snub to the puritans.[130] Other devices placed the queen at the centre of allegories of royal authority: a water pageant represented her as freeing the Lady of the Lake from a cruel knight; the device of a challenge to King Arthur was abandoned due to bad weather; towards the end, the gods again waited on her with gifts, and celebrated the concord and amity she brought in her train.[131]

The letter by the attendant R.L. then demonstrates the interplay in this entertainment of court and country, of magnificence and lowliness, regal and regional – much is written in a Warwickshire spelling and dialect – celebration and petition. It has also been suggested that it records other tensions. Though written in the name of R.L., the actual author, it has been argued, was William Patten, a retainer of Lord Burghley, and the text, it is suggested, discloses some of the disagreements between the queen's ministers, as well as differences between Elizabeth and her favourite.[132] Certainly another account of the Kenilworth entertainment by George Gascoigne, a confidant of Leicester, hints at criticism of Elizabeth's virginity and at the desirability of marriage; and it may be for this reason, rather than just the weather, that a pageant or masque of Diana and Iris was suspended and omitted from the entertainment.[133] Similarly, it would appear that the device of the rescue of the Lady of the Lake was recast to highlight Elizabeth the virgin herself, rather than Leicester, as the protector of chastity.[134] If there is something in the argument of a 'competition for representation', between the queen and her favourite and suitor, who may (it has been argued) have devised the entertainment to press his suit, the events at Kenilworth underlined the queen's control and the accounts suggest her direct intervention in the entertainments which, along with others, she perceived as articulating political positions and programmes. As the letter informs us, 3,000 to 4,000 people 'of various degrees' assembled each day to behold the queen and it was therefore vital that all pass in 'amity and obedience'.[135] Elizabeth resisted Leicester's implied proposal that she renounce her virginity for marriage. And the queen distanced herself from godly programmes: as well as authorizing the Coventry play, she touched to cure the king's evil – and presented herself to her people as 'one God, one Saviour, one faith, one Prince, one Sun, one Phoenix'.[136] As the letter concludes, all yielded to her imperial sway – or at least were presented as so doing.[137]

Our only account of Elizabeth's progress to Woodstock, to Sir Henry Lee's house, in the summer of 1576, was published, anonymously, ten years after the event, and is incomplete.[138] But in the pageant we can still deduce that a series of lovers in search of their amours, one of whom was struck blind in Venus's temple, were directed to a land where government was just and the most virtuous lady in the world ruled. There the lovers met and Hermetes recovered his sight, 'all which happened', a speech to Elizabeth put it, 'by virtue of your grace'.[139] The queen was then beckoned to follow the hermit into a house decorated as a rural bower, with flowers, trees and beasts, and a table shaped like a half-moon, a symbol of the queen which (as we saw) she wore as a jewel in her hair.[140] While Elizabeth sat for a banquet, the Queen of the Fairies was drawn in a chariot of state and addressed her as Virgin, single and singular in her perfection:

> your face, your grace, your goverment of state,
> your passing sprite whereby your fame is blowen:
> do knowe by certain skill you had no mate:
> and that no man throughout the world hath seene
> a prince that may compare with th'English Queene.[141]

As she left, accompanied by the Queen of the Fairies, Elizabeth was heralded as 'sacred saint/ in whom on earth the goddes in Heaven delighte'.[142]

Our narrator, who found in crucial scenes that 'the allegories are hard to be understood' and who could not read verses in Italian, seemed somewhat surprised at Elizabeth's appreciation of the pageant, for when the queen left she commanded that 'the whole in order as it fell should be brought to her in writing'; and using 'besides her own skill', as well as, the account speculated, 'the help of the devisers', she not only worked over the meaning but often recalled the entertainment with pleasure.[143] Indeed, there was evidently a sequel performed the next day. Here the gist was the Fairy Queen's counsel to Caudina, one of the earlier forlorn lovers, that she obey her father's will and abandon her amour, Contarenus. As Contarenus appreciated, what they were asked was to choose between 'countries good' and 'affections dazzling beames'.[144] In time, he concludes, 'You must regard the Commonweal's good plight and seeke the whole not only one to save'.[145] The Queen of the Fairies, whose own states 'from passions blind affects are ... free', commends his virtue, which (Caudina's maid adds) is that too of a 'vertuous Queene' who 'doth stately sceptre sway'.[146] The praise of Elizabeth as the resolver of all conflict, as the figure of Beauty and Virtue is obvious enough. It has also been suggested that Lee's romance deliberately countered Leicester's Kenilworth pageant by arguing the case for duty over affection.[147] But that theme also had relevance to the immediate situation of Elizabeth herself. Though negotiations were stymied, the possibility of Elizabeth's marriage to Alençon was not dead. The Queen of Fairies' speech therefore that 'no man throughout the world' might be compared with the queen may have spoken to, and questioned the wisdom of, the Alençon match as well as Leicester's last bid to marry the queen.[148] Whichever was the case, in celebrating chastity over passion, and duty over affection, the Queen of the Fairies probably spoke for the preference of Elizabeth – the true Fairy Queen.

The account of Elizabeth's 1578 progress was written by Thomas Churchyard, an ex-soldier, adventurer and professional writer, who wrote popular miscellanies and later in life secured the royal pension he had long sought.[149] In an epistle dedicatory to the queen's Attorney, Churchyard made clear his purpose in writing: that the pageant presented to her 'that is our triumph and earthly felicity' might be 'a mirror that . . . all the whole land may look into' and see a model to emulate.[150] 'I have penned,' Churchyard explained, 'for those people that dwell far off from the court that they may see with what majesty a prince reigneth and with what obedience and love good subjects do receive her.'[151] In particular, Churchyard (who helped devise some of the 'shows') wished to highlight the role of 'the common people' whose 'civil sort and courtesy is greatly to be commended'.[152] And, in a preface to the reader, he nicely identified the kinds of changes that Tudor, and especially Elizabethan, royal representation had brought about. Where, he suggested, some stubborn folk, jaded by familiarity, no longer behaved with due deference to their noble master, the people's reaction to the court on progress showed a 'new kind of reverence', indeed an eager desire to run out to see their sovereign.[153]

Though the advance notice of the queen's coming had been short, Churchyard had got to the city three weeks before the court to help prepare entertainments. After Elizabeth's entry on Saturday, 5 July and quiet rest on Sunday, Mercury was sent on Monday to call her abroad.[154] The next day, with 'as great a train' of commoners as courtiers present, a pageant of Venus and Cupid was staged.[155] Thrust out of heaven, Cupid runs to court for succour; finding none, he speeds to Chastity and her attending maids (Modesty, Temperance, Good Exercise and Shamefastness) who strip him of his cloak, which Chastity delivers to the Queen. While Cupid roams riotously, a philosopher counsels him to think of no gods but one, while Modesty sings the praises of a chaste life: 'Dame Chastitie is she that winnes the field' and the queen who has chosen chastity is a conqueror.[156] It is hardly surprising that the queen greeted the show with 'gracious words'.[157] Before the people of Suffolk was played out in a symbolic drama many of the themes of Elizabeth's own self-representation as Virgin, at a time when many were urging her to abandon her maiden status. What may have been a related pageant, of Manhood and Desert's unsuccessful striving for Beauty, was (as many were) rained off the day before the courtly train moved off towards Norwich.[158]

For the account of Elizabeth's *Joyful Receiving . . . into . . . Norwich*, we turn to Bernard Garter, a London citizen, anti-papal polemicist and poet, who helped to devise the civic entertainment for the royal party – perhaps another indication that provincial cities sought help from outside when arranging welcomes for the court and queen.[159] Rising to the extravagant language of masque in his dedication to the Lieutenant of the Tower, Sir Owen Hopton, Garter recalled the 'majesty of my prince which beautifieth her kingdom as the bright shining beams of beautiful Phoebus decketh forth the earth'.[160] In the 'terrestrial paradise' that Norwich became when graced with her presence, he continued, there had 'seemed but one heart in Queen, Council and communalty'.[161] The mayor, Sir Robert Wood, had set out to meet the queen on 16 August, accompanied by sixty bachelors and the figure of King Gurgunt who had built Norwich Castle.[162] Before a crowd that pressed around the train and cried out their welcome, Elizabeth replied to the ceremonial bestowal of a purse and the mace, as she had to several parliaments: that she desired only 'the hearts and true allegiance of our subjects'.[163] At the city gates, a royal arms was posted, with St George and a falcon (Elizabeth's badge), red and white roses, and with a verse that heralded 'our noble Phoenix deare' as the prince who extinguished division and strife – perhaps a reference to religious as well as dynastic division.[164] As she passed through the gate, Elizabeth found the first pageant which, in echo of her coronation entry, featured 'The causes of this commonwealth' – godliness, justice, obedience and labour. Pictures of looms and weavers and figures of women spinning and knitting presented to the court Norwich as a major city for cloth manufacture, which had overcome hardship through labour.[165] A second pageant featured the city with the biblical queens Deborah, Judith and Esther with Martia, a sometime queen of England. Here, the theme was praise of Elizabeth's promotion of true religion, as 'flower of grace' and 'prime of God's elect', whom the Lord had protected from enemies.[166] A few days later another show figured her as heir of male as well as female biblical rulers, as, like her half-brother Edward, another champion of the kingdom of Christ, drawn out of Josephus's history.[167] On the upper part of the structure, the history of Josephus was engraved, with verses describing Elizabeth as the Lord's chosen.[168] The Master of the city grammar school echoed Elizabeth's own words in giving thanks for a reign in which the word of God was preached and for a realm, unlike those of neighbours 'afflicted with most grievous wars', in peace and prosperity.[169] Elizabeth, as she had in London, called for silence while the Master's speech presented learning, property, peace and true religion as her gifts to all the nation, and, at its close, she gave him her hand to kiss.[170]

A masque after supper placed the queen in a pantheon of the classical gods, each of whom bestowed on her their gifts. The references to foes and critics (to combat whom Mars presented his weapons) disclosed some anxiety that peace was fragile and Elizabeth vulnerable; and, on the subject of marriage, the masque, lauding both chastity and the queen's amorous power, appears ambivalent – perhaps appropriately at a time when the duc d'Alençon was renewing his courtship of Elizabeth, as well as negotiating to aid the Dutch against Spain.[171] But if the city, a stronghold of godliness, in which a Dutch minister was chosen to address the queen, revealed some fears, the entertainment overall praised Elizabeth not only in her own terms, but in gendered language that hymned her as 'the mother and nurse of this whole commonwealth'.[172] 'How lamentable a thing it is,' a speech at her departure put it, in carefully gendered language, 'to pull away sucking babes from the breasts and bosoms of their most loving mother.'[173] Though the papists devised 'a thousand dangers', Elizabeth, as the sun the clouds, had driven them away 'and by Religion had restored the bright and glorious day'.[174] While subtly advancing its own economic interests and accomplishments, reminding the court of its reputation as a godly citadel, and urging the queen to advance the godly and suppress popish priests, the corporation of Norwich had reprised other representations of Elizabeth as the embodiment of classical virtues and descendant of biblical queens, as desired and chaste, as virgin mother and maiden queen, as (despite some 'very little' 'tumult') harbinger of Universal Concord.[175] Those – courtiers and civic dignitaries – who devised the pageant had counselled the queen. And, as she evidently did on such occasions, Elizabeth was said to have 'ravished the hearts of all' who had journeyed, inflamed with desire to behold her.[176]

Interestingly, after her victory over the Armada in 1588, Elizabeth did not undertake a triumphal progress. Persistent rumours of revived Spanish assaults kept her close to London or led her to tours of local fortifications on the south coast; and, it is suggested, she never resumed her journeys of the 1570s 'with her former enthusiasm'.[177] In the summer of 1591, the queen undertook a southern progress to Sussex and Hampshire, the longest stop on which was the final day she spent at Portsmouth whither she journeyed, according to the French ambassador, to inspect the fortifications.[178]

We have full contemporary accounts of the entertainments laid on for the queen that summer, at Cowdray in Sussex and at Elvetham in Hampshire. In the first case, Elizabeth's visit may have had a strategic, as well as social, purpose. Where Kenilworth was the home of not only Elizabeth's favourite but a champion of the godly cause, Cowdray was the seat of Sir Anthony Browne, first Viscount Montagu, a Catholic, who, though he had opposed anti-Catholic measures, had loyally supported Elizabeth, not least with a troop at Tilbury.[179] Since Elizabeth had no reason to doubt him, it is unlikely that the visit was an inspection, more probably a gesture of thanks and a display of her closeness to loyal English Catholics and publication of the loyalty she inspired in them. Uniquely, this entertainment was also related by the host Montagu himself, though it was printed and sold – 'by William Wright dwelling in Paul's Churchyard near to the French school' – in the usual way.[180] On 14 August, as Elizabeth entered, with her train, on to the bridge of Cowdray a figure, standing between two wooden posts and bearing a club in one hand and a golden key in the other, addressed her. It was prophesied, he explained, that the walls of the house would shake 'till the wisest, the fairest, and most fortunate of all creatures should by her first step make the foundation staid'.[181] Cowdray was presented as an allegory of the nation, which the queen had steadied and secured. As, taking the key, she began her sojourn, Elizabeth entered into a world in which praise was taken to its most exalted heights. Songs addressed her as a 'heavenly' creature, 'not framed of earthly molde', as 'Nature's glory', 'Goddess and Monarch of this happie ile'.[182] After dinner at the priory, a pageant of Peace and Wildness led Elizabeth to an oak, hung with the queen's and her nobles' arms – a symbol of her strength in the love of her subjects and of the normal defences of Sussex and the realm, which had recently routed her enemies.[183] The next day, as Elizabeth promenaded, another pageant ventured some critical comment on the times. An Angler by a fishpond punned on the ills of a 'nibbling world where every man lies bait for another', the merchants using deceit, the landlord racking rents.[184] Some who pretended love were dissimulators (it was a 'disguised world' where everyone was seeming to be true, which they were not), or worse 'carpers of state'.[185] The queen, however, was all virtue, the goddess to whom all paid tribute as the Angler did, presenting her with all the catch of the pond, as a sign of service and love – 'true hearted'.[186] A simple dance of the rural folk with pipe and tabor, in which Lord and Lady Montagu joined, performed the ideals of love and community which the entertainments had reaffirmed. Elizabeth departed; but, as the account of her visit concluded, 'the escutcheons on the oak remain', awaiting the monarch's return.[187]

From Sussex, the royal train progressed through Hampshire where the last visit was to the Earl of Hertford, at whose seat at Elvetham 300 artificers were set to work to create accommodations for the court and queen.[188] As well as the usual offices needed to provide for a court – spicery, pantry, laundry and wine cellar – Hertford commissioned a Great Hall especially for entertainment; and, though just built, the new structures were festooned with boughs, ivy and hazel-nuts to provide a rural setting.[189] As a special compliment to Elizabeth, between the house and a hill, Hertford had constructed a pond in the shape of a crescent moon, inside which were three islands shaped after a fish, a fowl and a snail.[190] Even before she arrived, that is, Elvetham, one of the earl's lesser residences, had been made into a homage to the queen, a representation of her own transformative power, as well as the builder's. Hertford rode out to meet Elizabeth on 20 September and escorted her with 300 men through the park, where a poet presented the queen with a volume and olive branch signifying the peace all wished for her.[191] In verses that the narrator translates 'because all our countrymen are not Latinists', the poet lauded

Elizabeth for her learning and beauty, as Augusta, another empress, 'more worthy than the gods'.[192] While the bard spoke, six virgins, three representing the queen and the other three the Hours, removed from the queen's path blocks 'which . . . were supposed to be laid there by the prince of envy'.[193] With typical grace, Elizabeth attended to the speech and received a scroll with the verse before following the virgin who strewed her way with flowers, singing the praise of the 'beauteous Queen of second Troy'.[194] Elizabeth, the virgins sang, had brought peace and harmony to a new British empire and to Nature itself, which rejoiced at her command.

The next day's planned entertainment was postponed on account of foul weather, but after dinner, a large canopy erected by the pond allowed the queen to view a water pageant. From a bower on the far side of the water, a 'pompous array' of sea creatures, Nereus (the prophet of the sea), Neptune, Oceanus and five tritons swam towards her, leading a pinnace.[195] Aboard the ship, as well as the sea nymph Neaera and Nereus, virgins played Scotch gigs (perhaps a gesture to Elizabeth's triumph over Mary, Queen of Scots). While Nereus addressed the queen as a 'faire Cynthia the Oceans Empresse', a scene on the pond represented the monster of enmity turned into a snail and the fort Neptune had raised for her defence.[196] And as sea nymphs hymned 'Elisaes matchlesse Grace', Sylvanus sprang from the woods with attendants to deliver his escutcheons, the emblem of Nature itself, to his princess.[197] Neaera, presenting Elizabeth with a jewel, lauds 'A sea borne Queene, worthy to govern kings'.[198] Sea and land pay homage to the Cynthia 'Nature Maid': 'on her', Neaera tells all, 'depends the future of thy boat', that is the ship of state.[199]

The next evening, before the start of a firework pageant on the water, Elizabeth was fêted with a banquet of a thousand dishes which featured castles and forts, as well as birds and beasts, in sugar work.[200] On the fourth day, the day of her departure, the fairies sang the praises of 'the fairest Queene,/That ever stood upon this greene', as the Graces, Hours and sea gods assembled with Sylvanus to sorrow at her leaving.[201] To Eliza, triumphant, who had triumphed over enemies and brought peace, 'every creature' paid homage.[202]

Our journey with the queen around some of her progress palaces records not only how the full royal show went on tour, but the extent to which, whatever the particularities or local circumstances, the personal and confessional agendas of the devisers, the themes of royal representation were repeated across the regions. Nor were they purely aristocratic entertainments. Time after time the pamphlet narratives tell of the ordinary folk who participated, travelled and 'swarmed like bees/when Prince abroad doth ride'.[203] Evidently, too, the allegorical entertainments which some have conceived as obscure or tedious did not surpass ordinary understanding. The texts of the progress pageants, and of commendatory verses delivered on such occasions, often written by quite ordinary men, were published, some in more than one edition, presumably for the market. In these texts, as with the prints and woodcuts of Elizabeth, we have not only documents of royal representation, but evidence of the consumption of those representations: documents of a cultural conversation by which the monarch was placed at the centre of everyone's gaze – and by the behaviour and desires of subjects as much as by official scripts or pamphlets. The person of Elizabeth, as well as the monarchy, had become a public site and text, represented and re-presented not only *to* but *by* the public – in ways that the first Tudor could not have imagined.

III

Queen Elizabeth's charisma and temperament served to foster a new cult of personality, but as a monarch she was also represented through her various public roles, notably as Supreme Head of the church and as the locus and source of justice. The emblems of the balance and the sword (an ancient attribute of Justitia) and of the book and the sword, the symbols of Tudor supremacy and Protestantism, were recurring motifs and figures in the images of the queen. And they were so because the church and justice themselves were, no less than the court, perceived as representations of true monarchy, of good and virtuous rule. However, while the rhetoric of representation was, and had to be, that of unity and concord, England was becoming ever more divided over notions of faith and justice, which Catholics and Protestants, and various groups within and outside the church, claimed for their cause. The history of these struggles – which is no less than the religious and political history of the age – cannot be our subject here. But what we do need to touch on is how, in these difficult circumstances, Elizabeth presented herself as Supreme Head and fount of Justice; and how she and her defenders sought, not always successfully, to eclipse others' appropriations and efforts to write representation differently.

The royal supremacy was itself a representation as well as a locus of royal authority. In 1561, official orders formalized what had been practice since at least the reign of Edward VI: the royal arms replaced the rood statues in every church in England.[204] A state emblem became a religious image and an earthly queen became integral to the service of worship of a divine Lord. The church and its rituals, the change signified, were to glorify the monarch as well as God and Christ. But, in the case of the church and religion perhaps more than in any other realm of government, the representation of royal supremacy involved, too, an accommodation of the beliefs and anxieties of subjects. If the rituals of church service and sermon were to perform as liturgies of state, queen and congregation, like queen and commonweal, had to be united – or at least have some sense that they were united. The rebellions under Edward VI and Mary had all clearly demonstrated the fragility of a church moulded only by the royal will or conscience. The Supreme Head needed, as far as possible, to govern a church which embraced the whole commonweal, so that religion served to strengthen, not subvert, royal authority. Each ruler, as George Bernard has argued, sought to establish his or her church, in changing circumstances, as a monarchical church, one that 'placed secular and political considerations of order above purely ecclesiastical and theological considerations . . .'.[205] And that involved a refusal to bow to factions and lobbies from courtiers and confessions and an insistence on a comprehension, on ambiguity and compromise, so as to exclude the minimum number. From the outset, while others tried to press her to unequivocal statement of her preferences, Elizabeth regarded equivocation on the details of faith as the mainstay of her supremacy.

Whatever her private and personal preferences, which remain a subject of controversy, Elizabeth's public exercise of her supremacy was early on characterized by caution, rather than any headlong rush to change. Count Helffenstein advised the Emperor Ferdinand in March 1559, that 'from the very beginning of her reign she has treated all religious questions with so much caution and incredible prudence that she seems both to protect the Catholic religion and at the same time not entirely to condemn and outwardly reject the Reformation'.[206] And, whatever his own preferences, Helffenstein saw the wisdom of such a course for a ruler: 'It was,' he wrote, 'in my opinion a very prudent action, intended to keep the adherents of both creeds in subjection.'[207] Elizabeth's first two proclamations on matters religious bear Helffenstein out. On 27 December 1558, reminding subjects that she exercised authority over the church to the end of 'quiet governance', she ordered the suspension of any preaching not taken from the gospel of the day and of any worship not ordained by law.[208] The next month, in announcing the regnal style the queen described herself as 'defender of the true, ancient and Catholic faith', without specifying what that might mean.[209] Even after a Protestant religious settlement was statutorily established by the queen in parliament, Elizabeth endeavoured to ensure that as many of her subjects as possible were embraced within it. In 1561, Elizabeth told an envoy from Scotland, that 'in the sacrament of the altar, some thinks a thing, some other'; for her part, 'whose judgement is best God knows'.[210] Elizabeth tried initially to incorporate the Catholic clergy into her settlement: in 1559 a proclamation ordered that tithes should still be paid to priests who did not administer communion in both kinds; and a grace appointed after a banquet at York, praying that Catholics might become godly teachers, hoped for their 'amendment not . . . their destruction'.[211] Early on in the reign, even the zealous Edmund Grindal, sensing the queen's desire to avoid division, preached at St Paul's a funeral sermon on the late Emperor Ferdinand, which was printed with royal privilege.[212] Though he raised the obvious point about the difference in religion, in an eirenic voice which echoed the queen's, Grindal praised him and his peaceable government: 'I am of St Augustine's mind,' he continued; 'whatsoever . . . tendeth to the edifying or increase either of faith or of charity is commendable'.[213]

There is no doubting that Grindal and other returning exiles had looked to Elizabeth for a different lead, and had hoped to use her supremacy for a fully reformed, unambiguously Protestant, church from which Catholics were excluded as reprobates and the disciples of Antichrist. From the very establishment of the Elizabethan settlement, they, many of her councillors and bishops, sought to unsettle it (as the queen saw it), and to end the ambiguity she seemed to favour. What aided them in part was the 1569 rising in the north and the papal excommunication of the queen the next year. As the godly did not cease to argue, such events demonstrated the potential disloyalty of English Catholics and seriously questioned Elizabeth's policy of comprehension. One senses that after 1570, to a degree greater than before, English nationalism became inseparable from Protestantism, as the papal excommunication marked English Catholics as potential fifth columnists. Certainly from the 1570s, the godly pressed their agenda even harder upon the queen and, importantly, endeavoured to define her representation as Supreme Head. In a sermon preached at Paul's Cross in 1578, the preacher John Walsall, denouncing the vestiges of popery in the land, called for a ministry of the true word of God.[214] Edward Dering also waged a long campaign for godly reform: in a sermon preached before Elizabeth in 1569, taking the biblical injunction uttered by the queen herself – that queens must be nursing mothers to the church – he pressed the duties of the magistrate to suppress superstition and advance God's word, and urged Elizabeth to 'take away your authority from the bishops'.[215]

As we well know, Elizabeth refused to give way to such pressure. What is interesting for the historian of royal representation, however, are the means deployed to sustain Elizabeth's authority as Supreme Head and a church settlement founded on order and concord. One measure was the queen's public emphasis on prayer over pulpit. In a speech to bishops and other clergy at Somerset Place, Elizabeth once remarked that there was more of value in one homily than twenty sermons, especially those sermons which excited disputes and division.[216] Elizabeth had very few court sermons preached in her presence; or at least few were printed for publication. By contrast, as we have seen, several volumes of prayers were published by John Day, the royal printer, and some with images of the queen at prayer in her closet were widely known as Queen Elizabeth's prayers. What is striking about these volumes is their silence on the crucial theological, and even liturgical, questions that divided Protestants – or for that matter Protestants and Catholics. In their very material form, as well as words, published prayers advertised Elizabeth's supremacy and authority.[217] At the end of the 1572 edition of *A Form of Common Prayer* a large engraving of a pelican feeding its young, flanked by Prudence and Justice, blazoned a familiar image of Elizabeth.[218] In 1585, another order of prayer for the queen's safety presented her as the protected chosen of Providence and the 'protector and defence of the blessed church'; and stipulated that prayers should be preceded by a sermon 'of the authority and majesty of princes' and the 'straight duty of obedience . . . required of all good and Christian subjects'.[219] Under the threat of the Armada, public prayers more stridently acclaimed Elizabeth as the chosen leader of 'the English Syon'.[220] A large royal arms faced the title page of the 1597 volume of prayer for the success of the navy – which opened with thanks to God for having blessed 'thy humble servant, our sovereign lady'.[221]

Whatever Elizabeth's preferences, the royal supremacy was unquestionably and increasingly presented as anti-papal. Anthony Anderson, who published his sermons with episcopal licence, probably had official approval for the image of the phoenix rising from the ashes which illustrated his anti-papal sermon presented at Paul's Cross on St George's Day 1581.[222] Anti-Romanism became part of the political culture of Elizabethan England: as William Segar put it in his *Blazon of Papists* dedicated to Queen Elizabeth, it was impossible to be a papist and a gentleman, for 'not one good subject is found among them all'.[223] The papist, a later treatise charged, was a politic atheist, who was equivocal in his allegiance to the queen.[224]

Yet, for all that events, as well as the relentless campaign of the godly, sharpened anti-Roman invective, Elizabeth remained committed to a church and to a supremacy which were different and separate from continental reformed Protestantism, indeed to a church that was, as far as possible, England as well as English. In recent years a large and contentious body of historical writing has debated whether it is appropriate to talk of an Anglican church in Elizabeth's reign.[225] But what Helffenstein early discussed as a prudently equivocal course remained the hallmark of Elizabeth's supremacy.[226] And, as episcopal appointments began to reflect her preferences, there was an increasingly audible discourse of a middle way, and of a monarchical church which was peculiar to the English people. In a sermon preached at Paul's Cross on Trinity Sunday 1571, Edward Bush proclaimed 'our gracious sovereign the queen's majesty . . . the principal pillar of the Church of England under Christ'.[227] Four years later, John Young, a future Bishop of Rochester, contemning those presumptuous people who 'hath a commonwealth, a church in his head . . .', urged restraint from meddling in religious controversy and obedience to the prince in all.[228] In 1587, John Bridges brought together the argument of earlier sermons in his massive *A Defence of the Government Established in the Church of England*.[229] Here, downplaying the differences within the church and commonwealth, Bridges defended ecclesiastical

authority, and the 'honesty and right of woman's regiment', and praised
Elizabeth for surpassing David, Solomon and Constantine in heading a
church in which 'we may be all fully united'.[230] Bridges's swipes at pretenders
to conscience and critics of church government were made more explicit in
Bancroft's sermon the next year, on the first Sunday of a new session of parliament. In a blistering attack that excoriated Presbyterians as enemies of state as
well as church, Bancroft lauded the doctrines and governance of the Church
of England and argued against any questioning of royal authority.[231]

The representation of Elizabeth as Supreme Head, then, was, despite the
reality of bitter confessional divisions, a representation of her as head of a
national church which advertised itself as comprehensive and united. In a
sermon to the Justices in Sussex, William Overton hoped all would join the
queen in fostering that unity and uniformity in religion which was, he considered, essential to the state; and even recognized that, unlike papists, English
Catholics were 'good subjects' to the queen and 'necessary members of the
commonwealth'.[232] Religious divisions by no means abated. Yet, as the horrific
accounts of continental religious wars began to circulate in England, it seems
that growing numbers became attached to a church which (founded in equivocation) had become what was perceived as a middle way that secured peace;
and to its Supreme Head.[233]

What we might, then, with contemporary warrant call the cult of
Anglicanism and the cult of Elizabeth came together in the sermons and services for her accession day which indeed became part of the liturgical as well as
festival calendar.[234] On 17 November 1587, preaching on Psalm 118, Isaac Colfe
presented Elizabeth as the cornerstone of the 'house of England', another David
or Judah, chosen and placed by God to advance his church.[235] In a sermon for
1599, published two years later, with a large fold-out royal arms and
commendatory verses to the queen, Thomas Holland, Regius Professor of
Divinity at Oxford, compared Elizabeth to the Queen of the South, of Matthew
12, verse 42, that is the Queen of Sheba whom she equalled in beauty, learning
and virtue.[236] Turning to the church and commonwealth's annual celebration
of 17 November, Holland recalled a day when, forty years before, the nation
had 'received a new light'.[237] The commemoration of 17 November, he
explained, honoured God and Elizabeth and the sermon reminded 'the auditory to give obedience to her majesty'.[238] Opposition to church and queen,
Holland acknowledged there was.[239] But 17 November had abrogated the feast
of St Hugh, as Elizabeth's birthday, 7 September, had eclipsed the commemoration of the eve of the Virgin's nativity.[240] The construction of an Anglican
church had been inseparable from the representations of Elizabeth as Virgin,
God's handmaid, bringer of Peace and Concord; and the queen's authority had
been strengthened by her headship of a church in England which had won the

affection of the people. Though never officially proclaimed by the church as a holiday, the rites of 17 November, known as 'queen's holy day', 'voluntarily continued by the religious and dutiful subjects of this realm' had come to symbolize the union of queen, church and nation.[241]

Central to Elizabeth's representation as Supreme Head was her famous unwillingness 'to make windows into men's souls': her disinclination to probe conscience or private faith, as opposed to public action.[242] Indeed, her government felt the need to give an explanation for the execution of two Catholic seminary priests in 1576, informing the nation of the avowed treason of missionaries to whom the queen had been inclined to show mercy, 'her majesty minding nothing less than that any of her subjects, though disagreeing from her in religion, should die for the same'.[243] Such an explanatory proclamation did not only reflect Elizabeth's concern to persuade loyal English Catholics of her *de facto* tolerance of their faith; it announced her mercy and clemency, attributes of royal justice.

Justice was both a constant virtue of good kingship and one the perception of which shifted with changing circumstances, and which had unquestionably been complicated by Reformation and religious division. Though few subjects questioned the laws and punishments against heresy, the Marian burnings had alienated even those of her English subjects who were not of strong Protestant convictions. From her succession to the throne, Elizabeth was careful to deploy the symbols and rhetoric of justice in her representation and to temper the rigour of the law and punishment with the language of mercy and love. The trial and the scaffold, she knew, were sites of royal representation; and the image of the sovereign as just ruler depended upon a perception that she was just, and on some shared (or negotiated) sense of which crimes merited, or did not merit, a harsh response.

One incident in 1578, in which Elizabeth displayed the royal clemency, became the stuff of a popular ballad, 'declaring the dangerous shooting of the gun at court'.[244] An unfortunate gunner, presumably firing a welcoming salvo, accidentally shot at the queen's barge and wounded one of her watermen, narrowly missing Elizabeth herself. The gunner was sentenced to death for endangering the life of the monarch. But Elizabeth, who had scurried to attend the wounded, sent a message to pardon the gunner on the scaffold – before the crowd assembled to witness the execution. At the proclamation of the queen's mercy and pardon, the people shouted with joy before the councillor led all in prayer for the queen. The accident had led many to contemplate what a parlous state the realm might have been in had the shot taken off the queen: the halcyon peace enjoyed by England 'might have turned to bloody wars'.[245] The next decade was to see not accidents but a number of deliberate attempts on Elizabeth's life, and the trial and public execution of Catholic conspirators. During the period after the papal bull and the mounting threat from Spain, the loyalty of English Catholics was vital but could not be taken for granted. Continental polemicists, and some in England, were quick to utilize the victims of justice, to figure them as martyrs, turning the tables on Foxe's account of the martyrs of Mary's reign, and appealing to a public many of whom remained sympathetic to the old faith. Though, therefore, Sir Thomas Smith boasted in *De republica anglorum* that in no place did malefactors 'go more constantly . . . and with less lamentation to their death, than in England', the theatre of justice was a highly contested site of representation, in which the queen and government had to make their case – in order to sustain the royal representation and authority.[246]

The case of Edward Campion presented the regime with a major difficulty.[247] Campion arrived in England, in June 1570, with his fellow Jesuit Robert Parsons, to place the Catholic mission on a new militant footing. Staunch Protestants in the Queen's Council took alarm and Elizabeth was persuaded to sign an act declaring any who endeavoured to induce a subject to withdraw allegiance by converting to Catholicism to be guilty of treason.[248] While the intention of the act, making proselytizing treason, was to avoid the appearance of persecuting in the name of religion, Campion and others insisted on their mission as a spiritual one – and published to win the hearts and minds of Catholic, and perhaps uncommitted, subjects. As Peter Lake and Michael Questier have argued, these moral narratives were struggles for representation in and to a public sphere, with both the Catholics and Protestants using the rhetoric of 'commonweal' as well as conscience, and the media of print, gossip and performance to air their case.[249] If, as they argued, 'from the moment that Campion's tract was circulated, the mission became a hugely public challenge to . . . the Elizabethan regime . . . and thus its claims to legitimacy', the trial was bound to be a crucial moment in the underpinning or unravelling of that legitimacy.[250] Campion was seized in mid-July and interrogated in the Tower, where, despite Smith's denials of the English use of torture, he was racked. In the months before his execution at Tyburn in December, pamphlet accounts on both sides tried to figure him, respectively, as innocent martyr or scheming traitor. *A Particular Declaration or Testimony of the Undutiful and Traitorous Affection Borne Against Her Majesty by Edward Campion* (1582) presented the government case.[251] Published by royal authority with a large royal arms, the *Declaration* was addressed to all 'good and faithful subjects'.[252] Acknowledging that other accounts of Campion's trial and execution were circulating, the pamphlet published his confession and answers to demonstrate 'how justly they were condemned for treason and not for points of religion'.[253] 'In general government propaganda that the priests merited death sentences as traitors seems to have been successful'; but the need to present the government case, so as to re-present Elizabeth as both just and wronged, was pressing.[254]

It was even more pressing when the case had to be made against Englishmen – and scions of ancient noble houses who traced their titles back to the Conquest. It was, as so often, Walsingham's spy network that fingered Francis Throckmorton as a go-between for France and Mary, Queen of Scots's plan for an invasion of England, in which the Earl of Northumberland was also implicated.[255] Northumberland at least spared the regime the discomforts of a trial and execution by committing suicide in the Tower. But the government still felt the need to publish the evidence of his treason and, in Throckmorton's case, to defend the queen's image of clemency and tolerance. A *Report* on Northumberland's case, published by the queen's printer, directly countered rumours that Northumberland had been wrongly detained and murdered in prison, and drew attention to Elizabeth's earlier mercy to him in his dealings with Mary, Queen of Scots.[256] The image of the merciful, beneficent queen whom one she had favoured cruelly deceived was essential for sustaining the royal image of mercy. Similarly A *Discovery of the Treasons* practised by Throckmorton was intended to fully document this offence and dispel false reports of royal cruelty and injustice – and to counter opponents of torture in treason trials by representing them as themselves 'friends to traitors'.[257]

In the case of Dr William Parry, the trial and scaffold became public sites of contention. Though arrested in 1584 for countenancing the death of the queen, the MP persistently denied his guilt, claiming his intention had been to infiltrate and entrap conspirators. In this case, at his trial and conviction, the queen's Vice-Chamberlain went so far as to require that 'for the satisfaction of this great multitude', he read his confession – which he did.[258] Later, however, Parry retracted his confession and, claiming that it was extorted and reasserting his innocence, 'fell into a rage and evil words with the Queen's Attorney General'.[259] At his sentence, Parry 'persisted still in his rage and ragingly there [in court] said he there summoned Queen Elizabeth to answer for his blood before God'.[260] And still 'before his execution he most maliciously and impudently' denied his guilt – which the official account offered to make manifest from his writings.[261]

Parry's behaviour demonstrated the tension and uncertainty involved in processes of justice and punishment which were supposed to represent royal authority and, in these cases, the royal supremacy also. Yet, for all that they were contested, official accounts of conspiracy and the presentation of Catholic activism as treason appear to have played an important role in sustaining loyalty to the regime. In Parry's case, it seems, the people were struck with horror and 'pursued him with outcries [of] "away with the traitor" '.[262] If this was indeed the reaction, Secretary Burghley's care that 'the fact of Dr Parry' be 'better published' paid dividends, for the Spanish envoy Mendoza thought that 'even amongst Englishmen' the belief was current that he was 'unjustly condemned'.[263] Certainly Thomas Nelson's *Discourse* against traitors, published in 1586, reported the joy and feasting in the streets when Thomas Babington and fellow conspirators were arrested – and indeed the letter of thanks sent by the queen for their loyalty.[264] *A Most Joyful Song*, published the same year as a broadside, illustrated with the heads of the 'late traitorous conspirators', described the many thousands who ran to see the captured felons, crying after them 'there go ye traitors false of faith' and 'there go the enemies of England' as the bells rang and bonfires were lit to celebrate their seizure:

> And thus the people still did cry, both men and women all,
> And children yong did shout aloude, and Traytors Traytors call. . . .

> To see these Traytors take so, their harts for ioy did spring,
> And to declare this perfect ioy, some ranne the Belles to ring.[265]

Behind the people's joy and shouts of abuse – the calling 'Traytors Traytors' – lay the efficacy of Elizabeth's self-presentation as a wronged, just and divinely protected queen, rather than the cruel persecutor she appeared in Catholic polemic.

Justice against subjects was one thing; against an anointed monarch quite another. Elizabeth herself was personally very reluctant to persecute Mary, Queen of Scots, despite the evidence of her involvement in conspiracy. And whilst the diplomatic considerations were paramount, the revulsion of the people also needed to be considered. Walsingham's spies had, however, confirmed written evidence of Mary's complicity in Thomas Babington's plot against Elizabeth's life, and the queen was at last persuaded to bring her to the trial and sentence that was eventually executed three months later. As well as persistent conciliar and parliamentary counsel, a number of pamphlets published in 1587 served to pressure Elizabeth to enact the sentence of death and to defend her decision as that of a just princess led by necessity to proceed against her cousin. They again point up the negotiations involved in the Elizabethan theatre of justice and in the representation of royal justice. The Plymouth schoolmaster William Kempe dedicated his *Dutiful Invective Against the Most Heinous Treasons of Ballard and Babington* to the Lord Mayor of London and 'to all loyal English subjects'.[266] Tracing in popular verse the cruel attempts against an Elizabeth who had promoted only the good of her subjects, Kempe identified Mary, the pope's disciple, as the instigator of them all.[267] She it was who sought to deprive Elizabeth of her crown and subvert religion, she whom a fair trial had justly convicted, she against whom a parliament had approved the sentence; she whom a merciful Elizabeth, after exploring all other options compatible with the nation's safety, had at last condemned to die. It was not only, Kempe asserted, a just decision: 'This is the end the Lorde appoints, for those that seeme to frowne/ Gainst his annointed whom he hath indued with regal crowne'.[268] Kempe, evidently slightly uneasy about justifying the sentence, prayed 'that a perfect love and duetie may take place/ Towards this peereles Prince' Elizabeth.[269]

Richard Crompton first aired his views on *The End of Traitors and False Conspirators Against the State* at the Sessions of the Peace in Staffordshire and was then urged to publish his address 'on a matter . . . much necessary for this present time'.[270] What, Crompton asked, would one not say to traitors who had plotted against a gracious queen, who was pious, 'of the right line and descent', 'not a foreigner . . . but one of our own nation', for whom thousands daily gave thanks?[271] Elizabeth had protected the true religion, passed good laws, exacted few impositions and expended all care on her subjects.[272] The proceedings against conspirators, he concluded, were for the good of all, and the sentence against Mary, Queen of Scots, the source of all evil treason, just.[273] Like Kempe, Crompton went to some lengths to point out that, had any other course guaranteed the queen's and realm's security, Elizabeth would have spared her life.[274] But there was none; and Mary's execution was greeted with bonfires and bells, 'whereby appeareth that the people were joyful that so dangerous an enemy to the Commonwealth was taken away'.[275] Crompton, in depicting treason as defeated by God and Mary as justly executed, represented Elizabeth as the Lord's chosen and as the careful guardian of her people who in turn responded with obedience and love. *A Defence of the Honourable Sentence and Execution of the Queen of Scots* (1587) was the most explicit attack on Mary and apologia for Elizabeth.[276] The treatise has been attributed to the poet and translator Maurice Kyffin, who published the same year a celebration of the queen's holiday and a eulogy on her reign, but his authorship has been questioned.[277] *A Defence* opens with a vitriolic attack on Mary who, like Joan, Queen of Naples, the author charged, strangled her husband, fostered schism and invited foreign forces into her country.[278] This was the ruler who had several times compassed the death of the virtuous counterpart of her vice, Elizabeth, 'and consequently was like to bring the whole realm in danger of a general massacre and present destruction, had not the clement and Almighty Lord of his unspeakable and accustomed goodness by a miraculous discovery preserved the same'.[279]

Like the other texts, *A Defence* asserted that Mary was justly sentenced.[280] Yet, 'to stop the evil speeches' of those who questioned the justice of the action, the author summoned the entirety of civil and canon law and the precedents of popes who had approved death sentences against emperors and princes.[281] The catalogue of examples, including that of Pope Urban, 'may serve', *A Defence* hoped, 'in the case of the Scottish queen to persuade any man that is not too far distempered in his judgement' – even Roman Catholics.[282]

And if law and precedent were not warrant enough, 'what man of reason in whom there is any natural love for his country ... would not counsel by justice to remove the Scottish queen' for the 'quiet and safety' of the kingdom?[283] Though here we sense an address to a continental audience, the pamphlet sets out also to persuade English Catholics, to appeal to national safety and sentiment and, again, to present Elizabeth as the chosen ruler whose natural clemency (we are told she endeavoured to spare her cousin) was suspended only by justice and necessity.[284] At a difficult moment in the maintenance of Elizabeth's image as tolerant, just, merciful ruler of *all* her subjects, English writers, Catholics as well as Protestants, with or without sanction, stepped in to represent her as she presented herself – and perhaps to help secure the obedience and loyalty that sustained her rule.

In many ways, the Armada resolved some tensions in the representation of Elizabeth, as in the politics of her reign. The Catholic invasion of which the godly had warned for years had happened, and yet English Catholic loyalty had been proved in a moment of crisis. After 1588, therefore, it was somewhat easier to present justice executed against popish conspirators as the act of a united nation. After 1588 intermittent intelligence continued to come in concerning plots on Elizabeth's life; but, after Mary's execution and Walsingham's death in 1590, the temperature of national anxiety was lowered. In 1594, however, a plot to take the queen's life was discovered and the queen's physician, Dr Roderigo Lopez, a Portuguese Jew, was charged with being involved with Spanish agents to poison her for a reward of 5,000 crowns.[285] There was some question about Lopez's guilt – he claimed to be an innocent agent; but his case, and execution played into representation of Elizabeth as 'miraculous[ly] conserved' against her enemies and as virtuous, triumphant and godly monarch.[286] *A True Report of Sundry Horrible Conspiracies of Late Time Detected* placed Lopez's treason in a narrative of Spanish attempts on Elizabeth. The pamphlet printed the conspiracies and other incriminating evidence 'under the handwriting of the offenders', clearly to dispel any doubts about the justice of the proceedings.[287] But the pamphlet manifested a new concern to present English Catholics as loyal. Despite Cardinal Allen's endeavours to use him in a plot to seize the crown, we are told, Lord Strange had remained a true subject.[288] Treasons, the pamphlet suggested, were hatched in Spain, at Brussels, or by Portuguese agents, rather than by Englishmen; but 'the Almighty God, the just avenger of such horrible wickedness' and a 'rewarder of piety and innocency' conserved Elizabeth as he scattered her enemies.[289]

The last act of royal justice performed on the scaffold did not, however, involve a foreign agent but an English nobleman, and a former royal favourite who had played a leading role in bringing Lopez to justice. Robert Devereux, Earl of Essex, had enjoyed a meteoric rise to favour and place which nevertheless fell short of an ambition that led him to defy royal orders and ultimately to plot rebellion.[290] Whilst his guilt was apparent, Essex was a popular figure who had assiduously worked the public; and though, at his own request, he was executed in private, his case drew widespread interest, and no little sympathy. The first Sunday after his execution (on 15 February 1601), therefore, the pulpit at Paul's Cross (by the end of Elizabeth's reign a familiar medium for public address) was given over to what the preacher William Barlow, a royal chaplain, called 'matter of state rather than divinity'.[291] Briefed by Cecil, Barlow, preaching on the text of Matthew 22, verse 21 ('Give unto Caesar'), described how the Jesuit Parsons corrupted the late earl, persuading him 'that it is lawful for the subject to rise against his sovereign'.[292] Careful in praising Essex's qualities, Barlow reported the earl's own admission on the scaffold that he was puffed up with vanity and scotched his claim that he had intended the queen no harm.[293] 'It was the most dangerous plot that was ever hatched within this land,' Barlow informed his auditors and readers, and the realm would have enjoyed no peace 'if he had been remitted'.[294] Appropriately anxious about Essex's popularity, Barlow endeavoured to undermine it by reporting the earl's contempt for them: 'he accompted,' the sermon claimed, 'your love to be . . . but vanity', and said 'that you were a very base people'.[295] The people, the pamphlet seemed concerned to stress, owed nothing to and needed to learn no lesson from the demagogic Essex: rather what his fall taught was that authority was to be obeyed and majesty honoured, especially that of a gracious queen whom God shielded from such audacious attempts.[296] The chaplain called on all to honour and praise her.

Between the lines of Barlow's sermon we detect an audible anxiety about the unpopularity of Essex's execution: a fear that rises to the surface in his free admission that it was 'given out that because we, being commended by authority, on the sabbath after the insurrection did describe the nature and ugliness of the rebellion, [we, the clergy] are become timeservers'.[297] Not only was the theatre of justice a complex and contested site of representation, the public was clearly reading and questioning royal representations of events; that is, its authority. Not least because of her own brilliant deployment of both majesty and popularity, Elizabeth was less the target of negative representations than Essex's rival and enemy Robert Cecil who was widely blamed for his death.[298] But hostility to Cecil expressed larger discontent which, when directed at the queen's principal minister, did not entirely spare the queen herself.

For all her skill as an actor on the stage of state, Elizabeth's performances as queen were enacted in a world of difference, division and discord. Though more than most rulers she succeeded in communicating a rhetoric of harmony, love and obedience, Elizabeth's representation was, throughout her reign, questioned, appropriated and contested by councillors, confessions and citizens. It is to counter-representations of the queen that we now turn.

CHAPTER 12

CONTESTING AND APPROPRIATING ELIZABETH

I

Elizabeth had at no time reigned without critics, opponents, those with different values, or agendas and policies which they sought to advance and publicize. Since some of those critics were members of the government, there was a struggle for royal representation within the court itself; but it was, we need to appreciate, a struggle which involved, like Elizabeth's own rhetoric and behaviour, appeal to the people.[1] We have examined the ways in which through words, symbols and performances, Elizabeth represented herself, and was represented, as the embodiment of virtue and godliness. That, of course, was by no means how all subjects saw her. The staunchest Romanists probably never fully accepted her legitimacy: most Catholics suffered some difficulties exercising their faith; the hotter sort of Protestants were frustrated at her refusal to lead a Protestant crusade in Europe and to build another Geneva in England; those, courtiers, nobles and aspirants, whose policies were not enacted or whose ambitions were frustrated murmured with discontent; economic difficulties and hardship, especially towards the end of the reign, led the populace into hostility and discontent.[2]

The relationship of discontent, murmur and opposition to the representation of Elizabeth is complex and circular. While on the one hand, the relentless promotion and publication of her monarchy reflected concerted efforts to win the contest for representation, on the other the publicity, the public-ness (to use a clumsy neologism) of Elizabeth made it necessary and possible for critics also to publish their different and counter-representations. Print, as Henry VIII's experience had shown, and Elizabeth's successors were to learn painfully, was not a royal prerogative. We have become familiar with the outpourings of print in late sixteenth-century England, which a simple count of imprints by year dramatically confirms.[3] As important, and less noticed, is the extent to which print became an increasingly popular medium, and one that fostered debate about government among circles below the political nation and elite.[4] 'There is,' wrote the son of a dyer and pamphleteer, Henry Chettle, 'many a tradesman of a worshipful trade yet no stationer who, who after a little bringing them up . . . takes into his shop some fresh men, and trusts his old servants of a two months standing with a dozen groats worth of ballads. In which, if they prove thrifty, he makes them pretty chapmen, able to spread more pamphlets by the state forbidden then all the booksellers in London.'[5] Print was evidently becoming a popular business; and, it would seem, a popular commodity. The entertainment for Elizabeth at Kenilworth featured one Captain Cox, a simple soldier who yet had at his fingertips the texts of ancient plays and histories, Virgil, the Shepherds' Calendar and Colin Clout, tales of Robin Hood, songs, ballads and almanacs.[6] A pamphlet of *News from the North* described one 'Piers Ploughman' entering an inn carrying a pile of books and then initiating a discussion on whether magistracy was ordained by God – which Piers doubted.[7] The assembled even go on to discuss the issue 'why poor men are not called to office of estate and government'.[8] *The Castle or Picture of Policy* (1581) similarly featured two common soldiers, 'poor and simple' debating 'policy and civil government' – though concurring on the excellence of princes.[9]

These were 'fictional' accounts, but our sense that they are drawn from social experience is confirmed by the testimony of foreigners, and the complaint of some English, that Elizabethans tended to read and discuss matters of government and state, even those subjects that were clearly *arcana imperii*, matters of state supposedly reserved for the consideration of the political classes. 'Who is there,' Bishop Young lamented in a 1575 sermon, 'almost be he of never so vile and base condition, what artificer, yea servant, prentice but he hath a commonwealth in his head and nothing in his mouth but the government of the commonwealth and the government of the church.'[10] Some even radically suggested that such debate might be the sign of a healthy commonweal. The prologue to the English translation of Chelidonius's *History of the Institution . . . of Princes* defended those 'books [which] do always frankly and with all liberty admonish us of those things which our friends . . . do suppress';[11] the English translation of *The Philosopher of the Court* proclaimed 'the commodity of true reports and faithful cou[n]ters [*sic*] of news is great and profitable to good life';[12] and the English edition of Patrizi's *Civil Policy*, published in 1576, insisted that 'it goeth not well in that commonweal . . . where citizens must live in that case that they dare not speak frankly or boldly those things which they think to be of their profit'.[13]

In a divided realm, in which people differed over what was for their profit – and still more their salvation – print and public debate became media for the critical discussion of the court, of royal policy, the institution of monarchy and, to some extent, of Elizabeth herself. Most obviously, Catholic and puritan polemicists waged print campaigns against the church and its Supreme Head. A translation of a *History of the Church of England*, published in 1565, though it bore the royal arms and a dedication to Elizabeth, advocated a rejection of the 'pretended religion of Protestants', a return to the old faith and the suppression of heresy.[14] More disturbingly for the government, Catholic treatises, written in the wake of rebellion, defended the Duke of Norfolk and Mary, Queen of Scots as true subjects misrepresented by false Protestant propaganda.[15] Whether imported from abroad or clandestinely printed in Britain, Catholic polemics continued to circulate and Catholic writers were ever ready to seize opportunities to publicize their cause.[16] In the case of the puritans, a persistent use of the press to critique the church and appeal for godly reformation developed into full advocacy of Presbyterianism and the radical populism of the Martin Marprelate tracts that led the regime to fear the overthrow of ecclesiastical and secular government.[17] Whatever their pulpit laments about popular ignorance, apathy or hostility, puritan polemicists wooed the people in genres of print that alarmed the state into hiring respondents, such as Thomas Nashe.[18] Moreover, the godly wanted a community in which, as well as faith, news and talk were shared in ways that officialdom feared were threatening. In 1579, William Overton warned the Sussex magistrates that the puritans 'do smell . . . of ill favoured smoke': 'they have their open meetings and solemn feastings together . . . amongst themselves with all freedom and liberty . . . talking and jesting at their pleasures of the state and of religion and so forth, whatsoever they list, to no good end, I warrant you, nor without unhappy meaning'.[19]

Thereafter, the Presbyterian campaign and especially the writings of Robert Browne struck not only at the royal supremacy but at the very foundations of allegiance to the sovereign.[20] As John Bridges argued in his *Defence of the Government . . . in the Church of England*, those who 'scatter[ed] abroad throughout the realm' books which slandered and reviled the church and government, hoping to 'win credit and pity with the common people', threatened all order and authority and fostered sedition.[21] Church government by elders rather than bishops, he insisted, undermined any princely government.[22] In a sermon delivered the year of the Armada, Richard Bancroft preached against the puritans by whom 'her majesty is depraved, her authority is impugned . . . civil government is called into question, princes prerogatives are curiously scanned, the interest of the people in kingdoms is greatly advanced and all government generally is picked at and condemned'.[23] Radical Calvinist literature advocating resistance to ungodly princes freely entered England from France; and though few puritan critics of the queen would have countenanced such opposition to Elizabeth, the insistent claims made in godly writings that conscience should have place before allegiance posed a fundamental challenge

to Elizabeth's reputation as God's handmaid and to her divine authority.[24] In
his famous *Theatre of God's Judgements*, the puritan divine and future schoolmaster to Oliver Cromwell, Thomas Beard, expounded a heavily qualified
theory of allegiance.[25] Though he acknowledged the duty owed to higher
powers, Beard proclaimed that 'the greatest monarchs in the world ought to be
subject to the law of God, and consequently the laws of men'; 'the laws ought
to be above the prince not the prince above the laws'.[26] And he exempted from
the duty of obedience, the realm of conscience and the service of God, undermining much of the foundation of royal supremacy and sovereignty.[27]

Such radical interrogation of sovereignty and obedience was aired not only
in puritan polemics. In recent years, scholars have identified in the action of
Elizabeth's councillors, and especially in the Bond of Association subscribed in
1584, a 'mixed polity' and even an imagining of the commonwealth without
the queen.[28] Other scholars have focused attention on a more secular literature
of political discussion and critique in Elizabeth's reign that, drawing on the
classics, praised republican virtues and constitutions as attractive alternatives
to monarchy.[29] Though there were probably few – if any – serious advocates of
a republic in England, such literature challenged representation of monarchy
as the God-given mode of government and implicitly Elizabeth's image as the
embodiment of virtue. As early as 1569, the English translation of Henry
Cornelius Agrippa's *Of the Vanity and Uncertainty of Arts and Sciences* publicized debate about democratic republics from the time of Athens.[30] Where
monarchists compared the king to the sun and to God, Agrippa argued, experience showed rather that 'the Venetians and the Swissters with their democ-
ratia flourish before all the sovereignties and seigneuries in Christendom'.[31]
Emperors and kings, the treatise continued, had been cruel and tyrannical
through the ages and now too many 'suppose that they were born and created
not for the people'.[32]

The publication in 1584 of Machiavelli's *Discorsi* in Italian certainly
acquainted the learned with arguments for republic over monarchy; and
pirate translations spread his ideas far beyond scholarly circles.[33] From
Scotland and France, books such as Buchanan's *De iure regni apud scotos* and
the *Vindiciae contra tyrannos* fused Calvinism with classical texts to argue for
a large measure of popular government.[34] And the translation of Guillaume
de la Perrière's *Mirror of Policy*, for all its traditional emphasis on order, aired
the pros and cons of elective monarchy.[35] La Perrière praised Venice, which
was held up as the model republic by all who advocated limited monarchy or
alternative government.[36] Lewes Lewkenor's translation of Contarini's
Commonwealth and Government of Venice, which praised the city in a prefatory verse as the 'Adriatic wonder', explained Venice and its constitution to
those readers not schooled in Italian.[37] In a preface to the reader, Lewkenor

asserted that 'out of this one commonwealth of Venice' one might 'gather and comprehend the fruit of all whatsoever other governments'.[38] Here, Contarini's work showed, was a commonweal in which laws not men were sovereign, where the multitude not one bore sway, and where the Doge, though possessing the 'resemblance of a monarchy', was 'deprived of all means whereby he might abuse his authority'.[39] Even after death, the Doge owed account to his subjects who, reviewing his rule, levied a penalty on his heirs if he were faulty and amended the republic's laws to prevent further abuses.[40] 'In everything,' Contarini wrote of Venice, 'you may see the show of a king but his authority is nothing.'[41] Interestingly, this is the polity the preface to the English reader describes as 'most excellent monarchy' – one which the rest of the world described as 'Virgin'.[42] To say the least that was audacious praise of a republic in the England of the Virgin Queen.

As well as the medium of Catholic and puritan polemics, and theoretical discussions of the nature and extent of authority, print was the organ of libels, satires and squibs against the government, and the stimulus to slander and gossip. The later years of Elizabeth's reign, as we have learned, gave birth to that new genre in England, the satire, which became a fashion among the Inns of Courts poets writing in the vein of Juvenal and Horace.[43] Critical satirical literature directed against the court circulated a discourse of corruption, ambition and greed which tarnished the image of virtue, chivalry and piety advanced by government apologists.

By 1596, even the loyal Thomas Churchyard, in *A Pleasant Discourse of Court and Wars* was lampooning a court that did not live up to its ideals.[44] 'The Court', Churchyard versed, was but 'a pleasant cage', a 'place of pomp and peril both' where 'ten thousand spend their time in vain'.[45] Not a few members of the court circle, such as John Harington, as well as a horde of wits outside, contributed to an often mordant literature of complaint which led Archbishop Bancroft to issue an edict forbidding the printing of 'satires or epigrams'.[46] Satires on the court also took the more popular, and at times more scabrous, form of libels. As early as 1573, a proclamation ordering the destruction of seditious literature included in the category 'infamous libels' which 'defamed . . . approved faithful servants and councillors' with 'manifest slanders' 'to the dishonour of her majesty to whom they are councillors'.[47] Three years later, another proclamation lamenting the 'infamous libels full of malice and falsehood' which had been 'spread abroad and set up in sundry places about the city and court . . .' expressed the government's frustration at its inability to touch the authors.[48] The publication of *A Gaping Gulf*, 'a heap of slanders and reproaches' against the regime, and later punishment of its author John Stubbs, or Stubbes, seems to have excited rather than stemmed the flow of libels.[49] By 1584, according to a proclamation, a multitude of 'false, slanderous, wicked, seditious, and traitorous books and libels' were being 'dispersed through this realm', intended to 'reproach, dishonour and foul with abominable lies' the queen's 'most trusty and faithful councillors'.[50] In the year of the Armada, the domestic threat of 'slanderous and traitorous libels . . . dispersed through this realm' exacerbated the anxieties of a government that worried about the loyalty of the people, as well as the force of Philip II's armies.[51]

Printed, or written, satires and libels drew on and performed in the oral culture of gossip and rumour which carried news of the court through the communities of the illiterate. Rumour, we have seen, disturbed the tranquillity of all Tudor governments and, for all its popularity, that of Elizabeth was no exception. 'Rumour still abrode he flies' ran a ballad of 1570;[52] and from Paul's Yard and the Exchange, rumour spread state business to the counties, parishes and alehouses: to a people who, in the words of the Lord Chancellor, were always more ready to receive bad rather than good report of government.[53] From the time of the northern rebellion in 1569, the government viewed rumour as the seedbed of rebellion.[54] As the 1570 *Homily Against Disobedience* put it, 'inward grudges, mutter and murmur' were 'inward treason . . . privily hatched in the breast', which later came to 'open declaration'.[55] And John Bridges warned his sovereign, in 1573, that malignants 'mutter and slander' her government.[56] Rumour and slander continued to haunt authority. In 1580, rumours of an invasion, 'by speech or writing . . . maliciously dispersed' circulated, disturbing the people.[57] By February 1587, the 'sundry lewd and seditious bruits . . . lately spread and carried abroad in many shires of the realm' by 'hue and cry' were feared to be 'stirring up such . . . humours as are apt to tumult and aberration'.[58] In the month of the arrest of the Earl of Essex, the queen had to act to try to check the 'undutiful words' and 'rumours against us and our government' which were running through the capital.[59] Still two months later, she heard that 'divers traitorous and seditious libels have of late been dispersed in divers parts of our city of London and places near the country adjoining . . . stirring up rebellion and sedition within our realm'.[60] The high strains of paeans to Gloriana were, throughout the reign, disturbed by the low hum of rumour and the murmur of discontent.

Though most rumours were vague, directed at general court corruption or at particular, unpopular ministers, Elizabeth herself was not immune from personal calumny and seditious talk. The queen of course always took attacks on her ministers personally – as tending to 'the destruction or ruin of some good estimation and fidelity towards her majesty'.[61] But from even before her succession, as recent scholarship has illuminated, Elizabeth was the butt of personal slander, which struck directly at her own self-representation: as godly handmaiden, virtuous princess and Virgin Queen. During the period of her residence as princess in the household of Catherine Parr and her husband

Lord Admiral Thomas Seymour, there were rumours of illicit sex and erotic play between Elizabeth and her stepfather, one of which went so far as to claim that she was pregnant by him. While Elizabeth loudly protested her innocence, in the absence of evidence subjects were left to believe whatever circulating account they chose, and as the daughter of a mother tried for sexual misconduct, Elizabeth did not entirely escape the taint of sexual impropriety.[62] As a recent historian of this incident opines, 'this area of Elizabeth's life provided a volatile space for speculation' – a space which not a few filled with lurid details drawn from their own imaginations or agendas.[63]

Not least because she made it prominent in her own representation, Elizabeth's sexuality and virginity were vulnerable to question and attacked by critics. As we have seen, reluctance to marry drew criticism from the queen's own confidants, councillors and parliaments, and critical concern about her failure to do so is audible in scores of pamphlets and tracts. But suitors and potential husbands brought their own problems: Elizabeth's behaviour with Alençon and Robert Dudley, Earl of Leicester excited unpleasant rumours, in the last case a suggestion not only of illicit sexual dalliance but of possible royal implication in the suspicious death of Dudley's first wife, Amy Robsart.[64] Scandalous tales that Elizabeth had borne a child by her lover freely circulated in England as well as Europe, and filtered down to the lowest social orders – even to the gossip of the likes of Mother Anne Dowe in a tailor's shop.[65] Ordinary folk referred to Elizabeth (as they had her mother) as a 'whore' and some even said openly that her fall from chastity (as it was alleged) disqualified her from being a monarch.[66] Sexual rumours about Elizabeth's affairs continued through the 1560s and into the next decade, when gossip also linked her with Christopher Hatton, Vice-Chamberlain of her household.[67] Stories of illegitimate children and affairs with other nobles followed Elizabeth to – and beyond – the grave: Elizabeth was said to have two children – or more – with Leicester, and envoys regularly reported rumours of pregnancies.[68] Often fuelled by concern and speculation over the succession, such tales played into the hands of Catholic and other opponents of the regime who doubtless promoted and embellished them, if they did not start them running.[69] The potential damage to the queen, of course, was inestimable. In a patriarchal society, as Elizabeth was the first to recognize, legitimacy was paramount – and all the more so for rulers. Those who questioned Elizabeth's virginity, no less than those who questioned Catherine of Aragon's, put her throne, and perhaps her life, at risk.

Ironically, rumours of royal lust went hand in hand with other demystifying tales about the royal body, suggesting the queen's incapacity for, or lack of interest in, sexual relations with men. Stories that Elizabeth had a genital abnormality which prevented sexual intercourse were repeated by no less a figure than Ben Jonson.[70] And, surely, in some agonized contemporary discussion of

Elizabeth's reluctance to marry and her professions of celibacy, we hear the *frisson* of lesbianism? Even Edmund Spenser seems to toy with some unnamed relations in the coupling of Britmart and Amoret, in book 4 of the *Faerie Queene*.[71] And, it has been interestingly suggested, Lyly's play *Sapho and Phao*, performed at court, for all its conventional praise, 'is invested with a certain innuendo' in its conjunction of the names of Diana and Sappho, the poet of Lesbos (to which England was also compared in his play *Midas*).[72] In the context of such discussions, the depicting of Elizabeth, in a number of literary texts, in an exclusively female entourage may take on a sexual charge. How far these hints of lesbianism were the stuff of court, or popular, talk, we cannot finally know. As Dorothy Stephens suggests, Spenser evokes 'a femininity just as secretive as the Eliza of the cult', and 'he allows women's alliances to trouble some of the poem's most resolutely trod paths, including those that lead toward matrimony'.[73]

Ambiguities concerning Elizabeth's sexuality and body also found expression in a discourse that figured her as hermaphrodite – as male and female. At some level, this echoed the queen's own representation. As Carole Levin has shown, and as we have seen, Elizabeth herself deployed a mixed language of male and female to represent her own authority, even figuring her physical body as hybrid – her 'heart and stomach' being male, whatever the frailty of her body.[74] Elizabeth's capacity to fuse such diverse virtues of both sexes was often a theme of panegyric. But this self-presentation, together with the cultural assumption of the 'monstrosity' of female rule, often led to critical figurations of Elizabeth as unnatural, un-female, Amazonian. John Knox himself had supported his diatribe against female regimes by references to the Amazons.[75] The queen was compared directly in 1588 with Penthesilea, the Amazon queen; and in the *Faerie Queene* Spenser linked Elizabeth with Penthesilea through Belphoebe.[76] Though Spenser may have sought to neuter the difficulties of female power, the pejorative associations with the Amazons remained.[77] As Mary Villeponteaux has argued, though Elizabethans would praise the Amazons as 'valiant', they remained monstrous as women, and abnormal and unnatural in their sexual behaviour. The legend of the Amazons amputating their right breast symbolized that 'unnaturalness', as did their cruelty to their own infants, which subverted all cultural expectations of maternity.[78] Moreover, such tales of monstrous women were 'the flip side of an image Elizabeth often promoted, that of herself as the mother of her people'.[79]

A cultural preoccupation with Elizabeth's body, her 'virginity', her sexuality, and even her sex, also produced a pornographic literature which hardly complemented the mystical images of Gloriana or the Platonic and Petrarchan ideals of Elizabethan chivalry. A recent, innovative essay goes further. Reminding us of the element of political critique in all Renaissance pornography, Hannah Betts has uncovered a current of sexually explicit literature that reflected hostility to Elizabethan government and the queen herself.[80] In Puttenham's popular *Arte of English Poesie*, she suggests, the exposure of the royal body is both sexual and political – a revelation of that most secret of state secrets under female monarchy, the cunt (often punned with 'quaint'). Sexually explicit figures of the female genitalia in some late Elizabethan verse 'suggest a certain hostility toward the cult of virginity by which the regime was characterised' and signal a graphic realism that punctures the majesty and sanctity of Elizabeth's representation.[81] 'Those secretes' that 'must not be surveyde with eyes' were political and gynae-cological; the publication of the one was an opening of access to the other.[82] As Betts argues, the virulently pornographic allusions to Elizabeth in this literature of the 1590s offer a case study in how 'every celebration of the queen's eternal reign invited a counter discourse'.[83]

Elizabeth's body and sexuality were sites of what remained an ambivalence towards female rule – and perhaps towards government itself. On the one hand, Elizabeth was the removed virgin and saint; on the other, she was a physical woman, the subject of complex physiologies and psychologies of desire and revulsion in early modern culture, which its pornographic litera-ture uniquely well evidences. Nor is it a coincidence that the vogue for such pornographic literature, like that for satire and the number of rumours circu-lating about Elizabeth's illegitimate children, reached a peak in the last decade of her reign. The question of the succession refocused critical attention on the sex of the queen and her sterile body, a queen who, as the nation's mother, had yet failed to provide the issue which would secure their future. And the queen's ageing body, displaying as the French ambassador graphically described it, the corruptions and decay of age, seemed to represent the government itself, in ways that were not positive.[84] Bitter factional rivalries at court which culminated in Essex's rebellion, continuing threats from Spain, the poverty of the crown which led to the extremely unpopular use of patents to raise money, harvest failures and the economic hardships that beset the realm all contributed to an enheightened social anxiety, exacerbated by fear that a disputed succession might lead to renewed civil war.[85] In these circum-stances, some of the figures and discourses of positive representation could be, and were, turned against the queen and her government.

The reign of Elizabeth I, to make an obvious point not often enough remem-bered, was a long one; and the near half-century of Elizabethan rule witnessed profound changes in society and culture which affected the performance of royal images and representations. In the queen's personal case, there were major turning-points when possible marriages were considered and aban-doned; and, it has been suggested, 'the period 1578–82 marked a crucial tran-sition between the years when Elizabeth might potentially marry and produce an heir and the years when it was certain that she would not do so'. [86] Events, such as the northern rebellion, the papal excommunication, the Armada and the Essex revolt dictated shifts in the representation of royal government as well as in policy. Longer-term changes – the quarrels between the Presbyterians and the church establishment, the passing of a generation of councillors such as Leicester and Walsingham – necessitated different official apologias as well as altered courses. By the end of the reign, there was not only a new world of print publicity, but a changed political culture: one in which, though still officially pejorative, the arts of politics and politicking were beginning to be acknowledged by readers of Tacitus and Lipsius, Livy and Machiavelli.[87] As Elizabeth herself put it, 'now the wit of the fox is everywhere on foot'.[88] The last decade of Elizabethan rule reveals the ambiguities of a society and polity in which the languages of chivalry and medievalism, even a 'secularised Catholic revival', reached their height at the moment of their final decline; and in which the most extravagant panegyrics of the queen vied with a 'literature of disillusionment'.[89] Throughout her long reign, 'Elizabeth acquired different aspects as she was required to fulfil various symbolic needs'.[90]

But by the 1590s, the gap between the representation and the perception of the reign began to unsettle the processes of symbolizing and signifying. As the discourse of Machiavelli and Tacitus drew attention to the art of dissimulation, representation itself became a complicated performance – the doubleness of which is brilliantly captured in plays like Shakespeare's *Henry V*, most probably first performed in 1599. The mysteries of the Virgin Queen were more than ever part of political discussion and debate, and hence no longer, as royal representations had sought to be, above the quotidian fray of politics. In this context, the increasingly iconic representation of the queen which we have observed in portraiture appears an orchestrated effort to remove and protect the mystery of power not only from the realities of politics but from a new world of realpolitik.

It is both the power of Elizabethan representation and the mounting tension between images of power and the realities of late sixteenth-century politics that inspired that most public medium of political debate – the theatre. Through the later decades of Elizabeth's reign, we hear a new and ubiquitous language of theatre used to describe social and political relations: 'every man', Bishop Young told his congregation in 1575, 'like . . . common players in plays and interludes playeth many parts'.[91] The monarch, wrote the author of *The History of the Institution of Christian Princes*, 'is as it were a theatre and glass, that all the world should behold'.[92] Probably because she had made the monarchy such a theatre and glass, Elizabeth was the first ruler to employ frequently the metaphor of regal government as theatrical performance: 'Princes, you know,' she told her parliament as though stating the obvious, 'stand upon stages, so that their actions are viewed and beheld of all men.'[93] Later, she shared the thought with James VI: 'We princes are set on highest stage, where looks of all beholders verdict our works.'[94] Like the explosion of print, the birth, and development as a full commercial business, of the theatre is inseparable from the success of Elizabeth in placing herself prominently in the public imagination, in publicizing power.

As a consequence, as numerous studies in the wake of New Historicism have argued, theatre was the principal site of meditation on power and the critical interrogation of politics. And it was a locus of the anxieties generated by a virgin queen and nursing mother who, as she aged, was going to leave her people without a sovereign. The vogue for history plays, in particular, evidenced both the success of the Tudors in establishing their dynasty and yet also the nation's anxieties about the succession, as Elizabeth's days neared their end. Whilst plays like *The Famous Victories of Henry V* rang with jingoistic nationalism and praise of charismatic rulers, the theatre also staged the rumours, plots and rebellions which had dogged Tudor rule, and, in the 1590s, the civil wars that had rent England in the fifteenth century and which, it was feared, might be rekindled on the death of Elizabeth.[95] Though the very titling of large number of plays after kings is another testament to the impact of Tudor monarchy on the cultural imaginary, history plays and 'king plays' also spread dialogue about the acceptable limit and abuse of power, about conscience and allegiance, obedience and resistance and, of course, reflection on the very nature of representation and royal performance.[96] Was Henry V a charismatic strong warrior prince or a Machiavellian dissimulator, and were both arts now essential to the exercise of rule? Do the court scenes in *King John* or *Richard II* celebrate royal magnificence or critique it as expense, deceit and misrepresentation? Were sacred sovereigns also often fallible men – and women? By posing such questions in a dialogic genre, theatre stimulated a larger dialogue. As Margot Heinemann put it, the history plays of the 1590s, 'fusing the popular dramatic tradition with new humanist or politique history ... helped both to create a consensus of support for a powerful monarchy and, paradoxically, to undermine it'.[97] The current emphasis on the capacity of even seemingly orthodox texts to be read as criticism is amply borne out by Elizabeth's own reading of *Richard II* as a dangerous comment on herself. 'I am Richard II,' she famously commented, 'know ye not that.'[98]

The last years of Elizabeth's reign saw a great number of plays that dealt specifically with the Yorkist and Lancastrian kings and with the civil wars from which the Tudors had rescued the crown and nation. The fear of renewed civil war on the death of the queen, a fear articulated by no less a figure than Francis Bacon, sent playwrights back to England's last civil conflict; perhaps, in Henry VII, they looked for a model for a new dynastic saviour who would found a great dynasty to replace that of the barren Virgin Queen. Thomas Lodge's *The Wounds of Civil War*, performed and published in 1594, was set in the Rome of the conflict between Antony and Pompey, but the theme of 'contentious brawls', not to mention the presence of the powerful Cleopatra, doubtless made this a text often read as a meditation on England's future fate.[99] John Speed's *Description of the Civil Wars of England*, a single sheet (possibly a wall chart) of the battles between Yorkists and Lancastrians, graphically addressed the same concern, which was also the theme of *The First Part of the Contention Betwixt The Two Famous Houses of York and Lancaster*, and *The True Tragedy of Richard Duke of York and The Death of Good King Henry VI*, plays which were published the same year.[100] In the process of revisiting civil war and aristocratic rebellion, drama staged kings opposed, deposed and murdered, and kings who were corrupt schemers as well as virtuous princes. Though in a decade nervous about disorder, much of the drama valued and valorized order and the monarchy which sustained it, the theatre's endorsement of royal authority was neither without qualification, nor absolute.

In *The True Tragedy of Richard III*, played before the queen, it was claimed in 1594, Lord Stanley, husband to the mother of the Earl of Richmond, addressed his stepson who was about to be king: 'My son, I glory more to hear what praise the common people gave of thee than if the peers by general full consent had set me down to wear the diadem.'[101] Richmond, now proclaimed Henry VII, told his people 'nor do I wish to enjoy a longer life than I shall live to think upon your love'.[102] His speech echoed the words of Elizabeth on several public occasions. And it nicely captured both the reciprocity of rule and the rapport with the people that, despite the discontent of the last years, Elizabeth had for the most part enjoyed. The rhetoric and imagery of love did not occlude criticism. Because the monarchy did not control discourse or the media, representation could be dangerous. But in the case of a skilful performer, the art of representation could translate even the discourse of accountability and reciprocity into enhanced power.

From the very outset of her reign to the end, Elizabeth skilfully performed the role of monarch, at a time when the performative dimension of power had never been more vital. And she used her sex and a language of affect which, like the earlier Tudor discourse of the commonweal, not only articulated ideals of order and harmony, but helped to sustain them. 'The good citizens of London' who, in the wake of the northern rebellion, 'could not contain their affections but . . . brake out into cries of hearty prayers for her grace . . . and thanks to God for her miraculous succession', bore witness to the powerful bond (what, we recall, Morrison had called the 'lovely bond') that Elizabeth forged with her people – and never lost.[103] Of course, there were, especially later in the reign, popular discontents and unrest, including grain riots in the mid-1590s.[104] We may find instances of ordinary subjects contesting not only Elizabeth's authority but the forms through which she represented it: rioters in Sussex in 1591 tore down the queen's arms; in 1589 a priest was found to have rubbed the image off the queen's coin.[105] But for all the hostility to the government or to particular ministers, whatever the grumblings or expressions of frustration, Elizabeth remained an object of the people's affections.

Interestingly, in the later years of her reign, treatises like Machiavelli's *Prince* questioned the whole basis of royal rule and royal representation that Elizabeth had embodied. The author of *The Prince*, which began to circulate widely in manuscript translation from the 1580s, proposed fear as a far more effective instrument of power than love and advised the ruler to practise feint and dissimulation, to deploy misrepresentation rather than representation. The end of the century gave rise to a new language of 'politics' and a brutal realism which challenged affective relations as the foundation of societies and status. Yet, even one of the leading figures of the new realpolitik, Justus Lipsius, tempered Machiavellian doctrine in one aspect. Though he pressed the need for rulers to practise prudence as well as virtue, Lipsius emphasized the importance of the love of the people for the successful government of the state.[106] Lipsius was of the view that 'majesty without force is unassured'.[107] But 'a reverent opinion of the king and his estate', 'good estimation' of the ruler was no less vital.[108] Writing the same year a treatise on the government of Ireland, dedicated to Elizabeth, Richard Becon, attorney for the province of Munster, argued 'it seemeth a matter very necessary that every magistrate should retain the art, skill and knowledge of persuading . . . the multitude'; 'the good will and consent of the people', he added, 'do promise no small security unto the magistrate'.[109] Four years later, in a proclamation declaring the reason for sending troops to Ireland, Elizabeth bore out Becon's advice. It was, she announced, 'always esteemed by us as the greatest surety to our royal state when our subjects' hearts are assured to us by the bonds of love rather than by forced obedience'.[110]

The art of representation in early modern England was the art of securing and sustaining those 'bonds of love'. Looking back over Elizabeth's reign in a sermon at Paul's Cross in 1599, Thomas Holland did not doubt that Elizabeth had sustained them. Preaching on 17 November, Holland recounted how the celebrations of the queen's accession day had arisen. Instituted in Oxford University, it was, he explained, 'followed by a voluntary current over all this realm'.[111] As we have seen, never an official holiday, 17 November was 'voluntarily continued by the religious and dutiful subjects of this realm' 'to express their sincere affections in joy to their sovereign'.[112] The unorchestrated spontaneity he conjured does not give the full picture. Service books of prayer praising the queen were provided for use in churches on 17 November; civic authorities in some cases ordered bell-ringing or attendance at festivities.[113] Official direction and popular desire – 'a meeting half way of the interests of government and people' – melded to make the day what it became: 'solemnised'.[114]

Elizabeth died a 'sacred' figure after a half-century of, if not meeting the people half way, then engaging them in a relation which was also an exchange. For that reason, above all other, she was 'solemnised' for decades, indeed centuries, after her death.

II

Elizabeth died on 24 March 1603 at her palace at Richmond. She had performed as queen to the last. In February 1603, Giovanni Carlo Scarametti reported to the Doge of Venice the audience he had obtained with the queen shortly after his arrival. 'The queen, who is in her seventy first year, is in excellent health.'[115] She was abreast of events, he continued, kept a personal eye on the navy and carefully played off France and Spain against each other. Clearly, even at her advanced age, Elizabeth's magnificence made an impact on him: she was, he reported, 'clad in taffety of silver and white, trimmed with gold; her dress was somewhat open in front and showed her throat encircled with pearls and rubies down to her breast . . . she had on a coif arched round her head and an imperial crown, and displayed a vast quantity of gems and pearls upon her person.'[116] Elizabeth was seated, enthroned, and surrounded by her leading councillors who attended uncovered, in a Privy Chamber full of worthies. By no means for the first time, the queen mixed warmth with stern words, raising the kneeling envoy with her own hands, only to assert that Venice had not treated her, a woman, with the respect that she had felt her due. Modestly returning to the inadequacies of her (excellent) Italian, Elizabeth, before dispatching Scarametti, gave him her hand to kiss.[117] The ambassador was charmed by her and even wrote of her 'never quite lost beauty', as well as her prudence and learning.[118] Within a week or two, however, things had changed drastically: the queen withdrew into melancholy, the illness was 'the first serious illness which she has had in the whole course of her life' – an illness from which she did not recover.[119]

In the flurry of events that unfolded over the next hours – notably the peaceful proclamation of James VI as king – Elizabeth's body was 'left . . . alone a day or two after her death, and mean persons had access to it', before being conveyed on a torchlit barge from Richmond to Whitehall, where it lay in state.[120] On 28 April, the queen's remains were conveyed to Westminster in a formal state funeral. It seems fitting that one account of Elizabeth's funeral was written by Henry Chettle, the pamphleteer and dramatist who, as a stationer, had published popular literature.[121] A more detailed account by the young poet Richard Niccols listed the huge (1,500 plus) procession that accompanied Elizabeth's hearse, led by 240 women and including nearly all the queen's household staff, legal officers, all the bishops and nobility, heralds and ambassadors.[122] Fitting because, for all the pomp of this cortège that accompanied to Westminster 'the lively [lifelike] picture of her Majesties whole body in her parliament robes with a crown on her head and a sceptre in her hand' atop the coffin, Niccols described popular mourning – of 'many thousand'.[123] Indeed, his account (which evidently sold well enough to start Niccols on a career as a writer) was written as if to place the reader who had not witnessed the event almost in the midst of the procession and proceedings. So, after listing the yeomen and sergeants and clerks and aldermen and esquires and pensioners, Niccols paused to say: 'Here Reader stay and if thou aske me whie/Tis to entreate thee beare them company'. 'Weepe,' he invited the reader, 'with these flowers of honour that drooping goe.'[124]

The injunction was hardly needed. The death of no monarch was greeted with so many verses and eulogies, in genres and forms popular as well as elite. The young undergraduate Richard Niccols may have had official patronage for his *Expicedium. A Funeral Oration upon the Death of the Late Deceased Princess*, published with a large royal arms. Yet, though he described her as 'greater than Alexander, a queen who enchanted with her beauty, who could not be described but in wonder and silence', Niccols doubted not that 'she lives as yet in the hearts of her grateful subjects'.[125] Similarly, the former headmaster of Merchant Taylor's School, Richard Mulcaster's *In mortem serenissimae reginae Elizabethae. Naenia consolans*, immediately appeared in translation, its title page illustrated with a phoenix rising from the ashes.[126] Mulcaster praised Elizabeth's learning (which 'did surmount her sex'), her bravery, her protection of the church and the state, and her provision of a successor 'to play the part in mothers losse'.[127] *An Elegy upon the Death of . . . Our Late Sovereign* lamented the passing of the 'lady of the fairy land, the phoenix of the world'.[128] In *Anglorum lacrimae*, Thomas Rogers and Richard Johnson remembered a queen whom they wrote, with pardonable exaggeration, all Europe termed celestial and all subjects loved.[129] Elizabeth, they praised, 'maintained her native Countries lawes' and 'ever sought her subiectes wronges to right'.[130] The author of *Eliza's Memorial*, cataloguing the blessings of her reign, not least peace and plenty, concurred with many other elegists that 'her subjects more for love than feare obei'd'.[131] Henry Petowe, showering a few poetic 'April drops . . . on the hearse of dead Elizabeth', whom he called 'the blessed queen of sweet eternitie', claimed the ordinary people simply would not believe that she was dead.[132]

The Poore's Lamentation for the Death of Our Late Dread Sovereign, recalling the joy at her coming to the throne after all the afflictions suffered under Mary, praised the Lord for sending a ruler whom 'the meanest sort did not despise', that is who valued the poorest of her subjects.[133] Thomas Churchyard's

Sorrowful Verses lauded her who had resisted mighty kings, 'great fame and glory got' and won 'worlds love and zeale'. Only her death, he closed, 'left us in a maze'.[134] The English, another panegyric put it, had lost 'our common parent'.[135]

As our flurry of brief quotations from a large outpouring of funeral verses evidences, on her death Elizabeth was often praised in terms and tropes through which she had represented herself and had been represented by others: as God's chosen, as Virgin, mother, as phoenix 'beloved', just princess, Judith, David, Deborah, Hester, 'Earth's true Astraea', who ruled with 'Reason's raine'.[136] Such panegyrics were not without different emphases, nor lacking in recognition that not all had been handled well. The anxiety about the fate of the realm after Elizabeth's death was audible in the funeral eulogies and in the paeans to her successor James. Real uncertainties about the future of 'orphaned lands' underlay the celebration of the new dynasty.[137] In John Fenton's lines describing the queen 'loving truth and hating reprobations', we hear the murmur of bitter religious divisions that gave the lie to idealizations of harmony and unity.[138] Several writers wondered whether there could ever be a reign like hers; some even began to ask, after Nature had perfected all her work in Delia (or Artemis) and she had died, 'now where's ... glory and ... maiestie?'[139] As in her lifetime, some of the qualities and positions for which Elizabeth was lauded were not those she would have emphasized. In death, as in life, her representation was not entirely in her control. Yet, for all that, the outpourings of sorrow and love for the queen and praise for a reign 'when prince and people mutually agree' offer striking testimony to the affective force of Elizabeth and the power of Elizabethan representation.[140] Elizabeth meant different things to different subjects, but her name, image and memory carried great authority long beyond the grave. 'All future ages shall admire her reign,' predicted the author of *Eliza's Memorial*.[141] His simple prophecy was to enfold in a myriad of posthumous representations of the queen – and in invocations, appropriations and counter-presentations which, for all their complexity, paid homage to her person and authority.

The frontispiece to *Sorrow's Joy*, a Cambridge volume lamenting 'our late deceased sovereign Elizabeth', has as its engraved title page the tomb of the queen. Though he moved the remains of Elizabeth from the crypt of Henry VII, James I built his predecessor a splendid monument, engraved with verses commemorating her victories abroad and the settling of peace and religion through prudent government at home.[142] Engravings of the monument circulated widely, some with accompanying verses adding to the praise of the late queen.[143] John Stow, the historian of London, and Thomas Fuller, author of *The Church History of Britain*, also inform us that representations of the Westminster tomb and other monuments to Elizabeth were erected in churches across the capital and country, inscribed with verses celebrating the victorious queen, 'a prince incomparable'.[144] Elizabeth, one monument proclaimed, 'in despite of death/Lives still ador'd'.[145]

The numerous engravings of Elizabeth produced after her death offer further evidence of the afterlife of a queen who had been, as one contemporary verse described her, 'in earth the first', now 'in heaven the second maid'.[146] As we have seen, Elizabeth's reign gave rise to a widespead desire to own images of monarchy, which began to be collected in popular volumes such as Richard Elstracke and Henry Holland's *Braziliologia*, a 'book of kings', first published in 1618.[147] But it was Elizabeth's image that dominated the market under the first two Stuarts, as woodcuts and engravings of the queen were used to illustrate books on nobility and honour, histories of the Netherlands, ecclesiastical histories and pamphlet polemics. Still in the 1640s, the London printseller Peter Stent had more than a dozen engraved portraits of Elizabeth I for sale.[148]

In no small part, these engravings and illustrations manifested a public affection for the queen which lasted decades beyond the grave. But as recent work has revealed, texts of memory and acts of commemoration carry ideological and political freight; and there can be no doubt that after her death Elizabeth became a means of articulating values and advocating programmes that were often critical of the persons and policies of her successors. In the case of Elizabeth's first historian, William Camden, although he received official patronage and encouragement for his *Annals* of the queen's reign, his account was, and was seen to be, in places critical of the first Stuart. Camden's praise of Walsingham (who had urged Mary of Scots's execution), more generally his celebration of Elizabeth's imperial expansion and victories, implied criticism of her successor.[149] After the domestic scandals of the Overbury murder and the outbreak of the Thirty Years War and eviction of James's daughter from the Palatinate, praise of Elizabethan successes pointed an ever greater contrast with what many saw as the weak pacifism of James I. Critics of James's pro-Spanish policies seized on Elizabeth, as had a party in her own reign, as champion of the Protestant cause. Engravings of the queen armed with a lance or trampling the seven-headed beast of Revelation with the Armada visible in the background figured the armoured Elizabeth as the defender of the word, just as Delaram's engraving, symbolically representing her as the woman of the Apocalypse, depicted her with a crown of stars, sun and moon.[150]

Radical critics of Stuart foreign policy found in Elizabeth the champion of their cause that she had never really been. In one 1624 tract, Thomas Scott, author of the infamous *Vox populi*, invoked the queen's memory for invective against James's pursuit of a Spanish marriage for Prince Charles. 'You had a queen in my time on earth,' the ghost of the Earl of Essex, Elizabethan champion of the Protestant cause, tells the nobles and commoners of England, 'who was … never wasteful in her private expenses but maintained armies and

garrisons . . . a well rigged navy; [who] assisted and lent money to her neighbouring states.'[151] In his pamphlet of the same year, the printer, merchant and
polemicist John Reynolds staged an imaginary 'consultation' between Henry
VIII, Edward VI, Mary, Elizabeth, Queen Anne of Denmark and Prince Henry,
in which Elizabeth was the vociferous spokeswoman against the Habsburgs for
the Protestant cause. 'How can,' she asks, 'King James say England and Scotland
is strong, when he fears the power of Spain and will not know . . . his own?' 'It
is an excellent thing,' she adds, 'for England to fight with Spaniards'; 'if King
James inherited my resolution . . . I would make Spain fear his sword.'[152]

As debates continued in Council, parliament and press, popular commem-
orations of Elizabeth grew to their greatest height. In John Taylor's *Memorial
of All the English Monarchs*, Elizabeth stood out as 'courageous, zealous,
learned, true' as the chaste princess, 'A Deborah, A Judith, A Susanna, A Virgin,
A Virago, A Diana'.[153] Celebrating 17 November became a mode of criticizing
the Jacobean regime.

If anything, the succession of Charles I, and his marriage to the Catholic
princess Henrietta Maria, brought the memory of Elizabeth, the scourge of
popery, into ever greater prominence. As David Cressy has noted, Elizabeth's
regnal anniversary on 17 November fell dangerously close to Charles I's
birthday on the 19th and that of his wife on 16 November, and the celebrations
for the three threw the rulers into sharp conjunction and contrast. Certainly,
Elizabeth remained a popular figure: in 1629 Thomas Brown translated
Camden's *Annals* as *The History of the Life and Reign of That Famous Princess
Elizabeth* with an engraved frontispiece, a dedication to Charles I, and a new
preface to the reader in which he closed by stating 'I will rather leave still her
Name for a terror to the Romanist faction'.[154] The playwright Thomas
Heywood, who had dramatized the queen's life on the Jacobean stage in his *If
You Know Not Me You Know Nobody*, re-published the two-part play in 1632–3
and in 1631 published a prose life, *England's Elizabeth*, which swiftly went to a
second edition.[155] Heywood's history of Elizabeth's life and troubles during her
minority carries an engraved frontispiece of the queen being crowned with a
celestial crown and pointing to a bible open at Psalm 66: 'If the Lord had not
been on my side . . .', she reflects, beneath a caption which reads 'Many daughters have done well but thou surpassest them all.' Heywood's praise of an
Elizabeth who saved the realm from popery might have been directed (as well
as to popular readers) to Charles's Catholic queen, as a model of the right faith.
Certainly, *A Chain of Pearls*, a memorial of the heroic virtues of Queen
Elizabeth, published the previous year, presented her as the embodiment of the
graces and female virtues of religion and chastity, prudence and temperance,
as a ruler who deemed her best treasure her people's love.[156] The 'perfect
phoenix' who ruled in Massinger's *Emperor of the East* 'by her example . . .

made a court' which might be a model for all – and one perhaps especially for Charles and Henrietta Maria.[157] 'England,' writes David Cressy, 'was never so conscious of Elizabeth as in the 1620s and 1630s'; and memories of Elizabeth led many to sense and speak of a decline from a golden past to a less glorious present.[158] 'Elizabethanism ... became increasingly identified with the opposition, with critics of Charles and his court.'[159] In 1639, there appeared an anonymous short history of *The Life and Death of Queen Elizabeth*, purportedly by one who had served her. Relating her birth and childhood, the history moves to the dark days of Mary's reign when 'Rome's tyranny the kingdom overran'.[160] During her sister's reign, the history relates, Elizabeth's life was in grave danger; but, guarded by Providence ('Preserv'd like Daniel in the lyons den'), she succeeded to rule.[161] As a queen, she built a strong navy, suppressed superstition, beat off England's enemies and reigned with the love of her Commons. 'She was a patron, and a pattern too,' the couplet sums her, 'To Show All Princes what and how to doe.'[162] It did not take a sage to grasp that one prince who might imitate her virtues was a king (Charles I) about to go to war with his own Protestant Scottish subjects, rather than popish enemies.

During the 1640s and '50s, the Queen Elizabeth who had elevated the Tudor monarchy to the heights of mystery was called upon to speak for Parliamentarian opponents of the king, for the Commonwealth and the Protectorate. The reissue of Robert Naunton's *Fragmenta Regalia, or Observations on the Late Queen Elizabeth Her Times and Favourites* may relate to the factional manoeuvres which were proposed on the eve of civil war as a means of bringing into royal councils those in whom parliament could place its trust.[163] The publication in January 1642 of Queen Elizabeth's Golden Speech to her 1601 parliament (the same month as the re-publication of a parliamentary speech of Henry VIII 'tending to charity and concord') may well have been part of the last efforts to avert the conflict sparked by Charles's attempted arrest of five MPs.[164] In 1643, parliament authorized publication of 'A Most Excellent and remarkable speech by the mirror and miracle of Elizabeth ... in the high court of parliament in the seventeenth year of her reign, wherein she fully expressed the duty of princes to their subjects', as well as the obligations of subjects to them.[165] The Golden Speech was reissued again in March 1648, perhaps, as Wedgwood suggests, as a critique of Charles, but also as an appeal to ancient ways against the threat of the army and the sword – and as part of the middle group's desire that spring to secure a 'long-sought settlement'.[166]

In the wake of the regicide and the establishment of a republic, it may not be surprising that there were few invocations of even so virtuous a Protestant monarch as Elizabeth. But the record is by no means silent. The years around 1650–1 saw the publication and re-publication of several texts of, or pertaining to, Elizabeth's reign: Robert Naunton's *Fragmenta* and *The Felicity of Queen Elizabeth and her Times* by Francis Bacon (1651), which announced the queen as 'the pattern of princes'.[167] Not least, the account of a queen 'whose sails swelled with pride . . . to the fear and astonishment of Europe' may have had something particular to say to a regime endeavouring to enforce the Navigation Act against naval rivals.[168]

It was for a holy crusade, rather than a mercantilist venture, that Oliver Cromwell invoked Elizabeth's name. Recalling 1588, a manifesto written for the Protector by John Milton held out the prospect of promoting the glory of God in the expedition to the West Indies. In his own speech to parliament, Oliver recalled 'Queen Elizabeth of famous memory' to argue for an aggressive foreign policy which she had so assiduously resisted.[169] Though he misappropriated her in so many ways, Cromwell, Dame Veronica Wedgwood argued, psychologically identified himself with a reign and queen who was already a legend in his childhood.

The memory of Elizabeth did not fade with the death of her self-appointed heir. The queen's Golden Speech was re-published – yet again – as the restored Commonwealth groped towards some kind of parliamentary settlement in 1659. The preceding year, Francis Osborne's *Historical Memoirs on the Reigns of Queen Elizabeth and King James* contrasted the 'splendour' of the 'incomparable Queen Elizabeth' with a rather less flattering portrayal of her successor.[170] Rewriting, too, a reign 'lovely, wise and successful', 'the felicity of which was never since matched', Osborne noted 'the bonfires and loud acclamations used *still* by the people on the day of her inauguration'.[171] The people were commemorating Good Queen Bess over fifty years after her death.

The Restoration of Charles II, for all the celebration of Stuart dynasty, by no means eclipsed Elizabeth. Famously, John Dryden's *Astraea Redux* deployed the name and memory of the Virgin Queen (Astraea) to laud a Charles II whom, like Elizabeth, Providence had protected and who was the object of 'our virgin love', as the 'crowds on Dover's strand' shouted their welcoming cheer. Back, like Elizabeth, from the wilderness, wise, mild, just, imperial, Dryden's Charles re-embodied the virtues of England's Eliza, as well as of his father the martyr. Like Charles the Martyr, however, the figure of Elizabeth was a symbol of virtue and authority and of the nation: a symbolic figure whom all needed to claim, and who, in consequence, became embroiled in the post-Restoration, and post-Revolution, politics of party.

During the crisis over the exclusion of the Catholic Duke of York from the succession and the so-called Popish Plot of 1678–81, Elizabeth was again invoked as a champion of Protestantism and parliaments. On the anniversary of her accession on 17 November 1681, *The Imperial Protestant Mercury* recalled the succession 'that put a period to established popery'.[172] Gilbert

Burnet's *History of the Reformation of the Church of England* appeared that year with an engraved illustration of the queen.[173] The next year Elizabeth as queen in parliament appeared as the frontispiece to the edition of Simonds D'Ewes's *Journals* of all the parliaments of her reign – as, no doubt, a pointed criticism of a Charles II who, in the wake of his victory over the Whigs at Oxford, ruled the rest of his life without summoning an assembly.[174] In the years of the so-called Tory reaction and their eclipse, the Whigs adopted and represented Elizabeth as a champion of their cause, with the hope of regaining popular support. Samuel Clarke's *History of the Glorious Life, Reign and Death of the Illustrious Queen Elizabeth Containing An Account By What Means the Reformation Was Promoted* presented the 'illustrious' queen as the protector of the faith at home and abroad, who earned 'the veneration and respect' even 'of the Great Turk himself'.[175] Illustrated throughout, Clarke's *History* was published in 1682 with a frontispiece of Elizabeth enthroned, flanked by Burghley and Walsingham, in a representation of good counsel. A second edition within a year testifies to the place of the queen in the national memory, as well as to the popularity of the nonconformist Clarke's biographies.

August 1688, the year of Revolution, saw the reissue of Camden's *History of Elizabeth* and the publication, with a half-length portrait, of Elizabeth's own thoughts on the issue of transubstantiation – together with speeches, prayers and thanksgivings of the 'gracious and godly queen'.[176] As Tony Claydon has demonstrated, the Williamite regime was swift to claim Elizabeth to support a break in the succession that placed William and Mary on the English throne. Presenting the story of English history as 'a series of heavenly deliverances', Whig histories figured William as the providentially appointed descendant of Elizabeth, as the ruler who formed 'a national covenant with the deity'.[177] During the 1690s, Elizabeth's Golden Speech to parliament was twice reprinted, along with new lives of the queen, written to advance the Whig cause. In 1693, Edmund Bohun, an apologist for the Revolution and licenser of the press, issued a *Character of Queen Elizabeth*, with an engraved frontispiece of Elizabeth and Mary II as 'queens of England'.[178] Not only did this image, accompanied with the motto 'Semper eadem', advertise a dynastic descent which served to temper the violent break of 1688, but Bohun, in his dedication to William and Mary, lauded the endowments and abilities of an Elizabeth whose example, it was argued, they followed.[179] Burnet followed two years later with his own *Essay on the Memory of the Late Queen*, which this time bore the portrait of Mary II alone, a ruler who had been 'the masterpiece of Nature'.[180] Sorrow at Elizabeth's death, Burnet consoled his reader, was now abated by the wise working of Providence which had provided another sovereign in her image, a second Mary who recalled her and re-presented her virtues.[181] *The Secret History of the Most Renowned Queen Elizabeth*, published in 1695, gestured towards that novelization of the past that was soon to transform the genres of both literature and history.[182] Indeed, in the late part of the century, several histories of Elizabeth's loves and the purported *Novels of Elizabeth*, translated from the French of Madame d'Aulnoy by Spencer Hickman in 1681, presented the queen as the author as well as subject of fiction.[183]

The return to the throne of a legitimate successor to the Stuart line, more importantly the succession of another woman, Anne, as queen regnant, refocused a great deal of attention on Queen Elizabeth as champion of the godly and as head of an Anglican church, English as distinct from continental in its Protestantism, and as imperial princess. For her own part, Queen Anne went to some lengths to appropriate her predecessor's name, image and authority. She took up for her own Elizabeth's motto 'Semper eadem'; Kneller painted her in a dress evocative of Elizabeth I; and engravings, bearing the motto, freely described her in words Elizabeth had made her own as the 'tender nursing mother to the church'. For all their obvious differences – Elizabeth the virgin, Anne ever pregnant with children who subsequently died in infancy – the two queens both represented the monarchy as a symbolic mother to their people. But, as Toni Bowers argued, the 'Second Elizabeth', as she was commonly known, failed to capture the nation's hearts like its first 'mother'.[184] Unlike Anne, Elizabeth was 'an icon, a sign of the nation'.[185] As well as confronting important cultural shifts which had complicated the performative power of symbols, Anne simply did not manipulate the rhetoric and signs of her representation as skilfully and effectively as Elizabeth.

It is Elizabeth who has stood through history as the great model not only of feminine monarchy, but of the most successful rule, latterly of powerful womanhood. As Jean Wilson put it, in a comparison which deserves further consideration, it was Elizabeth and Queen Victoria who 'have captured the public imagination as male sovereigns have not'.[186] Astute male leaders, however, have not been slow to appropriate her rhetoric and image of strength, and it is no coincidence that it was in the 1930s and '40s that a succession of male historians appear to have fallen in love with the queen. In our own time, Mrs Thatcher was frequently compared to Elizabeth I, in cartoon and popular print and in serious political discourse. More broadly, feminist politics has redirected attention to Elizabeth – sometimes simply as an early champion of the woman, more interestingly as a site of the complexities of female authority in sixteenth- and in twentieth-century patriarchal culture.

The history of the afterlife of Elizabeth, of the posthumous representation of her person and rule, is a history of ambiguity and contest. Throughout the years since her death, historical ages and agents have used her to validate causes quite alien to her sympathies as well as values she held dear. The struggle to appropriate her for myriad positions in some ways continued that contest for representation that characterized her own reign. The image of Elizabeth in her lifetime, as well as after her death, was often constructed and manipulated by others. Yet, the ubiquitous invocation of Elizabeth I testifies to the authority she was able to wield and to the centrality of her image and representation to that authority. In 1640, the author of a panegyric on the queen expressed the hope that 'never shall thy fame dye, Princely mayde'. Four centuries after her death, with the memory still fresh of another fairy princess who desired, like Elizabeth, to be 'Queen of hearts', and television producers attracting record audiences for programmes on her reign, it seems appropriate to conclude not only that his hope was granted, but many of Elizabeth's, too.

EPILOGUE

More than fifty years ago, the leading authority characterized the sixteenth century and in particular the age of Henry VIII as a period in English history that witnessed a 'Tudor revolution in government'.[1] In making his case, Sir Geoffrey Elton focused principally on the administration: on changes in the Council and the courts which made royal government, he argued, less personal, more bureaucratic and better equipped to deal with business. Other scholars questioned Elton's claims; in particular some historians of late medieval England doubted whether the government and central administration were fundamentally transformed by Henry or very different to those of his predecessors.[2] Yet a sense that the sixteenth century was a century of fundamental changes that led England from a medieval to a modern age has long been canvassed by historians of very different interests and perspectives.

Economic and social historians, for instance, have, since Marx and his English disciple R. H. Tawney, viewed the sixteenth century as one in which England emerged as a market economy and a society in movement and flux.[3] Backed by the formidable researches of Lawrence Stone, the sixteenth century began to be seen as an age of crisis for the old aristocracy and, by corollary, the age of the 'rise of the gentry'.[4] These theses in turn met with ferocious criticism which cautioned any scholar about making such large-scale claims: indeed, as a consequence, social historians turned to microstudies eschewing grand theses about the century.[5] Few, however, would deny that in economic and social terms, England was a very different country in 1600 to what it had been in 1500. Modern historians of London have demonstrated what the contemporary chronicler John Stow discerned and in some ways lamented: that in the capital, at least, a full market economy and market relations had eroded old economies, customs and relationships.[6] London had become a world centre of a commodity culture and, as playwrights along with

 by 1600

pamphleteers observed, status and identity had themselves become commodified in the process. As more and more gentlemen and women and fortune seekers spent time in the capital, the London effect, with which we are so familiar today, began to make its mark on other provincial cities and towns and even on the countryside to which the landed returned out of the metropolitan season. The rise and fall of the titled and landed, the social climbers and the gulls, was a principal subject of Tudor chatter and dramatic entertainment: the celebrity gossip of the sixteenth century.

Another revolution which most historians would acknowledge was that which took place in religion and the church. The sixteenth century opened with England as an orthodox Roman Catholic country and with Henry VII as a loyal son of the church, keen to advertise his piety and fidelity to Rome as the central qualities of virtuous kingship. His son went even further. Intervening in the greatest threat to the unity of the church and the authority of the papacy since the schism, Henry VIII vociferously denounced the teachings of Martin Luther and earned the title Defender of the Faith from an understandably grateful pope. Within a decade, however, Henry had embarked on the pursuit of a divorce which led him to a break from Rome and to assume the Supreme Headship of the church and to claim the status of God's lieutenant on earth. Henry had desired a vital but very particular outcome: a papal dispensation to divorce and remarry so as to sire a male successor. What in fact emerged from the 1520s and '30s was a revolution in church and state. Though Henry was, and in large measure remained, a Catholic in belief and liturgical practice, the rejection of the pope undermined the universal Catholic church in England. Moreover, though not himself Protestant, Henry's divorce, remarriage and campaign to convince others of the right of his course of action, and of his authority to pursue it, pushed him into the arms of Protestant sympathizers – literally in the case of Anne Boleyn, his mistress and second queen. Under Henry VIII, England was never officially (still less in reality) a Protestant country, but it was no longer a Roman Catholic country, nor a country united in religion. Under his two successors, the one staunchly Protestant, the other as committed to Rome, the legacy of Henry's divorce was played out and the hard facts of religious division (which everywhere on the continent had erupted into war) became inescapable.

Henry's break from Rome, as we know, had profound consequences for the monarchy as well as the church. In many respects, the crown was greatly strengthened. The dissolution of the monasteries which followed the break from Rome endowed Henry with a greater royal demesne than any monarch since the Norman Conquest. Had he not chosen to spend his new wealth on ambitious continental wars, Henry could have been the first ruler to 'live of his own', to fund the costs of government from his own landed income, in centuries. Secondly, the rejection of the papacy and the assumption of authority over the church ended a long history of tensions between the monarchy and papacy which had at times flared up to destabilize royal government – as in the case of St Thomas Becket. The Supreme Headship made Henry virtually a priest as well as a king, with divine powers to determine worship and faith in his realm, placing the so-called two swords of religious and secular power for the first time in one ruler's hands. On the other hand, as scholars have noted, the Reformation in some respects also weakened Henry and his successors. Though he insisted on his personal and divine authority, Henry could not bring about the changes needed to establish the supremacy alone. Not least, he needed the authority of statute law to enact and secure his authority: to remove appeals from Rome, to legalize his position and to pass draconian new treason laws intended to deter, and make it easier to punish, opponents of change. Thanks to the needs of Henry, then his heirs, to place on a statutory footing a succession of church settlements, parliaments, hitherto an occasional occurrence, became a regular part of Tudor government. While they formed a partnership with the crown, which in many ways further strengthened the monarchy, parliaments became part of royal government and MPs began to think of themselves as partners in government as well as occasional advisers to the sovereign. And, for all that they supported successive reformations, MPs had their own views which, as events were to show, often differed from the monarch's but which they insisted on expressing. Old Whig views about a rise of a revolutionary parliamentary opposition in the sixteenth century have been seriously challenged and we would not seek to revive them here.[7] But there can be no doubt that one of the unforeseen consequences of Reformation was the emergence of a more regular and self-confident parliament, which various interest groups and denominations could and did use to put pressure on the monarch. The Tudors were more powerful monarchs than their predecessors for centuries; but they were kings and queens who ruled with parliaments, in a partnership with the representatives of the people.

From the outset there were, as well as famous outspoken opponents of his actions such as John Fisher and Thomas More, very many ordinary subjects who doubted the right of Henry's divorce and break from Rome, or who even considered that he had sinned and was heterodox. Though rival aristocrats and aggrieved or hungry subjects had, throughout England's history, posed potential and actual threats to the monarch, Henry faced a new challenge: divided subjects and an ideological opposition which could not be appeased except by a fundamental change of direction and a surrender of authority. As, over the reigns of Edward and Mary, religious divisions intensified, the church, the Supreme Headship and religion were what most destabilized the

Tudor monarchy and threatened civil war. Within a few years of the death of the mighty Henry, the monarchy was plunged into what historians used to call a 'mid-Tudor crisis', which it was by no means certain it would survive.[8]

The economic, social and religious revolutions of the sixteenth century gave rise to a large number of rebellions and popular uprisings which shook the governments to the core. Earlier generations of historians, inclined to models of deference and little interested in any below the elites of past societies, tended to downplay the popular elements in these uprisings and instead to emphasize aristocratic and gentry leadership and concerns, which a feudal peasantry were merely led to follow.[9] More recent studies, however, have illuminated the nature and extent of popular discontents and a large degree of popular autonomy in the resort to action and riot.[10] The economic dislocations of an age of enclosure, the decline of resident and paternalist landlords and the shift to a market economy were, we know, all factors. But the dissolution of the monasteries caused spiritual as well as economic disruptions and the 1549 rising in the west was very much prompted by opposition to a new Prayer Book. As Geoffrey Elton long ago documented so magnificently and as Ethan Shagan's very different researches have confirmed, there was widespread popular opposition to the Reformation and to the reformations which followed it through the century.[11] Adding the vital concerns about the true faith and salvation in the afterlife to the daily anxiety about having food, the Reformation politicized the people and made them a force in politics.

Along with economic and social, religious and political revolutions, the sixteenth century was in England an age of technological revolution. At the beginning of the century, English printed books were few and ephemeral cheap print, in the form of pamphlets and broadsides, was virtually non-existent. During Henry VIII's reign, however, Lutheran pamphlets, illustrated with woodcuts, began to circulate and stimulated native production especially of what Tessa Watt termed works of popular piety.[12] Reformation and religious division and change were coterminous with the rise of print, and it is difficult to say confidently which came first. By mid-century they clearly stimulated each other, and by the late decades they took advantage of, as they further advanced, a growing literacy and the new market for books, along with other consumer objects. Print made all discussion and debate public, informed a public, and helped to fashion a public sphere of exchange and gossip about the formerly closed secrets of religion and state. By the end of the century, the appetite for news was insatiable and led to the appointment of paid reporters and informants, and early in the next century to news pamphlets and corantos or gazettes.[13] By 1600 even ordinary English men and women read or heard reported a great deal about their government, councillors and courtiers and their ruler; that by no means all of it was accurate does not change the fact. For the first time, by the end of the sixteenth century English people, especially in the cities and towns, were living in a media world – and so was their queen.

These fundamental changes we have sketched are not unfamiliar but they have been studied separately. One of the unfortunate consequences of the greater professionalization of, and specialization in, historical studies has been a growing divide between political and religious and social and economic historians; they even have their own textbook surveys. Moreover, there has been, at least until very recently, a divide between those, often described as traditionalists, who studied governments, nobles and gentry elites and those, more radical in their scholarly (and often political) preferences, who practised history from below, that is concentrated on the ordinary people, the poor and the marginalized. It hardly needs saying that such fragmentation has distorted the past, for elites and ordinary people did not live independently of each other and, given the centrality of religion in pre-modern societies, changes in worship, the organization of the church and the position of the clergy were, inevitably, social and economic changes too. As I have suggested, the Reformation – and reformations – of the sixteenth century were inseparable from, and related to, the other changes and developments which were transforming England.

What this study has argued is that the monarchy was at the very centre of all these revolutions, and is as central to histories from below as to administrative histories or accounts of 'high politics'. And it is central because the Tudors set out to make it so. One might be tempted to say that, compared with the beginning of the century, by the end of the sixteenth century the monarchy was unrecognizable. But it is the reverse which is true. Elizabeth, well before the end of her reign, was everywhere recognized and her image was circulated and reproduced in texts, on playing cards, and on plates. The sixteenth century had witnessed a revolution in representation: representation which responded to religious and political circumstances, new media opportunities and popular political awareness and which quickened social, political and constitutional changes; and – important but hardly studied – changes in the social psychology of sovereignty and subjectivity.

In his efforts to pressure the papacy and the church into granting him a divorce, Henry encouraged parliamentary and popular anticlericalism, which had a base, not least, in resentment at the economic costs of first fruits and tenths, tithes and other dues. And when he turned to arguing his own case for a divorce in print, Henry abandoned the Latin he had chosen to defend the Roman church against Luther and favoured a pamphlet dialogue written in accessible style, with homely references. Henry in order to argue for, then secure, his supreme authority over church as well as state appealed to patriotism and national sentiment. To some extent he formed it, and figured himself as the personification and embodiment of the nation: in speeches and writings, in portraits, on medals and coins and in pageants which reached to the people. The king and his advisers also formulated a new political idea, that of the commonweal, as an attempt to check the divisions brought about by economic and religious dislocations. Social improvement and religious reformation were presented as royal duties and achievements. Unlike the old Roman Catholic church which was universal and transnational, the commonweal and the new church of Henry VIII in England was a body of the nation, with the king as its head.

Though the consequences of his actions were ultimately to cause problems, Henry, in many respects, had more success in winning over ordinary subjects than counsellors and intellectuals. For all the documented opposition to him, he died and was remembered (as we saw) as a popular king. By his death, he had become a symbol of an emerging nation and his personal skill in representing himself had contributed much to the monarchy's making it through two decades of turmoil and danger.

Not least, Henry had papered over divisions with unifying discourses and images and had almost to the last refused to allow others to hijack them or the monarchy for a denomination. Edward VI and his advisers, however, had other priorities. The boy Edward wanted to be king not only of a nation and commonweal but of a godly commonwealth and chosen nation. Edward's representation was not as Solomon but Josiah, as a Protestant monarch who regarded it as his duty as Supreme Head to lead England out of darkness to the light of truth. In his efforts to do so, Edward branded the Tudor monarchy distinctly Protestant. And in Edwardian reiterations of commonwealth ideology, economic reform was presented also as evangelical reformation. Ethan Shagan has argued that, as a consequence, Protestant ideas were 'insinuated into [a] popular culture' which had tended to exhibit a conservative unease about doctrinal and liturgical change.[14] But the corollary is as important: the monarchy was being cemented to popularity and Protestantism in a way that threatened to render loyalty and allegiance the responses of only a party. Of course, Edward hoped and expected to bring the nation with him, to persuade the people to follow his faith. But, though he continued many of his father's representational vocabularies and tropes, Edward (and his councillors) appropriated them for what became a confessional monarchy.

His failure was manifest in the people's rejection of his organized coup to disinherit his half-sister and secure the succession of the Protestant Jane Grey. The will, that is the wishes as well as testament, of Henry VIII made loyalty to the monarch and the dynasty triumph over religious allegiance; even evangelicals supported Mary Tudor's claims. And Mary, as scholars now agree, might have restored a Roman Catholic church in England with full recognition of the papacy. Had she, that is, adapted for her desires the legacy of her father. Like Edward, however, though for a totally different faith, Mary presented herself as queen of her orthodox Catholic subjects and effectively left others to choose between conversion and quiet discontent or active resistance. Still worse, the central theme of Mary's representation was not her position as head of a church and nation but her role as a wife of a foreign prince whose father was the nephew of Henry's divorced first wife. In her words, her dress, her wedding ceremony, in pageants and portraits and on coins, Mary was represented as a wife to the (hated) Spaniard. One consequence was that her Catholic zeal, displayed in cruel persecutions as well as pious prayers and acts, became indelibly associated with the alien, the foreign, the un-English. While she did much to promote the social reforms and ideals of the commonwealthmen and, for example, acted to restore a sound currency, Mary did not succeed in reversing the association of reform with Protestantism or in being perceived as the head of an English church and nation. That others determined her posthumous reputation evidenced the extent of her failure to resume some control of the discourses and symbols that had become intrinsic to the validation of monarchy.

We recall that on the day of her coronation entry a citizen urged Queen Elizabeth I to remember her father, good old Henry VIII.[15] She did. More than that, she attempted to reappropriate, in what were very different circumstances, many of the strategies of her father's representation. Most significantly, she strove to make herself, as he had made himself but his successors had not, the embodiment of commonweal and nation, the centre of the subjects' imagining and the object of their love. The challenge was considerable in a realm now far more, and more deeply, divided than in her father's reign; and her sex, to say the least, added to her difficulties in forging, as had Henry, a corporeal, affective bond directly with the people. Elizabeth faced pressure from her councillors and her parliaments; she failed, as is now freely acknowledged, to solve or tackle key problems that were to beset the monarchy; she exposed England to the risk of invasion and civil war. But she succeeded – literally – spectacularly in the art of representation: she presented herself and was (and still is) perceived as the personification of England and Englishness. She did so because, unlike her half-sister and half-brother and even more than her father, she put image before policies or programmes. Many contemporaries complained (and many historians have concurred) that Elizabeth talked, hinted and half promised but did not resolve, implement or enact. In some ways that was the point of her representation: not to support a course (as Henry had needed his image to do) or to do, but to check competing pressures and to be, to symbolize, the whole nation: to be an icon. As I have argued, the queen skilfully negotiated the tensions between mystery and familiarity. Elizabeth, in order to retain some personal control, made herself, her body, her words, her person, the public's; and they reciprocated by regarding her as their queen and displaying her image on walls and household objects as their treasured possession. Elizabeth has a claim to be the first English ruler to make image the very essence of her authority. The risk, of course, of such a strategy, was that it made her authority no more than a representation, a performance – perhaps an illusion.

At the end of the sixteenth century, the Tudor monarchy had reached its apotheosis. But it was in thrall to a (potentially capricious) public opinion. The story of this volume is a story of the gradual enthralment of the monarchy to its subjects and a story of how the Reformation led to new modes of representing and figuring authority which served to make monarchy both sacred and yet constitutional.[16] After the break from Rome, every monarch had needed and sought to publicize himself or herself as sacred. But in publicizing themselves, they had demystified kingship, especially in the conditions of a print marketplace and commodity culture. While the ideal of the commonweal and developing national sentiment were promoted to enhance royal authority, in so far as they also emphasized the people and the nation (and the monarch's responsibility to both), they had implications that were, some might say, democratic and republican.[17]

In 1603, the queen and the monarchy stood, as never before, as Elizabeth was fond of saying, under a spotlight and on a stage. More than ever now, the future of the new dynasty and the monarchy in the next century would depend upon presentation, performance and popularity.

NOTES

Preface and Acknowledgements

1. I do not ignore, or wish to underestimate, the scribal publications, especially pamphlets, poems and squibs that we have come to recognize circulated broadly; but my emphasis remains on the printed texts and debates which often informed and responded to scribal media.
2. One press reader of the second volume urged just such a methodological discussion of the sort that opens this book.

1 Representing Rule: Terms, Premises, Approaches

1. See M. Howard, 'The Lessons of History', in Howard, *The Lessons of History* (Oxford, 1991), ch. 1.
2. S. H. Rigby, 'Marxist Historiography', in M. Bentley ed., *Companion to Historiography* (1997), ch. 36.
3. P. Burke, 'Strengths and Weaknesses of the History of Mentalités', in idem, *Varieties of Cultural History* (Cambridge, 1997), ch. 11.
4. See C. Geertz, *The Interpretation of Cultures* (1973); *Negara: The Theatre State in Nineteenth Century Bali* (Princeton, 1980). Scholars of early modern European ritual, such as Edward Muir, have clearly been influenced by Geertz who has, however, had curiously little impact on early modern English historiography; cf. below pp. 49–50.
5. D. Antonio, 'Virgin Queen, Iron Lady, Queen of Hearts: The Embodiment of Feminine Power in a Male Social Imaginary', in G. Pugliese ed., *The Political Legacy of Margaret Thatcher* (2003), pp. 199–213; J. Richards, S. Wilson and L. Woodhead eds, *Diana: The Making of a Media Saint* (New York, 1999); J. Walker, *The Elizabethan Icon: 1603–2003* (Basingstoke, 2004), pp. 201–8.
6. J. Plunkett, *Queen Victoria: First Media Monarch* (Oxford, 2003), p. 81.
7. The literature here is too large to reference. For examples, see J. F. Lyotard, *The Post-Modern Condition* (Manchester, 1984); D. Attridge, G. Bennington and R. Young eds, *Post-Structuralism and the Question of History* (Cambridge, 1987); R. Rorty, *Contingency, Irony and Solidarity* (Cambridge, 1989), introduction; H. White, *The Content of the Form: Narrative Discourse and Historical Representation* (Baltimore and London, 1987); F. R. Ankersmit, 'Historiography and Post-Modernism', *History and Theory*, 29 (1990), pp. 137–53.

8.   K. Sharpe, *Reading Revolutions: The Politics of Reading in Early Modern England* (New Haven and London, 2000), pp. 15–21. For a splendid example of a historian applying these techniques, see Ann Hughes, *Gangraena and the Struggle for the English Revolution* (Oxford, 2004); cf. my comments on Mark Knights below, p. 23.

9.   See R. Bowlby, *Shopping with Freud* (1993).

10.   See D. West, *Air Wars : Television Advertising in Election Campaigns, 1952–2004* (Washington, DC, 2005); M. Rosenbaum, *From Soapbox to Soundbite: Party Political Campaiging in Britain since 1945* (Basingstoke, 1997), ch. 2.

11.   N. Jones, *Soundbites and Spin Doctors: How Politicians Manipulate the Media – and Vice Versa* (1996).

12.   One cannot but recall John Major's evocation of warm beer, cricket and old ladies bicycling to church, a Conservative Party advertisement which owed much to TV's use of nostalgia in selling products such as Hovis bread.

13.   I take the phrase 'Securing Compliance' from the chapter title in P. Williams, *The Tudor Regime* (Oxford, 1979).

14.   For classic studies see R. Scribner, *For the Sake of Simple Folk: Popular Propaganda for the German Reformation* (Oxford, 1981); T. Watt, *Cheap Print and Popular Piety* (Cambridge, 1991); S. O'Connell, *The Popular Print in England 1550–1850* (1999).

15.   Cf. K. Sharpe, 'Representations and Negotiations: Texts, Images and Authority in Early Modern England', *Historical Journal*, 42 (1999), pp. 853–81; reprinted in Sharpe, *Remapping Early Modern England: The Culture of Seventeenth Century Politics* (Cambridge, 2000), pp. 415–59.

16.   T. C. Blanning, *The Culture of Power and the Power of Culture: Old Regime Europe 1660–1789* (Oxford, 2002), p. 5.

17.   J. Barrell, *Imagining the King's Death: Figurative Treason, Fantasies of Regicide 1793–1796* (Oxford, 2000).

18.   Plunkett, *Queen Victoria*, p. 65; A. Bell, *Spectacular Power in the Greek and Roman City* (Oxford, 2004).

19.   S. Lewis, *The Rhetoric of Power in the Bayeux Tapestry* (Cambridge, 1999); J. Watkins, *Representing Elizabeth in Stuart England: Literature, History, Sovereignty* (Cambridge, 2002), quotation, p. 2.

20.   Lewis, *Rhetoric of Power*, p. 78.

21.   Plunkett, *Queen Victoria*, p. 2.

22.   Bell, *Spectacular Power*, p. 247; W. Bagehot, *The English Constitution*, ed. M. Taylor (Oxford, 2001), p. 41. For all the importance of this study, Bagehot has tended to reinforce a disjuncture between the institutional and the 'dignified' or spectacular aspects of authority.

23.   E. H. Kantorowicz, *The King's Two Bodies: A Study in Medieval Political Theology* (Princeton, 1957).

24.   J. M. Bak, 'Introduction: Coronation Studies – Past, Present and Future', in Bak ed., *Coronations: Medieval and Early Modern Monarchic Ritual* (Berkeley, 1990), p. 10.

25.   See C. Levin, *The Heart and Stomach of a King: Elizabeth I and the Politics of Sex and Power* (Philadelphia, 1994), ch. 4; J. Walker ed., *Dissing Elizabeth: Negative Representations of Gloriana* (Durham, NC, 1998).

26.   Plunkett, *Queen Victoria*, p. 33. See for Edward II, C. Perry, 'The Politics of Access and Representations of the Sodomite King in Early Modern England', *Renaissance Quarterly*, 53 (2000), pp. 1,054–83; and for James I, D. Bergeron, 'Writing King James's Sexuality', in D. Fischlin and M. Fortier eds, *Royal Subjects: Essays on the Writings of James VI and I* (Detroit, MI, 2002), pp. 344–68.

27.   D. G. Hale, *The Body Politic: A Political Metaphor in Renaissance English Literature* (The Hague, 1971); L. Barkan, *Nature's Work of Art: The Human Body as Image of the World* (New Haven, 1975); K. Sharpe, 'A Commonwealth of Meanings: Languages, Analogues, Ideas and Politics', reprinted in Sharpe, *Remapping Early Modern England*,

pp. 111–13; K. Sharpe, *Criticism and Compliment: The Politics of Literature in the England of Charles I* (Cambridge, 1987), ch. 5.

28. Plunkett, *Queen Victoria*, pp. 140, 159.

29. P. Binski, *Westminster Abbey and the Plantagenets: Kingship and the Representation of Power, 1200–1400* (New Haven and London, 1995), p. 8.

30. Bell, *Spectacular Power*, p. 237 and *passim.*

31. Lewis, *Rhetoric of Power*, p. 72 and *passim.*

32. Ibid., pp. 131–3.

33. D. J. Sturdy, ' "Continuity" versus "Change" : Historians and English Coronations of the Medieval and Early Modern Periods', in Bak, *Coronations*, pp. 228–45, quotation, p. 239. See also Alice Hunt's forthcoming study, *Tudor Coronations and Tudor Drama: The Reformation and Representation of a Medieval Ceremony in Early Modern England* (Cambridge, 2008).

34. L. Schwoerer, 'The Glorious Revolution as Spectacle', in S. Baxter ed., *England's Rise To Greatness, 1660–1763* (Berkeley, 1983), pp. 109–50, quotation, p. 138.

35. Though there are countless studies of memory in modern history. See, for example, B. Niven, *Germans as Victims: Remembering the Past in Contemporary Germany* (Basingstoke, 2006); Ian McBride ed., *History and Memory in Modern Ireland* (Cambridge, 2001); P. Gray and K. Oliver eds, *The Memory of Catastrophe* (Manchester, 2004).

36. See P. Geary, *Phantoms of Remembrance : Memory and Oblivion at the End of the First Millennium* (Princeton, 1994). For one study of national memory in the early modern period, see P. Schwyzer, *Literature, Nationalism, and Memory in Early Modern England and Wales* (Cambridge, 2004).

37. Bell, *Spectacular Power*, p. 188.

38. Binski, *Westminster Abbey.*

39. Ibid., p. 140.

40. Ibid., p. 126.

41. H. Hackett, 'Dreams or Designs, Cults or Constructions? The Study of Images of Monarchs', *Historical Journal*, 44 (2001), p. 823.

42. See K. Sharpe, *Sir Robert Cotton: History and Politics in Early Modern England* (Oxford, 1979); D. Woolf, *The Idea of History in Early Stuart England* (Toronto, 1990).

43. See I. Backus, *Historical Method and Confessional Identity in the Era of the Reformation, 1378–1615* (Leiden, 2003), chs 4–6; A. G. Dickens and J. Tonkin, *The Reformation in Historical Thought* ((Oxford, 1985).

44. J. Brown, 'Enemies of Flattery: Velasquez's Portraits of Philip IV', *Journal of Interdisciplinary History*, 17 (1986), pp. 137–54.

45. H. Farquhar, 'Portraits of our Stuart Monarchs on their Coins and Medals', *British Numismatic Journal*, 5 (1909), p. 202.

46. P. Strohm, 'The Trouble with Richard: The Reburial of Richard II and Lancastrian Symbolic Strategy', *Speculum*, 71 (1996), pp. 87–111; quotation, p. 110.

47. Eamon Duffy, *The Stripping of the Altars: Traditional Religion in England, c.1400–c.1580* (New Haven and London, 1992).

48. K. Sharpe, ' "An Image Doting Rabble": The Failure of Republican Culture in Seventeenth-Century England', in K. Sharpe and S. Zwicker, *Refiguring Revolutions: Aesthetics and Politics from the English Revolution to the Romantic Revolution* (Berkeley and London, 1998), pp. 25–56, 302–11.

49. See below, pp. 276, 295.

50. J. Woodward, *The Theatre of Death: The Ritual Management of Royal Funerals in Renaissance England* (Woodbridge, 1997), pp. 67–86, 138–40.

51. See Walker, *Elizabethan Icon*; M. Dobson and N. Watson, *England's Elizabeth: An Afterlife in Fame and Fantasy* (Oxford, 2002); below pp. 464–73.

52. P. Collinson, ' "The State as Monarchical Commonwealth": "Tudor" England', *Journal of Historical Sociology*, 15 (2002), pp. 89–95; idem, 'The Monarchical Republic of Queen Elizabeth I', *Bulletin of the John Rylands Library*, 69 (1987), pp. 394–424.

53. Jstor, the digital archive of scholarly journals, describes *Representations*, which was published from Berkeley three years after the publication of Stephen Greenblatt's *Renaissance Self Fashioning*, as 'the best journal in interdisciplinary studies'.

54. Sharpe, *Reading Revolutions*, p. 12.

55. R. Chartier, *Cultural History: Between Practices and Representations* (Cambridge, 1988); idem, *On the Edge of the Cliff: History, Language and Practices* (Baltimore, 1977).

56. Lewis, *Rhetoric of Power*, p. 17.

57. Plunkett, *Queen Victoria*, p. 68.

58. Hackett, 'Dreams or Designs', p. 811.

59. J. Guy, *Thomas More* (2000).

60. M. Knights, *Representation and Misrepresentation in Later Stuart Britain: Partisanship and Political Culture* (Oxford, 2004).

61. Ibid., p. 15.

62. See also Sharpe, 'Sacralization and Demystification: The Publicization of Monarchy in Early Modern England', in J. Deploige and G. Deneckere eds, *Mystifying the Monarch: Studies on Discourse, Power, and History* (Amsterdam, 2006), pp. 99–115, 255–9.

63. Plunkett, *Queen Victoria*, p. 10.

64. Ibid., p. 8.

65. Watkins, *Representing Elizabeth*, introduction.

66. D. Kastan, 'Proud Majesty Made a Subject: Shakespeare and the Spectacle of Rule', *Shakespeare Quarterly*, 37 (1986), pp. 459–75.

67. *The Concise Oxford English Dictionary* defines propaganda as 'information, especially of a biased or misleading nature, used to promote a political cause or point of view'. The experience of twentieth-century propaganda may also have fostered a tendency among historians to regard representations as misleading or marginal to the real story of history.

68. P. Zagorin, *Ways of Lying: Dissimulation, Persecution, and Conformity in Early Modern Europe* (Cambridge, Mass., 1990).

69. Sharpe, *Remapping Early Modern England*, pp. 435–6.

70. K. Sharpe, 'Private Conscience and Public Duty in the Writings of James VI and I', in *Remapping Early Modern England*, pp. 160–1. And we should place James's own self-representation alongside his European reputation as a cunning dissembler.

71. A. K. McHardy, 'Some Reflections on Edward III's Use of Propaganda', in J. S. Bothwell ed., *The Age of Edward III* (York, 2001), pp. 171–92; cf. D. W. Burton, 'Requests for Prayers and Royal Propaganda under Edward I', in P. R. Cross and S. D. Lloyd eds, *Thirteenth Century England III: Proceedings of the Newcastle upon Tyne Conference* (Woodbridge, 1991), pp. 25–36.

72. S. Anglo, 'The Foundation of the Tudor Dynasty: The Coronation and Marriage of Henry VII', *Guildhall Miscellany*, 2 (1960), pp. 3–11; C. Levin, *Propaganda in the English Reformation: Heroic and Villainous Images of King John* (Lewiston, NY, 1988); Schwoerer, 'Glorious Revolution', p. 139.

73. P. Lindley in D. Gordon, L. Monnas and C. Elam eds, *The Regal Image of Richard II and the Wilton Diptych* (1997), p. 61.

74. E. Cavell, 'Henry VII, the North of England and the First Provincial Progress of 1486', *Northern History*, 39 (2002), pp. 187–208, quotation, p. 206.

75. See P. Burke, *The Fabrication of Louis XIV* (New Haven and London, 1992). Peter Burke's study is – typically of the author – a pioneering example of an engagement with a new cultural history of representations.

76. Blanning, *Culture of Power*, p. 47.
77. A. Johns, *The Nature of the Book: Print and Knowledge in the Making* (Chicago and London, 1998), ch. 2.
78. W. Leahy, *Elizabethan Triumphal Processions* (Aldershot, 2005), p. 63.
79. M. Homans, *Royal Representations: Queen Victoria and British Culture, 1837–1876* (Chicago, 1998), p. xix.
80. See, for example, Elizabeth's verse reflections on private desire and public duty in 'On Monsieur's Departure', in L. Marcus, J. Mueller and M.B. Rose eds, *Elizabeth I: Collected Works* (Chicago, 2000), pp. 302–3.
81. Leahy, *Elizabethan Triumphal Processions*, p. 63.
82. Plunkett, *Queen Victoria*, p. 75.
83. See E. Freund, *The Return of the Reader* (1987); S. Suleiman and I. Crossman eds, *The Reader in the Text: Essays on Audience and Reception* (Princeton, 1980); R. Darnton, 'First Steps towards a History of Reading', *Australian Journal of French Studies*, 23 (1986), pp. 5–30.
84. The classic formulation was W. Iser, *The Implied Reader: Patterns of Communication in Prose Fiction from Bunyan to Beckett* (Baltimore, 1980); cf. Iser, *The Act of Reading: A Theory of Aesthetic Response* (1978). See K. Sharpe and S. Zwicker eds, *Reading, Society, and Politics in Early Modern England* (Cambridge, 2003), introduction, pp. 1–37.
85. A. Marotti, *Manuscript, Print and the English Renaissance Lyric* (Ithaca, NY, 1995), p. 310.
86. Sharpe, *Reading Revolutions*, pp. 54–5.
87. D. J. H. Clifford ed., *The Diaries of Lady Anne Clifford* (Stroud, 1992), p. 52; H. Brayman Hackel, *Reading Material in Early Modern England* (Cambridge, 2005), pp. 221–41.
88. T. Eagleton, *Ideology: An Introduction* (1991), p. 195; The case study is of Sir William Drake: see Sharpe, *Reading Revolutions*, passim.
89. Knights, *Representation and Misrepresentation*, p. 47.
90. Above, n. 84; S. Fish, *Is There a Text in This Class? The Authority of Interpretive Communities* (Cambridge, Mass., 1980); A. Grafton and L. Jardine, ' "Studied for Action": How Gabriel Harvey Read his Livy', *Past & Present*, 129 (1990), pp. 30–78; W. Sherman, *John Dee: The Politics of Reading and Writing in the English Renaissance* (Amherst, Mass., 1995); Sharpe, *Reading Revolutions*.
91. See below p. 36.
92. For examples of work on the crowd following George Rudé's classic study of *The Crowd in the French Revolution* (Oxford, 1959), see T. Harris, *London Crowds in the Reign of Charles II: Propaganda and Politics from the Restoration until the Exclusion Crisis* (Cambridge, 1987); N. Rogers, *Crowds, Culture and Politics in Georgian Britain* (Oxford, 1998); N. Rogers, 'Crowds and Political Festival in Georgian England', in T. Harris ed., *The Politics of the Excluded, c1500–1850* (Basingstoke, 2001), pp. 233–64; A. Randall and A. Charlesworth eds, *Moral Economy and Popular Protest: Crowds, Conflict and Authority* (Basingstoke, 2000). On executions, see T. Laqueur, 'Crowds, Carnival and the State in English Executions, 1604–1868', in A. L. Beier, D. Cannadine and J. M. Rosenheim eds, *The First Modern Society: Essays in English History in Honour of Lawrence Stone* (Cambridge, 1989), pp. 305–55; R. S. Shoemaker, 'Streets of Shame? The Crowd and Public Punishments in London, 1700–1820', in S. Devereaux and P. Griffiths eds, *Penal Practice and Culture, 1500–1900: Punishing the English* (Basingstoke, 2004), pp. 232–57.
93. T. Cave, *The Cornucopian Text: Problems of Writing in the French Renaissance* (Oxford, 1979), quotation, p. 327.
94. Bell, *Spectacular Power*, p. 186.
95. P. Parshall, 'Prints as Objects of Consumption in Early Modern Europe', *Journal of Medieval and Early Modern Studies*, 28 (1988), pp. 19–36, especially p. 20.

96. Hackett, 'Dreams or Designs', p. 822. A friend displays in his toilet a portrait of Mrs Thatcher which dispenses toilet paper – not, I suspect, the intention of those at Conservative Central Office who issued the original poster.

97. Binski, *Westminster Abbey*, p. 84.

98. C. Burrow, 'The Experience of Exclusion: Literature and Politics in the Reigns of Henry VII and Henry VIII', in D. Wallace ed., *The Cambridge History of Medieval English Literature* (Cambridge, 1999), p. 816. David could also be read as an adulterous sinner and tyrant and so was a figure endlessly open to interpretation and appropriation for different purposes. I owe this observation to Greg Walker.

99. C. Edie, 'The Public Face of Royal Ritual: Sermons, Medals and Public Ceremony in Later Stuart Coronations', *Huntington Library Quarterly*, 53 (1990), p. 324.

100. Binski, *Westminster Abbey*, p. 86; Hackett, 'Dreams or Designs', p. 819.

101. Plunkett, *Queen Victoria*, p. 58, my italics.

102. Ibid., p. 198.

103. Ibid., p. 174.

104. N. McKendrick, J. Brewer and J. Plumb, *The Birth of a Consumer Society: The Commercialization of Eighteenth-Century England* (1982); J. Brewer and R. Porter eds, *Consumption and the World of Goods* (1993).

105. Blanning, *Culture of Power*, pp. 8–9.

106. Bell, *Spectacular Power*, p. 197.

107. M. Baxandall, *Patterns of Intention: On the Historical Explanation of Pictures* (New Haven and London, 1985), p. 47.

108. Parshall, 'Prints as Objects of Consumption', p. 34.

109. D. Bruster, *Drama and the Market in the Age of Shakespeare* (Cambridge, 1992); Jean-Christophe Agnew, *Worlds Apart: The Market and the Theater in Anglo-American Thought, 1550–1750* (Cambridge, 1986).

110. Sharpe, 'Sacralization and Demystification'; below, chs 10, 11.

111. For example, R. Elstracke, *Braziliologia: A Booke of Kings Beeing the True and Liuely Effigies of All Our English Kings from the Conquest Untill This Present* (STC 13581, 1618).

112. Sharpe, 'Sacralization and Demystification', pp. 107–10; below pp. 401–10.

113. Bell, *Spectacular Power*, p. 197. Linda Peck has curiously little to say about this aspect of consumption in *Consuming Splendour: Society and Culture in Seventeenth-Century England* (Cambridge, 2005).

114. Cf. P. Backscheider, *Spectacular Politics: Theatrical Power and Mass Culture in Early Modern England* (Baltimore, 1993).

115. H. Weber, 'Representations of the King: Charles II and his Escape from Worcester', *Studies in Philology*, 85 (1988), pp. 508–9.

116. J. Ogilby, *The Entertainment of His Most Excellent Majestie Charles II, in his Passage Through the City of London to his Coronation Containing an Exact Accompt of the Whole Solemnity, the Triumphal Arches, and Cavalcade . . .* (Wing O171, 1662); A. M. Broadley, *The Royal Miracle: A Collection of Rare Tracts, Broadsides, Letters, Prints and Ballads concerning the Wanderings of Charles II after the Battle of Worcester* (1912); M. Williams ed., *Charles II's Escape from Worcester : A Collection of Narratives Assembled by Samuel Pepys* (1967).

117. K. Sharpe, ' "Thy Longing Country's Darling and Desire": Aesthetic, Sex and Politics in the England of Charles II', in J. Alexander and C. MacLeod eds, *Politics, Transgression, and Representation at the Court of Charles II* (New Haven and London, 2007), pp. 1–32.

118. See Knights, *Representation and Misrepresentation, passim*; B. Cowan, *The Social Life of Coffee: The Emergence of the British Coffee House* (New Haven and London, 2005).

119. J. Habermas, *The Structural Transformation of the Public Sphere: An Inquiry into a Category of Bourgeois Society* (1989).

120. D. Zaret, *Origins of Democratic Culture: Printing, Petitions, and the Public Sphere in Early-Modern England* (Princeton, 2000); J. Raymond, *Pamphlets and Pamphleteering in Early Modern Britain* (Cambridge, 2003); P. Lake and S. Pincus, 'Rethinking the Public Sphere in Early Modern England', *Journal of British Studies*, 45 (2006), pp. 270–92. I am grateful to Peter Lake and Steve Pincus for stimulating discussions of this subject at the North American Conference on British Studies in 2004 and in personal communications.

121. Greg Walker argues for an aristocratic public sphere in the late 1530s. See G. Walker, *Writing under Tyranny: English Literature and the Henrician Reformation* (Oxford, 2005), p. 415. I would urge that it was also popular.

122. Cf. Blanning, *Culture of Power*, p. 7.

123. Adam Fox, *Oral and Literate Culture in England, 1500–1700* (Oxford, 2001); A. Fox and D. Woolf eds, *The Spoken Word: Oral Culture in Britain, 1500–1850* (Manchester, 2002).

124. See below, pp. 179–81, 236–9, 305–6, 456–9.

125. Levin, *Heart and Stomach of a King*; A. Bellany, *The Politics of Court Scandal in Early Modern England: News Culture and the Overbury Affair, 1603–1660* (Cambridge, 2002).

126. P.L. Hughes and P. Larkin eds, *Tudor Royal Proclamations* (3 vols, New Haven, 1964–9), II, no. 516, pp. 240–1, my italics.

127. Habermas, *Structural Transformation*, p. 161.

128. See M. McLuhan, *Understanding Media: The Extensions of Man* (1964), p. 7 and *passim*.

129. Plunkett, *Queen Victoria*, p. 164.

130. J. Whiting, *Commemorative Medals: A Medallic History of Britain from Tudor Times to the Present Day* (Newton Abbot, 1972), pp. 16–18; P. Seaby, *The Story of English Coinage* (1952).

131. See, for example, A. Globe, *Peter Stent, London Printseller circa 1642–65: Being a Catalogue Raisonné of his Engraved Prints and Books with an Historical and Bibliographical Introduction* (Vancouver, 1985).

132. A. Brock, *A History of Fireworks* (1949), chs 3, 4. Fireworks began in England in Elizabeth's reign (ibid., pp. 33–5).

133. Johns, *The Nature of the Book*; Fox, *Oral and Literate Culture*; E. Eisenstein, *The Printing Revolution in Early Modern Europe* (Cambridge, 1983). There has been too little consideration of perceptions of print.

134. B. Cummings, 'Reformed Literature and Literature Reformed', in Wallace, *Cambridge History of Medieval English Literature*, p. 831.

135. K. Sharpe and P. Lake eds, *Culture and Politics in Early Stuart England* (Basingstoke, 1994), introduction; Sharpe, *Reading Revolutions*, pp. 27–33.

136. Hackett, 'Dreams or Designs', p. 814.

137. Quoted in J. A. Knapp, *Illustrating the Past in Early Modern England: The Representation of History in Printed Books* (Aldershot, 2003), pp. 15, 21.

138. Binski, *Westminster Abbey*, p. 9.

139. I refer, of course, to Greenblatt's *Renaissance Self-Fashioning*, which I am surprised to discover has not been much *read* by historians.

140. Binski, *Westminster Abbey*, pp. 9, 200.

141. Plunkett, *Queen Victoria*, p. 87.

142. A. O. Lovejoy, *The Great Chain of Being* (Cambridge, Mass., 1936, 1948); E. M. W. Tillyard, *The Elizabethan World Picture* (1943).

143. See A. Patterson, *Reading between the Lines* (1993). Annabel Patterson's close historical criticism has been hugely influential but, again, is not as well known to historians.

144. A. Gannon, *The Iconography of Early Anglo-Saxon Coinage* (Oxford, 2003), pp. 100–1.

145. For an excellent discussion, see Q. Skinner, *Reason and Rhetoric in the Philosophy of Hobbes* (Cambridge, 1996), part I.
146. Below, pp. 105–6, 326–7.
147. I owe this observation to Julia Marciari Alexander.
148. Cf. the remarks in Sharpe and Zwicker, *Refiguring Revolutions*, introduction, especially pp. 1–2.
149. Gannon, *Iconography*, p. 186.
150. Bak, 'Introduction: Coronation Studies'.
151. E. Howe, 'Divine Kingship and Dynastic Display: The Altar Wall Murals of St Stephen's Chapel Westminster', *Antiquaries Journal*, 81 (2001), pp. 259–303.
152. Binski, *Westminster Abbey*, p. vii.
153. Hackett, 'Dreams or Designs', p. 816.
154. Lewis, *Rhetoric of Power*, p. 154; Binski, *Westminster Abbey*, p. vii.
155. Lewis, *Rhetoric of Power*, p. 3.
156. Plunkett, *Queen Victoria*, p. xix.
157. C. H. Mcilwain ed., *The Political Works of James I Reprinted from the 1616 Edition* (Cambridge, Mass., 1918); J. Sommerville ed, *King James VI and I : Political Writings* (Cambridge, 1994). The exception is edited by literary scholars, namely N. Rhodes, J. Richards and J. Marshall eds, *King James VI and I: Selected Writings* (Aldershot, 2003).
158. James I, *The Workes of the Most High and Mightie Prince, Iames by the Grace of God, King of Great Britaine, France and Ireland* (STC 14344, 1616).
159. See Epigrams IV in Ian Donaldson ed., *Ben Jonson Poems* (Oxford, 1974), pp. 8–9.
160. See D. Fischlin and M. Fortier eds, *Royal Subjects: Essays on the Writings of James VI and I* (Detroit, 2002).
161. M. Corbett and R. Lightbown, *The Comely Frontispiece: The Emblematic Title Page in England, 1550–1660* (1979), ch. 7, pp. 107–11.
162. See Fischlin and Fortier eds, *Royal Subjects* and J. Rickard, *Authorship and Authority: The Writings of James VI and I* (Manchester, 2007). I am grateful to Jane Rickard for allowing me to see parts of her important book prior to publication and for several stimulating discussions of James's writings. The completed book was published after my own manuscript went to press.
163. P. Herman ed., *Reading Monarchs Writing: The Poetry of Henry VIII, Mary Stuart, Elizabeth I, and James VI/I* (Tempe, Arizona, 2002); J. Summit,' "The Arte of A Ladies Penne": Elizabeth and the Poetics of Courtship', *English Literary Renaissance*, 26 (1996), pp. 395–422.
164. See C. Pemberton ed., *Queen Elizabeth's Englishings* (1899) and K. Sharpe,' "The King's Writ": Royal Authors and Royal Authority in Early Modern England', in Sharpe and Lake, *Culture and Politics*, pp. 117–38. For an important recent study see P. Burke and R. Po-chia Hsia eds, *Cultural Translation in Early Modern Europe* (Cambridge, 2007).
165. B. Weiser, 'Owning the King's Story: The Escape from Worcester', *Seventeenth Century*, 14 (1999), pp. 43–62; J. Callow, *The King in Exile: James II: Warrior, King and Saint, 1689–1701* (Stroud, 2004).
166. A. Lytton Sells ed., *The Memoirs of James II: His Campaigns as Duke of York, 1652–1660* (1962). Cf. K. Sharpe,' Whose Life Is It Anyway? Writing Early Modern Monarchs and the Case of James II', in K. Sharpe and S. Zwicker eds, *Writing Lives: Biography and Textuality, Identity and Representation in Early Modern England* (Oxford, 2008), pp. 233–52.
167. See above, n. 80.
168. P. Herman, 'Henry VIII and the Poetry of Politics', in Herman, *Reading Monarchs*, pp. 11–34; quotation, p. 17; below, pp. 88–90.
169. Herman, *Reading Monarchs*, p. 93.
170. J. Craigie ed., *The Poems of James VI & I*, (Edinburgh, 1955), introduction, pp. liv–lxi, 178, lines 5–6.

171. See, for example, J. Wormald, 'James VI and I, *Basilikon Doron* and *The Trew Law of Free Monarchies*: the Scottish Context and the English Translation', in L. Peck ed., *The Mental World of the Jacobean Court* (Cambridge, 1991), pp. 36–54. There is much more to be done on this subject.

172. J. Milton, *Eikonoklastes*, ed. M. Y. Hughes in *Complete Prose Works of John Milton*, Vol. III (New Haven and London, 1962), pp. 338–9.

173. James VI, *The Essays of a Prentise in the Divine Art of Poesie*, ed. E. Arber (1869).

174. 'For historians the messages from the past are in words and rarely in other media', J. Prown, *Art as Evidence: Writing on Art and Material Culture* (New Haven and London, 2001), p. 53.

175. Brown, 'Enemies of Flattery', p. 137.

176. R. Strong, *The Tudor and Stuart Monarchy: Pageantry, Painting, Iconography* (3 vols, Woodbridge, 1995–7).

177. 'Proceedings of a Conference on British Art in the Sixteenth and Seventeenth Centuries', 21 April 1965, on deposit in Huntington Library and Mellon Centre for British Art, London.

178. S. Foister, *Holbein in England* (2006); idem, *Holbein and England* (New Haven and London, 2004); S. Barnes, O. Millar, *et. al.*, *Van Dyck: A Complete Catalogue of the Paintings* (New Haven and London, 2003); T. Claydon, *William III and the Godly Revolution* (Cambridge, 1996).

179. The first successor to Strong was arguably David Howarth, *Images of Rule: Art and Politics in the English Renaissance, 1485–1649* (Basingstoke, 1997). There are also some good monographic studies which attempt to read visuals historically, for instance Malcolm Smuts, *Court Culture and the Origins of a Royalist Tradition in Early Stuart England* (Philadelphia, 1987); Lucy Gent ed., *Albion's Classicism: The Visual Arts in Britain, 1550–1660* (New Haven and London, 1995); A. McGregor ed., *The Late King's Goods: Collections, Possessions, and Patronage of Charles I in the Light of the Commonwealth Sale Inventories* (Oxford, 1989); and, importantly, the works of Simon Thurley: see, for example, *Whitehall Palace: An Architectural History of the Royal Apartments, 1240–1698* (New Haven and London, 1999); *Royal Palaces of Tudor England: Architecture and Court Life, 1460–1547* (New Haven and London, 1993).

180. Watt, *Cheap Print*.

181. M. Baxandall, *The Limewood Sculptors of Renaissance Germany* (New Haven and London, 1980); idem, *Painting and Experience in Fifteenth Century Italy: A Primer in the Social History of Pictorial Style* (Oxford, 1972); idem, *Patterns of Intention*.

182. Baxandall, *Painting and Experience*, preface, pp. 2, 152.

183. Ibid., preface; Baxandall, *Patterns of Intention*, p. 59.

184. Baxandall, *Painting and Experience*, p. 152.

185. Baxandall, *Patterns of Intention*, p. 125.

186. Ibid., p. 13; Prown, *Art as Evidence*. Material culture is now a very active field of research. Though it has not yet much influenced work in early modern studies in England, see R.M. Smuts, 'Art and the Material Culture of Majesty in Early Stuart England', in R.M. Smuts ed., *The Stuart Court and Europe: Essays in Politics and Political Culture* (Cambridge, 1996), pp. 86–112 and Eileen Ribeiro, *Fashion and Fiction: Dress in Art and Literature in Stuart England* (New Haven and London, 1995).

187. Binski, *Westminster Abbey*, p. 8.

188. Gannon, *Iconography*, p. 176.

189. There has been no systematic study of early modern medals. See Whiting, *Commemorative Medals*.

190. O'Connell, *Popular Print*, p. 31.

191. B. Thompson, 'Introduction: The Place of Henry VII in English History', in B. Thompson ed., *The Reign of Henry VII: Proceedings of the 1993 Harlaxton Symposium* (Stamford, 1995), pp. 1–10, especially p. 10.

192. J. L. Koerner, *The Reformation of the Image* (Chicago, 2004), p. 11. I owe this reference to the kindness of Ramie Targoff.
193. Ibid., p. 12.
194. O'Connell, *Popular Print*, p. 168.
195. W. Wynn Jones, *A Cartoon History of the Monarchy* (1978); K. Baker, *The Kings and Queens: An Irreverent Cartoon History of the British Monarchy* (1996). Elizabeth I was caricatured in prints circulating in the Low Countries but not in England.
196. S. Anglo, *Images of Tudor Kingship* (1992), quotation, p. 3; cf. idem, *Spectacle, Pageantry and Early Tudor Policy* (Oxford, 1969).
197. Anglo, *Images*, p. 109.
198. Ibid., p. 107.
199. See M. Bath, *Speaking Pictures: English Emblem Books and Renaissance Culture* (1994); P. Daly ed., *The English Emblem Book and the Continental Tradition* (New York, 1988).
200. Classic examples are D. Underdown, *Revel, Riot and Rebellion: Popular Politics and Culture in England 1603–1660* (Oxford, 1985); E. P. Thompson, ' "Rough Music": le Charivari Anglais', *Annales*, 27 (1972), pp. 285–312; M. Ingram, 'Ridings, Rough Music and the "Reform of Popular Culture" in Early Modern England', *Past & Present*, 105 (1984), pp. 79–113.
201. See M. Foucault, *The Archaeology of Knowledge* (1972); above, n. 4.
202. Cf. Leahy, *Elizabethan Triumphal Processions*, p. 35.
203. See James C. Scott, *Domination and the Arts of Resistance* (New Haven and London, 1990); idem, *Weapons of the Weak: The Everyday Forms of Peasant Resistance* (New Haven and London, 1985). I am grateful to Greg Walker for bringing Scott to my attention.
204. Bak, *Coronations*, p. 9.
205. Bell, *Spectacular Power*, p. 130.
206. Ibid., pp. 8, 244; Leahy, *Elizabethan Triumphal Processions*, p. 149.
207. Leahy, *Elizabethan Triumphal Processions*, p. 39; below, p. 170.
208. I. Gentles, 'Political Funerals during the English Revolution', in S. Porter ed., *London and the Civil War* (Basingstoke, 1996), pp. 205–24; J. Adamson, 'Essex: Apotheosis', on the funeral of the Earl of Essex. I am grateful to John Adamson for showing me this excellent chapter in advance of publication.
209. Gentles, 'Political Funerals', p. 207.
210. Ibid., p. 221.
211. For examples of approaches which have yet to fully influence studies of early modern English spectacles, see R. Mulryne and E. Goldring eds, *Court Festivals of the European Renaissance: Art, Politics and Performance* (Aldershot, 2002) and J. Mulryne, H. Watanabe-O'Kelly and M. Shewring eds, *Europa Triumphans: Court and Civic Festivals in Early Modern Europe* (2 vols, Aldershot, 2004). Malcolm Smuts has contributed to this subject in his essay on 'Public Ceremony and Royal Charisma: The English Royal Entry in London, 1485–1642', in A.L. Beir *et. al.* eds, *The First Modern Society: Essays in English History in Honour of Lawrence Stone* (Cambridge, 1989), pp. 65–93 and in his recent edition of James I's entry in *The Oxford Complete Middleton* (2007). But work in this field needs to be theorized and there is yet more that an emphasis on audience could add to even the most recent studies.
212. R. McCoy, *Alterations of State: Sacred Kingship in the English Reformation* (New York, 1992), pp. 58–60. Hunt questions the emphasis on the secular, see *Tudor Coronations*. Though her manuscript was completed after I had written my own, I am grateful to Alice Hunt for permitting me to see parts of her book in advance of publication.
213. Malcolm Smuts has brought to my attention his complementary views on 'Occasional Events, Literary Texts and Historical Interpretations' (in R. Wells and G. Burgess eds, *Neo-Historicism: Studies in Renaissance Literature, History and Politics* (Woodbridge, 2000), pp. 179–98) which I had not read.

214. Lois Schwoerer uses the same language of 'emotional catharsis' when discussing the impact of the firework display in 1688. See Schwoerer, 'Glorious Revolution', p. 138.

215. Bernadino De Mendoza to Zayas, 8 September 1578, *Cal. Stat. Pap. Spanish II, 1568–1579*, no. 524, p. 611.

216. *The Pleasant and Delightful History of King Henry 8th. and a Cobbler* (Wing P2530, 1670); *The Novels of Elizabeth, Queen of England Containing the History of Queen Ann of Bullen* (Wing A4221, 1680); R. Hutton, *Debates in Stuart History* (2004), pp. 137–42.

217. A. Lacey, *The Cult of King Charles the Martyr* (Woodbridge, 2003).

218. P. Monod, *Jacobitism and the English People, 1688–1788* (Cambridge, 1989).

219. F. Hepburn, *Portraits of the Later Plantagenets* (Woodbridge, 1986), pp. 1–2; S. Schama, 'The Domestication of Majesty: Royal Family Portraiture, 1500–1850', *Journal of Interdisciplinary History*, 17 (1986), pp. 155–83.

220. Below, pp. 163–4.

221. Bak, *Coronations*, p. 243.

222. Blanning, *Culture of Power*, p. 319.

223. Cited in ibid., p. 317.

224. Cf. Sharpe and Zwicker, *Refiguring Revolutions*, introduction.

225. Blanning, *Culture of Power*, p. 8.

226. Whiting, *Commemorative Medals*, p. 72.

227. J.C. D. Clark, *English Society 1688–1832: Ideology, Social Structure and Political Practice during the Ancien Régime* (Cambridge, 1985); idem, 'England's Ancien Régime as a Confessional State', *Albion*, 21 (1989), pp. 450–74.

228. E. Durkheim, *The Elementary Forms of the Religious Life* (New York, 1995), p. 215.

229. Plunkett, *Queen Victoria*, p. 122.

230. A. S. Williams, 'Panegyric Decorum in the Reigns of William III and Anne', *Journal of British Studies*, 21 (1981), pp. 56–67.

231. G. Ready, 'Mystical Politics: The Imagery of Charles II', in P. J. Korshin ed., *Studies in Change and Revolution* (Menston, 1972), p. 39.

232. Quoted in R. O. Bucholz, ' "Nothing But Ceremony": Queen Anne and the Limitations of Royal Ritual', *Journal of British Studies*, 30 (1991), pp. 288–323, at p. 312.

233. P. Monod, 'Painters and Party Politics in England, 1714–60', *Eighteenth Century Studies*, 26 (1993), pp. 367–98, especially pp. 391, 394–5.

234. Watkins, *Representing Elizabeth*, p. 173.

235. Ready, 'Mystical Politics', p. 40.

236. H. Farquhar, 'Portraits', p. 261.

237. Binski, *Westminster Abbey*, p. 8.

238. Blanning, *Culture of Power*, p. 4.

239. Baxandall, *Painting and Experience*, p. 151.

2 Founding a Dynasty, Forging an Image

1. S. B. Chrimes, *Henry VII* (1972); R. Lockyer, *Henry VII* (Harlow, 1997).

2. J. R. Lumby ed., *Bacon's History of Henry VII* (Cambridge, 1902), p. 5.

3. Ibid., pp. 11, 34.

4. Ibid., pp. 39–40.

5. Ibid., p. 98.

6. Ibid., p. 131.

7. Ibid., p. 168.

8. Ibid., p. 215.

9. G. Kipling, *The Triumph of Honour: Burgundian Origins of the Elizabethan Renaissance* (Leiden, 1977), quotation p. 4.

10. S. Gunn, 'Tournaments and Early Tudor Chivalry', *History Today*, 41 (1991), pp. 15–21.

11. B. Thompson ed., *The Reign of Henry VII: Proceedings of the 1993 Harlaxton Symposium* (Stamford, 1995), p. xiii.

12. Ibid., p. 8.

13. Ibid., pp. 169, 156.

14. N. Beckett, 'Henry VII and Sheen Charterhouse', in Thompson, *Reign of Henry VII*, pp. 117–32.

15. R. Marks, 'The Glazing of Henry VII's Chapel, Westminster Abbey', in Thompson, *Reign of Henry VII*, pp. 157–74.

16. F. Kisby, 'Courtiers in the Community: The Musicians of the Royal Household Chapel in Early Tudor Westminster', in Thompson, *Reign of Henry VII*, p. 239.

17. B. H. Meyer, 'The First Tomb of Henry VII of England', *Art Bulletin*, 58 (1976), pp. 359–67.

18. S. Anglo, *Images of Tudor Kingship* (Guildford, 1992), p. 20.

19. Kipling, *Triumph of Honour*, p. 58; P. Grierson, 'The Origins of the English Sovereign and the Symbolism of the Closed Crown', *British Numismatic Journal*, 33 (1965), pp. 118–34.

20. A. H. Smith, 'A York Pageant, 1486', *London Medieval Studies*, 1 (1948), pp. 382–98.

21. H. Ellis ed., *Hall's Chronicle Containing the History of England . . . to the End of the Reign of Henry VIII* (1809), pp. 426–8; J. C. Meacher, 'The First Progress of Henry VII', *Renaissance Drama*, 1 (1968), pp. 45–74.

22. Meacher, 'First Progress', p. 48.

23. E. Cavell, 'Henry 7, the North of England and the First Provincial Progress of 1486', *Northern History*, 29 (2002), pp. 187–208.

24. Ibid., pp. 206, 189.

25. Ibid., p. 189.

26. Ibid., p. 201.

27. B. Bevan, *Henry VII: The First Tudor King* (2000).

28. 'Henry VII', in *Oxford Dictionary of National Biography*.

29. Lumby, *Bacon's History of Henry VII*, p. 219.

30. Ibid., p. 221.

31. Ibid., p. 218.

32. http:answers.yahoo.com/questions/2qid=200606 18005902 Aauz8MZ

33. See the website Royalty.nu.

34. http://www.historylearningsite.co.uk/henry7.htm

35. Lumby, *Bacon's History of Henry VII*, p. 218.

36. S. Anglo, 'The Foundation of the Tudor Dynasty: The Coronation and Marriage of Henry VII', *Guildhall Miscellany*, 2 (1960), pp. 3–11, quotation p. 10; M. Van Cleve Alexander, *The First of the Tudors* (Totawa, NJ and London, 1981), p. 171.

37. Alexander, *First of the Tudors*, p. 165.

38. Ibid., p. 156.

39. Anglo, *Images of Tudor Kingship*, p. 3. The BBC poll was taken in 2002.

40. See K. Sharpe, 'Sacralization and Demystification: The Publicisation of Monarchy in Early Modern England', in J. Deploige and G. Deneckere eds, *Mystifying the Monarch* (Amsterdam, 2006), pp. 99–115, 255–9.

41. Lumby, *Bacon's History of Henry VII*, p. 7.

42. Ibid., p. 8.

43. Kipling, *Triumph of Honour*, p. 4.

44. Chrimes, *Henry VII*, p. 285.

45. Ibid., pp. 286–93.

46. In his monumental *The King's Reformation* (New Haven and London, 2005), pp. 240–1, 300, George Bernard casts doubt on the influence of Anne Boleyn on

Henry's religious policy. The point here is how she was perceived to have influenced him, whatever the reality.

47. Bernard, *King's Reformation*, pp. 228–43 and *passim*.
48. R. Strong, *Holbein and Henry VIII* (1967), p. 7.
49. M. Polito, *Governmental Arts in Early Tudor England* (Aldershot, 2005), p. 131.
50. H. Farquhar, 'Portraiture of our Tudor Monarchs on their Coins and Medals', *British Numismatic Journal*, 4 (1908), pp. 79–143, quotation, p. 91.
51. B. Cummings, 'Reformed Literature and Literature Reformed', in D. Wallace ed., *The Cambridge History of Medieval English Literature* (Cambridge, 1999), p. 824. See Cummings, *The Literary Culture of the Reformation: Grammar and Grace* (Oxford, 2002), part 2.
52. S. Anglo, 'An Early Tudor Programme for Plays and other Demonstrations against the Pope', *Journal of the Warburg and Courtauld Institutes*, 20 (1957), pp. 177–9, quotation, p. 179.
53. Cummings, 'Reformed Literature', p. 839; C. Levin, *Propaganda in the English Reformation: Heroic and Villainous Images of King John* (Lewiston, NY, 1988), p. 9.
54. Farquhar, 'Portraiture of our Tudor Monarchs', p. 91.
55. S. Foister, *Holbein and England* (New Haven and London, 2004), pp. 11–22.
56. Ibid., pp. 152–4; below, pp. 132–5.
57. Jane Seymour married Henry in May 1536 and died in October 1537. See below, pp. 135–7.
58. Foister, *Holbein*, p. 194.
59. Ibid., p. 195; below, p. 137.
60. Polito, *Governmental Arts*, p. 131.
61. R. McCoy, *Alterations of State: Sacred Kingship in the English Reformation* (New York, 2002), pp. x, 15.
62. See my discussion of *A Glass of the Truth*, below pp. 104–7.
63. Below, pp. 137, 184–5.
64. Polito, *Governmental Arts*, p. 131.
65. R. Morison, *An Exhortation to Styrre all Englyshe Men to the Defence of Theyr Countreye made by Richard Morysine* (STC 18110, 1529), sigs Bi^v–Bii.
66. J. Watts, ' "A New Ffundacion of is Crowne": Monarchy in the Age of Henry VII', in Thompson, *Reign of Henry VII*, p. 53.
67. Polito, *Governmental Arts*, p. 45.
68. Cummings, 'Reformed Literature', p. 823.
69. Polito, *Governmental Arts*, p. 41
70. E. Shagan, *Popular Politics and the English Reformation* (Cambridge, 2003), ch. 2; Bernard, *King's Reformation*, pp. 87–100.
71. See below, ch. 7, pp. 192–3, 228.
72. See below, ch. 12, pp. 457–60 and passim.
73. Below, ch. 8, pp. 268–70, 277–8.
74. J. Walker, *The Elizabethan Icon, 1603–2003* (Houndmills, 2004), p. 1.
75. Sharpe, 'Sacralization and Demystification'; R. Tittler, *The Reformation and the Towns in England: Politics and Political Culture, c.1540–1640* (Oxford, 1998).
76. See, for example, J. H. Salmon, *The French Religious Wars in English Political Thought* (Oxford, 1959).
77. S. P. Cerasano and M. Wynne Davies ' "From myself, my other self I turned": an Introduction', in Cerasano and Wynne Davies, eds, *Gloriana's Face: Women, Public and Private in the Renaissance* (Hemel Hempstead, 1992), pp. 12–14.
78. Below, ch. 9, pp. 330–3.
79. S. Logan, 'Making History: The Rhetorical and Historical Occasion of Elizabeth Tudor's Coronation Entry', *Journal of Medieval and Renaissance Studies*, 31 (2001), pp. 251–82; McCoy, *Alterations of State*, pp. 58–9.

80. W. P. Haugaard, 'The Coronation of Elizabeth I', *Journal of Ecclesiastical History*, 19 (1968), pp. 161–70.

81. D. Kastan, 'Proud Majesty Made a Subject: Shakespeare and the Spectacle of Rule', *Shakespeare Quarterly*, 37 (1986), pp. 459–75.

82. R. M. Smuts, 'Court-centered Politics and the Uses of Roman Historians, c.1590–1630', in K. Sharpe and P. Lake eds, *Culture and Politics in Early Stuart England* (Basingstoke, 1994), pp. 21–43.

83. J. Watkins, *Representing Elizabeth in Stuart England: Literature, History, Sovereignty* (Cambridge, 2002), ch. 3 and p. 39.

84. Ibid., Conclusion, pp. 220–9.

85. Walker, *Elizabethan Icon*, p. 1.

3 Writing Reformation

1. For long historians presented Henry as a malleable monarch, led by factions headed by ministers, noblemen, wives and mistresses. See, for example, G.R. Elton, 'King or Minister: The Man behind the Henrician Reformation', *Historical Journal*, 10 (1951), pp. 216–32; E. Ives, 'Faction at the Court of Henry VIII: The Fall of Anne Boleyn', *History*, 57 (1972), pp. 169–88; J.S. Block, *Factional Politics and the English Reformation 1520–1540* (Woodbridge, 1993); J.Guy, 'Henry VIII and His Ministers', *History Review*, 23 (1995), pp. 37–40. In his seminal biography, J. Scarisbrick portrayed Henry as much more in charge: J. Scarisbrick, *Henry VIII* (1968); and recently G. W. Bernard (who has always argued for Henry's dominant role) has provided extensive and persuasive documentation of the king's own direction of affairs. See G. W. Bernard, *The King's Reformation: Henry VIII and the Remaking of the English Church* (New Haven and London, 2005).

2. P. Griffiths, A. Fox and S. Hindle eds, *The Experience of Authority in Early Modern England* (1996); M.J. Braddick and J. Walter eds, *Negotiating Power in Early Modern Society* (Cambridge, 2001), pp. 1–42.

3. See G. W Bernard, 'The Tyranny of Henry VIII', in G. W. Bernard and S. J. Gunn eds, *Authority and Consent in Tudor England* (Aldershot, 2002), pp. 113–30; Greg Walker, *Writing under Tyranny: English Literature and the English Reformation* (Oxford, 2005).

4. K. Sharpe, 'Representations and Negotiations: Texts, Images and Authority in Early Modern England', *Historical Journal*, 42 (1999), pp. 853–81 (reprinted in K. Sharpe, *Remapping Early Modern England* (Cambridge, 2000), pp. 415–59); cf. Braddick and Walter, *Negotiating Power*, p. 13.

5. R. Strong, *Holbein and Henry VIII* (1967), p. 7.

6. S. Anglo, *Images of Tudor Kingship* (Guildford, 1992); Greg Walker, *Persuasive Fictions: Faction, Faith, and Political Culture in the Reign of Henry VIII* (Aldershot, 1991).

7. See above, Introduction, pp. 18–20.

8. Such a definition is itself problematic, for the leaders of Fascist parties believed, as did Hitler, in the truth of their propaganda. The word, however, is now inseparable from the notion of false information spread to mislead.

9. Indeed, the publicization of the king's conscience is one of the striking features of Henrician representation. See below, pp. 103–7.

10. Strong, *Holbein and Henry VIII*, p. 4.

11. J. N. King, *Tudor Royal Iconography* (Princeton, 1989), p. 15.

12. See above, pp. 10–11.

13. H. S. Croft, *The Boke Named The Governour Devised by Thomas Elyot, Knight* (2 vols, 1880), II, p. 198.

14. I take the phrase from the important chapter in P. Williams, *The Tudor Regime* (Oxford, 1979), ch. 11, p. 351.

15. King, *Tudor Royal Iconography*, pp. 19–42; above pp. 62–4.

16. St John 1:1.

17. Ecclesiastes 8:4.

18. M. T. Clanchy, *From Memory to Written Record: England 1066–1307* (2nd edn, Oxford, 1993).

19. K. Sharpe, *Reading Revolutions: The Politics of Reading in Early Modern England* (New Haven and London, 2000), pp. 27–34.

20. J. P. Carley, *The Libraries of King Henry VIII* (2000), pp. xxvi–xxviii, xxxvi–lxiv, 227–49; J. P. Carley, *The Books of King Henry VIII and His Wives* (2004), pp. 14–18, 26, 29, 31, 33, 53–80, 100–1, 104 and *passim*. See too, T. A. Birrell, *English Monarchs and Their Books: From Henry VII to Charles II* (1987), ch. 1.

21. D. Starkey ed., *The Inventory of Henry VIII: Society of Antiquaries MS 129 and British Library MS Harley 1419* (1998), nos 2339–54, 9676, 13711–48, pp. 72, 75, 206, 342; Carley, *Libraries of Henry VIII*, pp. xxxi–xxxiii, xxxix; Carley, *Books of Henry VIII*, p. 9.

22. Starkey, *Inventory*, no. 2542, p. 76; Thomas Berthelet's accounts also include blank bound books for the king to write in, Carley, *Libraries of Henry VIII*, pp. 232, 242.

23. Starkey, *Inventory*, nos 2339, 2348, 2352, 2391, pp. 71–2. Henry's *A Neccessarie Doctrine* was commonly referred to as 'The King's Book'; see below, p. 107.

24. T. Elyot, *The Dictionary of Syr Thomas Elyot Knyght* (1538), sigs Aii–Aiii^v. The 'Copy of the King's Gracious Privilege' faces sig. Aii.

25. P. Hughes and J. F. Larkin eds, *Tudor Royal Proclamations* (3 vols, New Haven, 1964–9), I, nos 216, 248, 272, pp. 317, 349–50, 373–6; 34 & 5 Henry VIII, c. 1 in A. Luders, T. E. Tomlins, J. France, W. E. Taunton, J. Raithby eds, *Statutes of the Realm, from Original Records and Authentic Manuscripts (1101–1713)* (11 vols, 1810–28), III, pp. 894–7.

26. 27 Henry VIII, c. 2, *Statutes of the Realm*, III, p. 532; see S. Lerer, *Courtly Letters in the Age of Henry VIII: Literary Culture and the Arts of Deceit* (Cambridge, 1997), p. 115.

27. Below, pp. 141–4.

28. Lerer, *Courtly Letters*, p. 87.

29. See A. Johns, *The Nature of the Book: Print and Knowledge in the Making* (Chicago, 1998), ch. 2; M. Rose, *Authors and Owners: The Invention of Copyright* (Cambridge, Mass., 1993); M. Woodmansee and P. Jazzi eds, *The Construction of Authorship: Textual Appropriation in Law and Literature* (Durham, NC, 1994); R. Chartier, *The Order of Books* (Cambridge, 1994), ch. 2.

30. Sharpe, *Reading Revolutions*, p. 40, n. 198.

31. Elyot, *Dictionary*, sig. Aiii^v.

32. R. W. Heinz, *The Proclamations of the Tudor Kings* (Cambridge, 1876), ch. 1.

33. See D. Starkey, 'Intimacy and Innovation: The Rise of the Privy Chamber, 1485–1547', in D. Starkey ed., *The English Court from the Wars of the Roses to the Civil War* (1987), pp. 71–118; Starkey, 'Representation through Intimacy: A Study in the Symbolism of Monarchy and Court Office in Early Modern England', in I. Lewis ed., *Symbols and Sentiments* (1977), pp. 187–224; Starkey, 'The King's Privy Chamber' (University of Cambridge Ph.D., 1973).

34. M. Trefusis, *Songs, Ballads and Instrumental Pieces Composed by King Henry VIII* (Roxburghe Club, Oxford, 1912); A. Lewis ed., *Henry VIII: Three Songs of His Own Composition* (1936); J. Blezzard, 'King Henry VIII: Performer, Connoisseur and Composer of Music', *Antiquaries Journal*, 80 (2000), pp. 249–71; J. Stevens, *Music at the Court of Henry VIII* (1962); D. Fallows, 'Henry VIII as a Composer', in C. Banks, A. Searle and M. Turner eds, *Sundry Sorts of Music Books* (1993), pp. 27–39.

35.   T. Stemmler, 'The Songs and Love Letters of Henry VIII: On the Flexibility of Literary Genres', in U. Baumann ed., *Henry VIII in History, Historiography and Literature* (Frankfurt, 1992), pp. 97–112.

36.   Cf. Blezzard, 'King Henry VIII', pp. 263–4.

37.   Stemmler, 'Songs', p. 78.

38.   Lewis, *Three Songs*, pp. 2–3.

39.   F. Macnamara ed., *Miscellaneous Writings of Henry the Eighth* (1924), p. 173.

40.   Ibid., p. 174.

41.   Stemmler, 'Songs', p. 99. In one legend holly is taken to be the tree of Christ's cross.

42.   Macnamara, *Miscellaneous Writings*, p. 178.

43.   Ibid., p. 176.

44.   Ibid., p. 180; P. C. Herman, 'Henry VIII of England', in *Dictionary of Literary Biography*, Vol. XXXII (Columbia, 1993), pp. 172–86; Herman, 'Henry VIII and the Poetry of Politics', in P. C. Herman ed., *Reading Monarchs Writing: The Poetry of Henry VIII, Mary Stuart, Elizabeth I and James VI/I* (Tempe, Arizona, 2002), pp. 11–34; P. C. Herman ed., *Rethinking the Henrician Era: Essays on Early Tudor Texts and Contexts* (Urbana, Ill., 1994); Professor Peter Herman is currently completing a book on *Royal Poetrie: Tudor–Stuart Monarchic Verse and the Early Modern Political Imaginary*. I am grateful to him for sending me his chapter on Henry VIII.

45.   Macnamara, *Miscellaneous Writings*, p. 180.

46.   Ibid., p. 176.

47.   Ibid., p. 173. My term gestures to Greg Walker's *Plays of Persuasion: Drama and Politics at the Court of Henry VIII* (Cambridge, 1991).

48.   Lerer, *Courtly Letters*, p. 90; see L. Jardine, *Erasmus, Man of Letters: The Construction of Charisma in Print* (Princeton, 1993).

49.   Lerer, *Courtly Letters*, pp. 93, 112–13.

50.   M. St Clare Byrne ed., *The Letters of King Henry VIII* (1936), pp. 56, 82; *Letters and Papers, Foreign and Domestic, Henry VIII* (23 vols, 1862–1932), Vol. IV part ii, no. 4597, p. 2003; See also, [Anon.] *The Love Letters of Henry VIII to Anne Boleyn* (1906), p. xl.

51.   St Clare Byrne, *Letters of Henry VIII*, p. 54; Macnamara, *Miscellaneous Writings*, p. 159 dates the letter early July 1527 but the date is uncertain.

52.   St Clare Byrne, *Letters of Henry VIII*, p. 71.

53.   Ibid., p. 70; *Love Letters*, pp. xxii–xxiii.

54.   St Clare Byrne, *Letters of Henry VIII*, pp. 57, 58, 70, Macnamara, *Miscellaneous Writings*, pp. 157, 158.

55.   St Clare Byrne, *Letters of Henry VIII*, pp. 68–9; Macnamara, *Miscellaneous Writings*, pp. 163–4.

56.   St Clare Byrne, *Letters of Henry VIII*, p. 85; *Love Letters*, pp. xxx, xlv.

57.   For the argument that Henry chose to abstain from sexual relations with his mistress, see Bernard, *King's Reformation*, pp. 6–9.

58.   St Clare Byrne, *Letters of Henry VIII*, p. 82; *Love Letters*, p. xxxix.

59.   Ibid., p. 57; Macnamara, *Miscellaneous Writings*, p. 157.

60.   St Clare Byrne, *Letters of Henry VIII*, p. 56; Macnamara, *Miscellaneous Writings*, p. 157; Lerer, *Courtly Letters*, p. 100.

61.   St Clare Byrne, *Letters of Henry VIII*, pp. 55–6; Macnamara, *Miscellaneous Writings*, pp. 160–1; Lerer, *Courtly Letters*, p. 94.

62.   'These are the tropes of love transformed into the ministrations of the courtier and diplomat. They give voice not to Henry as the King and master, but as servant and subject', Lerer, *Courtly Letters*, p. 94.

63.   St Clare Byrne, *Letters of Henry VIII*, p. 71; *Love Letters*, p. 11.

64.   St Clare Byrne, *Letters of Henry VIII*, p. xii.

65.   Ibid., pp. 10, 15–16, 21.

66. Ibid., pp. 277–82, 364–5.
67. Ibid., pp. 61–2.
68. Ibid., pp. 48, 149. On the importance of letters as a reward for service, see H. Ellis ed., *Hall's Chronicle Containing the History of England . . . to the End of the Reign of Henry VIII* (1809), p. 567.
69. St Clare Byrne, *Letters of Henry VIII*, pp. 149, 164.
70. Henry's letter to rebels in Yorkshire, ibid., pp. 150–5.
71. Ibid., p. 153; Henry to Ellerker and Bowes, ibid., pp. 155–7.
72. Henry VIII, *Literarum, quibus Inuictissimus Princeps, Henricus Octauus, Rex Angliae et Franciae, d[omi]n[us] Hyberni[a]e, ac Fidei Defensor Respondit, ad Quandam Epistolam Martini Lutheri, ad Se Missa[m] et Ipsius Lutheran[a]e quoq[ue] Epistol[a]e Exemplum* (STC 13084, 1526). The Latin work was the next year translated for English readers as *A Copy of the Letters Wherin the Most Redouted [and] Mighty Pri[n]ce, Our Souerayne Lorde Kyng Henry the Eight, Kyng of Englande . . . Made Answere vnto a Certayne Letter of Martyn Luther* (STC 13086, 1527), sigs Aii–Bi.
73. Ibid., sig. Avii.
74. Ibid., sig. Aviii.
75. 'We had intended to leave Luther to his rudeness without any further writing', sig. Avi^v; ibid., sigs Aviii, Aii–Aviii *passim*.
76. *An Epistle* (STC 13081.3, 1538), sigs Ai^v, Aii^v, Av.
77. Ibid., sig. A iiii.
78. Ibid., sig. Ai^v.
79. Ibid., sig. Ai^v.
80. Henry VIII, *A Necessary Doctrine and Erudicion for any Chrysten Man Set Furth by the Kynges Maiestye of Englande* (STC 5176, 1543), sig. Ovi^v.
81. St Clare Byrne, *Letters of Henry VIII*, p. 137, quoting Ecclesiastes 8: 4; *A Necessary Doctrine*, sig. Mv^v.
82. Hall, *Chronicle*, pp. 764–5; cf. p. 775.
83. Ibid., p. 526.
84. Ibid., p. 652.
85. Ibid., p. 764.
86. Ibid., pp. 742–4.
87. *The Noble Tryumphaunt Coronacyon of Quene Anne* (STC 656, 1533), sig. aii.
88. Hall, *Chronicle*, p. 757.
89. Ibid., pp. 754–5.
90. Ibid., p. 755.
91. St Clare Byrne, *Letters of Henry VIII*, pp. 418–22; Hall, *Chronicle*, pp. 864–6.
92. Hall, *Chronicle*, p. 744.
93. Ibid., p. 755.
94. Ibid., p. 764.
95. Hughes and Larkin, *Tudor Royal Proclamations*, I, p. xxiii; cf. Heinz, *Proclamations*, ch. 1.
96. Hughes and Larkin, *Tudor Royal Proclamations*, I, p. xxvi.
97. Ibid., p. xxvi.
98. The only study of either Tudor or Stuart royal proclamations is Heinz, *Proclamations*, which pays no attention to their rhetorical form or strategies.
99. Hughes and Larkin, *Tudor Royal Proclamations*, I, nos 66, 141; pp. 99–100, 211–12.
100. Ibid., no. 115, p. 168.
101. Ibid., no. 95, p. 141.
102. Ibid., no. 128, pp. 191–3.
103. Ibid., no. 75, pp. 122–3.
104. Ibid., no. 108, pp. 152–3.
105. Ibid., nos 168, 129, pp. 197, 245.

106. Ibid., no. 161, p. 236.
107. Ibid., no. 169, p. 246.
108. *The Late Expedicion in Scotlande Made by the Kynges Hyghnys Armye* (STC 22270, 1544), sig. Div.
109. Hughes and Larkin, *Tudor Royal Proclamations*, I, nos 98, 110, pp. 143, 155.
110. The first proclamation using the new title is 23 February 1522, ibid., I, no. 87, p. 135.
111. Ibid., no. 158, pp. 229–30.
112. Ibid., p. 230.
113. Ibid., no. 155, pp. 227–8.
114. Ibid., no. 186, pp. 270–1.
115. Ibid., nos 61, 63, 75, pp. 83, 85, 122.
116. On the developing idea of the commonweal, see Witney Jones, *The Tudor Commonwealth: 1529–1559: A Study of the Impact of the Social and Economic Developments of Mid-Tudor England upon Contemporary Concepts of the Nature and Duties of the Commonwealth* (1970); G. R. Elton, *Reform and Renewal: Thomas Cromwell and the Common Weal* (Cambridge, 1973); P. Fideler and T. Mayer, *Political Thought and the Tudor Commonwealth: Deep Structure, Discourse and Disguise* (1992).
117. Hughes and Larkin, *Tudor Royal Proclamations*, I, no. 140, pp. 209–11.
118. Ibid., no. 158, pp. 229–32.
119. Ibid., no. 129, p. 194.
120. Ibid., pp. 195–6.
121. E. Shagan, *Popular Politics and the English Reformation* (Cambridge, 2003), ch. 1.
122. See, for example, Hughes and Larkin, *Tudor Royal Proclamations*, I, no. 88, p. 136.
123. Ibid., no. 118, p. 174.
124. Ibid., no. 200, pp. 296–8.
125. Ibid., no. 191, pp. 284–6.
126. Ibid., no. 188, p. 279.
127. Ibid., no. 72, p. 106.
128. Bernard, *King's Reformation*, pp. 292–404; see especially p. 344; R. Hoyle, *The Pilgrimage of Grace* (Oxford, 2001).
129. Henry VIII's *Ansvvere to the Petitions of the Traytours and Rebelles in Lyncolneshyre* (STC 13077.5, 1536) is printed in St Clare Byrne, *Letters of Henry VIII*, pp. 141–4.
130. For the Statute of Uses, 27 Henry VIII c. 10, see *Statutes of the Realm*, III, pp. 539–42; E. W. Ives, 'The Genesis of the Statute of Uses', *English Historical Review*, 82 (1967), pp. 673–97.
131. St Clare Byrne, *Letters of Henry VIII*, p. 144.
132. Ibid.
133. Cf. Shagan's remarks on Henry's Amicable Grant, *Popular Politics*, p. 20.
134. Henry VIII, *Ansvvere Made by the Kynges Hyghnes to the Petitions of the Rebelles in Yorkeshire* (STC 13077, 1536) printed in St Clare Byrne, *Letters of Henry VIII*, pp. 150–5.
135. Ibid., p. 154.
136. Ibid.
137. Ibid., p. 151.
138. D. MacCulloch, *Thomas Cranmer: A Life* (New Haven and London, 1996), p. 179.
139. Above, ch. 2, p. 65.
140. Henry VIII, *Assertio septem sacramentorum adversus M. Lutherum* (first edition STC 13078, 1521). This has been translated with an introduction, see L. O'Donovan ed., *Assertio septem sacramentorum or Defence of the Seven Sacraments* (New York, 1908). I quote from the translation in Macnamara, *Miscellaneous Writings*, pp. 25–154; reference p. 38.
141. Scarisbrick, *Henry VIII*, p. 111.

142. Ibid., p. 112; O'Donovan ed., *Assertio*, pp. 53–93.

143. Ibid., p. 112.

144. Cf. Bernard, *King's Reformation*, pp. 238–9.

145. Scarisbrick, *Henry VIII*, pp. 112–13.

146. *Calendar of State Papers Venetian, III, 1520–6*, no. 210, p. 122.

147. Scarisbrick, *Henry VIII*, p. 113. The next royal success on this scale was Charles I's *Eikon Basilike* and one is led to wonder whether Charles, who followed the second Tudor in other matters, was influenced by Henry VIII's writing.

148. Macnamara, *Miscellaneous Writings*, p. 47.

149. Ibid., pp. 46, 57, 63, 97–9, 112–14 and 43–154 *passim*.

150. Ibid., p. 85.

151. Ibid., p. 92.

152. Ibid.

153. Ibid.

154. Ibid., p. 154.

155. Ibid., pp. 71, 86, 142.

156. Ibid., p. 150.

157. Ibid., p. 75.

158. Ibid., pp. 150, 154.

159. Carley, *Books of King Henry VIII*, p. 114; Scarisbrick, *Henry VIII*, p. 113.

160. Carley, *Books of Henry VIII*, p. 122.

161. St Clare Byrne, *Letters of Henry VIII*, p. 82; Macnamara, *Miscellaneous Writings*, p. 167. See V. Murphy, 'The Literature and Propaganda of Henry VIII's First Divorce', in D. MacCulloch ed., *The Reign of Henry VIII: Politics, Policy and Piety* (Houndmills, 1995), pp. 135–58, especially p. 148. Murphy takes the letter to refer to the book which Henry had a hand in composing for the trial of his marriage supervised by Wolsey and Campaggio, but there is no evidence and the letter may refer to the *Glass*.

162. J. Christopher Warner, *Henry VIII's Divorce: Literature and the Politics of the Printing Press* (Woodbridge, 1998), pp. 38–41.

163. *Letters and Papers of Henry VIII*, 5, no. 1338, p. 576.

164. W. Tyndale, *The Practice of Prelates: Whether the King's Grace May Be Separated from his Queen* . . . (Antwerp, 1530) in H. Walter ed., *Expositions and Notes on Sundry Portions of the Holy Scriptures Together with The Practice of Prelates* (Parker Soc., Cambridge, 1849), p. 246.

165. Henry VIII, *A Glasse of the Truthe* (STC 11918, 1532), sig. A2, 'To the Readers', my italics. Though Elton assigned the work to 1532, there has been a controversy over the date. See S. Haas, 'Henry VIII's Glasse of the Truthe', *History*, 64 (1979), pp. 65–72; MacCulloch, *Cranmer*, p. 57, n. 51; R. Rex, 'Redating Henry VIII's A Glass of the Truth', *The Library*, 7th Series, 4 (2003), pp. 16–27.

166. Henry VIII, *A Glasse of the Truthe*, sigs A2–A4.

167. Ibid., sig. A4^v.

168. Ibid., sigs C2–C2^v, C3^v–C4^v, D7^v–D8.

169. Ibid., sigs E8^v, F1^v–F2.

170. Ibid., sig. E5.

171. *Letters and Papers of Henry VIII*, 5, no. 1338, p. 576.

172. Henry VIII, *A Glasse of the Truthe*, sig. F1^v.

173. N. Pocock ed., *Records of the Reformation* (2 vols, Oxford, 1870–1), II, p. 422.

174. Bernard, *King's Reformation*, pp. 281–92, 498–505 and *passim*. A good account of Henry's apparent wavering is in MacCulloch, *Cranmer, passim*.

175. Scarisbrick, *Henry VIII*, p. 417.

176. Henry VIII, *A Necessary Doctrine and Erudition for any Chrysten Man Set Furth by the Kynges Maiestye of Englande* (STC 5173, 1543), sig. Piii.

177. *A Necessary Doctrine* has been curiously neglected. Bernard briefly discusses this work (*King's Reformation*, pp. 583–9) but, despite its title, the King's Book, does not consider it as a text of Henry's authority. MacCulloch gives it little attention except to present it as a sign of the archbishop's failure to win Henry to accept the doctrine of justification, MacCulloch, *Cranmer*, pp. 341–2

178. Henry VIII, *A Necessary Doctrine*, preface, sigs Aii–Aii^v.

179. Ibid., sig. Uiv (last page).

180. Ibid., preface, sig. Aiii.

181. Ibid., sig. Ii.

182. Ibid., sigs Dviii, Iv–Iv^v.

183. Ibid., sig. Dviii.

184. Ibid., sigs Dvii–viii, Mv.

185. Ibid., sigs Nii, Nvii^v.

186. Ibid., sigs Giv–v^v, Hiii^v.

187. Ibid., sigs Oiii^v–Ov^v.

188. Ibid., sig. Ri^v.

189. Ibid., sig. Ivii.

190. Ibid., sigs Svii–Tv.

191. Ibid., sig. Mv^v.

192. Warner, *Henry VIII's Divorce*, p. 85.

193. Ibid., p. 83. The actual relationship of being published by the royal printer or 'cum privilegio' to official views is complex and difficult to determine. Henry was the first to appoint a royal printer. But such works appear to have signified officially sanctioned views. I am grateful to George Bernard for discussions on this subject. See also P. Neville, 'Richard Pynson, King's Printer (1506–1529): Printing and Propaganda in Early Tudor England' (London University Ph.D., 1990). Cf. C. Clegg, *Press Censorship in Elizabethan England* (Cambridge, 1997), pp. 8–12.

194. J. Skelton, [*Elegy on the Death of Henry VII*] (STC 13075, 1509).

195. B. Lüsse, 'Panegyrical Poetry on the Coronation of King Henry VIII: The King's Praise and the Poet's Self-Presentation', in Baumann, *Henry VIII in History, Historiography and Literature*, pp. 49–78; M. Dowling, *Humanism in the Age of Henry VIII* (1986), ch. 1.

196. J. Skelton, 'A Lawde and Prayse Made For Our Sovereigne Lord The Kyng', in A. Dyce, ed., *The Poetical Works of John Skelton* (2 vols, 1843), I, pp. ix–xi.

197. Skelton, 'A Lawde', ibid., p. ix.

198. Ibid., p. x.

199. Ibid.

200. Ibid., p. xi.

201. Stephen Hawes, *A Ioyfull Medytacyon to all Englonde of the Coronacyon of our Moost Naturall Souerayne Lorde Kynge Henry the Eyght* (STC 12953, 1509); Wynkyn de Worde, *ODNB*; F. W Gluck and A. B. Morgan eds, *Stephen Hawes: The Minor Poems* (Early English Text Society, Oxford, 1974), pp. 85–91.

202. Gluck and Morgan, *Hawes: The Minor Poems*, lines 71, 95, pp. 87, 88.

203. Ibid., l.13, p. 85.

204. Ibid., ll. 62–3, p. 87. The woodcut is reproduced facing p. 85.

205. Ibid., ll. 111–12, 121–2, 137, pp. 88–9.

206. Ibid., ll. 153–4, p. 89.

207. Ibid., ll. 197–8, p. 91.

208. Ibid., l. 187, p. 90.

209. See for a later period, P. McCullogh, *Sermons at Court, 1559–1625: Religion and Politics in Elizabethan and Jacobean Preaching* (Cambridge, 1998).

210. See, for example, John Longland, *A Sermonde Made Before the Kynge his Maiestye at Grenewiche, vpon Good Frydaye* (STC 16796, 1538). Richard Morison's treatise, *A*

Remedy for Sedition (STC 18113.7, 1536) emphasizes the role of sermons in encouraging obedience, sigs Ciii–Cv; see below pp. 123–5.

211.   N.M. McClure, *The Paul's Cross Sermons* (Toronto, 1958), p. 14.

212.   See 'A Register of Sermons Preached at Paul's Cross', ibid., pp. 184–91.

213.   'The pulpit in Paul's churchyard was the most important vehicle of persuasion used by the government during the period 1534 to 1554', McClure, *Paul's Cross Sermons*, p. 20.

214.   Ibid., pp. 185, 187–9. On Crome, *ODNB*.

215.   McClure, *Paul's Cross Sermons*, pp. 188–9; Seton, *ODNB*.

216.   McClure, *Paul's Cross Sermons*, p. 189.

217.   Ibid., pp. 185–6.

218.   Ibid., p. 38.

219.   For a good general survey see A. Fox, *Politics and Literature in the Reigns of Henry VII and VIII* (Oxford, 1989), especially ch. 12.

220.   Croft, *The Boke Named The Governour*, II, p. 385. On chronicles and historical writing see F. J. Levy, *Tudor Historical Thought* (San Marino, 1967, reprinted Toronto 2004).

221.   See *The Cronycle, Begynnynge at the. vii. Ages of the Worlde with the Co[m]mynge of Brute, [and] the Reygne of all the Kynges with the Saynts and Martyrs that Haue Ben in the Lande* (STC 9984, ?1532); John Rastell, *The Pastyme of People: The Cronycles of Dyuers Realmys and Most Specyally of the Realme of Englond Breuely Co[m]pylyd* (1530). I owe this reference to the kindness of Greg Walker.

222.   The title page with Tudor royal arms and badges is repeated at the beginning of the second book that deals with kings since the Conquest.

223.   *Fabyans Cronycle Newly Prynted, wyth the Cronycl, Actes, and Dedes Done in the Tyme of the Reygne of the Moste Excellent Prynce Kynge Henry the vii.* (STC 10660; 2 vols, 1533). The quotation is from the full title and the royal arms are depicted as a frontispiece.

224.   Ibid., prologue, sig. Ai^v.

225.   Jürgen Beer, 'The Image of a King: Henry VIII in the Tudor Chronicles of Edward Hall and Raphael Holinshed', in Baumann, *Henry VIII in History*, pp. 129–50.

226.   King, *Tudor Royal Iconography*, pp. 21–2; *The Chronicle of Ihon Hardyng from the Firste Begynnyng of Englande, Vnto the Reigne of Kyng Edward the Fourth* (STC 12767, 1543).

227.   On the genre of politic histories, see Levy, *Tudor Historical Thought*, ch.7 and D. Woolf, *The Idea of History in Early Stuart England* (Toronto, 1990), pp. 105–6, 243–7.

228.   *The Vnion of the Two Noble and Illustrate Famelies of Lancastre [and] Yorke Beeyng Long in Continual Discension for the Croune of this Noble Realme with all the Actes Done in Bothe the Tymes of the Princes . . . Beginnyng at the Tyme of Kyng Henry the Fowerth . . . and so Successiuely Proceadyng to the Reigne of the High and Prudent Prince Kyng Henry the Eight.* It is interesting that where his first *DNB* biography regards Hall as a spokesman for the 'profound loyalty of the middle class', the *Oxford DNB* entry emphasizes his 'scepticism towards royal authority'. 'Edward Hall', *DNB* and *ODNB*. We await a full scholarly study of Hall. On Grafton and Cromwell, see Bernard, *King's Reformation*, p. 523.

229.   Anglo, *Images of Tudor Kingship*, p. 74.

230.   The quotation is part of the full title of the 1548 edition.

231.   Beer, 'The Image of a King', p. 147.

232.   Ibid., p. 140.

233.   *Hall's Chronicle*, p. 590.

234.   Ibid., p. 507.

235.   Ibid., p. 753.

236.   Ibid.

237. Cf. Beer, 'The Image of the King', p. 145.
238. *Hall's Chronicle*, p. 756.
239. Ibid., p. 759.
240. Ibid., pp. 775–80.
241. Ibid., p. 796.
242. See E. Jones, *The English Nation: The Great Myth* (Stroud, 1998), ch.1 and *passim*.
243. *Hall's Chronicle*, pp. 817–18.
244. Ibid., p. 828.
245. Quotation from 'Edward Hall', *DNB*.
246. Most famously in The Act in Restraint of Appeals, 24 Henry VIII c. 12, *Statutes of the Realm*, III, 427: 'Whereas by divers sundry old authentic histories and chronicles it is manifestly declared and expressed that this realm of England is an empire and so hath been accepted in the world, governed by one Supreme Head and king . . .'.
247. For example *Hall's Chronicle*, p. 759 where rumours were also described as 'the foolish communication of the people', adding a slur against class to that of gender.
248. *Hall's Chronicle*, pp. 696–7. See G. W. Bernard, *War, Taxation and Rebellion in Early Tudor England: Henry VIII, Wolsey and the Amicable Grant of 1525* (Brighton, 1986).
249. *Hall's Chronicle*, p. 697.
250. Ibid., p. 820.
251. Ibid., p. 823.
252. Walker, *Writing under Tyranny, passim*.
253. Clegg, *Press Censorship*, p. 9.
254. Ibid., p. 10; Hughes and Larkin, *Tudor Royal Proclamations*, I. no. 186, pp. 270–6, especially p. 272.
255. On Berthelet, see Warner, *Henry VIII's Divorce*, ch. 4; 'Thomas Berthelet', *ODNB*. It is possible that John Rastell briefly followed Pynson.
256. Warner, *Henry VIII's Divorce*, pp. 83, 87.
257. J. Lydgate, *This Present Boke Called the Gouernaunce of Kynges and Prync[es] Imprynted at the Co[m]maundement of the Good and Honourable Syre Charles Somerset Lorde Herbert* (STC 17017, 1511).
258. *The Preceptes Teachyng a Prynce or a Noble Estate his Duetie, Written by Agapetus in Greke to the Emperour Iustinian* (STC, 193, 1533) printed by Berthelet; the royal privilege is printed at the end.
259. Ibid., sig. aii.
260. Ibid., sig. aviii^v. There seems no obvious reason to find covert criticism in the tract, 'Thomas Paynell', *ODNB*.
261. P. Hogrefe, *The Life and Times of Sir Thomas Elyot, Englishman* (Ames, Iowa, 1967); S. Lehmberg, *Sir Thomas Elyot: Tudor Humanist* (Austin, 1960).
262. Walker, *Writing under Tyranny*, pp. 217–24.
263. Warner, *Henry VIII's Divorce*, p. 81.
264. T. Elyot, *Isocrates, The Doctrinall of Princis* (STC 14277, 1534), ff. 4, 14ᵛ.
265. Croft, *The Boke Named The Governour*, 'the proem', I, p. cxcii.
266. Ibid., pp. 13, 24.
267. Ibid., pp. 183–6, 290.
268. Ibid., pp. 256, 259–60.
269. Walker (*Writing under Tyranny*, ch. 8, pp. 141–80) discusses *The Governor* as a critique of kingship. It certainly places great emphasis on counsel ('the power of counsel is wonderful', Croft, *The Boke Named The Governour*, II, p. 432); but in 1533 that, of course, could be read as compliment to the king and evidently was so interpreted by Henry himself.
270. Croft, *The Boke Named The Governour*, I, p. 32; II, pp. 303, 335–6.
271. Ibid., I, p. 106.

272. Walker, *Writing under Tyranny*, p. 153. Lehmberg repeats his argument in his entry on Sir Thomas Elyot for *ODNB*.

273. Cf. Warner, *Henry VIII's Divorce*, pp. 71–2.

274. Ibid., pp. 73–4.

275. T. Elyot, *Image of Gouvernance Compiled of the Actes and Sentences Notable of the Moste Noble Emperor Alexander Severus* (STC 7664, 1541) sigs aii, bi. It may be significant that, for all the compliment to the king, this work was not printed by Berthelet and was dedicated not to Henry but to 'all the nobility' (sig. aii). For dating of and an analysis of Elyot's *Image*, see U. Baumann, 'Sir Thomas Elyot's *The Image of Gouvernance*: A Humanist's *Speculum Principis* and a Literary Puzzle', in D. Stein and R. Sornicola eds, *The Virtues of Language: History in Language, Linguistics and Texts* (Amsterdam, 1998), pp. 177–99; Walker, *Writing under Tyranny*, pp. 241–5, 247–56.

276. *Letters and Papers of Henry VIII*, 6, no. 562, p. 248.

277. On Elyot and the king's divorce, to which he was unsympathetic, see Walker, *Writing under Tyranny*, ch. 7. See too Murphy, 'Literature and Propaganda', p. 155.

278. See T. Mayer, *Thomas Starkey and the Commonweal: Humanist Politics and Religion in the Reign of Henry VIII* (Cambridge, 1989) ch. 7 and Mayer's entry on 'Thomas Starkey' for *ODNB*.

279. Mayer, *Thomas Starkey*, pp. 96–7; See T. Mayer ed., *Thomas Starkey: A Dialogue between Pole and Lupset* (Camden Soc. 4th Series, 37, 1989).

280. 'Richard Morison', *ODNB*. Curiously, there is no good modern biography.

281. Thomas Starkey, *An Exhortation to the People Instrucyinge Theym to Unity and Obedience* (STC 23236, 1536); 'Thomas Starkey', *ODNB*; Mayer, *Thomas Starkey*, pp. 216–27.

282. Starkey, *An Exhortation*, sigs aii–aiv.

283. Ibid., sig. Aiv.

284. Ibid., sig. Biii.

285. Ibid., sig. Biv^v.

286. Ibid. pp. 28, 32.

287. Ibid., pp. 58, 66.

288. Ibid., p. 69.

289. Ibid., p. 70.

290. Ibid., p. 83.

291. Ibid., p. 87.

292. Ibid., p. 83.

293. Ibid., p. 85.

294. Ibid., pp. 64–5.

295. [R. Morison], *A Remedy for Sedition Wherin are Conteyned Many Thynges Concernyng the True and Loyall Obeysance, that Comme[n]s Owe Vnto Their Prince and Soueraygne Lorde the Kyng* (STC 20877, 1536), sig. aiv.

296. Ibid., sig. aiv^v.

297. Ibid., sig. Biii.

298. Ibid., sigs Di, Div^v.

299. Ibid., sigs Civ–Di, Fii.

300. Ibid., sig. Gi.

301. Ibid., sig. Di. Jonathan Woolfson in the *ODNB* rightly observes that (not least through such language) *A Remedy* testifies to the government's belief that 'the opinion of relatively ordinary people could and should be manipulated by persuasion'.

302. R. Morison, *An Exhortation to Styrre all Englyshe Men to the Defence of Theyr Countreye. Made by Richard Morysine* (STC 18110, 1529), sigs Biv^v–Bii.

303. Ibid., sig. Bii. Morison's language not accidentally invokes the marriage service.

304. Ibid., sig. Bii.

305. Ibid., sigs Biii–Biv, Bv^v.
306. Ibid., sigs Bvi, Cii^v, Ciii^v.
307. Ibid., sigs Biv^v, Cv^v.
308. Ibid., sigs Dv–v^v. See II Esdras 11.
309. Morison, *An Exhortation*, sig. Dviii^v.
310. Ibid., sig. Ei.
311. S. Anglo, *Spectacle, Pageantry and Early Tudor Policy* (Oxford, 1969), p. 270.
312. Edward Walshe, *The Office and Duety in Fightyng for Our Countrey* (STC 25000, 1545), sig. Aiiii^v.
313. J. Bekinsau, *De supremo et absoluto regis imperio* (STC 1801, 1546). Beckinsau, a former student at Winchester as well as New College, was close to John Leland (*DNB*).
314. Walshe, *DNB*.
315. Perhaps because Beckinsau returned to Catholicism before his death in 1559 (*DNB*).
316. J. King, *English Reformation Literature: The Tudor Origins of the Protestant Tradition* (Princeton, 1982), pp. 48–9.
317. E. W. Dormer ed., *Gray of Reading: A Sixteenth Century Controversialist and Ballad Writer* (Reading, 1923), pp. 12–13.
318. Ibid., pp. 79–82.
319. Ibid., pp. 83, 95.
320. Ibid., p. 15.
321. Anglo, *Spectacle, Pageantry*, pp. 266–7.
322. D. Kastan, ' "Holy Wurdes" and "Slypper Wit": John Bale's *King Johan* and the Poetics of Propaganda', in Herman, *Rethinking the Henrician Era*, pp. 267–82, p. 269; D. Bevington, *Tudor Drama and Politics* (Cambridge, Mass., 1968), pp. 96–7. See too S. Baker House, 'Literature, Drama and Politics', in MacCulloch, *Reign of Henry VIII*, pp. 181–201 especially pp. 185–91.
323. J. H. Pafford ed., *King Johan by John Bale* (Malone Soc., Oxford, 1931), line 1343, p. 63; Kastan, ' "Holy Wurdes"; Greg Walker, *Plays of Persuasion: Drama and Politics at the Court of Henry VIII* (Cambridge, 1991), ch. 6.
324. Walker, *Plays of Persuasion*, p. 180.
325. C. Levin, *Propaganda in the English Reformation: Heroic and Villainous Images of King John* (Lewiston, NY, 1988).
326. Kastan, ' "Holy Wurdes", p. 278.
327. Walker, *Plays of Persuasion*, p. 182.
328. MacCulloch, *Cranmer*, chs 6, 7.
329. 34 Henry VIII c. 1, *Statutes of the Realm* III, pp. 894–7; Hughes and Larkin, *Tudor Royal Proclamations*, I, no. 240, pp. 341–2.
330. Walker, *Plays of Persuasion*, p. 21; Anglo, *Spectacle, Pageantry*, p. 203.
331. Carley, *Books of King Henry VIII*, p. 103. Thomas Cranmer reported this practice of Henry's to the German reformer Wolfgang Capito. Declaiming on a text pro and contra was, of course, an essential part of humanist education. See Q. Skinner, *Reason and Rhetoric in the Philosophy of Hobbes* (Cambridge, 1996), part I.
332. S. Greenblatt, *Renaissance Self Fashioning from More to Shakespeare* (Chicago, 1980), p. 13.
333. Hughes and Larkin, *Tudor Royal Proclamations*, I, no. 186, pp. 270–6; see p. 276.
334. Anglo, *Spectacle and Pageantry*, p. 267.

4 Images of Royal Supremacy

1. *OED*: 'recognition', especially meaning 4a and b; the first use of recognize to mean 'to know by means of some distinctive feature' is found in 1725.

2.   A. Luders, T. E. Tomlins, J. France, W. E. Taunton, J. Raithby eds, *Statutes of the Realm, from Original Records and Authentic Manuscripts (1101–1713)* (11 vols, 1810–28), IV, pp. 358–9.

3.   See Greenblatt, *Renaissance Self Fashioning* (Chicago, 1980), especially ch. 1; S. Orgel, 'The Royal Theatre and the Role of the King', in G. Lytle and S. Orgel eds, *Patronage in the Renaissance* (Princeton, 1981); P. Backscheider, *Spectacular Politics: Theatrical Power and Mass Culture in Early Modern England* (Baltimore, 1993). I am grateful to Dr Ross Parry for discussions of this subject.

4.   H. R. Trevor Roper, *Princes and Artists: Patronage and Ideology at Four Habsburg Courts 1517–1633* (1976).

5.   J. Peacock, 'The Politics of Portraiture', in K. Sharpe and P. Lake eds, *Culture and Politics in Early Stuart England* (Houndmills, 1993), pp. 199–228; cf. E. Chaney ed., *The Evolution of English Collecting* (New Haven and London, 2003).

6.   It is evident not least in the beginnings of collections of woodcut and engraved portraits of monarchs and of coins and medals.

7.   J. Rowlands, *Holbein: The Paintings of Hans Holbein the Younger* (Oxford, 1985), ch. 3, pp. 72–3, and p. 81; S. Foister, *Holbein and England* (New Haven and London, 2004), ch. 1 *passim*; idem, *Holbein in England* (Tate Exhibition Catalogue, 2006), pp. 17–77.

8.   Rowlands, *Holbein*, pp. 81–2; Foister, *Holbein and England*, p. 12.

9.   Rowlands, *Holbein*, pp. 87–8.

10.   Ibid., p. 88; Foister, *Holbein and England*, p. 13.

11.   Foister, *Holbein and England*, p. 16.

12.   W. A. Shaw ed., *Three Inventories of the Years 1542, 1547 and 1549–50 of Pictures in the Collections of Henry VIII and Edward VI* (1937), p. 33.

13.   D. Hoak, 'The Iconography of the Crown Imperial', in D. Hoak ed., *Tudor Political Culture* (Cambridge, 1995), p. 85.

14.   Ibid., p. 85; C. Lloyd and S. Thurley, *Henry VIII: Images of a Tudor King* (1990) pp. 53–4; D. Starkey ed., *Henry VIII: A European Court in England* (1991), pp. 50–1.

15.   S. Lerer, *Courtly Letters in the Age of Henry VIII: Literary Culture and the Arts of Deceit* (Cambridge, 1997), pp. 96–7; J. King, *Tudor Royal Iconography* (Princeton, 1989), p. 82; E. Auerbach, *Tudor Artists* (1954), p. 50.

16.   Ibid., pp. 25–6.

17.   Ibid., p. 35.

18.   Ibid., p. 37.

19.   Lloyd and Thurley, *Henry VIII: Images of a Tudor King*, p. 28.

20.   D. Starkey ed., *The Inventory of Henry VIII: Society of Antiquaries MS 129 and British Library MS Harley 1419* (1998), no. 10632, p. 238; cf. Shaw, *Three Inventories*, p. 35.

21.   See below pp. 141–3.

22.   J. King, 'Henry VIII as David: The King's Image and Reformation Politics', in P. C. Herman ed., *Rethinking the Henrician Era: Essays on Early Tudor Texts and Contexts* (Urbana, Ill., 1994), pp. 78–92, p. 80; Auerbach, *Tudor Artists*, p. 158.

23.   King, 'Henry VIII as David', p. 88.

24.   Ibid., p. 88; Foister, *Holbein and England*, pp. 153–4.

25.   Greg Walker, *Persuasive Fictions: Faction, Faith and Political Culture in the Reign of Henry VIII* (Aldershot, 1991), pp. 89–92.

26.   Cf. M. Levey, *Paintings at Court* (New York, 1971), p. 95.

27.   See O. Millar, *The Tudor, Stuart and Early Georgian Pictures in the Collection of Her Majesty the Queen* (1963), pp. 116–17.

28.   Rowlands, *Holbein*, p. 113; Foister, *Holbein and England*, p. 180.

29.   I take the translation from Rowlands, *Holbein*, p. 225.

30.   L. Montrose, 'The Elizabethan Subject and the Spenserian Text', in P. Parker and D. Quint eds, *Literary Theory/ Renaissance Texts* (Baltimore, 1985), p. 312.

31. Rowlands, *Holbein*, p. 113; cf. R. Strong, *Holbein and Henry VIII* (1967) pp. 35–54.
32. Strong, *Holbein and Henry VIII*, p. 39.
33. Foister, *Holbein and England*, pp. 191, 194.
34. Above, p. 91; Lerer, *Courtly Letters*, pp. 91–3.
35. Rowlands, *Holbein*, p. 116.
36. This is the usual account. Foister, however, argues that it was Cromwell not Holbein who was blamed for the disastrous marriage (Foister, *Holbein and England*, p. 203).
37. Walker, *Persuasive Fictions*, p. 84.
38. The painting, in the royal collection, was recorded in Elizabeth's reign as displayed in the Presence Chamber. For a brief discussion, see L. Montrose, *The Subject of Elizabeth: Authority, Gender and Representation* (Chicago, 2006), p. 25.
39. R. Strong, *Gloriana: The Portraits of Queen Elizabeth* (1987), p. 13.
40. S. Anglo, *Images of Tudor Kingship* (Guildford, 1992), p. 34.
41. Walker, *Persuasive Fictions*, p 75. I think Walker underestimates the propaganda of this portrait.
42. Anglo, *Images of Tudor Kingship*; see above, pp. 48–9.
43. Starkey, *Inventory*, p. x; below, p. 151.
44. I have made use of both the Witt Collection and the Huntington Library photo archives
45. Rowlands, *Holbein*, p. 236.
46. King, 'Henry VIII as David', p. 83.
47. Foister, *Holbein and England*, p. 162.
48. King, 'Henry VIII as David', pp. 80–2.
49. Walker, *Persuasive Fictions*, p. 86; Foister, *Holbein and England*, p. 159.
50. *The Byble in Englyshe of the Largest and Greatest Volume, Auctorysed and Apoynted by the Commaundemente of Oure Moost Redoubted Prynce and Soueraygne Lorde Kynge Henrye the. viii. Supreme Heade of this His Churche and Realme of Englande: to be Frequented and Used in Euery Churche w'in this his Sayd Realm* (STC 2073, 1541). The Bible was published with a royal coat of arms.
51. Stephen Hawes, *A Ioyfull Medytacyon to all Englonde of the Coronacyon of our Moost Naturall Souerayne Lorde Kynge Henry the Eyght* (STC 12953, 1509).
52. *The Noble Tryumphant Coronacyon of Queene Anne* (STC 656, 1533).
53. STC 12722, 12723; Anglo, *Images of Tudor Kingship*, p. 74.
54. Huntington Library, Richard Bull Granger Collection, II, no. 48.
55. D. Starkey, *The Reign of Henry VIII: Personalities and Politics* (1985), p. 125; Walker, *Persuasive Fictions*, p. 79. Walker dates the engraving to 1544; others to 1548.
56. See, for example, P. Glanville, *Silver in Tudor and Early Stuart England: A Social History and Catalogue of the National Collection, 1480–1660* (1990).
57. Starkey, *Inventory*, nos 10503, 10525, pp. 234–5.
58. M. Biddle and B. Clayre, *Winchester Castle and the Great Hall* (Winchester, 1983), p. 40.
59. Anglo, *Images of Tudor Kingship*, p. 15; H.M. Cautley, *Royal Arms and Commandments in Our Churches* (Ipswich, 1934); Henry VIII, *A Necessary Doctrine and Erudicion for any Chrysten Man Set Furth by the Kynges Maiestye of Englande* (STC 1543), sigs Li–iii.
60. Auerbach, *Tudor Artists*, p. 11.
61. Ibid., p. 14. On the scale of the royal works see H. Colvin, *The History of the King's Works*, IV (1982), pp. 128–40.
62. N. H. Nicholas ed., *The Privy Purse Expenses of King Henry the Eighth* (1827), p. 44; T. Mayer, 'On the Road to 1534: The Occupation of Tournai and Henry VIII's Theory of Sovereignty', in Hoak, *Tudor Political Culture*, p. 29.
63. J. Day, 'Primers of Honor: Heraldry, Heraldry Books, and English Renaissance Literature', *Sixteenth Century Journal*, 21 (1990), pp. 93–103; M. MacLagan, 'Genealogy

and Heraldry in the 16th and 17th Centuries', in L. Fox ed., *English Historical Scholarship in the 16th and 17th Centuries* (Oxford, 1956), pp. 31–48. Cf. M. Bath, *Speaking Pictures: English Emblem Books and Renaissance Culture* (1994).

64. H. S. Croft, *The Boke Named The Governour Devised by Thomas Elyot, Knight* (2 vols, 1880), I, pp. 139, 165.
65. Ibid, II, p. 24.
66. S. Thurley, *The Royal Palaces of Tudor England* (New Haven and London, 1993), p. 39.
67. Ibid., p. 49.
68. H. Ellis ed., *Hall's Chronicle Containing the History of England . . . to the End of the Reign of Henry VIII* (1809), pp. 786, 867.
69. Colvin, *King's Works*, IV, part II, pp. 79–82, 99–104, 132–40; Thurley, *Royal Palaces*, pp. 46, 186, 196; Auerbach, *Tudor Artists*, p. 14.
70. Colvin, *King's Works*, IV, part II, pp. 193–201.
71. Strong, *Holbein and Henry VIII*, p. 10.
72. Thurley, *Royal Palaces*, p. 102.
73. S. Anglo, *Spectacle, Pageantry and Early Tudor Policy* (Oxford, 1969), p. 165.
74. Ibid., pp. 165, 212.
75. Thurley, *Royal Palaces*, p. 101; cf. below, pp. 150–1.
76. Strong, *Holbein and Henry VIII*, p. 24.
77. Lerer, *Courtly Letters*, p. 96.
78. Huntington Library, Richard Bull Granger Collection, II, no. 86.
79. Starkey, *Inventory*, no. 8906, p. 174.
80. Ibid., nos 103, 641, 1317, pp. 10, 28, 45.
81. Ibid., nos 1461, 1990, pp. 49, 63.
82. Ibid., no. 12026, p. 273.
83. Ibid., nos 403, 453, pp. 21, 23.
84. Ibid., no. 9885, p. 217.
85. Ibid., nos 87, 88, 2055, 2131, 8990, pp. 9, 66, 67, 180.
86. Ibid., no. 156, p.12.
87. For example, ibid., nos 1329, 2059, 2998, 9085, pp. 45, 66, 69, 185.
88. Ibid., no. 1947, p. 62.
89. The cushion is ibid., no. 9798, p. 213.
90. Ibid., no. 3095, p. 85.
91. Ibid., no. 9431; p. 203. We recall the cartoon, above p. 144.
92. Ibid., nos 1094, 1238, 1410, 9015, 9016, 9171–7, 12101, 13072, pp. 39, 43, 48, 181, 189, 276, 312.
93. Ibid., nos 1094, 9307, pp. 39, 197.
94. Ibid., nos 114, 119, pp. 10, 11.
95. Ibid., nos 370, 536, 716, 786, pp. 20, 26, 30, 32.
96. Ibid., no. 12054, p. 274.
97. Ibid., no. 9365, p. 200.
98. See ibid., nos. 55, 9207, 11874–6, pp. 8, 191, 265.
99. Starkey, *Henry VIII: A European Court*, p. 131.
100. Starkey, *Inventory*, p. x.
101. Ibid., nos 37, 12321, pp. 6, 288.
102. Ibid., no. 9210, p.191. Absalom rose in rebellion against King David. See II Samuel, 14, 15.
103. Croft, *The Boke Named The Governour*, II, pp. 25–6.
104. Auerbach, *Tudor Artists*, pp. 30, 37; J. Harvey Bloom, *English Seals*, pp. 78–81.
105. Auerbach, *Tudor Artists*, p. 38.
106. Harvey Bloom, *English Seals*, p. 79; Auerbach, *Tudor Artists*, pp. 38–9.
107. Anglo, *Images of Tudor Kingship*, p. 117; E. Hawkins, *Medallic Illustrations of the History of Great Britain and Ireland to the Death of George II* (19 vols, 1904–11), I,

plates II, III, p. 7; A. Franks and H. Grueber, *Medallic Illustrations of the History of Great Britain* (2 vols, 1885), I, pp. 30–52.

108. Hawkins, *Medallic Illustrations*, plate I, 7; II, 7; Franks and Grueber, *Medallic Illustrations*, I, pp. 34, 48.

109. Franks and Grueber, *Medallic Illustrations*, I, pp. 44, 47; Huntington Library, Richard Bull Granger Collection, II, no. 11.

110. Franks and Grueber, *Medallic Illustrations*, I, p. 31; Huntington Library, Richard Bull Granger Collection, II, no. 11.

111. J. A. Muller ed., *The Letters of Stephen Gardiner* (Westport, Conn., 1993), p. 274.

112. Anglo, *Images of Tudor Kingship*, pp. 17–19.

113. Hoak, 'Iconography', in Hoak, *Tudor Political Culture*, pp. 66–70.

114. Ibid., p. 70; P. Grierson, 'The Origins of the English Sovereign and the Symbolism of the Closed Crown', *British Numismatic Journal*, 33 (1965), pp. 118–34.

115. C. Challis, *The Tudor Coinage* (Manchester, 1978), p. 66.

116. Ibid., p. 69.

117. Ibid., p. 220.

118. Ibid., p. 51.

119. Ibid., p. 71.

120. Jean Bodin listed coining as one of the inalienable prerogatives of the crown. See *The Six Books of the Commonwealth*, ch. X; 'As for the right of coining money, it is the same nature as law and only he who has the power to make law can regulate the coinage', J. H. Franklin, *On Sovereignty* (Cambridge, 1992), pp. 78–9.

121. Croft, *The Boke Named The Governour*, II, p. 36.

122. See J. Gould, *The Great Debasement: Currency and the Economy in mid-Tudor England* (Oxford, 1970), especially chs 1–3.

123. P. Hughes and J. F. Larkin eds, *Tudor Royal Proclamations* (3 vols, New Haven 1964–9), I, no. 197, p. 293. On 1540s campaigns see Potter, 'Foreign Policy', pp. 121–3.

124. Hughes and Larkin, *Tudor Royal Proclamations*, I, no. 228, p. 328.

125. Challis, *Tudor Coinage*, p. 92.

126. Ibid., p. 223.

127. Ibid., p. 224.

128. Ibid., p. 223.

5 Performing Supremacy

1. See below, pp. 173–4.

2. J. Lydgate, *This Present Boke Called the Gouernaunce of Kynges and Prync[es]*, (STC 17017, 1511), sig Cii$^\text{v}$.

3. H. Ellis ed., *Hall's Chronicle Containing the History of England . . . to the End of the Reign of Henry VIII* (1809), p. 520.

4. Ibid.

5. S. Anglo, *Spectacle, Pageantry and Early Tudor Policy* (Oxford, 1969), pp. 113–14.

6. Ellis, *Hall's Chronicle*, p. 674.

7. Anglo, *Spectacle, Pageantry*, p. 116.

8. D. Starkey ed., *The Inventory of Henry VIII: Society of Antiquaries MS 129 and British Library MS Harley 1419* (1998), no. 8384, p. 161. See Ellis ed., *Hall's Chronicle*, p. 862.

9. For a full account, see J. G. Russell, *The Field of the Cloth of Gold: Men and Manners in 1520* (1969).

10. See, for example, Starkey, *Inventory*, no. 8388, p. 161.

11. Ellis, *Hall's Chronicle*, p. 521.

12. See S. Howard, ' "Ascending the Riche Mount": Peforming Hierarchy and Gender in the Henrician Masque', in P. C. Herman, *Rethinking the Henrician Era: Essays on Early Tudor Texts and Contexts* (Urbana, Ill., 1994), pp. 16–39.

13. S. Thurley, *The Royal Palaces of Tudor England* (New Haven and London, 1993), p. 180.
14. Ibid., pp. 181–2.
15. Ibid., pp. 192–3. Henry had a reputation as a skilled archer, see Anglo, *Spectacle, Pageantry*, p. 154; Thurley, *Royal Palaces*, p. 70; Starkey, *Inventory*, nos 2564, 11972, 11977, 12017, pp. 76, 269, 272.
16. Ellis, *Hall's Chronicle*, p. 554.
17. A. Fox, *Politics and Literature in the Reigns of Henry VII and VIII* (Oxford, 1989), p. 232; *The Maner of the Tryumphe at Caleys and Bulleyn* (STC 4350, 1532).
18. M. St Clare Byrne ed., *The Letters of King Henry VIII* (1936), p. 29. A sense of the frivolity of pageantry in 1936 is quite understandable.
19. W. Readings, 'When Did the Renaissance Begin? The Henrician Court and the Shakespearian Stage', in Herman, *Rethinking the Henrician Era*, pp. 283–302, p. 287.
20. Ibid., p. 288.
21. Henry VIII, *A Necessary Doctrine and Erudicion for any Chrysten Man Set Furth by the Kynges Maiestye of Englande* (STC 1543), sig. Miiii.
22. Lydgate, *Gouernaunce of Kynges*, sig. Ci.
23. Ellis, *Hall's Chronicle*, p. 526.
24. Ibid., p. 580.
25. Ibid., p. 582.
26. Ibid., pp. 585–6.
27. S. Anglo, *Images of Tudor Kingship* (Guildford, 1992), p. 111; Starkey, *Henry VIII: A European Court in England* (1991), pp. 95–9. Ashmole describes Henry as 'that munificent increaser of the splendor of this most Noble Order', E. Ashmole, *The Institution, Laws & Ceremonies of the Most Noble Order of the Garter* (1672), p. 192. Throughout the study, Ashmole takes Henry VIII's statutes for the Garter as important in determining dress, ceremony and procedure.
28. Ellis, *Hall's Chronicle*, p. 598.
29. Ibid., p. 795.
30. Ibid., p. 598.
31. For the only study, see D. Dean, 'Image and Ritual in the Tudor Parliaments', in D. Hoak, *Tudor Political Culture* (Cambridge, 1995), pp. 243–71.
32. *Cal. Stat. Pap. Spanish*, IV, part 1, 1529–30, p. 323.
33. Dean, 'Image and Ritual', pp. 245–6.
34. Ellis, *Hall's Chronicle*, p. 506.
35. Ibid.
36. Ibid.
37. Ibid., p. 507. P. Fritz, 'From "Public" to "Private": The Royal Funerals in England', in J. Whaley ed., *Mirrors of Mortality: Studies in the Social History of Death* (1981), pp. 61–79, especially pp. 62–3. For a study of ceremonial procedures in later Tudor funerals, see J. Woodward, *The Theatre of Death: The Ritual Management of Royal Funerals in Renaissance England, 1570–1625* (Woodbridge, 1997).
38. Cf. C. Gittings, *Death, Burial and the Individual in Early Modern England* (1984), ch. 10.
39. Ellis, *Hall's Chronicle*, p. 506.
40. Ibid., p. 507.
41. Ibid., pp. 507–8.
42. Ibid., p. 511.
43. G. F. Beltz, *Original Records of the Form of Public Entry of King Henry the Eighth into Tournai* (1838); G. Cruickshank, *Army Royal: Henry VIII's Invasion of France in 1513* (Oxford, 1969).
44. Scarisbrick, *Henry VIII* (1968), p. 62; D. Potter, 'Foreign Policy', in D. MacCulloch ed., *The Reign of Henry VIII: Politics, Policy and Piety* (Houndmills, 1995), pp. 111–12.
45. See Russell, *The Field of the Cloth of Gold*.
46. Ellis, *Hall's Chronicle*, p. 604; Anglo, *Spectacle, Pageantry*, p. 139.

47. Ellis, *Hall's Chronicle*, pp. 604–22; Anglo, *Spectacle, Pageantry*, pp. 138–9.
48. Ellis, *Hall's Chronicle*, pp. 605, 611, 619–20.
49. Ibid., p. 620.
50. Ibid., p. 611.
51. Ibid., p. 634.
52. Anglo, *Spectacle, Pageantry*, p. 186.
53. Ellis, *Hall's Chronicle*, p. 637.
54. Ibid.
55. For description and analysis of the pageants, ibid., pp. 637–40; Anglo, *Spectacle, Pageantry*, ch. 5.
56. W. Lilly, *Of the Tryu[m]phe, and the Verses that Charles the Emperour, [et] the Most Myghty Redouted Kyng of England, Henry the VIII. Were Saluted With, Passyng Through London* (STC 15606.7, copy 5017, 1522), sig Bi^v and *passim*; Ellis, *Hall's Chronicle*, p. 637; Anglo, *Spectacle, Pageantry*, pp. 190–1, 201.
57. Anglo, *Spectacle, Pageantry*, p. 201.
58. Ibid., p. 204.
59. Above, note 56.
60. 'Why shoulde one write that eche man with his eye/ Dyd welbeholde and se wandering to and fro', *Of the Tryu[m]phe and the Verses*, sig. aii; cf. sig. aii^v.
61. The author of the account explains to those 'unlerned' as well as learned spectators. Ibid., sig. aii^v.
62. On the depth of the divisions, see Ethan Shagan, *Popular Politics and the English Reformation* (Cambridge, 2003).
63. Ellis, *Hall's Chronicle*, p. 798.
64. Ibid., pp. 798–804; Anglo, *Spectacle, Pageantry*, pp. 247–61.
65. *The Noble, Tryumphant Coronacyon of Queene Anne* (STC 656, 1533), sigs Aiii–Aiv; Ellis, *Hall's Chronicle*, p. 801.
66. Ellis, *Hall's Chronicle*, p. 801; *The Noble, Tryumphant Coronacyon*, sig. Aiv.
67. *The Noble, Tryumphant Coronacyon*, sig. Aiv^v; Ellis, *Hall's Chronicle*, pp. 801–2.
68. Ellis, *Hall's Chronicle*, pp. 801–2; *The Noble, Tryumphant Coronacyon*, sig. Av. Unlike Hall, the author translates the Latin for what was an unlearned audience of his account.
69. *The Noble, Tryumphant Coronacyon*, sig. Avi.
70. Above, ch. 4, p. 144.
71. Ibid., sigs Ai^v–Aii.
72. Anglo, *Spectacle, Pageantry*, p. 261.
73. J. Loach, *Edward VI* (New Haven and London, 1999), pp. 3–4.
74. Ellis, *Hall's Chronicle*, p. 833.
75. Ibid., pp. 834–6.
76. Ibid., pp. 506, 509, 640, 800.
77. *Of the Tryu[m]phe and the Verses*, sig. aii^v.
78. For an example of a pageant work remaining as a monument see *The Noble Tryumphaunt Coronacyon of Queene Anne*, sig. Av^v.
79. Above, ch. 3, note 302.
80. Ellis, *Hall's Chronicle*, p. 640.
81. Ibid., p. 836.
82. *The Noble Tryumphaunt Coronacyon*, sig. Aii. We note the repetition of 'all'.
83. Ellis, *Hall's Chronicle*, p. 509.
84. Ibid., p. 579.
85. Ibid., p. 756.
86. Ibid., p. 784.
87. J. Christopher Warner, *Henry VIII's Divorce: Literature and the Politics of the Printing Press* (Woodbridge, 1998), p. 61.
88. Anglo, *Spectacle, Pageantry*, p. 259.

89. Ibid.; *Letters and Papers. Henry VIII*, VI, p. 266. An excellent example of James C. Scott's concept of the 'weapons of the weak'; above, p. 50.

90. For a famous discussion of early modern ritual and carnival see M. Bakhtin, *Rabelais and his World* (Cambridge, Mass., 1968).

91. See E. Welsford, *The Court Masque: A Study in the Relationship between Poetry and Revels* (Cambridge, 1927), ch. 5; M. Twycross and S. Carpenter, *Masks and Masking in Medieval and Early Tudor England* (Aldershot, 2002), part II, especially pp. 164–83; ch. 13.

92. Ellis, *Hall's Chronicle*, p. 526.

93. Starkey, *Inventory*, nos 8663, 8664, p. 168; cf. pp. 166–7.

94. Ellis, *Hall's Chronicle*, pp. 566, 719.

95. Anglo, *Spectacle, Pageantry*, p. 223; *Cal. Stat. Pap. Venet. IV, 1527–1533*, p. 2.

96. S. Orgel, *Jonsonian Masque* (Cambridge, Mass., 1965), p. 29.

97. H. S. Croft, *The Boke Named The Governour Devised by Thomas Elyot, Knight* (2 vols, 1880), ch. xxii.

98. Ellis, *Hall's Chronicle*, p. 735; J. Rowlands, *Holbein: The Paintings of Hans Holbein the Younger* (Oxford, 1985), p. 117.

99. See above, ch. 3, note 33.

100. This aspect of the architectural changes awaits a full exploration.

101. Thurley, *Royal Palaces*, p. 198.

102. Scarisbrick, *Henry VIII*, p. 234; St Clare Byrne, *Letters*, p. 84.

103. Lydgate, *Gouernaunce of Kynges*, sig. Gii; The first English translation of Castiglione's *The Book of the Courtier* by Thomas Hoby appeared in 1561. The work, however, was well known in Italian and Latin editions in England. See P. Burke, *The Fortunes of The Courtier* (Cambridge, 1995), appendix 1, pp. 158–62; P. Burke, 'The Courtier Abroad: Or, The Uses of Italy', in D. Javitch ed., *The Book of the Courtier* (New York, 2002), pp. 388–400.

104. W. A. Shaw ed., *Three Inventories of the Years 1542, 1547 and 1549–50 of Pictures in the Collections of Henry VIII and Edward VI* (1937), pp. 61 ff.; Thurley, *Royal Palaces*, p. 80.

105. Thurley, *Royal Palaces*, pp. 70–3.

106. There were several other years when Henry was on progress for almost a fifth of the year. See N. Samman, 'The Progresses of Henry VIII', in MacCulloch, *Reign of Henry VIII*, pp. 59–74; Table 3.1, p. 63. See also D. Starkey ed., *Henry VIII: A European Court in England* (1991), pp. 118–23.

107. Ellis, *Hall's Chronicle*, p. 515.

108. Ibid.

109. Above, pp. 63–4.

110. Anglo, *Spectacle, Pageantry*, p. 21; *Letters and Papers, Henry VIII*, XII, part I, p. 519, no. 1118; S. Alford, 'Politics and Political History in the Tudor Century', *Historical Journal*, 42 (1999), p. 540.

111. Ellis, *Hall's Chronicle*, p. 842.

112. Ibid., pp. 599, 827.

113. Greg Walker, *Writing under Tyranny: English Literature and the English Reformation* (Oxford, 2005), *passim*; G. W. Bernard, 'The Tyranny of Henry VIII', in G. W. Bernard and S. Gunn eds, *Authority and Consent in Tudor England: Essays Presented to Cliff Davies* (Aldershot, 2002), pp. 113–29.

114. Anglo, *Spectacle, Pageantry*, p. 276.

115. For a classic study of the service–reward relationship, see J. H. Elliott, *The Revolt of the Catalans: A Study in the Decline of Spain, 1598–1640* (Cambridge, 1963), especially pp. 40–2.

116. F. W. Gluck and A. B. Morgan eds, *Stephen Hawes: The Minor Poems* (Early English Text Society, Oxford, 1974), p. 90, lines 185–6.

117. J. Loach 'The Function of Ceremonial in the Reign of Henry VIII', *Past & Present*, 142 (1994), pp. 43–68, p. 45.

118. Ellis, *Hall's Chronicle*, p. 510.

119. Ibid., pp. 510–11.

120. Ibid., p. 513.

121. Ibid., p. 526.

122. Nicholas, *Privy Purse Expenses*, pp. 16, 22, 41, 43, 46, 64, 71, 90, 93, 145, 150, 168, 214, 254, 273, cf. pp. 15, 20, 105.

123. See above pp. 17–18, 48 and, for a recent study of early modern England, Montrose, *The Subject of Elizabeth: Authority, Gender, and Representation* (Chicago, 2006).

124. Greg Walker, *Plays of Persuasion: Drama and Politics at the Court of Henry VIII* (Cambridge, 1991), p. 233.

125. Ellis, *Hall's Chronicle*, p. 539; Greg Walker, *Persuasive Fictions: Faction, Faith and Political Culture in the Reign of Henry VIII* (Aldershot, 1991), p. 16.

126. Ellis, *Hall's Chronicle*, p. 674.

127. Ibid., p. 591.

128. Ibid., p. 508.

6 Contesting Supremacy

1. See K. Sharpe, 'Sacralization and Demystification: The Publicisation of Monarchy in Early Modern England', in J. Deploige and G. Deneckere eds, *Mystifying the Monarch. Studies on Discourse, Power, and History* (Amsterdam, 2006), pp. 99–115.

2. See E. Shagan, *Popular Politics and the English Reformation* (Cambridge, 2003).

3. S. Mendyk, 'Early British Chorography', *Sixteenth Century Journal*, 17 (1986), pp. 459–81; idem, *'Speculum Britanniae': Regional Study, Antiquarianism, and Science in Britain to 1700* (Toronto, 1989); idem, 'Reformation, Civic Culture and Collective Memory in English Provincial Towns', *Urban History*, 24 (1997), pp. 283–300.

4. R. Titler, 'Political Culture and the Built Environment of the English Country Town, c. 1540–1620', in D. Hoak ed., *Tudor Political Culture* (Cambridge, 1995), p. 137.

5. Greg Walker, *Plays of Persuasion: Drama and Politics at the Court of Henry VIII* (Cambridge, 1991); idem, *Writing under Tyranny: English Literature and the English Reformation* (Oxford, 2005).

6. J. Christopher Warner, *Henry VIII's Divorce: Literature and the Politics of the Printing Press* (Woodbridge, 1998), pp. 118–20.

7. Ibid., pp. 125–33; Walker, *Writing under Tyranny*, pp. 100–19.

8. H. Ellis ed., *Hall's Chronicle Containing the History of England . . . to the End of the Reign of Henry VIII* (1809), p. 719.

9. Ibid.

10. A. Fox, *Oral and Literate Culture in England, 1500–1700* (Oxford, 2001).

11. Ellis, *Hall's Chronicle*, pp. 728, 754, 759.

12. Ibid., p. 784.

13. Ibid., p. 744.

14. Ibid., pp. 754, 759, 784; Warner, *Henry VIII's Divorce*, p. 113.

15. Ellis, *Hall's Chronicle*, p. 784.

16. P. Hughes and J. F. Larkin eds, *Tudor Royal Proclamations* (3 vols, New Haven, 1964–9), I, no. 168, p. 244.

17. Ellis, *Hall's Chronicle*, p. 784.

18. S. Jansen, *Political Protest and Prophecy under Henry VIII* (Woodbridge, 1991), pp. 29–34 and ch. 2, *passim*; G. R. Elton, *Policy and Police: The Enforcement of the Reformation in the Age of Thomas Cromwell* (Cambridge, 1972), pp. 54–5, 58–62, 71–3.

19. Jansen, *Political Protest*, pp. 47–8.
20. Ibid., p. 19.
21. Ibid., ch. 3.
22. Ibid., p. 67.
23. Ibid., pp. 67–8.
24. Ibid., pp. 57–61, 98–101.
25. Elton, *Policy and Police*, pp. 111, 243–8, 335–48, 399 and *passim*.
26. Jansen, *Political Protest*, p. 111.
27. Ibid., p. 144.
28. Ibid., p. 149.
29. ibid., pp. 58–60.
30. Ellis, *Hall's Chronicle*, p. 809; see G. W. Bernard, *The King's Reformation: Henry VIII and the Remaking of the English Church* (New Haven and London, 2005), pp. 87–100.
31. 33 Henry VIII. cap. 14 in A. Luders *et al.* eds, *Statutes of the Realm from Original Records and Authentic Manuscripts (1101–1713)* (11 vols, 1810–28), III, p. 850.
32. Jansen, *Political Protest*, p. 154.
33. *A Lamentation of the Death of the Moost Victorious Prynce Henry the Eyght Late Kynge of Thys Noble Royalme of Englande* (STC 13089, 1547), a one-page work.
34. Ibid.
35. The manuscript of W. Thomas, 'The Pilgrim: A Dialogue on the Life and Action of King Henry the Eight' is BL Add. MS 33383; it was published in Venice in 1552. See A. Daubant, *The Works of William Thomas* (1774). For a critical edition and commentary, see I.C. Martin, 'The Manuscript and Editorial Tradition of William Thomas's *The Pilgrim/ Ill Peregrino Inglese*'(University of Toronto Ph.D., 1999). This work is also briefly discussed in U. Baumann, ' "The Virtuous Prince": William Thomas and Ulpian Fulwell on Henry VIII', in U. Baumann ed., *Henry VIII in History, Historiography and Literature* (Frankfurt, 1992), pp. 167–93. See Greg Walker, *Writing under Tyranny*, pp. 5–7.
36. Baumann, 'Virtuous Prince', p. 176.
37. Ibid., p. 185.
38. J. Neale, *Queen Elizabeth* (1934), p. 59.
39. P. C. Herman ed., *Rethinking the Henrician Era: Essays on Early Tudor Texts and Contexts* (Urbana, Ill., 1994), p. 6.
40. See H. Müller, 'Shakespeare's *Henry VIII*: A Parable of Mutability', in Baumann, *Henry VIII*, pp. 203–22.
41. *The Pleasant and Delightful History of King Henry 8th. and a Cobler Relating How He Came Acquainted with the Cobler* (P2530, ?1670); *The Cobler Turned Courtier Being a Pleasant Humour between King Henry the Eight and a Cobbler* (C4782, 1680). There were many variant editions of *The History of the King and the Cobbler*, some in two parts, published in the eighteenth century.
42. Henry, that is, awaits the treatment recently given to Elizabeth in Julia Walker, *The Elizabethan Icon: 1603–2003* (Houndmills, 2004) and M. Dobson and N. Watson, *England's Elizabeth: An Afterlife in Fame and Fantasy* (Oxford, 2002).
43. J. King, *Tudor Royal Iconography* (Princeton, 1989), pp. 137–8.
44. Sir Walter Raleigh, *The History of World*, ed. C. A. Patrides (1971), pp. 56–7. I owe this reference to Baumann, *Henry VIII*, p. 69.
45. R. Perrinchief, *A Messenger From the Dead, or, Conference . . . Between the Ghosts of Henry the 8 and Charles the First of England* (E936/4, 1658).
46. Ibid., p. 10.
47. Readings, 'When Did the Renaissance Begin?' in Herman, *Rethinking the Henrician Era*, p. 288.
48. Ibid., p. 296.

49. G. Walker, *The Private Life of Henry VIII* (British Film Guides, 2003), p. 18. See also B. Bongartz, 'Henry VIII – The Moving Image: A Contribution to Four Biographical Movies about Henry VIII of England', in Baumann, *Henry VIII*, pp. 315–21.

50. Walker, *Private Life*, p. 45.

51. Ibid., p. 50.

52. Walker does not consider why Korda chooses Henry as a subject for this erotic *frisson*. I am grateful to Greg Walker for discussions of his study of the film.

53. F. W. Gluck and A. B. Morgan, eds, *Stephen Hawes: The Minor Poems* (Early English Text Society, Oxford, 1974), p. 85, line 14.

7 Representations of Edward VI

1. J. G. Nichols ed., *Literary Remains of King Edward VI* (2 vols, Roxburghe Club, 1857), p. cxlii; W. K. Jordan, *Edward VI: The Threshold of Power* (1970), pp. 21–3.

2. Jordan, *Edward VI*, p. 21.

3. J. Rowlands, *Holbein: The Paintings of Hans Holbein the Younger* (Oxford, 1985), catalogue no. 70, pp. 146–7.

4. Ibid., catalogue no. 35, pp. 235–6, plate 243.

5. K. Hearn, *Dynasties: Painting in Tudor and Jacobean England, 1530–1630* (1995), catalogue no. 113, pp. 49–50; O. Millar, *The Tudor, Stuart and Early Georgian Pictures in the Collection of Her Majesty the Queen* (1963), no. 44, pp. 64–5.

6. Rowlands, *Holbein*, p. 225.

7. Above, p. 139.

8. Hearn, *Dynasties*, p. 49.

9. See Nichols, *Literary Remains*, I, p. lxxxvi drawing on an account of the procession in College of Arms MSS I, 7, f. 29.

10. W. K. Jordan, *Edward VI: The Young King* (1968), pp. 348–9.

11. Jordan, *Edward VI: Threshold of Power*, p. 9.

12. Martin Bucer to Johannes Brentius, 15 May 1550, quoted in Nichols, *Literary Remains*, I, p. cxliv.

13. J. Loach, *Edward VI* (New Haven and London, 1999), pp. 153–5.

14. B. L. Beer ed., *The Life and Raigne of King Edward the Sixth by John Hayward* (Kent, Ohio, 1993), p. 37.

15. Ibid.

16. Report of England by Giacomo Soranzo, 18 August 1554, *Cal. Stat. Pap. Venet, V 1534–54*, no. 934, p. 535.

17. Edward to Queen Katherine, 12 May, 10 June 1546, Nichols, *Literary Remains*, I, p. 9.

18. Ibid., pp. 16–17, 21, 36.

19. Ibid., p. 9.

20. *Copies of Seven Original Letters from King Edward VI to Barnaby Fitzpatrick* (1772), p. 2.

21. Nichols, *Literary Remains*, I, pp. 117–27. 'Harsh kings are wicked rulers.'

22. Ibid., p. 121.

23. Edward to Somerset, 24 August 1546, ibid., pp. 47–8.

24. Stephen Alford writes that Edward began to absorb and deploy the 'vocabularies' of kingly authority but does not explore how he used them. See *Kingship and Politics in the Reign of Edward VI* (Cambridge, 2002), p. 160.

25. There is virtually no discussion of the chronicle in the two most recent studies, Alford's *Kingship and Politics* and C. Skidmore's popular biography, *Edward VI: The Lost King of England* (2007) which appeared after this chapter was drafted.

26. Jordan, *Edward VI: Threshold of Power*, pp. 23–7; Beer, *Life and Raigne*, p. 33. The chronicle is printed in Nichols, *Literary Remains*, II, pp. 209–474 and W. K. Jordan ed., *The Chronicle and Political Papers of King Edward VI* (1966). Though the Nichols

edition has very helpful annotation, I cite the Jordan text, which is more readily available.

27. Jordan, *Chronicle*, p. xix.
28. Ibid., p. 3.
29. Ibid., p. 4.
30. Ibid., pp. 8,10.
31. Ibid., p. 13.
32. Ibid., p. 34.
33. Ibid., p. 55; see D. MacCulloch, *Tudor Church Militant: Edward VI and the Protestant Reformation* (1999), pp. 36–9.
34. Jordan, *Chronicle*, p. 55. The phrase was inserted before 'but as a subject to obey'.
35. Ibid., p. 107; Jordan, *Edward VI: Threshold of Power*, p. 100.
36. Contrary to Jordan's statements about Edward's firm resolve removing any possibility of royal intervention to save Somerset, Hayward records that 'the lords did much help him to dispel any dampie thoughts . . . by applying him with great variety of exercises and sports', Beer, *Life and Raigne*, p. 147.
37. Jordan, *Chronicle*, pp. 64, 70, 72, 73, 75, 76, 85.
38. Ibid., p. 95, 14 November 1551.
39. Ibid., p. 116.
40. Ibid., p. 117.
41. Ibid., pp. 118–19.
42. Ibid., pp. 120, 122.
43. Ibid., p. 119.
44. Ibid., pp. 125, 132; see p. 144.
45. Ibid., p. 144.
46. Jordan, *Edward VI: Threshold of Power*, pp. 410–11.
47. For example, the change from 'These faults must be amended' to 'These sores must be cured' shows a concern with literariness which suggests an audience beyond the administration, ibid., p. 165. Other metaphors support that impression.
48. W. Jones, *The Tudor Commonwealth, 1529–1559: A Study of the Impact of the Social and Economic Developments of mid-Tudor England upon Contemporary Concepts of the Nature and Duties of the Commonwealth* (1970).
49. Jordan, *Chronicle*, p. 160.
50. Ibid., p. 161.
51. Ibid., p. 162.
52. Ibid.
53. Ibid., p. 164.
54. Ibid., p. 165.
55. Ibid., p. 166.
56. Ibid., p. 167.
57. *Pace* Jordan, *Edward VI: Threshold of Power*, p. 410.
58. 14 August 1551: 'Also appointed that I should come to and sit at Council, when great matters were debating, or when I would', Jordan, *Chronicle*, p. 76.
59. Ibid., pp. 168–73.
60. Ibid., p. xxv.
61. Ibid., p. xxvii.
62. Ibid., pp. 174–5.
63. Ibid., pp. xxviii, 176–80.
64. Ibid., p. 177.
65. Ibid., p. 179.
66. Ibid. John Harley's ecclesiastical career flourished under Edward VI and, having been appointed by the king in 1551 a prebend in Worcester Cathedral and royal chaplain, he was raised to the see of Hereford in 1552 ('Harley', *ODNB*).

67. Jordan, *Chronicle*, p. 180.
68. Ibid., pp. 114–15.
69. Ibid., pp. xxviii–xxxi, 181–4. See F.G. Emmison, 'A Plan of Edward VI and Secretary Petre for Reorganizing the Privy Council's Work, 1552–3', *Bulletin of the Institute of Historical Research*, 31 (1958), pp. 203–10.
70. Jordan, *Chronicle*, p. 182.
71. Ibid.
72. Ibid., p. 183. The imperial envoy Jehan Schefye notes Edward's new authority in Council in his dispatch of November 1552, *Cal. Stat. Pap. Spanish, X, 1550–2*, p. 592.
73. Jordan, *Chronicle*, p. 183.
74. In a 1552 memorandum on the appointment of committees of Council, Edward wrote 'I will sit with them once a week ... to hear the debating of things most important', Nichols, *Literary Remains*, II, p. 501.
75. Ibid, p. xxx.
76. Jordan, *Edward VI: Threshold of Power*, p. 455; Emmison, 'A Plan of Edward VI', p. 207.
77. Jordan, *Chronicle*, p. xxxi.
78. Ibid., pp. 187, and 185–90 *passim*.
79. These are printed in Nichols, *Literary Remains*, II, pp. 519–38. Jordan does not include them among the 'political papers' published with the *Chronicle*.
80. *Acts of the Privy Council*, II, 1547–50, p. 186; Nichols, *Literary Remains*, II, pp. 511–12; MacCulloch, *Tudor Church Militant*, pp. 30–2.
81. Nichols, *Literary Remains*, II, pp. 513–14; G. Townshend and S. R. Cattley eds, *The Acts and Monuments of John Foxe* (8 vols, 1837–41),VI, pp. 351–2.
82. Nichols, *Literary Remains*, II, p. 519.
83. Ibid., pp. 520–1. Edward crosses out the word 'saint' and describes George as a 'creature'.
84. Ibid., p. 522.
85. Ibid., p. 534.
86. Ibid., pp. 526, 528.
87. Ibid., p. 536.
88. Ibid., pp. 523, 531.
89. Cf. MacCulloch, *Tudor Church Militant*, pp. 32–5.
90. Nichols, *Literary Remains*, II, p. 514.
91. Ibid., I, pp. 206–8, quotation, p. 206.
92. Ibid., p. 206.
93. BL Add. MS 5464.
94. Nichols, *Literary Remains*, I, p. 173.
95. MacCulloch, *Tudor Church Militant*, pp. 26–30.
96. Ibid., p. 173; the dedication is dated the end of August, indicating that Edward had worked on the treatise for five months.
97. Nichols prints the French text. I cite the first English translation, Edward VI, *K. Edward the VIth His Own Arguments Against the Pope's Supremacy* (Wing E. 185, 1682), sigs B2–B6ᵛ.
98. Ibid., pp. 9–11, 26.
99. Ibid., p. 46.
100. Ibid., pp. 58, 61.
101. Ibid., pp. 66–7. Ezekiel 20: 18; Nichols, *Literary Remains*, I, p. 198.
102. Nichols, *Literary Remains*, I, p. 185.
103. *Edward the VIth His Own Arguments*, sig. B5.
104. Nichols, *Literary Remains*, I, p. 173; the copy is Cambridge University Library MS Dd. 12. 59.
105. Nichols, *Literary Remains*, I, pp. 173–4.
106. Jordan, *Edward VI: The Threshold of Power*, p. 26.

107. Edward VI, *A Message Sent by the Kynges Maiestie, to Certain of His People, Assembled in Deuonshire* (STC 7506, 1549).

108. See F. Rose-Troup, *The Western Rebellion of 1549* (1913); J. Sturt, *Revolt in the West: The Western Rebellion of 1549* (Exeter, 1987); P. Caraman, *The Western Rising, 1549: The Prayer Book Rebellion* (Tiverton, 1994); E. Shagan, 'Protector Somerset and the 1549 Rebellions: New Sources and New Perspectives', *English Historical Review*, 114 (1999), pp. 34–63.

109. P. Hughes and J. F. Larkin eds, *Tudor Royal Proclamations* (3 vols, New Haven, 1964–9), I, nos 337, 338, pp. 469–72.

110. *Cal. Stat. Pap. Dom, Edward, VI 1547–1553*, no. 302, p. 122, a revised edition of the first part of the *Cal. Stat. Pap. Dom. Edward VI, Mary, Elizabeth I, James I, 1547–1580*, corrects the earlier confusion. There are three copies in state papers.

111. P. F. Tytler, *England under the Reigns of Edward VI and Mary Illustrated in a Series of Original Letters* (2 vols, 1839), I, p. 182.

112. Jordan, *Chronicle*, pp. 13–15.

113. N. Pocock ed., *Troubles Connected with the Prayer Book of 1549*, p. 42.

114. Edward VI, *A Message*, sig. Aiii^v.

115. Ibid.,, sig. Avi^v.

116. Ibid., sig. Aviii.

117. Ibid., sigs Bi–Bii^v.

118. Ibid., sig. Biiii.

119. Ibid., sig. Biiii^v.

120. Ibid., sig. Bv.

121. Ibid., sigs Bvi–vii.

122. Ibid., sig. Bvii^v.

123. *Cal. Stat. Pap. Dom, Edward VI, 1547–1553*, pp. 122–4, quotation p. 122. Rose-Troup dates this answer to 24 July (*Western Rebellion*, p. 218; see appendix G, pp. 433–40).

124. Rose-Troup, *Western Rebellion*, pp. 433–4.

125. Ibid., p. 435. Henry VIII's Act of the Six Articles (1539) had upheld fundamental Catholic doctrines.

126. Rose-Troup, *Western Rebellion*, p. 436.

127. Ibid.

128. Ibid., p. 438.

129. Ibid., p. 439.

130. Ibid., pp. 439–40.

131. Rose-Troup, *Western Rebellion*, p. 218; Pocock, *Troubles Connected with the Prayer Book*, p. 42.

132. Hughes and Larkin, *Tudor Royal Proclamations*, I, no. 275, p. 381.

133. Ibid.

134. Ibid., no. 287, p. 393.

135. Ibid., nos 301 306, pp. 419, 424.

136. Ibid., nos 283, 294, 312, pp. 389–90, 408–9, 431–2.

137. Ibid., nos 294, 308, 311, pp. 409, 425–7, 430–1.

138. Ibid., no. 361, p. 495.

139. For example, ibid., nos 309, 367, pp. 427–8, 509–10.

140. 'An Exhortation Concerning Good Order and Obedience', in Thomas Cranmer, *Certayne Sermons, or Homelies Appoynted by the Kynges Maiestie, to be Declared and Redde, by All Persones, Vicars, or Curates, Euery Sondaye in their Churches, Where They Haue Cure. Anno 1547* (STC 13640, 1547), sigs Ri–Siv, quotation sig. Ri–Ri^v.

141. Hughes and Larkin, *Tudor Royal Proclamations*, I, no. 297, p. 413.

142. Thomas Cranmer, *Certayne Sermons, or Homelies* (STC 13647, 1551), sig. Aii.

143. Hughes and Larkin, *Tudor Royal Proclamations*, I, no. 303, p. 421.

144. Ibid., no. 331, p. 457.

145. Cranmer, *Certayne Sermons, or Homelies* (1547), sig. Aii.

146. Ibid., sig. Rii^v.

147. Ibid., sig. Si^v.

148. Hughes and Larkin, *Tudor Royal Proclamations*, I, no. 340, p. 474.

149. See ibid., nos 281, 329, pp. 387–9, 455–6.

150. Ibid. nos 337, 352, 371, 374, 378, pp. 469–70, 484, 514–15, 522–3, 528–9; quotation, p. 515.

151. Ibid., no. 371, p. 515.

152. Ibid., p. 517.

153. *All Such Proclamacion, As Haue Been Sette Furthe by the Kynges Maiestie* (STC 7758, 1551); *A Table To All the Statutes Made in the Tyme of the Most Victorious Reigne of Kynge Edward the Sixte* (STC 9545, 1553).

154. Cranmer's speech at the coronation of Edward VI in J. Edmund Cox ed., *Miscellaneous Writings and Letters of Thomas Cranmer* (Parker Society, Cambridge, 1846), pp. 126–7.

155. On the significance of the speech and oath see D. Hoak, 'The Coronations of Edward VI, Mary I, and Elizabeth I, and the Transformation of the Tudor Monarchy', in C. S. Knighton and R. Mortimer eds, *Westminster Abbey Reformed: 1540–1640* (Aldershot, 2003), pp. 114–51, especially pp. 146–8.

156. Ibid., pp. 126–7.

157. MacCulloch, *Tudor Church Militant*, pp. 24, 84.

158. G. Elwes Corrie ed., *Sermons of Hugh Latimer* (Parker Society, Cambridge, 1844), pp. 87–103.

159. Ibid., p. 91.

160. Ibid., p. 109.

161. Ibid., p. 215.

162. Ibid., p. 117.

163. Ibid., p. 118.

164. Ibid., p. 120.

165. Thomas Lever, *A Sermon Preached the Thyrd Sonday in Lent Before the Kynges Maiestie, and his Honorable Counsell, by Thomas Leauer* (STC 15547, 1550).

166. Ibid., sigs aiii^v, av.

167. See Alford, *Kingship and Politics*, pp. 34–43.

168. Erasmus, *The First Tome or Volume of the Paraphrase of Erasmus Vpon the Newe Testamente* (STC 2854.2, 1548), sigs Aii–bv; quotation, sig. Aii^v.

169. Ibid., sig. Aii^v.

170. Ibid., sigs Aiii, Aiv.

171. Ibid., sigs Avi^v, Bii^v.

172. Ibid., sig. Biii^v.

173. Thomas Wilson, *The Rule of Reason, Conteinyng the Arte of Logique, Set Forth in Englishe, by Thomas Wilson* (STC 25809, 1551).

174. Ibid., sig. Avi.

175. W. Patten, *The Expedicion into Scotlande of the Most Woorthely Fortunate Prince Edward, Duke of Soomerset, Uncle Unto Our Most Noble Souereign Lord ye Kinges Maiestie Edward the VI* (STC 19576.5, 1548), †iv^v.

176. Ibid., sig. Bv^v.

177. Ibid., sigs bviii, ciii^v.

178. Ibid., sig. pvi.

179. John Coke, *The Debate Betwene the Heraldes of Englande and Fraunce, Compyled by John Coke* (STC 5530, 1550)

180. Arthur Kelton, *A Chronycle with a Genealogie Declaryng that the Brittons and Welshemen are Linealiye Dyscended from Brute* (STC 14918, 1547). See W. O. Ringler,

'Arthur Kelton's Contributions to Early British History', *Huntington Library Quarterly*, 40 (1976–7), pp. 353–6.

181.   Kelton, *Chronycle*, sigs aii–aiv.

182.   Ibid., sigs aii, aiii.

183.   Ibid., sig. eii.

184.   Ibid., sig. aii^v.

185.   T. Lanquet, *An Epitome of Chronicles Conteining the Whole Discourse of the Histories As Well of This Realme of England, As All Other Countreis* (STC 15217, 1549), sigs Aii–Aiii^v.

186.   Ibid., ff. 89 ff.

187.   Ibid., f. 258^v.

188.   Ibid., ff. 270^v–271.

189.   Ibid., f. 283.

190.   Ibid., f. 291^v.

191.   *A Breuiat Cronicle Contaynynge all the Kinges from Brute to This Daye and Manye Notable Actes Gathered Oute of Diuers Cronicles from Willyam Conquerour Unto the Yere of Christ* (STC 9968, 1550), sig. Lii^v.

192.   Ibid., sigs Liii–iv.

193.   Johannes Carion, *The Thre bokes of Cronicles, Whyche John Carion . . . Gathered Wyth Great Diligence of the Beste Authours That Haue Written in Hebrue, Greke or Latine Whervnto Is Added an Appendix, Conteynyng All Such Notable Thynges As Be Mentyoned in Cronicles to Haue Chaunced in Sundry Partes of the Worlde From the Yeare of Christ. 1532. to Thys Present Yeare of. 1550* (STC 4626, 1550). Walter Lynne, a native of Antwerp, came to London in 1540 and was active in the book trade, especially in translating continental Protestant books. See Lynne, *ODNB*.

194.   Carion, *The Thre bokes of Cronicles*, sig. ccv.

195.   Ibid., sig. cclxxii.

196.   Ibid., sigs cclxxiv^v, cclxxix^v.

197.   Ibid., sig. cclxxix.

198.   Ibid., sig. cclxxiv^v.

199.   John Cheke, *The Hurt of Sedicion Howe Greueous It Is To a Commune Welth* (STC 5109, 1549). Curiously there is no modern scholarly biography of Cheke.

200.   Ibid., sig. Aiiii.

201.   Ibid., sigs Bvii^v, Cvi, Eii.

202.   Ibid., sigs Evi^v, Fiii.

203.   Ibid., sig. Fiii.

204.   Ibid., sig. Fvii.

205.   Ibid., sigs Fviii^v, Hiv.

206.   Ibid., sigs Cviii, Gvi^v, G vii^v.

207.   Crowley's publishing business was underwritten by the king's printer, Richard Grafton, but his strong anti-Catholic views pre-dated and appear independent of any official support. 'Crowley', *ODNB*.

208.   R. Crowley, *The Way to Wealth Wherein Is Plainly Taught a Most Present Remedy for Sedicion* (STC 6096, 1550), sig Av^v.

209.   Ibid., sig. Bv^v.

210.   *Ballad On the Defeat of the Devon and Cornwall Rebels of 1548* (STC 6795, 1549).

211.   Beer, *Life and Raigne*, p. 172.

212.   Cf. J.P.D. Cooper, ' "O Lorde Save the Kyng": Tudor Royal Propaganda and the Power of Prayer', in G. W. Bernard and S.J. Gunn eds, *Authority and Consent in Tudor England* (Aldershot, 2002), pp. 179–96.

213.   *A Prayer Sayd in the Kinges Chappell in the Tyme of Hys Graces Sicknes* (STC 7508, 1553). Ezechias was a strenuous religious reformer and pious king of Judah.

214.   Edward VI, *The Prayer of Kynge Edwarde the Syxte, Whiche He Made the .vi. of Iuly, Anno. M.D, Liii. and vii. of His Reygne, Thre Houres Afore His Death, To Hymself, His*

Eyes Beynge Closed, and Thynkyng None Had Heard Him (STC 7509, 1553). This publication of private prayer became an important mode of Elizabeth I's self presentation. See K. Sharpe, 'Sacralization and Demystification: The Publicisation of Monarchy in Early Modern England', in J. Deploige and G. Deneckere eds, *Mystifying the Monarch. Studies on Discourse, Power, and History* (Amsterdam, 2006), pp. 99–115; below pp. 330–3.

215. As MacCulloch suggests, Edward's lost sermon notes might have formed a complement to the diary. *Tudor Church Militant*, p. 23.
216. Jordan, *Chronicle*, pp. 32–3.
217. Ibid., p. 105.
218. *Copies of Seven Original Letters from King Edward VI to Barnaby Fitzpatrick*, p. 6.
219. Jordan, *Chronicle*, p. 57.
220. Ibid.
221. Ibid., p. 61.
222. Jordan, *Edward VI: The Threshold of Power*, p. 18.
223. Beer, *Life and Raigne*, p. 37.
224. Ibid. Roves or rovers are long-distance marks in archery.
225. *Letters . . . to Barnaby Fitzpatrick*, p. 8; Loach, *Edward VI*, pp. 153–4.
226. Loach, *Edward VI*, p. 155.
227. Soranzo's report on England, 18 August 1554, *Cal. Stat. Pap.Venetian, V, 1534–1554*, p. 535.
228. Advice sent by Scheyve, 12 May 1551, *Cal. Stat. Pap. Spanish, X, 1550–1552*, p. 293.
229. Jordan, *Chronicle*, pp. 35, 55, 66, 104; *Letters . . . to Barnaby Fitzpatrick*, p. 10.
230. Jordan, *Chronicle*, pp. 180, 188–9; cf. pp. 137–8.
231. Ibid., pp. 26, 59, 67, 119, 120.
232. Nichols, *Literary Remains*, I, p. xcii; Jordan, *Chronicle*, p. 83.
233. Jordan, *Chronicle*, p. 26.
234. Nichols, *Literary Remains*, II, p. 528.
235. Ibid., p. 346; Jordan, *Chronicle*, p. 84.
236. Beer, *Life and Raigne*, p. 144.
237. Nichols, *Literary Remains*, I, p. ccxi.
238. Jordan, *Chronicle*, p. 105
239. A. Feuillerat ed., *Documents Relating to the Revels at Court in the Time of King Edward VI and Queen Mary* (Louvain, 1914), pp. 41, 48–9, 85, 89, 116, 131, 134; for Edward's performances, see pp. 33, 47.
240. Beer, *Life and Raigne*, p. 144; Jordan, *Edward VI: Threshold of Power*, p. 99; *Cal. Stat. Pap. Spanish, X, 1550–1552*, p. 444.
241. *Cal. Stat. Pap. Spanish, 1550–52, X*, p. 444; Feuillerat, *Documents Relating to the Revels*, pp. 56, 77, 89–92.
242. Feuillerat, *Documents Relating to the Revels*, p. 89; S. Anglo, *Spectacle, Pageantry and Early Tudor Policy* (Oxford, 1969), p. 296; Loach, *Edward VI*, p. 148. 'They paraded through the court and carried, under an infamous tabernacle, a representation of the holy sacrament in its monstrance, which they wetted and perfumed in most strange fashion, with great ridicule of the ecclesiastical estate' (*Cal. Stat. Pap. Spanish, X, 1550–1552*, p. 444).
243. Nichols, *Literary Remains*, I, pp. lxxxv–lxxxvii.
244. Ibid., pp. xcv, cclxxvii, cclxxx. See also Hoak, 'Coronations', pp. 116, 122, 126 n. 45, 131–2, 133, 136, 141, 146–7.
245. Ibid., p. cclxxxi.
246. Ibid., pp. cclxxxi–ii.
247. Ibid., p. cclxxxii.
248. Ibid., pp. cclxxxiii–iv
249. Ibid., pp. cclxxxiv–vi.

250. Ibid., pp. cclxxxvi–vii. A curtana is a ceremonial sword; here it doubtless refers to the Sword of Mercy or Edward the Confessor's sword, a symbolically broken sword that is part of the traditional English regalia.
251. Ibid., p. cclxxxvii.
252. Ibid., p. cclxxxix.
253. Ibid., pp. cclxxxix–xc.
254. Ibid., p. cclxxxix.
255. Ibid., p. ccxci.
256. Ibid.
257. Anglo, *Spectacle, Pageantry*, p. 294.
258. Nichols, *Literary Remains*, I, pp. cclxxxii–iii.
259. Ibid., p. cclxxxvii.
260. Jordan, *Edward VI: The Threshold of Power*, p. 403.
261. Jordan, *Chronicle*, p. 36, 19 June 1550.
262. For example, ibid., pp. 93–4.
263. Ibid., pp. 72–3.
264. Ibid., p. 73.
265. Ibid., pp. 93–4.
266. Anglo, *Spectacle, Pageantry*, pp. 302–5.
267. *Historical Manuscripts Commission Salisbury*, I, p. 92; Jordan, *Chronicle*, p. 75; Loach, *Edward VI*, pp. 143–4.
268. Jordan, *Chronicle*, p. 13.
269. Ibid., p. 123; see pp. 137–43; *Cal. Stat. Pap. Dom. Edward VI, 1547–53*, no. 627, p. 238.
270. Jordan, *Chronicle*, pp. 137–43 *passim*.
271. Beer, *Life and Raigne*, p. 168.
272. *Letters . . . to Barnaby Fitzpatrick*, pp. 8–11.
273. Jordan, *Chronicle*, p. 137.
274. Jordan, *Edward VI: The Threshold of Power*, p. 534.
275. O. Millar, *Tudor, Stuart and Early Georgian Pictures in the Collection of Her Majesty the Queen* (1963), no. 44, pp. 64–5; K. Hearn, *Dynasties: Painting in Tudor and Jacobean England, 1530–1630* (1995), no. 13, pp. 49–50.
276. Hearn, *Dynasties*, p. 50.
277. Loach, *Edward VI*, p. 187.
278. E. Auerbach, *Tudor Artists: A Study of Painters in the Royal Service and of Portraiture on Illuminated Documents from the Accession of Henry VIII to the Death of Elizabeth I* (1954), pp. 77–8.
279. Ibid., pp. 75–6.
280. Loach, *Edward VI*, p. 188.
281. Auerbach, *Tudor Artists*, p. 81.
282. Ibid., pp. 81–3.
283. Ibid., pp. 86–7. See ibid., plate 26a.
284. Edward Hall, *The Union of the Two Noble and Illustrate Famelies of Lancastre [and] Yorke* (STC 12721, 1548); *Statutes Made in the Parliament, Begon at Westmynster, the. iiii. day of Nouember, in [the] First Yere of the Reigne of Our Most Dread Souereygne Lorde Edvvard the VI* (STC 9419, 1548); Nichols, *Literary Remains*, I, p. ccclvii; R. Luborsky and E. Ingram, *A Guide to English Illustrated Books, 1536–1603* (2 vols, Tempe, Arizona, 1998), I, p. 422, no. 1272.
285. Thomas Cranmer, *Catechismus, That Is To Say, A Shorte Instruction into Christian Religion for the Synguler Commoditie and Profyte of Children and Yong people* (STC 5993, 1548); Luborsky and Ingram, *Guide to . . . Illustrated Books*, pp. 305–6.
286. Cranmer, *Catechismus*, 'To the most excellent Prince Edward VI'.
287. John Bale, *Illustrium maioris Britanniae scriptorium* (STC 1295, 1548).

288. Luborsky and Ingram, *Guide to . . . Illustrated Books*, p. 47.

289. Alford, *Kingship and Politics*, p. 51.

290. National Portrait Gallery, no. 4165. See R. Strong, 'Edward VI and the Pope: A Tudor Anti-papal Allegory and its Setting', *Journal of the Warburg and Courtauld Institutes*, 23 (1960), pp. 311–13.

291. M. Aston, *The King's Bedpost: Reformation and Iconography in a Tudor Group Portrait* (Cambridge, 1993).

292. Hearn and Strong accepted Aston's redating (*Dynasties*, no. 31, pp. 75–6; R. Strong, *The Tudor and Stuart Monarchy: Pageantry, Painting, Iconography* (3 vols, Woodbridge, 1995), I, pp. 87–8); Loach questions Aston's case; see her review in *English Historical Review*, 111 (1996), pp. 704–5; idem, *Edward VI*, p. 187.

293. Nichols, *Literary Remains*, I, p. ccclx.

294. E. Hawkins, *Medallic Illustrations of the History of Great Britain and Ireland to the Death of George II* (19 vols, 1904–11), I, plate IV; A. Franks and H. Grueber, *Medallic Illustrations of the History of Great Britain* (2 vols, 1885) I, p. 56, no. 7; p. 57, no. 3.

295. Hawkins, *Medallic Illustrations*, I, plate IV; Franks and Grueber, *Medallic Illustrations*, I, p. 58, no. 9.

296. Ibid., I, p. 56, no. 6; Hawkins, *Medallic Illustrations*, I, plate III; Huntington Library, Richard Bull Granger Collection, II, no. 111^v.

297. J. Harvey Bloom, *English Seals* (1906), pp. 81–2; Nichols, *Literary Remains*, I, p. ccclx. An engraving of the seal can be seen in Francis Sandford, *A Genealogical History of the Kings of England and Monarchs of Great Britain* (Wing S651, 1677), p. 428.

298. Nichols, *Literary Remains*, II, pp. 534–5; above, pp. 202–3.

299. C. Challis, *The Tudor Coinage* (Manchester, 1978), p. 96. Latimer himself mocked the new debased coins, see R. Ruding, *Annals of the Coinage of Great Britain and its Dependencies, from the Earliest Period . . . to the Reign of Victoria* (3 vols, 1840), I, pp. 316–17; Jordan, *Edward VI: The Young King*, p. 396.

300. Challis, *Tudor Coinage*, p. 100.

301. Ibid., pp. 226–7, 257.

302. Hughes and Larkin, *Tudor Royal Proclamations* I, nos 321, 382; pp. 440–1, 535–6.

303. Jordan, *Chronicle*, p. 83.

304. Huntington Library, Richard Bull Granger Collection, II, no. 112.

305. Ibid. The inscription translates 'By thy cross save us, O Christ our Redeemer'.

306. Huntington Library, Richard Bull Granger Collection, II, no. 112. The references are to Proverbs 14: 27, Psalms 17: 3 and Psalms 131: 18.

307. Loach, *Edward VI*, p. 137.

308. Ibid., pp. 136–7; D. Starkey ed., *The Inventory of Henry VIII: Society of Antiquaries MS 129 and British Library MS Harley 1419* (1998), nos 3670–87, pp. 97–8.

309. D. MacCulloch, *Thomas Cranmer: A Life* (New Haven and London, 1996), part III; MacCulloch, *Tudor Church Militant*, ch. 2; Shagan, 'Confronting Compromise: The Schism and its Legacy in mid-Tudor England', in E. Shagan ed., *Catholics and the 'Protestant Nation'* (Manchester, 2005), pp. 49–68.

310. For the classic exposition of the reign as one of crisis see W. R. D. Jones, *The Mid-Tudor Crisis, 1539–63* (1973).

311. MacCulloch, *Tudor Church Militant*, pp. 106–7.

312. Hughes and Larkin, *Tudor Royal Proclamations*, I, no. 281, pp. 387–9.

313. Ibid., no. 303, pp. 421–3.

314. Ibid., no. 313, pp. 432–3.

315. Ibid., no. 329, pp. 455–6.

316. Ibid., p. 456.

317. Ibid., no. 337, p. 469.

318. Ibid., p. 469.
319. Ibid., p. 470.
320. Ibid., nos 344, 371, pp. 478–9, 517.
321. Ibid., no. 352, p. 484.
322. Ibid., no. 353, p. 485.
323. Ibid., no. 358, p. 491.
324. Ibid., no. 371, p. 517.
325. Ibid., p. 517.
326. For a study of this process see Adam Fox, *Oral and Literate Culture in England, 1500–1700* (Oxford, 2000); Ethan Shagan suggestively explores the reach of ideas of godly commonweal into popular culture. See E. Shagan, *Popular Politics and the English Reformation* (Cambridge, 2003), chs 7, 8. Cf. Shagan's discussion of the operation of rumour in the reign of Henry VIII, part II *passim*; E. Shagan, 'Rumours and Popular Politics in the Reign of Henry VIII', in T. Harris ed., *The Politics of the Excluded c. 1500–1850* (Basingstoke, 2001), pp. 30–66 and above pp. 179–80.
327. Hughes and Larkin, *Tudor Royal Proclamations*, I, no. 374, pp. 522–3.
328. Ibid., p. 523.
329. For a good discussion of the 'sites of convergence' and negotiations between the government and people, see Shagan, *Popular Politics*, p. 267 and ch. 7 *passim*.
330. MacCulloch, *Tudor Church Militant*, pp. 124–9; Shagan, *Popular Politics*, pp. 275–80.
331. Beer, *Life and Raigne*, p. 104. For a recent discussion of the Machiavellianism in Hayward's *Life*, see L.J. Richardson, 'Sir John Hayward and Early Stuart Historiography' (Cambridge University Ph.D. thesis, 1999).
332. Beer, *Life and Raigne*, p. 143.
333. Ibid., pp. 144–5.
334. Ibid., pp. 145–6.
335. Ibid., p. 145.
336. Ibid., pp. 146–8.
337. Ibid., p. 174.
338. Ibid., pp. 176–7.
339. MacCulloch, *Tudor Church Militant*, p. 18.
340. 'Mary was the single – and stubborn – impediment to all that the king wished for his realm in matters of faith', Jordan, *Edward VI: The Threshold of Power*, p. 264.
341. Ibid., pp. 253–4.
342. Ibid., p. 327.
343. Beer, *Life and Raigne*, p. 91.
344. See, for example, D. Hoak, 'Rehabilitating the Duke of Northumberland: Politics and Political Control, 1549–53', in J. Loach and R. Tittler eds, *The Mid-Tudor Polity c.1540–1560* (1980), pp. 29–51.
345. Nichols, *Literary Remains*, I, p. ccxxxiv.
346. For a later engraved portrait of Edward with inscription see ibid., p. cccliv.
347. Alford, *Kingship and Politics*, pp. 177–89 and ch. 6 *passim*.
348. W. P. Holden ed., *Beware the Cat and The Funerals of King Edward VI* (New London, Conn., 1963).
349. W. Baldwin, *The Funeralles of King Edward the Sixt Wherin Are Declared the Causers and Causes of His Death* (STC 1243, 1560).
350. Ibid., sig. Bvi.
351. Beer, *Life and Raigne*, p. 67.
352. Ibid., p. 31 and *passim*; ibid., introduction, p. 18.
353. Ibid., p. 107.
354. Ibid., pp. 66, 87.
355. Ibid., p. 169.

356.   Ibid.
357.   Ibid., p. 31.

8 Images of Mary Tudor

1.   The vilification, of course, began with Foxe's *Acts and Monuments*, the legacy of which has never quite been overcome. See D. Loades, 'The Reign of Mary Tudor: Historiography and Research', *Albion*, 21 (1989), pp. 545–58. One notes with regret that a recent study (E. Shagan ed., *Catholics and the 'Protestant Nation'*, Manchester, 2005) has no chapter on Mary and still too much perpetuates a Protestant bias.

2.   Revisionist studies of Mary began with D. Loades's *The Reign of Mary Tudor: Politics, Government, and Religion in England, 1555–1558* (1979) and J. Loach and R. Tittler eds, *The Mid-Tudor Polity, c.1540–1560* (1980). But the real revisionism followed in the wake of a radical challenge to the Protestant bias in English Reformation historiography. See, for example, C. Haigh, 'The Continuity of Catholicism in the English Reformation', *Past & Present*, 93 (1981), pp. 37–69; Haigh ed., *The English Reformation Revised* (Cambridge, 1987); Haigh, 'Revisionism, the Reformation and the History of English Catholicism', *Journal of Ecclesiastical History*, 36 (1985), pp. 394–405; idem, *English Reformations: Religion, Politics and Society under the Tudors* (Oxford, 1993); J. Bossy, *The English Catholic Community, 1570–1850* (1975); E. Duffy, *The Stripping of the Altars: Traditional Religion in England, c.1400–c.1580* (New Haven and London, 1992); Duffy, 'Mary', in P. Marshall ed., *The Impact of the English Reformation 1500–1640* (1997), pp. 192–231; and most recently and importantly, see E. Duffy and D. Loades eds, *The Church of Mary Tudor* (Aldershot, 2006).

3.   See J. Richards, 'Gender Difference and Tudor Monarchy: The Significance of Queen Mary I', *Parergon*, 21 (2004), pp. 27–46; idem, 'Mary Tudor as "Sole Quene"?: Gendering Tudor Monarchy', *Historical Journal*, 40 (1997), pp. 895–924.

4.   R. Garnett ed., *The Accession of Queen Mary, Being the Contemporary Narrative of Antonio de Guaras, A Spanish Merchant and Resident in London* (1892), pp. 87–8; D. MacCulloch ed., 'The *Vita Mariae Reginae* of Robert Wingfield of Brantham', *Camden Miscellany*, 38 (1984), p. 245.

5.   J. G. Nichols ed., *The Diary of Henry Machyn* (Camden Society, 42, 1858), p. 35; C. V. Malfatti ed., *The Accession, Coronation and Marriage of Mary Tudor As Related in Four Manuscripts of the Escorial* (Barcelona, 1956), pp. 7–8.

6.   Malfatti, *Accession, Coronation*, p. 10.

7.   MacCulloch, '*Vita Mariae*', p. 251; D. Loades, *Mary Tudor: A Life* (Oxford, 1989), p. 176.

8.   Loades, *Mary Tudor*, p. 176.

9.   Malfatti, *Accession, Coronation*, p. 8.

10.   Ibid., pp. 8–9.

11.   Garnett, *Accession of Queen Mary*, p. 88.

12.   Ibid., p. 90. Wingfield glosses over these early difficulties, MacCulloch, '*Vita Mariae*', p. 253.

13.   Garnett, *Accession of Queen Mary*, p. 90.

14.   Ibid., p. 91.

15.   J. G. Nichols ed., *The Chronicle of Queen Jane, and of Two Years of Queen Mary, and Especially of the Rebellion of Sir Thomas Wyat* (Camden Society, 48, 1850), p. 8.

16.   Again Wingfield wrote exaggerating how the Norfolk countryfolk 'everyday flocked to their rightful queen', MacCulloch, '*Vita Mariae*', p. 253.

17.   Garnett, *Accession of Queen Mary*, p. 91; MacCulloch, '*Vita Mariae*', pp. 253–5.

18.   MacCulloch, '*Vita Mariae*', p. 92.

19.   Garnett, *Accession of Queen Mary*, p. 94.

20.   MacCulloch, '*Vita Mariae*', p. 262.

21. Malfatti, *Accession, Coronation*, pp. 14–15.
22. Ibid., p. 14.
23. Ibid., pp. 14–15; MacCulloch, '*Vita Mariae*', pp. 261–2.
24. Malfatti, *Accession, Coronation*, p. 15.
25. Ibid., p. 16; MacCulloch, '*Vita Mariae*', p. 267.
26. Malfatti, *Accession, Coronation*, p. 19.
27. Ibid., p. 20; Garnett, *Accession of Queen Mary*, p. 96; Nichols, *Chronicle of Queen Jane*, p. 11; MacCulloch, '*Vita Mariae*', p. 265; P.L. Hughes and J.F. Larkin eds, *Tudor Royal Proclamations II: The Later Tudors* (3 vols, New Haven and London, 1966–9), II, no. 388, p. 3.
28. Malfatti, *Accession, Coronation*, p. 20.
29. Garnett, *Accession of Queen Mary*, p. 96.
30. Ibid.
31. Ibid.; Nichols, *Chronicle of Queen Jane*, pp. 11–12.
32. Garnett, *Accession of Queen Mary*, p. 97.
33. Nichols, *Chronicle of Queen Jane*, p. 14; MacCulloch, '*Vita Mariae*', p. 271.
34. MacCulloch, '*Vita Mariae*', p. 268.
35. Garnett, *Accession of Queen Mary*, p. 90; Loades rightly comments that 'it almost worked', *Mary Tudor* (1989), p. 183; ibid., pp. 172–3.
36. Wingfield relates the case of Lord Wentworth who after reflection, 'although he had pledged his fealty to Jane . . . his inner conscience constantly proclaimed that Mary had a greater right to the throne', MacCulloch, '*Vita Mariae*', p. 257.
37. Wingfield emphasizes the role of the people in securing Mary's succession ibid., pp. 253, 256; but, though obviously biased, he is supported in this by not only Guaras (Garnett, *Accession of Queen Mary*, p. 90) but also by Commendone (Malfatti, *Accession, Coronation*, pp. 8–9, 20). Cf. R. Tittler and S.L. Battley, 'The Local Community and the Crown in 1553: The Accession of Mary Tudor Revisited', *Bulletin of the Institute of Historical Research*, 57 (1984), pp. 131–9.
38. Malfatti, *Accession, Coronation*, p. 17.
39. Garnett, *Accession of Queen Mary*, p. 98.
40. Cf. Tittler and Battley, 'Local Community', p. 139.
41. The proclamation of Jane, as well as observing that their claims to the throne ended with their father's divorces, referred to the danger of Mary or Elizabeth marrying a foreign Catholic prince: 'And forasmuch also as it is to be thought, or at the least, much to be doubted, that if the said lady Mary, or lady Elizabeth should hereafter have and enjoy the said imperial crown of this realm and should then happen to marry with any stranger born out of this realm, that then the same Stranger having the government and the imperial crown in his hands, would adhere and practise, not onely to bring this noble free realm, into the tyranny and servitude of the Bishop of Rome, but also to have the laws and customs of his or their own native country . . . to be practised, and put in use within this realm, rather than the laws, statutes, and customs here of long time used'. *Jane, by the Grace of God Quene of England, Fraunce and Ireland, Defendor of the Faith, & of the Church of Englande* (STC 7846, 1553).
42. Nichols, *Diary of Henry Machyn*, p. 37.
43. 'Her majesty, now on foot, went round both divisions of the army speaking to them with exceptional kindness and with an approach so wonderfully relaxed as can scarcely be described . . . that she completely won everyone's affections', MacCulloch, '*Vita Mariae*', p. 265.
44. Penry Williams, *The Tudor Regime* (Oxford, 1979), ch. 11; E. Shagan, *Popular Politics and the English Reformation* (Cambridge, 2003).
45. Nichols, *Chronicle of Queen Jane*, p. 14.
46. Loades, *Mary Tudor* (1989), pp. 186–7.
47. *Cal. Stat. Pap. Spanish, XI, 1553*, p. 124.

48. Ibid., p. 129.
49. Ibid., pp. 130–1.
50. Ibid., p. 131.
51. Ibid., p. 132.
52. Ibid., pp. 134–5.
53. Loades, *Mary Tudor* (1989), p. 43.
54. F. Madden ed., *Privy Purse Expenses of the Princess Mary* (1831), p. cxxvii; see appendix II, clxxiii–iv.
55. The translation is in A. Prescott ed., *The Early Modern Englishwoman: A Facsimile of Essential Works Vol. 5: Elizabeth and Mary Tudor* (Aldershot, 2001). For the prayers, see J. Strype, *Ecclesiastical Memorials Relating Chiefly to Religion and the Reformation of It and the Emergencies of the Church of England, under King Henry, King Edward VI and Queen Mary the First . . .* (3 vols, 1733), III, pp. 288–90.
56. D. Loades, *Two Tudor Conspiracies* (Cambridge, 1965), pp. 59–62.
57. Ibid., p. 66.
58. The best account of the speech is in Malfatti, *Accession, Coronation*, part II, pp. 66–8; quotation, p. 66.
59. Ibid., p. 67.
60. Ibid.
61. Ibid.
62. Ibid., p. 68.
63. Ibid.
64. Ibid.
65. J. Proctor, *The Historie of Wyates Rebellion* (STC 20427, 1554), sig. Gvi; see below, p. 336.
66. Malfatti, *Accession, Coronation*, p. 68.
67. Paulina Kewes rightly notes the similarities between Marian and Elizabethan modes of representation. See P. Kewes, 'Two Queens: One Inventory', in K. Sharpe and S. Zwicker eds, *Writing Lives: Biography and Textuality, Identity and Representation in Early Modern England* (Oxford 2008), pp. 187–207.
68. Ibid., p. 68.
69. Proctor, *Historie of Wyates Rebellion*, sig. Gvi[v].
70. Ibid., sig. D1[v].
71. Ibid., sig.Gii[v].
72. Hughes and Larkin, *Tudor Royal Proclamations*, II, no. 388, p. 3.
73. Ibid., no. 390, pp. 5–6, my italics.
74. Ibid., p. 6. The words echo Henry VIII's own admonition to his subjects to avoid calling each other names.
75. Ibid., no. 391, pp. 8–9.
76. Ibid., no. 392, pp. 9–10.
77. Ibid., no. 396, p. 18.
78. Ibid., no. 398, pp. 21–6.
79. Ibid., p. 25.
80. Ibid., no. 399, p. 26.
81. Ibid.
82. Ibid., no. 401, p. 28.
83. Ibid., no. 402, p. 29.
84. Ibid., no. 497, pp. 35–8, quotation, p. 36; Nichols, *Diary of Machyn*, p. 50.
85. Hughes and Larkin, *Tudor Royal Proclamations*, II, p. 35.
86. Ibid., no. 417, pp. 48–9.
87. Ibid., nos 422, 443, pp. 57–60, 90–1.
88. See J. Loach, *Parliament and the Crown in the Reign of Mary Tudor* (Oxford, 1986).

89. Hughes and Larkin, *Tudor Royal Proclamations*, II, no. 403, pp. 30–1.

90. J. Seton, *Panegyrici in Victoriam illustrissimae. D. Mariae, Angliae, Franciae, & Hiberniae Reginae, &c. item in coronationem eiusdem sereniss. reginae, congratulatio* (STC 22258, 1553).

91. Ibid., sig. Ci.

92. Ibid., sig. Biii^v.

93. Ibid., sigs Biv, Cii.

94. Ibid., sigs Aiii, Ci, Ciii^v.

95. R. Beeard, *A Godly Psalme of Marye Queene Which Brought Us Comfort Al* (STC 1655, 1553). No pagination; see verses 30–5.

96. Ibid., verse 28.

97. Ibid., verses 29, 31.

98. Ibid., verse 34.

99. Ibid., verse 42.

100. 'Richard Beeard', *ODNB*.

101. The author and printer both freely announced themselves, as though not expecting the psalm to cause discontent.

102. Beeard, *Godly Psalme*, verses 10, 28, 32.

103. Ibid., verses 8, 34.

104. L. Stopes, *An Ave Maria In Commendation of Our Most Vertuous Queene* (STC 23292, ?1553).

105. For the story of Hester and Haman, see the Book of Esther, ch.7. There was an anonymous Tudor interlude of *Godly Queen Hester* which has been dated to the 1520s. See G. Walker, *Plays of Persuasion* (Cambridge, 1991), ch. 4, pp. 101–32. For Judith and Holofernes, see Judith 13: 9.

106. W. Forrest, *A Newe Ballade of the Marigolde* (STC11186, ?1553).

107. 'Forrest', *DNB* and *ODNB*. Forrest also wrote for the queen a long metrical account of the life of her mother, Catherine of Aragon, which he called *The History of Grisild the Second.*

108. A. Junius, *Philippeis, seu, In nuptias diui Philippi, aug. pii, max. & heroinae Mariae aug. felicis, inuictae, Regum Angliae, Franciae, Neapolis, Hierosolymorum, & Hiberniae, fidei defensorum* (STC 14861, 1554). The poem was published by Thomas Berthelet 'cum privilegio'.

109. Ibid., sigs Aii^v–Aiii.

110. Ibid., sig. Bi.

111. Ibid., sig. Aiiii. 'And also joins both peoples in a stable alliance'.

112. Ibid., sig. Ci^v.

113. Ibid., sig. Dii^v.

114. 'Admonitio ad aequum lectorem', ibid., sig. Div^v.

115. J. Heywood, *Balade Specifienge Partly the Maner, Partly the Matter, In the Most Excellent Meetyng and Lyke Mariage Betwene Our Soueraigne Lord, and Our Soueraigne Lady, the Kynges and Queenes Highnes* (STC 13290.3, 1554).

116. 'William Riddell', *DNB*. Riddell was dropped from the *ODNB*.

117. I am grateful to Greg Walker for pointing out the continuity of Heywood's service to Mary.

118. J. Cancellar, *The Pathe of Obedience Righte Necessarye For All the King and Quenes Maiesties Louing Subiectes, to Reade, Learne, and Use Their Due Obediences, to the Hyghe Powers* (STC 4564, ?1556).

119. Ibid., sigs Aiii^v–Aviii^v, quotation, sig. Aiiii.

120. Ibid., sig. Ciii.

121. Ibid., sig. Cv.

122. Ibid., sigs Dviii–Eii.

123. Ibid., sigs Cvii^v, Evi^v.

124. J. Christopherson, *An Exhortation to All Menne to Take Hede and Beware of Rebellion Wherein Are Set Forth the Causes That Commonlye Moue Men to Rebellion, and That No Cause Is There That Ought to Moue Any Man There Unto. With a Discourse of the Miserable Effectes that Ensue Thereof, and of the Wretched Ende that All Rebelles Comme to* (STC 5207, 1554).

125. Ibid., sig. Av^v.

126. ibid., sigs Avi^v–Avii, Bv^v–vi^v, Hvii^v.

127. Ibid., sigs Bvii, Cii^v, Ciiii.

128. Ibid., sigs Dii–iii.

129. Ibid., sig. Fi^v.

130. ibid., sigs Hiiii, Hvii^v, Iiii.

131. Ibid., sigs Iv^v–vi.

132. Ibid., sigs Li–ii^v.

133. Ibid., sigs Liv^v, vi^v.

134. Ibid., sigs Mviii–Ni.

135. Ibid., sig Oiiii.

136. Ibid., sigs Ovi^v, Ovii^v.

137. Ibid., sig. Ovi^v.

138. ibid., sig. Riiii.

139. Ibid., sigs Uviii and Ui–viii *passim*.

140. Ibid., sig. DDi^v.

141. Ibid., sigs DDvi, EEvii.

142. Ibid., sigs FFii–FFiii.

143. Ibid., sig. Riii.

144. See above, note 65.

145. Proctor, *Historie of Wyates Rebellion*, sig. av.

146. Ibid., sigs avi–viii.

147. Ibid., sig. Dvii^v.

148. Ibid., sigs Ei, Gii^v.

149. Ibid., sigs Lii, Gv^v–vi^v; above, pp. 252–3.

150. Ibid., sigs Ki–ii.

151. Ibid., sig. Kiiii.

152. Ibid., sig. Li^v.

153. Ibid., sig. Lv.

154. Ibid., sig. Mii.

155. Ibid., sig. Miiii.

156. Ibid., sig. Kvii^v.

157. Ibid., sig. Kvii.

158. Madden, *Privy Purse Expenses*, p. xci.

159. Ibid., p. clxxv.

160. Ibid., pp. cliiii–v.

161. K. Hearn, *Dynasties: Painting in Tudor and Jacobean England* (1995), p. 47. We recall the comments about the gloomy Christmas when Catherine of Aragon and her ladies were absent, above, Chapter 5, p. 170.

162. Madden, *Privy Purse Expenses*, pp. clv–vi.

163. Ibid., p. clvi.

164. Ibid., appendix III, pp. clxxv–vii

165. Hearn, *Dynasties*, p. 63.

166. Ibid., p. 66.

167. J. Woodall, 'An Exemplary Consort: Antonis Mor's Portrait of Mary Tudor', *Art History*, 14 (1991), pp. 192–224. See E. Drey, 'The Portraits of Mary I, Queen of England' (MA thesis, Courtauld Institute, 1990), pp. 33–50. The pendant may be a reliquary.

168. Courtauld B62/172. See *Country Life*, 13 June 1963, pp. 1,383–4.

169. Courtauld B56/185.

170. Woodall, 'Exemplary Consort', pp. 198–201; Hearn, *Dynasties*, p. 54.

171. Hearn, *Dynasties*, p. 54.

172. Woodall, 'Exemplary Consort', pp. 210–11.

173. 'He [Mor] copied the head of this queen ... a number of times on small panels, which he gave to great men', report of Van Mander, quoted by Woodall, ibid., p. 197.

174. P. Hendy, *The Isabella Stewart Gardner Museum Catalogue of the Exhibited Paintings and Drawings* (Boston, 1931), pp. 243–7.

175. Woodall, 'Exemplary Consort', p. 201; below, pp. 292–5.

176. L. Cust, 'The Painter HE (Hans Eworth)', *Walpole Society*, 2 (1913), p. 25 and plate VIII B.

177. Madden, *Privy Purse Expenses*, p. clxi.

178. Ibid., p. clxii, 'She to whom I the most excellent God allow to triumph over her enemies to rule the British people with righteous governance'.

179. J. King, *Tudor Royal Iconography: Literature and Art in an Age of Religious Crisis* (Princeton, 1989), pp. 191–2.

180. *The Lame[n]tacion of England* (STC 10015, 1558), pp. 7–8.

181. King, *Tudor Royal Iconography*, p. 116.

182. Ibid., p. 185. The image is reproduced as fig. 58.

183. Ibid., p. 219.

184. J. Heywood, *The Spider and the Flie: A Parable of the Spider and the Flie* (STC 13308, 1556). The series of nine woodcuts depicting Mary as God's handmaid who kills the (Protestant) spiders who have preyed on the (Catholic) flies commences at sig. Nniiii.

185. Ibid., sig. Qqii.

186. Beeard, *Godly Psalme* (Trinity College, Cambridge copy), sig. F.

187. Ibid., sigs Aiiii and full title.

188. E. Auerbach, *Tudor Artists: A Study of Painters in the Royal Service and of Portraiture on Illuminated Documents from the Accession of Henry VIII to the Death of Elizabeth I* (1954), p. 96 and plate 28.

189. Ibid., p. 98, plate 29.

190. Ibid., p. 99, plate 31.

191. Ibid.

192. See ibid., plates 32, 33.

193. *The Huntington Papers: Part I* (1926), p. 115. I owe my knowledge of this work to the kindness of Mary Robertson.

194. J. Harvey Bloom, *English Seals* (1906), p. 82.

195. Ibid., pp. 41, 83. This seal is illustrated in F. Sandford, *A Genealogical History of the Kings and Queens of England and Monarchs of Great Britain, &c. From the Conquest Anno 1066. to the Year 1707* (1707), p. 459.

196. See Huntington Library, Richard Bull Granger Collection, II, no. 147.

197. Franks and Grueber, *Medallic Illustrations*, I, p. 72, no. 20; pp. 73–4, nos 21, 22. See E. Hawkins, *Medallic Illustrations of the History of Great Britain* (1904–11), plate V.

198. Franks and Grueber, *Medallic Illustrations*, I, p.80, no. 37; Huntington Library, Richard Bull Granger Collection, II, no. 147. The legend reads 'For law, king and people' (literally 'crowd' or 'flock', with all its allusions to the ruler as good shepherd). Another (Franks and Grueber, *Medallic Illustrations*, I, p. 80, no. 38) figures Philip II as a pelican feeding its young, a favourite image of Elizabeth I.

199. Franks and Grueber, *Medallic Illustrations*, I, pp. 71–2, nos 17–19; 'Love preserves unity'.

200. Ibid., p. 74, no. 22.

201. C. Challis, *The Tudor Coinage* (Manchester, 1978), pp. 110–13, 116.
202. Ibid., p. 112; Malfatti, *Accession, Coronation*, p. 76; Huntington Library, Richard Bull Granger Collection II, no. 146ᵛ.
203. The legend is from Psalm 118: 23, 'This is the Lord's doing; it is marvellous in our eyes'.
204. 'We have made God our helper' The reference is perhaps to Psalm 17:3, Psalm 51:9 or Psalm 52:7.
205. Auerbach, *Tudor Artists*, p. 91; C. Hope, 'Titian, Philip II and Mary Tudor,' in E. Chaney and P. Mack eds, *England and the Continental Renaissance* (Woodbridge, 1990), pp. 53–65.
206. Christopherson, *An Exhortation*, sig. Viii.
207. Ibid.
208. King, *Tudor Royal Iconography*, p. 136; cf. pp. 184, 186.
209. Richards, 'Gender Difference'.
210. J. Murphy, 'The Illusion of Decline: The Privy Chamber, 1547–1558', in D. Starkey ed., *The English Court from the Wars of the Roses to the Civil War* (1987), pp. 141–6.
211. Madden, *Privy Purse Expenses*, pp. cxli, cxliii; Loades, *Mary Tudor* (1989), p. 119.
212. Madden, *Privy Purse Expenses*, pp. cxli–ii.
213. Ibid., p. cxlix.
214. Ibid., p. cx; above pp. 195–6.
215. ibid., p. cxi.
216. Murphy, 'Illusion of Decline', pp. 140–1.
217. Nichols, *Diary of Henry Machyn*, p. 79.
218. Ibid., pp. 80, 83.
219. Ibid., p. 84.
220. G. Douglas, *The Palis of Honoure Compyled by Gawayne Dowglas Byshope of Dunkyll* (STC 7073, 1553).
221. A. Young, *Tudor and Jacobean Tournaments* (1987), p. 30.
222. Malfatti, *Accession, Coronation*, p. 43. The words pre-empt what Elizabeth was reported as saying at Tilbury.
223. A. Feuillerat ed., *Documents Relating to the Revels at Court in the Time of King Edward VI and Queen Mary* (Louvain, 1914).
224. Ibid., p. 149.
225. Ibid., pp. 161, 164, 176, 184, 189.
226. Ibid., p. 181.
227. Ibid., pp. 166, 172, 225.
228. Ibid., pp.166, 172, 188.
229. 'Udall', *DNB* and *ODNB*.
230. G. Walker, *The Politics of Performance in Early Renaissance Drama* (Cambridge, 1998), ch. 5, pp. 163–95.
231. Feuillerat, *Documents*, pp. 149, 194, 289.
232. Eg. ibid., pp. 225, 226, 237.
233. Nichols, *Diary of Henry Machyn*, p. 61.
234. Garnett, *Accession of Queen Mary*, p. 100.
235. Nichols, *Diary of Henry Machyn*, pp. 39–40.
236. Above, pp. 48–51.
237. Nichols, *Diary of Henry Machyn*, p. 45.
238. Garnett, *Accession of Queen Mary*, pp. 115–19.
239. Ibid., p. 119.
240. Nichols, *Diary of Henry Machyn*, p. 45.
241. Malfatti, *Accession, Coronation*, p. 31.
242. The description is from Commendone, ibid., p. 32. The inscription praises Mary's renowned virtue and piety.

243. Ibid.
244. S. Anglo, *Spectacle, Pageantry and Early Tudor Policy* (Oxford, 1969), pp. 320–1.
245. Nichols, *Chronicle of Queen Jane*, pp. 29–30; Anglo, *Spectacle, Pageantry*, p. 321.
246. Nichols, *Chronicle of Queen Jane*, p. 30.
247. Garnett, *Accession of Queen Mary*, p. 120.
248. Ibid., p. 118.
249. Malfatti, *Accession, Coronation*, p. 33.
250. Nichols, *Chronicle of Queen Jane*, p. 31; Malfatti, *Accession, Coronation*, pp. 32–3; Garnett, *Accession of Queen Mary*, p. 120; J. R. Planche, *Regal Records : Or A Chronicle of the Coronation of the Queens Regnant of England* (1888), pp. 1–33.
251. Nichols, *Chronicle of Queen Jane*, p. 31; Garnett, *Accession of Queen Mary*, pp. 120–1.
252. Malfatti, *Accession, Coronation*, p. 153; see also, R. McCoy, ' "The Wonderful Spectacle": The Civic Progress of Elizabeth I and the Troublesome Coronation', in J. M. Bak ed., *Coronations: Medieval and Early Modern Monarchic Ritual* (Berkeley, 1990), pp. 218–19.
253. Nichols, *Chronicle of Queen Jane*, p. 31.
254. Nichols, *Diary of Henry Machyn*, pp. 45–6; Garnett, *Accession of Queen Mary*, p. 123.
255. Garnett, *Accession of Queen Mary*, p. 123.
256. Printed in Malfatti, *Accession, Coronation*, p. 82.
257. Ibid.
258. Ibid., pp. 82–3.
259. Ibid., pp. 83–4; J. Elder, *The Copie of a Letter Sent in to Scotlande of the Arivall and Landynge and Most Noble Marryage of . . . Philippe, Prynce of Spaine to the . . . Princes Marye Quene of England* (STC 7552, 1555), sig. Aiv^v.
260. Nichols, *Chronicle of Queen Jane*, appendix, p. 168.
261. Malfatti, *Accession, Coronation*, p. 85; Commendone twice compared the dais to a pulpit, ibid., pp. 51, 52. See A. Samson, 'Changing Places: The Marriage and Royal Entry of Philip, Prince of Austria, and Mary Tudor, July–August 1554', *Sixteenth Century Journal*, 36 (2005), pp. 762–3.
262. Malfatti, *Accession, Coronation*, p. 85; Nichols, *Chronicle of Queen Jane*, p. 168; Elder, *Copie of a Letter*, sig. Avi^v.
263. Elder, *Copie of a Letter*, sig. Avii.
264. Ibid., sig. Avii^v. Philip laid coins on the mass book, Malfatti, *Accession, Coronation*, p. 59.
265. Malfatti, *Accession, Coronation*, p. 87. Scholars adorned the palace doors with verses celebrating the marriage, Elder, *Copie of a Letter*, sig. Bii.
266. Malfatti, *Accession, Coronation*, p. 61. An account describes on one side of the hall 'a cupboard that reached the ceiling, full of vessels of gold and silver, more than a hundred and twenty of them', ibid., pp. 87–8.
267. Samson, 'Changing Places', p. 765; Malfatti, *Accession, Coronation*, p. 87.
268. Malfatti, *Accession, Coronation*, p. 88.
269. Elder, *Copie of a Letter*, sig. Bi.
270. Ibid., sigs Biii–iv.
271. Nichols, *Chronicle of Queen Jane*, p. 34. Another example of the 'weapons of the weak' and the opportunity presented even by rituals of encomium for protest.
272. Anglo, *Spectacle, Pageantry*, p. 326.
273. Elder, *Copie of a Letter*, sig. Bv.
274. Ibid., sig. Bvi^v; Nichols, *Chronicle of Queen Jane*, p. 78.
275. Nichols, *Chronicle of Queen Jane*, p. 79.
276. Ibid., pp. 78 n., 79; BL. Harleian MS 419 f. 131.
277. Elder, *Copie of a Letter*, sigs Bvi^v–vii; Nichols, *Chronicle of Queen Jane*, p. 80.
278. Nichols, *Chronicle of Queen Jane*, p. 80.
279. Elder, *Copie of a Letter*, sig. Bvii.
280. Nichols, *Chronicle of Queen Jane*, p. 147.

281. Elder, *Copie of a Letter*, sig. Bvii^v.
282. Ibid., sig. Bviii.
283. Anglo, *Spectacle, Pageantry*, p. 333.
284. Nichols, *Chronicle of Queen Jane*, p. 80.
285. Ibid.; Elder, *Copie of a Letter*, sigs Bviii^v–Ci^v.
286. Nichols, *Chronicle of Queen Jane*, p. 149; Anglo, *Spectacle, Pageantry*, p. 334 n. 3, citing S. R. Cattley and G. Townsend eds, John Foxe, *Acts and Monuments* (8 vols, 1837–41), VI, p. 558.
287. Elder, *Copie of a Letter*, sig. Ci^v.
288. Ibid.
289. Ibid.
290. Ibid., sig. Cii^v.
291. Ibid., sig. Ciii.
292. Ibid., sigs Ciii–iii^v; Anglo, *Spectacle, Pageantry*, p. 336.
293. Elder, *Copie of a Letter*, sig.Ciii^v–iv.
294. Ibid., sig. Civ.
295. Ibid., sig. Civ^v.
296. *Cal. Stat. Pap. Spanish, XIII, 1554–8*, no. 53, p. 43.
297. Elder, *Copie of a Letter*, sig. Cvi; Nichols, *Diary of Henry Machyn*, p. 74.
298. Elder, *Copie of a Letter*, sig. Cvi^v–vii^v.
299. Ibid., sig. Dvi^v.
300. Ibid., sigs Di^v–Ei.
301. Ibid., sig. Dvii^v.
302. Ibid., sig. Ev^v.
303. Ibid., sigs Evi–Fi, quotation Fi.
304. Ibid., sigs Evii, Fv.
305. Ibid., sig. Evii.
306. Nichols, *Diary of Henry Machyn*, p. 85.
307. Ibid., p. 137.
308. Ibid., p.159.
309. Ibid., pp. 59, 163,
310. Ibid., p. 49.
311. Ibid., p. 145.
312. Ibid., p. 146.
313. Madden, *Privy Purse Expenses*, p. cxliii.
314. Nichols, *Diary of Henry Machyn*, pp. 110, 114, 139, 168.
315. Ibid., pp. 93, 128, 142; *Cal. Stat. Pap. Dom. Mary I, 1553–8*, nos 205, 643, pp. 103, 290.
316. Nichols, *Diary of Henry Machyn*, p. 92.
317. Madden, *Privy Purse Expenses*, pp. liv, cxlix; Hughes and Larkin, *Tudor Royal Proclamations*, II, no. 392, pp. 9–10; Nichols, *Chronicle of Queen Jane*, p. 26; Malfatti, *Accession, Coronation*, pp. 37, 41, 68; Garnett, *Accession of Queen Mary*, p. 97.
318. Madden, *Privy Purse Expenses*, p. 10.
319. Malfatti, *Accession, Coronation*, pp. 97, 101.
320. Hughes and Larkin, *Tudor Royal Proclamations*, II, no. 390, pp. 5–8, quotation, p. 6.
321. Ibid., p. 5.
322. Ibid., no. 393.5, p. 12.
323. Nichols, *Diary of Henry Machyn*, p. 41; M. Maclure, *The Paul's Cross Sermons, 1534–1642* (Toronto, 1958), pp. 49–50.
324. J. Brooks, *A Sermon Very Notable, Fruicteful and Godlie Made at Paules Crosse the XII Daie of Noue[m]bre* (STC 3839, 15540).
325. Ibid., sig. Biv^v.
326. Ibid., sigs Cv, Cvii^v.

327. Ibid., sigs Cviii^v, Eiv–vii and *passim*.

328. Maclure, *Paul's Cross Sermons*, p. 198.

329. Nichols, *Chronicle of Queen Jane*, p. 54.

330. Christopherson, *An Exhortation*, sig. Rvi.

331. Nichols, *Diary of Henry Machyn*, pp. 69, 131.

332. *An Uniforme and Catholyke Prymer in Latin and Englishe, With Many Godly and Deuout Prayers, Newly Set Forth by Certayne of the Cleargye With the Assente of the Moste Reuerende Father in God the Lorde Cardinall Pole Hys Grace* (STC 16060, 1555).

333. J. Old, *The Acquital or Purgation of the Moost Catholyke Christen Prince, Edwarde the VI. Kyng of Englande, Fraunce, and Irelande &c. and of the Churche of Englande Refourmed and Gouerned Under Hym, Agaynst al Suche as Blasphemously and Traitorously Infame Hym or the Sayd Church, of Heresie or Sedicion* (STC 18797, 1555), sig. A4.

334. Ibid., sigs D3–E4.

335. Nichols, *Diary of Henry Machyn*, pp. 66–7.

336. Nichols, *Chronicle of Queen Jane*, pp. 82–3.

337. Hughes and Larkin, *Tudor Royal Proclamations*, no. 417 p. 48; above p. 297.

338. Nichols, *Diary of Henry Machyn*, p. 78.

339. Ibid., p. 80.

340. Ibid., pp. 84, 98.

341. Ibid., p.107.

342. Ibid., pp. 73, 79, 100, 101.

343. E.g. Hughes and Larkin, *Tudor Royal Proclamations*, II, no. 422, pp. 57–60.

344. Nichols, *Chronicle of Queen Jane*, p. 54.

345. Ibid., p. 25.

346. Garnett, *Accession of Queen Mary*, p. 101.

347. Ibid; W.K. Jordan and M.R. Gleason, 'The Saying of John Late Duke of Northumberland upon the Scaffold, 1553', *Harvard Library Bulletin*, 23 (1975), pp. 139–79.

348. Jordan and Gleason 'Northumberland', pp. 169–70.

349. Nichols, *Chronicle of Queen Jane*, p. 19

350. Jordan and Gleason, 'Northumberland', pp. 171–2.

351. Nichols, *Chronicle of Queen Jane*, pp. 18–19.

352. Malfatti, *Accession, Coronation*, p. 28.

353. Garnett, *Accession of Queen Mary*, p. 105.

354. Ibid.

355. Ibid., p. 107; *The Saying of John Late Duke of Northumberlande Uppon the Scaffolde at the Tyme of His Execution The. XXII. of Auguste* (STC 7283, 1553)(no pagination). See Jordan and Gleason, 'Northumberland', p. 174; and idem, 'The Saying of John Late Duke Northumberland', part II, *Harvard Library Bulletin*, 23 (1975), pp. 324–55, on accounts of the speech.

356. Garnett, *Accession of Queen Mary*, p. 108.

357. Malfatti, *Accession, Coronation*, p. 30.

358. Garnett, *Accession of Queen Mary*, p. 109.

359. Jordan and Gleason, 'Northumberland', part II, pp. 525, 353 and *passim*. The authors note the curious rarity of surviving copies of the official English edition (pp. 325–6).

360. See Loades, *Two Tudor Conspiracies*.

361. Nichols, *Chronicle of Queen Jane*, p. 63.

362. Ibid., p. 64.

363. Ibid., pp. 56–7.

364. See, for example, Foxe's account in Cattley and Townsend, *The Acts and Monuments of John Foxe*, VI, pp. 415–25.

365. Nichols, *Chronicle of Queen Jane*, pp. 69–70; T J. Howell ed., *Cobbett's Complete Collection of State Trials* (33 vols, 1816–28), I, pp. 861–70.

366. Nichols, *Chronicle of Queen Jane*, p. 69.
367. Ibid., pp. 72–3.
368. Ibid., p. 73.
369. Ibid.; cf. Proctor, *Historie of Wyates Rebellion*, sigs Kiiii–vi.
370. Nichols, *Chronicle of Queen Jane*, p. 74.
371. Ibid.
372. Nichols, *Diary of Henry Machyn*, p. 60.
373. Proctor, *Historie of Wyates Rebellion*, sigs Kiiii–vi.
374. For the report of François de Nouailles, see E. H. Harbison, *Rival Ambassadors at the Court of Queen Mary* (Oxford, 1940), p. 138, n. 2; Nichols, *Chronicle of Queen Jane*, p. 74.
375. *Cal. Stat. Pap. Venetian, VI, 1555–6*, no. 116, p. 94.
376. Harbison, *Rival Ambassadors*, p. 224; Loades, *Mary Tudor* (1989), p. 305.
377. Malfatti, *Accession, Coronation*, p. 49.
378. Proctor, *Historie of Wyates Rebellion*, sig. Bvii^v.
379. Malfatti, *Accession, Coronation*, p. 71.
380. Christopherson, *An Exhortation*, sig. Bvii.
381. Cancellar, *Pathe of Obedience*, sig. Cv.
382. Hughes and Larkin, *Tudor Royal Proclamations*, II, nos 389, 446, pp. 4, 93.
383. Ibid., p. 6; Malfatti, *Accession, Coronation*, p. 149.
384. In April 1554, the Danzig magistrates wrote to Queen Mary enclosing a libel against her and King Philip. The libel had been printed by order of an Englishman and hundreds of copies had been sent back to England. *Cal. Stat. Pap. Foreign, Mary, 1533–58*, no. 238, p. 105.
385. Hughes and Larkin, *Tudor Royal Proclamations*, II, no. 410, p. 41.
386. Nichols, *Diary of Henry Machyn*, pp. 42, 63, 64, 69, 71, 75, 150, 164.
387. Hughes and Larkin, *Tudor Royal Proclamations*, II, no. 466, p. 94.
388. *A Warnyng for Englande Conteynyng the Horrible Practises of the Kyng of Spayne, in the Kyngdome of Naples, and the Miseries Wherunto that Noble Realme Is Brought. Wherby All Englishe Men May Understand the Plage That shall Light Upon Them, Yf the Kyng of Spayn Obteyne the Dominion in Englande* (STC 10024, ?1555).
389. Ibid., sigs A2–6^v *passim*.
390. Ibid., sig. A7.
391. Ibid., sig. A8.
392. *A Trewe Mirrour Or Glase Wherin We Maye Beholde the Wofull State of Thys Our Realme of Englande Set Forth in a Dialogue or Communicacion Betwene Eusebius and Theophilus* (STC 21777, 1556). The work has been attributed to the martyr Laurence Sanders but the attribution seems unlikely.
393. Ibid., sig. Aviii^v.
394. Ibid., sigs Aviii, Bi.
395. Ibid., sigs Av^v, Bv.
396. J. Bradford, *The Copye of a Letter Sent by Iohn Bradforth to . . . the Erles of Arundel, Darbie, Shrewsburye, and Pembroke, Declaring the Nature of the Spaniardes, and Discovering the Most Detestable Treasons, Which Thei Haue Pretended . . . Agaynste . . . Englande* (STC 3504.5, 1555), sigs Aii–iv. On Bradford, see *ODNB*.
397. Ibid., sig. Ciii^v.
398. Ibid., sigs Cii, Cv, Gv^v.
399. Ibid., sig. Eiii.
400. Ibid., sig. Fiiii.
401. Ibid., sig. Dvi.
402. Wolfgang Musculus, *The Temporysour (That Is To Saye: The Obseruer of Tyme, Or He That Chaungeth With the Tyme.)*(STC 18312, 1555), sigs Aii, Aiv^v. The translator was Robert Pownall, an exile who was obviously drawn to what Andrew Pettegree describes as 'a work entirely typical of this phase of the exile, an admonition to those

true Christians who had remained behind in England to abandon their temporizing or "Nicodemism" and join the exodus abroad'. 'Parnell', *ODNB*.

403. R. Parnell, *An Admonition To the Towne of Callays* (STC 19078, 1557), no pagination. For the story of Athalia, see II Kings: 1–20.

404. Old, *The Acquital*, sig. A2 and *passim*.

405. Nichols, *Diary of Henry Machyn*, p. 59.

406. Ibid., p. 60.

407. Ibid., p. 86.

408. Ibid., p. 82.

409. Ibid., pp. 86–8.

410. Ibid., pp. 88, 101.

411. S. Gardiner, *De vera obedientia An Oration Made in Latine by the Ryghte Reuerend Father in God Stephan B. of VVinchestre, Nowe Lord Chauncellour of England, With the Preface of Edmunde Boner . . . Touching True Obedience* (STC 11586, 1553). Gardiner's loyal defence of the Henrician supremacy was first published in 1535.

412. Ibid., sigs Aii–vii.

413. Ibid., sig. Bii.

414. Ibid., sigs Lix–Lx^v. For advice on the power of the whore as a signifier, I am grateful to Dr Alexandra Lumbers.

415. W. Lauder, *Ane Compendious and Breue Tractate, Concernyng ye Office and Dewtie of Kyngis, Spirituall Pastoris, and Temporall Jugis* (STC 15314, 1556). On Lauder, see *ODNB*.

416. *Certayne Questions Demaunded and Asked by the Noble Realme of Englande, Of Her True Naturall Chyldren and Subiectes Of the Same* (STC 9981, 1555). Though it is described on the title page as 'Imprinted at London', it was almost certainly printed abroad and smuggled in; cf. note 384 above.

417. Ibid., sig. Aii.

418. Ibid., sig. Aii^v.

419. Ibid., sig. Aiii.

420. Ibid.

421. Ibid., sig. Aiii^v.

422. Ibid., sigs. Aiv–iv^v.

423. Ibid., sig. Bi.

424. Ibid., sig. Bi^v.

425. Ibid., sig. Bii.

426. Ibid., sig. Aiv.

427. Ibid., sig. Bi.

428. Ibid., sig. Aiv^v.

429. Ibid., sig. Bii^v.

430. Ibid.

431. J. Ponet, *A Shorte Treatise of Politike Pouuer and Of the True Obedience Which Subjectes Owe to Kynges and Other Ciuile Gouernours, With an Exhortacion To All True Naturall Englishe men* (STC 20178, 1556). There is no good modern edition. See B. Peardon, 'The Politics of Polemics: John Ponet's *Short Treatise Of Politic Power*, and Contemporary Circumstance, 1553–1556', *Journal of British Studies*, 22 (1982), pp. 35–49; B.L. Beer, 'John Ponet's *Shorte Treatise of Politike Power* Reassessed', *Sixteenth Century Journal*, 21 (1990), pp. 373–83.

432. 'Ponet', *DNB* and *ODNB*.

433. See J.H. Salmon, *The French Religious Wars in English Political Thought* (Oxford, 1959); Robert M. Kingdon, 'Calvinism and Resistance Theory, 1550–1580', in J. H. Burns and M. Goldie eds, *The Cambridge History of Political Thought, 1450–1700* (Cambridge, 1991), pp. 193–218.

434. Ponet, *Shorte Treatise*, sig. Av.

435. Ibid., sig.Bi^v.
436. Ibid., sig. Bii.
437. Ibid., sig. Bii^v.
438. Ibid., sig. Biii^v.
439. Ibid., sigs Cii, Cvii^v.
440. Ibid., sig. Cviii.
441. Ibid., sigs Diii–iv.
442. Ibid., sig. Dvii.
443. Ibid.
444. Ibid., sigs Dvii–vii^v.
445. Ibid., sig. Eiii.
446. Ibid., sigs Gi^v–Giii^v.
447. Ibid., sig. Gv^v.
448. Ibid., sigs Gviii–Hvii^v.
449. See Q. Skinner, *The Foundations of Modern Political Thought Volume II: The Age of Reformation* (Cambridge, 1978), part III, pp. 189–348.
450. Ponet, *Shorte Treatise*, sigs Bvii^v, Dvii, Iiv^v, Iviii^v.
451. Ibid., sigs Kvi^v, Kvii^v, Lv^v.
452. Ibid., sig. Miii.
453. Quotation, ibid., sig. Giii.
454. Ibid., sig. Ii.
455. Ibid., sig. Ivi^v.
456. Loades, *Reign of Mary Tudor* (1979), pp. 366–7; Loades, *Mary Tudor* (1989), pp. 276–7.
457. *Cal. Stat. Pap. Venet, VI (Part II), 1556–7*, no. 870, p. 1026; Loades, *Reign of Mary Tudor*, p. 366.
458. Hughes and Larkin, *Tudor Royal Proclamations*, II, no. 433, pp. 75–6.
459. Loades, *Reign of Mary Tudor*, pp. 225, 244, 391–3.
460. Nichols, *Diary of Henry Machyn*, p. 120.
461. *Cal. Stat. Pap. Venet, VI (Part II), 1556–7*, no. 743, p. 836.
462. Nichols, *Diary of Henry Machyn*, pp. 166–7.
463. Ambassadors were beginning to treat her as a queen; see Michiel's report on England, *Cal. Stat. Pap. Venet, VI (Part II), 1556–7*, no. 884, pp. 1,058–9.
464. *Cal. Stat. Pap. Venet, VI (Part III) 1557–8*, no. 1,285, p. 1,549.
465. Ibid.
466. Ibid.
467. J. Strype, *Ecclesiastical Memorials, Relating Chiefly to Religion, and the Reformation Of It, and the Emergencies of the Church of England, Under King Henry VIII. King Edward VI. and Queen Mary I* (3 vols in 6, Oxford, 1822), Vol. II (part II), pp. 536–50. At end, see *A Catalogue of Letters, Speeches, Proclamations, Records . . . Relating to the Reign* (1721), new pagination, pp. 277–87, no. xxxi.
468. *The Epitaphe Upon the Death of the Most Excellent and Our Late Quene Marie, Deceased, Augmented By the First Author* (STC 17559, ?1558). This work is Society of Antiquaries Broadside 46, of which I have seen a copy at the Huntington Library.
469. The Epitaphe is described as 'augmented by the first author' and there is a version with verses in praise of Elizabeth added.
470. Loades, *Mary Tudor* (1989), p. 332,
471. See J. Loach, 'Pamphlets and Politics, 1553–8', *Bulletin of the Institute of Historical Research*, 48 (1975), pp. 31–44; Loach, 'The Marian Establishment and the Printing Press', *English Historical Review*, 101 (1986), pp. 135–48; E. J. Baskerville, *A Chronological Bibliography of Propaganda and Polemic, 1553–1558* (American Philosophical Society, Philadelphia, 1979).
472. Baskerville, *Chronological Bibliography*, p. 30.

Part VI Prologue

1. See J. Watkins, *Representing Elizabeth in Stuart England: Literature, History, Sovereignty* (Cambridge, 2002).
2. Ibid.; C.V. Wedgwood, *Oliver Cromwell and the Elizabethan Inheritance* (1970); E. Bohun, *The Character of Queen Elizabeth* (Wing B3448, 1693). See below pp. 464–73.
3. Anne took Elizabeth's motto, 'Semper eadem' and dressed in gowns that recalled Elizabeth's; for Victoria and Elizabeth, see J. Plunkett, *Queen Victoria: First Media Monarch* (Oxford, 2003); J. Walker, *The Elizabethan Icon, 1603–2003* (Basingstoke, 2004), pp. 102–3, 112–13, 164, 178 and *passim*; M. Dobson and N.J. Watson, *England's Elizabeth: An Afterlife in Fame and Fantasy* (Oxford, 2002), figs 8, 27, pp. 72–6, 232, 251–5 and *passim*; J. Lynch, *The Age of Elizabeth in the Age of Johnson* (Cambridge, 2003), pp. 57–77; M. Peters, *Pitt and Popularity:The Patriot Minister and London Opinion during the Seven Years' War* (Oxford 1980) and 'Pitt the Younger', *ODNB*. D. Antonio, 'Virgin Queen, Iron Lady, Queen of Hearts: The Embodiment of Feminine Power in a Male Social Imaginary', in G. Pugliese ed., *The Political Legacy of Margaret Thatcher* (2003), pp. 199–213. Cf. below pp. 472–3.
4. J. Neale, *Queen Elizabeth* (1934).
5. See, for example, S. Bassnett, *Elizabeth I: A Feminist Perspective* (Oxford and New York, 1988); P. Berry, *Of Chastity and Power: Elizabethan Literature and the Unmarried Queen* (1989); C. Levin, *The Heart and Stomach of a King: Elizabeth I and the Politics of Sex and Power* (Philadelphia, 1994); S. Frye, *Elizabeth I: The Competition for Representation* (Oxford, 1993); S. Doran, *Monarchy and Matrimony: The Courtships of Elizabeth I* (1996). The quotation is from Francis Bacon, J. Spedding ed., *The Works of Francis Bacon* (14 vols, 1857–74), VI, p. 310.
6. For a classic revisionist study, see C. Haigh, *Elizabeth I* (Harlow, 1988).
7. David Starkey's 2000 Channel 4 Television programme on Elizabeth attracted record audiences. See D. Starkey, *Elizabeth: Apprenticeship* (2000).
8. E. M. W. Tillyard, *The Elizabethan World Picture* (1943).
9. Frye, *Elizabeth I*, pp. 1–21. Cf. Louis Montrose, 'Elizabeth was a privileged agent in the production of her royal image but she was not its master', in *The Subject of Elizabeth: Authority, Gender, and Representation* (Chicago, 2006), p. 2.
10. W. Leahy, *Elizabethan Triumphal Processions* (Aldershot, 2004); below pp. 430–6.
11. The extent to which Elizabeth controlled policy has been the subject of extensive recent debate. Stephen Alford and Paul Hammer have argued that councillors often 'bounced' the queen into measures to which she was not inclined: S. Alford, *The Early Elizabethan Polity: William Cecil and the British Succession Crisis, 1558–1569*, (Cambridge, 1998); P. Hammer, *The Polarisation of Elizabethan Politics: The Political Career of Robert Devereux, 2nd Earl of Essex, 1585–97* (Cambridge, 1999); cf. S. Adams, 'Eliza Enthroned: The Court and its Politics', in C. Haigh ed., *The Reign of Elizabeth* (Basingstoke, 1984), pp. 55–77. Natalie Mears, more persuasively in my view, restores the queen as the dominant figure, N. Mears, *Queenship and Political Discourse in the Elizabethan Realms* (Cambridge, 2005).
12. F. Smith Fussner, *The Historical Revolution: English Historical Writing and Thought* (1962).
13. M. MacLagan, 'Genealogy and Heraldry in the 16th and 17th Centuries', in L. Fox ed., *English Historical Scholarship in the 16th and 17th Centuries* (1956), pp. 31–48; L. Stevenson, *Praise and Paradox: Merchants and Craftsmen in Elizabethan Popular Literature* (Cambridge, 1984).
14. I. Archer, *The Growth of Stability: Social Relations in Elizabethan London* (Cambridge, 1991); idem, 'The Arts and Acts of Memorialization in Early Modern London', in J. Merritt ed., *Imagining Early Modern London: Perceptions and Portrayals of the City from Stow to Strype, 1598–1720* (Cambridge, 2001), pp. 89–113.

15. See above, Introduction and K. Sharpe, 'Sacralization and Demystification. The Publicization of Monarchy in Early Modern England', in J. Deploige and G. Deneckere eds, *Mystifying the Monarch. Studies on Discourse, Power, and History* (Amsterdam, 2006), pp. 99–115, 255–59.
16. An observation made by Sir Geoffrey Elton.
17. Tigurinus Chelidonius, *A Most Excellent Hystorie of the Institution and Firste Beginning of Christian Princes, and the Originall of Kingdomes* (STC 5113, 1571), p. 55.
18. H. Hackett, *Virgin Mother, Maiden Queen: Elizabeth I and the Cult of the Virgin Mary* (1994), Epilogue, pp. 235–41; G. Malynes, *Saint George for England, Allegorically Described* (STC 17226A, 1601), 'To the Loving Reader', sig. A6.

9 The Words of a Queen

1. J. Neale, *Queen Elizabeth I*, pp. 24–6; A. Somerset, *Elizabeth I* (1991), pp. 10–12.
2. Marguerite of Angoulême, *A Godly Medytacyon of the Christen Sowle, Concerninge a Love Towardes God and Hys Christe, Compyled in Frenche by Lady Margarete Quene of Naverre, and Aptely Translated Into Englysh By the Ryght Vertuouse Lady Elyzabeth Doughter To Our Late Souerayne Kynge Henri the VIII* (STC 17320, 1548). There is a facsimile with a brief introduction by A. L. Prescott ed., *Elizabeth and Mary Tudor* (*The Early Modern Englishwoman* Vol. V, Aldershot, 2001). Editions of the manuscript with commentary are Renja Salminen ed., *Marguerite de Navarre, Le Miroir de l'âme pécheresse* (Helsinki, 1979) and M. Shell ed., *Elizabeth's Glass* (Lincoln, Nebraska, 1993).
3. See Elizabeth's letter to Catherine Parr, 31 December 1544, in L.S. Marcus, J. Mueller and M. B. Rose eds, *Elizabeth I: Collected Works* (Chicago, 2000), pp. 6–7.
4. C. Pemberton ed., *Queen Elizabeth's Englishings* (Early English Text Society, 1899), pp. vii–viii.
5. Neale, though he refers to her translations of Isocrates and Sophocles, makes no mention of the later works (*Elizabeth*, p. 25); Wallace MacCaffrey recognized that they were later works but discussed them as part of her education and concluded that there was 'little evidence' that classical authors 'affected her practice of politics' (*Elizabeth I*, 1993, p. 7); Somerset correctly dates the Boethius but mentions it, along with her translations of Horace and Plutarch, only in the chapter on Elizabeth's childhood; the same is true of Neville Williams, *Elizabeth: Queen of England* (1967), p. 10. Even the editor, Pemberton, assesses the works as though they were scholarly exercises and, not considering the importance of dating, wonders that the queen could 'yet find inclination to undertake such tasks and time to devote to them' (*Elizabeth's Englishings*, p. xii).
6. [Henry Savile] *The Ende of Nero and Beginning of Galba: Fower Bookes of the Histories of Cornelius Tacitus* (STC 23642, 1591), 'To her most Sacred Majesty', sigs q2–q2ᵛ, my italics.
7. Ibid., sig. q2.
8. Pemberton, *Elizabeth's Englishings*, p. xi. The Clerk of the Signet was Thomas Windebank, who became Clerk of the Privy Seal in 1598.
9. Ibid., pp. ix–x.
10. H. Love, *Scribal Publication in Seventeenth-Century England* (Oxford, 1993); A. Marotti, *Manuscript, Print and the English Renaissance Lyric* (Ithaca, NY, 1995).
11. Marcus, *Elizabeth: Works*, p. xiii.
12. Janel Mueller and Joshua Scodel are preparing a scholarly edition of Elizabeth's translations which will add hitherto neglected pieces such as her rendering of Cicero's *Pro Marcello*.

13. *Nugæ Antiquæ: Being a Miscellaneous Collection of Original Papers, in Prose and Verse Written during the Reigns of Henry VIII, Edward VI, Queen Mary, Elizabeth, and King James by Sir John Harington* (2 vols, 1804), I, p. 109.

14. Camden, reporting the shock of Henri IV's conversion, described Elizabeth 'in her grief' seeking solace from several writings and added: 'sure I am that at this time she daily turned over Boethius his books De Consolatio and translated them handsomely into the English tongue', *The Historie of the Life and Reigne of the Most Renowned and Victorious Princesse Elizabeth* (STC 4500, 1630), book 4, p. 51.

15. Pemberton, *Elizabeth's Englishings*, pp. viii–xiii.

16. Ibid., p. 15.

17. Ibid., p. 66.

18. Ibid., p. 79.

19. E.g. ibid., pp. 51, 53.

20. Ibid., p. 120: 'there remains a sure liberty of will to mortal folks'; cf. p. 104: 'to such as reason have, a liberty of willing and denying is'.

21. Ibid., p. 15.

22. Ibid., p. 20.

23. A. Kernan, *The Cankered Muse: Satire of the English Renaissance* (New Haven, 1959).

24. Pemberton, *Elizabeth's Englishings*, pp. 122, 131, 136.

25. Ibid., pp. 122, 126, 136.

26. Ibid., p. 141.

27. Ibid., p. 140.

28. Ibid., pp. 130, 134, 137.

29. K. Sharpe, 'The King's Writ: Royal Authors and Royal Authority in Early Modern England', in K. Sharpe and P. Lake eds, *Culture and Politics in Early Stuart England* (Basingstoke, 1994), pp. 129–31.

30. Pemberton, *Elizabeth's Englishings*, p. 145.

31. Ibid., p. 143.

32. Marcus *et al.*, *Elizabeth: Works*, p. xx; S. May, *The Elizabethan Courtier Poets* (Asheville, NC, 1999), pp. 47–8. May calls one of the queen's poems a 'propaganda piece', p. 136n.

33. T. Churchyard, *A Handeful of Gladsome Verses, Given to the Queenes Maiesty at Woodstocke* (STC 5237, 1592), sig. B3.

34. Marcus *et al.*, *Elizabeth: Works*, p. 133.

35. See 'When I was fair and young', ibid., pp. 303–4.

36. Ibid., pp. 302–3.

37. Ibid., p. 300.

38. Ibid., p. 134.

39. Ibid.

40. Ibid., pp. 308–9.

41. Ibid., pp. 410–11.

42. Ibid., p. 302.

43. Churchyard, *Handeful of Gladsome Verses*, sig. B3.

44. *Precationes Priuat[ae] Regiae E.R.* (STC 7576.7, 1563); R. Day, *Christian Prayers and Meditations in English, French, Italian, Spanish, Greeke, and Latine* (STC 6428, 1569).

45. *Precationes*; Marcus, *Elizabeth: Works*, p. 135n.

46. Marcus *et al.*, *Elizabeth: Works*, p. 136.

47. Ibid., pp. 137–8.

48. Ibid., pp. 138–9.

49. Ibid., p. 141.

50. Ibid., p. 145.

51. Ibid., p. 150.

52. Ibid., p. 149.

53. Ibid., p. 142.
54. Ibid., p. 147.
55. Ibid., p. 159.
56. Ibid., p. 146.
57. Ibid., pp. 310–11.
58. Ibid., p. 311.
59. Ibid., p. 313.
60. Ibid., p. 319.
61. Ibid., p. 321.
62. Ibid., pp. 423–4.
63. Ibid., p. 424, probably a heading by Sir Thomas Egerton. Deborah was a judge of Israel and Theodosia a virgin martyr.
64. Ibid., p. 425 and n.1.
65. Ibid., p. 426.
66. Ibid.
67. Ibid., p. 427.
68. Ibid., p. 149.
69. Ibid., p. xiii.
70. The fullest modern collection is G. B. Harrison, *The Letters of Queen Elizabeth* (Westport, Conn., 1968). I have sampled from Marcus *et al.*'s more carefully edited collection.
71. Ibid., pp. 360, 361, 389, 399.
72. Ibid., p. 371.
73. Ibid., pp. 256–7.
74. Ibid., pp. 231–2.
75. Ibid., p. 361.
76. Ibid., p. 362.
77. Ibid., pp. 229–30.
78. Ibid., p. 284. Sir Amyas Paulet was guarding Queen Mary at Fotheringhay at the time of the Babington plot.
79. Ibid., pp. 399–400.
80. J. Bruce ed., *Letters of Queen Elizabeth and King James VI of Scotland* (Camden Society, 46, 1849); see, for a good example, Marcus *et al.*, *Elizabeth: Works*, pp. 372–4.
81. Marcus *et al.*, *Elizabeth: Works*, p. 380.
82. Ibid., p. 383.
83. Ibid., pp. 386–8.
84. Ibid., pp. 394–9.
85. *The True Copie of a Letter from the Queenes Maiestie, to the Lord Maior of London, and His Brethren Conteyning a Most Gracious Acceptation of the Great Joy Which Her Subjectes Tooke Upon the Apprehension of Divers Persons, Detected of a Most Wicked Conspiracie, Read Openly in a Great Assemblie of the Commons in the Guildhall of that Citie, the 22.day of August. 1586* (STC 7577, 1586).
86. Ibid., sig. Aii.
87. Ibid., sig. Aii^v.
88. Ibid.
89. V. Von Klarwill ed., *Queen Elizabeth and Some Foreigners* (1928), p. 59.
90. Marcus *et al.*, *Elizabeth: Works*, p. 88.
91. Janet Arnold, *Queen Elizabeth's Wardrobe Unlock'd* (Leeds, 1988), p. 8; Klarwill, *Queen Elizabeth*, p. 31.
92. *The Life and Death of Queene Elizabeth From the Wombe to the Tombe, From Her Birth to Her Burial* (STC 7587, 1639), sigs C3^v–4; cf. the version in Marcus *et al.*, *Elizabeth: Works*, pp. 58–60.
93. Marcus *et al.*, *Elizabeth: Works*, pp. 325–6.

94. Ibid., p. 326.
95. Ibid., p. 326 n.1; there is a copy in *Cabala, Mysteries of State in the Letters of the Great Ministers of K. James and K. Charles* (Wing C184, 1654), p. 260. Susan Frye critically examines the questionable reliability of the versions of the speech we have and the myths surrounding the occasion in 'The Myth of Elizabeth at Tilbury', *Sixteenth Century Journal*, 23 (1992), pp. 95–114.
96. T. Deloney, *The Queenes Visiting of the Campe at Tilsburie With Her Entertainment There to the Tune of Wilsons Wilde* (STC 6565, 1588); C. Levin, *The Heart and Stomach of a King: Elizabeth I and the Politics of Sex and Power* (Philadelphia, 1994), pp. 143–4; Marcus *et al.*, *Elizabeth: Works*, p. 326 n. 1.
97. The University of Warwick has been a launching site for several New Labour initiatives.
98. Marcus *et al.*, *Elizabeth: Works*, p. 87.
99. Ibid., pp. 88–9.
100. Ibid., p. 89.
101. Ibid., p. 88.
102. Ibid., pp. 89–91.
103. Ibid., p. 90.
104. See J. Nichols ed., *The Progresses and Public Processions of Queen Elizabeth* (3 vols, 1823), I, pp. 241–2.
105. Marcus *et al.*, *Elizabeth: Works*, p. 91.
106. Ibid., p. 327 n.1; Nichols, *Progresses*, I, pp. 149–60.
107. Marcus *et al.*, *Elizabeth: Works*, pp. 327–8.
108. Ibid., p. 328.
109. Ibid.
110. See L. Shenk, 'Turning Learned Authority into Royal Supremacy: Elizabeth I's Learned Persona and her University Orations', in C. Levin, J. Carney and D. Barrett-Graves eds, *Elizabeth I: Always Her Own Free Woman* (Aldershot, 2003), pp.78–96.
111. Henry VIII speech, 31 March 1543, G. R. Elton ed., *The Tudor Constitution* (Cambridge, 1982), p. 277.
112. Allison Heisch, 'Queen Elizabeth I: Parliamentary Rhetoric and the Exercise of Power', *Signs*, 1 (1975), pp. 31–55.
113. Marcus *et al.*, *Elizabeth: Works*, pp. 56, 59.
114. Ibid., p. 59.
115. Ibid., p. 70.
116. Ibid., pp. 70–2.
117. The reference was to Athenodorus.
118. Marcus *et al.*, *Elizabeth: Works*, p. 79.
119. Ibid.
120. Ibid., p. 93.
121. Ibid., p. 95.
122. Ibid.
123. Ibid., pp. 96, 97.
124. Ibid., p. 105.
125. Ibid.
126. Ibid.
127. Ibid., pp. 195–6, cf. version p. 107.
128. Ibid., p. 108.
129. Ibid., p. 169.
130. Ibid.
131. Ibid., p. 170.
132. Ibid., p. 182, speech of 29 March 1585.
133. Ibid., p. 182.

134. Ibid., pp. 182–3.
135. Ibid., p. 183.
136. Ibid., p. 187, speech of 12 November 1586.
137. Ibid., p. 197, reply of 24 November 1586.
138. Ibid., pp. 198–200.
139. Ibid., p. 200; Somerset, *Elizabeth* I, p. 433.
140. Ibid., pp. 328–30.
141. Ibid., p. 337, speech of 30 November, 1601. This speech was reprinted often in the seventeenth century (see, for example, Wing E528, E530, E534, E535; Thomason/669.f. 22[33])
142. Marcus *et al.*, *Elizabeth: Works*, p. 338.
143. Ibid., p. 341, version in papers of Sir Thomas Egerton.
144. Ibid., p. 338.
145. Ibid., p. 339.
146. Ibid., p. 341.
147. Ibid., p. 340.
148. This was one of the ways by which parliaments could act as points of contact between the government and the people; see G. R. Elton, 'Tudor Government: The Points of Contact. 1: Parliament', *Transactions of the Royal Historical Society*, 24 (1974), pp. 183–200.
149. Marcus *et al.*, *Elizabeth: Works*, p. 346.
150. Ibid., p. 347.
151. Ibid., pp. 346–51, quotations, p. 351.
152. Ibid., p. 351 n.1 citing the account in Sir Roger Wilbraham's Journal.
153. *A Booke Containing All Such Proclamations As Were Published During the Raigne of the Late Queene Elizabeth* (STC 7758.3, 1618), no. 40 has the first printed with royal arms dated 30 October 1561.
154. P. L. Hughes and J. F. Larkin, *Tudor Royal Proclamations* (3 vols, New Haven and London, 1964–9), II, no. 642, p. 446.
155. Ibid. III, no. 699, p. 13.
156. For example, ibid., II, nos 448, 529, pp. 99, 257.
157. Ibid., no. 451.5, p. 103.
158. For example, ibid., no. 463, p. 135.
159. Ibid., no. 467, p. 141.
160. Ibid., no. 556, p. 305.
161. Ibid., no. 680, pp. 518–21.
162. Ibid., no. 685, pp. 528–32.
163. Ibid., no. 520, pp. 246–7.
164. Ibid., no. 685, p. 529.
165. Ibid., p. 532.
166. Ibid., no. 467, p. 142.
167. Ibid., no. 568, p. 326.
168. Ibid., no. 570, p. 332.
169. Ibid., III, no. 737, p. 83.
170. Ibid., no. 817, p. 250. Cf. II, no. 568, p. 327.
171. Ibid., II, no. 642, p. 449; III, no. 786, p. 175. Cf. no. 814, pp. 241–5.
172. Ibid., III, no. 814, p. 242.
173. Ibid., nos 781, 812, pp. 165, 235.
174. Ibid., II, no. 642, p. 446.
175. Ibid., III, no. 798, p. 200.
176. Ibid., II, no. 580, p. 347.
177. *An Homelie Against Disobedience and Wylfull Rebellion* (STC 13679.2, 1570).
178. Ibid., sig. Bii^{v}.

179. Ibid., sig. Hiv^v.
180. Ibid., sig. Kii^v.
181. Ibid.
182. *An Homelie Against Disobedience and Wylfull Rebellion* (STC 13680, 1573), sigs Fii, G.
183. See, most recently, L. Montrose, *The Subject of Elizabeth* (Chicago, 2006); H. Hackett, *Virgin Mother, Maiden Queen: Elizabeth I and the Cult of the Virgin Mary* (1994); S. Frye, *Elizabeth I: The Competition for Representation* (New York, 1993); J. N. King, 'Queen Elizabeth I: Representations of the Virgin Queen', *Renaissance Quarterly*, 43 (1990), pp. 30–74; F. Yates, *Astraea: The Imperial Theme in the Sixteenth Century* (1975).
184. Tigurinus Chelidonius, *A Most Excellent Hystorie of the Institution and Firste Beginning of Christian Princes* (STC 5113, 1571).
185. Ibid., p. 16.
186. Ibid., pp. 17–18, 23.
187. Ibid., sig. Aii, pp. 18, 20.
188. Ibid., pp. 36, 157.
189. Ibid., sigs Aii–iv^v, pp. 36, 198.
190. J. Bridges, *The Supremacie of Christian Princes Over All Persons Throughout Their Dominions* (STC 3737, 1573). Bridges wrote in answer to the Catholic apologist Thomas Stapleton, but he went on to defend Elizabeth's supremacy against Presbyterians too: see 'Bridges', *ODNB*.
191. *A Forme of Christian Pollicie Drawne Out of French by Geffray Fenton* (STC 10793, 1574), p. 69. This was a translation of a French treatise by Jean Talpin rendered very much pertinent to English affairs by the dedication, sigs qii–qqi^v.
192. Ibid., pp. 12–13, 20, 24 and *passim*.
193. G. Gascoigne, *The Glasse of Gouernement: A Tragicall Comedie* (STC 11643A, 1575), published with licence.
194. Ibid., sigs Aiiii, Ciiii.
195. C. Merbury, *A Briefe Discourse of Royall Monarchie, As of The Best Commonweale Wherin the Subiect May Beholde the Sacred Maiestie of the Princes Most Royall Estate* (STC 17823, 1581). Merbury described himself as attending on the queen at court but we do not know in which, if any, office, 'Merbury', *ODNB*.
196. Merbury, *Briefe Discourse*, p. 1.
197. Ibid., pp. 11,19, 43 and *passim*.
198. Ibid., p. 43.
199. Ibid., full title and 'Merbury', *DNB*.
200. T. Smith, *De republica anglorum: The Maner of Governement or Policie of the Realme of England* (STC 22857, 1582), pp. 47, 118. Smith, a Secretary of State, may have described England as a 'mixed monarchy' but later attempts to read his treatise as an apologia for parliamentary sovereignty are highly misleading, see 'Smith', *ODNB*. Smith even argued that absolute royal power was necessary in war (pp. 7, 43).
201. J. Ferne, *The Blazon of Gentrie Devided Into Two Parts* (STC 10824, 1586).
202. Ibid., p. 144.
203. Ibid., p. 139.
204. Ibid., p. 141; 'Ferne', *ODNB*.
205. T. Floyd, *The Picture of a Perfit Common wealth Describing Aswell the Offices of Princes and Inferiour Magistrates Over Their Subiects, As Also the Duties of Subiects Towards Their Governours* (STC 11119, 1600). Interestingly, Floyd refers to Coriolanus (p. 8) and raises the spectre of civil war, 'the very root of all evil' (p. 297).
206. Ibid., p. 20.
207. Ibid., pp. 27, 187, 195 and *passim*.
208. 'No commonwealth can be rightly a commonwealth without a king', ibid., p. 2.
209. R. Mason, *Reasons monarchie* (STC 17621, 1602).
210. Ibid., pp. 69–70.

211. Ibid., p. 3.
212. Ibid., p. 87.
213. See, for example, the poem, 'The Minds Privilege' printed at the end [no pagination].
214. Ibid., p. 97.
215. J. Awdelay, *A Godly Ditty or Prayer to be Song Unto God for the Preservation of His Church, Our Queene and Realme, Against All Traytours, Rebels, and Papisticall Enemies* (STC 995, 1569).
216. J. Cheke, *The Hurt of Sedition, How Grievous It Is To A Common welth. Set out by Sir John Cheeke Knight, 1549. And Now Newly Perused and Printed the 14 of December 1569* (STC 5110, 1569). The edition was published with the royal arms.
217. T. Norton, *To the Quenes Maiesties Poore Deceiued Subiects of the North Countrey, Drawen Into Rebellion by the Earles of Northumberland and Westmerland* (STC 18682, 1569). A poet, translator, lawyer and MP, Norton worked loyally with Cecil to detect and discourage pamphleteering about the succession (*ODNB*).
218. Ibid., sig. Aiiii^v.
219. Ibid., sig. Bvii^v.
220. Ibid., sig. Div.
221. *A Ballad Reioycinge the Sodaine Fall, Of Rebels That Thought to Devower Us All* (STC 1326, 1570).
222. T. Bette, *A Newe Ballade Intituled, Agaynst Rebellious and False Rumours To the Newe Tune of the Blacke Almaine, Upon Scissillia* (STC 1979, 1570).
223. J. Barker, *The Plagues of Northomberland To the Tune of Appelles* (STC 1421, 1570).
224. T. Churchyard, *Come Bring in Maye With Me My Maye is Fresh and Greene: (A Subiectes Harte, An Humble Mind) to Serve a Mayden Queene. A Discourse of Rebellion, Drawne Forth for to Warne the Wanton Wittes How to Kepe their Heads on their Shoulders* (STC 5224, 1570).
225. Ibid., sigs Aiii–Aiii^v.
226. Ibid., sig. Aiii^v.
227. W. Kirkham, *Ioyfull Newes for True Subiectes to God and the Crowne the Rebelles Are Cooled, their Bragges Be Put Downe* (STC 15015, 1570).
228. J. Phillips, *A Frendly Larum, or Faythfull Warnynge to the True Harted Subiectes of England Discoveryng the Actes, and Malicious Myndes of Those Obstinate and Rebellious Papists* (STC 19870, 1570), sig. Aiiii^v.
229. Ibid., sig. Ciii^v.
230. Ibid., sig. Diii and *passim*.
231. *The Effect of the Declaration Made in the Guildhall by Mr Recorder of London* (STC 11036, 1571); above, p. 347.
232. Even just after the northern rebellion, Elizabeth issued a declaration stating that it was not her intention that subjects 'should be molested either by examination or inquisition in any matter ... of faith ... as long as they shall in their outward conversation show themselves quiet and conformable ... to the laws of the realm', Somerset, *Elizabeth*, p. 246.
233. W. Elderton, *A Balad Intituled, the Dekaye of the Duke* (STC 7552.5, 1572). Elderton was a well-known ballad writer with a prolific output, *ODNB*.
234. T. Nelson, *A Short Discourse Expressing the Substaunce of All the Late Pretended Treasons Against the Queenes Maiestie* (STC 18425, 1586).
235. Ibid., sigs Aiv–Aiv^v.
236. W. Kempe, *A Dutiful Invectiue Against the Moste Haynous Treasons of Ballard and Babington with Other Their Adherents, Latelie Executed* (STC 14925, 1587).
237. Ibid., sigs q2, q2^v, q4^v.
238. R. Crompton, *A Short Declaration of the Ende of Traytors, and False Conspirators Against the State & of the Duetie of Subiectes to Theyr Soveraigne Governour* (STC 6055, 1587).
239. Ibid., sig. Aiiii.

240. Ibid., sig. D4.

241. Ibid., sig. Di; cf. sigs Cii^v–Di *passim*.

242. W. Birch, *A Songe Betweene the Quene's Maistie and Englande* (STC 3079, 1564, entered 1558).

243. W. Blandie, *The Castle, Or Picture of Pollicy Shewing Forth Most Lively, The Face, Body and Partes of a Commonwealth* (STC 3128, 1581). Blandie was a loyal Catholic; M. Kyffin, *The Blessednes of Brytaine or a Celebration of the Queenes Holyday* (STC 15096, 1587), sig. A3^v.

244. R. Strong, 'The Popular Celebration of the Accession Day of Queen Elizabeth I', *Journal of the Warburg and Courtauld Institutes*, 21 (1958), pp. 86–103; D. Cressy, *Bonfires and Bells: National Memory and the Protestant Calendar in Elizabethan and Stuart England* (1989), ch. 4. See below, pp. 443–4.

245. Kyffin, *Blessednes of Brytaine*, sig. B3^v.

246. Ibid., sig. B1^v.

247. H. Constable, *Diana: The Praises of his Mistres, in Certaine Sweete Sonnets* (STC 5637, 1592), sig. D3^v. Constable answered Catholic attacks against Elizabeth but later converted to Catholicism in France (*ODNB*).

248. See, for example, the lament on social ills in the loyal Thomas Churchyard's *A Musicall Consort of Heavenly Harmonie . . . Called Churchyards Charitie* (STC 5245, 1595) and *A Mournfull Dittie on the Death of Certaine Judges and Justices of the Peace* (STC 15645, 1590); R. S., *The Phoenix Nest Built Up With the Most Rare and Refined Workes of Noble Men, Woorthy Knights, Gallant Gentlemen, Masters of Arts, and Braue Schollers* (STC 21516, 1593)

249. E. Hake, *A Commemoration of the Most Prosperous and Peaceable Raigne of our Gratious and Deere Soveraigne Lady Elizabeth* (STC 12605, 1575), sig. Biv.

250. F. Smith Fussner, *The Historical Revolution: English Historical Writing and Thought, 1580–1640* (1962); F. Levy, *Tudor Historical Thought* (San Marino, Calif., 1967); D. Woolf, *Reading History in Early Modern England* (Cambridge, 2000); A. Patterson, *Reading Holinshed's Chronicles* (Chicago, 1994).

251. *An Abridgement of the Chronicles of England, Gathered by Richard Grafton, Citizen of London. Anno Do. 1563* (STC 12148, 1563), sigs Bii–Biii.

252. Ibid., ff.165^v, 172.

253. *The Chronicle of Briteyn* (STC 12146, 1568), p. 1366; *A Chronicle at Large and Meere History of the Affayres of Englande* (STC 12147, 1569); *Graftons Abridgement of the Chronicles of Englande, Newely Corrected and Augmented, to Thys Present Yere of Our Lord, 1572* (STC 12152, 1572).

254. *Graftons Abridgement*, pp. 194, 215.

255. *The Historie of Cambria, Now Called Wales, A Part of the Most Famous Yland of Brytaine, Written in the Brytish Language Above Two Hundreth Yeares Past, Translated into English by H. Lhoyd Gentleman* (STC 4606, 1584). We recall, of course, that the Tudors were Welsh.

256. C. Ocland, *The Valiant Actes and Victorious Battailes of the English Nation* (STC 18777, 1585), title of third book after sig. Lii^v.

257. Ibid., p. 5.

258. W. Lambarde, *A Perambulation of Kent Conteining the Description, Hystorie, and Customes of that Shyre, Collected and Written (for the most part) in the Yeare 1570* (STC 15175, 1576). See S. Mendyk, 'Speculum Britanniae': Regional Study, Antiquarianism, and Science in Britain to 1700 (Toronto, 1989).

259. K. Sharpe, *Sir Robert Cotton, 1586–1631: History and Politics in Early Modern England* (Oxford, 1979), ch. 1.

260. [Anon., but assigned to Hayward in some copies] *The First Booke of the Preservation of King Henry the VII When He Was But Earle of Richmond, Grandfather to the Queenes Maiesty* (STC 13076, 1599), sig. C3.

261. Ibid., sigs D3^v–E2^v.

262. Ibid. sig. E2.

263. L. Lloyd, *The Triplicitie of Triumphes Containing the Order, Solempnitie and Pompe, of the Feastes, Sacrifices, Vowes, Games, and Triumphes Used Upon the Nativities of Emperours, Kinges, Princes, Dukes, Popes, and Consuls* (STC 16632, 1591), p. 22.

264. Ibid., p. 57.

265. H. Savile, *The Ende of Nero and Beginning of Galba: Fower Bookes of the Histories of Cornelius Tacitus* (STC 23642, 1591), sigs q3–q3^v, epistle to the reader. Savile also dedicated his work to the queen.

266. G. Botero, *Observations Upon the Lives of Alexander, Caesar, Scipio, Newly Englished* (STC 3397, 1602); G. Fenton, *The Historie of Guicciardin Containing the Warres of Italie and Other Partes* (STC 12459, 1599), sigs Aiii–Aiiii.

267. J. Speed, *A Description of the Civill Warres of England* (STC 23037, 1601).

268. T. Deloney, *Strange Histories, of Kings, Princes, Dukes, Earles, Lords, Ladies, Knights, and Gentlemen* (STC 6566, 1602).

269. R.M. Smuts, 'Court-centered Politics and the Uses of Roman Historians, c.1590–1630', in K. Sharpe and P. Lake eds, *Culture and Politics in Early Stuart England* (Basingstoke, 1994), pp. 21–43; 325–31; M. Peltonen, 'Citizenship and Republicanism in Elizabethan England', in M. van Gelderen and Q. Skinner eds, *Republicanism: A Shared European Heritage: Vol. II: Republicanism and Constitutionalism in Early Modern Europe* (Cambridge, 2002), pp. 85–106.

270. W. Painter, *The Palace of Pleasure Beautified, Adorned and Well Furnished, With Pleasaunt Histories and Excellent Novelles* (STC 19121, 1566), 'To the Reader'.

10 'The Portrait and Picture of the Queen's Majesty'

1. R.W. Scribner, *For the Sake of Simple Folk: Popular Propaganda for the German Reformation* (Cambridge, 1981); T. Watt, *Cheap Print and Popular Piety, 1550–1640* (Cambridge, 1991); R. Luborsky, R. Samson and E. M. Ingram eds, *A Guide to English Illustrated Books, 1536–1603* (2 vols, Tempe, Arizona, 1998).

2. L. Gent, *Picture and Poetry, 1560–1620: Relations between Literature and the Visual Arts in the English Renaissance* (Leamington Spa, 1981); Gent ed., *Albion's Classicism: The Visual Arts in Britain, 1550–1660* (New Haven and London, 1995).

3. Gent, *Picture and Poetry*, p. 38; the tag, from Horace's *De arte poetica*, has its roots in Aristotle's *Poetics*. See also R. W. Lee, *Ut Pictura Poesis, The Humanistic Theory of Painting* (New York, 1967).

4. Gent, *Picture and Poetry*, p. 40.

5. Ibid., p. 42.

6. M. MacLagan, 'Genealogy and Heraldry in the Sixteenth and Seventeenth Centuries', in L. Fox ed., *English Historical Scholarship in the Sixteenth and Seventeenth Centuries* (Oxford, 1956), pp. 31–48.

7. J. Ferne, *The Blazon of Gentrie Devided Into Two Parts* (STC 10824, 1586), sig. Aii^v.

8. Ibid., pp. 142–5.

9. Ibid., p. 290.

10. Ibid.

11. G. Legh, *The Accedence of Armorie* (STC 15391, 1591). This work was printed four times before the end of the century.

12. Ibid., p. 7.

13. Ibid., pp. 7ff.

14. See my discussion above concerning Anglo's scepticism about the capacity to understand these signs, pp. 48–9.

15. M. Bath, *Speaking Pictures: English Emblem Books and Renaissance Culture* (1994); P. Daly ed., *The English Emblem and the Continental Tradition* (New York, 1988). See

also Daly, 'The Place of the English Emblem Book in the Context of Continental Emblem Book Production to the Year 1700: A Chronological List of Editions of English Emblematic Works Published to 1700', in B. Westerweel ed., *Anglo-Dutch Relations in the Field of the Emblem* (Leiden, 1997), pp. 1–33.

16. G. Whitney, *A Choice of Emblemes, and Other Devises, for the Moste Parte Gathered Out of Sundrie Writers, Englished and Moralized* (STC 25438, 1586).

17. J. Manning, 'Unpublished and Unedited Emblems by Geoffrey Whitney: Further Evidence of the English Adaptation of Continental Traditions', in Daly, *English Emblem*, pp. 83–108, especially p. 101.

18. Part of full title; cf. 'To the Reader'.

19. Watt, *Cheap Print*, pp. 137–8, 192–3, 244–5, 351–3.

20. See [Anon.] *A Very Proper Treatise, Wherein Is Briefly Sett Forthe the Arte of Limming Which Teacheth the Order in Drawing [and] Tracing of Letters, Vinets, Flowers, Armes and Imagery* (STC 24252, 1573); R.K.R. Thornton and T.G.S. Cain, *A Treatise Concerning the Art of Limning* (Ashington, 1981).

21. P. Lomazzo, *A Tracte Containing the Artes of Curious Paintinge Carvinge Buildinge Written First in Italian by Io Paul Lomatius Painter of Milan and Englished by R.H Student in Physik* (STC 16698, 1598), 'To the Ingenious Reader', sigs qiii–qvi.

22. Ibid., p. 23.

23. Ibid., sig. qiv.

24. Ibid., p. 2.

25. Illustrations were appearing more frequently as finding aids. Lori Anne Ferrell is working on this subject.

26. T. Hariot, *A Briefe and True Report of the New Found Land of Virginia, of the Commodities and of the Nature and Manners of the Naturall Inhabitants* (STC 12786, 1590).

27. K. Sharpe, *Reading Revolutions: The Politics of Reading in Early Modern England* (New Haven and London, 2000), pp. 46–9; M. Corbett and R. Lightbown, *The Comely Frontispiece: The Emblematic Title-Page in England, 1550–1660* (1979), p. 43.

28. I studied the Huntington Library Richard Bull Granger Collection for several months.

29. W. Jaggard, *A View of All the Right Honourable the Lord Mayors of this Honorable Citty of London With the Personages* (STC 14343, 1601). Jaggard went on to print the fist folio of Shakespeare. *ODNB*.

30. T. T., *A Booke, Containing the True Portraiture of the Countenances and Attires of the Kings of England, from William Conqueror, Unto Our Soueraigne Lady Queene Elizabeth Now Raigning Together With a Briefe Report of Some of the Principall Acts of the Same Kings* (STC 23626, 1597).

31. Ibid., sig. F3ᵛ; *Baziliologia: A Booke of Kings Beeing the True and Lively Effigies of All Our English Kings from the Conquest Untill this Present, With Their Severall Coats of Armes, Impreses and Devises; and a Briefe Chronologie of Their Liues and Deaths, Elegantly Graven in Copper* (STC 13581, 1618). The engravings were by Renold Elstracke.

32. V. von Klarwill, *Queen Elizabeth and Some Foreigners* (1928), pp. 57–8.

33. L. S. Marcus, J. Mueller and M. B. Rose eds, *Elizabeth I: Collected Works* (Chicago, 2000), pp. 207, 209–12; cf. p. 35; see also Klarwill, *Queen Elizabeth*, pp. 52, 64, 112, 227 for other examples of Elizabeth's interest in portraits.

34. P. L. Hughes and J. F. Larkin eds, *Tudor Royal Proclamations* (3 vols, New Haven and London, 1964–9), II, no. 469, pp. 146–7.

35. Ibid., no. 683, p. 526.

36. Elizabeth to Alençon, c. June 1581, Marcus *et al.*, *Elizabeth: Works*, p. 250.

37. Ibid., p. 35.

38. Above, pp. 138–9.

39. J. Arnold, 'The "Pictur" of Elizabeth I When Princess', *Burlington Magazine*, 123 (1981), pp. 302–4.

40. J. Arnold, *Queen Elizabeth's Wardrobe Unlock'd* (Leeds, 1988), p. 4.

41. The adage was 'You must endure what cannot be altered', see Marcus *et al.*, *Elizabeth: Works*, p. 36.

42. My reading strongly dissents from E. Pomeroy, *Reading the Portraits of Queen Elizabeth* (Hamden, Conn., 1989), pp. 3–6. L. Montrose (whom I read after writing) gestures to a similar interpretation, *The Subject of Elizabeth: Authority, Gender, and Representation* (Chicago, 2006), pp. 28–32.

43. R. Strong, *Gloriana: The Portraits of Queen Elizabeth* (1987), p. 59; K. Hearn, *Dynasties: Painting in Tudor and Jacobean England, 1530–1630* (1995), p. 63.

44. See, for example, R. Strong, *Portraits of Queen Elizabeth I* (Oxford, 1963), p. 56, no. 7 and plate IV; idem, *Gloriana*, pp. 58–9.

45. Strong, *Gloriana*, p. 59.

46. Hughes and Larkin, *Tudor Royal Proclamations*, II, no. 516, pp. 240–1.

47. Strong, *Gloriana*, p. 59.

48. Hearn, *Dynasties*, no. 33, p. 79.

49. Strong, *Gloriana*, p. 61.

50. O. Millar, *The Tudor, Stuart and Early Georgian Pictures in the Collection of Her Majesty The Queen* (1963), no. 58, p. 69.

51. Strong, *Gloriana*, p. 65; Hearn, *Dynasties*, no. 29, pp. 73–4.

52. Strong, *Gloriana*, p. 66.

53. S. Alford, *The Early Elizabethan Polity: William Cecil and the British Succession Crisis, 1558–1569* (Cambridge, 1998), ch. 8 and *passim*.

54. Ibid., p. 69.

55. The painting is at Sudeley Castle, Winchcombe, Gloucestershire. The following interpretation is my own and differs from earlier accounts. Cf. Montrose, *Subject of Elizabeth*, pp. 57–61.

56. Above ch. 4, pp. 134, 143.

57. Montrose has suggested that the left background to Mary and Philip may depict scenes of Rome, *Subject of Elizabeth*, pp. 59–61.

58. Strong, *Gloriana*, p. 74.

59. Ibid., p. 79.

60. Ibid., pp. 79–80. On the Phoenix Portrait, see Hearn, *Dynasties*, no. 34, p. 80.

61. Arnold, *Queen Elizabeth's Wardrobe*, p. 23.

62. Strong, *Gloriana*, p. 80.

63. See ibid., plate 47.

64. S. Olderr, *Symbolism: A Comprehensive Dictionary* (1986), p. 101.

65. U. Becker, *The Continuum Encyclopaedia of Symbols* (New York, 1994).

66. S. Anglo, *Images of Tudor Kingship* (1992), p. 82.

67. National Portrait Gallery, no. 2082.

68. Strong, *Gloriana*, p. 85. See Arnold, *Queen Elizabeth's Wardrobe*, fig. 27, p. 24.

69. Strong judges that 'no other face pattern of the queen was to be so widely disseminated', *Gloriana*, p. 89.

70. Cf. Arnold, *Queen Elizabeth's Wardrobe*, p. 328.

71. Pomeroy, *Reading Portraits*, p. 38, though she offers little analysis.

72. Olderr, *Symbolism*, p. 100.

73. Becker, *Continuum Encyclopaedia*.

74. Hearn, *Dynasties*, no. 100, p. 153

75. Strong, *Gloriana*, pp. 95–9.

76. Ibid., p. 97; S. Frye, *Elizabeth I: The Competition for Representation* (Oxford, 1993), p. 70; again my interpretation is followed by Montrose, *Subject of Elizabeth*, pp. 125–7.

77. See C. Levin, *The Heart and Stomach of a King: Elizabeth I and the Politics of Sex and Power* (Philadelphia, 1994), ch. 4; below, ch. 12, pp. 457–9.

78. Montrose, *Subject of Elizabeth*, p. 126.
79. Strong, *Gloriana*, p. 96.
80. For this version, now in Siena, see Hearn, *Dynasties*, no. 40, p. 85.
81. Strong, *Gloriana*, p. 101.
82. 'Hatton', *ODNB*.
83. An inscription on the left reads: 'Weary I rest and, having rested, still am weary'.
84. See the illustration of the impresa of Charles V in Strong, *Gloriana*, fig. 91, p. 105.
85. Ibid., pp. 101–7; Hearn, *Dynasties*, p. 85.
86. C. H. Wilson, *Queen Elizabeth and the Revolt of the Netherlands* (1970); R. B. Wernham, *Before the Armada: The Growth of English Foreign Policy 1485–1588* (1966).
87. See Hearn, *Dynasties*, no. 42, p. 87.
88. The painting, in a private collection, is reproduced in Hearn, *Dynasties*, no. 41, p. 86.
89. J. E. Cirlot, *A Dictionary of Symbols* (1962), p. 84: Becker, *Continuum Encyclopaedia*.
90. Hatfield House; see Strong, *Gloriana*, p. 113.
91. Ibid.
92. Ibid., p. 115.
93. Below, p. 398.
94. W.T. MacCaffrey, *Elizabeth I: War and Politics, 1588–1603* (Princeton, 1992), pp. 123–6, 139 and *passim*; S. Doran, *Elizabeth I and Foreign Policy* (2000), pp. 54–5; Strong, *Gloriana*, p. 113.
95. Hearn, *Dynasties*, no. 43, p. 88.
96. Ibid., p. 88.
97. Strong, *Gloriana*, p. 131.
98. The pendant pearl placed at the queen's groin symbolizes her chastity, see L. Gent and N. Llewellyn, *Renaissance Bodies: The Human Figure in English Culture c.1540–1660* (1990), p. 14. Cf. Montrose, *Subject of Elizabeth*, pp. 145–7.
99. See also, R. Helgerson, *Forms of Nationhood: The Elizabethan Writing of England* (Chicago, 1992).
100. Hearn, *Dynasties*, no. 45, pp. 89–90; Strong describes Lee as his 'principal patron', *Gloriana*, p. 135.
101. Strong, *Gloriana*, p. 137.
102. Arnold, *Queen Elizabeth's Wardrobe*, p. 43.
103. It was an emblem used in connection with accession day tilts and was also worn on Lee's sleeve in his portrait, Hearn, *Dynasties*, p. 90.
104. Hatfield House; Strong, *Gloriana*, pp. 157–61.
105. Cf. Arnold, *Queen Elizabeth's Wardrobe*, p. 81.
106. F. Yates, *Astraea: The Imperial Theme in the Sixteenth Century* (1975), pp. 215–19.
107. See P. E. J. Hammer, *The Polarisation of Elizabethan Politics: the Political Career of Robert Devereux, 2nd Earl of Essex, 1585–1597* (Cambridge, 1999).
108. Arnold, *Queen Elizabeth's Wardrobe*, p. 82.
109. Strong, *Gloriana*, p. 159.
110. Genesis 9: 11–17; Becker, *Continuum Encyclopaedia*.
111. Becker, *Continuum Encyclopaedia*. There are several depictions in sixteenth-century art of Christ with a rainbow as his judgment seat (Revelation 4: 2–3), notably Bosch's famous altarpiece in Vienna. See also the illustration of Christ on a rainbow in Jean de Mandeville, *Reysen und Wanderschafften durch das Gelobte Land* (Basel, 1481).
112. Matthew 13: 16–17.
113. R. Graziani, ' "The Rainbow Portrait" of Queen Elizabeth and its Religious Symbolism', *Journal of the Warburg and Courtauld Institute*, 35 (1972), pp. 247–59.
114. Ibid., p. 258.
115. Strong, *Gloriana*, p. 153.
116. Elizabeth's stomacher points directly down to Worcester.

117. R. Strong, *The Cult of Elizabeth* (1977), ch.1, especially pp. 17–46.

118. Ibid., pp. 36–7.

119. Ibid., pp. 28–30.

120. The white and style of Elizabeth's as well as Anne's dress and the composition of the canvas lead the viewer to compare the two women to, of course, the queen's advantage.

121. Levin, *Heart and Stomach*, ch. 2 and p. 28.

122. Strong, *Cult of Elizabeth*, p. 27.

123. See, for example, National Portrait Gallery, no. 5175.

124. Hearn, *Dynasties*, p. 90; Strong, *Gloriana*, p. 140.

125. *Acts of the Privy Council XXVI, 1596–7*, p. 69, July 1596. See Montrose, *Subject of Elizabeth*, p. 221.

126. *Acts of the Privy Council XXVI, 1596–7*, p. 69.

127. Strong, *Gloriana*, p. 147.

128. E. Auerbach, *Tudor Artists: A Study of Painters in the Royal Service and of Portraiture on Illuminated Documents from the Accession of Henry VIII to the Death of Elizabeth I* (1954), p. 109.

129. Ibid., p. 121; see F.M. O'Donoghue, *A Descriptive and Classified Catalogue of Portraits of Queen Elizabeth* (1984), no. 27, p. 31.

130. R. Strong, *Artists of the Tudor Court: The Portrait Miniature Rediscovered 1520–1620* (1983), pp. 10–11; cf. Strong, *The English Renaissance Miniature* (1983), ch. V.

131. Strong, *Portraits of Queen Elizabeth*, no. 2, p. 89.

132. Strong, *Artists of the Tudor Court*, p. 10.

133. Ibid., p. 11; cf. N. Mears, *Queenship and Political Discourse in the Elizabethan Realms* (Cambridge, 2005), p. 249.

134. As Elizabeth Pomeroy observes, 'both the giver and the receiver affirmed public loyalty and private affection', *Reading Portraits*, p. 28.

135. Strong, *English Renaissance Miniature*, nos 92, 99, 146, pp. 83, 87, 120; Strong, *Portraits of Queen Elizabeth*, no. 19, p. 97.

136. Strong writes of an industrial production, *Artists of the Tudor Court*, p. 12; Hilliard executed over 170 miniatures, Pomeroy, *Reading Portraits*, p. 21. The fairly elementary instruction offered in *A Verie Proper Treatise Wherein is Briefly Set Forth the Art of Limning* (STC 24252, 1573) also suggests a wide audience.

137. Strong, *Artists of the Tudor Court*, p. 12.

138. Cf. K. Sharpe, 'Sacralization and Demystification: The Publicization of Monarchy in Early Modern England', in J. Deploige and G. Deneckere eds, *Mystifying the Monarch. Studies on Discourse, Power, and History* (Amsterdam, 2006), p. 109. As I write, Woolworths has announced its commissioning of a souvenir plate for the (yet to be announced) engagement of Prince William.

139. S. O'Connell, *The Popular Print in England, 1550–1850* (1999), ch. 3 and p. 84; A. Griffiths, *The Print in Stuart Britain, 1603–1689* (1998), introduction, pp. 13–14.

140. O'Donoghue, *Descriptive and Classified Catalogue*, p. xiii; A. M. Hind, *Engraving in England in the Sixteenth and Seventeenth Centuries*, Vol. I: *The Tudor Period* (1952), pp. 35–6, 258–80.

141. Auerbach, *Tudor Artists*, p. 109.

142. Strong, *Portraits of Queen Elizabeth*, nos. 7, 9, 11, p. 107.

143. Hind, *Engraving*, I, p. 67.

144. Andreas Vesalius, *Compendios a totius anatomie delineatio, aere exarata: per Thomam Geminum* (STC 11718, 1559); O'Donoghue, *Descriptive and Classified Catalogue*, no. 9, p. 38; Strong, *Portraits of Queen Elizabeth*, engraving no. 4, p. 106; Hind, *Engraving*, I, p. 46, plate 18.

145. 'Geminus', *ODNB*; Hind, *Engraving*, I, pp. 39–48.

146. Strong, *Portraits of Queen Elizabeth*, p. 106; cf. paintings nos 8–11, p. 56 and figs 8, 9, p. 55.

147. Ibid., no. 5, p. 106; Hind, *Engraving*, I, pp. 47–8, plate 18.

148. Strong, *Portraits of Queen Elizabeth*, p. 106.

149. Hind, *Engraving*, I, p. 65.

150. Ibid., I, p. 69; M. Parker, *et al.*, *The Holie Bible* (STC 2099).

151. Parker's Bible removed the notorious Geneva Bible notes, some of which hinted at the limited powers of kings.

152. J. N. King, *Tudor Royal Iconography: Literature and Art in an Age of Religious Crisis* (Princeton, 1989), pp. 233–4, and fig. 75.

153. Strong, *Portraits of Queen Elizabeth*, p. 107.

154. Ibid., engraving no. 7, p. 107; cf. paintings nos 12, 21, 22, pp. 57–8; Hind, *Engraving*, I, pp. 72–3, plates 36, 37.

155. C. Saxton, *Atlas of the Counties of England and Wales* (STC 21805.1, 1579); Hind, *Engraving*, I, pp. 73–4; Strong, *Gloriana*, fig. 82, p. 98; Marcus *et al.*, *Elizabeth: Works*, p. 166; Helgerson, *Forms of Nationhood*, ch. 3; S. Tyacke and J. Huddy, *Christopher Saxton and Tudor Map Making* (1980).

156. King, *Tudor Royal Iconography*, p. 155 and fig. 50.

157. J. Dee, *General and Rare Memorials Pertayning to the Perfect Arte of Navigation* (STC 6459, 1577); Corbett and Lightbown, *Comely Frontispiece*, pp. 49–56; Strong, *Gloriana*, pp. 91–3; King, *Tudor Royal Iconography*, pp. 238–41.

158. Dee, *General and Rare Memorials*, sig. Ai.

159. Hind, *Engraving*, I, p. 263, plate 139; Strong, *Portraits of Queen Elizabeth*, p. 111.

160. Hind, *Engraving*, I, p. 263; Strong, *Portraits of Queen Elizabeth*, engraving no. 17, p. 111; Arnold, *Queen Elizabeth's Wardrobe*, fig. 189, p. 124.

161. Strong, *Gloriana*, p. 114.

162. Hind, *Engraving*, I, p. 264; see plate 139; Strong, *Portraits of Queen Elizabeth*, engraving no. 18, p. 111. It is significant that this version was acquired by the British Museum from the French Protestant Church.

163. Hind, *Engraving*, I, pp. 283–4, plate 146; Strong, *Portraits of Queen Elizabeth*, engraving no. 21, p. 113.

164. Hind, *Engraving*, I, pp. 284–5, plate 144.

165. Ibid., pp. 265–7, plate 161; Strong, *Portraits of Queen Elizabeth*, engraving no. 30, p. 114; Psalms 35:1.

166. Hind, *Engraving*, I, pp. 264–5; Strong, *Portraits of Queen Elizabeth*, engraving no. 29, p. 114; plate E29, p. 116.

167. Hind, *Engraving*, I, p. 264, plate 145.

168. Lomazzo, *Artes of Curious Paintinge*, sig. qiiii.

169. J. Day, *Christian Prayers and Meditations in English, French, Italian, Spanish, Greeke, and Latine* (STC 6428, 1569); idem, *A Booke of Christian Prayers, Collected Out of the Auncient Writers* (STC 6429, 1578).

170. T.I., *A Joyful Song of the Royall Receiving of the Queenes Most Excellent Maiestie Into Her Highnesse Campe At Tilsburie in Essex* (STC 14067, 1588). Interestingly, the illustration in the upper left corner of this broadsheet emulates those on plea rolls.

171. Hind, *Engraving*, I, p. 182, plate 103(b); Strong, *Portraits of Queen Elizabeth*, p. 111. Strong identifies the portrait type as derived from Saxton's atlas. The translation of these images from elite to popular culture would repay careful study. See also the image of the queen in Stephen Gosson, *Pleasant Quippes For Upstart Newfangled Gentle-women* (STC 12096, 1595).

172. Hind, *Engraving*, I, p. 182, no. 1.

173. *A Fourme of Praier with Thankes Giving to be Used Every Yeere, the 17. of Nouember, Being the Day of the Queenes Maiesties Entrie to her Reigne* (STC 16479, 1576, 1578); *An Homelie Against Disobedience and Wylfull Rebellion* (STC 13679, 1570).

174. O'Donoghue, *Descriptive and Classified Catalogue*, p. 104; A. Wyon, *The Great Seals of England, From the Earliest Period to the Present Time* (1887), pp. 76–7.

175. Arnold, *Queen Elizabeth's Wardrobe*, p. 61, fig. 104; Wyon, *Great Seals*, pp. 77–8.
176. Strong, *Gloriana*, p. 109.
177. Strong, *Artists of the Tudor Court*, p. 122.
178. Ibid.
179. E. Auerbach, *Nicholas Hilliard* (1961), pp. 182–3, plates 175 a,b.
180. Strong, *Artists of the Tudor Court*, p. 71.
181. Though it appears that Elizabeth had planned a third version; see, N. Blakiston, 'Nicholas Hilliard and Queen Elizabeth's Third Great Seal', *Burlington Magazine*, 90 (1948), pp. 101–7.
182. O'Donoghue, *Descriptive and Classified Catalogue*, medal no. 1, p. 93; A. Franks and H. Grueber, *Medallic Illustrations of the History of Great Britain* (2 vols, 1885), I, p. 90, no. 1; E. Hawkins, *Medallic Illustrations of the History of Great Britain* (1904–11), plate VI. Strong questions the early date assigned to these but on no conclusive evidence (*Portraits of Queen Elizabeth*, p. 136).
183. Strong, *Gloriana*, p. 82.
184. O'Donoghue, *Descriptive and Classified Catalogue*, medal no. 4, p. 93; Franks and Grueber, *Medallic Illustrations* I, pp. 99–100, nos 22–4; Hawkins, *Medallic Illustrations*, plate VII; Hughes and Larkin, *Tudor Royal Proclamations*, II, no. 471, p. 150.
185. Strong, *Portraits of Queen Elizabeth*, medals nos 1, 2, p. 134; Franks and Grueber, *Medallic Illustrations*, I, p. 120, no. 57; Hawkins, *Medallic Illustrations*, plate VII.
186. Franks and Grueber, *Medallic Illustrations*, I, pp. 116–17, nos 48–9; Hawkins, *Medallic Illustrations*, plate VIII.
187. Franks and Grueber, *Medallic Illustrations*, I, p. 117, no. 49; Hawkins, *Medallic Illustrations*, plate VIII.
188. Strong, *Portraits of Queen Elizabeth*, medal no. 3, pp. 134–6; Franks and Grueber, *Medallic Illustrations*, I, p. 124, no. 70; Hawkins, *Medallic Illustrations*, plate VIII; H. Farquhar, 'John Rutlinger and the Phoenix Badge of Queen Elizabeth', *Numismatic Chronicle*, 3 (1923), pp. 270–3.
189. 'Haddon', *DNB*.
190. Hawkins, *Medallic Illustrations*, I, plate IX; Strong, *Portraits of Queen Elizabeth*, medal no. 13, p. 138.
191. Hawkins, *Medallic Illustrations*, plate IX; Franks and Grueber, *Medallic Illustrations*, I, p. 133 nos 86, 87; Strong, *Portraits of Queen Elizabeth*, medal no. 14, p. 138.
192. Hawkins, *Medallic Illustrations*, plate IX; Franks and Grueber, *Medallic Illustrations*, I, p. 134, no. 90.
193. Hawkins, *Medallic Illustrations*, plate X; Franks and Grueber, *Medallic Illustrations*, I, p. 142, no. 104.
194. Hawkins, *Medallic Illustrations*, plate XI; Franks and Grueber, *Medallic Illustrations*, I, p. 154, no. 129.
195. Hawkins, *Medallic Illustrations*, plate XI; Franks and Grueber, *Medallic Illustrations*, I, pp. 144–5, no. 111. Another medal was inscribed 'It came, it went, it was', again suggesting the direction of Providence in defeating the Armada, p. 146, no. 113.
196. Hawkins, *Medallic Illustrations*, plate X; Franks and Grueber, *Medallic Illustrations*, I, p. 147, no. 115.
197. Hawkins, *Medallic Illustrations*, plate XI; Franks and Grueber, *Medallic Illustrations*, I, p. 148, no. 119.
198. Hawkins, *Medallic Illustrations*, plate XI; Franks and Grueber, *Medallic Illustrations*, I, pp. 154–5, nos 129–31.
199. Strong, *Portraits of Queen Elizabeth*, medal no. 17, p. 138
200. Hawkins, *Medallic Illustrations*, plate XIII; Franks and Grueber, *Medallic Illustrations*, I, p. 177, no. 177; p. 181, no. 184; Strong, *Portraits of Queen Elizabeth*, medal nos 22, 23, p. 140.
201. Levin, *Heart and Stomach*, p. 134.

202. Above, p. 404.
203. T. Smith, *De republica anglorum: The Maner of Governement or Policie of the Realme of England* (STC 22857, 1582), p. 45.
204. *The Summarie of Certaine Reasons Which Have Moved the Quenes Maiestie to Procede in Reformations of Her Base and Course Monies* (STC 9184, 1560); M. Kyffin, *The Blessednes of Brytaine* (STC 15096, 1587), sig. A4.
205. Hughes and Larkin, *Tudor Royal Proclamations*, II, no. 480, pp. 169–70; III, no. 805 pp. 222–4.
206. Ibid., II, no. 533, pp. 263–4.
207. Klarwill, *Queen Elizabeth and Some Foreigners*, p. 227.
208. C. E. Challis, *The Tudor Coinage* (Manchester, 1978), p. 229.
209. Strong, *Portraits of Queen Elizabeth*, coin no. 1, pp. 141, 143.
210. Psalm 118: 23.
211. Strong, *Portraits of Queen Elizabeth*, coin no. 2, p. 141; see G. C. Brooke, *English Coins* (1954), plate xliii (2).
212. Strong, *Portraits of Queen Elizabeth*, coin no. 17, pp. 142–3.
213. Richard Bull Granger Collection, III, no. 22; R. Lobel, *Coincraft's Standard Catalogue of English & UK Coins 1066 to Date* (1999); H. Seaby, *Coins of England and the United Kingdom* (1978), no. 2579, p. 156; 'Hammered Coin Inscriptions and Their Meanings' (http://www.psdetecting.com/Inscriptions-ElizabethI-&-JamesI.html)
214. Challis, *Tudor Coinage*, pp. 229–31.
215. Ibid., p. 292.
216. Ibid., p. 300.
217. Ibid., pp. 145, 266.
218. Above, ch. 4, pp. 148–52.
219. A. J. Collins ed., *Jewels and Plate of Queen Elizabeth: The Inventory of 1574* (1955). See chs 1–3, pp. 3–131 *passim*.
220. Ibid., p. 115.
221. For example, ibid., nos 154, 155 pp. 308–9.
222. Ibid., nos 44, 478, 740, 1,453, pp. 277, 370, 415, 557 and *passim*.
223. Ibid., nos 1,497–1,509, 1,547, pp. 570–1, 580.
224. Ibid., no. 1,578, pp. 590–1.
225. I. Dunlop, *Palaces and Progresses of Elizabeth I* (1962), p. 97.
226. Collins, *Jewels and Plate*, p. 102.
227. Ibid., Arnold, *Queen Elizabeth's Wardrobe*, p. 75; cf. J. Arnold, *'Lost From Her Majesty's Back': Items of Clothing and Jewels Lost or Given Away by Queen Elizabeth I between 1561–1585, Entered in One of the Day Books Kept for the Records of the Wardrobe of Robes* (Wisbech, 1980).
228. Arnold, *Queen Elizabeth's Wardrobe*, p. 74.
229. Ibid., p. 72.
230. Ibid. See Book of Nehemiah, especially ch. 13.
231. Arnold, *Queen Elizabeth's Wardrobe*, p. 71.
232. Ibid., p. 76.
233. Ibid., p. 75.
234. Ibid., p. 71.
235. Levin, *Heart and Stomach*, p. 134.
236. Strong, *Portraits of Queen Elizabeth*, pp. 128–9.
237. Ibid., cameo no. 7, p. 129.
238. For example, Hughes and Larkin, *Tudor Royal Proclamations*, II, nos 464, 493, 494, 495, 496, 601, 646, pp. 136, 187–91, 192, 195, 202, 381, 454; III, nos 697, 786, pp. 3, 174.
239. Pomeroy, *Reading Portraits*, p. 72.
240. Arnold, *'Lost From Her Majesty's Back'*, p. 9.
241. Arnold, *Queen Elizabeth's Wardrobe*, pp. 82, 85.

242. Ibid. p. 85.
243. For example, ibid. p. 290; see Stowe Inventory, ibid., pp. 251–334 *passim*.
244. Ibid., p. 300, item 61.
245. Ibid., p. 305, item 120.
246. Above, ch. 8, p. 292.
247. Arnold, *Queen Elizabeth's Wardrobe*, p. 122.
248. Ibid., pp. 123–8, especially p. 124.
249. Ibid., p. 123.
250. Ibid., pp. 142–4.
251. Ibid., p. 143; P. Stubbes, *The Anatomie of Abuses Containing a Description of Such Notable Vices and Enormities, as Raigne in Many Countries of the World, but Especiallie in This Realme of England* (editions published in 1583, 1585, 1595).
252. See above, ch. 9, p. 337 n. 95.
253. Frye, *Elizabeth I*, p. 13.
254. Levin, *Heart and Stomach*, p. 91.
255. Ibid., ch. 5, pp. 91–120.
256. Above, ch. 7, p. 308.
257. Levin, *Heart and Stomach*, p. 111.
258. Ibid., p. 116.
259. Ibid., pp. 123–5, 128, figs 7, 8.
260. *Cal. Stat. Pap. Spanish, IV, Elizabeth, 1587–1603*, pp. 17–18.

11 'Viewed and Beheld of All Men': Queen Elizabeth and the Performance of Majesty

1. Above, introduction, pp. 48–52.
2. Louis Montrose writes of a real presence replaced by a royal presence, L. Montrose, *The Subject of Elizabeth: Authority, Gender and Representation* (Chicago, 2006), p. 83.
3. Montrose only slightly exaggerates when he opines that 'few monarchs can have ascended the throne with a more questionable, lurid or violent pedigree than did Elizabeth Tudor', ibid., p. 37.
4. Cf. G. W. Bernard, 'The Church of England, *c.* 1529–*c.* 1642', *History*, 75 (1990), pp. 183–206.
5. *The Passage of Our Most Drad Soveraigne Lady Quene Elyzabeth Through the Citie of London to Westminster the Daye Before her Coronacion Anno 1558* (STC 7590, 1559). See also Sidney Anglo, *Spectacle, Pageantry and Early Tudor Policy* (Oxford, 1969), pp. 345–59; Roy Strong, 'The 1559 Entry Pageants of Elizabeth I', in Strong, *The Tudor and Stuart Monarchy: Pageantry, Painting, Iconography II, Elizabethan* (Woodbridge, 1995), pp. 33–54.
6. *Passage*, sig. Aii.
7. Ibid.
8. Ibid., my italics.
9. Ibid., sigs Aii–Aii^v.
10. Ibid., sig. Aii^v, my italics.
11. Ibid.
12. Ibid., sigs Aiii–Aiii^v.
13. Ibid., sigs Aiiii–Aiiii^v.
14. Ibid., sig. Bi.
15. Ibid., sigs Bi–Bi^v.
16. Ibid., sig. Bi^v.
17. Ibid., sig. Bii^v.
18. Ibid., sigs Biii–Biiii.

19. Ibid., sig. Biii.
20. Ibid., sig. Biiii^v.
21. Anglo, *Spectacle, Pageantry*, p. 348.
22. Grafton had worked on the Great Bible, 'Grafton', *ODNB*.
23. *Passage*, sig. Ci.
24. Ibid., sig. Ci; Matthew 5: 1–11.
25. *Passage*, sig. Ci^v.
26. Ibid.
27. Ibid.
28. Ibid., sig. Cii.
29. Ibid.
30. Ibid., sigs Ciiii–Di^v.
31. Ibid., sig. Cii.
32. Ibid., sig. Ciiii^v.
33. ibid., sigs Di–Di^v.
34. Above, ch. 8, p. 276.
35. Above, ch. 8, p. 293.
36. *Passage*, sig. Di^v.
37. Ibid., sig. Ciiii^v.
38. Ibid., sig. Diii.
39. Ibid., sig. Diiii.
40. The English Bible that Henry VIII was depicted as presenting *to* his people.
41. *Passage*, sigs Ei–Ei^v.
42. Ibid., sig. Eii.
43. Ibid.
44. Ibid., sig. Eiii^v.
45. Ibid., sigs Eiiii–Eiiii^v.
46. Ibid., sig. Eiii.
47. H. Hackett, *Virgin Mother, Maiden Queen: Elizabeth I and the Cult of the Virgin Mary* (1994), p. 47.
48. Ibid.
49. T. Lanquet, *An Epitome of Chronicles Conteyninge the Whole Discourse of the Histories as Well of this Realme of England, as al Other Cou[n]treys, with the Succession of their Kinges* (STC 15217.5 1559), sig. Gggg5; R. Fabyan, *The Chronicle of Fabian Whiche He Nameth the Concordaunce of Histories, Newly Perused* (STC 10664, 1559), pp. 566–70.
50. L. Lloyd, *The Triplicitie of Triumphes* (STC 16632, 1590), pp. 56–7.
51. V. von Klarwill, *Queen Elizabeth and Some Foreigners* (1928), p. 159.
52. I. Dunlop, *Palaces and Progresses of Elizabeth I* (1962), pp. 36–7.
53. Ibid., p. 36.
54. Ibid., p. 37.
55. W. Segar, *The Booke of Honor and Armes* (STC 22163, 1590), pp. 90, 100.
56. *The Philosopher of the Court, Written by Philbert of Vienne in Champaigne, and Englished by George North* (STC 19832, 1575), p. 52.
57. Klarwill, *Queen Elizabeth and Some Foreigners*, p. 336. We await a full study of the protocol of the Elizabethan court.
58. Ibid., p. 379.
59. Ibid.
60. Ibid., p. 386.
61. T. Smith, *De republica anglorum The Maner of Governement or Policie of the Realme of England* (STC 22857, 1582), p. 47.
62. Dunlop, *Palaces and Progresses*, p. 61.
63. Ibid., p. 109.
64. Klarwill, *Queen Elizabeth and Some Foreigners*, pp. 95, 228.

65. Ibid., pp. 336–7.
66. Ibid., p. 338.
67. Ibid., p. 322.
68. Ibid., p. 323.
69. Ibid. p. 394.
70. Ibid., p. 59; E. Pomeroy, *Reading the Portraits of Queen Elizabeth* (Hamden, Conn. 1989), p. 39.
71. J. Arnold, *Queen Elizabeth's Wardrobe UnLock'd* (Leeds, 1988), p. 99.
72. Though see L. Montrose, ' "Eliza Queen of Shepherds" and the Pastoral of Power', *English Literary Renaissance*, 10 (1980), pp. 153–82; Montrose, *Subject of Elizabeth*, though Montrose writes surprisingly little about love games in this study.
73. R. McCoy, *The Rites of Knighthood: The Literature and Politics of Elizabethan Chivalry* (Berkeley, 1989), p. 3.
74. J. Wilson, *Entertainments for Elizabeth I* (Woodbridge, 1980), p. 28.
75. Ibid., p. 29.
76. T. Hughes, *Certaine Devises and Shewes Presented to Her Maiestie By the Gentlemen of Grayes-Inne at Her Highnesse Court in Greenewich, the Twenty Eighth day of Februarie in the Thirtieth Yeare of Her Maiesties Most Happy Raigne* (STC 13921, 1587), quotation, p. 46.
77. H. Goldwel, *A Briefe Declaration of the Shews, Devices, Speeches, and Inventions, Done & Performed Before the Queenes Maiestie, & the French Ambassadours, at the Most Valiaunt and Worthye Triumph . . . on the Munday and Tuesday in Whitson Weeke Last, Anno 1581* (STC 11990, 1581).
78. Ibid., sig. Avii^v.
79. Ibid., sig. Ci^v.
80. W. Segar, *Honor Military, and Civill Contained in Foure Bookes* (STC 22164, 1602), p. 200. See A. Young, *Tudor and Jacobean Tournaments* (1987), appendix, pp. 201–5.
81. Ibid. and Segar, *The Booke of Honor and Armes*, p. 99.
82. Segar, *Honor Military, and Civill*, p. 197; Young, *Tudor and Jacobean Tournaments*, p. 202.
83. Young, *Tudor and Jacobean Tournaments*, pp. 33–7; R. Strong, *The Cult of Elizabeth* (1977), ch. 5, especially pp. 137–50.
84. Segar, *Honor Military, and Civill*, p. 217.
85. Above ch. 7, pp. 202–3, 221.
86. Strong, *Cult of Elizabeth*, pp. 167–8.
87. Arnold, *Queen Elizabeth's Wardrobe*, p. 21; Strong, *Cult of Elizabeth*, figs 80–3, pp. 170–1; cf. Strong, 'Queen Elizabeth and the Order of the Garter', in Strong, *Tudor and Stuart Monarchy*, II, pp. 55–86.
88. Strong, *Cult of Elizabeth*, p. 165.
89. Strong, 'Elizabeth and Garter', p. 61.
90. Klarwill, *Queen Elizabeth and Some Foreigners*, p. 378.
91. Ibid., pp. 375–8.
92. Strong, 'Elizabeth and Garter', p. 65.
93. Strong, *Cult of Elizabeth*, p. 183.
94. G. Peele, *The Honour of the Garter Displaied in a Poeme Gratulatorie* (STC 19539, 1593), sig. Ci and *passim*; R.S., *The Phoenix Nest Built Up With the Most Rare and Refined Workes of Noble Men* (STC 21516, 1593), pp. 12–15; 'Peele', *DNB*, *ODNB*.
95. Peele, *Honour of the Garter*, sig. C4.
96. Ibid., sigs B2^v, C1, C3.
97. G. Malynes, *Saint George for England, Allegorically Described* (STC 17226A, 1601).
98. Ibid., sigs A6–A6^v.
99. Ibid., sig. A2^v.
100. Ibid., sig. A8.

101. For all his salutary caution, there is a danger that Anglo encourages a return to such a view in S. Anglo, *Images of Tudor Kingship* (1992). See above, introduction, pp. 48–9.

102. Wilson, *Entertainments for Elizabeth*, p. 31.

103. Klarwill, *Queen Elizabeth and Some Foreigners*, p. 378.

104. Ibid.

105. Richard Harrington, *A Famous Dittie of the Joyful Receiving of the Queens Moste Excellent Maiestie, By the Worthy Citizens of London the XII Day of Nouember, 1584 At Her Graces Comming to Saint James* (STC 12798, 1584).

106. Klarwill, *Queen Elizabeth and Some Foreigners*, p. 328.

107. W. Jaggard, *A View of All the Right Honourable the Lord Mayors of this Honorable Citty of London With the Personages* (STC 14343, 1601), engraved portraits with no pagination; see that for Sir Richard Saltonston, skinner, 1597.

108. Edward Hake, *A Commemoration of the Most Prosperous and Peaceable Raigne of our Gratious and Deere Soveraigne Lady Elizabeth* (STC 12605, 1575), sig. Ciii^v.

109. C. Levin, *The Heart and Stomach of a King: Elizabeth I and the Politics of Sex and Power* (Philadelphia, 1994), p. 28: D. Cressy, *Bonfires and Bells: National Memory and the Protestant Calendar in Elizabethan and Stuart England* (1989), ch. 4, pp. 50–66.

110. *Cyvile and Uncyvile Life: A Discourse Very Profitable, Pleasant, and Fit To Bee Read of All Nobilitie and Gentlemen* (STC 15589.5, 1579).

111. Ibid., sig. Giv^v.

112. See F. Heal, *Hospitality in Early Modern England* (Oxford, 1990), especially ch. 3.

113. Wilson, *Entertainments for Elizabeth*, p. 38.

114. M. H. Cole, *The Portable Queen: Elizabeth I and the Politics of Ceremony* (Amherst, Mass., 1999), appendix 1, pp. 180–201.

115. Ibid., appendix 6, pp. 206–25.

116. Elizabeth to Valentine Dale, ambassador in France, 15 March 1574, L. S. Marcus, J. Mueller and M. B. Rose eds, *Elizabeth I: Collected Works* (Chicago, 2000), p. 227; Dunlop, *Palaces and Progresses*, pp. 116–17.

117. Dunlop, *Palaces and Progresses*, pp. 116–17.

118. Cole, *Portable Queen*, p. 204.

119. See W. Leahy, *Elizabethan Triumphal Processions* (Aldershot, 2005) and above, introduction, pp. 51–2.

120. P. Williams, *The Tudor Regime* (Oxford, 1979), p. 351.

121. W. Patten, *A Letter Whearin Part of the Entertainment Untoo the Queens Maiesty at Killingwoorth Castle, in Warwick Sheer, in this Soomerz Progress 1575 Is Signified: From a Freend Officer Attendant in the Coourt, Unto his Freend a Citizen and Merchaunt of London* (STC 15191, 1585); J. Nichols, ed, *The Progresses and Public Processions of Queen Elizabeth* (3 vols, 1823), I, pp. 426–523.

122. Patten, *A Letter*, pp. 7–9.

123. Ibid., p. 10.

124. Ibid., pp. 11–13.

125. Ibid., pp. 13–14.

126. Ibid., p. 15.

127. Ibid., p. 16; K.L. Parker, *The English Sabbath: A Study of Doctrine and Discipline from the Reformation to the Civil War* (Cambridge, 1988), ch. 3, pp. 41–91. Parker underplays the divisions within the church over Sabbath observance. Cf. J. T. Dennison, *The Market Day of the Soul: The Puritan Doctrine of the Sabbath in England* (Lanham, MD and London, 1983).

128. Patten, *A Letter*, pp. 20–1. The episode recalls Henry VIII's magnanimous gesture when at a joust a lance splintered his helmet (above ch. 5, p. 158). One wonders whether it was meant to.

129. Patten, *A Letter*, pp. 21–3.

130. Ibid., pp. 33–9.

131. Ibid., pp. 42–3, 53–6, 59–63.
132. S. Frye, *Elizabeth I: The Competition for Representation* (Oxford, 1993), pp. 63–5.
133. Ibid., p. 63; the interpretation is supported by Leahy, *Elizabethan Triumphal Processions*, pp. 115–24.
134. Frye, *Elizabeth*, pp. 68–9; Leahy, *Elizabethan Triumphal Processions*, p. 118.
135. Patten, *A Letter*, p. 63.
136. Ibid., pp. 38, 44, 73.
137. Ibid., p. 73.
138. *The Queenes Maiesties Entertainement at Woodstock* (STC 7596, 1585); A. W. Pollard ed., *The Queen's Majesty's Entertainment at Woodstock, 1575* (Oxford, 1903); Nichols, *Progresses*, I, pp. 553–99.
139. *The Queene Maiesties Entertainment*, sig. B3ᵛ.
140. Ibid., sig. B4.
141. Ibid., sig. C1.
142. Ibid., sig. C2ᵛ.
143. ibid., sigs B4ᵛ, C1, C3.
144. Ibid., sig. F2ᵛ.
145. Ibid., sig. F3ᵛ.
146. Ibid., sigs E4ᵛ, G3.
147. Wilson, *Entertainments for Elizabeth*, pp. 119–20; Hackett, *Virgin Mother*, pp. 153–4.
148. *Entertainement at Woodstock*, sig. C1.
149. T. Churchyard, *A Discourse of the Queenes Maiesties Entertainement in Suffolk and Norffolk With a Description of Many Things Then Presently Seene* (STC 5226, 1578); Nichols, *Progresses*, II, pp. 134–214.
150. Churchyard, *Discourse*, sigs Aii–Aiii.
151. Ibid., sig. Aiiiᵛ.
152. Ibid.
153. Ibid., sigs Biᵛ–Bii.
154. Ibid., sigs Biii–Ciᵛ.
155. Ibid., sigs Civᵛ–Diᵛ.
156. Ibid., sigs Di–Dii.
157. Ibid., sig. Diᵛ.
158. Ibid., sigs Eiii, Eiv–Eivᵛ.
159. B.G., *The Joyfull Receyving of the Queenes Most Excellent Maiestie Into Hir Highnesse Citie of Norwich the Things Done in the Time of Hir Abode There and the Dolor of the Citie at Hir Departure* (STC 11627, 1578).
160. Ibid., sig. Aii.
161. Ibid., sigs Aii–Aiiᵛ.
162. Ibid., sigs Aiii–Aiiiᵛ.
163. Ibid., sig. Biiᵛ.
164. Ibid., sig. Biiiᵛ.
165. Ibid., sigs Biv–Bivᵛ.
166. Ibid., sigs Bivᵛ–Ciiiᵛ.
167. Ibid., sigs Di–Diᵛ.
168. Ibid., sig. Dii.
169. Ibid., sigs Diiiᵛ–Divᵛ.
170. Ibid., sig. Ei.
171. Ibid., sigs Eiiiᵛ–Fi; cf. sig. Fivᵛ.
172. Ibid., sigs Civ, Fiv.
173. Ibid., sig. Fiiiᵛ.
174. Ibid., sig. Gii.
175. Ibid., sigs Biv, Fiv–Fivᵛ. Montrose identifies the anti-papal polemics of the progress pageants, see *Subject of Elizabeth*, ch. 6.

176. B.G., *Joyfull Receyving*, sigs Aii, Aiii^v.
177. Cole, *Portable Queen*, p. 161.
178. Ibid.
179. Wilson, *Entertainments for Elizabeth*, pp. 86–7; 'Anthony Browne, First Viscount Montagu', *ODNB*. See Nichols, *Progresses*, III, pp. 90–8.
180. *The Speeches and Honorable Entertainment Given to the Queenes Maiestie In Progresse at Cowdrey in Sussex, By the Right Honorable the Lord Montacute, 1591* (STC 3907.7, 1591).
181. Ibid., p. 2.
182. Ibid., pp. 3–4.
183. Ibid., p. 6.
184. Ibid., p. 9.
185. Ibid., pp. 10–11.
186. Ibid., p. 11. Wilson interprets the Angler scene as a Christian allegory, *Entertainments for Elizabeth*, p. 87.
187. Wilson, *Entertainments for Elizabeth*, p. 95.
188. *The Honorable Entertainement Gieuven to the Queenes Maiestie in Progresse, at Elvetham in Hampshire, By the Right Honorable the Earle of Hertford, 1591* (STC 7583, 1591); Wilson, *Entertainments for Elizabeth*, pp. 96–118; Nichols, *Progresses*, III, pp. 101–22.
189. *Honorable Entertainement*, sigs A2^v–A3.
190. Ibid., sigs A3–A3^v.
191. Ibid., sig. A4.
192. Ibid., sigs B2^v–B3^v.
193. Ibid., sig. B3^v.
194. Ibid., sig. B4.
195. Ibid., sigs C1–2.
196. Ibid., sig. C2^v–C3.
197. Ibid., sigs C4–C4^v.
198. Ibid., sig. D1^v.
199. Ibid.
200. Ibid., sig. D4.
201. Ibid., sig. E1^v.
202. Ibid., sig. E2.
203. T. Churchyard, *A Handeful of Gladsome Verses Given to the Queenes Maiesty at Woodstocke this Prograce* (STC 5237, 1592), sig. C1.
204. Hackett, *Virgin Mother*, p. 65. The substitution had begun in Edward VI's reign but was now revived and became common parish practice.
205. Bernard, 'Church of England', p. 188.
206. Klarwill, *Queen Elizabeth and Some Foreigners*, p. 47.
207. Ibid.
208. P. L. Hughes and J. F. Larkin, *Tudor Royal Proclamations* (3 vols, New Haven, 1964–9), II, no. 451, pp. 102–3.
209. Ibid., II, no. 451.5, p. 103.
210. Marcus *et al.*, *Elizabeth: Works*, p. 62.
211. Hughes and Larkin, *Tudor Royal Proclamations*, II, no. 484, pp. 109–11; *A Speciall Grace Appointed to Have Been Said After a Banket at Yorke* (STC 7599, 1558), sig. eiii.
212. E. Grindal, *A Sermon At the Funeral Solemnitie of the Most High and Mighty Prince Ferdinandus, the Late Emperour of Most Famous Memorye Holden in the Cathedrall Churche of Saint Paule in London, the Third of October, 1564* (STC 12337, 1564).
213. Ibid., sig. Diii^v.
214. J. Walsall, *A Sermon Preached at Pauls Crosse by Iohn Walsal, One of the Preachers of Christ His Church in Canterburie, 5 October 1578. And Published at the Earnest Request of Certeine Godlie Londoners and Others* (STC 24995, 1579).

215. E. Dering, *A Sermon Preached Before the Queenes Maiestie the 25 Day of Februarie by Mayster Edwarde Dering, in Anno. 1569* (STC 6701, 1572); quotation sig. Eii. The biblical reference was to Isaiah 49: 23. A client of Archbishop Parker's, Dering went on to be a puritan with connections to Presbyterians, *ODNB*.

216. Marcus *et al.*, *Elizabeth: Works*, p. 178.

217. Cf. N. Mears, *Queenship and Political Discourse in the Elizabethan Realms* (Cambridge, 2005), pp. 165–6.

218. *A Fourme of Common Prayer to be Used, and So Commaunded by Auctoritie of the Queenes Maiestie, and Necessarie for the Present Tyme and State 1572, 27. Octob.* (STC 16511, 1572), last page.

219. *An Order of Praier and Thankes-giving, for the Preseruation of the Queenes Maiesties Life and Salfetie* (STC 16516, 1585), sigs A1ᵛ, A4 and *passim*.

220. H.R., *[A Prayer for Assistance Against the Armada]* (STC 12576, 1588), one page.

221. *Certaine Prayers Set Foorth by Authoritie to be Used for the Prosperous Successe of Her Maiesties Forces and Navy* (STC 16528, 1597), sig. Bi.

222. A. Anderson, *A Sermon Preached at Paules Crosse, the 23 of Aprill, Being the Lords Day, Called Sonday, 1581* (STC 570, 1581). Anderson was a stalwart defender of the Prayer Book and established church, *ODNB*.

223. W. Segar, *The Blazon of Papistes* (STC 22162, 1587), sig. Diii.

224. J. Hull, *The Unmasking of the Politike Atheist* (STC 13935, 1602).

225. Nicholas Tyacke, for example, all but renounces the term Anglican which he uses in quotation marks; see Tyacke, 'Anglican Attitudes: Some Recent Writings on English Religious History, from the Reformation to the Civil War', *Journal of British Studies*, 35 (1996), pp. 139–67.

226. Klarwill, *Queen Elizabeth and Some Foreigners*, p. 47.

227. E. Bush, *A Sermon Preached At Pauls Crosse On Trinity Sunday, 1571* (STC 4183, 1576), sigs Giᵛ–Gii.

228. J. Young, *A Sermon Preached Before the Queenes Maiestie, the Second of March, An. 1575* (STC 26110, 1576), sig. B8ᵛ.

229. J. Bridges, *A Defence of the Government Established in the Church of Englande for Ecclesiasticall Matters* (STC 3734, 1587). Bridges, a royal chaplain, answered Presbyterian attacks on the church; he was promoted to the bishopric of Oxford by James I, *ODNB*.

230. Bridges, *Defence*, pp. 710, 763, 1,401 and *passim*.

231. R. Bancroft, *A Sermon Preached at Paules Crosse the 9 of Februarie Being the First Sunday in the Parleament, Anno. 1588* (STC 1346, 1588). Bancroft explicitly praised the Church of England, which he contrasted with that of Scotland.

232. W. Overton, *A Godlye, and Pithie Exhortation Made to the Judges of Sussex* (STC 18925, 1579), sig. Bviᵛ.

233. In 1603, Henry Chettle was to reflect that Elizabeth had secured a church and faith which 'keepeth place in the midst', *Englandes Mourning Garment Worne Here by Plaine Shepheardes in Memorie of Their Sacred Mistresse, Elizabeth* (STC 5121, 1603), sig. D4: 'For in religion as in other things, there hath been an extreme erring from the truth, which like all virtues . . . keepeth place in the midst; so hath she established the true Catholic and apostolical religion in this land, neither mingling with multitudes of idle superstitions, nor yet wanting true honour and reverence for the ministry in laudable and long received ceremonies'.

234. Cressy, *Bonfires and Bells*, p. 53.

235. I. Colfe, *A Sermon Preached on the Queenes Day Beeing the 17. of November 1587. at the Towne of Lidd in Kent* (STC 5552, 1588), sigs B1ᵛ, B7ᵛ and *passim*.

236. T. Holland, *[[H]-e panegurìs] D. Elizabethae Dei Gratia Angliae Reginae: A Sermon Preached in Pauls Church at London the 17 of November in the Yeare of Our Lord 1599* (STC 13596.5, Oxford, 1600). See sig. B1ᵛ.

237. Ibid., sig. K2.
238. Ibid., sig. I 2ᵛ.
239. He referred to 'seditious spirits' and equated them with puritans such as Reynolds who questioned the propriety of the celebrations for Elizabeth, ibid., sigs H–H3.
240. Cressy, *Bonfires and Bells*, p. 58.
241. Ibid., p. 50; Holland, *Sermon*, sig. N4.
242. The words, often thought to be Elizabeth's, were probably by Sir Francis Bacon (*Oxford Dictionary of Quotations*).
243. Hughes and Larkin, *Tudor Royal Proclamations*, II, no. 680. pp. 518–21.
244. 'A Newe Ballad Declaryng The Daungerous Shootyng of the Gunne at the Court', *Harleian Miscellany*, vol.10 (1813), pp. 272–4.
245. Ibid., p. 274.
246. Smith, *De republica anglorum*, p. 85. For a magisterial study of the Elizabethan scaffold as a site of religious contest, see P. Lake, *The Antichrist's Lewd Hat: Protestants, Papists and Players in post-Reformation England* (New Haven and London, 2002), ch. 7.
247. Lake, *Antichrist's Lewd Hat*, pp. 255–62.
248. A. Somerset, *Elizabeth I* (1997), p. 389.
249. P. Lake and M. Questier, 'Puritans, Papists and the "Public Sphere" in Early Modern England: The Edmund Campion Affair in Context', *Journal of Modern History*, 72 (2000), pp. 587–627.
250. Ibid., p. 607.
251. *A Particular Declaration or Testimony, of the Undutifull and Traiterous Affection Borne Against Her Maiestie by Edmond Campion Iesuite, and Other Condemned Priestes Witnessed By Their Owne Confessions* (STC 4536, 1582).
252. Ibid., sig. Aiii.
253. Ibid., sig. Aiiiᵛ.
254. Somerset, *Elizabeth*, p. 393; Lake, *Antichrist's Lewd Hat*, pp. 260–2 is less sanguine.
255. A. Haynes, *Walsingham: Elizabethan Spymaster and Statesman* (Stroud, 2004); 'Henry Percy, Eighth Earl of Northumberland', *ODNB*.
256. *A True and Summarie Reporte of the Declaration of Some Part of the Earle of Northumberlands Treasons Deliuered Publiquelie in the Court at the Starrechamber by the Lord Chauncellour and Others of Her Maiesties Most Honourable Priuie Counsell, and Counsell Learned, by Her Maiesties Special Commandement, Together with the Examinations & Depositions of Sundrie Persons Touching the Maner of His Most Wicked and Violent Murder Committed Upon Himselfe With His Owne Hand, in the Tower of London, the 20 Day of Iune, 1585* (STC 19617, 1585). The report specifically states that 'lest through the sinister means of such persons as be evil affected to the present estate of her Majesty's government, some bad and untrue conceits might be had as well of the cause of the Earl's detainment as of the means of his death, it was . . . thought necessary to have the truth thereof made known' (sig. Aiii).
257. Q. Z., *A Discoverie of the Treasons Practised and Attempted Against the Queenes Maiestie and the Realme, by Francis Throckmorton Who Was For the Same Arraigned and Condemned In Guyld Hall, In the Citie of London, the One and Twentie Day of May Last Past* (STC 24050.5, 1584), quotation, sig. Civᵛ. The mention of judgement in Guildhall may have been intended to emphasize due process.
258. 'William Parry', *ODNB*; *A True and Plaine Declaration of the Horrible Treasons, Practised by William Parry the Traitor, Against the Queenes Maiestie, The Maner of his Arraignment, Conviction and Execution, Together With the Copies of Sundry Letters of His and Others, Tending to Diuers Purposes, for the Proofes of His Treasons* (STC 19342A, 1585), anon. but published by the royal printer 'cum privilegio'; quotation, pp. 29–30. The titles of all these pamphlets disclose a sensed need to prove things to a broad public.
259. Ibid., pp. 34–5.

260. Ibid., p. 38.

261. Ibid., p. 39; see 'an addition', pp. 40–5.

262. Ibid., p. 38.

263. *Cal. Stat. Pap. Dom. Elizabeth, 1581–90*, p. 229; *Cal. Stat. Pap. Spanish, Elizabeth, III, 1580–6*, p. 535.

264. Thomas Nelson, *A Short Discourse Expressing the Substaunce Of All the Late Pretended Treasons Against the Queenes Maiestie* (STC 18425, 1586). Though there is no evidence that this was an official publication, the balladeer and printer Nelson wrote an epitaph on Walsingham, *ODNB*.

265. T. D. [now assigned to Thomas Deloney], *A Most Joyfull Songe Made in the Behalfe Of All Her Maiesties Faithfull and Loving Subiects Of the Great Joy Which Was Made In London At the Taking Of the Late Trayterous Conspirators* (STC 6557.6, 1586).

266. W. Kempe, *A Dutiful Invectiue Against the Moste Haynous Treasons of Ballard and Babington With Other Their Adherents, Latelie Executed, Together, With the Horrible Attempts and Actions of the Q. of Scottes and the Sentence Pronounced Against Her at Fodderingay* (STC 14925, 1587).

267. Ibid., sigs q3–q3^v.

268. Ibid., sig. q4.

269. Ibid., sig. q4^v.

270. R. Crompton, *A Short Declaration of the Ende of Traytors, and False Conspirators Against the State & of the Duetie of Subiectes To Theyr Soveraigne Governour: and Wythall, Howe Necessarie Lawes and Execution of Justice Are, for the Preservation of the Prince and Common wealth* (STC 6055, 1587).

271. Ibid., sigs Aiiii–Aiiii^v.

272. Ibid., sigs Bi–Biiii, *passim*.

273. Ibid., sig. Cii^v.

274. Ibid., sig. Ciiii.

275. Ibid., sig. Di.

276. *A Defence of the Honorable Sentence and Execution of the Queene of Scots Exempled with Analogies* (STC 17566.3, 1587). The Old STC gave this as STC 15098 and indicated Kyffin as author.

277. 'Maurice Kyffin', *DNB*.

278. *A Defence*, sigs A1–A2.

279. Ibid., sig. B2.

280. Ibid., sig. C4.

281. Ibid., sigs D1, D4^v.

282. Ibid., sigs E2, K4^v.

283. Ibid., sigs K3, K4–K4^v.

284. Ibid., sig. C4.

285. D. Green, *The Double Life of Doctor Lopez: Spies, Shakespeare and the Plot to Poison Elizabeth I* (2003).

286. *A True Report of Sundry Horrible Conspiracies of Late Time Detected to Haue (By Barbarous Murders) Taken Away the Life of the Queenes Most Excellent Maiestie Whom Almighty God Hath Miraculously Conserved Against the Treacheries of Her Rebelles, and the Violences of Her Most Puissant Enemies* (STC 7603, 1594).

287. Ibid., pp.4–7, 23.

288. Ibid., p. 18.

289. Ibid., pp. 23–4.

290. P. E. J. Hammer, *The Polarisation of Elizabethan Politics: The Political Career of Robert Devereux, 2nd Earl of Essex, 1585–1597* (Cambridge, 1999); 'Robert Devereux, 2nd Earl of Essex', *ODNB*.

291. W. Barlow, *A Sermon Preached at Paules Crosse, on the First Sunday in Lent . . . 1600 With a Short Discourse of the Late Earle of Essex His Confession and Penitence, Before*

and At the Time of His Death (STC 1454, 1601), sig. A3. On Cecil's orchestration of the sermon following Essex's rebellion, see *Cal. Stat. Pap. Dom. Elizabeth, 1598–1601*, pp. 598–9; *HMC Salisbury*, XII, p. 201.

292. Barlow, *A Sermon*, sig. B5ᵛ.
293. Ibid., sigs C2ᵛ–C3.
294. Ibid., sig. E1.
295. Ibid., sigs D6–D6ᵛ.
296. Ibid., sigs B6–B6ᵛ, C6, E1. It is worth noting that Barlow mentioned Coriolanus as one 'who might make a fit parallel for the late earl' (sig. C3ᵛ).
297. Ibid., sig.B7ᵛ.
298. P. Croft, 'The Reputation of Robert Cecil: Libels, Political Opinion and Popular Awareness in the Early Seventeenth Century', *Transactions of the Royal Historical Society*, 6th series, 1 (1991), pp. 43–69. Several ballads praised Essex, even after his execution; see, for example, *A Lamentable Dittie Composed Upon the Death of Robert Lord Deuereux Late Earle of Essex Who Was Beheaded in the Tower of London, Vpon Ash Wednesday in the Morning, 1601. To the Tune of Welladay* (STC 6791, 1603).

12 Contesting and Appropriating Elizabeth

1. See S. L. Adams, 'Favourites and Factions at the Elizabethan Court', in J. Guy ed., *The Tudor Monarchy* (1997), pp. 253–76; Adams, 'Eliza Enthroned? The Court and its Politics', in C. Haigh, ed., *The Reign of Elizabeth I* (Basingstoke, 1984), pp. 55–77; Adams, *Leicester and the Court: Essays on Elizabethan Politics* (Manchester, 2002); J. Guy ed., *The Reign of Elizabeth: Court and Culture in the Last Decade* (Cambridge, 1995); S. Alford, *The Early Elizabethan Polity: William Cecil and the British Succession Crisis, 1558–1569* (Cambridge, 1998); P. Hammer, *The Polarisation of Elizabethan Politics: The Political Career of Robert Devereux, 2nd Earl of Essex, 1585–1597* (Cambridge, 1997); N. Mears, *Queenship and Political Discourse in the Elizabethan Realms* (Cambridge, 2005) best addresses the appeal to a world beyond the court and metropolis.
2. See J. A. Sharpe, 'Social Strain and Social Dislocation', in Haigh, ed., *Reign of Elizabeth I*, pp. 192–211 and *Reign of Elizabeth, passim*.
3. See J. Raymond, *Pamphlets and Pamphleteering in Early Modern Britain* (Cambridge, 2003) figs 1, 2, pp. 164, 167 and chs 3–4 *passim*.
4. This is, of course, the undercurrent to P. Lake, *The Antichrist's Lewd Hat: Protestants, Papists and Players in Post-Reformation England* (New Haven and London, 2002) and the subject of his research on the Elizabethan and early Stuart public sphere. I am grateful to Peter Lake for stimulating and helpful discussions of this subject.
5. H. Chettle, *Kind-harts Dreame Conteining Five Apparitions, With Their Invectiues Against Abuses Raigning* (STC 5123, 1593), sig. C2ᵛ.
6. W. Patten, *A Letter Whearin Part of the Entertainment Untoo the Queens Maiesty at Killingwoorth Castle, in Warwick Sheer, in this Soomerz Progress 1575 Is Signified: From a Freend Officer Attendant in the Coourt, Unto his Freend a Citizen and Merchaunt of London* (STC 15191, 1575), pp. 34–5.
7. T. F., *Newes from the North: Otherwise Called The Conference Between Simon Certain and Pierce Plowman* (STC 24062A, 1585), sigs Bii–Di and *passim*. The common folk names suggest a popular audience and no surprise that Everyman might be debating such topics.
8. Ibid., sig. Kiᵛ.
9. W. Blandie, *The Castle, or Picture of Pollicy Shewing Forth Most Lively, the Face, Body and Partes of a Commonwealth* (STC 3128, 1581), ff. 2–2ᵛ, 9ᵛ–10, 14ᵛ–15 and *passim*. For all its pronouncements of simplicity, this treatise was printed by John Day with privilege (at end). 'William Blandy' [or Blandie], *ODNB*.

10. J. Young, *A Sermon Preached Before the Queenes Maiestie, the Second of March, An. 1575* (STC 26110, 1576), sig. C1.

11. Chelidonius, *A Most Excellent Hystorie Of the Institution and Firste Beginning of Christian Princes, and the Originall of Kingdoms* (STC 5113, 1571), p. 4.

12. *The Philosopher of the Court, Written by Philbert of Vienne in Champaigne, and Englished by George North* (STC 19832, 1575), p. 22. Counters probably means recounters.

13. F. Patrizi, *A Moral Methode of Civile Policie Contayninge a Learned and Fruictful Discourse of the Institution, State and Government of a Commonweale. Abridged Oute of the Commentaries of the Reverende . . . Franciscus Patricius, Byshop of Caieta in Italye. Done Out of Latine into Englishe, By Rycharde Robinson, Citizen of London. Seene and Allowed* (STC 19475, 1576), p. 63.

14. *The History of the Church of Englande Compiled by Venerable Bede, Englishman. Translated Out of Latin into English by Thomas Stapleton Student in Divinite* (STC 1778, 1565), p. 3. Stapleton published a vast amount of Catholic polemic from his exile in Douai, *ODNB*.

15. See, for example, John Leslie, *A Treatise of Treasons Against Q. Elizabeth, and the Croune of England Divided into Two Partes: Whereof, the First Parte Answereth Certaine Treasons Pretended, That Never Were Intended: and the Second Discovereth Greater Treasons Committed, That Are By Few Perceiued* (STC 7601, Douai, 1572). (Leslie was imprisoned after Norfolk's rebellion for his support for Mary, Queen of Scots, *ODNB*.)

16. P. Lake and M. Questier, 'Puritans, Papists and the "Public Sphere" in Early Modern England: The Edmund Campion Affair in Context', *Journal of Modern History*, 72 (2000), pp. 587–627.

17. Raymond, *Pamphlets and Pamphleteering*, ch. 2, pp. 27–52; Lake, *Antichrist's Lewd Hat*, pp. 505–20, 521–37, 550–5; J. Black, 'The Rhetoric of Reaction: The Martin Marprelate Tracts (1588–89), Anti-Martinism, and the Uses of Print in Early Modern England', *Sixteenth Century Journal*, 28 (1997), pp. 707–25.

18. Lake, *Antichrist's Lewd Hat*, pp. 563–76; J. Andersen, 'Thomas Nashe and Popular Conformity in Late Elizabethan England', *Renaissance and Reformation*, 25 (2001), pp. 25–44.

19. W. Overton, *A Godlye, and Pithie Exhortation, Made to the Judges of Sussex . . . By William Ouerton, Doctor of Divinitie, and One of the Queenes Maiesties Justices Appoynted For the Peace* (STC 18925, 1579), sigs Di, Dvi.

20. B.R. White, *The English Separatist Tradition from the Marian Martyrs to the Pilgrim Fathers* (Oxford, 1971), especially ch. 3.

21. J. Bridges, *A Defence of the Government Established in the Church of Englande for Ecclesiasticall Matters* (STC 3734, 1587), pp. 10, 35 and *passim*.

22. Ibid., book 11, pp. 861–951; book 14, pp. 1,141ff.

23. R. Bancroft, *A Sermon Preached at Paules Crosse the 9 of Februarie Being the First Sunday in the Parleament, Anno. 1588* (STC 1346, 1588), p. 87.

24. J.H. Salmon, *The French Religious Wars in English Political Thought* (Oxford, 1959).

25. T. Beard, *The Theatre of Gods Judgements: Or a Collection of Histories Out of Sacred, Ecclesiasticall, and Prophane Authours Concerning the Admirable Judgements of God Upon the Transgressours of His Commandements* (STC 1659, 1597). This work went into several editions. See G.F. Waller, 'The Popularization of Calvinism: Thomas Beard's *The Theatre Of God's Judgements* (1597)', *Theology*, 75 (1972), pp. 176–87.

26. Beard, *Theatre of Gods Judgements*, pp. 12–13 and *passim*.

27. Ibid., ch. 5, p. 231.

28. J. Guy, 'Monarchy and Counsel: Models of the State', in P. Collinson ed., *The Sixteenth Century, 1485–1603* (Oxford, 2002), pp. 133–6; P. Collinson, 'The Monarchical Republic of Queen Elizabeth I', *Bulletin of the John Rylands Library*, 69 (1987), pp. 394–424; Alford, *Early Elizabethan Polity*, pp. 111–16; A. McLaren, *Political Culture in the Reign*

of Elizabeth (Cambridge, 1999), pp. 237–41. Mears warns against the excesses of such arguments, *Queenship*, pp. 95–9.

29. R. M. Smuts, 'Court Centered Politics and the Uses of Roman Historians, *c.* 1590–1630', in K. Sharpe and P. Lake eds, *Culture and Politics in Early Stuart England* (Basingstoke, 1994), pp. 21–43; M. Peltonen, 'Citizenship and Republicanism in Elizabethan England', in M.van Gelderen and Q. Skinner eds, *Republicanism: A Shared European Heritage: Vol. 1. Republicanism and Constitutionalism in Early Modern Europe* (Cambridge, 2002), pp. 85–106; M. Peltonen, *Classical Humanism and Republicanism in English Political Thought, 1570–1640* (Cambridge, 1995), ch. 2.

30. *Henrie Cornelius Agrippa, of the Vanitie and Uncertaintie of Artes and Sciences, Englished by Ia. San. Gent* (STC 204, 1569). There was another edition in 1575.

31. Ibid., f. 77.

32. Ibid.

33. *I Discorsi di Nicolo Machiavelli, Sopra la Prima Deca di Tito Livio* (STC 17159.5, London, 1584); F. Raab, *The English Face of Machiavelli* (1964), ch. 2, especially pp. 51–76; S. Anglo, 'The Reception of Machiavelli in Tudor England: A Reassessment', *Il Politico*, 31 (1966), pp. 127–38.

34. G. Buchanan, *De Iure Regni Apud Scotos Dialogus* (STC 3973, 1579); *Vindiciae Contra Tyrannos: Sive, de Principis in Populum, Populíque in Principem, Legitima Potestate* (STC 15211, 1579); Salmon, *French Religious Wars*.

35. G. La Perrière, *The Mirrour of Policie* (STC 15228, 1598).

36. Ibid., sigs Bi–iii, Div^v.

37. *The Commonwealth and Government of Venice, Written by the Cardinall Gasper Contareno, and Translated out of Italian into English, by Lewes Lewkenor Esquire* (STC 5642, 1599), p. 4.

38. Ibid., sigs A1–3.

39. Ibid., pp. 37–42.

40. Ibid., p. 157.

41. Ibid., p. 43.

42. Ibid., sigs A2^v–3.

43. A. Kernan, *The Cankered Muse : Satire of the English Renaissance* (New Haven, 1959); J. Peter, *Complaint and Satire in Early English Literature* (Oxford, 1956).

44. T. Churchyard, *A Pleasant Discourse of Court and Wars with a Replication to Them Both, and a Commendation of All Those That Truly Serve Prince and Countrie* (STC 5249, 1596).

45. Ibid., sigs A1–A1^v.

46. Smuts, 'Court Centred Politics', p. 21; P. Collinson, 'Ecclesiastical Vitriol: Religious Satire in the 1590s and the Invention of Puritanism', in Guy, *Reign of Elizabeth*, p. 153.

47. P. L. Hughes and J. F. Larkin, *Tudor Royal Proclamations* (3 vols, New Haven, 1964–9), II, no. 598, pp. 376–9.

48. Ibid., II, no. 612, pp. 400–1.

49. Ibid. II, no. 642, pp. 445–9; J. Stubbes, *The Discoverie of a Gaping Gulf Whereinto England Is Like to be Swallowed by Another French Mariage, if the Lord Forbid Not the Banes, By Letting her Maiestie See the Sin and Punishment Thereof* (STC 23400, 1579).

50. Hughes and Larkin, *Tudor Royal Proclamations* II, no. 672, pp. 506–8.

51. Ibid., III, no. 699, pp. 13–17.

52. *A Newe Ballade Intituled, Agaynst Rebellious and False Rumours To the Newe Tune of the Blacke Almaine, Upon Scissillia* (STC 1979, 1570).

53. J. Phillips, *A Frendly Larum, or Faythfull Warnynge to the True Harted Subjectes of England* (STC 19870, 1570), sig. Avi; *A True and Summarie Reporte of the Declaration of Some Part of the Earle of Northumberlands Treasons Deliuered Publiquelie in the Court at the Starrechamber by the Lord Chauncellour and Others of her Maiesties Most Honourable Privie Counsell* (STC 19617, 1585), sig. Aii^v.

54. *The Effect of the Declaration Made in the Guildhall* (STC 11036, ESTC S121998, 1571), sigs Biiii–Biiii^v.

55. *An Homilie Against Disobedience and Wylfull Rebellion* (STC 13680.6, 1570), sig. Fii.

56. J. Bridges, *The Supremacie of Christian Princes Over all Persons Throughout their Dominions* (STC 3737, 1573), sig. qiii.

57. Hughes and Larkin, *Tudor Royal Proclamations*, II, no. 650, pp. 469–71.

58. Ibid., no. 688, pp. 534–5.

59. Ibid., III, no. 808, pp. 230–2.

60. Ibid. no. 810, pp. 233–4.

61. Ibid. II, no. 612, pp. 400–7.

62. S. Cavanagh, 'The Bad Seed: Princess Elizabeth and the Seymour Incident', in J. Walker ed., *Dissing Elizabeth: Negative Representations of Gloriana* (Durham, NC, 1998), pp. 9–29.

63. Ibid., p. 23.

64. Walker, *Dissing Elizabeth*, pp. 44, 86.

65. Levin, *Heart and Stomach of a King*, pp. 75–6.

66. Ibid., p.77 and ch. 4 *passim*

67. Ibid., p. 79.

68. Mears, *Queenship*, pp. 219–24.

69. Levin, *Heart and Stomach of a King*, pp. 80–1.

70. Ibid., pp. 85–7.

71. Spenser, *Faerie Queene*, book 4, canto 1.

72. P. Berry, *Of Chastity and Power: Elizabethan Literature and the Unmarried Queen* (1989) pp. 123–4.

73. D. Stephens, 'Into Other Arms: Amoret's Evasion', in J. Goldberg, *Queering the Renaissance* (Durham, NC, 1994), pp. 190–217, quotation at p. 211.

74. Levin, *Heart and Stomach*, ch. 6, pp. 121–48.

75. H. Hackett, *Virgin Mother, Maiden Queen: Elizabeth I and the Cult of the Virgin Mary* (1994), pp. 164–5; Berry, *Of Chastity and Power*, pp. 68–9.

76. W. Schleiner, '*Divina Virago*: Queen Elizabeth as an Amazon', *Studies in Philology*, 75 (1978), pp. 163–80.

77. Berry, *Of Chastity and Power*, pp. 162–3.

78. M. Villeponteaux, ' "Not as women wonted be": Spenser's Amazon Queen', in Walker, *Dissing Elizabeth*, pp. 209–25, especially pp. 213–14.

79. Ibid., p. 215.

80. H. Betts, ' "The Image of this Queene so Quaynt": The Pornographic Blazon 1588–1603', in Walker, *Dissing Elizabeth*, pp. 153–84.

81. Ibid., p. 164.

82. Ibid., p. 167.

83. Ibid., p. 176.

84. J. Arnold, *Queen Elizabeth's Wardrobe UnLock'd* (Leeds, 1988) pp. 7–8; Guy, *Reign of Elizabeth*, pp. 1–19.

85. Hammer, *Polarisation of Elizabethan Politics*; Guy, *Reign of Elizabeth*.

86. Hackett, *Virgin Mother*, p. 126.

87. See, for example, the lines from Thomas Churchyard's *A Musicall Consort of Heavenlie Harmony* (STC 5245, 1595), p. 9:

> Fine Machevill, is now from Florence flown
> To England where, his welcome is too great,
> His busie books are heare so red and known
> That charitie, therby hath lost her heat.

88. I. Dunlop, *Palaces and Progresses of Elizabeth I* (1962), p. 56.

89. Hackett, *Virgin Mother*, pp. 161, 163.
90. Ibid., p. 164.
91. Young, *A Sermon Preached*, sig. C1ᵛ.
92. Chelidonius, *A Most Excellent Hystorie*, p. 55.
93. L. S. Marcus, J. Mueller and M. B. Rose, eds, *Elizabeth I: Collected Works* (Chicago, 2000), p. 189.
94. Ibid., p. 383.
95. *The Famous Victories of Henry the Fifth Containing the Honourable Battell of Agincourt, As It Was Plaide by the Queenes Maiesties Players* (STC 13072, 1598).
96. D. Kastan, 'Proud Majesty Made a Subject: Shakespeare and the Spectacle of Rule', *Shakespeare Quarterly*, 37 (1986), pp. 459–75; cf. above, ch. 1, pp. 17–18.
97. In A. Braunmuller and M. Hattaway, eds, *The Cambridge Companion to English Renaissance Drama* (Cambridge, 1990), p. 177.
98. P. Ure ed., *Richard II* (The Arden Shakespeare, 1956), p. lix.
99. T. Lodge, *The Wounds of Civill War Lively Set Forth in the True Tragedies of Marius and Scilla* (STC 16678, 1594), quotation sig. H1ᵛ.
100. J. Speed, *A Description of the Civill Warres of England* (STC 23037, 1600); *The First Part of the Contention Betwixt the Two Famous Houses of Yorke and Lancaster with the Death of the Good Duke Humphrey* (STC 26100, 1600). This has been assigned to Shakespeare; *The True Tragedie of Richarde Duke of Yorke and the Death of Good King Henrie the Sixt* (STC 21006A, 1600).
101. *The True Tragedie of Richard the Third* (STC 21009, 1594), sig. H4.
102. Ibid., sig. H4ᵛ.
103. *The Effect of the Declaration*, sig. Cii.
104. See J. A. Sharpe, 'Social Strain and Social Dislocation', in Guy, *Reign of Elizabeth*, pp. 192–211.
105. L. A. Montrose, *The Subject of Elizabeth: Authority, Gender, and Representation* (Chicago, 2006), pp. 176, 184; cf. 177.
106. J. Lipsius, *Six Bookes of Politickes or Civil Doctrine, Written in Latine by Iustus Lipsius: Which Doe Especially Concerne Principalitie; Done into English by William Iones Gentleman* (STC 15701, 1594).
107. Ibid., p. 82.
108. Ibid., pp. 78, 108.
109. R. Becon, *Solon His Follie, or a Politique Discourse, Touching the Reformation of Common-weales Conquered, Declined or Corrupted* (STC 1653, 1594), pp. 26–7.
110. Hughes and Larkin, *Tudor Royal Proclamations*, III, no. 798, pp. 200–2.
111. T. Holland, *Paneguris D. Elizabethae, Dei Gratiâ Angliae, Franciae, & Hiberniae Reginae: A Sermon Preached at Pauls in London the 17 of November Ann. Dom. 1599* (STC 13597, Oxford, 1601), sigs a2–b2ᵛ, N4.
112. Ibid., sigs N4, O4ᵛ.
113. R. Strong, *The Cult of Elizabeth* (1977), p. 121.
114. Ibid., p. 123; Hackett, *Virgin Mother*, p. 87.
115. *Cal. Stat. Pap. Venetian IX, 1592–1603*, no. 1132, p. 529.
116. Ibid., no. 1135, pp. 531–2.
117. Ibid., pp. 532–4.
118. Ibid., no. 1169, p. 565.
119. Ibid., no. 1162, p. 558.
120. A. Somerset, *Elizabeth I* (1991), p. 569.
121. H. Chettle, *Englands Mourning Garment Worne Heere by Plaine Shepheards, in Memorie of Their Sacred Mistresse, Elizabeth; To the Which Is Added the True Manner of her Emperiall Funeral* (STC 5122, 1603), sigs E4ᵛ–F2ᵛ.
122. R. Niccols, *Expicedium [sic]. A Funeral Oration, Upon the Death of the Late Deceased Princesse of Famous Memorye, Elizabeth by the Grace of God, Queen of England,*

France and Ireland Wherunto is Added, the True Order of Her Highnes Imperiall Funeral (STC 18520, 1603). On Niccols, see *ODNB*.

123. Ibid., sigs B4, C3.

124. Ibid., sig. C2.

125. Ibid., sigs A3–B1ᵛ.

126. R. Mulcaster, *In Mortem Serenissimae Reginae Elizabethae. Naenia Consolans* (STC 18251, 1603); Mulcaster, *The Translation of Certaine Latine Verses Written Uppon Her Maiesties Death, Called A Comforting Complaint This Onely Way I Could Declare My Thankefull Mind* (STC 181252, 1603).

127. Mulcaster, *Translation*, sigs A2, A3ᵛ.

128. J. Lane, *An Elegie Upon the Death of the High and Renowned Princesse, Our Late Soveraigne Elizabeth* (STC 15189, 1603), sigs A3, A4ᵛ and *passim*; 'Lane', *ODNB*.

129. T. Rogers and R. Johnson, *Anglorum Lacrimae In a Sad Passion Complayning the Death of Our Late Soveraigne Lady Queene Elizabeth* (STC 14671, 1603), sig. A3ᵛ.

130. Ibid., sig. B1.

131. Anthony Nixon, *Elizaes Memoriall. King Iames his Arriuall* (STC 18586, 1603), sig. A3ᵛ; 'Nixon', *ODNB*.

132. H. Petowe, *Elizabetha Quasi Vivens Eliza's Funerall. A Fewe Aprill Drops, Showred on the Hearse of Dead Eliza* (STC 19804, 1603), sigs A3ᵛ, B3 and *passim*.

133. *The Poores Lamentation for the Death of Our Late Dread Soveraigne the High and Mightie Princesse Elizabeth, Late Queene of England* (STC 7594, 1603), sig. B1ᵛ.

134. T. Churchyard, *Sorrowfull Verses Made on [the] Death of Our Most Soveraigne Lady Queen Elizabeth, My Gracious Mistresse* (STC 5256, 1604), one page.

135. *Sorrowes Ioy. Or, A Lamentation for Our Late Deceased Soveraigne Elizabeth* (STC 7598, 1603), p. 2.

136. H. Chettle, *Englandes Mourning Garment Worne Here by Plaine Shepheardes; in Memorie of their Sacred Mistresse, Elizabeth* (STC 5121, 1603), sig. F1; Churchyard, *Sorrowfull Verses*.

137. *Sorrowes Ioy*, p. 10.

138. J. Fenton, *King Iames His Welcome to London With Elizaes Tombe and Epitaph, and Our Kings Triumph and Epitimie* (STC 10798, 1603), sig. A2ᵛ; cf. sig. B4ᵛ. Chettle even referred to late 'railings against princes', *Englandes Mourning Garment*, sig. B2.

139. Thomas Newton, *Atropoïon Delion, or The Death of Delia with the Teares of Her Funerall: A Poeticall Excusiue Discourse of Our Late Eliza* (STC 18513.5, 1603), sig. B4. Newton was a translator and clergyman, *ODNB*.

140. Diana Primrose, *A Chaine of Pearle. Or A Memoriall of the Peerles Graces, and Heroick Vertues of Queene Elizabeth, of Glorious Memory* (STC 20388, 1630), p. 7. A nice example of how Elizabeth was later held up as a model of loving government.

141. Nixon, *Elizaes Memoriall*, sig. C1.

142. For the verses, see F. M. O'Donoghue, *A Descriptive and Classified Catalogue of Portraits of Queen Elizabeth* (1984), p. 154; though cf. J. Walker, 'Bones of Contention: Posthumous Images of Elizabeth and Stuart Politics', in Walker, *Dissing Elizabeth*, pp. 252–76.

143. See R. Strong, *Gloriana: The Portraits of* Queen Elizabeth (1987), p. 45.

144. Ibid., p. 43; Walker, 'Bones of Contention', p. 258.

145. Strong, *Gloriana*, p. 43.

146. See O'Donoghue, *Descriptive and Classified Catalogue*, nos 47–287, pp. 47–91; BL Add. MS 4712, in hand of Sir Robert Cotton.

147. Above, p. 362; R. Elstracke, *Braziliologia: a Booke of Kings Beeing the True and Likely Effigies of all our English Kings from the Conquest* (STC 13581, 1618).

148. A. Globe, *Peter Stent, London Printseller circa 1642–65: Being a Catalogue Raisonné of his Engraved Prints and Books* (Vancouver, 1985).

149. See H. R. Trevor Roper, *Queen Elizabeth's First Historian: William Camden and the Beginnings of English 'Civil History'* (1971); D. Woolf, 'Two Elizabeths? James I and the Late Queen's Famous Memory', *Canadian Journal of History*, 20 (1985), pp. 167–91.
150. Strong, *Gloriana*, figs 182, 185.
151. T. Scott, *Robert Earle of Essex his Ghost, Sent from Elizian to the Nobility, Gentry, and Communaltie of England* (STC 22084A, 1642), p. 15.
152. J. Reynolds, *Vox Coeli, or, Newes from Heaven of a Consultation There Held by the High and Mighty Princes, King Hen.8. King Edw.6. Prince Henry. Queene Mary. Queene Elizabeth, and Queene Anne* (STC 20946.6, 1624), pp. 37, 43, 48.
153. Quoted in D. Cressy, *Bonfires and Bells: National Memory and the Protestant Calendar in Elizabethan and Stuart England* (1989), p. 133.
154. W. Camden, *Tomus Alter, & Idem: or The Historie of the Life and Reigne of That Famous Princesse, Elizabeth* (STC 4498, 1629), dedication to King Charles.
155. T. Heywood, *Englands Elizabeth Her Life and Troubles, During her Minoritie, From the Cradle To the Crowne* (STC 13313, 1631).
156. Primrose, *Chaine of Pearle*.
157. Quoted in A. Barton, *Ben Jonson, Dramatist* (Cambridge, 1984), ch. 14, especially pp. 312–13.
158. Cressy, *Bonfires and Bells*, p. 134.
159. Barton, *Jonson*, p. 312.
160. *The Life and Death of Queene Elizabeth from the Wombe to the Tombe, from her Birth to her Burial* (STC 7587, 1639), sig. A6.
161. Ibid., sig. B1^v.
162. Ibid., sig. B7.
163. R. Naunton, *Fragmenta Regalia, or Observations on the Late Queen Elizabeth, Her Times and Favorits Written by Sir Robert Naunton* (Wing N250, 1641).
164. *Queene Elizabeths Speech to her Last Parliament* (E534, 1642).
165. *A Most Excellent and Remarkable Speech Delivered by that Mirrour and Miracle of Princes, Queen Elizabeth of Famous Memory, in the Honourable the High Court of Parliament* (E531, 1643).
166. *Queen Elizabeth's Speech to her Last Parliament, Made 30. November. 1601* (E535, 1648); C. V. Wedgwood, *Oliver Cromwell and the Elizabethan Inheritance* (1970), pp. 5–6; D. Underdown, *Pride's Purge: Politics in the Puritan Revolution* (Oxford, 1971), pp. 94–5.
167. F. Bacon, *The Felicity of Queen Elizabeth and Her Times With Other Things* (Wing B297, 1651).
168. Ibid., p. 14.
169. Wedgwood, *Oliver Cromwell*, p. 21.
170. F. Osborne, *Historical Memoires on the Reigns of Queen Elizabeth and King James* (Wing O515, 1658), 'To the Reader' [n.p.].
171. Ibid., pp. 103, 107–8, my italics.
172. Cressy, *Bonfires and Bells*, p. 140.
173. G. Burnet, *The History of the Reformation of the Church of England* (Wing B5798, 1681).
174. S. D'Ewes, *The Journals of All the Parliaments During the Reign of Queen Elizabeth* (Wing D1250, 1682).
175. S. Clarke, *The History of the Glorious Life, Reign, and Death of the Illustrious Queen Elizabeth Containing An Account By What Means the Reformation Was Promoted* (Wing I462, 1682), sigs A1–4.
176. Camden, *History* (Wing C363A, 1688); *Queen Elizabeth's Opinion Concerning Transubstantiation* (Wing E532, 1688).
177. T. Claydon, *William III and the Godly Revolution* (Cambridge, 1996), p. 127.
178. E. Bohun, *The Character of Queen Elizabeth* (Wing B3448, 1693).
179. Ibid., sig. A4.

180. G. Burnet, *An Essay on the Memory of the Late Queen* (Wing B5784, 1695), p. 4.
181. Ibid., pp. 19, 30–1.
182. *The Secret History of the Most Renowned Q. Elizabeth and the E. of Essex* (Wing S2345, 1695).
183. See, for example, *The Novels of Elizabeth Queen of England* (Wing A4221,1680); *The History of the Most Renowned Queen Elizabeth, and her Great Favourite, the Earl of Essex In Two Parts. A Romance* (Wing H2173, 1700); *The Secret History of the Duke of Alencon and Q. Elizabeth a True History* (Wing S2341, 1691).
184. T. Bowers, 'Queen Anne Makes Provision', in K. Sharpe and S. Zwicker eds, *Refiguring Revolutions: Aesthetics and Politics from the English Revolution to the Romantic Revolution* (Berkeley and London, 1998), pp. 66–8.
185. Ibid., p. 67.
186. J. Wilson, *Entertainments for Elizabeth* (Woodbridge, 1980).

Epilogue

1. G. R. Elton, *The Tudor Revolution in Government: Administrative Changes in the Reign of Henry VIII* (Cambridge, 1953).
2. G. L. Harriss and P. Williams, 'A Revolution in Tudor History?' *Past & Present*, 31 (1965), pp. 87–96.
3. R. H. Tawney, 'The Rise of the Gentry, 1558–1640', *Economic History Review*, 11 (1941), pp. 1–38.
4. L. Stone, *The Crisis of the Aristocracy, 1558–1641* (Oxford, 1965).
5. H. R. Trevor Roper, *The Gentry, 1540–1640* (1953); 'The Elizabethan Aristocracy: An Anatomy Anatomized', *Economic History Review*, 2nd ser., 3 (1951), pp. 279–98.
6. I. Archer, 'The Nostalgia of John Stow', in D. Smith, R. Strier and D. Bevington eds, *The Theatrical City: Culture, Theatre and Politics in London, 1576–1649* (Cambridge, 1995), pp. 17–34; idem, 'John Stow, Citizen and Historian', in I. Gadd and A. Gillespie eds, *John Stow (1525–1605) and the Making of the English Past: Studies in Early Modern Culture and the History of the Book* (2004), pp. 13–26; idem, *The Pursuit of Stability: Social Relations in Elizabethan London* (Cambridge, 1991); S. Rappaport, *Worlds Within Worlds: Structures of Life in Sixteenth-century London* (Cambridge, 1989).
7. W. M. Mitchell, *The Rise of the Revolutionary Party in the English House of Commons, 1603–29* (1957). The whole revisionist movement in early Stuart studies began as a critique of such arguments.
8. W.R. D. Jones, *The Mid-Tudor Crisis, 1539–63* (1973).
9. M.E. James, 'Obedience and Dissent in Henrician England: The Lincolnshire Rebellion 1536', *Past & Present*, 48 (1970), pp. 3–78; G. R. Elton, 'Politics and the Pilgrimage of Grace', in B.C. Malament ed., *After the Reformation: Essays in Honor of J.H. Hexter* (Manchester, 1980), pp. 25–56. There remains an emphasis on gentry direction in R. Hoyle, *The Pilgrimage of Grace and the Politics of the 1530s* (Oxford, 2001).
10. E. Shagan, *Popular Politics and the English Reformation* (Cambridge, 2003); idem, 'Rumours and Popular Politics in the Reign of Henry VIII', in T. Harris ed., *The Politics of the Excluded, c.1500–1850* (Basingstoke, 2001), pp. 30–66. For a recent discussion, see G. W. Bernard, *The King's Reformation: Henry VIII and the Remaking of the English Church* (New Haven and London, 2005), ch. 4, especially pp. 293–404.
11. G. R Elton, *Policy and Police: The Enforcement of the Reformation in the Age of Thomas Cromwell* (Cambridge, 1972); Shagan, *Popular Politics*.
12. T. Watt, *Cheap Print and Popular Piety, 1550–1640* (Cambridge, 1991).
13. N. Mears, *Queenship and Political Discourse in the Elizabethan Realms* (Cambridge, 2005), chs 5, 6 *passim*; C.J. Sommerville, *The News Revolution in England* (New York,

1996); J. Raymond, *Pamphlets and Pamphleteering in Early Modern Britain* (Cambridge, 2003); R. Cust, 'News and Politics in Early Seventeenth-century England', *Past & Present*, 112 (1986), pp. 60–90; F.J. Levy, 'How Information Spread among the Gentry, 1550–1640', *Journal of British Studies*, 21 (1982), pp. 11–34.

14.   Shagan, *Popular Politics*, p. 280 and ch. 8 *passim*.

15.   Above ch. p. 423.

16.   I owe this nice formulation to the kindness of Tom Buhler.

17.   Above, pp. 236–40, 313, 321–2; cf. A. McClaren, *Political Culture in the Reign of Elizabeth I: Queen and Commonwealth 1558–1585* (Cambridge, 1999).

INDEX

/

169 pageants present H8 as ruler lurd by ppl
Ig crowds enhance the authority & the performa
& the presentation g the day left
    impression

170   pageant & festival acknowledge
      reciprocity betw. monarch & ppl

170   interwoven initials g H8 & Anne
      as H.A. H.A.

171   The Masque (for whitehall P.
                              chap)

173   qty g H8s royal progresses
"took the royal show on the road."

177   something like a public sphere
      began during the Henrician Revolution
      conscious g being in the public arena

p182 - H8 as Brand — 183 "good King Hal

p184   Shakespeare's H8 replech
visual pageantry g his reign

185 - still reigns in the court g memory

189 H8 as personal monarch √
      family monarch

222 Edward 6's reign also filled w/ pageantry

228 E6 the Tudor most rep'd in drawings & pictures

228- talk about plea roles.

245 "~~pleoel~~ proclamation, patruet & pageant"

246 Mary lost control of her own representation

250 most impt issue in early modern politics - succession to the throne

251 Mary advised to "from a suitable match..." to alleviate the problems of female govt."

319- Elizabeth Tudor - ~~memo~~ engrained her image in the public memory

320 diff't. parties fought over representation of E1.

321 - mid-16th c. emergence of a market society & consumer culture.

322 public sphere hungry for news & images, "teeming marketplace of print." & emerges

336. Eliz's speeches "second only in renown to W. Churchill"

344 Eliz I's proclamations

348 " rep'd in more forms of print by than any other previous monarch

349 Most speeches, proclamations etc emphasized Eliz divine right of kingship

350 also fashionable to exalt the monarchy in leterature late 16th C, and Catholics as un-English & also it was anti-papist

354 fostered a "culture of obedience"... fashioned by in by elite & popular apologias for monarchy
personal, familiar & even intimate — have EI is rep'd "sweet Bessy" (1st royal annivr celebrat)
in 1570, annual commemoration of her coronation began — rep'd as a (418) second sun, sent to dispel the clouds —

355- all accompanied by growth in interest in English history/heritage —

356- Society of Antiquaries founded abt 1586 —
356- Eliz also praised as "the world's diamond Virgin Queen, God's handmaid, leader of golden age —

358 EI hired 1st English portraetist - Hilliard cultural classes became more int'd in visual art

359 obsession w/ heraldry in the Eliz Age to re-establish importance of family lineages

359- def. of heraldy as a system of
signifiers re: virtues, graces, family
359- meaning of coronation jewels (each one!)
360 relatedly, emblems interwoven w/the
material culture of the Renaissance,
not just elite texts; extended into pop cult too
(pamphlets, fables, broadsides, ballads)
illustrations in books
much stressed links of visual w/ authority/power

⚡361 reproduction of authority figs became a
commercially viable enterprise
1597 - 1st book of illustrations of Eng monarchs
36 started a trend— mainly pics, little text

365- market for coronation pics of Eliz even tho
bad pics
37 Hilliard begins to transform the image 1570-
pelican & phoenix pntngs   1572-

374 Darnley portrait-sexual as woman but
also as Queen
382- Ditchley portrait- symbolizes
Queen's authoritarian dominance —
literal embodiment of the nation

8 ft tall picture - she stands on a map of England

387 began to be painted as youthful eventho old

388 "face frozen as a timeless mask"

389 miniatures take off late 1500s as quality
of mass production - ☆
response to desire to have image of the Q
after Armada victory (also woodcuts/~~etchings~~)

(389) EARLIEST EXMPLE Royal souvenir
porcelain - plate of EI w/ motto
in Mus of London

→ (engravings)

1580s - copperplate engraving in
England becomes viable living

1563 govt sught to control "graving
and printing" images

1589 - 1st engraved image q EI

(394) - EI engravings in Bibles

397 - Shift q image q EI from Queen to Empress
after success of Drake's voyages -

401 - 1st monarch 2B depicted on set of playing
cards

402 - royal seals, medals, coins -
commemorative medals greatly ↑ during EIs
reign (404)

412 - Eliz gave jewels of her rep'sentation

1570s- cameos of the Q became popular- avail. to any who could purchase them.
412) clothes assigniffers & sumptuary laws gave up them-
   had over 3000 dresses upon death
She became a "moving allegorical tableau" -
415) when wished to assert authority, referred to.
   herself by the masculine naun prince and king
417) performances demonstrate her possession of
the "common touch" - (DIANA) "genius for public
performance (418) - rituals require supportive audiey processing
(418): REBRANDING as term   (419) Coronation pageants
                                    Jan 14 1559
424 "elevated courtly
   ceremonial into rituals of worship for her persm"
425 comb. of "mysterious majesty & common humanity"
discourse of chivalric love in court helped dispel
the problems w/ her unmarried state .revived
Edward II's tilting turnaments- link to K. Arthur
427 Order of Garter - origin is in Holy Trinity / Catholic
   symbolism
tilts were public events if the entry fee fee
could be paid (428)

430- Elizabeth's "progresses" - cut a wide
swath thru rural England.
         See notes pp 430- end on actual
455 satire, new genre   pages